Irish Rugby
1874–1999
A History

IRISH RUGBY
1874–1999
A History

EDMUND VAN ESBECK

GILL & MACMILLAN

Gill & Macmillan Ltd
Goldenbridge
Dublin 8
with associated companies throughout the world
www.gillmacmillan.ie

0 7171 2930 6
Index compiled by John Loftus
Print origination by Design Image
Colour separations by Typeform Repro
Printed in Spain

A catalogue record is available for this book from the British Library.

1 3 5 4 2

CONTENTS

FOREWORD

IT IS A PRIVILEGE TO WRITE A FOREWORD to this book on the occasion of the 125th anniversary of the Irish Rugby Football Union and I warmly congratulate the author, Edmund van Esbeck, affectionately known to everyone as 'Ned'.

The book is an admirable addition to the literature on the game of rugby. It is full of analysis and detail as one would expect from the writer and I commend it to devotees of rugby. I shall be suitably brief in this foreword so that the reader will not be delayed on his way to better things.

The history of Irish rugby in its many aspects is contained within this volume. Importantly, the successes enjoyed and the disappointments suffered by the national side and the Irish rugby fraternity are vividly and lucidly recalled and the great feats and achievements of the legendary characters of the game in Ireland can be relived through the pages of this book.

After August 1995 the game was transformed when the International Rugby Board declared it to be open. The ensuing difficulties and complexities, and the Union's solutions to the problems which emerged, are central to the latter part of the book. As a consequence, rugby in Ireland was guided successfully into the professional era and the solid foundations laid will, I believe, stand the test of time and yield a rich harvest in the years ahead.

It would be remiss of me if I did not refer to what, in common with many others, I consider to be a matter of powerful significance which has been interwoven in the fabric of our game from one generation to the next — and that is the co-operation and unity of purpose of those involved in the game from all parts of Ireland over the 125 years of the Union's existence. The evidence of that co-operation and unity which have played such a crucial role in the history of the Union is thoroughly catalogued throughout these pages and it is one of the great strengths of Irish rugby of which the Union can be justly proud.

It is said style makes the distinction between reading material and literature. Ned has written with his customary style. For form and substance this book is one to be read and I wish it all good fortune.

W.S.H. Lavery
President
Irish Rugby Football Union

PREFACE

WHEN OVER 25 YEARS AGO I had the privilege to write the official history of the IRFU, I stated that I owed a considerable debt to the many people who helped me in that onerous task.

I now reiterate my thanks to those people as the text of *One Hundred Years of Irish Rugby* is incorporated in this book with some amendments as a result of further research and information that became available.

I have set out in the book to make this a comprehensive record of all Ireland teams at every level (those teams are listed in the Appendices) and to trace the evolution and development of the game in Ireland.

The task of compiling this information was formidable and I was fortunate in having the total support and invaluable assistance of two men in particular, Willow Murray and Des Daly. I want to express my gratitude to both. Willow, a former Leinster interprovincial player and indeed provincial coach, has been a constant support, a man with a deep knowledge of and love for the game, and one who with an extensive collection of memorabilia. Des is another with a great passion for rugby. He keeps meticulous records. His help was invaluable and the statistics that are included on the universities were compiled by him.

I got tremendous support and encouragement from Billy Lavery, the current IRFU president and his immediate predecessor in that onerous office, Noel Murphy, together with former presidents Syd Millar and Bobby Deacy. I want to thank them as well as Philip Browne, the secretary-treasurer of the IRFU, Martin Murphy, the IRFU administrative officer, George Spotswood, the IRFU rugby administrator, and Gerard Carmody and Ann MacSweeney of the IRFU staff. I got maximum co-operation from the staff at Lansdowne Road and complete access to the IRFU records.

I owe an immense debt to my wife Mary for her forbearance, understanding and encouragement during the time I spent writing the book and compiling the statistics. I would also like to thank my two daughters Mary and Geraldine and son Declan for their interest and encouragement.

The following publications were invaluable sources of reference, *The Phoenix Book of International Rugby Records* by John Griffiths, the *Playfair Rugby Annuals*, the *Rothmans Rugby Yearbooks* and the *Who's Who of International Rugby* by Terry Godwin.

I have endeavoured to make this a record of Irish rugby based on the information and records available to me and hope I have faithfully discharged the brief entrusted to me by the IRFU. In conclusion I want to thank Michael Gill of the publishers Gill & Macmillan, their managing editor, Deirdre Greenan and Dara McEvoy of Design Image.

Edmund Van Esbeck

CHAPTER 1

ELLIS'S INDISCRETION AND THE IRISH CONNECTION

DAWN BROKE SOMBRE AND MURKY over the city of London on 15 February 1875. A clinging grey mist pervaded the suburbs and thickened to the consistency of a dirty fog within the heart of the great city. No one unused to the urban gloom of the English Industrial Revolution could have viewed such a dawn without feelings of dismay; and to a little group of Irishmen who surveyed the cheerless scene from the windows of the Golden Cross Hotel, that morning must have seemed singularly grim and forbidding. But their minds were occupied with more important matters than the unpromising prospects of the weather.

A match had been arranged for two o'clock that afternoon between the rugby players of England and Ireland. And if that was a matter of some indifference to the great majority of London's teeming millions, it was, none the less, a historic occasion, for it marked Ireland's first venture into international competition on the rugby field.

Ireland's sporting prowess was already very well known in an England then in the middle of the Victorian era. The Irish were regular and by no means unsuccessful competitors at Wimbledon; in the field of athletics they had long since revealed an ability to compete on level terms with the best that Britain had to offer, while, as *Saunders' News Letter* put it, 'There is no crew more feared at Henley as the Dublin Four, who have thrice had their names inscribed on the Visitors' Cup.' Whatever the result of their match against England, the Irish rugby team of 1875 had the heavy responsibility of maintaining their country's established reputation as a sporting nation.

In 1871, rugby football had entered the arena of international competition when England met Scotland at Raeburn Place, Edinburgh. From the moment that this game took place, the thought was exercising the minds of the rugby fraternity in Ireland generally and the students of Trinity College, Dublin, in particular, that Ireland, too, should take her place among the rugby-playing nations of the earth.

Ireland's appearance at the Oval, Kennington, was then the culmination of a dream nurtured in Trinity where, at the annual general meeting of the football club on 24 October 1874, it had been decided to set up an executive committee with the short-term objective of drawing up a team to meet England that season and with the long-term aim of establishing the game on a properly organised basis throughout the country. Both objectives were attained. The first was accomplished, without undue difficulty, in collaboration with a union that had been formed in Belfast immediately after Trinity's initiative had established the Irish Football Union in Dublin. The Irish team that played at Kennington was therefore the product of a co-operative venture between the north and south of Ireland. This set a pattern which has endured for a century: by crossing great political, religious and social divides it has been possible to recruit successive rugby teams on an all-Ireland basis.

History records that the weather that February day in 1875 cleared up dramatically. The state of the ground at the Oval still bore testimony to the drenching rain that the people of London had endured during the preceding week and it may have proved a deterrent to the players, but it did not prevent the game from taking place. History also records that England won by two goals and a try to nothing and that 3,000 people came to see how proficient the Irish were in this new art of football called rugby.

The roots of football in its various and assorted forms ran deep in the heritage of those who represented both Ireland and England that day at the Oval, but the distinctive features of this version of the game as it was then practised have been attributed to an indiscretion by a boy at Rugby School in 1823.

Whether legend or fact, it is generally accepted that it all started when the 16-year-old William Webb Ellis, while playing in a Bigside game on the Close at Rugby School, caught the ball and, instead of claiming a mark, ran forward with the ball in his hands. His action, if not strictly illegal, breached the accepted conventions of the game at that time, and the other players may well have given him abuse rather than applause. However, as a result of that act, Ellis has been given the credit for creating the distinctive features from which rugby football was later to evolve.

Many eminent and learned historians of rugby have closely examined the suggestion that Ellis was responsible for initiating the game. The claim made on his behalf has survived all their curiosity and ingenuity, as it has survived that of the present writer. So before we turn to the development and growth of the rugby game in Ireland, it may be of interest to consider Ellis and his background in some detail and to investigate, in particular, his alleged connection with Ireland.

William Webb Ellis

One theory popularly held in Ireland is that Ellis was born in the county of Tipperary. A different theory favours Manchester. However, no firm documentary evidence has yet been uncovered to bear out either theory. Rugby School cannot confirm his place of birth; nor can Oxford University, within whose walls he was to continue his studies; nor can the Church of England, which he was later to serve as an ordained minister.

The entry under his name in the *Alumni Oxonienses, 1715–1886* refers to his father as being 'of Manchester, gent.', and on the return which Ellis made for the 1851 census he gave his place of birth as Manchester. This is strong evidence, but it may not be conclusive. Although we cannot be sure where Ellis was born, we do know for certain the month and year of his birth — November 1807.

Thanks to Irish researchers, we know that Ellis's father, James, married Ann Webb, of Bristol, at St Peter's Church, Exeter, in 1804 and that at that time James Ellis was in the British Army. He served in the 18th Royal Irish Regiment and, at a later date, in the First Dragoon Guards. It was while he was with the latter regiment that he served in Dundalk, Clonmel, and Dublin in the year in which William was born, 1807. In 1808 he was posted to the regimental depot in Manchester, before going to the Peninsular War in the following year.

Thus at the time of William's birth there was a definite connection with Ireland, as indeed there was with Manchester. His subsequent statement that Manchester was his birthplace was conceivably born of expediency or perhaps even simple ignorance. Irregular and inaccurate census returns in the middle of the nineteenth century were by no means a rarity, especially by some Irishmen who found fame and fortune in England and chose, for their own personal reasons, to conceal their origins.

James Ellis died while his son was still a small boy. After buying a commission in the 3rd Dragoon Guards for the sum of £735 on 14 September 1809, he was killed in the battle of Albuera on 16 May 1812, receiving a posthumous commendation for his gallantry. After the death of her husband, his widow Ann was left with two young sons, William aged 5, and Thomas aged 8. She was granted a pension of £10 per annum for each of her sons and subsequently moved to live in Rugby, presumably so that the boys could qualify for education at Rugby School on the grounds of local residence. William eventually entered Rugby School in 1816 and remained there until 1825 when he was admitted to Brasenose College, Oxford. After enrolling at Oxford, his sporting interests no longer included football, but he clearly had a talent for cricket. He represented Oxford University against Cambridge in 1827 and scored twelve runs in the match at Lord's.

Ellis took his BA degree in 1829 and two years later his MA. He was later ordained a minister of the Church of England, serving in Albemarle Street, London, and St Clement Dane's, where there is a plaque erected to his memory. The *Church of England Directory* establishes that he was later Rector of Chipping Ongar in Essex and at the same time priest-in-charge of the parish of Laver Magdalen in the same county. The *Church of England Directory* also clearly discounts another belief that he served as Rector of St George's, Hanover Square, London. Further research at the Public Record Office in London has failed to produce a census return for him in 1861 or 1871 from any of the areas in which he ministered at those times.

Not a great deal is known of Ellis's life, and indeed the circumstances of his death and place of burial had an air of mystery about them until 1959, when Ross McWhirter traced his grave to caveau no. 957 in the Cimetière des Vieux, Château Menton, in the south-east corner of France. McWhirter suggests that Ellis was probably spending part of the winter on the Riviera, as did many Englishmen of means at that time. It is a suggestion that warrants the greatest respect, for if it was his custom to winter in France, it would account for the absence of census returns in 1861 and 1871.

Certainly the discovery of his grave aroused tremendous enthusiasm in France, and the man who is credited with starting the rugby game was, and still is, duly honoured by the French Rugby Federation, who tend his grave. Ellis died a bachelor and left the sum of £9,000, a substantial fortune in those days when, as Disraeli said, the world was for the few and the very few.

While some information is available about his career in the Church of England, there is no evidence that once he left Rugby School he took any interest whatsoever in the development of football in any of its various forms. Nor does he seem even to have been aware that shortly before his death the game's first administrative body, the Rugby Football Union, was formed in London. Those who were in Rugby School at or around the same time as Ellis have said that he was not especially adept at or keen on football. If this is true, his indiscretion may well have sprung from sheer boredom, and it would therefore not be surprising if the subsequent developments of the game failed to interest him.

Ellis was the author of a number of works on religion, and one sermon he preached was of sufficient moment to warrant a mention in the *Illustrated London News.*

It is perhaps more interesting to record that he also wrote a poem on beer. The partiality of rugby men towards this particular drink has been proverbial for generations, and Ellis's work was undoubtedly inspired by the virtues of ale as a palatable beverage. Many will agree that he had his priorities right.

There is no doubt that the years between Ellis's celebrated 'indiscretion' in 1823 and his death in 1872 were crucial to the development of rugby football. Indeed, there was a tremendous upsurge of interest in sport generally throughout Britain and Ireland during this period, a factor due in no small measure to the immense amount of social reform that was then taking place. Sport began to take on distinctive and organised forms; and before Ellis died administrative bodies were in existence to legislate on rugby football and association football. And in 1884 the Gaelic Athletic Association was formed in Ireland to propagate the gaelic form of football and the ancient and noble art of hurling. The fraternity that existed between the various 'gaelic' and 'non-gaelic' groups can be gauged from the sporting backgrounds of two of the founders of the Gaelic Athletic Association, Michael Cusack and George St J. McCarthy. McCarthy had played rugby for Ireland and Trinity, while Cusack was a player of no mean skill and apparently a coach of some ability while teaching at Blackrock College and at his own school, Cusack's Academy.

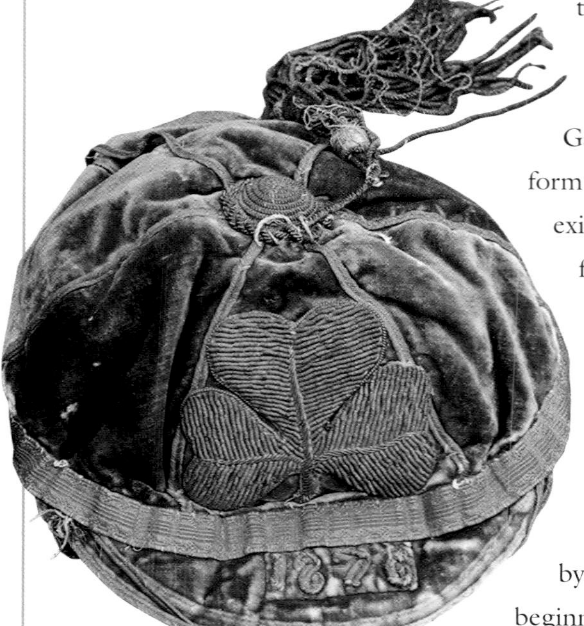

AN IRISH CAP FROM THE EARLY DAYS

A number of publications, including *A History of Football* (1954) by Morris Marples, make it quite clear that different types of football were beginning to develop during the middle of the nineteenth century, and some interesting information about rugby as a distinctive form is to be found in an article by Matthew Bloxham (1805–88) which appeared in *The Meteor* (the Rugby School magazine) in the issue of 10 October 1876. Bloxham was a contemporary of Ellis at Rugby, but left the school before the celebrated 'indiscretion'.

Thomas Hughes, author of the classic *Tom Brown's Schooldays* which immortalised Rugby School, also provided valuable evidence on the evolution of rugby. Hughes's first year at Rugby was 1834 and, according to him, running with the ball was not then forbidden but it was 'not prudent'. The practice grew, however, and by 1840 it was an accepted part of the game. Hughes was captain of Bigside in 1841–42, by which time the debatable question of running with the ball had been finally settled.

In 1846 the first laws for rugby football were drawn up at Rugby School. Similar forms of football were certainly being played in other English public schools at this time, but the laws as practised by each school were very far from being uniform for a long time after 1846. Sir Montague Sherman in *Football, its History for Five Centuries* arrived at the very plausible conclusion that each particular school had its own rules, which were often modified to meet the size of the playground available.

An exhaustive enquiry into the early history of the game was carried out by the Old Rugbeian Society in 1895. The report issued by the society produced, among other things, signed statements and letters, a number of drawings and maps of Rugby Close, the 1846 laws and the revised laws of one year later. Regarding the all important question of the game's true origin, the society found that: 'In 1820 the form of football in vogue at Rugby was something approximating more closely to association than what is known as rugby football today. And that at some date between 1820 and 1830 the innovation was introduced of running with the ball; that this was in all probability done in the latter half of 1823 by Mr W. Webb Ellis.'

That is probably as near to the truth as anyone will ever come. Whether England or Ireland can rightly claim his birthplace, to William Webb Ellis belongs the credit for having 'in all probability' invented the game of rugby football.

CHAPTER 2

EARLY DAYS IN IRELAND

MR MORRIS MARPLES, who has carried out detailed research into the origins of football in all its forms, confesses that he is unable to trace the game back beyond the seventh and eighth centuries in England. However, in his *History of Football* he suggests that the modern football games may have had their beginnings among the Celtic peoples.

Football was definitely popular in Britain during the fourteenth century and was considered a sufficient threat to the status quo to warrant a ban by a royal proclamation proscribing certain sports in 1365. Ireland followed where England led, and within twelve months the Irish authorities issued a similar edict as part of the Statutes of Kilkenny. What effect these bans had on the populace is difficult to assess; their regular reiteration suggests that they were fairly ineffective. It is, however, significant that the proclamation of Kilkenny differed in one important aspect from the 1365 decree of Henry III in that it substituted hurling for football. Unless we are to assume that football was unknown in Ireland at this time, it is clear that it was not considered by the rulers of the day as a threat to the status quo of Irish society.

By the sixteenth century football was still considered to be of too little consequence to have an adverse effect on the compulsory military training of the population. In a decree by the mayor and aldermen of Galway in 1527 it was specifically exempted from a general ban when the people were ordered not to play with the stone or the shot, but urged to practise with the longbow and to hurl the dart or spear. It was further ordered that 'at no tyme to use ne occupye the hurlinge of the litill balle with the hookie stickies or staves, nor use no hande balle to play without the walls, but only the great foote balle'.

It seems that the 'great foote balle' continued to enjoy popularity in England during the next century, despite the vigorous efforts of authority to discourage it; but if it was equally popular in Ireland, those who ruled continued to tolerate it, either because they did not know how wide the practice was, or because they saw fit to ignore it.

By the middle of the seventeenth century, there is evidence that a football match was played in the Slane area of County Meath. In a poem written by Séamus Dall Mac Cuarta (1647–1732) he described a match played on the south bank of the Boyne in the townland of Fennor. The poem, entitled 'Imirt na Boinne', suggests that the author was present when his side from the Boyne Valley defeated a team from the area south of the town of Drogheda. It is of more than passing interest to note that carrying the ball was one feature of the play.

John Dunton, an Englishman who found Ireland a good source of material for his literary works, described football in the later years of the seventeenth century in Ireland as being played only in the small territory called Fingal, near Dublin. Dunton came to Ireland in 1698 and apparently travelled quite extensively. His *Conversation in Ireland*, in which his account of football appears, was published in 1699. He recorded that the players of Fingal 'tripped and shouldered very handsomely'. But he also drew the conclusion that even the best of the participants would not come off well if pitted against the exponents who operated in Moorfields, London, a sporting arena of no small consequence. Later references confirm that football was indeed played in the area of Fingal but, unlike the present day when sporting events are fully chronicled by the press, not many writers saw sufficient romance in sport to deem it worthy of their attention either in prose or verse.

There is evidence that football was played on quite a large scale in Ireland throughout the eighteenth century. One intriguing example of this is a poem written in 1780 by Edward Lysaght (1763–1810) in which he describes football as he saw it played in College Park. The pitch was presumably situated on the strip of ground that lies adjacent to Nassau Street. Lysaght's treatment of his theme is very revealing. He suggests that the wealthy refrained from indulging in such pursuits as football, a comment that supports the contention of a succession of historians that football was frowned upon by the aristocracy in Ireland as well as across the channel.

Lysaght was an interesting character. Born at Bird-Mill, County Clare, he was the son of John Lysaght, who was related to the noble family of Lisle. His mother was a cousin of Lord Eyre of Eyrecourt, County Galway. By his genealogy he would certainly be regarded as one of the gentry. His father died when Edward was young and the family fell into straitened circumstances. Lysaght entered Trinity in 1779. In 1784 he enrolled at the Inner Temple as a law student. He was also a student at St Edmund's Hall, Oxford, where he took his MA. He was subsequently called to the English Bar before returning to Ireland. In Ireland, Lysaght was also called to the Bar and went on the Munster Circuit. He was very active in the Volunteer organisation, and used his considerable talents as orator and writer to assist the movement. He wrote a large number of poems and songs, his best known work being 'The Man who led the Volunteers'. He is also credited with the authorship of 'The Rakes of Mallow' and 'Kitty of Coleraine'. The circumstances which led to the poem about football throw an interesting sidelight on the general attitude towards the game in 1780.

In Trinity in Lysaght's student days fellow commoners thought that they were superior beings to pensioners. Every evening the pensioners played football in College Park. The fellow commoners were above taking part in such vulgar pursuits. A pensioner, whose name, according to the conventions of eighteenth-century satirical verse, appears semi-disguised as 'C-lf-rd', was vain enough to associate entirely with fellow commoners and never played football until one evening he accidentally deigned to do so. Scarcely had he made his attempt on the field when some of his fellow students, indignant at his past folly, tripped up his heels, to the no small gratification of the assemblage present and much to the mortification of the unfortunate C-lf-rd. That night Lysaght wrote a short poem called 'Impromptu', a copy of which appeared in every student's letterbox the next morning. The poem read:

Dear C-lf-rd play football no more I entreat;
The amusement's too vulgar, fatiguing and rough;
Pursue the conduct you followed of late;
And I warrant, ere long, you'll get kicking enough.

References to sport in Ireland became much more frequent in the press of the nineteenth century, and although the amount of space and detail devoted to football was very small, it is enough to show that it was played in various forms throughout the country, though we cannot be absolutely specific about any of these forms. The inter-parish game played across fields and in the open country was in all probability the most common form. Here we are reminded of Ellis and the question of whether he was influenced by what he might just possibly have seen in the Tipperary area.

One of the games most popular in south Munster and especially in the Kerry area was *cad*. Thanks to the work of the Rev. Liam Ferris, parish priest of Ballylongford, County Kerry, until his death in 1972, we can be fairly specific about its rules, the type of ball used, and other details.

Fr Ferris wrote a treatise on the game and carried out wide research into its origins. A letter written by him on the subject which appeared in *The Irish Times* on 23 January 1968 is worth reproducing in full.

THE GAME OF CAD

Sir,

The carrying ball game called Cad was played by all branches of the Celtic race; Gaelic, British, Welsh, Cornish and Gallic. Cad was thus far more extensive and by millennia more ancient than hurling, which was confined to the Gaels of Ireland and Scotland.

There are two varieties of Cad; Cross-country Cad (Interparish) and Field Cad (definite space and number of players).

Dineen's dictionary quotes Ballyferriter as retaining the expression '*ag imirt Caid*' for 'playing football'.

In Britain during the eighteenth century the carrying game of Cad was dropped through the influence of half a dozen great public schools, including Rugby. It was replaced by the kicking game, later called soccer, whose rules were definitely formulated by the Football Association in 1867.

In Ireland, however, up to 1885, there was not even a whisper against the carrying game of Cad. Not only so, but Cad was re-introduced into Britain through Irish influence. An English boy, William Webb Ellis, learned the game from his cousins in Tipperary and by running with the ball restarted it at Rugby School in 1823.

His action was later called 'inspired insubordination' and the old game of Cad was once more re-established within the decade, though the Rugby Union was founded only in 1871. The word Cad means the scrotum of the bull, the bag containing its testicles. With extraordinary tenacity, the Rugby Union has retained the shape.

The GAA was established in 1884, but it was only in the following year that the

> Clareman, Cusack, introduced the kicking game which he called 'Gaelic'. It merely modified the soccer rules of 1867 slightly by allowing the use of the hands.
>
> With the powerful new organisation at his back, Cusack, by the stroke of a pen, killed the thousand-year-old game of Cad. It was not quite dead, however, but it gave what was probably its last gasp in Castleisland three years later in 1888 in a match between the two out-parishes of Cordal and Scartaglen.
>
> Cusack's kicking game may be the wonderful thing which through powerful propaganda it is alleged to be. But to call the kicking game 'Gaelic' pretending thereby that it is traditional football, is nothing but the veriest impudence, paralleled only by Whateley's calling his primary school national.
>
> Irish traditional football is Cad, now improperly called 'Rugby'. It would be a gracious act for the GAA to admit an error which has lasted only a lifetime and to restore the national game of Cad once more to its position of honour.

After writing the letter Fr Ferris said that he, like many others, was relying on hearsay when he pointed out that Ellis had learned the game of cad from his cousins in Tipperary.

Yet it is worth taking a more detailed look at the game of cad, for certainly there were marked similarities between it and rugby football. The outer case of the ball was inflated by a natural bladder so that its shape was not round, but elongated in the manner of the later rugby ball. The cross-country version of the game was usually played between parishes, with the issue often apparently being disputed in a day-long duel, the object of the exercise apparently being to take the ball home. The field version was much more akin to rugby, and in this, trees bent in the shape of an arch were used as goals. Fr Ferris even discovered a very old man from the south Kerry area who clearly remembered having seen the game played and who actually claimed to have taken part in the game himself when a youth.

It is by no means impossible that Irish boys attending English public schools brought back to Ireland something of what they had seen and learned on the sports fields of their academies, and that the games they introduced in vestigial form evolved into what we know today as rugby football. Time has, however, kept most of its secrets about the absolute origins of football in Ireland and elsewhere. But we do know that football had been played in Ireland for many hundreds of years before the beginning of the nineteenth century. We also know that it incorporated carrying and running with the ball. Could those Irish boys have brought with them to their English schools something of what they had seen and played while at home?

CHAPTER 3

TRINITY LEADS THE WAY: 1854–74

DUBLIN IN THE 1850s presented a face very different to that of the thriving, bustling city we know today. It is possible, with the aid of old drawings, photographs and maps, to re-create an impression of the city as it appeared in the early days of what has sometimes been called the Grand Victorian era. But there are still tangible reminders of the past, and a careful inspection of the vicinity of Trinity College reveals the sharp contrast of the multi-storey office blocks side by side with houses that still display all the elegance of Georgian architecture at its most perfect. Trinity College itself is a place of contrasts, the intermingling of the old and the new, in its buildings and in its character. It was here, in the year 1854, that the earliest recorded Irish rugby club was founded.

GRAFTON STREET IN THE NINETEENTH CENTURY

The Trinity club's foundation date of 1854 makes it the second oldest rugby club in the world: only Guy's Hospital can claim seniority. For reasons that are difficult to explain, one seldom finds acknowledgment in rugby reference books to Trinity's true year of origin.

Football traditions in Trinity, of course, go back far beyond 1854, a point made clear by Edward Lysaght's poem. As in Lysaght's time, the sporting scene in Trinity in the middle of the nineteenth century was largely influenced by Irish boys returning from English public schools. As is pointed out in the centennial history of the club published in 1954 — an event incidentally in which the centrepiece of the celebrations was appropriately a match against Blackheath, a founder member of the Rugby Union in 1871 and a leading influence — several of the early members of the Trinity club had been entered at the college some years before the club was officially formed. The earliest known members of the club included many from Cheltenham and Rugby schools and the first three listed all entered Trinity in 1848, six years before the club was formed. W. Stackpool and E. Lloyd were both Cheltenham boys, while E. S. Forester was educated at Mr Ryder's School.

The first public reference to the existence of a club in Trinity is, according to the records, a notice which appeared in the Dublin *Daily Express* on Saturday, 1 December 1855, to the effect that a game would take place that day at two o'clock between original and new members of the club. It was signed by Robert Henry Scott, the new club's first officer. Scott, born in Dublin in 1833, was, significantly, an Old Rugbeian. He entered Trinity in 1851, became a classical scholar in 1853 and First Moderator in Experimental Physics in 1855. He held the joint offices of honorary secretary and treasurer until 1856.

As is perhaps indicated by the teams selected to play in the match of December 1855, one of the club's main initial difficulties was in finding opponents, and for several years the members had to be content to play games organised within the college with Freshmen taking on the Rest; those with initials 'A' to 'M' facing those that remained; the Football Club v the Boat Club (a fixture which survived until 1874); Rugby and Cheltenham boys v The Rest; and English-educated boys v Irish-educated boys.

The first record of a match against outside opposition, if outside it can be called, is of a match against the 'Wanderers' in 1860. Those Wanderers were not the club that bears that name today, though they, like Trinity, can claim a record that goes back over a hundred years, having been founded in 1869. The Wanderers of 1860 were apparently a collection of former students of Trinity. It is worth noting, too, that the Wanderers formed in 1869–70 had a decidedly Trinity influence as well. The connection between the two Wanderers must, however, be left in the realms of speculation and imagination.

Charles Barrington

The match was, at any rate, deemed worthy of an advertisement in the press of the day. The *Dublin Evening Packet* of 27 November 1860 carried a notice signed by Anthony Traill, honorary secretary of the Trinity club, and *The Irish Times* of 6 December 1860 carried a report of the match, stating that darkness called a halt to the proceedings and that the game would be resumed on the following day.

The honorary secretary must have been a powerful figure in those distant days, for it was not until 1863–64 that Trinity elected a captain; to Richard Traill goes the distinction of being the first holder of that office. He led the club until 1864–65 and was succeeded by A. M. Dobbs, who also held the office for two seasons, and then A. F. Graves who was captain in 1866–67.

The next man to lead Trinity was Charles Barrington who was in control in 1867–68. His influence was to stretch far beyond the confines of the close circle around which the club's affairs revolved. Barrington was a member of a distinguished Irish family, whose old residence, Glenstal Abbey, just outside Limerick city, is now a rugby academy of some standing. Barrington, later Sir Charles, died on 12 August 1943 in Botley, near Southampton, at the age of 95. His maternal uncle, Charlie West, is believed to have been the person on whom Thomas Hughes based the character East in *Tom Brown's Schooldays*, and Barrington had himself also been a pupil at Rugby School.

Barrington was captain of Trinity for three years, with Richard M. Wall, honorary secretary since 1865–66, continuing in that post when Barrington took over the leadership on the field. Barrington was obviously a man of administrative as well as playing ability; together with Wall, he drew up a set of laws that bore many similarities to those Blackheath — one of the founding clubs of the Rugby Union — had drafted in 1863. In a letter written in 1931 to Dr Edward Watson, a Trinity stalwart to the day he died in 1947, Barrington vividly recalled working on the laws with Wall in 1867, though they were not, of course, presented until the annual general meeting of the club in October 1868. Needless to say they were passed.

Barrington's arrival at Trinity coincided with a general expansion and reorganisation of the club. There was a big increase in the membership and a second XV was formed. With the arrogance that comes from a superiority that is total, Trinity decided that any team that wished to play their First XV must first prove their worth by defeating their second string. In 1867 the Seconds played St Columba's College, which still maintains a thriving rugby tradition, with enthusiastic participation in the Leinster Schools Cups to this day. Hume Street School and Dungannon School also played Trinity Seconds in this period, so rugby had spread its net to Ulster, and within a short period to points south and west as well.

The reorganisation of the Trinity club in 1867–68 ensured that proper records were kept from the year 1867. It was in 1868 that the club colours of red and black were officially adopted and they still survive. Honours caps were first awarded in 1868, an innovation that was, apparently, also decided at that momentous meeting at which the rules were passed. The caps were red and black, quartered, with a gold shamrock embroidered on the front. Opponents for these stylishly equipped players were, unfortunately, still hard to find.

Rugby football was beginning to spread in Ireland and the laws passed at that meeting in 1868 had important repercussions on the expansion of the game within the next six years. Clubs began to emerge that were to contribute handsomely to Irish rugby; indeed, many of them are still contributing over a century later.

Wanderers (1869) had their motivating force in Richard Milliken Peter, later to play an important role in the setting up of the first administrative body in Ireland. Other clubs formed at about this time include Lansdowne (1872), variously known as the Irish Champion Athletic Club and Lansdowne Road, Dungannon (1873), and Queen's College, Cork (1874). But it is possible that UCC may be denying themselves seniority, for recently a printed copy of the Rugby Football Laws as played in Queen's College, Cork, in 1872 came to light. Carlow (1873) and Ballinasloe (1875) are still prospering, and Cork FC and Cork Bankers made a significant contribution before time took its toll of them, as it did of several others such as Arlington, Phoenix, Engineers, Monaghan, Scott's Military Academy, Merrion, Kingstown, Kingstown School and Bray.

'The Pioneers', Dublin University 1866

The Jesuit colleges of Belvedere and Clongowes Wood had their own set of laws in those early days; latterly they follow those laid down by the ruling body. Tullabeg College, near Tullamore, the sister college of Clongowes with which it was amalgamated in 1886, also played football. Football was the winter game in Tullamore until the canal froze, whereupon skating took over. The type of football played in Tullabeg and Clongowes until 1890 was neither rugby nor soccer: it was a game which resembled the field cad referred to by Fr Ferris in his letter to *The Irish Times*. The game was played under what are variously called the 'Jesuit rules' or the 'Catholic College rules'. Another early starter was Portora Royal School, near Enniskillen, County Fermanagh, and this school sent out and is still sending out some of Ireland's finest rugby players.

At the time the Barrington laws were introduced, rugby in the Belfast area was non-existent, but cricket was a thriving sport, and nowhere more so than in the North of Ireland Cricket Club, which had been formed in 1859. At this period Mr John Lawrence operated as a well-known supplier of sports equipment in Grafton Street, Dublin. He was also a keen sports enthusiast and annually produced a handbook on cricket. Lawrence quickly recognised how rugby football was spreading and reproduced 'The Laws of Foot Ball as played at Trinity College, Dublin' in his handbook, which was avidly read and digested by members of the North of Ireland Cricket Club.

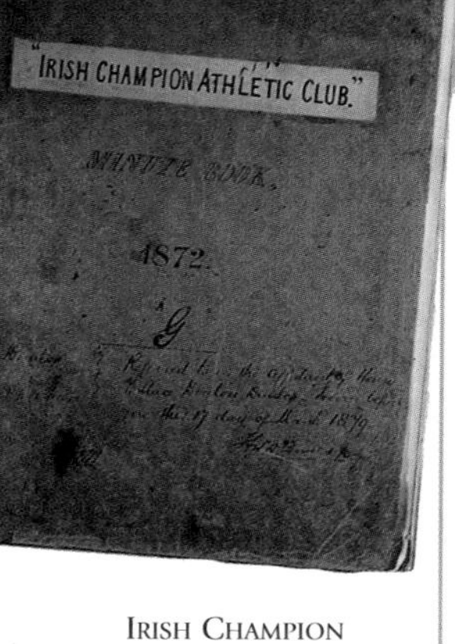

Irish Champion Athletic Club minute book

That handbook and the boys coming home to Belfast from the English public schools were profound influences in the Belfast area and, in particular, rugby in and around the North of Ireland Cricket Club's ground at Ormeau. To those influences could be added yet another, E. H. Moeran, a cricketer of repute but also a rugby enthusiast, who was willing and able to inspire others with his love of the game. The fact that a rugby section of the North of Ireland Cricket Club was formed in the autumn of 1868 is not without significance. At the time, several of the cricketers objected strongly to this invasion, but their objections were brushed aside as this extract from the *Belfast News-Letter* of 27 November 1868 reveals.

The North of Ireland Foot Ball Club

> The idea of establishing this club originated a short time ago with some members of the North of Ireland Cricket Club, who had been at English schools and who knew and appreciated the game. Great difficulties lay in their way. Few in this part of the world had ever seen the rugby game played, still fewer had ever played it. After some hesitation the consent of the North of Ireland Cricket Club was gained to permit the erection of goals on the lower part of their ground and about a month and a half ago the North of Ireland Foot Ball Club played its first practice match. Since that time many new members have been enrolled.
>
> Saturday is the club match day and the following have been elected to form a committee: P. M. Dudgeon, R. H. Orr, J. T. Reade, J. M. Sinclair, and E. H. Moeran, honorary secretary and treasurer.

Moeran was to North, the name by which the club is known throughout the rugby world, what Barrington was to Trinity, and the fact that he was a leading bowler with the cricket club no doubt gave him the influence and the standing needed to propagate the rugby cause.

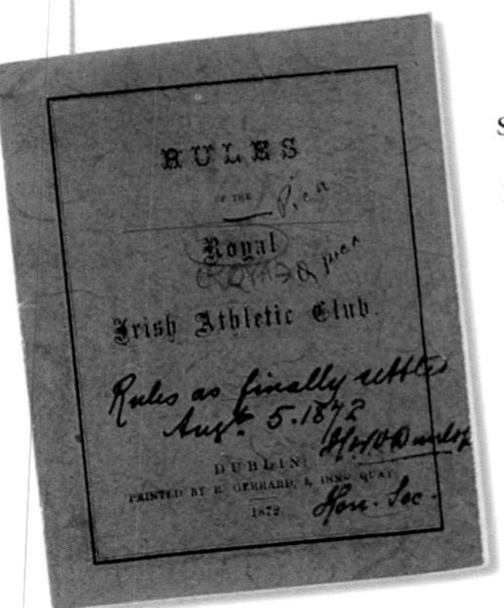

Athletic Club rule book

Like Trinity, North found it difficult to find opposition, but, unlike Trinity, did not impose such qualifications as beating the Second XV before getting a match against the First XV. The formation of a rugby club in Queen's University in the autumn of 1869 gave North their first outside opposition, and on 16 January of the following year the clubs met for the first time at Ormeau. The match apparently went on for three days, Queen's fielding eighteen players to North's thirteen, which probably accounted for the fact that Queen's got the first score, McIllreavy getting a try and J. M. Sinclair converting. That try, however, was a long time coming, for it did not occur until the second day of the match, which was not until 23 January. Queen's finished that afternoon leading by a goal to nil. Hostilities were resumed a week later and the account in the *Belfast News-Letter* of 1 February does not tell all, but it reveals much.

> The match was finished on Saturday last, the third day of play. The club [North] won the toss and selected the upper goal, the wind being in their favour. At the end of the first half hour the club had obtained two points and the sides changed goals. The College then pressed their opponents more vigorously making five points in succession. Shortly before four o'clock, Mr W. Bottomley succeeded in obtaining a touch down for College and Mr Sinclair secured a goal by a well directed kick. The College had made a goal on the previous Saturday, and as their opponents had made none, victory was theirs.

The indications are that the laws as practised in Belfast were not exactly orthodox even for those times, but it was a good start.

In the next few years the shortage of opponents was acute, but interest was maintained and more players were learning the game. Eventually North looked outside the Belfast area for opposition and readily found it in Dublin and Scotland in the 1871–72 season. In the interim North fulfilled fixtures with Queen's University and the Royal Schools at Dungannon and Armagh.

On 16 December 1871, North and Trinity met for the first time. The match was fifteen a side and was played at Ormeau. Trinity won by one goal and one touch down to nil. A week later the first match between Scottish and Irish clubs took place when North entertained West of Scotland and lost by a goal to nil. By 1873–74 North had embarked on a Scottish tour, during which they lost to Glasgow Academicals. By this time the game had spread to the RA Institution and Methodist College in Belfast, where masters were included in the school team. Meanwhile Trinity had opened their fixture list to more than North, for in 1873–74 they travelled to the Dingle Club, Liverpool, where they drew the game. All these connections with England and Scotland which were being established by Trinity and North were to have beneficial results in the near future.

The game was spreading in Dublin and Belfast and to points south and west, but it was not until 1875–76 that Wanderers had earned the right to meet Trinity's First XV. In the north the establishment of clubs such as Windsor, Ulster, Belmont, Lisburn and Albion, all now defunct, helped in no small way to establish the rugby traditions of the province of Ulster where, undoubtedly, North made the biggest contribution of all.

CHAPTER 4

TWO UNIONS: 1874–75

OUR STORY HAS BROUGHT US ONCE AGAIN to that fateful day, 15 February 1875, when Ireland for the first time put an international rugby team in the field. The season of 1874–75 was the most significant in the history of the game in Ireland, for it saw the formation of the Irish Football Union, the game's first administrative body in this country. It is interesting to note that this momentous development was brought about as a direct result of pressure from England.

England and Scotland had been engaged in the field of international combat since 1871. It was therefore only natural that with two clubs of the calibre of Trinity and North, both of whom had sampled the delights of cross-channel football, the thought should cross the minds of their officials that Ireland too should be represented in the international arena. In 1873–74 Trinity made valiant attempts to arrange a match against England, but the principal stumbling block was England's objection to the fact that there was no national administrative body in Ireland.

27 Trinity College

Following the annual general meeting of the Trinity club in October 1874, it was decided to call a meeting of the 'principal clubs' with a view to forming an executive. It was even announced after the Trinity annual general meeting that an international between England and Ireland would 'very probably be played' in London in the not too distant future. With the Trinity influence so strong among such 'principal clubs' as Wanderers and Lansdowne, there was no difficulty in making the arrangements for the gathering and it took place, according to the *Irish Sportsman and Farmer* of 12 December 1874, at 1.30 p.m. on the afternoon of 7 December in the rooms of George Stack at No. 27 Trinity College.

A great deal of rubbish has been written and spoken about that meeting. The lack of any surviving minutes probably accounts for the accretions of myth and legend that have been perpetuated about it — an unfortunate characteristic of much of the early history of Irish rugby.

The assembly that gathered in Stack's rooms consisted of Messrs Barlow (in the chair), Stack, Peter, Casement, Walsh, Neill, Malet, Ogilby and Robinson. Many of these men played a major part in subsequent developments. Richard Milliken Peter probably emerges as the key figure in the early days of Irish rugby administration, though he was later to

George Hall Stack, the first Irish captain

sever his connections with the game and to depart under a cloud. He was a clerk in the offices of the Commissioners of Church Temporalities in Ireland and in addition to being a skilful and enthusiastic rugby player, he was also a leading figure on the rowing, yachting and swimming scenes in Ireland.

The match against England was discussed and Saturday, 6 February, and Monday, 8 February, were suggested as possible dates for the game but, significantly, it was decreed that 'no firm decision could be taken until an executive was formed'. It was, however, decided that this task would take place one week later at John Lawrence's rooms at 39 Grafton Street.

Wanderers certainly took due note and they called a meeting for Thursday, 10 December, and appointed Messrs Peter and Barlow as their representatives. They duly took their places in Lawrence's rooms at 3.30 p.m. on the afternoon of Monday, 14 December 1874. So too did others. George Hall Stack represented Trinity, and he was joined by Richard Galbraith. Engineers were represented by H. D. Walsh and D. Neill, and they were joined by J. D. Ogilby and G. Burke (Lansdowne), H. Adams and W. H. Wilson (Bray), C. Murphy and E. Galbraith (Portora), W. Smyth and W. Beatty (Dungannon), and A. P. Cronyn and J. Cronyn (Monaghan).

As befitted the status of the captain of Trinity, Stack was in the chair. Peter was elected honorary treasurer and Walsh took over the onerous duties of honorary secretary. A working committee of five members was elected to carry out the day-to-day chores connected with arranging the match against England, which had been the specific purpose in calling the meeting. Messrs Stack, Barlow, E. Galbraith, R. Galbraith and A. P. Cronyn were elected to this committee.

It was decided that the administrative body should be called the Irish Football Union and that all clubs adhering to the rugby code should be invited to join. An immediate recruit was the Kingstown club, though they were not represented at the inaugural meeting. It must be added, too, that Trinity had a more than adequate representation, for several of those who were there in the interests of other clubs and paid their £1 entrance fee could be said to have had a dual commitment. Notable among these were Edgar Galbraith, Arthur Cronyn, who spread his talents around liberally, and Walsh. All three were included in the first Irish team as representatives of Trinity.

Shortly after the establishment of the IFU, a circular was issued stating the aims of the new body and announcing, in a clever example of persuasive democracy: 'The meetings of the IFU are at present held in the metropolis, but this arrangement, it is hoped, will in future years be exchanged if provincial clubs so desire, for some other plan which will enable them to make their wishes better understood and more effectively carried out.'

The formation of the IFU was not exactly greeted with euphoria in the corridors at Ormeau, or so we are told by the leading rugby journalist of the day, one Jacques McCarthy. McCarthy was a man of wit and wisdom; he was also, alas, too often indebted to his memory for his 'facts' and to his prejudices for his jests. Certainly his assertions about the game in the early days do not stand up to historical investigation, not least with regard to the administrative set-up.

In 1892 a Church of England clergyman, the Rev. Frank Marshall, produced a monumental work on rugby entitled *Football, the Rugby Union Game*. Marshall's book was for long accepted as the authoritative source on the early years of the game. It must be pointed out, however, that the chapter on Ireland, written by McCarthy, is largely responsible for the many inaccuracies about the early history of Irish rugby. It is surprising, too, that many who have down the years poured scorn on McCarthy's accuracy, or rather his lack of it, have, none the less, slavishly followed his opinions and accepted them as fact wherever it has been convenient to do so.

McCarthy's conclusion that rugby administration in Ireland began with a split is probably the most widely repeated of all the myths about Irish rugby. Two unions there certainly were in the early days; but a split there was not.

It is not the intention to take McCarthy's assertions here and attempt to disprove them one by one, but we must briefly examine McCarthy's version of the story of how the Northern Football Union of Ireland came into being on 13 January 1875.

In his account in Marshall's book, McCarthy suggests that after Wanderers and North had met in a match at Ormeau on 28 November 1874, 'a dreadful row arose when North won the game and questioned the right of those in Dublin to form an "Irish Football Union" without first consulting Belfast. They had shown that day they were the better footballers and furthermore had more money and more enthusiasm.'

If that row arose, then North were a little ahead of their time, for the actual foundation of the IFU was still a fortnight away. Furthermore, an account of the match appearing in the *Irish Sportsman and Farmer* on 5 December states that Wanderers were 'most hospitably received'. In retrospect that phrase has a lot of significance.

So much for McCarthy's story and for the one subsequently written by J. W. Whitehead in the 1925 edition of Marshall, which basically follows the McCarthy line, even asserting that the North members 'there and then formed their own union'.

That they did not do. Certainly the rugby fraternity in Belfast, and the North club in particular, did not take kindly to Dublin running the show, but the notice convening the inaugural meeting of the Northern Football Union of Ireland was more placatory than recriminatory. It read:

> The lovers of football in Belfast and neighbourhood have under consideration what steps should be taken with regard to the success of the Irish Football Union and the establishment of annual international matches between three kingdoms. It has been decided to call a meeting for 13 January to see what course should be adopted.

The *Belfast News-Letter* of 14 January 1875 records what steps were decided upon; in that edition the following report appeared.

NORTHERN FOOTBALL UNION OF IRELAND

> At a meeting largely attended by representatives of the various clubs in this district in the Linen Hall Hotel last evening, Mr Combe, captain of North of Ireland Football Club in the chair, it was resolved, on the motion of Mr Heron, seconded by Mr McDonald that, in order to secure a proper representation of Northern clubs, and in general to support and encourage the game, a union for this district be formed, to be named the 'Northern Football Union of Ireland'. It was also decided on the proposal of Mr Shaw, seconded by Mr Cochrane, that the question of Northern clubs competing in the coming international match to be played in London early in the year, be left to the working committee of the Northern Union to confer with the Irish Union in Dublin and to report to a further meeting.

That notice does not tell all about the circumstances and events surrounding the formation of the union in Belfast, but it effectively kills many legends. The most notorious of these is the suggestion that Ulster saw itself as a rival body to the Dublin administrators. Nor does the report bear out the ridiculous contention that anything other than full support would be given to the Dublin initiative for the match against England. Such 'facts' belong more to the faulty memory and fertile imagination of Jacques McCarthy than to the annals of rugby history.

There may indeed have been a row after Wanderers visited North in November. Perhaps in the heat of the moment the North players decided to form their own union. But they obviously had second thoughts on the whole matter, not least because, out of consideration for the other clubs in the Belfast area, they were scarcely justified in going it alone; and, furthermore, an Irish team was going on to the field and North wanted to be represented on it.

THE FIRST PRESIDENT 1874–76, THE DUKE OF ABERCORN

On 12 January 1875, the eve of the big Belfast meeting, a working committee of the IFU convened at No. 8 Trinity College. The earliest extant minutes of the union date from this meeting. It is recorded that Edgar Galbraith laid before the committee a letter to the effect that the Lord Lieutenant of Ireland, the Duke of Abercorn, had agreed to become president of the union. Such matters as the jerseys to be worn by the Irish team and the printing of a circular were also discussed.

Meanwhile Peter, at the instigation of the committee, had already sent out another circular appealing for funds, and the *Freeman's Journal* of 30 December 1874 took up the cry from the heart. In a leading article it commended the proposed international match to its readers. 'We anticipate with pleasure the future encounters of our Irish youths with their compeers of the sister countries', stated the article, which ended by appealing to 'the practical sympathy of their fellow countrymen of all shades and degrees'. The combined efforts of Peter and the *Freeman's Journal* no doubt had a big bearing on the fact that £30 was raised by public subscription. This money went a long way towards sending the first Irish twenty to London.

Jacques McCarthy in his account of how the first Irish team was picked claims that it was agreed that each union would nominate ten men, thus ensuring an even balance. That, in fact, was not at all how the first Irish team was selected.

On 22 January a meeting of the IFU was held at which was read a letter from A. G. Guillemard, honorary secretary of the Rugby Union, confirming that the match against England would be played at Kennington Oval on Monday, 15 February 1875. George Stack then proposed that:

> In order to guarantee that the Northern clubs' interests would be duly regarded in the selection of the international twenty, that the Irish Union shall nominate seven men to play on the twenty, and the Northern Union a like number and that each Union would then submit the names of ten further players each from which the remaining six players would be chosen.

The Northern Union accepted the proposal with a slight amendment: for some obscure reason they proposed that each union would submit the names of eleven players from which the remaining six players would be chosen to complete the team. The Northern Union enclosed the names of their selected seven, but Stack, obviously a man of character as well as scholarship, would not allow the names of the seven northern players to be read at a meeting of the IFU on 3 February until after the IFU had chosen their seven.

Stack himself was one of the seven selected by the IFU. Joining him were W. Smyth, M. Barlow, E. Galbraith, A. P. Cronyn, F. Hewson and R. Galbraith. It is interesting to record that all but Smyth did in fact line out at the Oval. By a strange coincidence six of the north's original selections also played: R. Walkington, R. Bell, W. Ash, A. Combe, J. MacDonald and W. Gaffikin. The odd man out was G. Shaw. After the seven southern players had been chosen, B. Casement, H. Robinson, H. D. Walsh, J. Magennis, J. Shannon, H. Adams, R. Greer, J. Myles, J. Allen and A. W. Cuscadden were nominated for further consideration, the IFU here waiving its right to submit a total of eleven names. The remaining six places on the team would be picked by a subcommittee of six, three from each union, and Stack, Peter and R. Galbraith were chosen to represent Dublin interests when the team was finalised in London.

Myles, Allen, Casement, Magennis and Walsh eventually made the team, as did H. Cox of Trinity, which meant that the IFU eventually had twelve men on the field at the Oval, of whom no fewer than nine were from Trinity College. Wanderers had three representatives in M. Barlow, J. Allen and H. Hewson, NIFC had six representatives, Windsor one, and Methodist College one. It is not recorded how this balance eventually materialised.

To Stack went the honour of being Ireland's first captain — and a richly deserved distinction for the man who had been one of the leading figures in setting up the match and who was not averse to putting his hand into his pocket to support the cause in practical terms. Stack, as well as being a man of means and a footballer of considerable skill, was also well endowed intellectually. He took his MA in 1875, having entered Trinity in 1870 after being educated in Raphoe, County Donegal. He was, sadly, not destined to live long enough to see more organised Irish teams in the field, for he died unexpectedly and apparently under tragic circumstances in November 1876.

The First Irish 'Twenty' who played England at The Oval in Kennington, Monday, 15 February, 1875

Whatever fate was to befall him two years later, he was in vigorous good health when he led his side out at the Oval. The Irishmen were attired that day in green and white-hooped jerseys, white knickerbockers and green and white-hooped stockings. Jacques McCarthy, however, was not impressed by the display of his fellow countrymen. 'What an enterprise and what a twenty,' he wrote. 'They had never previously seen each other. H. L. Robinson and the celebrated "Darky" Smyth, the two best backs in Dublin University, were absentees, although their names were on the cards sold about the Oval.' One must wonder about McCarthy's assertion once more, for while Smyth was an original selection for the game, Robinson was not deemed worthy of being named among the seven first choices by the IFU. But dignity in defeat was not one of McCarthy's characteristics, a fact made very clear in many of his subsequent offerings on Ireland's early efforts in the field of international competition.

England won the game by two goals and a try to nil, and contemporary reports suggest that the defeat could in large part be attributed to a complete inability to match the England teamwork, an understandable situation when one considers that England had the benefit of three games against Scotland. The Irish kicking was, apparently, very bad as well. McCarthy's sweeping condemnation was not, however, re-echoed in other publications such as *Bell's Life*, the *News-Letter*, *The Irish Times* and the *Freeman's Journal.*

A certain A. T. Mitchell was, apparently, the scourge of the Irish. It was he who scored the first try, an effort that was not converted, for, as the *Freeman's Journal* reported, the try was 'almost on the touchline and the place by Fraser failed'.

England led by that try at half-time and immediately after the interval laid siege to the Irish line, forcing the Irish to touch down four times in succession, before A. Cronyn, who was apparently one of the Irish heroes of the day, made a dashing run towards the England line. But Nash then dropped a goal for England, and that was followed by a try from Cheston to which Pearson added the goal points.

That evening the Irish players were entertained to dinner by the Rugby Union at St James's Hall. The *News-Letter* records that though Ireland lost, they 'won the respect of the conquerors'.

The assessment of the game as given in *Bell's Life* was that Bell, Cronyn and Galbraith (though it did not specify which of the Galbraiths) had all tackled well but, added the commentator, 'Ireland has much to learn in the matter of tactics and play. However, we have no doubt that when an English twenty first plays in the Emerald Isle, a wonderful improvement in the form shown on Monday will be evident to all.'

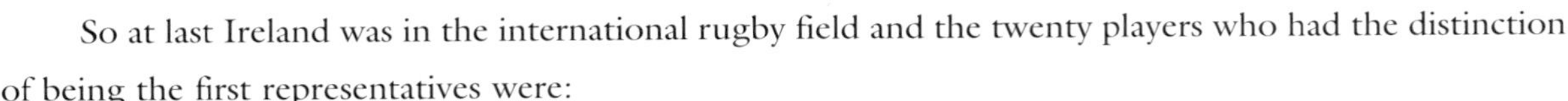

So at last Ireland was in the international rugby field and the twenty players who had the distinction of being the first representatives were:

Backs:

E. Galbraith (Dublin University)
R. B. Walkington (NIFC)

Threequarter backs:

E. McIlwaine (NIFC)
R. Galbraith (Dublin University)

Half-backs:

A. P. Cronyn (Dublin University)
G. H. Stack (Dublin University) Capt.
R. Bell (NIFC)

Forwards:

J. Allen (Wanderers)
G. Andrews (NIFC)
W. Ash (NIFC)
M. Barlow (Wanderers)
B. Casement (Dublin University)
A. Combe (NIFC)
W. Gaffikin (Windsor)
J. Myles (Dublin University)
H. L. Cox (Dublin University)
F. T. Hewson (Wanderers)
J. MacDonald (Methodist College)
J. Magennis (Dublin University)
H. D. Walsh (Dublin University)

Many of these men were playing out of position, but in those days this was not a rare occurrence.

The first international out of the way, the IFU and the Northern Football Union turned their attention to other things. The IFU began thinking about arranging a return match in Dublin, while the Northern Union tried to organise a match against a team from Dublin. Their invitation was rejected at a meeting of the IFU on 3 March, a meeting incidentally at which the first Munster club became affiliated to the Dublin body, the honour of this seniority going to the Rathkeale club.

Within a short time two other teams came into the union, Arlington and Scott's Military Academy. In the interest of accuracy it must be pointed out that the inclusion of Rathkeale, Scott's Academy and Arlington in the list of founder-members in the 1892 edition of Marshall is erroneous. The minutes of the general meeting of the IFU held on 19 March 1875 clearly state that as 'Rathkeale, Arlington and Scott's Academy had all joined the union so late in the year, their subscriptions be considered their subscriptions for the following season'.

The minutes of that meeting also record that when everything was paid, the union showed a credit balance for the year of £2 1*s.* 3*d.*, not a bad performance when one considers that it had necessitated public subscription to send the Irish twenty to the Oval.

The working committee for the 1875–76 season was also elected: Walsh was again honorary secretary and Peter honorary treasurer, with Stack and Richard Galbraith completing the line-up. It was decided, however, that this committee would resign and a new one be elected at the beginning of the season 'should any important clubs join the union in the interim'. The necessity did not arise, but other happenings of some moment were at hand.

CHAPTER 5

A DUBLIN INITIATIVE: 1875–79

THE OFFICIALS OF THE IFU did not sit back and enjoy the sun during the summer months of 1875. They wanted a single controlling body for the whole country, and with that aim in view they sent the following proposals to the Northern Football Union.

1. That the annual meeting take place in rotation in the north (Belfast), in Dublin and in the south (suppose Limerick). The business of the meeting would be the election of officers and a working committee for the year.
2. That trial matches take place in each of the above-named places; and
3. That as a full attendance of the working committee on the occasion of the selection of the Irish team was desirable, that expenses of the various members be paid by the union.

Irish Football Union.

GRAND INTERNATIONAL MATCH.

IRELAND v. ENGLAND,

PLAYED AT THE

LEINSTER CRICKET GROUND, RATHMINES,

On **MONDAY, DECEMBER 13th, 1875.**

ENGLAND.

Backs.	
S. H. Login	Royal Naval College.
A. W. Pearson	Blackheath.
Three-quarter-backs.	
C. R. Gunner	Marlboro' Nomads.
A. J. Mitchell	Oxford University.
Half-backs.	
C. W. H. Clark	Liverpool.
W. E. Collins	Old Cheltonians.
Forwards.	
F. Luscombe, Captain	Gipsies.
J. Brewer	Gipsies.
C. C. Bryden	Clapham Rovers.
A. Bulteel	Manchester.
J. A. Bush	Clifton.
J. D. Graham	Wimbledon.
H. J. Graham	Wimbledon.
J. Green	Manchester.
W. H. H. Hutchinson	Hull.
E. Kewley	Liverpool.
E. E. Marriott	Manchester.
M. W. Marshall	Blackheath.
E. B. Turner	St. George's Hospital.
C. L. Verelst	Liverpool.

IRELAND.

Backs.	
H. Moore	Windsor.
R. Walkington	North of Ireland.
Three-quarter-backs.	
E. W. Hobson	Dublin University.
B. N. Casement	Wanderers.
Half-backs.	
A. P. Cronyn	Dublin University.
R. Bell, Captain	North of Ireland.
Forwards.	
D. T. Arnott	Lansdowne-Road.
W. Ash	North of Ireland.
C. Andrews	North of Ireland.
W. Cuscaden	Bray.
R. Galbraith	Dublin University.
R. Greer	Kingstown School.
H. L. Cox	Dublin University.
J. Ireland	Windsor.
J. Macdonald	Methodist College.
E. MacIlwaine	North of Ireland.
R. Maginniss	Dublin University.
W. Finley	North of Ireland.
H. D. Walsh	Dublin University.
G. J. Wentry	Dublin University.

PROGRAMME FOR IRELAND V ENGLAND, LEINSTER CRICKET GROUND, RATHMINES

The proposals did not meet with a ready response from Belfast, and Dick Bell, the honorary secretary of the Northern Football Union, informed Dublin that amalgamation for this season was not considered possible.

Meanwhile, England suggested 13 December as a likely date for the first international in Dublin, and at a meeting of the working committee of the IFU that proposal was accepted. The date of 13 December had also been suggested by Bell as the most suitable occasion for the first interprovincial match between Leinster and Ulster. Bell also suggested that a subcommittee consisting of five members from each union would pick the team to meet England following the interprovincial. This was accepted by Dublin with the proviso that the claims of Munster and Connacht players be also considered. This is, incidentally, the first reference to Connacht in the official records, though there is no record of any Connacht clubs being affiliated to the IFU at this time.

The interprovincial was fixed for 27 November at the Ormeau grounds. Now all that remained was to find a suitable venue in Dublin for the match against England. The IFU had originally turned to Trinity, but College Park was not deemed suitable so the net had to be cast wider. The Nine Acres at Phoenix Park was then proposed and for a time came under active consideration. Then Henry William Doveton Dunlop, honorary secretary of the Irish Champion Athletic Club, who was also a Trinity graduate and an athlete of repute, offered the Lansdowne Road ground, on which he had a lease from the Earl of Pembroke, but his letter of proposal was rejected out of hand on 5 November, in spite of Dunlop's persistent efforts to induce the committee to reconsider their decision. Lansdowne Road, it was claimed, was 'quite inadequate for an international rugby match'. Subsequent events were to give that decision a hollow ring.

The choice of venue for this historic occasion eventually fell on the Leinster Cricket Ground at Rathmines, and after negotiations the ground was secured at a rent of £10. Although Trinity had been unable to provide a ground, they came to the assistance with ropes, posts and a flag-pole. So now all was ready for the big day, even down to the booking of the Antient Concert Rooms for the after-match dinner at a cost of £5. There remained, however, the matter of the interprovincial and, even more important, the selection of the Irish team. Both events took place on the weekend of 27–29 November.

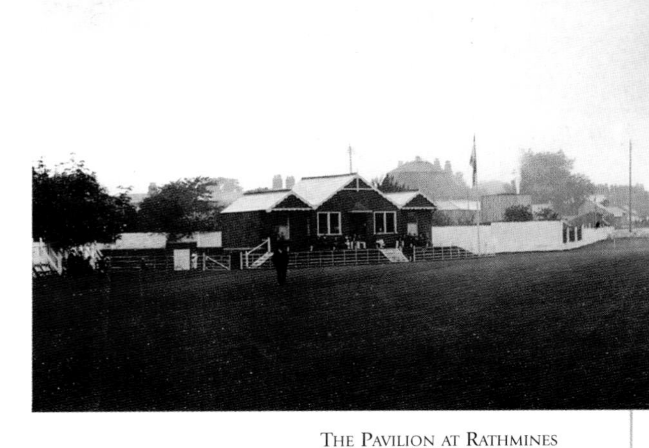

The Pavilion at Rathmines

Leinster and Ulster faced each other at Ormeau on Saturday, 27 November, and the fiercely held belief in Belfast that they were the superior football beings was borne out by the result: Ulster one goal, Leinster nil. Trinity supplied eleven of the Leinster twenty, Wanderers six, Lansdowne, Bray and Kingstown one each. The familiar names of Galbraith, Walsh, Cox, Casement and Barlow appeared in the Leinster team. A notable absentee was Stack, but the *News-Letter* recorded that Leinster also missed the services of Mr Cronyn ('one of Ireland's finest men behind the scrummage'), Mr Higginson, Mr O'Connor and Mr Wilson. Thus a built-in excuse was readily available to explain away defeat. For Ulster, the NIFC was represented by twelve players, Windsor seven and Methodist College one — a suitable commentary on where exactly the strength of Ulster rugby was vested. Ulster had seven of the players who had represented Ireland at the Oval in their team: Walkington, Bell, Ash, Andrews, McIlwaine, Gaffikin and MacDonald. A contemporary report rhapsodises: 'The morning broke beautifully and the day was one of the finest that could possibly be expected. It was just cold enough to make sealskin jackets and ulster coats comfortable.'

The Leinster Cricket Ground, Rathmines, the first home venue

A crowd of a thousand turned up at Ormeau, a record number for a match in Belfast according to the *News-Letter*, whose representative was much taken by the appearance of the Leinster players in their 'Shetland coloured jerseys and harp, white knickerbockers and club stockings'. Ulster wore white jerseys with the red hand as a crest, white knickerbockers and red stockings. Only the knickerbockers have changed to this day.

Ulster scored early through Heron and the try was converted by Walkington. Heron was president of the Northern Football Union, and he must have been in a tranquil mood when he presided at the after-match dinner in the Linen Hall Hotel, Belfast.

The vigorous efforts of the players and the after-match celebrations obviously took their toll, for it was not until Monday that the five representatives from the IFU joined their five comrades from the Northern Union to select the Irish team to play England. Seventeen of those selected in Belfast eventually took the field at Rathmines when Ireland, needless to say with the full blessing of the IFU, was led for the first time by an Ulsterman, Dick Bell. Twelve of those who had played at the Oval were again in the Irish side; while Ulster had the captaincy, Leinster still had the majority representation, eleven to nine, when Ireland lined out at Rathmines.

When the Irish team, led by Bell, ran on to the Rathmines ground, their uniform was very different to that which they had worn at the Oval. This time Ireland wore navy blue knickerbockers, blue stockings and white jerseys, and for the first time had the shamrock as a crest. The fact that England, too, wore white jerseys did not apparently lead to any confusion, and it certainly did not detract from the merit of England's performance.

Ireland, apparently, showed much improvement in their play from the initial engagement, but England were too strong and too clever for the home representatives and won convincingly by one goal and one try to nothing. Thousands had turned up to witness the spectacle, though their presence is not borne out by the gate receipts which totalled only £22 9*s*. As the admission fee had been set at a shilling (ladies admittedly being granted free access), large numbers must have gatecrashed the proceedings.

Some consideration had also been given to organising a match against Scotland, and the arrangements were left in the hands of the Northern Union. However, after Dublin had agreed to the game taking place in February, Bell wrote saying that the game would not take place but failed to give a reason.

Once again the IFU managed to show a profit on the year's workings, and Peter reported a credit balance at the end of the season of £4 17*s*. 2*d*. The accounts also reveal that he had managed to get the Leinster Cricket Club to reduce the rent from the original £10 to £7 10*s*.

The match against England was now firmly established on an annual basis, but when in November 1876 the Rugby Union informed the IFU that the forthcoming game at the Oval would be fifteen a side, the suggestion was greeted with something approaching outrage and was summarily rejected. The reduction in the number of players had complications for the two Irish unions other than the fact that any deficiency in playing skill could be more easily disguised when there were forty players on the field.

Negotiations were completed on a more satisfactory basis for the second interprovincial between Leinster and Ulster, and Henry William Dunlop's persistence that Lansdowne Road was a suitable venue for representative rugby was regarded when the match was fixed for the ICAC ground. The terms of the agreement between Dunlop and the IFU are interesting. Dunlop agreed either to let the ground for £5 or to charge no ground rent but share the expenses of the game and the gate receipts. The IFU chose to accept the latter proposition.

The weather was not very kind for the first interprovincial match to be played in Dublin; the afternoon of 16 December 1876 saw no let-up in the torrential rain that had fallen throughout the morning but, as *The Irish Times* reported, 'the Interprovincial match — Leinster versus Ulster — did actually come off despite the inclemency of the weather, and the general impression in the city that the game could not possibly take place.' *The Irish Times* also records that Leinster deservedly won by a goal and a try to two tries. After the game the representatives of the two unions met in the Arcade Hotel, Suffolk Street, Dublin, for the purpose of selecting the Irish team to meet England at the Oval on 5 February 1877. The Rugby Union had by this time secured the grudging approval of the Irish as to their stipulation concerning the numerical strength of the two teams. Fifteen a side they wanted, and fifteen a side they would get.

Ulster's suggestion that the interprovincial, too, be played fifteen a side had been adopted, and the northern committee's initiative in arranging a game against Scotland to be played at Ormeau on 19 February 1877 was also readily endorsed by the IFU. Ireland set off for the Oval once more, and yet again defeat was their portion, this time by two goals and two tries to nil. The score margins in these international defeats were widening and the worst fears about the reduction in playing strength were proved to have solid foundation. Ireland had only three survivors from their first international match, Richard Galbraith, Walkington and Cox.

After seeing the debacle at the Oval, the joint selection subcommittee retired to the Charing Cross Hotel to pick the team to meet Scotland. Surprisingly, only four of those who played against England were dropped, but when the team lined out against Scotland at Ormeau, it in fact showed seven changes from the side that lost at the Oval. The changes were not, however, for the better as Ireland was overwhelmed by six goals and two tries to nil, scarcely an auspicious start to the series.

THE IRISH TEAM 1877. THE FIRST FIFTEEN A SIDE INTERNATIONAL.

On the home front, however, many important developments were under way. Munster were about to enter the field of competition. A challenge was issued by the Limerick club and accepted by the IFU at a meeting on 2 March 1877, and the date for the first Leinster v Munster game was fixed for 24 March, with College Park as the venue. This time, however, the weather intervened in full force, and so bad was the day that the game had to be postponed to Monday, 26 March. Munster put up a brave fight, but Leinster prevailed by one goal to nil.

Munster was represented for the first time at a meeting of the IFU when C. B. Croker of Limerick attended the annual general meeting of the union on 15 October 1877, a meeting at which Harry Walsh resigned as the honorary secretary, and the post was taken over by Dr William Neville.

Less than a fortnight later an even more important event occurred when the first specific moves were made towards an amalgamation with the Northern Football Union. At a special meeting of the IFU on 29 October 1877 it was decided to call a committee meeting for the following Thursday, 1 November, to draw up a scheme for amalgamation. It was also agreed to call an extraordinary meeting of the union with a view to getting the scheme adopted.

The committee met, in fact, on 2 November and drew up the following scheme for amalgamation with the Northern Union.

1. That the union be called the Football Union of Ireland.
2. That branches in connection with the union be established in Leinster, Ulster and Munster to manage the affairs of the clubs in these provinces.
3. That the committee of the union consist of nine members, three to be elected from each branch annually on or before 20 October each year and that within a fortnight after their election, they elect a secretary and treasurer.
4. That when possible this committee shall meet in Dublin.
5. That each club pay an annual subscription of half a guinea to defray the expenses of the union.

The scheme was adopted with slight amendment at the extraordinary meeting held at 63 Grafton Street on 7 November, and things looked set fair for the big union between north and south. But Belfast hedged on the issue and a dispute arose between the two unions about the date for the match against Scotland that season. There was further insistence by the IFU that it was now time that Munster got a say in the running of the national side, and Munster having agreed to meet Leinster at College Park in Dublin on 26 January, the IFU suggested that the north send representatives to attend that game. Leinster once again beat Munster, this time by one goal and a try to nil. But the NFU was not represented at the game.

The cool atmosphere between north and south was eased somewhat when the Northern Union requested a date for the Leinster-Ulster game and also informed Dublin that arrangements for the match against Scotland had fallen through. It was news greeted with some dismay by the IFU committee. However, they suggested 2 March as a likely date for the interprovincial and also took the opportunity to remind the Ulstermen that they had not yet received a reply to their suggestion that Munster be represented at future meetings to select an Irish side. Ulster agreed to 2 March as the date for the interprovincial, with Belfast as the venue. Ulster won the match by two goals to nil.

The IFU had several weeks earlier quietly arranged for a visit from England for 11 March. A meeting was held in Belfast to discuss this forthcoming fixture and to select the Irish team. The IFU minutes record that H. L. Robinson, H. Murray, W. Neville, R. M. Peter and F. Kidd represented Leinster and Munster at this meeting.

The presence of the Munster delegates may have irritated the Ulstermen, for the proceedings became heated. Dick Bell, who was in the chair, at one stage threatened to leave the meeting, but his better judgment prevailed in the end, no doubt on the grounds that anything might have happened had he left the room. After a lengthy discussion, the team was finalised. Significantly enough, it contained no fewer than three Munster players: E. Croker, W. Griffiths and J. J. Keon, all of Limerick. Griffiths and Croker were in the side that eventually lined out.

William Dunlop, seeing that all was now ready for the fray, again offered Lansdowne Road for the game against England, but this time at slightly elevated terms. (It was, after all, an international!) The union agreed to Dunlop's terms that he be paid £5 and half of any profit over £50 after the deduction of expenses.

Only one player now survived from the 1875 game against England at the Oval. This was R. B. Walkington who played at full-back and captained the Irish side that day at Lansdowne Road. The story of the game was the old familiar one — another defeat, this time by two goals and a try, and once again Ireland failed to score. Five matches in international competition had failed to yield even one score, but reports of the after-match dinner, which was held at the Shelbourne Hotel, do not suggest that the Irishmen allowed any cloud of depression to settle over them because of this latest reverse.

In October 1878 the IFU again opened negotiations with the Northern Football Union for an amalgamation. This time the south decided to use Munster as their lever, suggesting that if Ulster persisted in standing in the way of the establishment of a single legislative body, then Munster could feel entitled to form a Munster Branch and claim equal representation at all future meetings of selection subcommittees. With Cork and Limerick football clubs both affiliated to the IFU, the suggestion carried some weight. Cork had three representatives at the annual general meeting of the IFU, held on 4 November 1878, and one of their representatives, William Goulding, was elected on what was termed 'a new executive committee' which replaced the old working committee. A nice balance was preserved when J. G. Cronyn of Limerick also found a place.

Dublin kept a firm hold on the Cork connection, and Wanderers and Trinity arranged to visit Cork for matches early in December. It was decided that this would be an opportune time to play the first interprovincial in Cork. The southern public were therefore now to have their full-scale rugby festival, with Wanderers taking on Cork FC on Saturday, 30 November, Trinity facing Cork on Monday, 2 December, while Leinster would meet Munster on Tuesday, 3 December. Cork managed to draw with Trinity but lost to Wanderers, and Munster lost to Leinster by one goal and three tries to nil.

The proceedings of that programme in Cork did not go unnoticed in the northern metropolis, and a meeting of the executive committee of the IFU held in Neville's rooms at No. 9 Trinity College on 25 November 1878 was attended by none other than Dick Bell. His errand was, according to the minutes, 'to learn the views of the IFU with respect to amalgamation and to assist in drawing up a general scheme'. After lengthy discussion, the following rules emerged.

1. That the union be called the Irish Rugby Football Union.
2. That its objects shall be to promote and foster the game of rugby football in Ireland and to arrange international and interprovincial matches.
3. That branches in connection with this union be formed in Leinster, Ulster and Munster respectively, to manage the affairs of the clubs in these provinces belonging to the union.

4. That the committee of the union shall consist of eighteen members, six from each province to be elected annually, on or before 1 November, and that within a fortnight of their election they shall proceed to elect a president, two vice-presidents, an honorary secretary and honorary treasurer out of their own body.
5. That in case of any member of the committee retiring during the term of office, that branch of the union which he represented shall fill the vacancy so caused.
6. That the annual subscription of each club belonging to the union shall be £1 and that there shall be an entrance fee of one guinea.

It was further agreed by the committee that Munster, until they had either drawn or won a match against Ulster or Leinster, should only have four representatives on the committee, the two places to be left vacant in the interim.

These proposals were accepted by the north with one amendment to rule 6, which was that clubs at present belonging to either union would not have to pay the entrance fee. At a meeting of the IFU on 11 January 1879 it was agreed to accept the Ulster amendment. The same meeting also finalised arrangements for a double-bill interprovincial programme at Lansdowne Road on Friday, 16 January, when Ulster would meet Munster for the first time, and Saturday, 17 January, when Ulster and Leinster would renew their rivalry.

A dinner was planned for the Saturday night in the Royal Arcade Hotel and it was also decided that members of the Munster team could attend 'provided that they paid their own share'.

The outcome of the games was a double victory for Ulster, Leinster this time losing by one goal to nil. The papers of the day heralded the new set-up as the formation of the Irish Rugby Football Union. Alas, they were ahead of their time, for the amalgamation was still twelve months away. In the intervening period there were occasions when the prospect of the great union looked to be in great jeopardy. Indeed, the first signs of Ulster dissent came the day before Ulster met Munster, when at a meeting of the IFU a letter from the honorary secretary of the Northern Union was read informing the meeting that the NFU did not intend that the rules for amalgamation should come into force that season (1878–79), particularly with regard to the selection of the Irish team. The minutes record:

> After much discussion, it was unanimously agreed to remonstrate with the Northern Union upon this apparent breach of faith and to point out to them the injustice done to Munster in refusing its players a place on the committee of selection, while playing them on terms of equality. In case the NFU persisted in their refusal, it was agreed that the IFU should agree to the old method of selection for the Irish XV to play against England that season, but should refuse to play the Scotch match in conjunction with the Northern Union unless the XV for it was chosen by a committee arranged on the new system.
>
> H. L. Robinson, G. Nugent, R. M. Peter, F. Schute and W. Neville were then selected to act as the members of the committee of selection on behalf of the IFU. In case no Munster representative was allowed on the committee, it was agreed that the two last-named representatives would retire from the meeting in favour of W. J. Goulding and J. C. Cronyn of Munster.

It was in this slightly sensitive atmosphere, then, that Munster met Ulster for the first time the following day.

After the Leinster v Ulster game, the committee of selection met in the Royal Arcade Hotel to select the Irish team to meet England at the Oval on 3 February 1879. R. B. Walkington, J. A. MacDonald, E. Hughes, J. R. Bristow and W. Finlay represented the NFU and, just as they had threatened, they refused to admit any representative from Munster to the meeting. True to their word, Messrs Neville and Schute retired from the proceedings, their places being taken, as planned, by Goulding and Cronyn. Notice was formally given to the representatives of the NFU that the IFU would not consent to play Scotland unless the team was picked by a committee representing all three provinces as agreed under the scheme of amalgamation.

Scotland v Ireland
1879

The team to meet England was chosen without the assistance of the Ulstermen, but fate was to deal Ulster a kind hand when the match against England had to be postponed because of frost and the NFU suggested that the team originally selected to play against England now line out against Scotland in Belfast on 7 February 1879. The Northern Union also proposed that after the match in Belfast an amalgamated committee of the three provinces, six representatives from Ulster and Leinster and four from Munster, should meet to draw up rules for the guidance of the IRFU, which should come into force at the commencement of the following season.

With the long-cherished union now in peril, the IFU agreed to these proposals at a meeting in Dublin on 12 February. The date of the match against England was also fixed at this meeting for 24 March.

The withdrawal of J. Heron and J. Cuppaidge from the team that met Scotland made way for the advent of Goulding and A. Archer of Trinity to the Irish team, which once again maintained its undesired tradition by losing and failing to score. After the match a meeting was held in the Linen Hall Hotel in which all three provinces participated and, according to plan, drew up the rules for the guidance of the IRFU. Suffice it to say that they made only very minor amendments to the regulations originally accepted by both major bodies.

Ireland made their now customary unsuccessful excursion to London where, even though they played ten forwards and five backs, they failed to contain the opposition who won easily by three goals and two tries to nil.

CHAPTER 6

A NEW BEGINNING: THE 1880s

THE LAST MEETING OF THE IFU took place on 28 October 1879 at 63 Grafton Street, premises owned by John Lawrence, who had also been the host five years earlier when the inaugural meeting had been held, on that occasion at 39 Grafton Street.

The new union was finally a fact of life. The inaugural general meeting of the IRFU was held at 63 Grafton Street at noon on 5 February 1880. William Neville was elected president, with Richard Bell and William Goulding as vice-presidents, thus creating a nice balance of three provinces. Peter was elected the first honorary secretary, while Edwin Hughes from Ulster was entrusted with the office of honorary treasurer. The Leinster representatives were Neville, Peter, F. Kennedy, G. P. Nugent, G. Scriven and F. Schute. Ulster's six were Bell, J. MacDonald, Hughes, W. T. Heron, H. C. Kelly and G. M. Shaw, while William Goulding, William Kelly, T. Harrison and J. J. Keon were looking after Munster's interests.

At the time of the IRFU's foundation Ireland had played seven matches, lost them all and had failed to register even one score. Now with one controlling body and the game expanding at club level, surely the first score, if not the first victory, would not be too long delayed.

By a happy coincidence the first try for Ireland came in the inaugural year of the first union, and to a Trinity student, John Loftus Cuppaidge, went the distinction of scoring it. Cuppaidge was a medical student who subsequently set up practice in Queensland and lived to recall his singular feat until 1934. His effort did not, however, preface a long career in the Irish jersey, for he was capped but once subsequently in a match against Scotland that same year.

That Ireland's first try should have been scored by a Trinity player and at Lansdowne Road was of course fitting and contemporary reports reveal that Cuppaidge grounded the ball right between the England posts. Those reports also inform us that R. B. Walkington, despite his international experience at the time, 'was shaking like a leaf' while he was taking the kick. Not surprisingly, he missed, an omission of some consequence at a time when a goal was considered superior to any number of tries. England went on to win the match by a goal and a try to a try. On 14 February that year Scotland were hosts to Ireland for the first time and the match followed a familiar pattern when in Glasgow Scotland won by three goals and two tries to nil.

Munster had the honour of providing the IRFU with the president in 1880–81 when William Goulding defeated Richard Bell in a ballot for the office. Goulding was to have the distinction of presiding over the first Irish victory dinner for the big breakthrough was at hand. It came on 19 February 1881 when Ireland defeated Scotland by a dropped goal to a try at Ormeau.

Jacques McCarthy, who had been singularly unimpressed after another defeat by England, displayed an appreciative pen when he recorded that famous victory.

> Although Scotland were warm favourites, the odds against Ireland had been reduced in rather odd fashion, however, for several of the original Scottish XV had to be replaced at the last moment owing to the secession of a section of Edinburgh players who felt aggrieved at the committee's choice of captain.

After revealing, and not for the first time, his dislike of Belfast, graphically illustrated by his remark that 'by as yet some unexplained miracle the amphibious inhabitants of the Northern Athens were favoured by a fine day', McCarthy went on to state that Ireland should have won, but did not turn first-half superiority into tangible benefit on the scoreboard so that at half-time there was no score, a situation that continued until five minutes from the end when disaster struck in the shape of a Scottish try. McCarthy described the effort as follows:

> McMullan, of Cork, making a mis-catch at a long kick, placed the whole of the Scottish team on-side and Graham, who was leaning against the Irish goalpost, rubbing his shin, after a recent hack, leisurely limped over the line and touched the ball down. Nothing could be more galling or tantalising than this; but some slight relief was forthcoming when Begbie missed the kick which was as easy as possible.
>
> Only five minutes remained, could we now win? Surely we deserved it as we had been up on the Scottish line all day and thrice compelled them to touch down in defence with very narrow escapes. The spectators became simply hysterical and never ceased shouting from this to the very end.

Their exhortations were rewarded, however. McCarthy graphically described the winning score in the last minute.

> J. W. Taylor got possession immediately after the drop out and with all his team attending him, ran up to the Scottish 'twenty-five', where he passed to 'Merry' Johnston, who returned him the leather on the very verge of the Scottish line.
>
> Here it was heeled out from the scrummage to Johnston, who, amidst vociferous profanity, missed his pick-up, and Campbell, darting in, shot the ball into touch ten yards down.
>
> Barney Hughes, however, rapidly realised the situation and threw it out to Taylor before the Scots could line up, and Taylor transferred to Johnston, who quicker than you could think or write, tossed to Bagot, who dropped the ball over the Caledonian bar.
>
> Such frantic excitement as these lightningly executed triumphant movements evoked was never previously seen, and men and women and children embraced each other indiscriminately.

The spell of sorrow was broken and we returned to Dublin by the five o'clock train supremely happy. So Ireland had won a match at last and the fifteen noble players who achieved that first victory were:

R. E. McLean (Dublin University)
J. C. Bagot (Dublin University)
H. R. Spunner (Wanderers)
A. J. Forrest (Wanderers) Capt.
D. Browning (Wanderers)
J. W. Taylor (Queen's College, Belfast)
J. A. MacDonald (Queen's College, Belfast)
R. W. Hughes (NIFC)
W. W. Pike (Kingstown)
M. Johnston (Dublin University)
J. Johnstone (Ulster)
W. Finlay (NIFC)
H. Purdon (NIFC)
A. R. McMullan (Cork)
H. B. Morell (Dublin University)

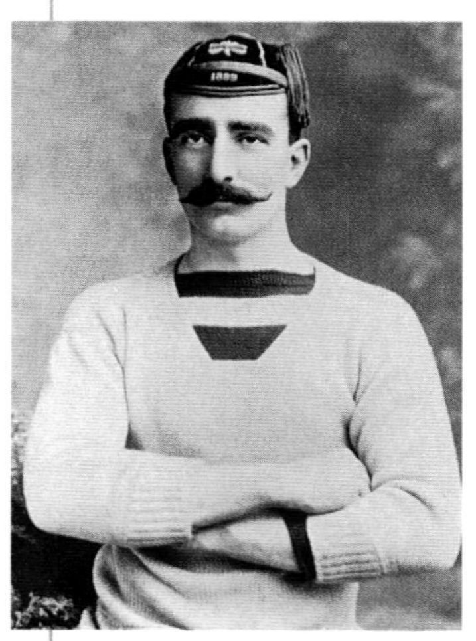

Edward G. Forrest

The team was led by A. J. Forrest of Wanderers, and while McCarthy made reference to the fact that Scotland were not at full strength, it is worthy of note that of the Irish team elected for that season by open ballot among the members of the union, no fewer than five of the Irish side that beat Scotland were originally only named as substitutes: McLean, McMullan, J. Johnstone, Purdon and Morell.

That victory was to have a sequel at the annual general meeting of the union in Dublin on 17 December 1881. When the accounts were presented it was discovered that there was only £23 4*s.* 7*d.* in the kitty and that the sum of £24 5*s.* was still due to the Imperial Hotel, Belfast, for the dinner to the Scottish team. Worse still, a balance of £8 5*s.* 6*d.* was also due to the Shelbourne Hotel, Dublin, for an international dinner given to the England team that had conceded that try to Cuppaidge in February 1880. The IRFU now faced something of a financial crisis; indeed, money troubles were to beset the union for the next decade. The only reward received by the fifteen heroes who had beaten Scotland was a bill from the union for one guinea each. There is no record that any of them ever paid it.

Dublin University 1881–82 team, winners of the inaugural Leinster Senior Cup

That meeting in December 1881 also saw Dick Bell sever his connection with the IRFU. No reason was given for his resignation; possibly he may have been discouraged by his defeat in the 1880 election for the presidency. So Bell, who had done so much in the organisation of the Northern Union and the IRFU, was destined never to be honoured with the supreme office.

A similar fate was to befall R. M. Peter, whom Jacques McCarthy had described as 'the father of Irish rugby', a title that was perhaps rather exaggerated. Peter severed his connection with his club, Wanderers, and the IRFU in 1882 after a dispute about a match report he wrote in *The Irish Times*. Shortly before he departed from the rugby scene, he attempted unsuccessfully to organise a national cup competition and even went as far as drawing up the rules for what he termed the 'Irish Rugby Football Union Challenge Cup'. His project was not, however, greeted with any great enthusiasm and it fell through. Peter was, however, more successful in Leinster, where he had been very active as a club representative for both Wanderers and Dundalk.

The Leinster Branch realised the potential of such a competition within its own province and established the Leinster Senior Cup in 1882. Not unexpectedly, Trinity won the inaugural tournament and retained the cup for the following two seasons before Wanderers broke their monopoly in 1885.

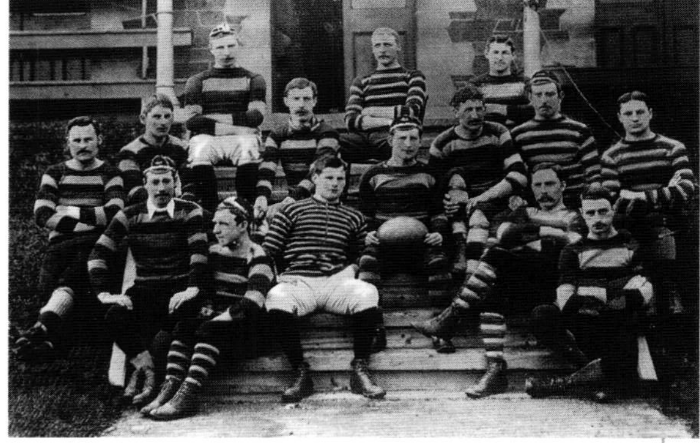

North of Ireland FC, first Ulster Senior Cup Winners 1885

It is to Ulster, however, that the credit for initiating cup football in Ireland belongs, for as early as 1875–76 the Ulster Schools Cup was established. Armagh Royal School were the first winners, beating the Royal Academical Institute by a dropped goal to nil in the second replay, after the teams had played two scoreless draws.

Leinster followed the Ulster lead in 1887 when they too started a senior schools cup, with Blackrock College the first winners. The eighties may not have been a particularly auspicious decade for Ireland's performances on the playing field, but it was none the less a period of tremendous development on the home front. The Ulster Senior Cup was started in 1884–85 and, as might be expected, NIFC were the first winners, while Munster and Connacht soon followed suit, Bandon winning the first Munster Senior Cup in 1886, and Galway Town taking the inaugural Connacht title in 1896. Cup football has ever since been an integral part of the game in Ireland, and the last two months of each season are always a period of frenzied activity in the field of competitive rugby.

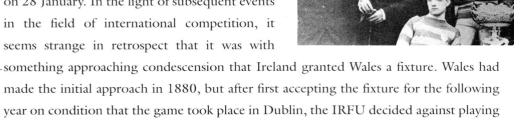

Blackrock College team that won the inaugural Leinster Schools Senior Cup 1887

In 1882 Ireland met Wales for the first time, the game taking place at Lansdowne Road on 28 January. In the light of subsequent events in the field of international competition, it seems strange in retrospect that it was with something approaching condescension that Ireland granted Wales a fixture. Wales had made the initial approach in 1880, but after first accepting the fixture for the following year on condition that the game took place in Dublin, the IRFU decided against playing the game.

Munster did, however, undertake a Welsh tour in 1881, led by William Goulding. They played three matches: one against Newport, which they lost, one against a South Wales XV, which they also lost, and they ended their campaign on a successful note by defeating Neath. It was an effort that earned a severe reprimand from the ruling body, for Munster had not sought permission from the IRFU, and Wales had

Leinster Senior League medal

taken the opportunity to count the victory by their South Wales XV over Munster as a win for Wales over Ireland.

Perhaps Ireland's attitude to the first match against the principality can best be put into perspective by the fact that only four of the selected team turned out at Lansdowne Road on 28 January 1882. Ireland duly paid the penalty, losing by two goals and two tries to nil.

A week later, also at Lansdowne Road, Ireland achieved her best result yet against England, a draw, two tries each. It was a game that aroused more than a little controversy, to say nothing of the ire of that trenchant critic, Jacques McCarthy.

> Without any possibility of contradiction, Ireland won by a goal and a try to two tries, but the official result was a draw. This was the famous Pike cum Nugent match, Pike the player winning it, while Nugent the umpire lost it. McLean kicked a goal for Ireland off a try by Taylor, but Dr Nugent decided that it was no goal. Stokes scored for Ireland immediately after the kick-off, but Walkington missed the kick, then Hunt got in for England, Rowley missing. W. N. Bolton (an Irishman by the way) then scored for England and finally M. Johnson got a try which was virtually scored by Taylor. Off this McLean kicked the goal above referred to and which was disallowed by Nugent amidst universal dismay.

So a draw it was, despite McCarthy's claims. Even so, the result was encouraging for Ireland, though it was to prove no deterrent to Scotland, who exacted due retribution for their defeat the previous season by gaining a victory of two tries to nil in Glasgow.

The annual general meeting for 1882–83, held on 20 January 1883, was not without its dramatic moments. At the outset of the meeting, the statement of accounts was rejected on the grounds that 'they were quite unintelligible', and J. Atkinson, the honorary secretary for the previous season who had resigned the post prior to the 1883 meeting, was requested in his absence to furnish a detailed account of his stewardship. A special committee was set up to investigate the accounts and instructed to take 'whatever steps they deemed necessary for the recovery of any balance they found due'.

History does not record what they found or what steps they took. Meanwhile the Imperial Hotel in Belfast was still seeking the money due for the dinner to Scotland in 1881 and the union was still seeking one guinea from each of the players who had taken part in the game.

Dublin Hospitals Cup medal

Munster, who in 1880 had beaten Leinster and had thus enjoyed equal representation on the committee, provided the treasurer when William Goulding was appointed in succession to Atkinson, while the new president was George Scriven, by now qualified as a doctor from Trinity. Still at the height of his playing career, he was not only elected president of the union, but was also appointed captain of the Irish team for the season. As the union committee still picked the team on a system of ballot, Scriven had the unique distinction of being president of the union, captain of the Irish team and chairman of selectors in the same season. H. C. Cook took over as honorary secretary. Showing a fine appreciation of the possibilities contained in the decision to set up an investigating committee on the financial position, Cook promptly informed all and sundry that he was accepting the honorary secretary's position on the strict understanding that he would not be held in any way responsible for outstanding debts.

That the union's difficulties, financial and otherwise, got a thorough airing in the press of the day was evident when, at the general meeting the following season, A. R. McMullan proposed that in future the press be barred from reporting the proceedings of the union's meetings. Despite strong support from Cook for this motion, the committee, showing a fine regard for the democratic process, rejected it, so McCarthy and his ilk were not to be denied free access to any contentious material. Rather less democratic, perhaps, was the reduction of the representation of each province from six to five during the season.

Scriven had led Ireland against England and Scotland in the previous season, but the match arranged against Wales had been dropped. The failure to honour the fixture against Wales was the subject of a lively debate. Cook informed the meeting that the Irish players were just not interested in travelling to play Wales and that he found it quite impossible to raise a team to make the journey to Cardiff. At this juncture it was proposed and carried that any man who played in the Welsh match only would not be awarded an international cap. Then making an impassioned plea that a truly representative side should be sent to Cardiff in March 1884, the president said that every effort must be made to select a team worthy to met Wales. However, those sentiments did not deter the union from deciding unanimously that while Ireland would fulfil its commitment in 1884, Wales would thereafter be dropped from the international schedule.

The 1883–84 season was the first year in which a complete international programme took place, with the four home countries meeting each other. England won in Dublin and Scotland won in Edinburgh in 1884. But, once again, the union had extreme difficulty in getting a really representative team to travel to Cardiff — so much difficulty, in fact, that Cook, who travelled in his capacity as honorary secretary, is listed as having played. Even then, in order to field fifteen players Ireland had to borrow two players. These were both Newport players — H. M. Jordan and J. McDaniel. Jordan subsequently played for Wales against England and Scotland the following year and against Scotland in 1889, but McDaniel never again achieved the distinction of playing at international level.

Ireland team v Scotland 1884

Although it has been confirmed that Jordan and McDaniel did play, and McDaniel subsequently became a vice-president of the Bath club and often spoke of the day he played for Ireland, what has not been established with clarity is who the two Ireland players were who are credited with caps but who did not play. Such reports of the match as are available all list the Ireland team and do not include Jordan and McDaniel. Cook is also listed as captain, but that too is incorrect. The team was in fact captained by D. F. Moore.

One name listed in the team, R. O. N. Hall, is also incorrect. There is very substantial evidence that this, in fact, was William Hallaran, and the name and initials of Hall were coined from the name of Hallaran. William Hallaran was a divinity student at that time in Trinity College and may well have had his own specific reasons for not playing under his name. Hallaran, subsequently a minister in the Church of Ireland, had the satisfaction of seeing his son Charles play for Ireland in the 1920s.

While one cannot with certainty state who did not play, credit must be given to the two Welshmen. Consequently, the team listed in the appendix for that match includes the two Welshmen.

J. A. MacDonald's game for Ireland against Scotland in 1884 was his last and severed the final connection with the first twenty, which had included the Ulsterman. It was in view of his sterling service to Ireland that he was given the captaincy for 1884, having stated that this would be his last year in international football.

Ireland's difficulties in Cardiff were not the only problems that beset the rugby world that season. When England met Scotland at Blackheath, a dispute arose in the course of the game that had major repercussions. While Ireland was not directly involved, the referee at Blackheath was George Scriven, who had added the distinction of being an international referee to his other achievements. Sir Rowland Hill, one of the leading legislators of the era, and a legendary figure in the Rugby Union, summed up the incident thus: 'In the course of play, the ball was knocked back by a Scotsman (ruled so by the referee G. Scriven, a well known Irish player), one of the English team secured it and a try was scored. The Scotsmen claimed that the knocking back was illegal.'

The English and the Scots were unable to reach an agreement on the matter and so in 1884–85 Scotland did not meet England. There the matter rested until Ireland considered the matter at the general meeting of the IRFU held on 11 December 1885.

W. J. Moore proposed and R. G. Warren seconded a successful motion, 'That the honorary secretary be directed to write to the honorary secretaries of the English and Scottish Unions stating that an International Board would be very useful for the settlement of international disputes.' England and Scotland consented and a conference was held in Dublin on 6 February 1886. As a result of its deliberations, Scotland awarded the 1884 match to England on the understanding that England would join an international board composed of an equal number of representatives of each of the four unions. Thus was born a body that has since been the ruling authority of the game. And while, like many other great institutions, it had its teething troubles, it was founded on an Irish initiative, a fact which is scarcely ever mentioned in rugby reference books.

But the 1884–85 season was in many other ways a momentous one for Ireland. At the annual meeting of 1885 the honorary treasurer, William Goulding, was able to report that at long last the financial position was improving, the union now having a credit balance of £20 8*s.* 4*d.*

It was at this meeting, too, that the clubs attached to the Irish Provincial Towns Rugby Union, which had been formed some years earlier by a few provincial clubs, were finally brought in under the senior body. They had applied to the IRFU the previous season for amalgamation and were informed that they should affiliate to the respective branches in their area. With the exception of Dundalk, all the clubs concerned were in Ulster.

It was in 1885 also that the province of Connacht made an attempt to form its own branch, although there were only four clubs in the province. The meeting decided that if a fifth club should be formed in Connacht, the province would have the right to form their own branch and be given representation on the union committee and admitted to the interprovincial programme. In the meantime a Monkstown FC proposal that Galway Grammar School, Ballinasloe, Connacht Exiles and Queen's College, Galway, be elected to membership of the IRFU was accepted. It was the start of what proved to be a long hard road for administrators in the west and it was not really for another fifty years that the objectives envisaged that December day in 1885 were brought to full fruition.

Finally, at the same meeting the design for the crest on the Irish team jerseys was changed to the shamrock pattern that Irish teams have worn ever since, and Scriven was elected once again as president of the union, the only man in history to have been appointed to that office twice, with a break between the two terms of service.

During this season the Irish team actually played Scotland twice, which in some ways made up for the fact that the Scots did not meet England at all. Ireland was led for the first time by a Munsterman, W. G. Rutherford, and lost to England by two tries to a try in Manchester on 7 February. For some undefined reason, five of the Irish players refused to play: L. Kidd, H. M. Brabazon, R. Nelson, J. Forrest and J. J. Johnston. The match against Scotland at Ormeau on 21 February lasted exactly fifteen minutes and was called off because of bad weather. Scotland insisted on a return match to be played in Edinburgh; it took place in March, and Ireland, badly depleted, lost the game by two tries and one goal to nil.

The season of 1885–86 saw things return to normality. England had a full programme of games, but rumblings of discontentment were still evident as the International Board was still not framed to England's liking. At a meeting in October 1886 England decided to change the scoring system, allowing three points for a penalty goal, where previously a penalty did not count. But the other countries would not go along with England's wishes and for a time it looked as if England would be without a fixture in 1887. Indeed, the IRFU called a special meeting on 29 November 1886, when it was proposed by J. F. Blood (Leinster) and seconded by S. Harris (Leinster) that 'It would not be advisable to play England in Dublin in 1887.' The proposal was defeated by thirteen votes to three. The meeting also decided that the old system of scoring would operate and England subsequently agreed to that principle. This was, incidentally, the first meeting of the IRFU at which Connacht was officially represented, and one of their three delegates was none other than Jacques McCarthy.

The subject of Sunday rugby was also raised at that special meeting when Kincora FC, a recently formed Munster club, wrote to request a union ruling on the subject and were informed that there was nothing in the laws of the IRFU which prohibited Sunday play. The matter was accordingly referred back to the Munster Branch.

England came to Lansdowne Road on 5 February 1887, which turned out to be a memorable day for Ireland. On twelve previous occasions Ireland had faced England, and with the exception of the draw in 1882 it had been one defeat after another. Ireland put a young side into the field, a team that in fact contained ten new caps, and at long last England were humbled. Ireland not only won, scoring two goals, but for the first time did not concede a score. Jacques McCarthy was ecstatic. He opened his article in *Sport* of the following week thus:

> Ladies and gentlemen — with your kind permission and attention I shall now sing you a few verses of a little parody on Joe Coburn's original favourite 'Two Lovely Black Eyes'. Ahem! Mr Conductor, will you oblige please?
>
> Two goals off two tries,
> Oh, what a surprise;
> Were ever Englishmen leathered like this?
> Two goals off two tries.

Ireland team v England 1887

McCarthy's great rival 'Green and Gold' who operated for the *Irish Sportsman* was, however, even more jubilant for he had greeted the announcement of the team with far greater confidence than had McCarthy. 'Green and Gold', looking ahead to the game against Scotland, had this to say:

> Gentlemen of the Irish fifteen, thus far by means of play that was grand, you have marched on despite impediment. England, the erstwhile successful boar, whose ravenous appetite had swallowed up our teams, gave our poor country a taste that rudely cropped its ripened hopes of fair prosperity, is now even chockfull of bile.
>
> St Patrick, who after all was a gentleman, has caught St George between wind and water and the latter eminent personage is now weeping by the waters of Babylon with a leg on each side of his tail. You have licked the Saxon and you have done it nobly. Now you face the representatives of brown heath and shaggy wool, oaten cakes and Islay whisky. Having settled St George and Merrie England, are you going to play second fiddle to Bonnie Scotland? Gentlemen, you have begun well and your country looks to you to go on and finish the work. I say then in the familiar but immortal words of the Iron Duke, 'Up guards and at them', break the thistle as you have plucked the rose and plant on the heights of victory the great immortal shamrock.

One suspects that 'Green and Gold' saw infinitely more in Ireland's win than a victory on the rugby field over England. Not even McCarthy could equal the invective of his tirade, though he did have a good try. Their exhortations were, however, all in vain, for Scotland put a stop to Ireland's Triple Crown ambitions, and Wales, with whom Ireland had resumed negotiations, followed by winning as well that season. Yet victory over England was something to shout about, especially when little confidence had been expressed in the young side that had been elected by the IRFU committee.

McCarthy had been at his vitriolic best when describing the team selection for *Sport*. He declared that four of the selected side were unfit through injury and that the selection meeting 'all wound up with a hot battle for the last place, which finally went to the Munsterman John Macaulay after his portrait, war paint and all, had been handed around the room'. But McCarthy had a vivid imagination and did not hesitate to bend the facts in the interest of a good story and readable copy. He concluded his assessment of the team selection by remarking: 'All the mischief was now done, the Irish XV for 1887 had been elected. And directly after the team had been made known, R. M. Bradshaw offered to put down £50 as a guarantee and pick an outside fifteen which would play as well as the chosen one.' McCarthy asserts that Bradshaw formally challenged the Irish XV but that E. McAlister, who that day was elected honorary secretary of the union and was later to emerge as a distinguished legislator, was unable to get the latter together, so that the bet fell through. Suffice it to say that the IRFU minutes of the proceedings do not bear out McCarthy's statements; indeed, if Bradshaw was even present at the meeting, it was not in an official capacity.

It is instructive to look a little more closely at the achievements of that little-fancied Irish team which by its victory wrote a glorious chapter in the history of rugby in Ireland. Robert G. Warren was captain that day. As a youngster of 21, he had come into the Irish side in 1884 against Wales and in all won fifteen caps. His service on the field was invaluable and he could be said to have been the first really accomplished back that Ireland produced. He was destined to have an even more distinguished career as a legislator, serving on the IRFU committee for over fifty years and holding the posts of honorary secretary of the International Board from 1897 to 1933 and president of the union in 1895–96.

Legend has it that another player, John Macaulay (who figured in McCarthy's alleged 'portrait' incident) had arranged to get married that weekend. Having taken all his annual leave, it was the only way he could think of to get time off from an employer not apparently well disposed towards sport. Macaulay was to play in only one more international but, like Warren, he later became a distinguished legislator.

Ireland, apparently, beat England 'fore and aft' and Warren, who was playing at half-back, must have given his threequarters a good service, for two of them, C. R. Tillie (Dublin University) and R. Montgomery (Queen's College, Belfast), scored the tries, both of which were converted by Dave Rambaut (Dublin University).

'Green and Gold's address to the troops did not have the desired effect when Scotland, a week later, won convincingly by two goals and two tries to nil in Belfast.

The restoration of the game against Wales that season did not result in any further glory for the Irish, but it was, none the less, a historic occasion, for the game, played at Birkenhead, is the only international on record to have been contested at a neutral venue. Birkenhead was chosen to save Ireland expense, being an infinitely more convenient location than Cardiff or Swansea. Wales won the game by a dropped goal to three tries, all of them scored by Montgomery.

None of the other home countries played England in 1888. At a meeting of the English Union in March 1887, invitations were sent to Ireland, Scotland and Wales to attend a meeting at which the laws of the game would be discussed. When no replies were received from the other three unions by September 1887, England decided that the interests of international rugby would be best served if they played their future internationals according to the laws of the country in which the matches took place. The IRFU at a special general meeting on 20 September 1887 showed independent spirit and its contempt for the whole affair by deciding that they would not send any delegates to a meeting of the Rugby Union, 'having no wish to interfere with the laws of the game in England and that we should retain our right of legislating on the rules to govern the game in this country'.

A meeting of the International Board in Crewe on 5 December 1887 decided that 'All international matches must be played under rules approved of by the International Board, in terms of which no international match with England can take place until the English Rugby Union agrees to join the International Board.' England recognised that decision for what it was and finally accepted the principle that the International Board would become the lawmakers for the game generally.

The vexed question of scoring continued to cause dissension, and again in 1889 England did not meet any of the home countries. The method of scoring that obtained since 1875 was still good enough for the IRFU, but at a general meeting in January 1888 the Irish Union ruled that a match should be decided on a majority of points. A try would count as two points; a goal from a try (the try not to count) as four points; and a dropped goal or a goal from a free as three points. In 1892 these values were altered by reducing a goal from a free to one point. By 1894 the IRFU had agreed to assimilate the scoring in international matches to that adopted by the other unions. A try was now to count as three points; a goal from a try (the try not to count) as five points; a dropped goal as four points; and a penalty goal or a goal from a mark as three points. And that was how the scoring stood until 1948 when the dropped goal was reduced in value to three points.

The period of the late eighties and early nineties could be said to have been the second great period of development within the game. In addition to scoring values, many other practices were under constant consideration. These included alterations in the line-up of the backs, originally introduced by the Welsh when they experimented with four threequarters. Another highly contentious question, which still arouses a fair share of controversy, was the role of the wing forward.

When the Irish team was being elected for the 1888 matches, the question of wing forward play was raised by E. McAlister and W. Stokes. There was also a request that the press should not report any details about the picking of the team, a request that the irrepressible McCarthy did not comply with, as the following passage from *Sport* illustrates.

> Messrs Stokes and McAlister spoke strongly against the pest of the wing forward, but Mr Warren (note R. G.) was just as fervent in favour of it. He was mainly the man to be considered, or at least one of them, and gave personal reasons for his opinions. In the end it was as much as could be done to prevent two wing men from being decided on.

Nothing daunted, Ireland picked the team to meet Scotland and Wales. The match against Wales on 3 March at Lansdowne Road was, in fact, the first that took place as the game against Scotland was postponed until 10 March because of frost.

There was not much confidence in the Irish side as Wales had already beaten Scotland and were regarded as 'a tricky lot'; their tactics had certainly incurred the wrath of the termagant critic McCarthy, who wrote:

> Scotland was simply swindled out of the match. There is not the least use in using nice words when dealing with such shabby subterfuges as those which were adopted by the Welsh.
>
> To put the case in a nutshell, they got a surprise try early in the first half and then killed the remainder of the time by lying down on the ball, kicking out of play and every other trick and dodge that the rules have not provided against, as prostitution of a noble, fair and chivalrous game. . . . Since Ireland was swindled out of her first game with Wales, I have fought tooth and nail in these columns to have the Ireland and Wales fixture abandoned and I think I have a few converts to my view now.

But the match and its result had a truly remarkable effect on McCarthy's previously held views. Ireland won by two goals and a try to nil, and he decided that these Welsh were not so bad after all. 'If we are always to meet Welshmen like these,' he conceded, 'even though they may be better players, and beat us, they will be welcome for I never saw a more gentlemanly lot on a field.'

R. G. Warren again led the side and proved to be one of the heroes of the day, together with the Monkstown back M. Carpendale, who apparently had a hand in every score. Warren had obviously got his way with regard to the wing forward, for T. Shanahan (Waterford) apparently played in the role of a rover. Carpendale, Warren and Shanahan shared the scoring between them. The Irish side also included

D. B. Walkington at full-back. He regularly wore a monocle when playing. It was his habit to take off the monocle when making a tackle and then replace it.

The team that defeated Wales for the first time included six of those who had shared in the win over England the previous season. Walkington was one of the six. The full team was:

D. B. Walkington (Dublin University)
C. R. Tillie (Dublin University)
D. F. Rambaut (Dublin University)
M. J. Carpendale (Monkstown)
R. G. Warren (Lansdowne) Capt.
J. H. McLaughlin (Derry)
H. J. Neill (NIFC)

E. Stoker (Wanderers)
F. O. Stoker (Wanderers)
W. G. Rutherford (Lansdowne and Clanwilliam)
T. Shanahan (Lansdowne and Waterford)
C. M. Moore (Dublin University)
J. Moffatt (Albion)
R. Mayne (Albion)

W. Ekin (Queen's College, Belfast)

The victory over Wales did not inspire a performance of similar moment against Scotland at Raeburn Place a week later, when Ireland lost by a goal to nil.

The annual general meeting of the IRFU for 1889 was an eventful occasion. Proposals that Munster's representation be reduced to three and Connacht's to two were successfully resisted, as was a motion from Ulster that the Irish XV in future be picked by subcommittee. Connacht were struggling on with the aid of annual subsidies out of union funds; nevertheless, this meeting saw the election for the first time of a Connachtman, Richard Biggs, to the presidency.

The season of 1888–89 was notable for the visit of the first team from overseas, when a side from New Zealand, led by Joe Warbrick and named the Maoris, came to these shores. An Irish team was selected to meet them, although its members were not awarded international caps. Playing Ireland on 1 December 1888, the Maoris won by four goals and a try to a goal and a try, but lost to both Wales and England (the latter's only international engagement of the season). Ireland also lost to Scotland in Belfast but beat Wales in Swansea, so the eighties which had opened with Ireland seeking her first international win, closed on a note of victory. The win against Wales in Swansea, Ireland's first victory on foreign soil, was a good omen for the nineties.

Irish cap 1889

CHAPTER 7

THE GAY NINETIES AND GLORY

THE GATE RECEIPTS OF £210 that had been taken at Lansdowne Road for the match against England in 1887 did much to put the union's finances on a sound footing. Meanwhile the workings of the union were beginning to take on a much more efficient aspect. The new president for 1890 was Frederick Moore, a leading figure in Wanderers and one of three brothers who had played for Ireland. Frederick was in four Irish teams between 1884 and 1886; he was capped for the first time at the age of 27, and while his international career was now over, he continued to assist his old club until 1901 when he was 41. He was, too, the first member of Wanderers to be elected to the presidency of the union. Frederick's younger brother Frank had also been capped four times, while a third brother, Malcom, who assisted Trinity, won three caps and was in the first Irish team to beat Wales in 1888. Frederick Moore, who was knighted in 1911, proved to be an able president and under his guidance the union flourished.

When the nineties dawned, Ireland had played thirty-two matches, won four, drawn one and lost twenty-seven, and one game against Scotland had been abandoned. Not a very auspicious record, but the performances on the playing field did not really reflect the progress the game was making internally.

The four seasons between 1890 and 1893 were not exactly vintage years for Ireland in the field of international competition. In twelve matches, Ireland only managed to get one win (against Wales) and two draws (one each against Wales and Scotland). In 1893 England won readily enough by two tries to nil at Lansdowne Road, Ireland played a scoreless draw with Scotland in Belfast, and lost rather unluckily by a try to nil against Wales in Llanelli. There were, however, definite signs by this time that things were improving.

A revisionary committee had already been set up under Moore's presidency in order to facilitate changes in teams selected by the whole union committee, but the idea of forming an autonomous body to pick the Irish team had also been exercising the minds of the union, particularly the Ulster Branch, for some time, and an experiment with a rather unwieldy committee of nine in addition to the president of the union was subsequently approved. It was not until October 1892, however, that the specific words 'selection committee' were mentioned. Bob Warren proposed that a committee, 'called a selection committee' and consisting of six members, two each from Munster, Leinster and Ulster, be established. The first record of a selection committee operating appears in the minutes for the annual meeting in January 1894, a meeting at which J. Redmond Blood, the president for the previous year, presided. Blood, Bob Warren (Leinster), R. Garret and R. Stevenson (Ulster) and J. Hook and H. McOstrich (Munster) were appointed selectors. Their appointment coincided with Ireland's first Triple Crown triumph. Scotland had won the Triple Crown in 1890–91, England in 1891–92 and Wales in 1892–93;

Sir Patrick Dun's Hospital Cap

in the case of both Wales and Scotland it was their first time to capture the coveted trophy. Ireland was very much the poor relation then, which probably accounts for the fact that they were quoted at odds of 5-1, or so a contemporary informs us, when they faced England at Blackheath.

Wales had been experimenting with four threequarters for the previous ten years and had used them successfully in 1893. It was probably in the natural order of things that Ireland should follow suit.

The Irish selectors, like many of their successors, decided to put their faith in experience when they named the side to meet England. The team contained three new caps, all in the pack. They were Tom Crean of Wanderers, George Walmsley of Bective Rangers, and the NIFC man Jim Lytle, whose brother John was one of the veterans of the Irish side, having been capped first in 1889. But John Lytle was not the only experienced campaigner in the Irish eight that day. The captain, E. Forrest of Wanderers, had also been in the team on various occasions since 1889. The pack was completed by John O'Conor of Bective Rangers, Charles Rooke of Trinity and Harry Lindsay, another Trinity man. O'Conor and Rooke in particular had built up tremendous reputations since their appearances on the international scene in 1890 and 1891 respectively. Both were to play their full part in Ireland's triumph.

John O'Conor, member of 1894 Triple Crown winning team

But the class and experience were not confined to those up front. Ireland had a threequarter line of Willie Gardiner, Sam Lee, Lucius Gwynn and H. G. Wells. Lee had come into the side in 1891 and had been a tower of strength ever since. He was highly regarded by the leading critics of the day, notably by that prolific rugby writer E. H. D. Sewell, for many years rugby correspondent of the *Evening Standard* and the author of numerous books, who declared him to have been among the greatest threequarters he saw before or since, an opinion shared by another respected critic of the era, W. J. Townsend Collins, who wrote under the pen-name of Dromio. At half-back Ireland had the combination of Ben Tuke (Bective Rangers) and Trinity's W. S. Browne, two players who apparently had the ability and intellect to use threequarters when it was prudent and ignore them when it was not.

Writing about the 1894 series many years later, John O'Conor recalled the Triple Crown triumph.

> Although it was a famous victory when we beat Wales in Belfast, I must admit it was not a great match.
>
> In those days handling was not developed to the extent that came later. The game was left almost entirely to the forwards and the scrums were grim affairs, with all their forwards giving the full weight to the shove. There were no specialised positions such as hooker or wing forward, and every forward was expected to be an accomplished hooker. First up, first down was the rule. The backs were used mainly in defence.

We got off to a good start when beating England by a dropped goal and a try to a try at Blackheath and thus had the satisfaction of scoring the first Irish victory over England on English soil.

Generally we were pleased with the performance of the side which was not a particularly hefty one — I was the heaviest at 13½ stone — but all the players were tall and speedy. That English game was also notable for the fact that it was the first time Ireland used four threequarters. Until then we had played nine forwards.

We had a full-back problem that year and after the English match Sparrow (Trinity) was replaced by Grant (Bective) who had started the season in his club's second XV.

He played very soundly against both Scotland and Wales. Walmsley broke a leg before the Scottish match and Bond of Derry replaced him in the pack, but we got through against Scotland by a goal to nil, Wells getting the all important try. But Wells was injured for the big day against Wales in Belfast and Dunlop of Trinity replaced him on the wing.

The Lagan had overflowed on to the Ormeau ground shortly before the Triple Crown match and the pitch was in a frightful condition for the match. The mud was over our ankles and it was almost impossible to keep a foothold. But we were less affected by the conditions than Wales. We relied on fast foot rushes to keep their defence in trouble and prevented their backs from developing attacks.

The conditions and the ability of our forwards to maintain a non-stop onslaught won us the day. John Lytle got the only score of the game in the early stages, when he kicked a penalty goal from in front of the posts. That kick won us the Triple Crown.

In all, Ireland used 17 players in the three matches; the heroes who carved out that first crown and championship triumph were:

P. J. Grant (Bective Rangers)
R. Dunlop (Dublin University)
L. H. Gwynn (Dublin University)
S. Lee (NIFC)
W. Gardiner (NIFC)
H. Lindsay (Dublin University)
J. N. Lytle (NIFC)
J. H. O'Conor (Bective Rangers)
A. T. Bond (Derry)
B. Tuke (Bective Rangers)
W. S. Browne (Dublin University)
E. G. Forrest (Wanderers) Capt.
T. Crean (Wanderers)
C. V. Rooke (Dublin University)
W. Sparrow (Dublin University)
H. G. Wells (Bective Rangers)
G. Walmsley (Bective Rangers)

Bond and Grant replaced Walmsley and Sparrow after the English match. Dunlop came in for Wells for the match in Belfast, so twelve of the players were engaged in all three matches.

O'Conor's reference to wing forwards is especially relevant, for Rooke apparently brought a new dimension to the game in this respect during his career, which saw him help Ireland to another

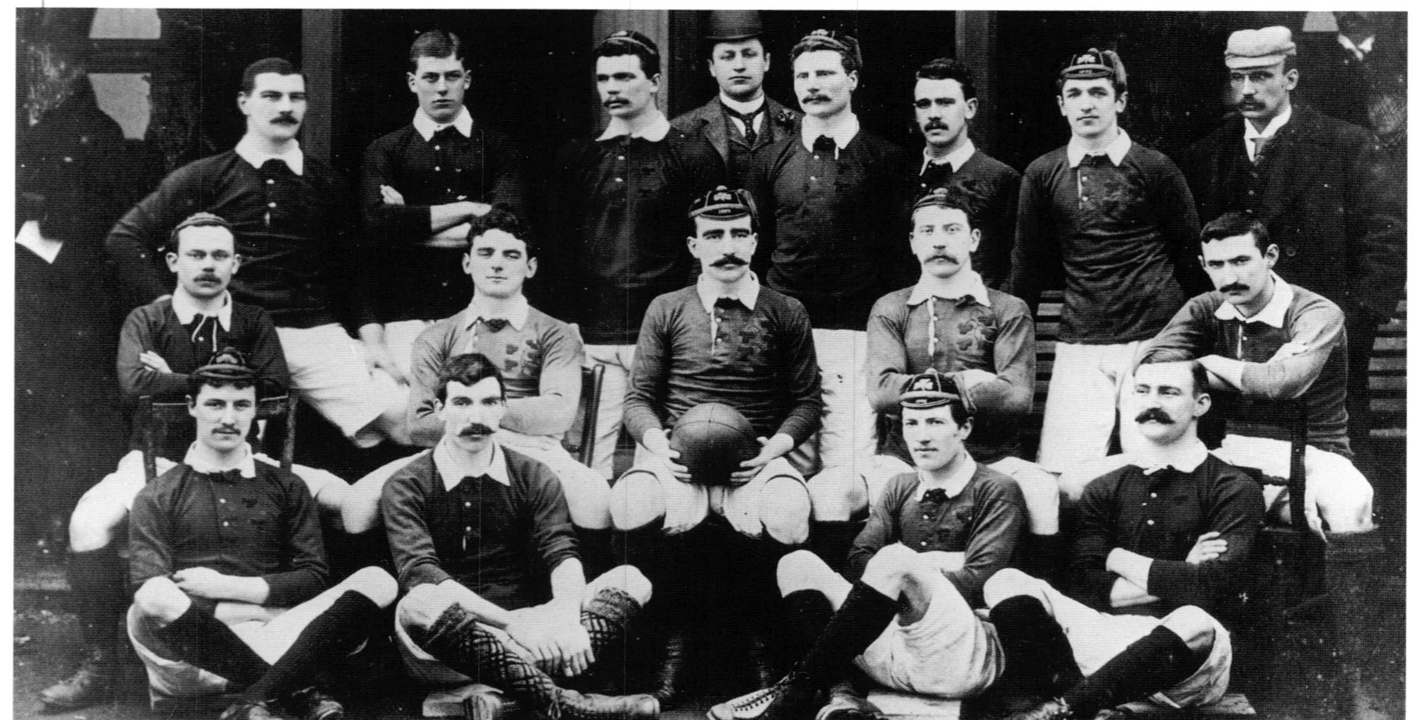

IRELAND 1894 TRIPLE CROWN WINNERS

championship success in 1896 before he retired from the game the following season. He subsequently became a minister in the Anglican Church and died in Wellington, New Zealand, in 1936. Charles Vaughan Rooke did not exploit the possibilities of the wing forward position quite as far as an illustrious player who was to follow shortly after he left the playing field, the legendary New Zealander, Dave Gallagher, but he impressed Dromio more. It is interesting to note that neither of these players impressed that great judge of rugby, E. H. D. Sewell.

The first Triple Crown success and the outright win in the championship that went with it were greeted with tremendous enthusiasm in Ireland and nowhere more so than within the IRFU itself. It was decided that the players who had participated in the three games would be given special presentations to mark their achievement, but someone had second thoughts on the issue and at a meeting of the committee held in December 1894 it was decided not to proceed with the matter, no doubt on the grounds that their amateur status might be violated, a consideration that will have a familiar ring for many present-day rugby players.

The 1894–95 season was notable for much, not least the fact that, despite having nine of the Triple Crown heroes in the side for the three internationals, Ireland lost every game, thus going from zenith to nadir in record time. Munster lost their second selector that season on the grounds that their club strength was inferior to that of Leinster and Ulster; indeed, at one stage in the early season the Munster Branch stood suspended by the union for non-payment of club affiliation fees. Either by accident or design they did manage to pay the sum of £6 which ensured that all was forgiven in time for the championship.

Three notable additions to the Irish strength that season were the Magee brothers, Louis and Joe, and Andrew Clinch. Both Clinch and Louis Magee were to play significant parts in subsequent triumphs, even if their initial appearances against England at Lansdowne Road were not marked by any signs of impending greatness.

LOUIS MAGEE, LED IRELAND TO TRIPLE CROWN WIN IN 1899

The following season, Ireland used only sixteen players. Gardiner, Lee, Crean, O'Conor, Jim Lytle, Lindsay and Charles Rooke of the Triple Crown-winning combination were still on active service. Louis Magee was now firmly established at half-back. James Sealy, later to have a distinguished career as an administrator, came into the pack against England, who were warm favourites, having destroyed Wales by 25 points to nil at Blackheath.

But England could perform no similar demolition job on Ireland, who took control of the proceedings from an early stage and, with tries by Sealy and T. H. Stevenson, won by 10 points to nil.

There was one change made for the match against Scotland. G. McAllen of Dungannon RS was brought in for Fulton at full-back. McAllen's selection made him the first schoolboy to play for Ireland. He was aged 18 years and 2 months when he made his first appearance against Scotland at Lansdowne Road. Regrettably, his debut was not marked by an Irish success, and against the predictions of most and the desires of all in Ireland, Scotland managed to get away with an honourable 0-0 draw. However, that result enabled Ireland to go on to achieve their second triumph within two years for, fielding an unchanged side, they secured the championship by defeating Wales by 8 points to 4 in Dublin, Jim Lytle and Tom Crean getting tries.

The strength of the Irish side was subsequently reflected in the fact that no fewer than six of the sixteen who had shared in it were selected for the British and Irish team to tour South Africa in the summer of 1896. In all there were nine Irishmen on that tour: the six who had shared in the championship triumph were Louis Magee, Larry Bulger, Jim Sealy, Andrew Clinch, Tom Crean and Andrew Meares; they were joined by Louis Magee's brother Jim, who was never capped for Ireland at rugby but who was an international cricketer, Robert Johnston (Wanderers) who had played twice for Ireland in 1893, and the as yet uncapped Trinity man C. V. Boyd. Availability rather than ability was often the yardstick for the early touring teams, but nine representatives was, none the less, a singular tribute. These were the first Irish rugby players to tour abroad, for the 1888 team that toured Australia and New Zealand did not contain any Irish representatives.

The 1896 team to South Africa was led by the Cambridge Blue, J. Hammond, and played four Test matches, winning three and losing one. Bulger, Crean, Louis Magee, Clinch and Sealy played in all four Tests, Meares played in three, while Jim Magee and Johnston played in two, and Boyd in one. This was no mean contribution.

Both Crean and Johnston were to go back to South Africa within a short time, but on a very different mission. Both fought in the same regiment in the Boer War three years later, and both were also awarded the highest military decoration, the Victoria Cross, for valour.

That match against Wales in 1896 was the last Crean played for Ireland, but the nucleus of the previous season's championship side was still at hand, and they opened the new season's campaign by defeating England by 13 points to 9 at Lansdowne Road. For this match two brothers, Mick and Jack Ryan from Cashel, County Tipperary, came into the Irish pack for the first time. The Ryans were members of the Rockwell College club, where a famous contemporary of theirs who also wore the college's blue and white jersey with distinction was Éamon de Valera, a full-back and centre of some calibre.

An 8-3 defeat by Scotland in Edinburgh terminated Ireland's championship aspirations and also their international programme for that season as neither Ireland nor Scotland met Wales.

The question of payment for 'broken time' had been creating difficulties in the north of England since 1886. Differences of opinion reached a critical point at a general meeting of the English Union in September 1893, when it was proposed that players be allowed compensation for bona fide loss of time. The proposal was not carried, and the issue continued to cause trouble, with the result that in 1895 twenty-one clubs broke away and formed what subsequently became the Rugby League.

It was against that background then that what has become known as the 'Gould dispute' occurred. It caused a major problem for the International Board that culminated in Scotland and Ireland refusing to play Wales in 1897, and Scotland again refusing to meet Wales the following year.

Arthur Gould, a magnificent Welsh centre who had just retired from international football, was to be the recipient of a house from his admirers, but the board stepped in to bar the presentation. The Welsh RU did not accept that the board had jurisdiction in the matter. However, Gould himself declined the offer and eventually Wales, after resigning from the board, was permitted to rejoin in February 1898 on the specific condition that they recognised its bye-laws.

In 1897 Ireland lost an outstanding administrator, Eddie McAlister, honorary secretary of the union from 1886 and also honorary secretary of the International Board from 1887 until his untimely death in 1897. He was succeeded as honorary secretary of the union by Charles Ruxton, who occupied the position until 1925, and as honorary secretary of the board by another Irishman, Robert Warren, who held that position until 1933. McAlister was only the first in a long line of Irishmen to act in that capacity for the board,[1] for when Warren resigned in 1933 he was followed by Harry Thrift (1933–56), who in turn was succeeded by Eddie Kirwan (1956–71).

Ireland's campaign in 1898 opened against England at Richmond, and after a 9-6 defeat, Sam Lee retired from the international scene. Scotland then won by 8 points to nil in Belfast. With cordial relations now resumed with the Welsh, the match was arranged for Limerick on 19 March. It is the only international that has been played in that great rugby city, and it ended in a Welsh victory by 11 points to 3.

Thus the omens did not look good for the closing season of the nineteenth century, and when Ireland faced England at Lansdowne Road in the opening match of the 1899 campaign not one of the 1894 Triple Crown team remained. Andrew Clinch of the 1896 championship-winning side had also departed, so that the most experienced members of the pack were the Ryan brothers, James Sealy and W. G. Byron. Fulton was still at full-back and, of course, the incomparable Louis Magee was at half-back to lend his talents and experience. One of the newcomers for that England game was a schoolboy at Campbell College, J. B. Allison. The combination of the old and the new proved potent enough to resist

[1] For a full list of Irish representatives on the International Board, see Appendix 3.

the demands England put on it at Lansdowne Road, where Ireland won by a try, scored by Magee's half-back partner, G. C. Allen, and a penalty goal.

While injuries had severely restricted the selectors' scope for the match against England, that did not account entirely for the fact that only two of the seven backs who faced England were in the side against Scotland at Inverleith. The pack showed three changes, including the recall of Jim Lytle, thus re-establishing a connection with the 1894 Triple Crown team. A. D. Meares of Trinity was given his first cap and Tom Little of Bective Rangers, who had played against Wales the previous season, was also brought back. Ireland won by three tries to nil, with E. F. Campbell of Monkstown, C. Reid of NIFC and James Sealy making the scores.

IRELAND V WALES IN LIMERICK 1898 — THE ONLY INTERNATIONAL PLAYED IN LIMERICK

So Ireland went on to tackle Wales, this time at Cardiff, where they had never won. For this match, which was fixed for 18 March, Ireland made two changes in the pack, McIlwaine and C. H. Moriarty coming in for McGown and Lytle; it was to be Moriarty's only Irish cap. Behind the scrum George Harman, who had played against England but was injured at the time of the Scottish match, was recalled in the centre, and G. C. Allen resumed his half-back partnership with Magee, Barr of Methodist College being omitted. Many years later the game and its background was described by Mick Ryan in the *Rockwell College Annual.*

> You know the feeling a player has when his team has reached a cup final — a feeling of satisfaction for having done so well, and a feeling that if this game is lost, all that was hitherto gained is quite undone; that the hard training, the gallant deeds and the plucky defence have gone for nothing.
>
> Such a feeling intensified is what a player has when it comes to a chance of winning the Triple Crown. Would all our previous efforts be for nothing or would we emerge victorious?
>
> Wales had studied the Irish methods and at 'a council of war' had selected and constructed their team and prescribed their tactics with a view to frustrating the Irish forwards.
>
> The fact that the game was played in Cardiff proved to be no small matter. The rails of the enclosure gave way and an unruly crowd took up whatever positions they chose. They crowded on the touch and goal lines and at times it seemed an impossibility for Ireland to score; as one reporter said afterwards, 'Wales had a thousand full-backs, some of whom came up even to the "twenty-five".'
>
> Play had to be stopped time and again to clear the field. The Cardiff police had apparently just received new uniforms which they were not going to trust to the mercy of the mob. They simply kept out of the way and even the horse police declined to go on the ground.

Our team had been changed out of recognition and only five of us had played in both the English and Scottish games: Louis Magee, James Sealy, Billy Byron, Jack and myself. Influenza had done a lot of the damage with regard to the many changes made during the season.

We were accorded a hearty welcome when we came on to the field, then Wales, led by Bancroft, came to the strains of 'Men of Harlech'. By that time the spectators had practically taken possession of the field and it was obvious that a start could not be made until they were cleared.

That took a considerable time and both teams withdrew while it was being done. Nearly half an hour was lost before the ground was playable.

At last we were off. It was desperate stuff. We got away from the first scrum on a good rush and 'Blucher' Doran kicked ahead, but Skrimshire fielded and brought play back to midfield.

The Welsh threequarters tried some flashy movements, but Butler and Campbell tackled splendidly. Frees were numerous to both sides and we had a few chances of penalty goals, but luck was decidedly against us.

After play was held up, when the spectators invaded the pitch, Wales were very dangerous on the resumption. We were beaten back to our own line, but Butler saved the situation with a beautiful punt to touch at halfway.

Then it was our turn to attack. Sealy made a splendid opening and passed to me. I saw the line within easy distance, but alas heard the referee whistle for an infringement. Wales cleared, but only for a while until Sealy tackled Nicholls in possession inside the Welsh 'twenty-five'. Scrum; we will have this ball back or die. Ah! we've done it.

Allen picked up and set the whole back line in motion. Doran took his pass in masterly fashion and romped past the opposition.

During the interval, the mob again invaded the pitch and more time was lost before the game could resume. Louis Magee had to go around with Mr Turnbull, the referee, and beg the over-enthusiastic ones to move back.

The second half was thrilling. Wales, not beaten by Doran's try, opened up some brilliant movements, Nicholls and Llewellyn made great efforts to score, and twice we were forced to touch down. Skrimshire broke through to be taken down by Butler, while Magee eased the pressure twice in succession by good runs.

Still Wales pinned us inside our own 'twenty-five' and it seemed as if nothing could prevent a score. And then came the most exciting incident of the game.

Lloyd whisked the ball out to Nicholls. Straight through all opposition he went, swerved and transferred to Skrimshire, who seemed to have a perfectly clear field. He had lightning speed and there appeared to be nothing to prevent him scoring between the posts. Suddenly Magee flashed up and dived for his heels. Amidst frantic cheers from the Irish supporters, Skrimshire came down and lost the ball.

After that, the game was ours. We stormed the Welsh defence, but it was remarkably sound. We were still on the Welsh line when the final whistle sounded. The Triple Crown was ours.

Twenty-four players helped to achieve that second Triple Crown success for Ireland and, as Mick Ryan pointed out, only five players participated in all three matches. The players (with Triple Crown appearances shown in brackets) were:

T. Ahearn (Queen's College, Cork) (E)
G. C. Allen (Derry and Liverpool) (E W)
J. B. Allison (Campbell College) (E S)
A. Barr (Collegians) (S)
W. H. Brown (Dublin University) (E)
W. G. Byron (NIFC) (E S W)
E. F. Campbell (Monkstown) (S W)
I. G. Davidson (NIFC) (E)
G. P. Doran (Lansdowne) (S W)
J. Fulton (NIFC) (E)
G. Harman (Dublin University) (E W)
T. J. Little (Bective Rangers) (S W)
J. H. Lytle (NIFC) (S)
L. M. Magee (Bective Rangers) Capt. (E S W)
A. D. Meares (Dublin University) (S W)
C. H. Moriarty (Monkstown) (W)
H. C. McCoull (Albion) (E)
T. McGown (NIFC) (E S)
J. E. McIlwaine (NIFC) (E W)
P. O'Brien-Butler (Monkstown) (S W)
J. C. Reid (NIFC) (S W)
J. Ryan (Rockwell College) (E S W)
M. Ryan (Rockwell College) (E S W)
J. Sealy (Dublin University) (E S W)

A happy footnote to that victory is that it could still be recalled by one of the Irish players, George Harman, in the summer of 1974 when he celebrated his hundredth birthday at his home near Looe in Cornwall.

So despite the gloomy forecasts by the journalists of the day that Ireland would be struggling that season, the second Triple Crown and third championship were brought back in triumph. The words of the *Freeman's Journal* of 2 January 1899 have a hollow ring in retrospect: 'The trials in Dublin and Belfast must be regarded as unsatisfactory and where an Irish XV is going to come from is purely a matter of enterprising conjecture.'

The year 1899 saw the outbreak of the Boer War and much other conflict in the world, but in Ireland at least it was made memorable by twenty-four men in green. The president of the union in that triumphant season was John Moore, a man who gave almost forty years' service on the union committee and who was an International Board representative from 1892 to 1927. Lucius Gwynn, Sam Lee and John Macaulay were on the selection committee, and Macaulay was still there thirty-one years later. He first served in 1895–96 and sat on the selection committee for no fewer than twenty-six seasons.

Ireland v Scotland 1899

A combined British and Irish team set off in the summer of 1899 for Australia. It contained three Irishmen, two of whom, 'Blucher' Doran and Tom McGown, had helped to win the Triple Crown. The third member of the Irish contingent was the Trinity player E. Martelli, who is not listed as having played for Trinity at first team level. But he did play at senior level for Wanderers and subsequently became an international referee.

IRELAND TEAM THAT TOURED CANADA 1899

But an event of even greater significance took place in September 1899 when an Irish team set sail for Canada. It was led by J. G. Franks (Dublin University), who had won three caps as a forward in 1898, but the only Triple Crown hero in the side was Ian Davidson of NIFC, who had played against England. 'Blucher' Doran's brother Bertie, one of three brothers to play for Ireland (a third brother, Eddie, having won two caps in 1890), was also in the party. Irish rugby has long been noted for its strong tradition of fraternity (in the original meaning of the word as well as in the commonly accepted sense), as is demonstrated by the fact that two other sets of brothers, the Boyds and the Rowans actually took part in the Canadian tour. The full party of seventeen players was:

J. C. LEPPER (NIFC)
P. C. NICHOLSON (DUBLIN UNIVERSITY)
T. A. HARVEY (DUBLIN UNIVERSITY)
R. R. BOYD (LANSDOWNE)
J. BYERS (NIFC)
J. S. MYLES (DERRY CITY)
I. G. DAVIDSON (NIFC)
H. A. MACREADY (DUBLIN UNIVERSITY)
J. STOKES (LANSDOWNE)
H. A. BOYD (DUBLIN UNIVERSITY)
R. STEVENSON (DUNGANNON)
B. W. ROWAN (LANSDOWNE)
F. DINSMORE (NIFC)
I. GROVE-WHITE (DUBLIN UNIVERSITY)
B. W. DORAN (LANSDOWNE)
J. G. FRANKS (DUBLIN UNIVERSITY)
A. C. ROWAN (LANSDOWNE)

The tour was sponsored by 'Duke' Collins, a native of Dublin living in Toronto, and apparently no voice was raised in objection to an act of sponsorship. Whatever the cost or the profits (if any), there is no record in the IRFU accounts of the tour for the 1899–1900 season or for the following term.

The team sailed to Halifax, and arrived a couple of days before the outbreak of the South African War. The Irishmen played eleven games, winning ten and losing one. The games took place in Halifax, Montreal, Ottawa, Brockville, Peterborough, Quebec, Toronto and Hamilton. The sole Irish defeat was suffered in Halifax at the hands of a combined side picked from seven cruisers of the Atlantic Fleet and the Province of Nova Scotia. The Irish played a man short in the game, as J. Sproule Myles, later to serve as a member of Dáil Éireann for East Donegal, broke a leg in the early stages of an earlier match in Toronto. This accident, combined with other injuries, left the Irish with only fourteen fit players. Myles's injury necessitated a protracted stay in Canada and he did not arrive home until late in December, the remainder of the party having returned over a month earlier.

The Canadian tour was the closing chapter in the story of Irish rugby in the nineteenth century. Ellis had started something more than a scientific exercise that day at Rugby School in 1823. There had been many faltering steps *en route* to two Triple Crowns and three championship triumphs for Ireland, but surely the gayest day of the gay nineties had been 18 March 1899 in Cardiff.

CHAPTER 8

A NEW CENTURY: 1900–14

COMPARISONS BETWEEN THE GREAT SIDES of different eras are always difficult, not only because of the lapse in time, but even more because of the game's constant evolution. The great success enjoyed by Ireland in the nineties made it difficult for those who followed and wore the green jersey in the early 1900s, and if the period between 1900 and the Great War did not herald achievement of similar moment, there were occasional displays of brilliance and some Homeric battles were won and lost. The championships of 1906 and 1912 were the high points in the story of Irish rugby in this period.

It was, too, a period of advancement at home, with the Triple Crown triumph in 1899 giving the spur for many new clubs to emerge. The First All-Blacks came and went, leaving a trail of destruction behind them. The First Springboks came too and if not quite as successful as the New Zealanders, they added a further dimension to the rugby game in these islands.

Ireland opened the challenge for the Triple Crown against England at Richmond in 1900 with a team which had been built around the nucleus of the previous season's championship side. Louis Magee was still at half-back; Doran, Allison, Reid and Campbell, the threequarters, had all worn the Irish jersey previously, as had full-back O'Brien-Butler. The Ryans, James Sealy and Meares were in the pack, and to their strength was added the newcomers Jack Coffey, Fred Gardiner, Sam Irwin and P. Nicholson, the last of whom had toured in Canada.

Sam Lee, who had played with many of them, was president of the union. His term of office did not get off to a very auspicious start when England won by 15 points to 4, with Allison getting Ireland's solitary score, a dropped goal. A draw with Scotland at Lansdowne Road and defeat by Wales in Belfast left Ireland at the bottom of the championship table. The wheel of fortune seemed to have turned full circle back to the gloomy days of 1895.

It was a bad start to the new century. The year 1900 saw Wales take over as Triple Crown and championship winners, their Crown victory being only the first of five which they were to achieve within the space of eleven seasons. Ireland alone of the four nations failed to win a Triple Crown between 1900 and 1914; Scotland won it three times in this period and England twice, statistics that seem to point to the fact that Ireland was very much the sick man of the rugby scene. Yet statistics can be misleading, for of the fifty-four matches Ireland played in the fifteen seasons preceding the Great War, twenty-one were won, including six against England, six against Scotland, three against Wales and six against France. Two games were drawn, against Scotland in 1900 and against England in 1910, while New Zealand and South Africa (twice) proved beyond the range of Ireland's capabilities.

LINE OUT ACTION FROM IRELAND V WALES 1902

In those fifteen seasons there flourished some of the most distinguished players ever to wear the Irish jersey. Magnificent forwards such as Fred Gardiner, Jack Coffey, Alf Tedford, C. E. 'Ellie' Allen and George Hamlet are all unforgettably associated with that era. Tedford, who arrived on the scene in 1902, was to make a tremendous impact on forward play, while Hamlet, who made his debut in the same season, wore the green jersey with honour on no fewer than thirty occasions. Nor was all the talent contained in the heart of the scrum, for there flourished backs of equally high quality in E. D. Caddell, James Cecil Parke, an international lawn tennis player of world renown, Harry Thrift, the flamboyant Basil Maclear, Alex Foster, Harry Read and the incomparable Dickie Lloyd, described by E. H. D. Sewell in *Rugger: the Man's Game* as 'an ace at all three aspects of kicking, punt, drop and place. For sustained accuracy, I never saw anything like the kicking achievements of this boy from Portora School. His accuracy was phenomenal.'

That victory by Wales in the 1900 Triple Crown series was the preface to a run of four successive victories over Ireland, the gloom being broken by wins over England at Lansdowne Road in 1901 and 1903 and a 5-0 success against Scotland in 1902. By the time of the England-Ireland match of 1904 the Ryan brothers, 'Blucher' Doran and J. Fulton were all that remained from the glorious nineties. Louis Magee was also still on active service but was recovering from injury at the time of the encounter at Blackheath. England won that day by 19 points to nil, and the match signalled the end of international rugby for Jack Ryan. Mick played in the 19-3 defeat by Scotland at Lansdowne Road, as did another pair of brothers, James and Joe Wallace, who had gained their first caps in the game against England. The game against Scotland proved to be the last international for both Mick Ryan and James Wallace, but Joe was there when Ireland faced Wales in Belfast in 1904 and played his full part in a great Irish success.

A TOUCH JUDGE'S FLAG FROM 1904

Louis Magee came back for the game against Wales, at full-back Ireland had a newcomer, Mossy Landers from the recently formed Cork Constitution club, and there was another new cap on the wing, Harry Thrift.

This has been described as Tedford's match, and quite apart from his contribution of two tries, he proved the scourge of a remarkably talented Welsh team that included Teddy Morgan, Willie Llewellyn and Dickie Owen. A notable absentee was Gwyn Nicholls, but Wales did not attribute their 14-12 defeat so much to Nicholls's absence as to the 'blindness' of the referee, Mr Crawford Findlay from Scotland.

The scene for a thrilling climax was set in the first half, at the end of which Ireland led by 6-3, Tedford and Joe Wallace getting tries and Teddy Morgan replying with one for Wales. After Wales equalised in the second half with a try by Gabe, Ireland lost their left wing, C. G. Robb, and Joe Wallace went on to the wing. Robb returned to the fray but was barely able to walk, and Wales took advantage of the situation to score two tries, after which Robb left the field for good. With a 12-6 lead and Ireland reduced to fourteen men, nothing other than a Welsh win could be envisaged. But the Welshmen had reckoned without Tedford and his colleagues in the forward line, and a magnificent seven they proved.

Thrift signalled his entry into international football by scoring a try. Its circumstances were somewhat controversial, but it could hardly be allowed to hold up the game at such a crucial and thrilling moment. Now within striking distance and playing like men possessed, the Irish forwards, brilliantly nursed by Magee, were subduing the Welsh eight. A great passing movement initiated by Magee reached Wallace, who was hemmed in; but he cross-kicked, the Welsh full-back Winfield misfielded it, and Tedford grabbed the ball and went in under the posts. The winning conversion was a formality for Landers.

With Limerick having seen one international and with Dublin and Belfast on the regular schedule, the clubs in Cork decided that it was time that an international match took place in the southern capital, and the win over Wales in Belfast gave added impetus to the demand. The Cork Constitution and Cork County clubs put a request to the union that the match against England in February 1905 should be played in Cork, but the proposition was rejected out of hand at a meeting of the union committee on 29 March 1904, and the match against England was fixed for Lansdowne Road on 11 February. It was also pointed out at the meeting that no request had been made from the Munster Branch. That omission was quickly rectified, however, and when the committee met again on 11 May, they had before them a letter from the Munster Branch asking that the previous decision be reconsidered. Once again the appeal fell on deaf ears. No doubt the fact that the number of clubs in Munster had decreased from thirteen to six was a weighty part of the argument for refusing to play another international in the province. But other Munster demands met with a more positive response, for at that meeting Garryowen, now becoming a force in Munster rugby, was granted a sum of £250 towards obtaining a lease on a ground in Limerick. At that meeting, too, Connacht, after yet another period in the wilderness, was granted official branch status once again, as there were now five clubs in the west: Galway Town, Old Galwegians, Queen's College, Galway Grammar School and St Ignatius' College.

Irish team takes the field v England at Mardyke, Cork, 1905

The Munster clubs were by no means prepared to abandon so readily their case for providing an international venue. If their numerical strength had dwindled, their resolution was not impaired, and they knew their union laws. A requisition summoning a special meeting of the union committee to consider yet again the playing of the match against England in Cork was immediately prepared by the Munster

Branch and signed in accordance with union laws by the honorary secretaries of five clubs. On 24 August 1904 the IRFU honorary secretary, Charles Ruxton, sent the following circular to all members.

> I beg to inform you a special meeting of the Council will be held on Saturday the 10th day of September 1904, at the Hibernian Hotel at 8 p.m., for the consideration of the following requisition from the Munster Branch of the IRFU.
>
> 'We the undersigned honorary secretaries of Munster clubs affiliated to the IR Union hereby request you to convene a special meeting of the Council of the Union for Thursday, August 25th in accordance with rule 9, for the purpose of considering the application of the Cork County and Cork Constitution clubs to have the international match, England v Ireland, of 1904–05 played on the new grounds of these clubs, situate at the Wellington Bridge, Mardyke Walk, Cork.'

The necessary £5 was enclosed in accordance with rule 9 and the requisition was signed by George Hutchinson, honorary secretary of Constitution, A. E. Bennet (Limerick County), J. M. O'Sullivan (Garryowen), E. Mason (GPO) and George J. Daly (Cork County).

Suddenly the vociferous opposition to Cork as a venue for an international was stilled, with scarcely a dissenting voice. Munster had won the day and the match was fixed for Cork. There was one stipulation, however: Munster had to guarantee the union the sum of £200. The accounts for the season reveal that they met their obligations; and so the Mardyke, a ground that enshrines so much that is best in Munster rugby, became the scene of a famous Irish victory over England. Strangely enough, it was to be an Englishman who proved the main instrument of the Saxon debacle.

If ever there was a case of revenge being sweet, it was Maclear's international debut that February day in Cork. An English officer in the Royal Dublin Fusiliers, Maclear was stationed in Fermoy, County Cork, a circumstance that did not prevent his occasional appearance for Blackheath. With the international season approaching, the eyes of the English and Irish selectors were turned towards him, and it was his rejection by one of England's most famous legislators that gave him to Ireland. In January 1905 Maclear played for Old Bedfordians against Old Paulines at the Richmond Athletic ground. An interested spectator at the match was Sir Rowland Hill who, having seen Maclear convert eleven tries and score two, then pronounced the verdict, 'Not good enough, no opposition to test his true ability.'

So the way was clear for Ireland and when the team to meet England was announced, Maclear was named in the centre. It was the first of eleven appearances for Ireland, and in each of his three games against England he was on the winning side.

At full-back for Ireland that day in Cork was Mossy Landers, later to become an Irish selector and respected rugby correspondent of the *Cork Examiner*. Landers himself played a noble part in Ireland's great victory — the biggest over England up to that time and a record that was to stand for another forty-two years. Many years later he recalled that famous match in the following account.

> The Mardyke ground was part of the site of the Cork Exhibition at the turn of the century. When the Exhibition closed in 1903, negotiations between the Exhibition committee and those three

> great sportsmen, Frank Morrogh, John Reese and Alderman P. H. Reade, resulted in the Mardyke grounds being handed over to Cork County and Cork Constitution as joint tenants.
>
> The 'Dyke' was soon in excellent condition and in 1905 came the outstanding event in the history of rugby in Cork — the international between England and Ireland. Ireland won by 17 points to 3, after one of the greatest displays ever put up by the wearers of the green.
>
> I have some outstanding memories of this game, the first being that it was Basil Maclear's initial game in international football. In between my own spells of work at full-back, I watched the Cork County man as he flashed up the field time and again — always dangerous to the English defence — and I came to the conclusion (to which I still hold) that he was the greatest back Ireland ever had. . . .
>
> Incidentally I might mention that the Irish team that year and the side that defeated Wales the previous season, in spite of gloomy critics, included at least three forwards who had played for their provinces as backs.
>
> For instance Alf Tedford and Fred Gardiner played as backs for Ulster and Joe Wallace was an excellent half-back both for Trinity and Leinster.
>
> 'Ellie' Allen and Moffatt of Old Wesley got tries just before half-time, both made by Maclear, who got among the tries himself after the interval, adding the goal points to supplement tries by Joe Wallace and Moffatt again.

Landers is not alone in his opinion of the Irish performance that day, for E. H. D. Sewell in a description of the game says that Maclear's opponent, S. F. Cooper, later to become secretary of the Rugby Union, spent the day 'stern-chasing'.

It was a record day all round for the attendance was 12,000 and the gate receipts were £900, which left the Munster Branch smiling and some red faces in the corridors of power in Dublin. The match was also notable for the new stand which had been specially erected for the occasion. In his description of this stand Landers wrote:

> The stand was probably the most unique ever used for an international match. It was made possible by the generosity of the local brewers, Beamish and Crawford and J. J. Murphy. They lent the committee hundreds of empty barrels — large and small.
>
> The whole stand was bound very securely with thick strong wire and it was passed perfectly safe by the official engineers the day before the match. Thousands of spectators occupied the stand, as the structure ran along the whole length of each touchline outside the paling.

Ireland went to Inverleith to meet Scotland, fortified by that great victory and, not unnaturally, with an unchanged side. With Coffey, Tedford and Joe Wallace at their brilliant best in the Irish pack and Maclear again stamping his class on the proceedings, Ireland won easily by a goal and two tries to a goal, with Tedford, Wallace and Moffatt gaining the tries and Maclear adding one conversion. So the Triple Crown beckoned yet again, and the campaign was carried on to Welsh soil.

With Wales having defeated both England and Scotland, this was a Triple Crown match for both contestants. The stakes could not be higher on 11 March in Swansea. Wales were at the height of their power, seeking their fourth Crown in six seasons, with Gwyn Nicholls, Rhys Gabe, Owen Llewellyn and Morgan to give the class behind the scrum and the hardy miners from the valleys up front to slog it out with Tedford and his comrades. The Welsh back division was probably the greatest produced in the world up to that time. Many will argue that it has never been surpassed.

Ireland made one change, James Parke, who had been injured for the earlier matches, coming into the centre in place of A. D. Harvey (Wanderers). But the mighty Welsh combination of class behind and aggression up front proved too much for a gallant Irish side that lost by 10 points to 3.

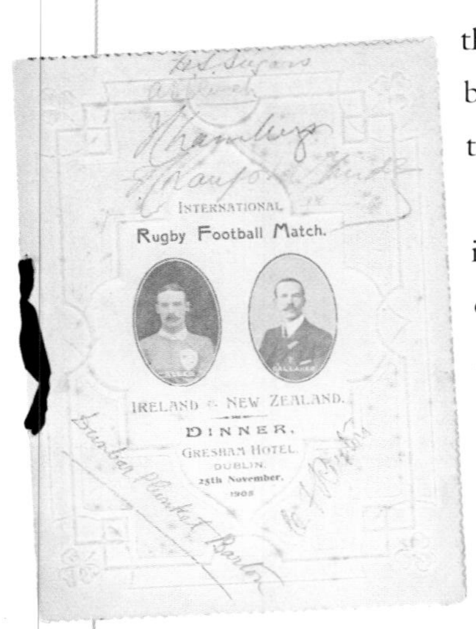

Ireland v New Zealand, 1905, dinner menu card

Ireland had a huge following that day at St Helen's ground. The contingent from Cork included the Barrack Street band. A violent storm had given them a rough crossing, but not even the loss of some of their instruments overboard could dim their enthusiasm as they marched proudly through the streets of Swansea.

On six further occasions in a span of just over thirty years Wales were to prove an insurmountable final obstacle for Ireland's Triple Crown hopes. But if Wales claimed world supremacy after that win in 1905, the claim was about to be disputed by a team from New Zealand.

The First All-Blacks, captained by an Irishman, Dave Gallagher, came to Britain in September 1905 an unknown quantity. They played in Ireland, England, Scotland and Wales, participating in thirty-three matches, thirty-two of which they won; they scored 830 points and conceded only 39; twenty-four of their opponents failed to score against them and the only game they lost, to Wales in the twenty-eighth game of the tour, provoked a controversy that still goes on. They brought a new concept to the game and gave birth to a legend that grew rather than diminished with the passing of the years.

The New Zealand team opened their tour in a sensational fashion that gathered momentum as the tour progressed. They beat Devon by 55 points to nil at Exeter, a result that was greeted with such scepticism by the news agencies that the result was reversed in the belief that it was wrong. But it was all too true, and Cornwall were the next to fall victims to the awesome brilliance of the invaders.

As the tour progressed, the full realisation of the true powers of the tourists shook the complacent rugby world in Britain and Ireland, and the IRFU decided that, in view of the results achieved by the invaders, it would be prudent to play a special trial match before Ireland met them on 25 November. Munster were also on the tour schedule, and a request from New Zealand that the game fixed for Limerick on 28 November might be cancelled as they wanted a week's rest before they met England four days later was rejected out of hand by the IRFU.

When the New Zealanders arrived in Dublin for the game against Ireland their record stood: played 21, won 21; points for 646, points against 22. Their tactical appreciation, superb physical fitness and astonishing teamwork had destroyed all opposition, including Scotland, who had the unenviable privilege of meeting them in the first international.

New Zealand raised again the question of the function of the wing forward, a thorny subject which had exercised the minds of rugby pundits and legislators for a decade, but this time the All-Blacks raised the controversy to a new pitch when Gallagher, who filled the role, also put the ball into the scrum. Accusations that he was putting 'bias' on the ball and committing sundry other acts, such as obstruction, were levelled, and not all the accusations were coming from the conservative elements in the game. They scarcely troubled Gallagher and his men, who drew record crowds at every match they played, a circumstance that influenced the IRFU to make the international in Dublin an all-ticket game, the first in international rugby history.

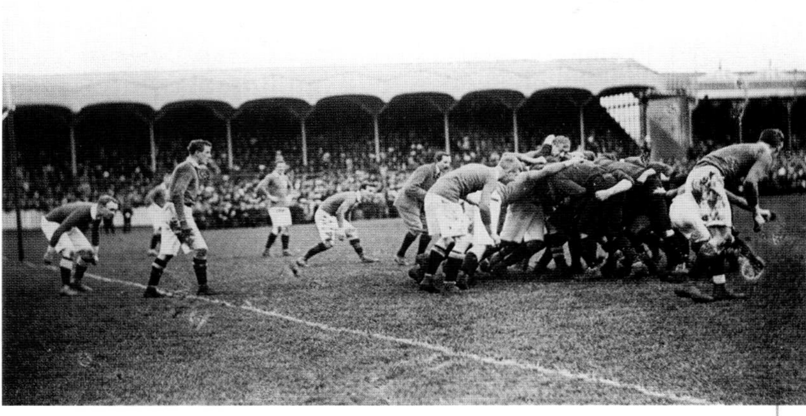

Ireland v Wales at Balmoral, 1906

Ireland called on all her tried and true warriors for the match against the All-Blacks, and H. J. Millar (Monkstown) and Moffatt were the only players missing from the side that had lost in Swansea. Moffatt was replaced by C. G. Robb, who had played in all four games in 1904, while H. S. Sugars of Trinity came in for Millar. It was Sugars' first cap, and a tough baptism it proved for him.

The Irish put up a tremendous display in the first half, but eight minutes before the interval R. Deans, a threequarter who was setting the rugby scene alight by his prowess, got in for a try, which full-back Wallace converted. Wallace achieved similar feats in the second half when Deans and A. McDonald ran in further tries to give New Zealand a 15-0 win in a performance that embellished still further their legendary prowess. No wonder Wallace said after the tour: 'The best time I had personally on the whole tour was in Ireland. The Dublin people gave us a grand reception.' Similar sentiments were to be voiced sixty-eight years later by a New Zealand side, but under less happy circumstances.

An injury sustained while playing against Scotland had prevented Gallagher from participating in the match against Ireland, but his absence made little difference on that occasion or against Munster three days later in Limerick.

Basil Maclear was the only one of the Munster team who had played in the international, and in fact that match in Limerick was Maclear's fourth appearance against the tourists as both Blackheath and Bedford had summoned his services earlier in the tour — not with any great profit, for Blackheath lost 32-0 and Bedford went down by 41-0. Maclear was to suffer a similar fate in the Munster colours, for the All-Blacks scored 33 points that day in Limerick when Munster got the now customary total against them of nil.

The extent of the touring side's impact on the Irish population was illustrated by a contemporary report of their arrival in Limerick, where 'Loyalists and Nationalists alike turned out to meet the New Zealand team at the railway station on their arrival from Dublin.'

Later touring teams were to have a much harder passage when they encountered Munster on their own territory; but if the Munster team of 1905 did nothing else, they created history by being the first interprovincial team in Ireland to play a touring team.

A member of the Munster back line was Dickie Magrath, who later won one cap for Ireland and was president of the IRFU in 1921–22. He lived to the ripe old age of 95, and recalling the First All-Blacks in 1970, two years before his death, he stated that they were 'unquestionably the greatest rugby team of all time'. The full Munster team that lined out in Limerick was:

A. Quilligan (Garryowen)
A. Newton (Cork County)
B. Maclear (Cork County)
W. O. Stokes (Garryowen)
J. Wallace (Garryowen)
S. Hosford (Cork Constitution)
J. Lane (Lansdowne and Limerick)
M. White (Queen's College, Cork)
R. Magrath (Cork Constitution)
J. McQueen (Queen's College, Cork)
J. O'Connor (Garryowen)
J. Reeves (Cork County)
A. Acheson (Garryowen)
W. Churchwards (Cork County)
R. Welphy (Queen's College, Cork)

It fell to Wales to lower the All-Blacks' colours, but the match at Cardiff is still a matter of dispute for New Zealanders still contend, nearly seventy years later, that Deans scored a legitimate try which was disallowed by the referee, J. D. Dallas of Scotland. Dickie Magrath, who was present at the match, concurred with the New Zealanders' opinion.

The New Zealanders returned home, leaving behind them a new appreciation of the art of rugby football, but those who sought to emulate their tactics did not always do so with beneficial effects. The mixed blessings of the All-Blacks' influence were particularly apparent in Ireland.

The wiles and strategy employed by Gallagher became something of an obsession with some members of the Irish rugby fraternity, and when Ireland faced England in Leicester in February 1906 it was decided to play only seven forwards, with Maclear being given a roving commission. Ireland got away with it against a weak English side, winning by 16 points to 6. Tedford, once again in magnificent form, scored two tries, and Bill Brooke Purdon signalled his advent to international football at half-back getting a further try. Maclear's contribution was seven points — a try and two conversions.

The quality of opposition encountered against Scotland at Lansdowne Road was of an altogether different calibre. The Scottish pack, which included such notables as Pat Munro and 'Kimo' Simpson, capitalised to the full on Ireland's new methods and won by 13 points to 6.

Wales, meanwhile, had beaten England and Scotland, and so came to Belfast with the Triple Crown in their sights yet again. Describing the Belfast match in *Rugger: the Man's Game*, E. H. D. Sewell wrote:

> About the only certain thing concerning Irish rugby is its uncertainty. As an example, was there an Irishman anywhere, on that March morning in 1906, which heralded the greatest victory recorded in rugby's stirring history, who would have risked a ha'penny that the Irish team, if playing one short throughout the second half and two short for the last ten minutes of it, would beat that Welsh side?

The Irish team that walked on to the field at Belfast in 1906 was:

C. Henebry (Garryowen)	C. E. Allen (Derry and Liverpool) Capt.
B. Maclear (Cork County)	A. Tedford (Malone)
F. Casement (Dublin University)	H. G. Wilson (Malone)
J. C. Parke (Dublin University)	H. J. Knox (Dublin University)
H. Thrift (Dublin University)	J. Coffey (Lansdowne)
E. D. Caddell (Wanderers)	F. Gardiner (NIFC)
W. B. Purdon (NIFC)	Joe Wallace (Wanderers)

M. White (Queen's College, Cork)

The half-back Purdon was carried off just before half-time with a broken leg, at a time when Ireland led by 8 points to 3, Harry Thrift having scored a try which Fred Gardiner converted, with Joe Wallace adding another try and Teddy Morgan getting one for Wales. Joe Wallace took over at half-back, and the ever eager Tedford, Jack Coffey and their colleagues on the Irish forward line pressed on, magnificent in the face of adversity.

With about ten minutes to go, further disaster came Ireland's way when Tommy Caddell had to retire with a broken ankle, and Fred Gardiner joined Wallace at half-back. Nothing daunted, Ireland added a further try through Maclear, who that day wore his customary white kid gloves, though he had also added a khaki puttee for good measure as if in anticipation of a great occasion. All Wales could muster in a last assault was a solitary try, and so once again Belfast and the Irish had proved the stumbling block to the principality, reawakening vivid memories of a similar result two seasons previously.

That was Gwyn Nicholls's last game for Wales. In his pre-match address to the Irish team, the captain, 'Ellie' Allen, had told his men to pay Nicholls the compliment of tackling him on every conceivable occasion. Allen had also apparently informed the Irish selectors that he did not want to lead the side if Ireland persisted with the ploy of playing only seven forwards. He got his wish and Ireland accomplished what Sewell described as 'the greatest of all wins in international or any rugby. None can snatch that laurel from the Shamrocks, though botanists may cavil.'

Menu card, Ireland v South Africa 1906

By an extraordinary coincidence, the total number of caps won by each of the two teams came to 202.

Belfast was to be the scene of Ireland's next appearance in the international arena, and when the First Springboks came to Britain and Ireland in the early season of 1906–07 the Ulster crowd was once again treated to a magnificent match. However, this time the ending was not so happy, for South Africa won by 15 points to 12, with the winning try coming two minutes from the end when A. C. Stegmann pierced the Irish cover. That match was notable for one of the greatest tries ever scored, with Maclear running from his own 'twenty-five' after an Irish back movement had broken down. He gathered the ball, and jumped a Springbok tackle. Then swinging for the open country, he was engaged by

S. Joubert, the South African full-back, but Maclear disposed of the challenge with a superb hand-off and completed his assignment with a try halfway between the posts and corner flag. Douglas Morkel, one of the famous South African rugby family, was in the South African side that day and kicked a penalty goal; indeed, he was to kick himself to rugby immortality on that tour.

A 17-4 win over England at Lansdowne Road in February 1907 augured well for Ireland's Triple Crown hopes, but the team's progress in that direction came to a summary halt when Scotland won by 15 points to 3 at Inverleith. Worse was to follow, however, for Wales extracted full retribution for recent indignities by defeating Ireland by 29 points to nil in Cardiff. It was Maclear's last match and an inglorious exit for one of the great threequarters of an era when there were many talented backs in international football. Maclear was killed in the 1914–18 War.

But the year 1907 was a significant one in Irish rugby for developments other than Maclear's departure from the Irish team. In December 1906 the honorary treasurer of the IRFU, Harry Shepperd, died unexpectedly and his death brought a complication for the union that was later turned into a shrewd stroke of business from which Irish rugby followers have derived the utmost benefit. Shepperd's death set in action a chain of events which eventually led to the establishment of the Lansdowne Road ground as the mecca of Irish rugby.

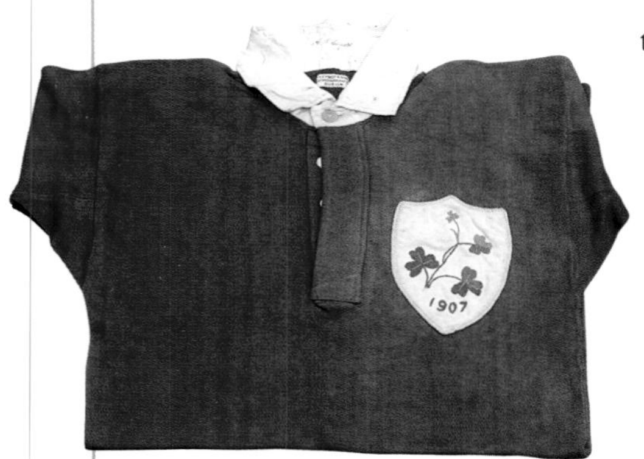

H. S. Sugar's jersey 1907

Lansdowne Road holds a special place in the hearts of all rugby men. It is not alone an aristocrat among the great rugby grounds of the world, formidable territory for the invader and the home of two of Ireland's oldest clubs, Wanderers and Lansdowne, it is also an integral part of Irish rugby history. To all Irishmen the name is magic, but all too many are vague as to its true origins as a rugby ground.

To Henry William Dunlop goes the major credit for its early development; happily, he lived to see his initial humble multipurpose stadium of the early 1870s grow to achieve the status of national headquarters. Some years before Shepperd died, he had acquired the lease of the ground, which had previously been held by Dunlop from the Pembroke estate. With Shepperd the lessee, Lansdowne Road was secure as a rugby stadium. At a meeting on 4 January 1907 the IRFU decided to purchase the lease and paid the representatives of the late Mr Shepperd £200 for his interest in the ground. A new lease for a term of fifty years was negotiated with Lord Pembroke at an annual ground rent of £50.

Now secure in their tenancy, the union undertook a major rebuilding and planning programme. It was decided to alter the ground layout, which then ran from east to west, to a north-south alignment. Plans were drawn up for a covered stand on the west side of the ground and an uncovered stand to the left of it. The total cost of the project came to over £6,000, and the whole job was completed in time for the visit of Scotland in February 1908. Ireland celebrated the occasion with a win.

Almost twenty years later a new stand was built on the east side of the ground and that, too, got its first baptism with a game against Scotland in 1927. Unfortunately, the roof had not been put on, and the day was marked by a prolonged torrential downpour that is still vividly remembered by many who had the 'pleasure' of sitting in it. The West Stand built in 1908 served admirably until 1955, when the union decided to build the modern two-tier structure which straddles the railway line that carries passengers along the busy suburban route to Blackrock, Killiney and Dun Laoghaire and all places south-east of Dublin.

Dunlop had originally conceived Lansdowne Road as a stadium to meet almost the entire sporting requirements of the capital. Under his careful guidance, it served that need, too. Not only was there a cinder track for athletics, but the complex also included a cricket pitch, football ground and tennis courts. He built a stand to seat four hundred, and by the mid-1870s the ground was the regular location of the Irish athletics championships, lawn tennis championships and club rugby matches. By this time it had also become established as the home of the Lansdowne Football Club, founded in the midst of his other sporting pursuits by Dunlop and known variously as the Irish Champion Club and Lansdowne Road.

LANSDOWNE F.C. CAP

Many years after Dunlop's death international athletics events were to take place there again, and in the late 1950s a crowd of up to 40,000 saw Ronnie Delaney, a rugby player of no mean ability, take on the cream of Britain's runners and display the athletic prowess that earned him an Olympic gold medal in 1956 in the 1,500 metres. In recent years Lansdowne Road has also been a regular venue for international and European Cup soccer matches.

In 1880 Wanderers became co-tenants of the ground, and soon it became an almost exclusive rugby preserve. Dunlop, as he sat and watched his beloved Lansdowne grow in stature, must often have reflected on the fact that it had once been rejected as quite unsuitable for an international rugby game.

Despite the glory of the win over Scotland in 1908, the acquisition of the ground by the union did not herald a period of particular distinction for Ireland on the international front, and apart from a draw with England in 1910, Ireland lost every game against the other home countries up to 1911.

There was, however, some consolation to be found when France were entertained for the first time in 1909. England had been playing France since 1906 and recording big scores against these newcomers to international rugby. Wales brought France on to their fixture list in 1908 and Ireland then decided to follow suit. The first match took place at Lansdowne Road on 20 March 1909. Most of those who had played such a noble part in the great victories over Wales in the middle of the decade had gone, but two notables who remained behind the scrum were Harry Thrift and James Parke. Fred Gardiner, too, was in the pack, together with George Hamlet. Whatever the deficiencies of the Irish team at this time (and contemporary reports leave no doubt at all that there were many), Ireland coasted home against France by 19 points to 8. This was Fred Gardiner's last international, and having before the game announced his decision to retire, he and his colleagues were most anxious that the occasion be marked by a score from the old warrior. He duly got a try — and converted it for good measure. Thrift and Parke, too, made their last appearances in the Irish jersey that day, and Thrift later described his grand finale as a 'light-hearted affair'. Unlike Fred Gardiner, Thrift did not celebrate with scores, but there is no evidence that he was aware of his impending retirement. Parke, however, collected five points with a penalty goal and conversion.

International rugby, like all other sporting events, was having to compete in this era with the new wonder of the age, the cinema, though the attraction in the Round Room of the Rotunda of 'Perfection New Living Pictures' hardly accounts for the meagre attendance that turned up to see the French, who drew a gate of only £399 13*s.* 6*d.*, as opposed to the England match which enriched the union funds to the extent of £1,201.

Post-match photograph, Ireland v France 1910

The win over the French was repeated in Paris the following season at the Parc des Princes, while a draw with England was a reasonable reward for Ireland's first visit to Twickenham, which was opened for the first time that season. Two youngsters came into the Irish team for the first time that day at Twickenham, and while they performed with a reasonable degree of distinction, few recognised in the play of the Irish half-backs Dickie Lloyd and Harry Read, both of Trinity, that this combination would later make such a profound impact. Lloyd was the dominant figure, not only of this powerful new partnership, but of the whole Irish team; he may not have been a great contributor to the fluid movement of his threequarters, but he was a master kicker and his skill as a strategist and tactician was unparalleled. He was a product of Portora Royal School which only twelve months earlier had sent out what is still believed by many to be the best school team ever seen in Irish rugby. They not alone destroyed all opposition at their own level, but took on and defeated senior club sides. A measure of their true brilliance can be gleaned from the fact that in Lloyd's time they had supplied the whole Ulster Schools back line in a team that had defeated Leinster by the record score of 72 points to nil.

R. A. Lloyd and H. M. Read, Ireland's first specialised half-backs

The advent of Lloyd and Read, later to become president of the IRFU, gave an entirely new shape to the Irish team. Previously the half-backs had a fluid role, each operating at scrum-half and out-half. With George Hamlet an inspiring forward and captain, the Irish pack, which also included Tom Smyth of Malone who had led the British and Irish side to South Africa in 1910, laid on the kind of possession on which Lloyd and Read thrived.

The 1911 campaign opened well for Ireland, who defeated England in Dublin by a try to nil, Tom Smyth getting the all important score. Lloyd demonstrated all his considerable talents against Scotland at Inverleith on 25 February, converting two of the four tries Ireland scored in a great 16-10 victory. With Wales having beaten both England and Scotland, Ireland's game in Cardiff on 11 March was the Triple Crown final of that season.

Munster team v Leinster 1912

It was, however, Wales who won the day, proving themselves far too accomplished for their Irish opposition. It was their sixth Triple Crown victory in the space of eleven seasons. The 16-0 result tells its own tale. There was, however, consolation for Ireland when once again they defeated France by 25 points to 5 a fortnight later in Cork. That game was the last of thirty appearances George Hamlet made for Ireland, a world record for a forward at that time.

Lloyd took over the leadership of the side in the following year and the initial match against England did not promise great hopes for the immediate future, ending in a 15-0 defeat. However, against Scotland, Lloyd dropped a goal and kicked a penalty, and Alex Foster, a forceful threequarter who had come on the scene two years earlier, also got a try in a 10-8 win. Welsh power had been curbed that season by England and it was further diminished when Ireland won by 12 points to 5 in Belfast; that victory, combined with an 11-6 win over France in Paris, enabled Ireland to share the championship with England.

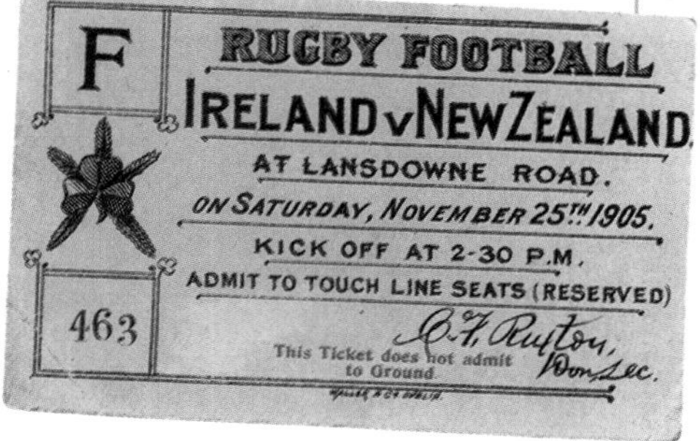

Ticket for the first all-ticket match in rugby history

A more doubtful distinction was not far away, however, for the visit of the South Africans, the Second Springboks, brought a defeat of record proportions at Lansdowne Road on 30 November 1912. Ireland lost that day by 38 points to nil. This was not alone the biggest defeat ever inflicted upon Ireland, but also upon any country in the realms of international competition up to that time. Not even France in their faltering advent to the top echelons had suffered a similar indignity.

The match against South Africa was due to be refereed by Mr Potter Irwin, a noted official of the day, but when he was unable to make the journey, the whistle was taken over by Mr J. Tulloch, a past president of the Scottish Union and an official well known to the Lansdowne Road clientele. However, Mr Tulloch had to retire midway through the proceedings and Fred Gardiner took over as referee while the Springboks wove their by now familiar patterns of destruction. Ireland's net return in two seasons consisted of two wins over France and one over Scotland.

CHAPTER 9

WAR CALLS A HALT: 1914–23

RUGBY PLAYERS ENLISTING AT LANSDOWNE ROAD FOR SERVICE IN THE GREAT WAR

So shall you, when morning comes
Rise to conquer or to fall.
(*Sir Henry Newbolt*)

AT MIDNIGHT ON 4–5 AUGUST 1914 Britain declared war on Germany and for the next four years the talk was not of Lloyd or Poulton Palmer. The battles on the international front were fought not with an oval ball but by mechanised armies that wrought the greatest devastation ever known to mankind. Among the hundreds of thousands who fell were many rugby men. Nine Irish internationals lost their lives: J. T. Brett, R. B. Burgess, E. C. Deane, W. V. Edwards, B. Maclear, V. McNamara, R. S. Smyth, A. L. Stewart and A. S. Taylor. These were only a few among the numerous Irish players who were killed or permanently disabled in that great conflict. Many who survived brought back with them decorations and honours earned on the battlefields of France, Gallipoli and elsewhere.

The disruption of rugby football caused by the Great War was accentuated when the uneasy peace in Ireland was shattered by the Easter Rising in 1916, which also brought much death and destruction. The storm clouds that gathered over the country did not clear until 1923, when the Irish Free State was set on a firm footing.

Just as so many rugby men had, in response to their sense of duty and the call of their leaders, fought and died in the war against German aggression, so also there were others, fewer in number, who took up arms in the cause of Irish independence. Some, notably Kevin Barry of UCD Rugby club, died for the cause. Fortunately the friendships and good fellowship of Irish rugby men were not affected by differing loyalties and political sympathies, and this great sporting bond continues to be a bright feature in the most gloomy times.

One sad casualty was the president of the IRFU, Frederick Browning, who had presided over the union meeting in September 1914 which decided that all club games and representative matches should be suspended for the duration of the war. Consequently, only school competitions and interprovincial school matches kept public interest in the game alive. Browning was tragically killed when his unit of the Veterans' Corps, returning to Beggar's Bush Barracks after a route march on Easter Monday 1916, was fired upon by outposts from Commandant Éamon de Valera's garrison in Boland's Mills, under the mistaken impression that the advancing men were combat troops. It was a sorrowful incident, and a grim quirk of history that the president of the union should have lost his life in a confrontation, however remote and undesigned, with another man who played and loved rugby football.

The Great War ended in 1918 but turbulent clouds hung over Ireland for four years as the 'Troubles' continued, to be succeeded by a civil war. Yet despite the great difficulties the game went on in Ireland, although it was virtually confined to the schools in the season of 1918–19. There were only five schools playing the game in Munster that season, and only two or three in Connacht. The position in Leinster and Ulster, however, was much healthier and immense interest was taken in the schools cup competitions in those provinces. There was also considerable activity in the university colleges. In Dublin an unofficial league competition included teams from UCD, the College of Science, Blackrock College, St Mary's, Merrion and Trinity South Africans. The competition was unfinished after UCD and Trinity had played two exciting drawn finals in College Park.

The Trinity South Africans included many fine players, including Jan Van Druten, subsequently to become one of the greatest of Springbok forwards. He continued to play for Trinity until 1923. There was strong public opinion in favour of his being selected for Ireland, as would have happened in England and Scotland, but the Irish Union adhered to what may be termed its strictly 'racialist' policy in such matters. Irish blood, however diluted, is considered a necessity.

In the season of 1919–20, club competitions and a full international programme were once again restored. A notable addition to the senior club scene in Leinster was that of University College, Dublin. This outstanding club was later to give many great players to the Irish side and was destined to make a signal contribution to the game generally.

When Ireland faced England at Lansdowne Road on 14 February 1920, football in Ireland was still in a parlous state, and the Irish selectors had some difficulty finding fifteen players of international calibre.

Some of the selections in that season have with at least an element of truth been described as 'truly Gilbertian' choices. Yet despite all the obstacles and restriction of choice, the first game in the international sphere bade fair to produce a surprise of the first magnitude.

Weak in playing strength, but not apparently in will, Ireland could still call on the genius of Lloyd. His brilliance and a personal contribution of eight points left Ireland ahead by 11 points to nil with just thirty minutes to go, even though faced by an England team led by one of her most distinguished rugby sons, W. J. A. Davies. But at this critical juncture and, alas, not for the first time, the Irish forwards cracked, and England were the masters in the final reckoning, winning by 14 points to 11.

Ireland v England 1920

The season had not begun well, but Irish optimism was still high. However, the downward trend continued in the later games of the season, when Ireland were thrashed 19-0 by Scotland and 28-4 by Wales in Cardiff. The final indignity came in Dublin on 3 April, when France beat Ireland for the first time and did so in comprehensive fashion with a result of 15 points to 7. That was Lloyd's last match for Ireland and he was partnered at half-back by another great veteran Stan Polden, who had played three times before the war and whose career had extended over a period of twenty years. He was later to play a very active part on the administrative side of the game, being an Irish selector for eleven years and president of the union in 1933–34.

The inglorious beginning to the post-war campaign on the international front prefaced some further dismal days ahead, but all was not on the debit side during that 1919–20 season for the internationals of that season brought forth two players who were later to stamp their vigorous presence on the international scene.

Whether in desperation or by conviction that he was the best man for the job of full-back, the selectors had finally picked Ernie Crawford, at that time a veteran of 28 years, for the game against England. His debut was characterised by a splendid display in the art and craft of full-back play. A Belfastman resident in Dublin and a member of the Lansdowne club, Crawford went on to win thirty caps for Ireland and shared in many of the considerable triumphs that his club was to enjoy during a magnificent spell in the twenties.

In the game against France, George Stephenson, a youth who had started the season in the Queen's University third XV, won his first cap in the centre. From that April day in 1920 until he received an injury in February 1929 Stephenson played in every game, a truly remarkable sequence. His reputation in an international career that saw him win forty-two caps, a world record that stood for a quarter of a century, was built mainly on his defensive powers and his ability as a place kicker.

With the advent of Crawford and Stephenson and despite the departure of Lloyd, the nucleus of a formidable back line was formed but the strength in depth was not at hand, and the next few years were ones of trial and error. A 9-8 win over Scotland was the only reward during the 1920–21 season, which saw the arrival on the international scene of yet another Irish back of quality, Denis Cussen, but the shortage of youthful talent was emphasised by the fact that two other pre-war stalwarts, Alex Foster and Harry Jack, played in the championship series.

There was one other pre-war stalwart, however, still chasing the ball with vigorous pursuit and renewed enthusiasm. This was Billy Collopy of Bective Rangers, who had played against England in 1914 and in the three subsequent matches that season. He was to remain on the scene for some time yet.

IRISH AND FRENCH TEAMS LINE UP PRIOR TO 1921 INTERNATIONAL IN PARIS

Billy Collopy's father had played for Ireland in 1891, and this is only one example of those strong family traditions that were such a noticeable characteristic of top-class Irish rugby in the 1920s. A sizeable list of illustrious fathers, sons and brothers could be compiled for this period. George Stephenson was joined by his brother Harry during that 1921–22 season, and Billy Collopy was soon to be accompanied by his brother Dick. 'Jammie' Clinch, a forward of some substance who, like his famous father, Andrew ('Six Hundred') Clinch, was never referred to by his baptismal appellation, was about to emerge on the international scene and leave his stamp as a wing forward of quality and determination (not to mention wit). From the north would come the Hewitts, Frank and Tom, and up from Tipperary the Pikes, Ted and Victor, two of the eleven children of a Tipperary clergyman, who saw five of his sons play for Leinster and two for Ireland, with a couple of near misses in Andrew and Robert. The name McVicker was to appear in an Irish team for the first time in 1922 when Sam from Queen's University played in all four matches. His career was eclipsed, however, by two more of the clan, Jim and Hugh, who came into the side in 1924 and 1927 respectively.[1]

Dick Collopy had joined his brother Billy in the Irish pack in the 1922–23 season, and after Ireland had lost to England and Scotland, 'Jammie' Clinch made his debut against Wales at Lansdowne Road and shared in a 5-4 win which was only Ireland's third success in the post-war era. But a new dawn was breaking: many of the boys who had played with distinction in the schools cups in the years immediately after the war were now emerging as players of international quality, and the difficulties that had beset the game in Connacht and Munster in particular were receding. In 1923-24 Ireland won two of the four matches played, and from this point on great things began to happen.

Club football had received a major stimulus in the organisation of a national competition in 1922. A cup presented by a rugby enthusiast, Mr Robert Bateman, was contested at the end of the season between the winners of the respective cup campaigns in the provinces. Not surprisingly, Lansdowne were the first winners in 1922.

On the international front, Ireland, having lost to both England and Scotland, faced Wales in Cardiff with the knowledge that they were long outsiders. Desperate situations often preface what could be called

[1] For a full list of fathers, sons and brothers who have played for Ireland, see Appendix 9.

a gamble rather than a calculated risk and the Irish selectors' choice for the game in Cardiff could certainly be put into the category of a gamble of major dimensions. In desperation the selectors picked a 19-year-old schoolboy from Belfast, Frank Hewitt, to play at out-half. The name Hewitt came into the international sphere in the grand manner, for Frank's elder brother Tom was also chosen for his first cap in the same game, being named on the left wing. The paternal instincts of a bygone age were reflected in the choice of another new cap in the forward Bob Collis, whose father had played for Ireland in 1884. And Ernie Crawford, who had been dropped for the match against Scotland, was recalled to the position of full-back.

Within fifteen minutes Tom Hewitt celebrated his elevation to international status by scoring a great try and Crawford signalled his return by kicking the goal points to put Ireland five points up. This was a good start, but better was to follow. Less than five minutes later Harry Stephenson ran diagonally across the field from his own line and when faced by two Welsh defenders passed to Tom Hewitt. He held the ball for only a fraction of a second before giving a return pass to Stephenson, who got in at the right corner, and even when Crawford hit an upright with the conversion attempt, Irish joy was not dimmed.

With Frank Hewitt giving a masterly display at out-half and the Irish forwards playing with spirit and skill, opportunity was strictly limited for the Welsh who, however, shortly before the interval laid siege to the Irish line. They were helped by a superiority in the tight scrums, and intense pressure culminated in Cliff Richards getting an unconverted try for Wales. The interval score of 8 points to 3 in Ireland's favour suggested the Welsh were in for a struggle and the spectators for a memorable spectacle when hostilities were resumed.

A few near misses were all Ireland had as a reward for a lot of pressure early in the second half, and it was Wales who scored first with a dropped goal, so the whole issue hung on a single point. Forty thousand Welsh voices rose in chorus to urge on their countrymen. But a cruel surprise was in store for them. About twenty minutes before the final whistle, Frank Hewitt received a perfect pass from his scrum-half Joe Clarke and he proceeded to make a tremendous run. He beat Griffiths, one of the Welsh half-backs, and then sold two glorious dummies before crossing for a gem of a try beside the posts. The conversion was a formality, but the thrills were not over yet.

Wales rallied, and one of the Welsh pack, Pugh, got in for a try. The score now stood at 13 points to 10 in Ireland's favour; time was running out and the Irish pack was tiring rapidly. The crisis point was at hand and it came in the form of a splendid run by Welsh winger Rowe Harding, who seemed certain to score. Harry Stephenson raced across from the other wing to head Harding off. In an amazing burst of speed, the Irishman shortened the gap with every stride and then, staking all on a last despairing leap, took Harding down a yard short of the Irish line.

It was a glorious tackle, the closing thrill of a memorable struggle. The victory was the first that Ireland had won on Welsh soil since Louis Magee's team had travelled to that same Cardiff pitch exactly a quarter of a century before to take the Triple Crown. Their successors could now feel that they had earned the right to regard themselves as the equals of their legendary forebears. Their day of glory was a milestone in the history of Irish rugby, for it marked a turning point in Ireland's international fortunes.

CHAPTER 10

THE DAWN OF A NEW ERA: 1924–29

NOW FREE FROM POLITICAL STRIFE, the people of Ireland had more time to devote to sport. Rugby in particular enjoyed greater popularity than ever before. In 1923 the IRFU purchased a new ground in the Ravenhill district of Belfast for the sum of £2,300. The ground was enclosed and a stand built at a cost of £15,500, an adequate commentary on how the union finances had improved. A paid administrative assistant, Rupert W. Jeffares, had already been appointed by the union, and in 1924 he was carrying out secretarial duties under the direction of the honorary secretary, C. Ruxton. In the following year the office of honorary secretary was discontinued and Rupert Jeffares was appointed secretary of the union. With the game spreading and administration imposing increasing demands on honorary officers, Jeffares's appointment was a logical development. He was to occupy the position for twenty-six years and to see many changes take place in the committee room and on the field of play. In this latter respect the opening years of Jeffares's reign coincided with a period of brilliance for Ireland unmatched since the glorious days of the gay nineties.

The 1924–25 season opened with a visit to the home countries by the Second All-Blacks. Ireland was the first country to feel the weight of their talents when, on 1 November 1924, New Zealand, later to reach a peak of perfection that earned them the title of the 'Invincibles', was hard put to defeat a gallant Irish side that lost by 6 points to nil, a penalty goal and a try. That Irish performance took on added significance when New Zealand subsequently beat Wales by 19-0, England by 17-9 and France by 30 points to 6 and ended with a tour record of played 30, won 30. The fact that Scotland did not play the All-Blacks hardly seemed to matter.

Time had at last caught up with Billy Collopy and he was gone when Ireland faced the challenge of the championship in 1925. There was, however, a notable new recruit in the Irish team that defeated France by 9 points to 3 in Paris. He was yet another product of Trinity College, and of Anglo-Irish stock. His name was Mark Sugden.

CIGARETTE CARDS FROM THE 1920S

Sugden's career had been one of some success when he played for Trinity and Leinster as a threequarter. His advent to the scrum-half position came out of need rather than of conviction when Trinity found themselves short of a scrum-half one afternoon and Sugden was drafted to fill the gap because of the reluctance of others to take over those duties. Never was opportunity taken to such devastating effect. Sugden went from strength to strength and even on that day in Paris had not yet revealed the whole range of his talents, though he certainly demonstrated sufficient ability to be retained for an important assignment against England at Twickenham.

One of the two new caps in the forward line for that game was George Beamish, later to earn distinction as an air ace and no little reputation on the golf links. (His brother Charles was later capped too.) The second newcomer to the pack was a former captain of Campbell College, William Fraser Browne, better known by the soubriquet of 'Horsey', a name spoken with reverence in every rugby-playing nation. Once a threequarter of indifferent skill, he found his true vocation in the pack, and prior to his departure to the British Army training camp at Sandhurst, he was already a player of personality, courage and skill. Ruthless tackling was his *métier*. His advent to the Irish side was a protracted business on the grounds that some of the selectors thought him too small and light for the demands of international competition.

Browne helped Ireland to a 6-6 draw with England at Twickenham, the first time since 1911 that England had failed to win against the Irishmen. H. Wakelam in his book, *The Game Goes On*, probably summed up this encounter correctly when he wrote: 'The game was marked by the happy and strange phenomenon of an Irish pack of forwards sticking it out to the last and finishing with something in reserve.' Certainly Wakelam is correct when he says that with this pack modern Irish forward play came into being; Browne, as much as any and more than most, deserves the credit for its creation. His subsequent matches were characterised by his courage, and while lack of weight and height took toll of his stamina throughout a career that was all too short, he was to share in some great matches and moments in his international appearances that spanned three years and gained him twelve caps.

Jamie Clinch kicks to touch v Wales in Cardiff 1924

In 1926 Ireland beat England, Scotland and France before Swansea proved the graveyard of Triple Crown hopes yet again. This was the third time since 1905 that Wales had foiled the Irish Triple Crown effort.

That draw against England in 1925 did not presage any deeds of moment against Scotland, who won readily enough by 14 points to 8 at Lansdowne Road; but a 19-3 win over Wales at Ravenhill was the prelude to greatness which was to be tangibly rewarded in the following year. On that day in Belfast, Sugden had a new partner at half-back, his Leinster colleague Eugene Davy, then a student at University College, Dublin. Sugden and Davy made their contribution to that historic win over Wales, and they were to be the linchpin of a great Irish back line in 1926.

The back line of that season was arguably the greatest ever fielded by an Irish side. Sugden, the master of the dummy, was the scrum-half supreme; Davy, the complete footballer, took over at the half-back position; Ernie Crawford, who mixed subtlety of movement with sarcasm of tongue and was never afraid to use both attributes, was at full-back; Denis Cussen, first capped in 1921, still retained the pace that made him a sprint champion; George Stephenson and Frank Hewitt,

now moved into the centre, had Tom Hewitt outside them on the left; while J. H. Gage of Queen's University, who had the distinction of also being capped for South Africa, was included in the side against Scotland when Frank Hewitt was unable to play.

In the pack, Bradley was the experienced man of the front row, and the campaign also saw A. M. Buchanan, Charlie Hanrahan and C. Payne gain their first caps. James McVicker, who had spent much of his career as a threequarter with a junior club in Belfast, had developed into a second row of substance after joining Collegians in 1924, and beside him was another newcomer in J. L. Farrell of Bective Rangers. S. J. Cagney played in all four games, but C. F. Hallaran, now a well-tried veteran, was dropped after the English match. 'Horsey' Browne was unable to play against France or England, but appeared against Scotland and Wales, while Clinch was still very much in the picture mapping out territory of forward play never previously traversed. Great in defence, Clinch had the distinction, if that it may be called, of playing in thirty matches for his country without scoring a single try and without impairing his unimpeachable reputation — a salutary lesson for some present-day players.

Ernie Crawford

A notable absentee from the Irish pack in 1926 was George Beamish, who was out of action with a serious leg injury. His absence, combined with the unavailability of Browne, probably accounted in part for a sluggish display by the Irish forwards against France, who were, none the less, defeated by 11 points to nil in Belfast. There was little evidence in this game of the brilliance that lay ahead.

Still without the formidable pair, Ireland nevertheless reached the pinnacle against England in 1926, a performance and a match that many assert was the greatest they had yet seen. The events are worthy of at least a brief description. England took an early lead when their out-half Kittermaster cut through and laid on a try for his half-back partner Arthur Young. T. E. Francis converted: 0-5 to England. The England full-back Catcheside was caught in possession by Cussen, dropped the ball, and George Stephenson was presented with a try: 3-5. A splendid English movement culminated in H. G. Periton getting a try, and Francis was again on target with the conversion: 3-10. Obstruction against England and

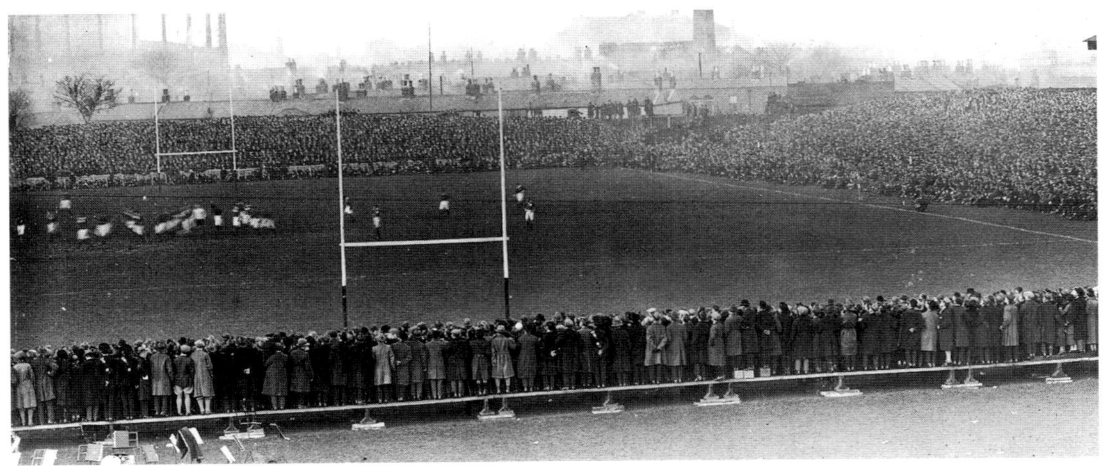

Ireland v Scotland at Lansdowne Road 1925

a long-distance penalty goal was kicked by Stephenson, who was given the kick by the captain, Crawford, against advice from the crowd. At half-time the score was 6-10 to England, and then, after the interval, Sugden began to weave his pattern of magic.

Twice within the space of five minutes Sugden outwitted the English defence with swerve and dummy and twice Stephenson kicked the goals from the same mark, a yard from the touchline, after Cussen had capitalised on Sugden's ploys: 16-10 to Ireland. Then, near the end of the game, Haslett, a new cap in the English side, broke through from a line-out to get a try for England and Francis added the goal points. So it was 16-15 and all to play for. An English attack was foiled and Cussen, instead of finding a safe touch, kicked across the field. An English defender was deceived by the flight of the ball and failed to field it, but Frank Hewitt, following up quickly, did get it and ran in for a try that assured a win for Ireland by 19 points to 15.

J. D. Clinch's cap

Now, having beaten England in a victory that was acclaimed by an Irish invasion of the Lansdowne Road ground, it was on to Scotland and Murrayfield, the new home of the Scottish Rugby Union. Ireland brought more than a victory over England to Murrayfield; they also brought with them the innovation that had marked out that game against England on 13 February as historic for a reason which had nothing to do with its being the occasion of the first Irish defeat of the Saxons for fourteen years. On that day in Dublin, Ireland had worn numbered jerseys for the first time, and they were similarly clad for their initial visit to Murrayfield. The game was played under appalling conditions which were a test of endurance rather than skill. Ireland won on both counts, with a movement between Stephenson, Clinch, Davy and Gage producing the only score of the game, a try in the last minute.

Crowd at Lansdowne Road railway gates 1925

Davy's defensive qualities were seen at their best that day, while Crawford played with the utmost steadiness in conditions calculated to test the mettle of a full-back. Now the last hurdle was to come at Swansea yet again; the result was an 11-8 win for Wales, a bitter disappointment to the Irish team but a just tribute to the strength of the Welsh pack. Yet it was a close-run game which nearly turned into a win for Ireland, as Tom Hewitt was only inches from his objective with a last-minute drop at goal which, had it gone over, would have given Ireland a one point victory. (At that time the drop had the inflated value of four points.)

So Triple Crown honours were missed literally by inches, and a share in the championship with Scotland was the rather poor substitute for what might have been. The game against Wales marked the close of Tom Hewitt's career, and his brother Frank retired in the following season. These were premature retirements that may have cost Ireland the glory that looked imminent but which was not to materialise in the immediate future.

While chance had made Sugden a scrum-half, so also it cost him his place for Ireland's first match the following season. Paul Murray, a young and versatile back, was making an impression in his games for Wanderers, but with Sugden secure on the Leinster team, Murray's chances of representative honours in the scrum-half position seemed limited in the extreme. But an injury to an Ulster player in the match against Leinster in December 1926 gave Murray an unexpected opportunity to display his talents. He was called into the Ulster side during the match and played with sufficient authority to displace Sugden in the selectors' favours when the team to meet France was picked. An 8-3 win in Paris did not help Murray keep Sugden out for long, however, for he was recalled against England at Twickenham, a match in which Hugh McVicker made his international debut alongside his brother Jim. It was not, alas, an auspicious partnership, for Ireland lost by 8 points to 6.

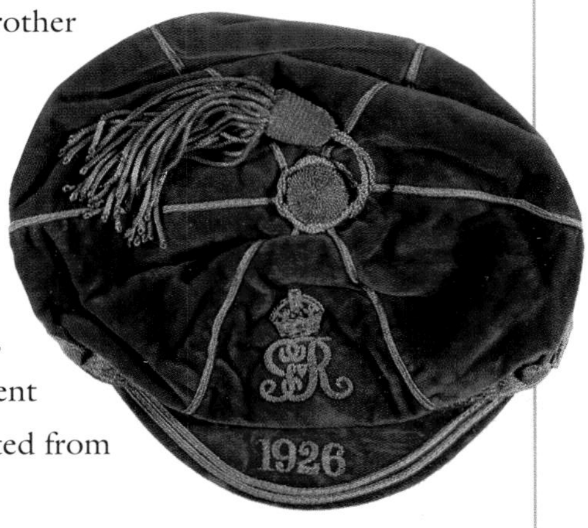

Wins over Scotland and Wales followed that season, which marked the end of Crawford's international career and the advent to the Irish team of two threequarters of great merit, Jack Arigho, one of a splendid Lansdowne back line, and J. B. Ganly of Monkstown. The game against Scotland was played at Lansdowne Road in atrocious conditions; this was the day already referred to, when patrons in the new East Stand received a severe drenching. Subsequent incumbents of the stand have viewed proceedings in greater comfort, well protected from the weather.

In the 1928 series of internationals Sugden and Davy were prominent at half-back and George Stephenson's solid presence still dominated the threequarter line. 'Horsey' Browne, 'Jammie' Clinch, Ted Pike and Charlie Hanrahan were experienced members of the pack, in which George Beamish, who had been out of action for the previous two seasons because of injury, was also a conspicuous and formidable figure. With men such as these in the team, it is small wonder that Ireland won against Wales in Cardiff, against Scotland at Murrayfield, and against France in Belfast. However, they lost to England and to the touring team from New South Wales, and England took the 1928 Championship.

The great side assembled in the mid-twenties was, however, breaking up; but while no Triple Crown or outright win in the championship had been accomplished as a testimony to their undoubted ability, many of them, including George Stephenson, Beamish, Sugden, Davy, Clinch and C. T. Payne, were still together when Ireland at last laid the Twickenham bogey on 13 February 1929. It was a victory achieved against a background of misfortune in the shape of an injury in the early stages to Stephenson, who fractured several ribs. If fate had not always smiled benignly on Ireland at Twickenham and elsewhere, they hung on grimly to win a historic victory over England by 6 points to 5, with Davy and Sugden scoring the tries that saw Ireland home on the strength of a magnificent forward effort.

Paul Murray was back in the Irish side, but in the centre, and his contribution that day, like those of Davy and Sugden, was complementary to the forwards' efforts. And Stephenson, always magnificent in defence, won the game for Ireland with a great saving tackle in the dying minutes despite his broken ribs. The victory, not unnaturally, was greeted with euphoria, and Twickenham, by no means unused to the theatrical especially when Wales played there, was the scene of overflowing Irish emotions. (The seat cushions proved a handy wherewithal for releasing the pent-up feelings.)

Now a Triple Crown beckoned again, but Scotland called a halt to those aspirations when they won surprisingly a fortnight later at Lansdowne Road, where the crowd actually overflowed on to the pitch throughout the game, a circumstance that deprived Ireland of at least one score when Jack Arigho was unable to ground the ball near the posts after scoring an early try. Stephenson was still an absentee because of his rib injury, the first game he had missed since 1920, but he was back again for the game against Wales in Belfast, when Morgan Crowe also came into the side in place of Paul Murray. Another new arrival in the Irish team which faced Wales that year was Mark Deering, a fine forward from the Bective Rangers club. By a strange coincidence, Crowe's brother Phil and Deering's brother Séamus were later to make their debuts on the same Irish team against England in 1935.

Cigarette cards from the 1920s

So the twenties, which had opened with the game in such an uncertain state in Ireland, closed on an altogether different note. The achievements at international level were reflected in a growth domestically that bordered on the dramatic. At the close of the 1929 season there were no fewer than 160 clubs and 59 schools affiliated to the IRFU. Nowhere was the strength more pronounced than in Munster, where in 1920 the game was in a perilous condition. Munster could now boast of having 54 clubs and 10 schools. In Connacht, too, where the struggle to survive had gone on for so long, the situation had improved immeasurably: there were now 15 clubs and 5 schools playing rugby in the province. In Leinster and Ulster, where the main strength of the union had always lain, the improvement was steady if less dramatic. Leinster had 45 clubs and 25 schools, while there were 46 clubs and 19 schools affiliated to the Ulster Branch.

Ireland had also made a significant contribution to international rugby in 1923, when Ellis's exploits of a century before were celebrated with a game that saw six players from Ireland join forces with nine from Scotland to meet a combined England-Wales team. It was an excellent game, worthy in every way of the event it commemorated. England-Wales won by 21 points to 16. A similar game took place at Twickenham in October 1929 when, to honour the memory of one of England's most famous sons, Sir Rowland Hill, Scotland-Ireland exacted revenge by winning an exhilarating match by 20 points to 13. Paul Murray, Eugene Davy, Mark Sugden, George Beamish, Michael Dunne (a Lansdowne forward who had made his mark on the international scene the previous season), C. T. Payne and J. L. Farrell all displayed their talent and skills to great effect that day at Twickenham.

A most important feature of the twenties was the emergence of organised associations of referees, which both recruited new aspirants and vastly improved the general standard of refereeing. In earlier days it had often been the case, particularly in junior games, that a referee was conscripted haphazardly from the touchline spectators. It was vitally important as the game spread that referees should be available on an organised basis. Ulster and Leinster took the lead in this vital work, and the names Wallace Harland, Sam Donaldson, Tom Bell, Jim 'Cocky' Rowlands and Billy Jeffares can be gratefully remembered. Munster soon followed, being inspired by Dickie Magrath, himself an international referee of the pre-war era. Not long afterwards a Connacht association was formed. The fruits of this pioneering work were clearly seen in the later emergence of Irish referees of world stature, such as Ham Lambert, Michael Dowling, Ray Williams, Kevin Kelleher and Paddy D'Arcy.

CHAPTER 11

CONTROVERSY AND ACHIEVEMENT: 1929–39

WALES, WHO HAD THREE TIMES SINCE 1905 foiled Irish Triple Crown aspirations, were unquestionably the bane of the Irish team in the thirties, a decade, nevertheless, of some considerable achievement and no little controversy within the corridors of power of the IRFU administration.

Growth and expansion invariably bring with them attendant problems, and there were those in Irish rugby who rightly felt that the game's administration needed overhauling. Old traditions die hard in rugby, as elsewhere, and while those charged with the responsibility of guiding the game within the country had contributed handsomely, it was time for changes and not all of them were palatable to those in power.

The growth of the game in Munster and Connacht brought with it major problems, not least in respect of playing accommodation. In an effort to cater for an ever increasing playing population, Munster and Connacht led a call for Sunday rugby. Although it was a reasonable request, it did not meet with favourable reaction from the more conservative element of the IRFU, and initially the attempt was resisted strongly. But Munster and Connacht were not alone, for there were strong voices in Leinster too who saw that if there was to be healthy development and progress, then the rigid views of those who resisted the call for Sunday rugby would have to be challenged and overcome. The challenge was made, and the contentious issue was eventually resolved.

The first rumblings of discontent, ironically, did not centre round Munster or Connacht, but around a provincial competition in Leinster, the Midland League. The union refused to allow any games under its jurisdiction to be played on Sunday and several times reiterated that stand. The whole issue was therefore ready to be aired openly, and in October 1929 a deputation from Connacht and Munster met the union and explained their difficulties. The union refused to review their attitude and, in so ruling, offered as one of their reasons for forbidding Sunday play the quite extraordinary allegation that, according to reports that had reached them, the behaviour of players and spectators at games that had taken place on Sunday strengthened them in their resolve to oppose such games. But the matter was far from over.

CIGARETTE CARDS OF IRISH PLAYERS FROM THE 1930S

University College, Dublin, asked the union to investigate Sunday play, proposing that a special committee be appointed to look into the structure of the game, particularly in Munster and Connacht. Unfortunately the union saw no reason to do so and the request was turned down. But matches were taking place on Sundays, including the universities tournament, the Dudley Cup. The demands were growing and culminated in a special general meeting of the union being called in January 1930 to investigate the whole question of Sunday play.

Compromise eventually solved the problem at the meeting in January, as it could have done much earlier. The proposal that averted what was certainly building up to crisis point came from Sam Lee, the man who in the nineties had played so many distinguished games for Ireland. The union decided that 'League and cup matches and all friendly matches shall be played on weekdays except by the special permission of the branch or branches to which the competing clubs belong.'

The establishment of the Irish Free State in the early twenties had left the union in the position of governing the game for one island which contained two separate political entities. It is not surprising, therefore, that the next controversy that afflicted the committee centred on what flag should be flown at international matches, as Ireland played both in Belfast, which was politically part of the United Kingdom, and in Dublin, the capital of the Free State. The question was resolved in 1925 by the union designing a special flag of its own. But there were many who felt that when Ireland played at Lansdowne Road, she should do so under the national flag. It was not a request that met with the approval of all the committee, perhaps an understandable position among a body of men who shared a common interest in rugby but whose political outlooks were diverse in the extreme.

Connacht raised the issue again in January 1932 in a letter to the union, asking if it was the intention to fly the Irish flag at future international matches at Lansdowne Road. The union, no doubt wishing to maintain a nice balance, replied that the flag which had been designed in 1925 and which incorporated the arms of the four provinces was the only flag flown at Ireland's home international matches, and that it was not intended to depart from this procedure.

But the call for the flying of the national flag was taken up by the press and by many of the clubs. Yet again, University College, Dublin, lent its weight to the argument. More important, the Minister for External Affairs in the Free State government asked to meet the president of the union on the matter. That meeting resulted in the union, without a dissenting voice, deciding on 5 February 1932 that in future the national flag would be flown alongside the union flag at all international matches at Lansdowne Road. So an issue that had initially raised the passions of many inside and outside the game was resolved yet again with the fine balance that has maintained the unity of purpose within the game in Ireland, even if that balance has not been matched in the political arena.

There is no doubt that the union committee of the period comprised people who had done splendid work for the game. They had seen it through a period of crisis in the aftermath of the Great War and had presided over its organisation and development. They were men with distinguished records of service on the field and in the council chamber, men such as R. G. Warren, Stan Polden, Jack Coffey, Harry Thrift, Fred Strain, John Macaulay and Andrew Clinch. Yet it was none the less true that to a large extent the union had been geared to a common viewpoint and, perhaps, to principles that were too rigid. Nowhere was the common bond of thought more pronounced than in the selection committee. John Macaulay had served no fewer than twenty-six times on it starting in 1895 and was still there in 1930. Stan Polden had been a member of every committee from 1922 to 1931 and was back again in 1932 for a further period of two years. John Warren, like Polden a distinguished legislator, held office for twelve years from 1922/23 to 1933/34.

Change was needed within the union and the clamour for it came from outside, notably from Leinster, where once again the UCD club were the architects of the dramatic changes that took place within the Leinster executive in the mid-thirties, and subsequently the wind of change blew, with beneficial results, through the IRFU executive committee and selection committees. The new school of thought, which had been frowned upon by the establishment as too radical, none the less represented the views of the majority of the players and clubs within the game.

The new set-up in Leinster brought renewed vigour and impetus to the game both within the province and in a more general aspect. It was reflected in the selection committee for the 1934–35 season when Leinster's representatives were Paul Murray and G. P. Sarsfield Hogan.

P. F. Murray kicking goal against Wales at Cardiff 1932. E. C. Ridgeway placed the ball

Murray had just retired as a player, having represented Ireland nineteen times in three different positions, centre, out-half and scrum-half. He had also toured New Zealand with the Lions in 1930. He was to make a contribution of similar moment on the administrative side, eventually serving as president of the union in 1965–66.

Sarsfield Hogan had been a leading figure in setting the UCD club on the road to success when the college entered senior ranks in 1919, nine years after its foundation. A threequarter of high class, he was on the first UCD team to win the Leinster Senior Cup in 1924 and subsequently a member of the great Lansdowne side of the twenties. His playing career did not follow a similar course to that of Murray, but the ultimate honour, an international cap, only just evaded him, for he played in two final trials and was several times on the panel of reserves for Ireland. His term of service as an administrator was both long and distinguished. His election to the selection committee in 1934 was the preface to a career that culminated in his election to the presidency of the union in 1948. Two years earlier he had been appointed one of Ireland's representatives on the International Board and he remained a member of that body until he retired in 1971. Hogan's period of service on the board featured some revolutionary and very beneficial changes in the laws of the game on which he was considered one of the world's leading authorities.

There were many other able men who came into the administrative sphere at branch and union level during that period of transition in the mid-thirties. One of these was Judge C. F. Davitt, and he too succeeded to the union presidency in 1936–37.

Connacht, too, came into the interprovincial fold in its own right, and for the first time established fixtures with all the other provinces on an annual basis, though it was not until 1947 that Connacht competed officially in the Interprovincial Championship, thereby giving the annual series the status of an all-Ireland fixture. Connacht had long been blessed with dedicated souls who kept rugby football going within the province despite great difficulties. Foremost among them was Henry Anderson. He was the first Connachtman to be capped for Ireland, receiving that honour four times between 1903 and 1906 while a member of the Old Wesley club. At the annual general meeting of the union in October 1937, Connacht gained direct representation to the union committee for the first time since the old haphazard days of the nineteenth century. Henry Anderson was nominated as Connacht's representative, and a worthy one he proved to be. In 1946 he was elected to the union's highest office.

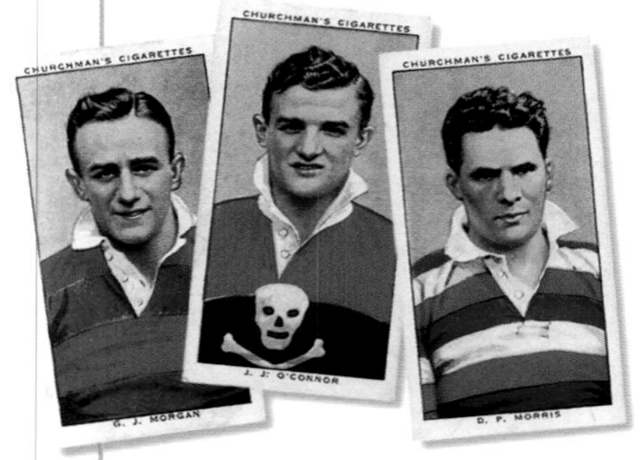

CIGARETTE CARDS FROM THE 1930S

At that meeting in October 1937 the changing administrative scene was reflected in a lively debate on the constitution of the committee, but a proposal to increase the direct representation of Leinster, Ulster and Munster from one to two members and reduce the elected representatives from eight to four was rejected.

While circumstances and events had brought about the retirement of some of the old established figures of the union in this period, it was time itself that caught up with one of the most remarkable rugby careers of all, that of Robert G. Warren, the former captain of Ireland and a player of considerable ability. Warren had attended his first IRFU meeting in 1885 and had an unbroken spell on the committee until, in 1936, he announced his resignation but agreed to act as one of Ireland's representatives on the International Board. He had acted in that capacity since 1877 and had been honorary secretary of the board from 1897 to 1933, being succeeded in that office by Harry Thrift. R. G. Warren thus served on the union committee for fifty-one years. He had seen many changes, and none of these was more important, dramatic or effective than those that had taken place during his closing years on the committee. His period on the International Board spanned forty-nine years, during which he had as his fellow Irish representatives men whose contribution to the game generally and to Irish rugby in particular cannot easily be measured: J. B. Moore (1892–1927), Andrew Clinch (1928–36), Eddie McAlister (1886–97), H. C. Sheppard (1897–1906) and, in the closing years, Fred Strain (1932–46) and Harry Thrift (1931–56).

The thirties, in retrospect, added up to one of the most significant periods in Irish rugby history, but all the drama was not confined to the council chamber. The changes at executive level took place against a playing record for Ireland of near misses, great successes and the winning of the championship for the first time since 1899. The long, barren spell was broken by a fine Irish combination in 1934–35.

By that time France had departed from the championship scene which she had first entered in 1909–10. The break with the four home unions came in March 1931 when, against a background of allegations of rough play and professionalism, it was decided that fixtures against France would be discontinued.

Before that championship triumph for Ireland in 1935, the team had contested two Triple Crown finals, in 1930 and 1931. Ironically, Ireland lost to France in both seasons, but beat England and Scotland before Wales yet again proved the stumbling block.

In 1930 a team that still included George Stephenson, with Eugene Davy in the centre and Paul Murray at out-half, beat England by 4 points to 3 at Lansdowne Road, and Scotland by 14 points to 11 at Murrayfield. The match against Scotland on 22 February was notable for a brilliant performance from

Davy, who scored three tries in the space of thirty minutes. Stephenson's career ended with the following match against Wales at Swansea, where Wales won by 12 points to 7.

The following season, Ireland, with an all-Lansdowne threequarter line of Ned Lightfoot, Eugene Davy, Morgan Crowe and Jack Arigho, defeated Scotland by 8 points to 5 in Dublin. They had earlier accounted for England at Twickenham by 6 points to 5, a match that completed a hat-trick of victories over England. The Lansdowne threequarters were still together when Ireland faced Wales in Belfast in March, but the combination was not effective enough to deal with the opposition, and Wales won by 15 points to 3.

IRELAND V ENGLAND 1930

Leading figures in the pack now were two notable players from Cork, Noel Murphy from the Constitution club and Jack Russell from University College. 'Jammie' Clinch was still around too, while Jack Siggins from Collegians had come into the side in 1931. The latest of the Pike brothers, Victor, also made his debut that season. And George Beamish was still on hand to lend his experience to that of Clinch and Farrell from Bective.

A great South African team under the leadership of Benny Osler came to Dublin and beat Ireland on 19 December 1931. This was 'Jammie' Clinch's last game for Ireland, by which time Mark Sugden had departed and Paul Murray was now established at scrum-half. Murray's half-back partner was Larry McMahon, who had made his first appearance as a centre against England in the previous season and who subsequently gathered twelve caps in an international career that extended until 1938. There are many who still find it difficult to understand why McMahon's career was frequently interrupted at the whim of the selectors, for he was a centre of the highest class.

Ireland figured in a three-way tie with England and Wales in the 1932 series, when the outstanding feature of the season was a magnificent display against Scotland at Murrayfield. Ireland won by 20 points to 8. Lightfoot scored two tries that day, and Murray converted all four Irish tries. Michael Dunne, who had missed the 1931 season, was a leading figure in the pack that dismissed the Welsh challenge by 12 points to 10 at Cardiff.

Murray's career ended the following season when in his last match he helped Ireland to defeat Wales by 10 points to 5, an unexpected victory since Ireland had previously lost to both England and Scotland. Ireland had been wonderfully served at scrum-half since Sugden had made his initial appearance in 1925. Sugden and Murray had shared the position between them for eight seasons for all but one match, the game against England in 1932, when the Limerickman, Danaher Sheehan, then playing with London Irish, partnered Eugene Davy.

Murray's retirement brought to the scrum-half position another great player and one who was to remain in the national side until 1939. This was George Morgan, who was initially attached to the

Clontarf club and who was later a leading figure in establishing Old Belvedere, a senior-ranking club composed of past pupils of his old school. Morgan's first season in the Irish jersey was something of a traumatic experience, however, for in 1934 Ireland lost all three matches and Davy's international career ended with the game against England.

In 1935 there were four new caps against England: Phil Crowe in the back line and three new forwards, P. J. Lawlor and Séamus Deering (Bective Rangers) and H. J. Sayers (Lansdowne) in the pack. The new formula did not add up to a potent force, and England won by 14 points to 3. Morgan's partner at half-back was Aidan Bailey, who had made his debut in the previous season while still a schoolboy at Presentation College, Bray.

For the match against Scotland, Bailey was restored to his proper position in the centre, and another Hewitt, Victor, a brother of Frank and Tom, came in at out-half for his first cap. Jack Siggins, the Irish captain, led a pack of forwards that included herculean workers in Deering, Bob Greaves and Sammy Walker, all recent additions to the front line. Ireland won by four tries to a goal, the tries being scored by Joe O'Connor of UCC, Lawlor, Ernie Ridgeway and George Morgan.

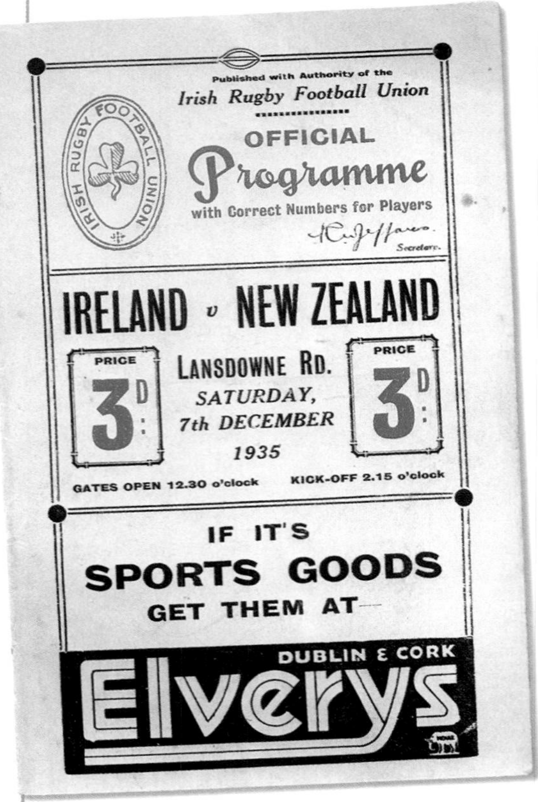

Only one change was made for the match against Wales on 9 March 1935: Jack Doyle of Bective Rangers came in on the wing for Dave Lane of UCC. The Irish pack was again magnificent, but the feature of the match was the manner in which Bailey put the great Welsh centre Wilfred Wooller out of the game. Two penalty goals, one each by Siggins and Bailey, gave Ireland a 6-0 interval lead. Doyle celebrated his first and, as it transpired, his only cap by getting a try and Wales's only achievement that day was a penalty goal. So Ireland won the championship for the first time in thirty-six years, and the Ravenhill crowd suitably acclaimed the feat. Theirs would be the privilege again when next the title was captured, but that was some time ahead.

The Third All-Blacks came on tour the following season and Ireland failed to register their first win over a touring team, losing by 17 points to 9, despite the fact that there were sixteen Irishmen on the field, for the referee that day was an Irishman, Billy Jeffares, son of the IRFU secretary and one of a long line of distinguished Irish referees. One such referee was Kevin Kelleher, who established an all-time record in taking charge of no fewer than twenty-three international matches before his retirement from the international scene in 1972.

A narrow victory but a victory none the less over England (by 6 points to 3 in Dublin) and Scotland, beaten with greater ease by 10 points to 4 at Murrayfield, set the stage for another Triple Crown match against Wales in Cardiff in 1936. Cardiff, where four years earlier Ireland had foiled Welsh Triple Crown hopes, was no happy hunting ground for Ireland, who travelled as reigning champions. And while Wales could not win the coveted title, having been held to a draw by England, victory in the match would give them the championship.

The Arms Park was packed to capacity for the game, with thousands locked outside the gates. The game was better in the expectation than the realisation, however, for it was decided by a penalty goal kicked by the Welsh full-back Vivian Jenkins after only twelve minutes' play.

The Irish forwards worked tremendously hard to open the way for the backs, but all the endeavours of Deering, Russell, Siggins, Walker and their comrades proved in vain, and the Welsh goal was the only score of a most disappointing encounter.

RUGBY FOOTBALL UNION.
England v. Ireland
Saturday, February 13th, 1937, at Twickenham
Kick-off 2.45 p.m.
ENTRANCE ROW SEAT
EAST P 12 97
Lower Stand
(See plan on back, which shows how to reach your Seat).
Price - 10/-
(including Tax and Admission to Ground)
OFFICIAL PROGRAMMES INSIDE the Ground ONLY.
Engineer Commander R.N., Secretary, R.F.U.
IMPORTANT—Kindly occupy your seat by **2.30** *p.m.*

Wales and Scotland were both defeated in 1937, when George Cromey took over the out-half position, but England took the Triple Crown and the championship. Their 9-8 win over Ireland at Twickenham was surrounded by controversy. England had scored a try in doubtful circumstances, the ball appearing to go out of play, but A. Butler, the England right wing, immediately went in for a try, which gave England the lead. That advantage was short lived, as Fred Moran, an Irish sprint champion who had come into the team the previous season, gained an equalising score following a great passing movement. Within ten minutes Ireland was in the lead: George Morgan paved the way for Moran to cross for a second try, to which Aidan Bailey added the points from the touchline. With ten minutes' play remaining, Peter Cranmer reduced the lead with a penalty goal for England. And then, five minutes from the end, came the incident that provoked the controversy and gave England the winning try.

H. V. Sever, the England left wing, put in a great dash down the wing. As he grounded the ball, he was bundled into the corner flag by the combined efforts of Vesey Boyle and Fred Moran. The referee, Mr J. W. Faull of Wales, was unable to decide whether or not Sever had been bundled into touch in goal and the Irish linesman, Stan Polden, was asked to adjudicate. He decided that Sever had scored a legitimate try. Recalling the incident many years later, Stan Polden was adamant that Sever had grounded the ball before being knocked into touch in goal. So victory went to England.

In the 1937–38 season Ireland suffered a humiliating 36-14 defeat by England at Lansdowne Road. This was to be Scotland's season, for both the Triple Crown and championship went to them — they have not won either since — and Ireland took the wooden spoon after losing to Wales in Swansea. But better days were ahead.

The Lions went to South Africa in the summer of 1938, travelling under the leadership of Sammy Walker. That, however, did not deter the selectors from dropping Walker for the game against England in 1939. It was, nevertheless, a useful-looking side that travelled to Twickenham. Charlie Teehan, a young hooker from UCC, and J. Ryan of UCD were brought into the pack, while at full-back the selectors opted for the diminutive Lansdowne man, Con Murphy. Among the experienced members of the team, Harry McKibbin, who had toured in South Africa, was partnered in the centre by Des Torrens of Bohemians, and Fred Moran and V. J. Lyttle were on the wings. Like the half-backs Cromey and Morgan, all had played in the international arena previously. The pack was fortified by the presence of Blair Mayne, a tremendously strong forward and a boxer of repute, and Dave O'Loughlin, who had made his mark as a forward in the previous season.

H. J. 'Mike' Sayers of Lansdowne and Aldershot Services had been on the scene for some time, while his back-row colleagues, Sinclair Irwin and Robert Alexander, were established internationals, Alexander since 1936 and Irwin since the match against Scotland in the previous season. Sinclair Irwin was following in his father's footsteps, for Sam Irwin had played for Ireland nine times between 1900 and 1903 and was president of the union in 1935–36. In that respect, too, Sinclair was to emulate his father, for he attained the presidency in 1969–70. Harry McKibbin, his colleague that day, had the distinction of being elected president of the IRFU for the centenary season (1974–75) and is one of Ireland's representatives on the International Board.

Paul Murray meets the Duke of York, Twickenham 1929

It was the combined efforts of McKibbin and Irwin that gave Ireland a 5-0 victory over England at Twickenham on 11 February 1939, Irwin scoring the try and McKibbin converting.

While it was a success gained against the expectations of most, it was thoroughly deserved, and the same team was named to meet Scotland at Lansdowne Road. One change was necessary before the game as D. Tierney of UCC was forced to withdraw; his departure brought in Tommy Headon of UCD for his first cap. In conditions of rain and mud, Ireland won convincingly by 12 points to 3. McKibbin kicked a penalty goal, Torrens and Moran scored tries, and Mike Sayers marked a Scottish drop-out and then dropped a goal from the mark, a rarity at the best of times but a truly remarkable feat in the prevailing wind and rain. It was the first score of that nature in international football for eight years, and only the eleventh in international rugby. A crowd of 35,000 was present to witness the novelty.

A crowd of 30,000 packed into Ravenhill on 11 March to see an Irish side that showed just one alteration from the team that had beaten Scotland. Vesey Boyle was recalled on the left wing. The spectators did not, however, see an Irish victory, for the Irish forwards were outplayed and Wales won. However, in spite of the disappointment, the future looked bright and there would be other opportunities in the years that lay ahead. But the opportunity to contest another Triple Crown was not to come for another seven years. Seven times in all had Wales foiled Ireland at the last obstacle, and four of those frustrations had been suffered since 1930.

CHAPTER 12

EUROPE ERUPTS: 1939–46

THE POLITICAL SITUATION IN EUROPE had for several years been clouded by a growing menace as Germany made territorial demands on some of her neighbours. What many expected finally occurred on the first Sunday of September 1939, when Britain declared war on Germany. Éire was not involved but a war situation was not one in which international rugby could be played.

The proposed tour of Australia to Britain and Ireland scheduled for the autumn of 1939 was cancelled and, in common with the other unions, Ireland lost £1,050, their share of the guarantee towards the Wallabies' tour expenses. The Australians returned home without playing a match. All official internationals were cancelled for the duration of a war that lasted until 1945 and ravaged mankind to a degree never previously known.

Cork Constitution Connetts 1943. This photograph includes five IRFU Presidents: Teddy Magrath, Dickie Magrath, Noel Murphy Sr, Noel Murphy Jr and Tom Kiernan

The effect of the previous conflict in 1914–18 had been to stifle effectively all rugby other than in the schools. This time the series of cup campaigns in the provinces, with the exception of Ulster, continued throughout the war and brought in some much-needed revenue, but the Bateman Cup, suspended in 1939, was never again contested.

There were also Services internationals in Britain, including a four-countries match at Richmond in December 1939. Such games as an Irish XV v Defence Forces gave an opportunity to players who would in ordinary circumstances have worn the Irish jersey in full internationals. In 1942 further spice was added to the representative scene when an Irish XV met the British Army at Ravenhill. It was the first of five such matches that took place and it was not until the last of the games, in December 1945, that the Irish side managed to win, beating the British Army by 19 points to 3. These games gave tremendous experience to Irish players who were later to form the backbone of the national side when full internationals were resumed in 1947, while some of those who had distinguished themselves in the Irish jersey in the period immediately before the war also figured in the series.

Yet many fine players were deprived of the ultimate distinction because of the war, notably Austin Carry, a splendid out-half who played for Trinity and Old Wesley, Des Thorpe of Old Belvedere, a

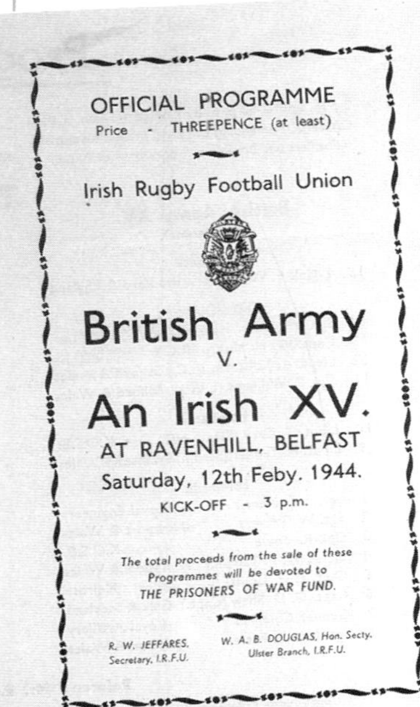
OFFICIAL PROGRAMME
Price - THREEPENCE (at least)

Irish Rugby Football Union

British Army
v.
An Irish XV.
AT RAVENHILL, BELFAST
Saturday, 12th Feby. 1944.
KICK-OFF - 3 p.m.

The total proceeds from the sale of these Programmes will be devoted to THE PRISONERS OF WAR FUND.

R. W. JEFFARES, Secretary, I.R.F.U.
W. A. B. DOUGLAS, Hon. Secty. Ulster Branch, I.R.F.U.

scrum-half who just missed a cap, Hugh Greer, an accomplished back from NIFC , Jack Guiney of Bective Rangers, and his namesake, Jack Guiney of Clontarf.

The war in Europe ended in 1945 and international rugby reverted to civilian control in Britain, where the Services had organised what games had been possible during the war period. When international rugby was resumed in 1946 with unofficial internationals there were many missing faces. Two of the Irish side of 1939, Robert Alexander and Mike Sayers, were killed in 1943. C. F. Hallaran, a sterling forward of the twenties, was killed in 1941, while P. B. Coote, who had won one cap in 1933, lost his life in the same year. J. B. Minch of Bective Rangers, capped five times in 1913 and 1914, also fell in 1943, and there were many others. On the home front, the union's affairs had been guided by John Warren, elected president in 1938, until he too died in 1945.

In 1946 there was a full programme of matches and, happily, France had now returned to the fold. The 1946 games were not, however, recognised as full internationals, so those that participated in them did not get caps. Ireland's first assignment was against France at Lansdowne Road in January 1946. France's return to the international scene did not bode well for the Irish, who lost by 4 points to 3. The French side that lined out at Lansdowne Road in 1946 showed no signs of being the products of a ravaged and hungry land. It included two giant second-row forwards, A. Soro and R. Moga, both of whom played a major role in Ireland's defeat. That day the Irish crowd got a first glimpse of a back-row forward in the French team, Jean Prat, later to leave his imprint on the rugby scene by his brilliant application and execution of line-out technique and other facets of wing forward play.

Ireland lost to England by 14 points to 6, while Scotland and Wales also applied sufficient pressure on the Irish XV to win. And if Britain had felt the hardships of war and the severity of food rationing, there was as yet enough rugby talent around to ensure that the 1947 championship would not be conceded to a team from across the Irish Sea.

Rugby football in its first season after the war, 1945–46, owed a great debt to a touring party of New Zealand soldiers. They played as the 'Kiwis' but wore the black jerseys for so long associated with the All-Blacks, and they added lustre to the proud traditions of New Zealand football, reviving happy memories of All-Black teams by their standard of play. The Kiwis played two games in Ireland, beating Ulster by 10 points to 9 in a splendid game at Ravenhill on 14 November. Three days later they faced Leinster at Lansdowne Road. The game ended in a 10-10 draw and provided a magnificent match. It was a splendid performance by Leinster against a team that succeeded in beating Wales, England and France twice subsequently.

Meanwhile, the IRFU had elected Henry Anderson as president for 1946 and all was back to normal on the domestic front. The task was now to build up a team for a worthwhile Triple Crown challenge.

CHAPTER 13

THE GOLDEN YEARS: 1947–52

One crowded hour of glorious life
Is worth an age without a name.
(T. O. Mordaunt)

ALMOST HALF A CENTURY HAD PASSED since Ireland's last success when, once again, an Irish team set out in quest of the Triple Crown. Those forty-nine years of waiting had seen much disappointment and frustration, most of it inflicted by Wales. But the crowded hour of glory was at hand, and it came in Belfast on 13 March 1948, when Wales was defeated by two tries to nil. That win gave Ireland the Triple Crown and, for the only time in history, the grand slam victory over all the home countries and France. It did not give Ireland the international championship, for when Ireland took the field at Ravenhill the result of the championship contest had already been decided.

Ireland had used twenty-six players during the 1946 campaign of unofficial internationals. Only three of the players, Con Murphy the full-back, wing Fred Moran and Dave O'Loughlin of the forwards, had been capped in the pre-war era. But while that 1946 campaign proved one of no joy for Ireland, it did provide valuable experience for the players, two of whom were to make such an impact in the immediate future. By coincidence, they were both medical students, one from Belfast and one from Dublin. Jack Kyle from Queen's University and Karl Mullen from the Old Belvedere club played in the positions of out-half and hooker respectively on the Irish side that by its victory over Wales in 1948 wrote the preface to a tale of glory that has become known as the golden years of Irish rugby. Mullen and Kyle played together on an Irish side for the first time against the British Army in December 1945. Later that season they got a better appreciation of the international atmosphere during the unofficial contest against France, England, Wales and Scotland. Mullen played in all four matches in 1946, while Kyle played in those against France and England.

Mullen was already a top-class international hooker in 1947 and when given the opportunity to lead the side the following season, he proved a splendid captain and a great tactician at a time when the tactics employed by the Irish side were very much a matter for the captain. Mullen's name will always be identified with Ireland's golden years, during which he gave ample proof of his qualities of leadership and of his depth of thought and ability to analyse the potential of his own team and the strengths and weaknesses of the opponents. He brought a new dimension to the Irish captaincy and was a worthy successor to two of the shrewdest Irish captains of an earlier age, Louis Magee at the turn of the century and Ernie Crawford in the 1920s. And any comparison must take account of the fact that the evolution of the game may have made Mullen's task more difficult than those of his two illustrious predecessors.

Kyle, every inch an athlete, stamped his class and authority on the international scene in 1947 when the championship series was resumed and if, as yet, the greatness soon to emerge was not revealed in all its full bloom during the 1947 campaign, the potential was there for all to see.

In January 1947 international rugby was restored to the calendar in its full official form when France met and beat Scotland in Paris. Ireland's first match that year was against France in Dublin on 25 January, and the journey from representative to international rugby was not smoothly made by the Irish, who lost by 12 points to 8. Con Murphy of Lansdowne was the only player who survived from the pre-war era. Although Ireland lost, there were plenty of players in the Irish side that day who would be around in sunnier times. Barney Mullan, on the left wing, had come from the same club, Clontarf, as that flier Fred Moran, whom the war deprived of anything up to twenty more caps. Kyle was at out-half, and the nucleus of a great pack was on view, with Karl Mullen being propped on one side by M. F. Neeley and on the other by a formidable figure in stature and accomplishment, John Christopher Daly, who for much of the war period had been engaged in battles of a very different nature on the high seas. Colm Callan, a tough and uncompromising second row from Lansdowne, Bob Agar from Malone and Bill McKay, another medical student from Queen's University, all wrote the preface to greater things that day before the enthusiastic gathering that had assembled at Lansdowne Road.

The French did not in those days attract the capacity attendances that gathered at the shrine when England and Wales were the visitors, though later French teams were of sufficient skill to be greeted by the 'house full' sign in Dublin.

The defeat by France induced no feeling of depression among Irish supporters or panic decisions among the Irish selectors for the next assignment, the match scheduled against England at Lansdowne Road on 8 February. Ireland brought in a newcomer on the right wing, Bertie O'Hanlon of Dolphin, and his was one of many fine contributions to an Irish victory of historic proportions. His play was clearly of sufficient character and skill to suggest that greater things were at hand.

Ireland won by 22 points to nil, and there never had been, nor has there been since, an Irish victory over England by so wide a margin.

The Irish forwards had hustled and harried the French a fortnight earlier before eventually yielding territory and possession to a heavier French eight, who capitalised on an injury to Karl Mullen. But in the match against England there was no injury, and from start to finish the Irish pack gave England a roasting. Kyle, partnered by his university colleague Ernie Strathdee, was magnificent at half-back and the backs responded splendidly to the service laid on for them. Barney Mullan with two tries, two conversions and a penalty goal contributed thirteen points to Ireland's total. O'Hanlon scored two tries and McKay one.

After this great victory Con Murphy's long and successful career as a full-back, small in size but a giant in performance, came to an end. He was replaced by Dudley Higgins and the captaincy passed to J. D. Monteith, one of the Irish centres.

Fortified by that astounding win over England, Ireland faced Scotland at Murrayfield a fortnight later and justified the confidence they carried. In bitter cold and on a snow-bound pitch, Barney Mullan's unconverted try in the closing stages proved decisive.

That victory at Murrayfield set up a Triple Crown opportunity yet again, and Ireland's task against Wales was to be at Swansea, where Ireland had not won since 1889, five years before their first Triple Crown success. Ireland included a new cap for the game, Michael Lane of UCC, who made his debut as a centre, although his experience and talents were more suited to the wing. Once again Swansea proved a place of doom and gloom for Ireland and her supporters. Ireland did reasonably well in the first half, at the end of which there was no score. Then W. E. Tamplin of Cardiff landed a penalty goal for Wales, who held the lead in precarious fashion until the genius of Haydn Tanner, the brilliant Welsh scrum-half, was utilised to open the way for a try near the end. So Wales had managed to blight Irish hopes once more, and for the fifth time since 1930 and for the eighth time in all. But the Welsh sceptre was soon to be removed from over the Irish head. Ireland would lay the Swansea bogey, and many of the players who walked dejectedly from the St Helen's ground were soon to return to the territory and not have to make the journey to the pavilion by their own resources when the battle was over.

The Australian team which visited Britain, Ireland and France in the 1947–48 season came as the Third Wallabies but they were, in fact, only the second fully representative side from Australia, for the Second Wallabies came and went in 1939 without playing a match. One of the 1939 team, W. M. McLean, came back in the autumn of 1947 as captain of these first post-war tourists. A broken leg sustained in the sixth match of the tour ended McLean's active participation for the duration, but despite his absence Australia beat England, Scotland and Ireland.

That match against Ireland in Dublin on 6 December proved a bitter disappointment, for Ireland were comprehensively beaten by 16 points to 3. Not even the stimulus of an early penalty goal kicked by Kevin Quinn, a player who for some reason could not reveal in international games the full extent of his immense talents, succeeded in lifting the Irish. The Australians also played Ulster and Munster and found that both these teams, especially the latter, provided much stiffer opposition to their ability than had the national side.

Neither O'Hanlon nor Mullan, each of whom had contributed so handsomely the previous season, were in the Irish side. The wings were Des McKee, later in the season to solve a problem in the centre, and Kevin O'Flanagan, an all-round sportsman of truly astonishing versatility, if not every man's idea of the complete rugby player. O'Flanagan was also a soccer international and a champion athlete, and he later turned his attention to golf with no little success. His brother Michael later also made one appearance for a later Irish side and he, too, was a soccer international. Thus if the O'Flanagan brothers both had a short tenure in the Irish rugby team, the fact that both were capped at rugby and soccer was a unique double.

Ireland met France at Colombes on New Year's Day 1948 in the first match of the international championship and surprisingly gained a decisive victory by two goals and a try (13 points to 6). Less than a month previously, ten of those who played at Colombes had been in the side against Australia. But the display in Paris was in complete contrast to the performance against Australia. Barney Mullan was back in

the threequarter line, as was O'Hanlon, and the centre positions were taken by McKee and the Garryowen man Paddy Reid, who had made his debut against Australia. In the pack Colm Callan was recalled to the second row, and among other changes was the inclusion of a new cap at wing forward, Jim McCarthy of Dolphin. His arrival had an instant impact on the quality of play, and on that day he formed with Bill McKay a useful partnership that was to become devastatingly effective when the back row unit included the Old Belvederian Des O'Brien. McKay was a tackler of the highest quality, McCarthy an opportunist who brought a new concept to wing forward play and who was to prove the principal agent of Kyle's plan for breaching the opposing cover. The team lacked penetration in the centre but played to the strength of a superb pack of forwards.

That win in Paris was the prelude to the finest accomplishments in the whole history of Irish rugby. The teamwork of the Irish side was at almost its greatest pitch of perfection and was ready to be exploited to the full, first by Jack Kyle and later by Karl Mullen. The finishing touches to the team's composition were made when Mullen took over in time for the next game against England, when Kyle was able to achieve the desired dominance by his superb improvisation and by skilfully manipulating his forwards' rhythm and control.

The terminology of rugby, like much else, has changed today. In 1948 there was no talk of 'second-phase attack' or of 'good ball'. Ireland won two Triple Crowns by what today would be termed second-phase attack but which then was referred to as a magnificent pack of forwards, as well as the ability of others to eliminate error and grab opportunity when it presented itself in the shape of penalty goal chances and try-scoring opportunities — to say nothing of the sheer genius of Jack Kyle, surely among the greatest of all rugby players.

In Jim McCarthy, Ireland had the ideal ally to Kyle once the ball came back on the Irish side. Barney Mullan (like George Norton in the following year) was a place kicker who had full mastery of his craft. Daly, injured early in the season, was recalled for the game against England, and despite the win over France, Strathdee lost the scrum-half berth to Hugh de Lacy and the captaincy to Karl Mullen. Des O'Brien came in at No. 8, Daly was restored to the front row in place of Jim Corcoran of UCC, and Jack Mattsson of Wanderers was at full-back.

D. R. Gent, the former English international who was for many years a highly respected rugby correspondent for *The Times*, was one of many impressed by Ireland's 11-10 win over England at Twickenham on 14 February 1948. 'A great Irish side this and a great victory', he wrote. McKee, Kyle and McKay scored tries and Mullan converted one, and that was enough for the needs of the hour.

Scotland at Lansdowne Road was the next assignment, and the visiting side included no fewer than three pre-war internationals, one of whom, W. C. Murdoch, had first been capped in 1935. Ireland restored Dudley Higgins to full-back and had Michael O'Flanagan in the centre for Paddy Reid. Victory for Ireland against Scotland meant that Ireland would win the championship irrespective of how they fared later against Wales. And victory came, following a faltering and nervous first half. Kyle scored a magnificent try which assured success after Barney Mullan had given Ireland the lead with a similar effort after the interval. So Ireland were champions for the first time since 1935 and the championship was won at Lansdowne Road for the first and only time in history.

Ireland faced the supreme test when they lined out at Ravenhill against Wales in front of a capacity crowd of 30,000 on 13 March 1948. Had there been room to accommodate another 100,000, it is safe to assume that the capacity would still have been stretched to the limit, such interest was there in the game. A championship had been won, and Ireland were meeting Wales for the Triple Crown and the grand slam. Karl Mullen, recalling what it was like in the Irish dressing-room that March day, said:

Jack Kyle scores against England 1949

> We were tense and anxious, yet I knew, and the players knew, we could win. The whole team discussed tactics, the Welsh strengths and what we thought were their weaknesses. And that was a procedure that we always went through. Every man had his say, it was an important part of the pre-match preparations in a side whose hallmark was team spirit. Forward supremacy was all important and we knew we had to win in the pack if victory was to be ours. The atmosphere was tremendous. The realisation that we could win the Triple Crown came first, I think, after the win over England at Twickenham. The main worry we had before the match in Belfast was that things might go wrong on the day and that old Welsh bogey would assert itself once more.
>
> We decided on a policy of seeking to win through our forwards and the genius of Jack Kyle, undoubtedly one of the great players of any era. A plentiful supply of possession for the Welsh, we felt, would probably mean disaster for they had a splendid back line and we feared three players in particular, Haydn Tanner, Bleddyn Williams and Ken Jones.
>
> A little incident just after the kick-off inspired great confidence in me. Barney Mullan took a penalty that went just over the Welsh full-back Frank Trott's shoulder and trickled into touch near the Welsh line. For some reason, I felt then that this was going to be our day.
>
> There is a widely held belief that apart from Kyle, our back line was not good. It is an opinion that I do not subscribe to. Kyle was certainly the master outside the scrum, but the defensive qualities of the backs were excellent, and that day in Belfast Paddy Reid and Des McKee were magnificent in defence and did not give Bleddyn Williams an inch. Our defence behind the scrum was invariably good, even if the attacking ability was a little limited.

At half-time the score was 3-3, with Bleddyn Williams having scored a great try to bring Wales level after Barney Mullan had given us the lead with a try when he took a long pass from Kyle in full flight. Rhys Stephens had been giving us a lot of trouble in the line-out and Jimmy Nelson was given the job of subduing him. Nelson well and truly performed his task. The 'council of war' we held at the interval gave us a lift and we were, I believe, the better team in the second half.

When J. C. Daly got the try in the second half that gave us the lead, the whole team played like men possessed. In the closing stages Kyle used the touchline superbly and we felt that we had only to avoid doing something rash. We held out to the final whistle and when that went, there was, initially, only a dim realisation that we had won the Triple Crown.

Dim the realisation may have been, but within seconds Karl Mullen and his fourteen heroes had to bear the full brunt of long-pent-up emotions. Few in the crowd at Ravenhill had seen Ireland's last triumph forty-nine years earlier. Souvenir hunters of a historic victory made Chris Daly the primary target, and as he left the field shoulder high the shirt was stripped from his back. Daly, who had started the season with a bad injury that threatened to end his career, was not to play for Ireland again as he turned professional after the Triple Crown triumph. As a league player he revealed the athletic ability that had made him a priceless asset to Ireland.

That match against Wales was not vintage rugby, but it was a champagne occasion, a long-cherished dream realised. It was a just reward for effort and ability, for determination and character.

Ireland, Grand Slam winners in 1948

Nine of the team in Belfast had played in all four matches in the championship: Bertie O'Hanlon, Des McKee, Barney Mullan, Jack Kyle, A. A. McConnell (a strong and durable prop from Collegians), Colm Callan, Karl Mullen, Jim McCarthy and Bill McKay. Three more had played in the three Triple Crown matches: Jimmy Nelson, Des O'Brien and Chris Daly. Dudley Higgins, injured for the game against England, had played against France, Scotland and Wales; Paddy Reid had played against France, England and Wales; Hugh de Lacy against England and Scotland; and Ernie Strathdee against France, after which game he was surprisingly dropped in favour of de Lacy, though he was recalled for the Welsh match. Jack Mattsson, Mick O'Flanagan, Ernie Keeffe, a fine forward from Sunday's Well who was yet another player deprived by the war of further honours, Jimmy Corcoran and Bob Agar had all played in one game each, Mattsson against England, and Agar, Corcoran and Keeffe against France.

Thus twenty-four players contributed to Ireland's success and attained a level of achievement without equal either before or since. It was the privilege of a Corkman, the late Teddy McGrath, to be president of the union in that season of triumph, one that gave a tremendous stimulus to the game in Ireland. Meanwhile as Karl Mullen's men carved out their path of glory, time caught up with four stalwarts who had served nobly in an earlier age. In the space of six weeks, and at the height of Ireland's glory, four Irish internationals died: John Fulton, who had played against England in the 1899 Triple Crown-winning year and who had in all played sixteen times for Ireland, Mossie Landers, like Fulton an accomplished full-back in the early 1900s, Bertie Doran, one of three brothers from the Lansdowne club to play for Ireland, and Eddie McCarthy, who was in the Irish team against Wales in Limerick in 1898. They may not have been in full accord with all the concepts of the game as played in 1948, but they would undoubtedly have appreciated Mullen's men and rejoiced in their deeds.

Ireland opened the 1949 campaign in the role of defending champions, secure in the knowledge that the great majority of the championship-winning team was still at hand. Two exceptions were Chris Daly and Paddy Reid, both of whom joined the Rugby League. Once again they were team-mates, but in the cause of the Huddersfield club.

Ireland included four new caps for the first assignment of the 1949 campaign. One of the newcomers who faced France at Lansdowne Road on 29 January was full-back George Norton. His advent to international status did not have happy consequences on his initial appearance, but the benefits of his presence would be gained in the immediate future. With Daly gone, there was a vacancy at prop forward and the selectors turned to another Munsterman, Tom Clifford from the Young Munster club, and a very fortunate choice he turned out to be. The international careers of the other two caps were of shorter duration. Tom Cullen, at scrum-half, made his only international appearance that season against France. Two seasons earlier he had been selected for the international side but was unable to play. The fourth newcomer to the side came into the problem spot on the team, the centre. He appeared to have a most unlikely background, for he was a Roman Catholic priest. Father Tom Gavin of London Irish did not have a lengthy or distinguished international career, but is unique in so far as he is the only Catholic priest ever to have been capped for Ireland.

It was once again a case of the unpredictable Irish when France were entertained in 1949. Ireland had opened the previous season by being well beaten by the Australians, and yet had gone on to take the

Triple Crown and the championship. This time a French team which had lost earlier to Scotland travelled to Dublin and won by two goals and two dropped goals (16 points) to three penalty goals (9 points), a scoreline that revealed almost the full range of the scoring system, but one that was an anticlimax for the Irish after their previous fine performances. George Norton kicked all three penalties for Ireland. Had the game taken place in the previous season, Ireland's margin of defeat would have been two points wider, but the International Board, in its wisdom, had reduced the value of the dropped goal from four points to three, a happy decision that went some way towards putting that particular facet of scoring into something approaching its proper perspective in relation to the try.

Despite the reverse against France, Ireland once again went on to win the championship and the Triple Crown, with which legendary honour the French were not of course concerned.

From the French match onwards, Ireland had the best pack of forwards, notably in the set scrums, in support of the outstanding hooker of the age, Karl Mullen, and the best out-half, Jack Kyle. The Kyle-Strathdee partnership was restored for the game against England, a match in which the threequarter line was moderate, with Gavin unable to provide the thrust the line needed. The wing positions were occupied by O'Hanlon and Mick Lane who, having been capped in 1947 as a centre, now found his natural environment. Clifford, a forward in the typical Munster mould, tough and uncompromising, proved an able ally to Mullen in the front row.

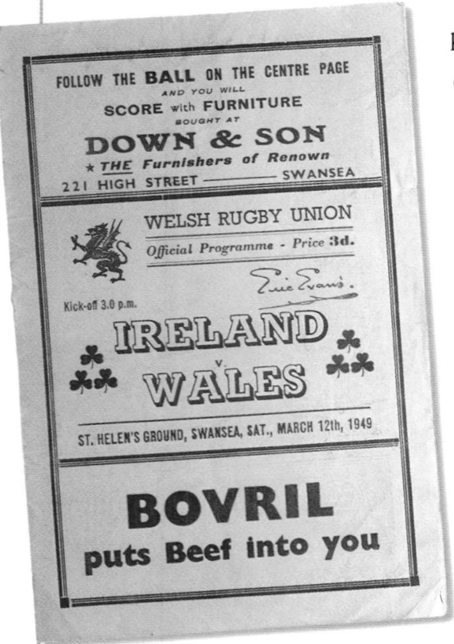

Norton's three penalty goals against France had made no difference to the end product, but such was not the case against England. He kicked two in the first half of that match when a try by O'Hanlon gave Ireland a 9-5 lead at the interval. Norton brought his points total to seventeen in two matches when he converted a second-half try by Des McKee, and Ireland won comfortably by 14 points to 5. And if the Irish display was not of a quality that appeared to presage another title, the win over England was important, not least in psychological terms.

Callan and McConnell were both omitted for the game against Scotland at Murrayfield. Ireland also replaced Gavin, bringing in a youngster from Queen's University, Noel Henderson. He had been a brilliant schools player and emerged on the senior representative scene that season in the Ulster team. His first cap against Scotland was the start of a brilliant international career that extended over the next decade, and his presence in the 1949 series turned a moderate threequarter line into what was at least now an ample force. In the pack Bob Agar took over from Callan in the second row and Les Griffin of Wanderers came in at prop for McConnell.

By the time Ireland reached Murrayfield, Scotland had championship aspirations, having beaten both France and Wales. However, they proved no match for the Irish side. George Norton again made a rich contribution, scoring a penalty goal and two conversions. The Kyle-McCarthy combination bedevilled the Scots, McCarthy getting both the Irish tries. Scotland's only reply was a penalty goal.

Ireland took an unchanged side to Swansea on 12 March for a match in which both the Triple Crown and the championship were at stake. The Welsh side had shown erratic form and their selectors

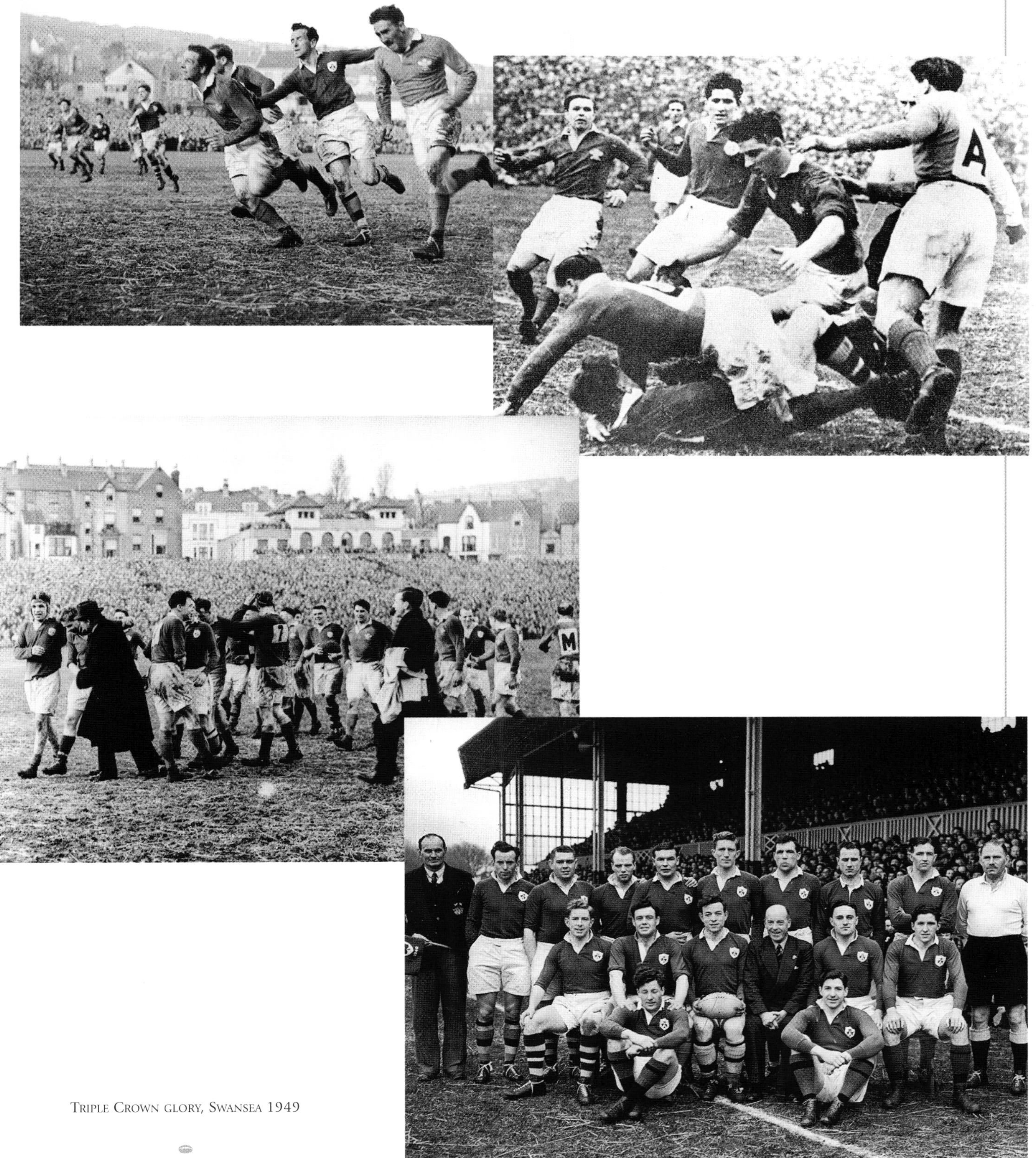

Triple Crown glory, Swansea 1949

had therefore brought back the experienced Billy Cleaver for Glyn Davies at out-half. The first half was scoreless, but after the interval Kyle began a brilliant tactical movement which culminated in a try for Ireland, scored, as so often, by McCarthy. Norton then converted it to register the full five points. It was the only score of the match. The Triple Crown was Ireland's once again.

Ireland owed much to McCarthy that day for, quite apart from his try, he did a most effective spoiling job on the Welsh half-backs. Kyle had made a remarkable blind side break which he turned to full account by a cleverly lofted kick inwards over the heads of the converging defence. McCarthy's speed of thought and movement did the rest. Jumping high for the ball just short of the Welsh goal-line, he defeated the desperate efforts of several defenders to prevent him from scoring.

The try was the reward for enterprise and thought, qualities that epitomised the play of McCarthy and (even more so) of Kyle. Kyle not only possessed excellent hands and a fine turn of speed, but he also had the facility for knowing just the right moment to seek and make the breaks. He was the outstanding back of that entire championship series in which Ireland used nineteen players. Only three times previously had the Triple Crown been won by the same country in successive seasons: England won it in 1913 and 1914 and achieved the double again in 1923 and 1924, as did Wales in 1908 and 1909.

It was a happy Irish party that returned to their headquarters at Porthcawl to celebrate the victory and to enjoy the festivities arranged by the president of the union, Sarsfield Hogan, who had been a selector when Ireland had won the championship fourteen years earlier. George Norton had more reason than most for celebration, for he could reflect on a contribution of twenty-six out of the forty-one points Ireland had scored in the championship. That total was a record for an Irish player in one season and stood until 1973, when Ireland's out-half Barry McGann contributed twenty-eight points, also in four matches, though one of these was against New Zealand.

The 1950 international season was surrounded by a time-worn argument about the eligibility of players. The controversy basically concerned England, who fielded what amounted to a Dominions team liberally sprinkled with South Africans and including one All-Black. The question of proper qualification had never been solved, or indeed really faced, except by Ireland. Agreement of a kind was reached towards the end of the season, when it was decided that no overseas player could be offered a cap once he had played for his own country, but that hardly settled the matter, especially at a time when the number of outstanding Dominion players resident in Britain was increasing rapidly. Ireland thus remained in almost splendid isolation by the IRFU's long-standing unwritten agreement to select only players of Irish birth (or at least one Irish parent) who had never appeared in a trial for another country.

On the playing field, Wales relieved Ireland of both Triple Crown and championship, and Ireland achieved a win and a draw in the four matches. It was little consolation to Ireland that Wales paid her the compliment of imitation, winning the series by close co-operation among the forwards and halves, supported by the opportunism of those behind. One notable divergence from Irish practice, however, was that Wales possessed adroitness in the centre that had not been at Ireland's disposal. Nowhere was it used more effectively than at Ravenhill on 11 March 1950, when Wales won by 6 points to 3, Ken Jones and Malcolm Thomas getting tries for Wales, while George Norton kicked a penalty goal for Ireland.

Ireland's first match of this season was played in arctic conditions in Paris. Ireland included two new caps, J. H. Burges, a scrum-half from Rosslyn Park, and the Instonians man Des McKibbin, whose selection to the prop forward position strengthened still further the family tradition in Irish rugby, for his brother Harry, the centenary president, had been a centre for Ireland and the Lions before the war.

It was a penalty goal by Burges in the last minute that earned Ireland a draw after France had held on grimly to a three point lead, established by means of a dropped goal by their out-half P. Lauga. Lauga had taken three drop shots at goal during that first half; apart from the one that counted, another also went over the bar, but as the whistle had gone for off-side, the goal was disallowed. Adding some weight to the opinion that Ireland had been extremely lucky were the facts that Jean Prat had missed a penalty from in front of the posts and the full-back R. Arcalis had hit a post with a superb drop kick in the second half. It was an unimpressive start to Ireland's championship defence and Jim McCarthy's absence was sorely felt.

An injury to Des McKee, which forced him to leave the field for good at half-time, was something that Ireland could not afford against England at Twickenham, and Bill McKay's removal from the pack to fill the void at centre was another change that the Irish pack could ill afford. England won the match, yet the margin of their victory was a narrow one, 3 points to nil. Nevertheless, it ended all hopes of the hat-trick of championship and Triple Crown successes that so many had expected Ireland to achieve.

Ireland, with three new caps in the side, demolished Scotland by 21 points to nil at Lansdowne Road a fortnight later, an event that did not go unnoticed in Wales, whose team did not face the prospect at Ravenhill with any degree of equanimity. As it transpired, Wales won, and deservedly so, but had to endure periods of intense danger before getting home by two tries to a penalty goal. Jim McCarthy was back after missing three games through injury, but this time Wales managed to circumvent the Kyle-McCarthy link.

In the summer of 1950 the first British and Irish side to go on an overseas tour since the war left for New Zealand, and Ireland's accomplishments in the recent past were reflected in the choice of Karl Mullen as captain. Eight Irishmen accompanied him. George Norton, Michael Lane, Noel Henderson and Jack Kyle were among the backs, a clear indication of the selectors' awareness that not all the talents of the Triple Crown sides were hidden in the heart of the scrum. Tom Clifford, Jimmy Nelson, Bill McKay and Jim McCarthy were the Irish representation in the forward line-up.

Not for those tourists the quick jet-flight that takes today's teams across the world in little more than a day. They went by boat and had to endure a rough passage on the initial stages of the voyage. On the field the demands were no less severe and New Zealand won the Test series by three games to nil, with one drawn. George Norton broke an arm while playing against Southland at Invercargill during the sixth match of the tour and took no further part in the proceedings. Karl Mullen was also injured and did not play in the third and fourth Tests.

The 1950–51 season was one in which the form of the participants varied to an astonishing degree throughout the series. But for Ireland all ended happily, for the title was regained. Mullen again proved an able captain and his educated footwork ensured a smooth service for Kyle, who still revealed the form that had captivated the New Zealand public, perhaps the most discerning critics in the rugby world. Kyle was a real match-winner and match-saver.

When Ireland played France at Lansdowne Road on 29 January 1951 fortune was on the side of the home team. The side included four new caps: C. S. Griffin on the right wing, R. R. Chambers in the centre, J. H. Smith of Queen's University at prop, and John O'Meara of UCC at scrum-half. O'Meara was in the side after the original choice, Hubie McCracken, had withdrawn because of an attack of pleurisy. They were surrounded by experience and expertise, and tries by Jimmy Nelson and Tom Clifford and a penalty goal from Noel Henderson saw Ireland safely through by one point (9-8).

Ireland selected the same side for the game against England at Lansdowne Road, but Michael Lane had to withdraw because of a broken rib. His defection brought in a new cap, the Queen's University player Harry Millar. It also brought to a total of five the Queen's University representation on the side. (The other four were Henderson, now firmly established in the centre, Kyle at out-half, and Bill McKay and Smith in the pack.) Des McKibbin, operating in the second row, kicked a penalty goal in the second half and that sufficed to decide the issue in a game notable for excitement rather than quality.

An injury to George Norton after fifteen minutes of the match against Scotland at Murrayfield did not augur well for Ireland's Triple Crown chances, but Millar played heroically at full-back and, with McKay on the wing, the seven Irish forwards performed splendidly. But once again it was primarily Kyle's brilliance that saw Ireland through. He opened the way for the match-winning try ten minutes from the end, and Des O'Brien applied the finishing touch to Kyle's break. McKibbin missed the conversion, but Ireland held on to a 6-5 lead. Noel Henderson had dropped a goal in the first half which had cut Scotland's advantage at the time to 5-3. It was no mean achievement to leave Murrayfield with victory after playing for sixty-five minutes with fourteen players.

That was Norton's last appearance for Ireland. His place for the Triple Crown match against Wales went to Aengus McMorrow of Garryowen; McMorrow, who played for Connacht, was the first man from that province to be capped in the post-war era. Tom Clifford, too, had gone and McKibbin had moved to the front row for the game against Scotland. J. R. Brady of CIYMS came into the second row to form a new partnership with Paddy Lawlor of Clontarf. A 3-3 draw against Wales in Cardiff on 10 March gave Ireland the championship, but not the Triple Crown. Norton's absence was never more sorely felt, for three kickers failed to score with chances ranging from the reasonable to the simple. The scoring pattern was decided in the first twenty minutes with Ben Edwards kicking a penalty for Wales and Kyle equalising with a great try for Ireland. The second half was a battle between the forwards, with the monotony broken by the attempts of Kyle and his opponent on the Welsh side, Cliff Morgan, to find a way through tight defensive cover. That was the first confrontation between Kyle and Morgan, later to emerge as one of the game's great outside-halves.

The golden years were over now, but despite a defeat at the hands of the Fourth Springboks in Dublin on 8 December, Ireland went to Colombes and defeated France by 11 points to 8 early in 1952.

Ireland's performance against the Springboks had been of reasonable dimensions, and with Clifford now back in the pack and a most promising second row from Ulster, Robin Thompson, having made an impressive debut against South Africa, Ireland looked capable of taking any opposition up front. And Kyle was still a master of his craft at out-half. Tries by Henderson and McCarthy, a penalty goal from Henderson and a conversion by a new cap, Jack Notley, added up to more than the French could handle. The victory nurtured hopes that were not, however, realised.

The match against England was scheduled to take place at Twickenham on 9 February but was postponed to 29 March because of the death of King George VI. So Scotland was to provide the next examination for Ireland in Dublin on 23 February and with Notley now in the centre and two new caps, Mick Dargan of Old Belvedere at flank forward and Archie O'Leary of Cork Constitution in the second row, Ireland met the needs of the occasion and won by 12 points to 8.

Lansdowne Road on 8 March provided proof that Ireland had reached the end of a glorious era, for Wales completely outplayed the home side and won even more decisively than the 14 points to 3 on the scoreboard suggested. It was Karl Mullen's last match for Ireland, for he lost his place for the rearranged game against England at Twickenham on 29 March. His replacement, Robin Roe, proved a worthy successor as hooker. Ireland gambled with five new caps at Twickenham for in addition to Roe there were two newcomers in the pack, Paddy Kavanagh and Billy O'Neill, both from UCD, the club which also provided a new wing, Mick Hillary. The name Bailey figured on an Irish side yet again when Noel Bailey of Northampton was picked for the threequarter line.

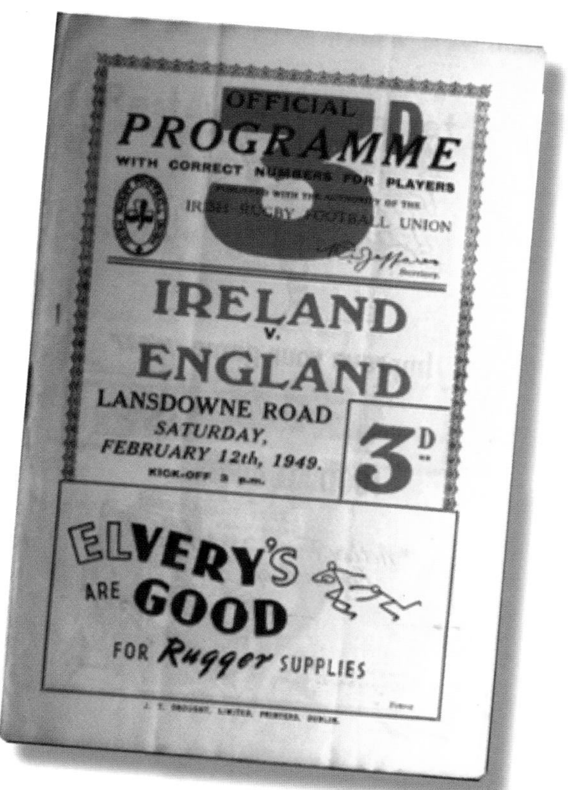

Des O'Brien took over the leadership from Mullen, but his tenure of office did not start in the winning vein, as England defeated Ireland by 3 points to nil. The whole did not add up to a memorable season for Ireland, but there had been satisfactory features. The high spot of the season had undoubtedly been the win at Colombes. This took on added significance later, for twenty years were to elapse before an Irish team was able to manage a similar feat at that ground. Munster, too, had put up a tremendous display against the Springboks, maintaining their great tradition of fighting qualities against touring sides.

CHAPTER 14

LOW-INTENSITY OPERATIONS: 1952–59

ONLY ONCE IN HISTORY HAD AN IRISH TEAM embarked on an overseas tour. Fifty-three years after that initial crusade an Irish side, captained by Des O'Brien and with Sarsfield Hogan as manager, undertook the second mission, this time to Argentina. It was not unexplored rugby territory, for three times previously the English Rugby Union had sponsored tours, while two years before the Irish visit the full strength of France had played Argentina at Buenos Aires. Several leading players such as Mullen, Kyle and Henderson were not available for inclusion. If Kyle's absence did nothing else, it gave an opportunity to the man who had stood in his shadow for Ulster and Ireland, the Instonians out-half John Hewitt. Hewitt was later to gain the elusive Irish cap, but a total of four appearances for Ireland hardly bore testimony to an ability that would have been more widely recognised had he not been unfortunate enough to be of the same era as Kyle. Hewitt later had the task of sorting out similar difficulties himself as chairman of the Irish selection committee in 1973–74.

Those whose task it was to choose the party for the Argentine in 1952 originally settled on a combination that included fourteen internationals, but defections reduced the number of capped players who eventually travelled to thirteen, one of whom, Michael Dargan, was not an original choice. The party also included a referee, Mr O. B. Glasgow, and, as secretary to the manager, Billy Jeffares, who was soon to succeed his father R. W. Jeffares as secretary of the IRFU. The team and officials left Dublin on 20 July. The first match was played in Santiago, Chile, and resulted in a 30-0 win for the Irish.

IRFU touring team, Argentina and Chile, 1952

Argentina was in a sombre mood when Ireland's rugby tourists arrived in Buenos Aires, where the people were still mourning the recent death of Eva Perón, the wife of the Argentinian president, an event that had threatened to put the tour in jeopardy.

Ireland, plagued by injuries and with limited scoring power, won six, drew two and lost one of the nine matches played. This was quite a respectable performance against unexpectedly strong opposition. Ireland won one and drew one of the two Test matches and ended the tour with a record of having scored 126 points and conceding 43. John Hewitt was the star performer among the Irish backs in a side that lost some prestige by a defeat early in the tour but largely regained it before the expedition ended.

For the players and officials the tour was a most enjoyable experience and the 'Shamrocks', as the team was called, served a worthy purpose in supporting the game in South America. The large Irish community in Buenos Aires was pleased to have a chance of seeing and supporting a national team from the homeland.

The South American journey over, the prospects on the home front were not reviewed with a confidence similar to that which had preceded the championship series in recent years. The doubts in the minds of the Irish supporters were confirmed in a series in which Ireland used nineteen players and awarded nine new caps. Ireland beat France and Scotland, but could only draw with England and lost to Wales. Among the newcomers to the side was yet another forward in the true Munster tradition, Tom Reid of Garryowen, a splendid back row from UCD, Ronnie Kavanagh, and a wing from Bective Rangers, Maurice Mortell. Kavanagh's elevation added still further to the growing list of brothers who had been honoured for Ireland. He had laid his claims while in the Argentine, where he was accompanied by his brother Paddy, who had been capped in 1952.

Des O'Brien had gone and Kyle had taken over the leadership. McCarthy was still present and John O'Meara remained a fine link at scrum-half. But together with Mullen, O'Brien, Clifford and McKay, O'Meara played his last game against France in 1952. Now that these fine players were to be seen no more in the green jersey, much of the old zest was gone and as yet had not been recaptured. Nevertheless, a feature of the 1953 campaign was a resounding 26-8 win over Scotland; and Murrayfield, where once Eugene Davy had scored three tries and Paul Murray had kicked four conversions, witnessed another scoring feat by an Irishman when Séamus Byrne, a wing from UCD, signalled his entry to the international sphere by scoring three tries. It was not, however, the prelude to a long and distinguished career for he was capped but twice subsequently.

Jack Kyle scoring against France, Belfast, 1953

The Fourth All-Blacks came in the autumn of 1953, and the Irish got a glimpse of a powerful pack of forwards and one of the greatest of all full-backs, Bob Scott. They also got another beating from the New Zealanders. But the distinguished visitors, like so many touring teams before them, had discovered Munster territory to be ground where not an inch was given, and it took a last-minute try to avert the Munster challenge.

An Ireland team now took the field for the first time without the assistance of Kyle, for when England were encountered at Twickenham on 13 February 1953 Kyle had to withdraw because of injury. So at last John Hewitt got his chance. Despite Kyle's continued absence, Hewitt was omitted for the remaining games against Scotland (won 6-0 in Belfast) and Wales (lost 12-9 in Dublin). Ireland therefore ended the season with one win and four defeats, used twenty-seven players and awarded eight new caps, including a full-back later to give distinguished service, Paddy Berkery of Lansdowne and Garryowen.

Ireland achieved less than promised over the next three seasons. Kyle and Henderson were still in the team, but McCarthy had retired in 1954. In 1955 a young centre from Old Belvedere came on the scene in a match against France. Tony O'Reilly's red hair made him easy to identify on the field, while his physique made him a difficult opponent to stop. If he promised more than he attained in the Irish jersey, he emerged as one of the stars of the Lions tour to South Africa in the summer of 1955, when once again the Lions were captained and managed by Irishmen, Robin Thompson and Jack Siggins respectively. The side also included five Irish players, Thompson, Tom Reid and Robin Roe among the forwards, and O'Reilly and Cecil Pedlow, a recent recruit to the Irish side, among the backs.

SCOTLAND—IRELAND				ENGLAND—WALES	
15	R. W. T. CHISHOLM, Melrose—Scotland	FULL BACKS		1	P. M. DAVIES, Cambridge Univ. and Llanelly (W.)
		THREE QUARTERS			
14	A. R. SMITH, Cambridge Univ.—Scotland	RIGHT WING	LEFT WING	5	J. ROBERTS, Old Millhillians (E.)
13	A. C. PEDLOW, Queen's Univ.—Ireland	RIGHT CENTRE	LEFT CENTRE	4	M. C. THOMAS, Newport—Wales
12	A. J. O'REILLY, Old Belvedere—Ireland	LEFT CENTRE	RIGHT CENTRE	3	W. P. C. DAVIES, Harlequins—England
11	J. S. SWAN, Coventry—Scotland	LEFT WING	RIGHT WING	2	K. J. JONES, Newport—Wales
		HALVES			
10	J. W. KYLE, N.I.F.C.—Ireland, Captain	OUTSIDE		6	C. I. MORGAN, Cardiff—Wales, Captain
9	A. F. DORWARD, Gala—Scotland	SCRUM		7	R. E. G. JEEPS, Northampton (E.)
		FORWARDS			
1	H. F. McLEOD, Hawick—Scotland			8	C. C. MEREDITH, Neath—Wales
2	R. ROE, Richmond—Ireland			9	B. MEREDITH, Newport—Wales
3	P. J. O'DONOGHUE, Bective Rangers—Ireland			10	W. O. WILLIAMS, Swansea—Wales
4	J. R. BRADY, C.I.Y.M.S.—Ireland			11	J. PROSSER, Pontypool (W)
5	P. J. LAWLOR, Clontarf—Ireland	Referee:		12	R. H. WILLIAMS, Llanelly—Wales
6	J. T. GREENWOOD, Dunfermline—Scotland	M. SERGE SAULNIER (F.F.R.)		13	V. G. ROBERTS, Harlequins—England
7	T. E. REID, London Irish—Ireland	KICK-OFF 2.30 P.M.		14	I. D. S. BEER, Harlequins—England
8	A. ROBSON, Hawick—Scotland			15	R. E. SYRETT, Wasps (E.)

Touch Judge: T. ELLIOTT (S.R.U.)

Touch Judge: D. L. SANDERS (R.F.U.)

Thompson and Siggins could reflect on a splendid tour during which their side drew the Test series by two wins to two and ended with a record of eighteen wins and a draw from twenty-four matches. O'Reilly amassed sixteen tries, a record number, and ended the tour as top scorer.

On the provincial front, the 1955–56 season was marked by Connacht's consolidation as a first-class rugby power. The reward for their honest endeavour and dedication was gathered in the form of a share in the interprovincial championship in 1956, when they divided the spoils with Ulster, having beaten Munster by 10 points to 3 in Cork to record their first victory on Munster soil. Connacht lost to Leinster, but ended the season with a splendid 6-3 win over Ulster at Ravenhill, where two years earlier they had scored their first victory away from home.

No really worthwhile challenge was mounted by Ireland for the Triple Crown and championship during the remainder of Kyle's career, which came to an end in 1958 against Scotland in Dublin. Kyle won his forty-sixth cap that day to establish a world record of international appearances in matches involving the International Board countries and France. And if Kyle did not play at his brilliant best, at least he ended on the winning side. He had a new partner now, Andy Mulligan, who had come on the scene in 1956, thus becoming the eighth man to partner Kyle in international rugby.

Irish team and officials arriving in Cardiff for match v Wales in 1957

A month previously Kyle had been a member of the first Irish team to beat a touring side when Australia were defeated by 9 points to 6 at Lansdowne Road. John O'Meara was recalled for the game after two seasons out of international rugby, and Ireland had six new caps in their side, including four who were later to render sterling service. One was the latest of the Hewitt clan, David. His father Tom had proved his worth in the 1920s and the son further embellished the family tradition. Among the five newcomers to the

pack was Noel Murphy, another son of a famous father, also named Noel, who had been a stalwart in the Irish pack of the 1930s. Noel Junior would go on to earn forty-one caps and captain his country. Two other new men were also future Irish captains, Bill Mulcahy in the second row and Ronnie Dawson, the hooker, for whom the honour was indeed at hand.

Dawson scored a try for Ireland on his debut against Australia, as did Pedlow. But the match was won for Ireland by the veteran Noel Henderson, who scored the all important try that decided the issue in the closing minutes. Ireland had at last beaten a touring side and Kyle, who had been the biggest single contributor to the unprecedented run of success between 1948 and 1951, was appropriately in the first Irish side to accomplish such a historic victory. Henderson, his able right-hand man in so many of the glorious battles fought and won during the golden years, was the captain. The Irish team that beat Australia in 1958 was:

P. J. Berkery (London Irish)
A. J. F. O'Reilly (Old Belvedere)
N. J. Henderson (NIFC) Capt.
D. Hewitt (Queen's University)
A. C. Pedlow (CIYMS)
J. W. Kyle (NIFC)
J. A. O'Meara (Dolphin)
B. G. M. Wood (Garryowen)
A. R. Dawson (Wanderers)
P. J. O'Donoghue (Bective Rangers)
J. A. Donaldson (Collegians)
W. A. Mulcahy (UCD)
N. A. Murphy (Cork Constitution)
J. R. Kavanagh (Wanderers)
J. B. Stevenson (Instonians)

It was no easy task to follow Kyle. The job fell to a player from Bohemians, Michael English, who was given a veteran partner in John O'Meara. Sadly, O'Meara ended his international career against Wales in 1958 by being carried from the field on a stretcher midway through the second half, after having scored a try, which together with a penalty goal from Henderson gave Ireland a 6–0 interval lead. But weight of numbers up front and the speed and thrust of the Welsh backs proved too much for Ireland, who conceded three tries in the second half. And, with Henderson in the full-back position, the season ended with an 11-0 defeat in Paris.

Noel Henderson scores winning try against Australia, Lansdowne Road, 1958

The aura of greatness that surrounded the Irish team at the outset of the 1950s was not attendant upon the side that represented Ireland in the series of 1959. But if the side itself could not be classed as great, it contained great players. The leadership was given to Ronnie Dawson, the first sign of the team selectors' recognition of his depth of thought, tactical appreciation and knowledge of the game. Those attributes would grow with experience and be applied in a different capacity at a later date when international rugby came to take on a new meaning and when the strategy and indeed the very idiom of the game underwent a dramatic change.

Dawson was supported by two strong and able performers in Syd Millar and Gordon Wood, and if Ireland did not have the best team in 1959, they had probably the best front row, and arguably the best pack, since the Mullen era. Mulcahy and a new cap, Gerry Culliton, both of whom were to enjoy protracted careers, were in the second row, while Noel Murphy had the experience and craft of Ronnie Kavanagh and the exuberance and courage of a Connachtman, Tony O'Sullivan, as his back row colleagues.

The back line that faced England at Lansdowne Road in 1959 had a less settled look about it. Henderson was still filling in at full-back. O'Reilly was in the centre with another Connacht debutante, John Dooley, while the wings were occupied by the experienced Pedlow and Niall Brophy, a fast and intelligent player who had enjoyed a brilliant schools career in the colours of Blackrock College and who was now a student at UCD. He had made a quiet entrance to the Irish side the year before, but greater things were in the offing. English and Mulligan were at half-back.

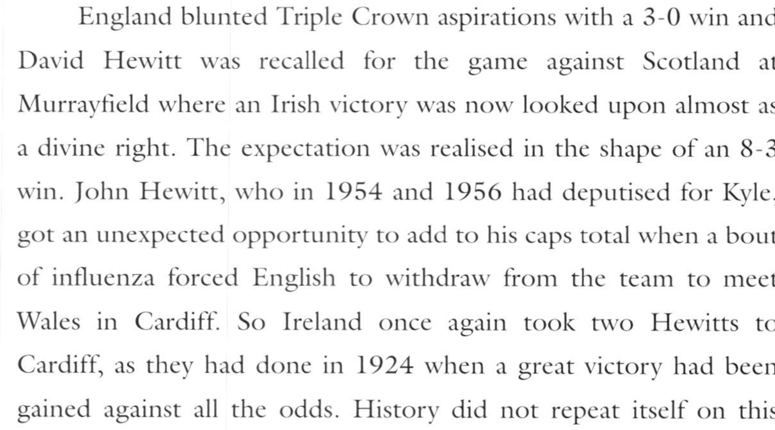

Action from Wales v Ireland, Cardiff, 1959

England blunted Triple Crown aspirations with a 3-0 win and David Hewitt was recalled for the game against Scotland at Murrayfield where an Irish victory was now looked upon almost as a divine right. The expectation was realised in the shape of an 8-3 win. John Hewitt, who in 1954 and 1956 had deputised for Kyle, got an unexpected opportunity to add to his caps total when a bout of influenza forced English to withdraw from the team to meet Wales in Cardiff. So Ireland once again took two Hewitts to Cardiff, as they had done in 1924 when a great victory had been gained against all the odds. History did not repeat itself on this occasion, however, as Wales won a narrow 8-6 victory.

But it was not Wales who were the dominant force of the season. That honour belonged to France who, under the shrewd leadership of Lucien Mias, came to Dublin on 18 April as champions for the first time in history. They had beaten Scotland and Wales and drawn with England, and the five points thus amassed left them in an impregnable position. Victory over Ireland was naturally expected not alone by France but the rugby world at large, who now at last recognised France for what she was, a major rugby power.

Dawson and his forward colleagues kept up a sustained and furious attack that completely disconcerted the French pack and prevented them from weaving the pretty patterns that had destroyed earlier opposition. The backs responded, none more so than the 19-year-old new cap in the centre, Kevin Flynn of Wanderers. Flynn it was who made a brilliant break that laid on a try for Brophy during the first half. Then English, now restored to full health and vigour, scored a dropped goal which gave Ireland a 6-0 interval lead.

There was no way back for France when David Hewitt landed a penalty goal and a try from left wing J. Dupuy. A conversion from P. Lacaze was the only French consolation. So the fifties ended on a victorious note for Ireland. Noel Henderson made the last of his thirty-eight appearances in the Irish jersey, and with his retirement the last tangible link with the golden years was gone.

After the close of the European rugby season the Lions went to New Zealand and Australia. They travelled under the leadership of Ronnie Dawson, just as almost ten years earlier they had been led by another Irish captain and hooker. The strength of the Irish pack was emphasised by the fact that Dawson was one of five Irish forwards selected, the others being prop forwards Gordon Wood and Syd Millar, second row Bill Mulcahy and wing forward Noel Murphy. Tony O'Reilly, David Hewitt, Niall Brophy and Mick English were also included, while Andy Mulligan was sent out on an errand of mercy after the team had been hit by injuries. There were two serious casualties: English had to retire from the side after three games, and Brophy after only one. Tony O'Reilly, in contrast, played in more matches than any other player, twenty-four in all, and collected the massive haul of twenty-two tries. David Hewitt was top scorer, however, with 106 points, made up of twenty conversions, ten penalty goals and three tries. The Lions lost a wonderful Test series by three games to one, winning the last of the four internationals. They visited Canada on the way home.

So the fifties came to a close. There had been major changes at Lansdowne Road with the West Stand being completely reconstructed and the capacity of the ground increased to just over 50,000. Rupert Jeffares, the first secretary of the union, retired in 1951 and was succeeded by his son Billy, and it was Billy who helped organise the four-countries match that took place on 31 December 1955 to celebrate the opening of the new West Stand. The ceremony was performed by the president of the union, Harry Read, a man who had rendered such distinguished service on the field of play in an earlier and less organised era. England-Wales beat Ireland-Scotland by 18 points to 15. What was more important, the quality of the game was entirely in keeping with the occasion.

The fifties also saw the retirement of Harry Thrift as honorary secretary of the International Board. He announced his official departure from active participation at the board's annual meeting at Edinburgh on 17 March 1956. He was succeeded by yet another Irishman, Eddie Kirwan. Harry Thrift's connection with the game had extended over half a century; he had played a major role in the development of the game and was an international figure as a player and legislator. The IRFU marked his retirement by presenting him with a silver salver and the presidents of the English, Welsh and Scottish unions, together with the vice-president of the French Federation, were present at the ceremony which took place on the morning of the four-countries match in Dublin.

Rowland Hill of England, Aikman Smith of Scotland, Horace Lyne of Wales and R. G. Warren of Ireland had all played major roles in moulding rugby football. Harry Thrift was worthy to be ranked with that distinguished quartet. He died in February 1958. Another great Irish rugby man, John Macaulay, had died a few months earlier at the age of 91.

CHAPTER 15

A MOMENTOUS DECADE: THE 1960s

PRIOR TO 1960 RUGBY FOOTBALL could be said to have had four great periods of development: the early days of international rugby when faltering yet decisive steps were taken; the closing years of the nineteenth century and the opening years of the twentieth when backs at last became more than agencies of defence and when Welsh influence was brought to bear on threequarter play and Irish influence on the distinctive role of each half-back; the period between the two world wars when forward play took on a new meaning; and the aftermath of the 1939–45 War when international rugby became a highly organised sector of the game and the first really great ball-carrying forwards emerged. Here the French influence was probably the predominant factor. Yet when future generations come to study the game and its evolution, the happenings in the sixties will be seen as having been truly momentous.

It was in this period that the short tour by individual countries came into its own as modern travel facilities put practically every part of the world within reach in little more than a day. It was also in this decade that substitutes were first permitted in international and representative football. But above all it was the time when the coach came into his own, when new tactical concepts were born and a new terminology evolved. Time will tell whether all the innovations were for the better, but on balance the evidence thus far is that the majority of the changes made rugby football a better game to play and a better game to watch.

The improvements were manifest in the game in Ireland as elsewhere, and if no Triple Crown or championship was won during the sixties, the players who wore the national jersey did so to a large degree with distinction. Historic victories were recorded, two overseas tours undertaken, and great players emerged on the scene. Two of them stayed in the game long enough to shatter, in turn, the cap record set by Jack Kyle.

Tom Kiernan, a member of a Cork rugby family with a long tradition in the game, came into the Irish team against England at full-back in the match at Twickenham in 1960. He went on to play fifty-four matches for Ireland before his international career ended at Murrayfield in 1973. Yet that record number of appearances lasted no longer than twelve months before it was broken in 1974 by the Ballymena second row forward Willie John McBride, Kiernan's colleague for so long in the Irish side. Kiernan retired from international rugby as the most capped full-back in history, having also established two other landmarks that are likely to stand for a long time to come: he scored 158 points for Ireland, more than any other player, and he led his country on a record number of twenty-four occasions.

McBride was first capped against England in 1962 and was still present in 1973–74 to lead the national side. The previous year he set a record of forty-three consecutive appearances in international rugby, eclipsing the record held by the great Scottish prop forward Hugh McLeod, who made the last of forty successive appearances in 1962.

To the names of this distinguished pair could be added yet another, that of Michael Gibson, who while a student at Cambridge University came into the Irish team at out-half in 1964 and for a long time bade fair to equal the degree of proficiency attained by Jack Kyle in that onerous position. Gibson was later switched to the centre, a position in which he also achieved world status.

Kiernan, McBride and Gibson formed a mighty triumvirate, dominating the era which had produced them.

Kiernan was the only one of the three who was a member of the Irish party that toured South Africa in the summer of 1961.

In the previous winter the Fifth Springboks had come to Britain and Ireland and had escaped from Lansdowne Road with a victory that came in injury time by means of a push-over try. They had also been given very hard games by Munster and Leinster, so there was some reason for optimism when the Irish party set out in May 1961. If the Irish hopes were not fully realised, the tour was, nevertheless, a major success, and there were to be happier consequences four years later when the South Africans returned the compliment with a short tour of Ireland and Scotland in 1965.

The Irish touring team of 1961 was led by Ronnie Dawson, and Noel F. Murphy, once a respected international player, was the manager. One of the players he had under his guidance was his son, Noel A. Murphy. Ireland played four games, won three and lost one, which was, admittedly, the most important engagement, the international. Ireland scored fifty-nine points and conceded thirty-six in the four matches; Kiernan contributed forty-four, including all eight that Ireland scored in a 24-8 international defeat.

All but one of the team that played in the international had been capped previously, the exception being the Queen's University back Ken Houston. But even with such experience in the back line as that embodied in the presence of Tony O'Reilly and Andy Mulligan, and with the solid defensive qualities of a recent recruit to international rugby, Jerry Walsh of UCC in the centre, Ireland could not provide an effective answer to their opposition. The South Africans' tremendously strong and able pack proved altogether too formidable for an Irish eight that included Dawson, Syd Millar, Gordon Wood, Bill Mulcahy and Noel Murphy, all five of whom had toured New Zealand with the Lions in 1959.

Despite the presence of so many fine players, Ireland could not mount a really serious challenge for the honours on the home front, suffering, as they have so often done, from being short of just a few really good players that would complete a competent line-up. Yet they had a good representation on the Lions team that toured South Africa in the summer of 1962: Tom Kiernan, Niall Brophy and David Hewitt in the back positions, and Syd Millar, Bill Mulcahy and Bill McBride among the forwards. It was the first of five Lions tours for McBride, but was not attended by the glory that followed later for the Ballymena man on other foreign soil.

A six-strong Irish representation for this tour had hardly seemed likely at one stage in 1962, notably after a visit to Twickenham, to which location the Irish selectors decided to take nine new caps. Ireland took a fearful 16-0 hammering and some who shared in the experience were not destined to have the responsibility of wearing the green jersey again. Two of the forwards who had to endure a tough baptism that February day were still considered good enough, however, to be selected for Ireland in 1973: one was McBride and the other a prop forward, Ray McLoughlin.

Time was when a prop was a prop. McLoughlin, however, begat an era when the defined lines of duty were specifically separated into tight and loose head. And it was in the latter role that he established a worldwide reputation, not alone for his physical attributes and his ability to use them in the cause of his side, but as a thinker on the game and a wily strategist. His reputation in that direction reached its zenith when he took over the leadership of the Irish side in 1965, a year that promised at last to see the Triple Crown returned to Irish soil, though Wales, not for the first time, ended all thoughts in that direction.

McLoughlin's scientific approach had not yet fully asserted itself, however, when Ireland met England at Twickenham in February 1964. Ireland's win that day was their first victory at Twickenham since 1948. The 18-5 win ended the losing sequence in the grand manner, and no one contributed more richly to the victory than Michael Gibson, who had experienced a moment of equal brilliance on the same pitch two months earlier when he had inspired a Cambridge victory over Oxford. He performed a feat of similar moment for Ireland on this his first appearance in the national side. Ireland led by 3 points to nil at half-time through a try by Noel Murphy, but when that great forward 'Budge' Rogers had got a try for England after the interval and John Willcox converted it, the Irish began to think in terms of the Twickenham bogey again. The doubts were reinforced when Kiernan missed an easy kick, but it was to take more than a bogey to keep the Irish from claiming their rights against England this time.

Kevin Flynn, who as a 19-year-old youngster had made such an impressive debut against France in 1959 but to whom fate had dealt some unkind hands in the shape of injuries in the intervening period, was Gibson's able ally this time. He started the Irish blitz that came in the final fifteen minutes by getting a try which Kiernan goaled. Now all was forgiven the Corkman. Then Gibson stamped his genius on the hour. He pierced the English defence with a break from near his own 'twenty-five'. The ball was transferred inside to centre Jerry Walsh after a diagonal run. Walsh changed the direction of the attack from left to right and the movement ended with the Irish right wing Pat Casey scoring a try almost under the posts after the English defence had been disconcerted yet again by a change in direction. It was a score to rank with Basil Maclear's effort against South Africa more than half a century earlier. Flynn completed a day of glory by scoring for the second time near the end, and Kiernan once again landed the conversion. This time the cushions did not fly to herald the Irish triumph when no-side was called, but thoughts of a Triple Crown were uppermost in the minds of the huge Irish following, who saw at last the man they believed to be the logical successor to Kyle.

That win, following a fine effort against the Fifth All-Blacks in Dublin the previous December, did not condition the Irish mind to accept easily the anticlimax that ensued. Ireland was beaten by Scotland in Dublin for the third successive time, and this was followed by further defeats by Wales and France. Ireland had again exercised her almost unique facility for going from the sublime to the ridiculous in the shortest possible time, and ended the season at the bottom of the championship table.

When Ireland opened their 1965 championship programme against France in Dublin on 23 January, they did so under a new captain, Ray McLoughlin, whose prowess as a prop forward was quite exceptional. Ronnie Dawson had gone, having made his last appearance against France in Paris the previous April. Dawson had surprisingly been dropped for the match against Wales, being one of four players who had to pay the penalty for the defeat by Scotland. Two other distinguished heads rolled too, those of Kiernan and Syd Millar. Kiernan's absence was not prolonged, however, for his successor, Fergus Keogh, failed, as so many others before had subsequently failed to match the Corkman's all-round accomplishments. Kiernan was back for the game against France in 1965, when the hooking duties were entrusted to a young medical student from Queen's University, Belfast, Ken Kennedy. This was the start of another long career. Length of service was indeed a characteristic of many of the players who made their mark in the sixties.

It has been said of McLoughlin that he brought a new dimension to the captaincy of Ireland and killed once and for all any remnants of the old *laissez-faire* attitude to preparation and tactics. His contribution and tactical appreciation were certainly of major proportions, but it would appear wrong to claim that his was the initial breakthrough in this direction. While McLoughlin's approach to this task was certainly thorough and scientific, it has been argued by his critics that some of his methods were too rigid in concept and not workable by the players at his disposal. Karl Mullen had proved fifteen years earlier that he too was an accomplished strategist as well as a great hooker and he made his point tell with two Triple Crowns and three championships. Ronnie Dawson was not as well endowed as Mullen with regard to his team's strength in depth, yet he was another before the McLoughlin era who had been fastidious in his approach to the job as Ireland's captain — to such outstanding effect when he had led the Lions in New Zealand. Kiernan, also, in his long reign had made a valuable contribution.

McLoughlin did not enjoy a long term of office as captain of Ireland, perhaps because he tried to do too much too soon, perhaps because he was unable to command the ultimate success for which he so zealously strove. What is not in doubt is that McLoughlin's approach would be totally in accord with the game as it is played today and perhaps his greatest accomplishment is that he helped to prepare the way for many of the traumatic changes that followed in the wake of his leadership.

Ray McLoughlin's captaincy was not rewarded in the shape of a Triple Crown. As it transpired, Ireland, after beating England and Scotland in 1965, failed yet again to Wales at the final hurdle, losing in Cardiff by 14 points to 8. For both teams it was a Triple Crown occasion, for Wales had previously beaten England and Scotland.

The atmosphere at the Arms Park is at any time demanding on the visitor, but on 13 March 1965 it was positively electric, a circumstance that was probably a contributory factor in Kiernan missing an early penalty from in front of the posts. The kick was taken against a background of booing, not the customary silence afforded a penalty-taker. It was a disappointing match, not least in terms of the result. Ireland was in with a chance until five minutes from time, at which stage Wales led by 11 points to 8, but Terry Price, the Welsh full-back, landed the penalty goal that finished the contest and gave Wales the Triple Crown. Not everyone was satisfied with the tactics of either team.

Less than a month later, Ireland, with McLoughlin as captain, had a much more rewarding experience when the first international victory over South Africa was achieved at Lansdowne Road on 10 April. South Africa had come on a five match tour of Ireland and Scotland. They opened their itinerary in Belfast on 3 April and managed to get away with a draw against a Combined Provinces side. But they were to learn a lesson that others who engaged on similar short tours had endured before them, that the time for preparation for the international games during the long official tour is an invaluable asset in ironing out deficiencies and building up team spirit. No such opportunities are available to quick-striking raiders.

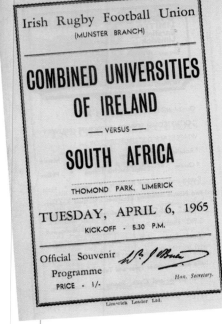

Three days after the Belfast match South Africa met the Combined Universities, some of whose best players, such as Tom Kiernan, Roger Young, Pat McGrath, Ken Kennedy, Ray McLoughlin and Bill Mulcahy, were not available by the wish of the Irish selectors. It was thus all the more remarkable that this depleted team, captained by Jerry Walsh of UCC, earned the distinction of being the first Irish XV to beat the South Africans. In view of the number of times that Munster had unluckily failed to beat touring teams, it was appropriate that the win should have come on Munster soil. It was a most exciting match, during which every university player performed with distinction. South Africa met unexpected resistance from their smaller and lighter opponents who, incidentally, wore red jerseys in order to avoid confusion with the Springboks' green.

The Universities led 6-0, 6-5, 12-5 and 12-10, and managed to hold out desperately in the closing minutes. The South Africans got enough possession of the ball to win a dozen matches, but the Universities deserved victory for their sheer courage and opportunism. Tony Hickie (penalty goal), Eamonn McGuire (try), John Murray (dropped goal) and Mike Grimshaw (try) scored for the Universities, while Tommy Bedford got both tries for the Tourists, one in each half, both of which were converted.

Programme for match in which an Irish side scored first victory over the Springboks

At the subsequent dinner the chairman of the Irish Universities Rugby Union, Sarsfield Hogan, praised South Africa for their most sporting acceptance of their unexpected defeat. Avril Malan, the captain, replied: 'We are glad to hear Mr Hogan's words because we Springboks have very little practice in how to behave as losers.' It was a reasonable enough comment at the time.

The Universities team that recorded that historic win at Thomond Park, Limerick, was:

A. Hickie (UCD)	M. Carey (UCD)
M. Lucey (UCC)	M. Argyle (Dublin University)
J. C. Walsh (UCC) Capt.	A. Moroney (UCD)
M. Grimshaw (Queen's University)	M. Leahy (UCC)
W. Glynn (UCD)	O. Waldron (UCC)
J. B. Murray (UCD)	J. Davidson (Queen's University)
M. Whiteside (Queen's University)	H. Wall (UCD)

E. McGuire (UCG)

Ireland could scarcely have asked for a better stimulant than that given in Limerick and McLoughlin and his colleagues responded by defeating the Springboks by 9-6 at Lansdowne Road on 10 April. Jerry Walsh was the only player who shared in both triumphs; the Universities selection had been restricted to players who were not engaged in the international, but the Irish selectors had conceded that the Universities should not be deprived of their captain.

Conditions were not ideal for the game, even though it took place in the middle of April. An appreciable wind blew and the odd shower of rain made control and ball handling difficult. South Africa had the benefit of the wind in the first half, but it was Ireland who opened the scoring. Scrum-half Roger Young, who had come into the side that season, kicked the ball over the South African line and Pat McGrath, one of the Irish wings, got his hand to it before any of the Springboks could touch down to safety. South Africa then drew level with a penalty goal, but despite sustained pressure, the Irish defence was not breached during the opening period, at the end of which the sides were level at 3-3.

With the wind behind them in the second half, Ireland looked set to strike gold, but it was South Africa who scored again, centre W. J. Mans getting an unconverted try. Tom Kiernan soon brought the sides level, however, with a penalty kick, and when Mike Gibson went over for a try the acclamation that greeted the effort turned to despair when play was recalled for an apparent infringement.

But Irish supporters were not denied a grand finale. It came through the agency of a wonderful penalty kick by Tom Kiernan. There was a breathless moment of suspense while the ball was in flight and an explosion of thunderous acclamation when it reached its objective. It was enough: South Africa had been beaten twice within the space of five days, and by Irish opposition. And if that was an unlikely happening in the days of Danie Craven and Benny Osler, it hardly mattered to the 45,000 Irish supporters who were in Lansdowne Road in April 1965. Some of them had probably seen Osler and Craven weave their own particular brand of magic in the distant past; this time the spell was not strong enough for the needs of the occasion.

Ireland made the now accustomed unrewarding journey to France for the first match in 1966, a game in which Willie John McBride got a new partner in the strong and durable Connachtman, Mick Molloy. Molloy proved a worthy successor to Bill Mulcahy, whose international career had ended the previous season. A draw with England at Twickenham was a reasonable if not a fair return from a game that Ireland had dominated territorially. Similar dominance had been exerted previously to no effect whatsoever.

Ireland were then defeated by Scotland for the fourth successive time at the Lansdowne Road ground. There were several alterations to the team selected to meet Wales, including a change in the captaincy, Tom Kiernan taking over the job from Ray McLoughlin — a selectorial decision that may have cost McLoughlin the leadership of the Lions side that went to New Zealand that summer. The Welsh match also saw the return on the right wing of the Lansdowne player Alan Duggan, who had been capped twice in 1964 but had been overlooked subsequently. He did not score that day in Ireland's surprising but welcome 9-6 win, but his try-scoring feats in later matches enabled him to establish an Irish record.

The Fifth Wallabies came to Britain and Ireland in the autumn of 1966, and though they proved good enough to beat Wales and England, Ireland once more registered a win over a touring team by beating Australia by 15 points to 8 on 21 January 1967 at Lansdowne Road. Mike Gibson dropped two goals, Duggan got the first of the eleven tries he scored for Ireland, and Tom Kiernan, making his twenty-eighth appearance at full-back for Ireland, kicked a penalty goal.

Four days later at Musgrave Park, Munster at last got the long-sought and well-deserved win over a touring team when they beat the Australians by 11 points to 8, thereby becoming the first Irish province to win against a side from overseas. Kiernan kicked eight of the eleven points Munster scored, and John Moroney of London Irish and Garryowen and subsequently an international, scored a try. The Irish side that day was led by Noel Murphy, who also had the distinction of captaining the Munster team that had defeated the Wallabies.

Willie John McBride gains possession against Wales 1967

Murphy remained in charge throughout the 1967 championship series. After losing to England at Lansdowne Road, Ireland won against Scotland at Murrayfield, where Murphy scored the decisive try and Kiernan landed the conversion for a 5-0 win. Ireland then went to the Cardiff Arms Park and won by 3 points to nil, Alan Duggan getting the only score the match produced.

Meanwhile, the results of the other international matches had ensured that the Ireland-France match at Lansdowne Road on 15 April would decide the championship. As a result of the win in Cardiff, there was considerable confidence backing Ireland's chances of taking the title for the first time since 1951.

Roger Young gets his Irish back line moving against Wales, Cardiff, 1967

As it transpired, the celebrated kicking ability of the Camberabero brothers, Guy and Lilian, effectively countered the Irish challenge, and France deservedly won by 11 points to 6. Noel Murphy was named as captain of the Irish team to tour Australia, and an official party of twenty-four members, with two officials, Eugene Davy as manager and Des McKibbin as assistant manager, left Dublin Airport on 22 April. Murphy, however, was not able to accompany them and so Kiernan took over the leadership.

Ireland accomplished the main business of the six match itinerary in magnificent fashion when on 13 May they beat Australia by 11 points to 5 in Sydney. That was the first, and to date the only, win achieved by Ireland in a full-scale international overseas. After losing heavily by 21 points to 9 to New South Wales on the same Sydney ground a week previously, thought and application for the international were needed. The position was slightly complicated because of a thigh injury to one of the centres, Barry Bresnihan, who had come into the Irish team in 1966. Pat McGrath, normally a wing, was placed at centre and the veteran Niall Brophy went on the left wing. There was one new cap in the pack, Terry Moore of Highfield, and his performance that day suggested that many more caps would follow in the immediate future, but it was not until 1973 that he was again included in an Irish team. Kiernan, meanwhile, was making his thirty-third appearance in the full-back position for Ireland, and by so doing equalled the world record held by the great Welshman, W. J. Bancroft.

Brendan Sherry, the Irish scrum-half, got Ireland off to a good start by creating the opening from which Jerry Walsh scored a try and Kiernan added the goal points. Just after the interval Kiernan dropped a goal. Australia reduced the deficit to 8-5 with a try by their clever scrum-half, Ken Catchpole, and the veteran J. K. Lenehan converted. But the suspense lasted for only four minutes as McGrath quickly capitalised on good work by Duggan to stretch Ireland's lead to 11-5; and that was the final score. Ireland ended the tour with a record of four wins from six matches and a points total of 119, with 80 being registered against.

An outbreak of foot and mouth disease in Britain caused the cancellation of the international between Ireland and the Sixth All-Blacks, which was due to take place in December 1967. It was unfortunate in every way, not least in that Irish followers were deprived of seeing one of the greatest rugby combinations ever to visit Britain and France. The All-Blacks played fifteen matches, won fourteen and drew one; and they beat England, Wales, France and Scotland in the international engagements.

So when the championship campaign started, Ireland did not have the advantage of a match as was the case with the other participants. Ireland lost to France in Paris (as usual) and were deprived of a win against England when Bob Hiller, the English full-back, kicked a last-minute penalty goal from the right touchline to earn his side a 9-9 draw. Hiller that day struck the first of many blows he was later to inflict on the Irish. A win over Scotland at Lansdowne Road was not entirely unexpected, but the 9-6 victory over Wales in Dublin provided both excitement and controversy.

Ireland, with a penalty goal from Kiernan and a dropped goal from Gibson, led 6-3 well into the second half. Then Gareth Edwards, the Welsh scrum-half, took a drop at goal that apparently went wide of the left-hand upright. To the astonishment of the capacity crowd, the referee, Mr M. H. Titcomb of England, deemed Edwards's kick good, and it was a decision that for a few moments threatened to have dire consequences in the form of an invasion of the pitch by a section of the crowd. But the incident ceased as quickly as it had begun and the game was restarted without undue delay. The Irish players showed no outward signs of dissatisfaction with the decision, but it was a bitter blow.

But Ireland won in the end when Mick Doyle, a flank forward who had seen service with UCD and Cambridge University and had first been capped in 1965, got a try just before the end of the match. Justice was done.

Doyle had been joined for the game against England by his brother Tommy from the Wanderers club; they are the most recent of the many sets of brothers to play for Ireland.

Kiernan was subsequently chosen to captain the Lions team in South Africa, and Ronnie Dawson was appointed coach and assistant manager. That appointment epitomised the new approach to the game that had been adopted by the home countries, where coaching at national level was now looked upon as a necessity. Wales had shown the way with the appointment of David Nash as coach to their national side in 1967, and the other countries were soon to follow the lead. Such happenings as squad training sessions, unknown in earlier times, soon became commonplace, with national selectors summoning groups of players to assemble at weekends so that tactics and stratagems could be perfected. Despite the appointment of an Irishman as coach to the 1968 Lions in South Africa, the idea had not as yet fully caught on in Ireland, nor was it altogether acceptable to many of those who ran the game, mainly because of fears that the status and authority of the captain would be diminished or at least misunderstood.

Kiernan and Dawson were accompanied by seven Irish players: Barry Bresnihan, Mike Gibson, Roger Young, Syd Millar, who that season had again found favour with the Irish selectors after four years in the wilderness, Bill McBride, Mick Doyle, and Ken Goodall, a No. 8 forward of top quality. Goodall had come into the Irish side that season and had made an immediate impact. He joined the Lions as a replacement during the tour but was injured in the first game he played and took no further part in the proceedings.

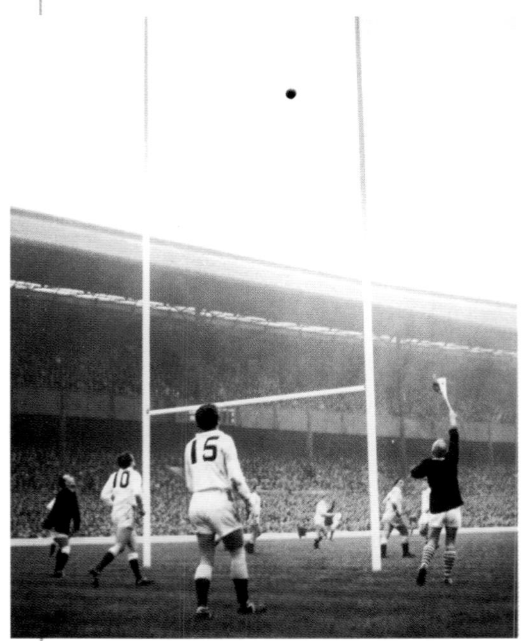

A Tom Kiernan penalty goal against England, Twickenham, 1968

One significant example of the changes that were being implemented in the game was the International Board's decision in March 1968 that in future replacements would be allowed for seriously injured players during the course of official trial games and international representative matches involving touring teams. The Lions South African tour saw the first such replacement, and to Barry Bresnihan went the distinction of being the first substitute in representative football when he came on for Mike Gibson fifteen minutes from the end of the opening game of the tour against Western Transvaal.

The Lions did not win the Test series, but they did win fifteen of the twenty matches they played and drew one, the second Test. Kiernan scored eighty-four points in thirteen matches to set another record for a Lions player in South Africa, and his contribution of thirty-five points in the Test series accounted for all but three of the points the Lions amassed in the internationals.

In October 1968 Australia came on a five match tour of Ireland and Scotland, and once again Ireland won the international by 10 points to 3. This game gave Irish followers a first glimpse of top-class rugby under an experimental rule that a player could only kick directly to touch from inside the twenty-five yard lines. The game was not a good advertisement for the experiment. That match apart, the new law speeded up the game appreciably on a general level and was subsequently incorporated into the laws on a permanent basis. Substitutes, kicking laws and coaches truly had the wind of change blown through the game.

Ireland had not as yet appointed a coach to the national side when the 1968–69 season opened, but coaching was gradually becoming an accepted principle within the country, and nowhere more than in Leinster, where since 1964 an annual course had been run at the Butlin's Holiday Camp at Mosney, County Meath. Ronnie Dawson was one of the prime movers in the project and he had a willing and able accomplice in Judge Charles Conroy, the then honorary secretary of the Leinster Branch and president of the union in 1972–73. Desmond Scaife, who succeeded Judge Conroy as Leinster honorary secretary in May 1972, was another leading advocate and did an immense amount of work in the organisation of the course, which is still run annually and is attended by many of the game's leading authorities from other lands, notably Wales and France.

Wales also had a coach in 1969, the job having passed from David Nash to a former Welsh captain and scrum-half, Clive Rowlands, and he mobilised them for their Triple Crown and championship victories, two distinctions earned over Ireland's head as the result of the decisive game in the series between Wales and Ireland at Cardiff Arms Park on 8 March 1969.

Ireland had failed to beat France for the quite astonishing period of eleven years, but the trend was finally arrested at Lansdowne Road on 25 January 1969. Ireland was without Mike Gibson, who had fractured his jaw in the final trial, and the out-half position was taken over by Barry McGann, who had been a brilliant schools player at Presentation College, Cork (Kiernan's old academy), and who was now attached to Lansdowne. McGann made a great debut and Ireland won by 17 points to 9, a victory that equalled one record and established another.

Only once before, in 1948, had Ireland won four matches in succession, and now the win over France had brought a similar run of success, following wins over Scotland and Wales in the 1968 championship and the victory over Australia in October 1968. The second record was an individual one created by a wing threequarter. John Moroney, who had played at out-half for his club, London Irish, had been selected on the left wing for the game against France and scored fourteen points, made up of three penalty goals, a try and a conversion. McGann, with a dropped goal, completed the seventeen points. Moroney's scoring spree broke the previous individual record set in 1948 by Barney Mullan with thirteen points. The same game was also the first match in which Ireland made a substitution, Mick Hipwell of Terenure College coming on during the second half for Noel Murphy, who had retired injured.

England, with Hiller in his usual kicking form, gave Ireland a hard time of it in Dublin before a 17–15 win for Ireland stretched the winning sequence to five games, and once again Ireland had to take advantage of the substitution law, Colin Grimshaw of Queen's University coming on during the second half for Roger Young at scrum-half.

Things were distinctly promising now. The five successive wins became a record sixth when Scotland proved no match for Ireland at Murrayfield. Tries by Alan Duggan, his third in two matches against the Scots, Mike Gibson, Barry McGann and Barry Bresnihan and two conversions by John Moroney gave Ireland a 16-0 win.

Ireland did pay a price for that win, however, for Ken Goodall was injured and replaced by Mick Hipwell, who thus picked up two caps as a replacement to add to the four he had collected between 1962 and 1968. He was named in an otherwise unchanged team to travel to Wales for the game at Cardiff Arms Park on 8 March.

TOM KIERNAN INTRODUCES PRINCE OF WALES TO IRISH TEAM, CARDIFF, 1969

The Welsh programme of matches had been disrupted that season, so that when they faced Ireland it was only the second match of their championship programme. It was, however, the one they knew they had to win. The build-up to the game was tremendous, nowhere more so than in Wales, where Ireland's progress had been watched with respect and, one suspects, some trepidation. Despite the tremendous popular interest in the game, it was played before a crowd of only 25,000 as major reconstruction work in the Arms Park had severely limited its capacity. Proposals that the game be taken to some other venue (Twickenham and Lansdowne Road were widely canvassed) had met with no response from the Welsh Rugby Union.

Suggestions had gone around that the Irish forwards were living dangerously throughout the championship, and imagination became intermingled with fact, which was that Ireland had incurred several penalties throughout the series. The great majority of them had been for line-out infringements, basically of a technical nature, and some for retreating at the back of the line, a law that was subsequently amended.

To what extent reputation preceded Ireland to Wales one can only guess, but within ten minutes of the start there occurred an incident that ruined the game and left Noel Murphy lying stunned after being the recipient of a punch from a Welsh forward, who broke from a ruck to dispatch his message. Assertions that the blow was the result of provocation were simply post-mortem efforts to whitewash a blatant foul and do not merit serious consideration. The referee, Mr McMahon of Scotland, warned and penalised the offender, but he did not send him off, presumably on a merciful application of the 'first offence' rule. Many thought it would have been better for the image and reputation of international rugby if the referee had been more severe.

Ireland did not win, nor on the balance of play did they deserve to do so, and a highly talented Welsh side took the honours by the convincing margin of 24 points to 11.

It was Noel Murphy's last match and it was regrettable that a magnificent international career, in which he won forty-one caps and went on two Lions tours, should have ended in such an unsatisfactory manner.

Wales went on to beat England and take the Triple Crown, and a draw in France gave them the championship as well, with one point to spare over Ireland. Wales had clearly demonstrated the value of coaching, and the other home countries were not long in following the lead at national level.

CHAPTER 16

TOURS AND TORMENTS: 1970–71

IN THE AUTUMN OF 1969 THE IRFU decided that the national team would be the better for the appointment of a coach and, not surprisingly, one of those who had preached the coaching gospel louder than most, Ronnie Dawson, was given the task of moulding the Irish side to meet the demands of the modern concept of rugby football. His first assignment was to prepare the Irish side for the international against the Sixth Springboks in Dublin on 10 January 1970.

The Sixth Springboks, under the captaincy of the great scrum-half D. J. de Villiers, faced problems that none of their predecessors had been forced to face. They were most unlucky in the matter of injuries, and wherever they went they were greeted by crowds demonstrating against the policy of apartheid. But these were only two of the factors that made their task difficult. The third, despite all that has been written about demonstrations against South African government policy, was probably far more important. Rugby in Britain and Ireland, through the 'coaching revolution', meant that the Springboks met sides that were better prepared than at any time in the game's history. The home countries had at last discovered that the elimination of error and the ability to capitalise on opponents' mistakes had been the stock in trade of the overseas tourists, especially those that came from South Africa and New Zealand. And now they were able to reply to the challenge of these sophisticated foreign teams in like manner.

The first really fruitful application of this newly acquired knowledge came in the third match at Newport, which the Welsh club side won by 11 points to 6. By the time the South Africans reached Ireland they had lost four games, including the international against England.

It was a strange-looking Lansdowne Road that greeted the visitors. The terraces behind the goals were empty and the pitch was well protected by barbed wire to keep out unwelcome invaders. The result of the game was a closely fought draw. South Africa, strong in the forward line but, with the exception of de Villiers, not very potent behind the scrum, almost won and almost lost.

Ireland were 5-3 up at half-time, Duggan scoring a try and Kiernan converting, with H. O. de Villiers gaining a penalty goal for South Africa. In the second half P. J. Greyling scored a try for South Africa and de Villiers again found the range to put the visitors 8-5 ahead. The advantage was maintained until the eighth minute of injury time, when Alan Duggan kicked deep into the South African 'twenty-five'. With the Irish in full pursuit, the South African full-back had no option but to lie on the ball in front of his posts. He saved a try which would almost certainly have been converted, but he gave Kiernan the opportunity to level with a simple kick from the ensuing penalty. Five years earlier a kick by Kiernan had had more serious consequences for the South Africans.

One of three new caps in the Irish side for the game was a wing forward from UCD, Fergus Slattery, who lived up to the promise he revealed on his initial outing in the Irish jersey.

With Dawson at the helm, there was hope of a new dawn, bringing with it a change of fortune, but there was no evidence forthcoming that it was in the immediate offing when Ireland lost by 8 points to nil in Paris. At Twickenham Bob Hiller once again broke the heart of the Irish challenge with two superb drop goals that gave England a 9-3 win. But better times were round the corner.

A 16-11 win over Scotland brought a welcome change in the pattern the season appeared to be taking, but hardly prefaced great things when Wales came to Lansdowne Road in search of the Triple Crown. Nevertheless, Ireland destroyed the Welsh team of all the talents and amazed the rugby world, not because they won, but by the margin of their win — 14 points to nil.

ALAN DUGGAN SCORING A TRY AGAINST WALES, LANSDOWNE ROAD, 1970

The Welsh forwards were completely overwhelmed, and the great half-back partnership of Gareth Edwards and Barry John was played out of the game. All the scoring came in the second half during which Wales collapsed before the Irish onslaught. Barry McGann started the Welsh decline with a well-taken drop goal, and then Alan Duggan scored a wonderful try to which Tom Kiernan added the conversion. Before the end Ken Goodall, one of the stars in a great Irish pack, added a second try, and again Kiernan converted. There were doubtless a few inquests in the valleys that night, and no little celebration in Dublin. Retribution for the previous season's defeat at Cardiff Arms Park had been exacted. Goodall's talents were not to be at Ireland's disposal again, for he turned to Rugby League before the start of the following season.

Ireland went back to the Argentine in August 1970; the party consisted of twenty-three players, with Kiernan as captain, Dawson as coach, and the IRFU president, Pete Patterson, as manager. The experiences of Wales and Scotland, who had recently met defeat in the Argentine, testified to the strength of the game in Buenos Aires and its neighbouring towns, so the fact that Mike Gibson, Roger Young, Fergus Slattery and Ken Kennedy were unable to go on the tour weakened the strength considerably.

Ireland played seven matches and won four, but two of the three defeats came in the two Test matches, the first of which proved to be a torrid affair during which two players, one from each team, were sent off the field. The Argentine won the match by 8 points to 3, and in the last game of the tour, the second Test, they won by 6 points to 3. Ireland also lost to an Argentine C selection by 17 points to nil.

There were many difficulties, not least a spate of injuries, the most serious of which was incurred by wing Bill Brown who had made his international debut against South Africa in January. Brown broke a leg in the sixth match. Earlier in the tour back row forward Ronnie Lamont, another international, had been forced to spend four days in hospital recovering from severe concussion. Other casualties were Barry McGann, Tom Grace, the UCD wing at that time uncapped, Syd Millar, the most experienced of the forwards, and Paddy Madigan, a hooker from the Old Belvedere club who had been Ken Kennedy's understudy in the Irish squad for the previous two seasons.

All the games were played in Buenos Aires, with the exception of one game in Rosario, and the Irish found the conditions trying and some of the refereeing decisions strange. It added to the difficulties that the tour took place in August, three months after the close of the previous season, so that Ireland had to face players who were match hardened since April.

Yet the greatest subject of controversy connected with this most unsatisfactory tour was not the events on the field, but an incident which occurred on the journey home. On the pretext of misconduct, but apparently in an effort to cover up some other airline difficulty, the Irish party was ordered off the plane at Rio de Janeiro and compelled to wait some days in the city until alternative flights could be arranged. The IRFU, having fully investigated the matter, issued a strong statement repudiating the suggestion that there had been misconduct or any other reason justifying the arbitrary and inexplicable action taken by the airline or the Brazilian authorities.

Having eclipsed Jack Kyle's record of forty-six caps in the memorable triumph over Wales in 1970, Kiernan was again the choice as Ireland's captain and full-back for the match against France in 1971. He did not see the season out. A broken bone in his right leg caused him to retire in the second half of the match, which Ireland drew, and he was replaced by Barry O'Driscoll, a Manchester-based doctor who played for Connacht. It seemed the end of Kiernan's international career.

England came to Lansdowne Road and once again Bob Hiller brought about the destruction of the Irish by kicking three penalty goals to give England a 9-6 win. Not since Oliver Cromwell had Ireland been harried to a similar degree by an Englishman. Ireland failed to stop Wales winning the Triple Crown, going down by 22 points to 9 in Cardiff after scoring a meritorious 17-5 win at Murrayfield.

England celebrated her centenary season, the highlight of which was a wonderful four-countries match at Twickenham. Things had come a long way since England had met Scotland at Raeburn Place a hundred years before.

The build-up to the Lions tour of New Zealand in the summer was in direct contrast to the preparation for the first rugby international of all. But those who invented the rugby game reasserted their superiority through the medium of their successors who, for the first time, won the Test series. Wales supplied the coach and captain in Carwyn James and John Dawes respectively, and Ireland supplied six players. Mike Gibson was the only Irish back in the party, but there were five forwards, Seán Lynch, Ray McLoughlin, who had made a return to the Irish side after five years' absence in 1971, Willie John McBride, making a record fourth tour, Fergus Slattery and Mick Hipwell.

McLoughlin and Hipwell had to leave the tour halfway through the campaign because of injuries and for that reason did not play in any of the Tests. Slattery was chosen for one Test but could not play, also because of injury, but Gibson, McBride and Lynch (who had come into the Irish team in 1971) all played in the four Tests.

CHAPTER 17

A SAD AFFAIR AND A HAPPY SEQUEL: 1972–74

IRELAND'S FACILITY FOR RECALLING seasoned campaigners has largely been a profitable exercise through the years. When the Irish team travelled to Paris in 1972 there were two in the side whose international careers had at one time appeared to be over. Kiernan had returned to his old position at full-back, having shaken off the effects of the leg injury that might have caused a lesser man to opt out for good. Kevin Flynn, who had last played in 1966 and first played for Ireland in 1959, had shown enough of his former skill while helping Leinster to win the interprovincial championship to earn the favours of the selection committee.

The Irish team that faced France in Colombes was an odd mixture of the old and the new. On the one hand there were Kiernan, Flynn, Gibson, McLoughlin, Kennedy and McBride, whose combined total of caps amounted to over two hundred, while on the other, there were no fewer than five new caps. They were Tom Grace on the right wing, Wallace McMaster on the left, John Moloney at scrum-half, Con Feighery in the second row and Stewart McKinney at wing forward. The blend proved a potent mixture, however, and for the first time in twenty years Ireland won at Colombes and did so convincingly by 14 points to 9.

Yet again the call for change in the laws of the game had been answered by the International Board, who had elevated the value of a try to four points at their meeting in Edinburgh the previous March. The decision made no difference to the match result in Paris, but the wisdom of it was soon evident.

KEVIN FLYNN SCORING WINNING TRY AGAINST ENGLAND AT TWICKENHAM, 1972

Having laid the bogey at Colombes, Ireland took an unchanged side to Twickenham. This time not even the presence of Bob Hiller could deprive the Irish who, however, left their winning effort until almost too late. With just five minutes to go, Ireland was trailing by 12 points to 7 and, needless to say, Hiller had made his personal contribution in the form of eight points. Ireland's last hope appeared to be gone when Mike Gibson missed a penalty goal, but an England player knocked the ball on behind his own line, and from the ensuing scrum McGann dropped a neat goal. Then Flynn made his presence felt when everyone except the most important person, the referee, thought that time was up. A scrum near the English 'twenty-five', a deft pass from Moloney to McGann, who transferred to Flynn, and the veteran cut his way through the English midfield defence for a classic centre try. It mattered not whether Kiernan could add the goal points; but he did, and Ireland thus won by 16 points to 12. Now England knew how Ireland had felt on innumerable occasions.

It transpired that Ireland had disposed of England and rid themselves for ever of the menace of Bob Hiller at the same time. Hiller was dropped for England's next match against France and subsequently announced his retirement from international football. He had kicked forty-one points in five appearances against Ireland, and the Irish were therefore not exactly sorry to see him go.

Shortly before the game against England there had been rumours and rumblings that Scotland and Wales were not prepared to travel to Dublin to fulfil their engagements. The reason given was political instability in Dublin. For those in Ireland who were totally familiar with the true position, the suggestions were nothing short of baffling. Parts of Ulster, notably Derry and Belfast, had certainly borne the brunt of political and civil unrest since 1969. Many soldiers, policemen and civilians had been killed, the most recent tragic incident having been the deaths of thirteen people in Derry when British Army units opened fire. One of the consequences of that tragedy was that some members of a protest march in Dublin succeeded in burning down the British Embassy. Although Dublin and the Republic of Ireland remained otherwise peaceful, the attack on the embassy naturally angered and alarmed some people in Britain.

Two days before Ireland met England the four home unions met in London and decided that there was no reason why the game between Scotland and Ireland scheduled for Lansdowne Road on 26 February 1972 should not take place. That appeared to end the doubts. But two days after the Irish victory at Twickenham the Scottish Rugby Union informed the IRFU that they did not intend to travel to Dublin. If the Irish could not understand the Scottish fears, they nevertheless made a determined attempt to allay them. Six members of the IRFU, led by the president of the union, Dom Dineen, travelled to Edinburgh on 16 February in an effort to get the Scottish Union to change its previous decision. The Irish delegation included Judge Charles Conroy, vice-president of the IRFU, Tommy O'Reilly, the union's honorary treasurer, Harry McKibbin and Sinclair Irwin, Ireland's two representatives on the International Board, Ronnie Dawson, and Bob FitzGerald, the union secretary who had taken over the duties of secretary-treasurer of the union in 1964 after the death of Billy Jeffares.

The persuasive powers of this formidable team, which included men eminent in public life as well as in the rugby world, succeeded in getting the SRU to reconsider their earlier decision, but after a further meeting of the Scottish Union on 17 February, Mr John Law, the SRU secretary, read a prepared statement to the effect that Scotland would not travel to Dublin out of consideration for the safety of their players and supporters. It was a bitter disappointment to Ireland who, having won their first two games away from home for the first time since 1948, appeared at last to have a wonderful chance of bringing off the Triple Crown-championship double with their two home games.

Fears that Wales would follow the Scottish lead were realised ten days later, and once again the same delegation travelled to Cardiff and met the Welsh committee. This time it was the turn of the Welsh secretary, Mr Bill Clement, to issue a statement which echoed that made by Mr Law in Edinburgh. Wales offered to play the game in Cardiff or at a neutral venue. The IRFU, feeling that it was Dublin or not at all, rejected the proposal.

Even at the height of the political troubles and violence in Ireland after the 1914–18 war, international rugby fixtures had been played. In this context, the failure of Scotland and Wales to come to Dublin occasioned great surprise and not a little resentment among Irish rugby supporters. For its part, the IRFU adopted a cool and dignified stance.

Friends are needed in times of stress, and in France Ireland found a friend with whom affinity had begun long after the forming of the old friendships between the home unions. France was willing to oblige one of the family of rugby nations and came to Dublin and met Ireland on 29 April, when the French team got the warm-hearted reception they deserved from the attendance of almost 30,000. It mattered little that Ireland won; it mattered a great deal that the game took place.

In view of the decisions of the Welsh and Scottish Unions and the refusal of British clubs to travel to Ireland, there was a lot of speculation about whether or not the Seventh All-Blacks would travel to Ireland for the four games that were on their itinerary in the 1972–73 season. However, all doubts about the intentions of the New Zealanders were removed when their manager, Ernie Todd, announced that they intended to travel to Ireland and fulfil their two part programme, against Leinster and Ulster in November 1972 and against Ireland and Munster in January 1973.

Tom Grace scores equalising try against New Zealand, Lansdowne Road, 1973

The New Zealanders won a great match against Leinster in Dublin and the following day travelled to Belfast to prepare for the game against Ulster; if Ravenhill was forbidden territory to others, the New Zealanders saw no reason why they should not honour their commitment to play there. They duly arrived, were given a tremendous reception and won into the bargain.

They travelled back to the Republic in January, and Ireland achieved her best result against them by drawing 10-10 on 10 January. A draw was a fair result to a splendid game, but Ireland almost snatched a historic win in the closing minutes. Tom Grace scored a dramatic equalising try in the right-hand corner within no more than an inch of the dead ball line, and Barry McGann's conversion was off target by inches. Four days previously a penalty goal in injury time had given the New Zealanders a 3-3 draw with Munster at Musgrave Park.

The All-Blacks, like the Springboks before them, found rugby in the home countries a more highly organised exercise than at any time in history. In addition, they were perhaps not as good as their illustrious predecessors, and their team had become noticeably unsettled by what they felt to be an unsympathetic attitude towards them during the early part of the tour. Ireland will, however, always remember the Seventh All-Blacks with affection and gratitude. They lived up to the principles on which rugby was nurtured and has prospered. They came, they saw, and they came back again.

The president of the English Rugby Union, Dick Kingswell, made it clear in January 1973 that it was his union's intention to bring a team to Dublin to play Ireland on 10 February 1973. Some feelings were expressed in England that the example of Scotland and Wales should be followed, and it was rumoured that some players had expressed doubts about playing in Dublin. The English Union was, however, unanimous in its resolve to play the match unless the Irish Union advised them otherwise, and they duly arrived at Lansdowne Road with their chosen team.

For over a century the happenings on the field of international rugby have stirred men's emotions, but it is doubtful if there was ever a more moving or emotional scene than that at Lansdowne Road when the English side ran on to the field. The entire concourse to a man stood and applauded the English team for five minutes. It was a wonderful sight and a wonderful sound. It was a great occasion for Dick Kingswell and his committee, and an even greater one for rugby football. It was hardly material that Ireland won a close match in which England missed more chances than they took.

Tom Kiernan scores a try against Scotland, Murrayfield, 1973, in his last international for Ireland

The matches against Scotland and Wales took place according to plan in 1973. Ireland lost both games, but finished the season with a 6-3 win over France.

Syd Millar had taken over the position as coach to the Irish team at the start of the season, a season in which Tom Kiernan ended his international career after he won his fifty-fourth cap at Murrayfield. He left the international field with the dignity that he had always shown on it, and one of his last acts in an Irish jersey was to wave his right arm in the air to signal that the final Scottish drop at goal was good. It was the farewell of a great player and a great captain. Willie John McBride, who had won his fiftieth cap in the game against England, took over the leadership of the Irish side, and Tony Ensor replaced Kiernan in his position on the field.

Scotland celebrated their centenary and Ireland played a full part in the celebrations. There was a generous complement of Irish players in the combined Scotland-Ireland team that defeated England-Wales in the centrepiece of the celebrations. Mike Gibson and Tom Grace scored five tries between them.

In an international seven-a-side tournament at Murrayfield, Ireland surprised not only the opposition but most observers by reaching the final in a form of rugby that is not widely practised in the country. England won the competition by beating Ireland in the closing seconds of a magnificent final.

The autumn of 1973 brought new and most welcome visitors in the Fijians and the Argentinians. The Fijians brought their own brand of fluent football to Lansdowne Road in September, where Leinster were hosts and victors in an attractive game. The Argentinians chose Ireland and Scotland for their first visit to Europe in October. They played four matches in Ireland. The tour opened with a game against Munster at Thomond Park and once again Munster drew with a touring team. Connacht entertained a touring side for the first time at the Sports Ground in Galway, and here the Argentinians recorded their only win of the four engagements they undertook in Ireland. It came as a welcome boost four days before the match against Ireland at Lansdowne Road and in the aftermath of a defeat by Ulster at Ravenhill. Ireland, who had won one, drawn one and lost two of four Test matches against the Argentinians in their two visits to that country, evened the score by recording a convincing victory.

Two great Irish captains, Willie John McBride and Ray McLoughlin

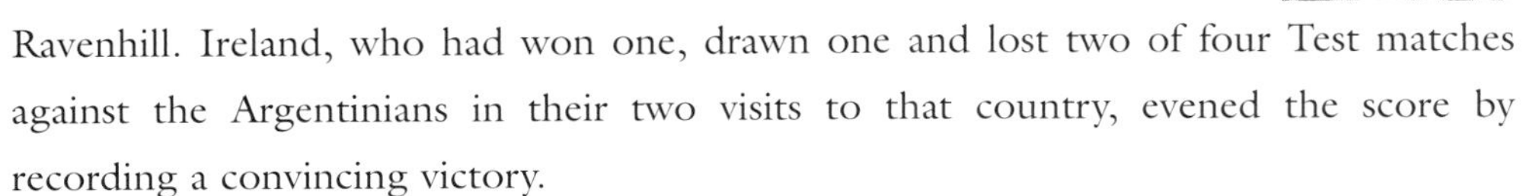

CHAPTER 18

CELEBRATION OF A CENTURY

IT IS NOT AN UNREASONABLE CLAIM to say that any institution that survives and prospers over 100 years must have been well served by its members. And in the case of Irish rugby that membership embraced the entire island of Ireland. It included all sections of political and religious persuasions. That loyalty had been put to severe tests in the years gone by and would again in the years ahead. When the IRFU started out on the centenary celebrations it was a vastly changed scene from the humble origins of the organisation founded on faith and the initiative of the very few one hundred years previously.

HARRY MCKIBBIN, CENTENARY PRESIDENT OF IRFU, 1974–75

But the visions and hopes of the founding fathers had come to fruition as the Irish rugby family set out on the celebrations. Rugby had prospered on the commitment of successive generations of people who had a passion for a game that grew, if not dramatically, then steadily.

Life in the later part of the twentieth century was very different from that in the same period of the nineteenth century. Bell's telephone, for instance, came into being in 1876, a new fangled contraption that was perfected as the years went by and made communications so much easier. It was to play an important part in the reporting and consequently the propagation of rugby and all sports. Mechanisation, convenience of travel and indeed electrification were perfected with the passing of time. Then came the radio and television and both were profound in helping to bring the game to a worldwide audience and very important as rugby evolved.

Organised rugby grew with the nation. With the advent of air travel, no longer did it take weeks to cross the world as had been the case when rugby touring was in its formative years. The spartan nature of the sporting stadia was transformed, as were spectator facilities. The game had survived two world wars and many other conflagrations.

But when the IRFU centenary celebrations got under way, it was at a green cathedral in the suburbs of Dublin 4 that the multitude gathered, Lansdowne Road, as they had first gathered in 1878 for the initial international played at the oldest international ground in the world — a tangible link with the past, an old friend dressed in its splendid best in celebration.

The president of the IRFU was Harry McKibbin, a man from a renowned rugby family, a son of Ulster, a former international and a Lion in 1938. If his career on the field was distinguished, so also his contribution at administrative level and his rounded abilities, affable manner and generosity of spirit found ideal expression in the highest forum of the game, the International Rugby Board, as one of Ireland's representatives.

His was a happy choice and came after another great administrator, Sarsfield Hogan, decided that age was not on his side when the suggestion was made that he would occupy the presidential chair in centenary year. He had been president of the IRFU in 1948–49 and had given magnificent service to the game. So it was to McKibbin that the union turned and he filled the office with immense distinction.

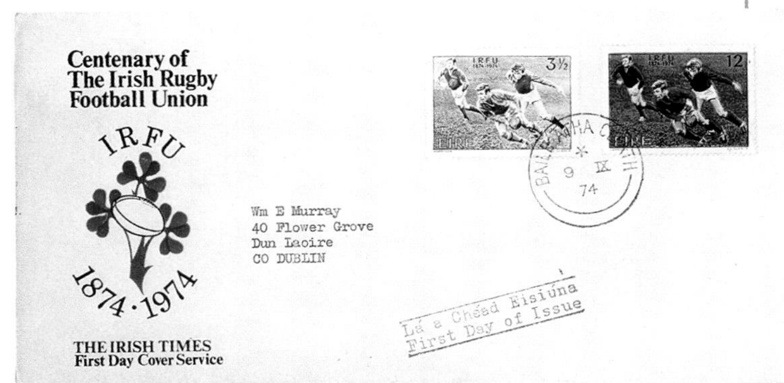

The celebrations opened at Lansdowne Road on 7 September 1974 when the Ireland team played a President's XV. That was a cosmopolitan selection drawn from seven countries. The flags of every club affiliated to the IRFU were flown and while the weather was not in a very benign mood that afternoon, it did not dampen enthusiasm. Appropriately, the proceedings opened with an ecumenical service.

The match itself was as symbolic as it proved to be competitive and ended in an 18 all draw. The IRFU decided that full caps would be awarded for the match, an appropriate gesture for so notable an occasion.

The Wolfhounds, an Irish touring team on the lines of the famous Barbarians, undertook a tour of the four provinces and players from all the major rugby nations were in the Wolfhounds squad, with the exception of New Zealand.

A visit from the famous All Blacks was a central part of the celebrations. That tour opened on another famous rugby ground, the Mardyke in Cork, the home ground of University College Cork and a venue in the long ago for international rugby. The first opposition for the All Blacks was provided by the Irish Universities, a fitting tribute to the contribution the universities had made to Irish rugby.

The All Blacks played against all four provinces and won every match. The Universities proved to be the toughest opposition the tourists faced in the run-up to the international at Lansdowne Road which took place on 23 November. The match against Connacht had a very special significance in that it was the first time that Connacht had met a major touring team.

That All Blacks side was captained by Andy Leslie, a fine back row forward who was later to have considerable involvement with Irish rugby as a very influential coach with the Garryowen club. He also, for a time in 1992–93, acted as an adviser to the IRFU on game development and game structure in Ireland. The coach to the side was J. J. Stewart and the manager Noel Stanley.

The tour was something of a rehabilitation exercise for the All Blacks. They had lost a series to the Lions for the first time three years previously and the team that toured Britain and Ireland in 1972–73 was far from a vintage All Blacks squad. But they had put the series loss and some indifferent form behind them. In their typically efficient manner they had rectified their deficiencies, notably their scrummaging, and they proved far too accomplished for an Ireland side minus the services of Mike Gibson, who had been such a thorn in their side for the Lions in 1971. The Ireland team that afternoon further strengthened the family bonds so pronounced in Irish rugby. James Crowe, a student at UCD, came in for Gibson and by so doing emulated the achievement of his father Morgan who had played for Ireland in 1929. Another university student Pat Parfrey from UCC was also capped that afternoon.

A medical doctor, he later made a significant contribution to the London Irish club before emigrating to Canada, and his deep knowledge of the game was of immense help to the Canadians when he became coach to their national side.

The 15-6 defeat by the All Blacks did not dampen enthusiasm about Ireland's prospects of retaining the International Championship. There was a vast reservoir of experience in the Ireland team with the Lions contingent of 1974 on hand in a team led again by Willie John McBride. Hopes of another championship win were elevated when Ireland defeated England 12-9 at Lansdowne Road in a game that was of mediocre standard. But the primary objective, a win, had been attained. The season was notable for the advent to the international stage of Willie Duggan, a superb No. 8 from Kilkenny who was a member of the Blackrock College club, and for the start, too, of the international career of hooker Pat Whelan from Garryowen who had been Ken Kennedy's understudy over the previous few seasons.

Ireland team that played England, 1974

Billy McCombe, who had won his first cap at outside half against France in Paris seven years previously while a student at Trinity College, was recalled to the colours after seven years' absence. Now with Bangor, McCombe was to retain his position throughout the 1975 championship.

But it was a championship series that was to prove significant for Ireland and to mark the end of the international road for some great players who had served Ireland so well for so long. Scotland outplayed Ireland at Murrayfield to dent championship and kill Triple Crown hopes. Time and circumstances took their inevitable toll on some of the Ireland players and with no rest in the aftermath of the 1974 tour to South Africa, fatigue was at times evident.

Yet there was to be a great moment in the career of one of the truly all time greats of Irish rugby, McBride. Ireland played very well to defeat France 25-6 in the third match of the championship and McBride scored a try, the only try he scored for Ireland in his 63 cap international career. It was acclaimed by the crowd with the enthusiasm that would have marked a Grand Slam triumph.

Ken Kennedy had been recalled for the match against France and Ireland gave a first cap to a young flanker, Mick Sherry, a former captain of UCD and now with Lansdowne. In the aftermath of the win over France, Ireland went to Cardiff to meet Wales in confident mood.

But from an early stage it was obvious that Ireland just did not have the resources to match a brilliant Welsh team who won 32-4. Ireland's solitary score came from Duggan in the closing moments. The

Welsh backs ran riot that afternoon and Wales scored five tries, four of them from the backs. The Welsh were to go on in the years immediately ahead to unprecedented glory. For some of the Irish it was the last hurrah. We would not again see McBride, Ray McLoughlin or Kennedy in an Ireland jersey; nor indeed centre Dick Milliken, whose career was regrettably cut short by a severe ankle injury.

COMBINED IRELAND AND PRESIDENT'S TEAMS, IRFU CENTENARY MATCH, 1974–75

There was, however, to be a last appearance for McBride as captain of a representative side at Lansdowne Road. He led the combined Ireland-Scotland team against England-Wales in a special centenary match at Lansdowne Road on 19 April, and appropriately Ireland-Scotland won.

That night the centenary banquet was held in Dublin and the gathering included personalities from the world of rugby. The occasion was marked by two outstanding speeches, one from Wavell Wakefield (Lord Wakefield of Kendall), one of the great figures of rugby, and another from the then president of Ireland, Cearbhaill Ó Dálaigh.

TERRY MOORE IN ACTION AGAINST NEW ZEALAND, CENTENARY SEASON, 1974–75

There was, too, a very special element to the centenary year that would prove to be highly significant in the years ahead. For the first time Ireland fielded a team at schools international level. The Ireland Schools played the England Schools at Lansdowne Road on 29 March. England won that match 6-3. It was to be the start of continuous Irish participation in the realm of schools international rugby, something that, strangely, had been resisted by successive generations of IRFU committees.

Another special event to mark the centenary season was an All Ireland club competition at Thomond Park between the cup winners from the four provinces. The final, a superb match, ended in a 9-9 draw between St Mary's College and Garryowen, but St Mary's took the title as they had scored a try, the defining difference in the event of a draw. Bangor and Galwegians were the other participants.

Thus the centenary season ended and Ireland faced into the next 100 years. The many changes that had taken place during the previous 100 years as the game evolved had been considerable, but what subsequently happened in the world of Rugby Union was within twenty years to be a revolution that few if any of those who had guided Rugby Union's destiny for a century could have envisaged. But that was some way ahead, although Irish rugby was to face its own difficulties in the period immediately after the centenary season. As the second century approached, society was changing radically and rugby would not be immune to aspects of those changes, nor indeed some of the ills of society.

CHAPTER 19

TRIALS AND TRIUMPHS

THE PERIOD BETWEEN 1975 AND 1979 WAS, in some respects at least, an accurate summation of Irish rugby, which so often in a short space of time moved from the indifferent to the glorious, put another way, poor performances followed by great and unexpected victories. Unpredictable was an accurate enough description. The four year period between 1975 and 1979 could accurately be described as trials and triumphs. But the trials in this period were to come before the triumphs.

Even before a ball was kicked in the 1975–76 season, Irish rugby suffered an unexpected blow at administrative level. Dr Jim Keane, from Athlone, who has been so supportive a vice-president to Harry McKibbin, took over the presidential chair at the end of June, and died twelve days later.

Jim Keane had served Connacht and Irish rugby well. He had been president of the Connacht Branch for two years 1965–66 and again the following season and in 1967 became one of Connacht's representatives on the IRFU committee. He served on that committee for eight years, six as a direct representative from his province and two as junior and senior vice-president. It was decided in honour of his memory that the office would not as such be filled in 1975–76, with the senior vice-president Dudley Higgins taking over most of the presidential duties.

On the field there were some historic happenings. After much debate and consideration and following the recommendations from the selection committees of the previous few seasons, it was decided that Ireland would enter the realm of B international rugby. The arguments of the pro and anti lobbies were both understandable. But it was felt that with Ireland's limited playing population it would be difficult for Ireland to field what would in effect be two international teams. What strengthened those against the concept was that capped players could not be selected at B level. That imposed its own burdens on the selection committee and the task of selecting a team was entrusted to the senior selection committee.

With several great players having bade farewell to the international scene, the Ireland coach Syd Millar, the man who had masterminded the 1974 Lions triumph in South Africa, also stood aside after his three years in charge of the national team. He had been the central figure in that triumph in South Africa and had coached the Ireland team that won the championship in 1974, the first such success for Ireland since 1951. His had surely been a truly magnificent contribution as player and coach.

His successor was Roly Meates, a man who had coached Trinity College and Leinster and a noted enthusiast and one for long dedicated to the coaching concept. He had played for Trinity and for Wanderers and had also played for Leinster. He had been a contender for the Irish coaching berth three years previously but Millar had been preferred at that time. Now Meates's chance had come and he embraced it with immense enthusiasm and no little hope.

Meates was not, in fact, a member of the five man Ireland selection committee as Millar and Dawson had been as one of their province's representatives. It was, too, a very changed selection committee from the previous season. The only survivor from the previous year was Joe Fanagan, who was chairman of the five. Two former internationals, Niall Brophy and Noel Murphy, came in representing Leinster and Munster respectively. Ken Reid and Roy Saunders were Ulster's representatives. They faced a difficult task, and as events transpired, a difficult season.

The B international against France was played at Lansdowne Road on 6 December 1975. Ireland won the match 9-6 with all the points coming from kicks. And kicks and punches were exchanged freely in a match more noted for the fact that four players were sent off, two from each side, than any quality in the play. The English referee Alan Welsby whistled a sombre tune all through and, if his strict and at times eccentric interpretations of the law did little to aid continuity, none the less he could defend his decisions to send off four players.

Within a few weeks of that match, Ireland faced Australia at Lansdowne Road. That was Meates's first big test. He and the selection committee came up with a rather peculiar mixture seeking to replace players who had retired and some others who were out of form with a blend of experience and youthful promise. It was an amalgam of the old and the new. It did not, however, prove to be a potent mixture under the leadership of Mike Gibson, who had taken over as captain from McBride. Two youngsters were chosen at half-back, Ollie Campbell and John Robbie, both of whom would later leave their mark, but not that afternoon. Mick Molloy was recalled to the international scene after three years' absence to partner Moss Keane in the second row.

Mike Gibson, Ireland's most capped player (69), in action for the Lions in South Africa, 1974

Ireland brought in five new caps for that match, Ian McIlrath, a centre from Ballymena, Campbell, Robbie, hooker John Cantrell from UCD, and Feidhlim McLoughlin, a brother of Ray at prop. McLoughlin had played most of his rugby with the Northern club in England but had also been in the Connacht side since 1969. At 34, he was the oldest player to win a first cap for Ireland. Ireland lost to the Australians 20-10 and could have no complaints.

That result underlined Ireland's problems which were to assert themselves as the season progressed. A visit to Paris was next on the agenda and that proved to be a chastening experience as Ireland went down to a then record 26-3 defeat. But that match was to see a young prop from Trinity College, Philip Orr, make his debut on the national team and, although that afternoon he scarcely revealed just what lay ahead, he went on to win 58 caps for his country, a record for an Ireland prop, in a magnificent international career that spanned eleven years. Barry McGann was recalled at outside half, having last played in 1973, Phil O'Callaghan was recalled at tight head prop and a young second row from Shannon, Brendan Foley, also won a first cap. Shay Deering was recalled at flank forward with Fergus Slattery losing out.

Willie John McBride gains possession against Wales, Cardiff, 1975

Mike Gibson was unhappy in the role of captain and that responsibility was taken over by Tom Grace for the visit of Wales to Dublin. Two more newcomers were called in for that match, Donal Canniffe, who had been an outstanding member of a fine Cork Constitution side at scrum-half and who later gave very distinguished service to Lansdowne, and Ronnie Hakin from the CIYMS club in Ulster in the second row. Yet again Ireland were comprehensively beaten, this time by 34 points to 9, and that defeat precipitated further changes for the visit to Twickenham.

Joe Brady, a centre from Wanderers, was given a chance at Twickenham and he was joined by two more new caps in Steve Blake-Knox from Trinity on the left wing and Harry Steele from Ballymena at No. 8. That afternoon Ireland yet again revealed their ability to defy the odds and played extremely well in beating England 13-12, with Grace getting a try and McGann two penalty goals and a dropped goal. It was Ireland's fifth consecutive win over England and there was hope that Ireland had put the bad days behind when Scotland came to Dublin for the final match of the championship in March. John Moloney was recalled at scrum-half for Canniffe and Willie Duggan, unavailable for the match in Twickenham because of injury, replaced Steele. Larry Moloney from Garryowen came in at full-back for Tony Ensor. Moloney had won a cap as a replacement for Pat Lavery against Wales. Ireland lost 15-6 and so had won just one of five matches.

It was scarcely the best preparation for a tour to New Zealand and Fiji arranged for the summer, and the general belief before the tour was that Ireland could face a very torrid time on what was the first visit of an Ireland side to New Zealand. This was, in fact, only Ireland's sixth overseas tour in over 100 years.

Kevin Quilligan from Garryowen was appointed manager of the team. He was a man of considerable experience, having had a long and illustrious playing career with Garryowen and Munster and at administrative level had served on the Munster Branch and IRFU with some distinction. He and Meates together with Grace as captain formed a good management team. Bob O'Connell, a founder of the Old Belvedere club and a very distinguished doctor, travelled as medical officer.

The Ireland squad for the tour included only two uncapped players, Tom Feighery, a prop forward from St Mary's College who had also played with UCD, and Emmet O'Rafferty, a second row from Wanderers. John Moloney was omitted and Canniffe and Robbie were the scrum-halves.

Ireland started the tour well with a 19-4 win over South Canterbury. Another win followed against North Auckland. Then Ireland lost 13-10 to Auckland, but that defeat was directly attributable to a very bad mistake by the referee. A 22-16 win over Manawatu was followed by an 18-4 loss to Canterbury and Ireland then defeated Southland in Invercargill in a bad-tempered match. So Ireland went into the Test with a record of four wins from six matches. Canniffe and Deering were both injured. Canniffe broke an ankle in training and Deering sustained a very severe shoulder injury against Canterbury. Robbie McGrath, an uncapped scrum-half from Wanderers, was flown out to replace Canniffe and the experienced Jim Davidson from Dungannon flew out to replace Deering.

Ireland did quite well in the Test and, had penalty chances been taken, could well have surprised New Zealand in Wellington, but New Zealand won 11-3, a rather flattering margin. The tour ended with a visit to Suva in Fiji and, in a remarkable match played on a ground with frogs jumping around the playing surface and some incredible refereeing, Ireland none the less won 8-0.

So Meates's first year in charge had ended with five defeats from six matches at international level, but the tour to New Zealand had kindled hope that Ireland might have turned the corner. Ireland had used eleven new caps in the season, a telling statistic in relation to the difficulties the selectors and Meates faced.

Ireland's first match in 1977 was against Wales in Cardiff and that proved yet another humbling experience as Ireland lost 26-9. The match in Cardiff was refereed by Scotsman Norman Sanson and he sent Willie Duggan and Geoff Wheel, of Wales, off the field in the 38th minute. It was a controversial decision. Duggan's dismissal was the first time an Ireland player had been sent off in such a full international, and to date, happily, the only such instance.

New caps were brought in, changes made, but Ireland ended the championship by being whitewashed. Two of the new caps, Alistair McKibbin, son of the centenary president, and Jimmy Bowen had both been on the Ireland Schools side in 1975. Meates worked hard but success did not come his way. Ireland had played ten internationals under Meates, lost nine and won one. He was to pay the price for that and was replaced by former Ireland captain Noel Murphy, who had coached both his club, Cork Constitution, and Munster. In fact, Murphy operated with a selection committee unchanged from the previous season.

IRISH FORWARDS COVER V ENGLAND, 1977

The Lions went to New Zealand in the summer of 1977 and Ireland's poor performances were reflected in the composition of the Lions squad. Only three Irish players were chosen. They were Gibson, Philip Orr and Willie Duggan. Prior to the start of the tour, Moss Keane was called into the squad as a replacement for Geoff Wheel, who had to withdraw.

Ireland's first match under Murphy was against Scotland in Dublin on 21 January 1978 and that match saw Ireland end the barren spell with a 12-9 victory. It marked the start of the international careers of some players who later left their mark upon the scene. Foremost in this respect was outside half Tony Ward. He had been a pupil at St Mary's College, Rathmines, and a very accomplished schools player. He was also a very good soccer player and had been capped for Ireland at youth level in that discipline and had, in fact, signed for Shamrock Rovers in the League of Ireland. A student in Thomond College, Limerick, he had been prevailed upon to join Garryowen and made an immediate impact helping the club to win the Munster Senior Cup in 1975. He was subsequently capped for Munster and, after playing for the Ireland B team on two occasions, he was called into the Ireland team against Scotland and was partnered by John Moloney, who was restored to the team and was now captain in place of Tom Grace whose international career ended with that match. Mike Gibson was recalled for the match against France and played on the right wing throughout the series. Grace subsequently had to retire because of a knee injury, but he had contributed very significantly to Ireland at a difficult period.

Ward was one of five new caps in the team against Scotland including yet another member of the Ireland 1975 Schools team, Donal Spring, and a flanker John O'Driscoll. He was a medical doctor in Manchester who had played for Manchester and London Irish. His older brother Barry had been capped for Ireland at full-back at the start of the decade. John went on to have a superb career for Ireland and the Lions. Ward's innate football skill was displayed to telling effect on his debut and he kicked two penalty goals and a conversion as Ireland won a tense match with Stewart McKinney getting a try after he had come on as a replacement for O'Driscoll who was injured. Ireland lost by a point to France in the Parc des Princes in a match played on a frozen surface that was in reality dangerous. A one point defeat was cruel return for Ireland. Ireland lost to Wales by 20-16 in a very good match on 4 March and the season ended with a 15-9 loss to England in Twickenham. In sharp contrast to the previous seasons, Ireland had in fact used only 19 players throughout the championship. One win from four matches was an imbalanced return for the Irish and Ward ended the season with 39 points, a record for a player in the championship. He was subsequently named 'European Player of the Year'.

Mike Gibson announced his retirement prior to the 1978–79 championship, but as events subsequently transpired, it was to be a premature announcement. The All Blacks came on a tour of Britain and Ireland and on 31 October 1978 met Munster at Thomond Park.

MUNSTER TEAM THAT BEAT NEW ZEALAND, THOMOND PARK, 1978 — ONLY IRISH TEAM EVER TO BEAT NEW ZEALAND SIDE

MUNSTER BRANCH I.R.F.U.
Munster v. New Zealand
THOMOND PARK, LIMERICK
Tuesday, 31st October, 1978
KICK-OFF 3.00 p.m.
Admission to Ground 80p
№ 10401
Hon. Secretary
Notwithstanding the issuing of this Ticket—the Munster Branch, I.R.F.U., reserves the right to refuse admission to the Ground at its absolute discretion.

It was a historic occasion as Munster, revealing all their traditional fire and courage against touring teams, allied those attributes to tremendous tackling and a perceptive tactical awareness to fashion a famous victory, winning by 12 points to nil. The pack was magnificent in that match and Canniffe was a superb captain and tactician at scrum-half. Ward was at his brilliant best as Munster outplayed the All Blacks and held them scoreless.

The All Blacks were well aware of the problems they could face against Munster, whose exploits against touring teams had not gone unheeded by the tourists who had had such a narrow escape in Musgrave Park six years previously. The All Blacks consequently selected a team of Test strength for the match. Munster had four internationals in their back line, Larry Moloney, Ward, Canniffe and Seamus Dennison, who had won a cap in 1973 and two more in 1975. In the pack Pat Whelan, Donal Spring, Brendan Foley and Moss Keane represented a quartet of internationals and they were surrounded by four more who knew their business, two of whom were subsequently to be capped, flanker Colm Tucker and prop Gerry McLoughlin from Shannon.

From the outset it was clear that Munster, superbly drilled by coach Tom Kiernan, had an inner belief that they could win. Dennison set the trend early on with a great tackle and Munster never wilted in any area of the field. Ward dropped a goal, kicked a penalty and converted a try scored by flanker Christy Cantillon. Munster had seized the initiative from the outset and long before the end of the match it was obvious that the much cherished win over New Zealand would be attained. At the end of the match the ground erupted. The players were mobbed by the delirious crowd of 12,000.

Tony Ward kicks a goal against Scotland at Lansdowne Road, 1978

The following Saturday, Ireland went into the match against the All Blacks in a very confident mood. Shay Deering was recalled on the flank and named as captain, and Ward was partnered at scrum-half by Colin Patterson from Ulster. But Ireland could not show the kind of form and concentration that Munster had revealed and New Zealand won the match. And although it was an injury time try which clinched their 10-6 win, they deserved their victory.

Despite the defeat there was optimism that Ireland would do well in the championship. France represented the initial test at Lansdowne Road. Ireland brought in a new cap at full-back, Dick Spring, older brother of Donal and later to become a leading political figure in Ireland, and Colm Tucker won his first cap on the flank in a team led by Fergus Slattery and which included another new cap in the Trinity College No. 8, Michael Gibson.

Ireland drew 9-9 with France and yet again Ward was the scorer with three penalty goals. His kicking was invaluable and he brought a new dimension to this aspect of the game, a facet in which Ireland had a very costly deficiency prior to Ward's arrival on the scene. Ireland went to the Arms Park and, after a great match, Wales won 24-21. Both

teams scored two tries, with Wales getting one from second row Alan Martin in very fortunate circumstances in a mix-up between Spring and Patterson, both of whom played well that afternoon. It added to Ireland's frustration that 21 points had been scored against Wales, a record at the time, and yet Ireland lost.

Ireland played England with a team that showed two changes from the side that had lost in Cardiff. Moss Finn, another member of the first Ireland Schools team of 1975, was on the right wing for Terry Kennedy, who had won his first cap against New Zealand. Willie Duggan returned to the team on the flank in place of Tucker. Ireland won the match 12-7 and did so even more comprehensively than that score suggests.

The last match of the championship was against Scotland in Murrayfield and it marked the return of Mike Gibson. He was prevailed upon to have second thoughts about his availability. He was not an original selection and was brought into the squad as a precaution because of a doubt about Alistair McKibbin's fitness. Kennedy had been restored to the wing for Finn. As events transpired McKibbin passed a fitness test, but Kennedy was ruled out the day before the match because of a bout of influenza, and Gibson was chosen to play on the wing. At full-back Ronnie Elliott of Bangor replaced Dick Spring. Ireland drew a rather untidy match played in high wind 11 points all. Ward was again named 'European Player of the Year'.

At administrative level the IRFU was looking closely at the development of the game and it was felt that this was an area that needed attention. With this as the objective, a Game Development officer was appointed for the first time with specific terms of reference. The union appointed George Spotswood to the position in January 1979.

That appointment and indeed the establishment of a game development committee came as a result of the recommendations of the IRFU Coaching subcommittee. There had been a keen awareness over the previous years that proper organised coaching was of paramount importance. Men who exercised immense influence in this area were Judge Charlie Conroy, Des Scaife and Ronnie Dawson, to mention just three. In fact the first national coaching course as such was held in Clongowes Wood College in 1976. But courses had been held at Butlin's Holiday Camp in Mosney, County Meath, for some years prior to that inaugural national effort in Clongowes.

The national team, the provinces and the clubs had by that time firmly embraced the coaching concept, but it needed co-ordination and leadership from the union. It was Spotswood who directed that course in Clongowes. He brought to it a wide embracing experience.

He had played for Dungannon, a club with which his family had been closely associated. He had also played at outside half for Ulster. He had coached Dungannon, Malone, the Ulster Under 21 and junior sides and for three years the Ulster Senior team. He was a teacher in Regent House School at the time of his appointment which came under the direction of the Game Development Committee chaired by Ewart Bell. Spotswood thus brought to his new and onerous tasks a deep involvement in the game and an appreciation of what was required. His appointment was the initial step that precipitated major changes in the area of game development.

CHAPTER 20

SUCCESS AND CONTROVERSY IN AUSTRALIA

THERE IS NO DOUBT THAT after the dismal record of 1976 and 1977, Ireland had now turned things round under Murphy. Ireland had won one, drawn two and lost one of their championship matches in 1979. The next test was a tour to Australia in the summer of 1979. Ireland had visited Australia in 1967 and won the Test match on that tour. The 1979 tour embraced two Tests, a considerable challenge for the Irish.

Ward had established a tremendous reputation in his two seasons on the international scene and many rated him among the best backs in the game. That was certainly the view expressed by the All Blacks and by Carwyn James, the man who had coached the 1971 Lions to Test series success.

But he had his detractors on the home front. Some felt he was getting too much publicity. He certainly got a lot, but his arrival had coincided with a marked change in Ireland's performances and also with the vastly increased coverage rugby was getting on television, radio and in the newspapers.

Ward had undoubtedly helped lift the scene, people related to him, even those who were not particularly interested in rugby. That seemed to upset the more conservative elements in the game and some members of what one might term the rugby establishment. But there were those on the IRFU who realised his value to the side and to the game.

The man chosen as manager of the Ireland team in Australia, Jack Coffey, was not an admirer of Ward. He had been president of the IRFU in 1977–78 and had been a very good player for the Lansdowne club and came from a family that had made a very significant contribution to the game. His father was a former international, a former president of the IRFU and long-standing rugby official.

A man from the old and conservative school, some of Coffey's comments prior to the tour made it explicitly clear that he was not well disposed to Ward. Perhaps Ward was too accessible to the news media and one ill advised photograph in a British tabloid newspaper certainly did do Ward a lot of damage and was ready ammunition for his detractors.

Ward was chosen for the Australian tour and the second outside half selected was Ollie Campbell, the man who had gained his only cap to date against Australia over three years previously. Campbell had spent much of the season recovering from an injury, but returned to play for his club, Old Belvedere, in the Leinster Senior Cup. He had played splendidly in that campaign. Slattery was captain of the side coached by Murphy and yet again Bob O'Connell was named as medical officer. Mike Gibson, having made his unexpected return to the international scene against Scotland, made himself available for the tour and was duly chosen. Donal Spring, the younger Michael Gibson, Dick Spring and Alistair McKibbin were unavailable.

THE MOST SUCCESSFUL IRELAND TOURING TEAM, AUSTRALIA, 1979. BOTH TESTS WERE WON

The squad included eight uncapped players, but by the time the tour was over several of those had attained international honours and a few of them were to leave a very profound impact on the scene in later years.

The tour got off to a very bad start off the field and a very good start on it. Prop forward Ned Byrne was knocked down by a car two nights before the first match and sustained a badly fractured leg. He was replaced by Mick Fitzpatrick. Ireland won the first match against Western Australia in Perth very easily by 35-9. Campbell played in that match. He was, in fact, off form with his place-kicking that day, but not so as the tour progressed. Ireland defeated ACT in the second match 35-7 and Ward scored a record 19 points. Next up was New South Wales and Ward was again outside half and contributed eight points. The Irish side was well in control in that match but New South Wales scored two late tries as the result of uncharacteristic defensive mistakes by Gibson who played on the wing.

The fourth match was against Queensland, then the most powerful provincial side in Australia, and Campbell played in that game and played superbly. He scored Ireland's 18 points in an 18-15 win. The first Test was next on the schedule and there was a lot of speculation about the composition of the side. Both Ward and Campbell had played very well on the tour. Ward was the man in possession, but there were ominous comments being made that he would be dropped in favour of Campbell. Bearing in mind Ward's track record, such an occurrence scarcely seemed conceivable. There were suggestions, too, that Campbell might be played in the centre. The years were catching up on Gibson and in any case he had played on the wing against Scotland and against New South Wales. Alfred McLennan had been injured and unable to play against Queensland and John Moloney had been named on the right wing. He had the pace and the defensive skill to make a good job of the position and he was chosen for the Test.

Ward had played well, at times extremely well, in every match in the Ireland jersey. His form on tour was equally good. Campbell had qualities that could have been used to effect in the centre. The tour management opted to play Gibson in the centre and Campbell at outside half, thus dropping Ward. The news of Ward's demotion was received with astonishment at home. The ominous comments prior to the team announcement had proved correct.

It was very hard on Ward and indeed also on Campbell, a first-class footballer, tremendous tackler and the most inoffensive of men. Ward was shattered when he was told he was dropped. The manner in which he was told, too, left something to be desired. The squad had travelled to Surfers Paradise outside Brisbane for a training session and the team was due to be announced at the session. But Ward got a tip-off on the coach going to Surfers Paradise that he was dropped. His Garryowen club-mate Pat Whelan told him of his omission after Whelan had been told by one of the journalists on the tour that he understood that Ward had been omitted.

Ollie Campbell — a prolific kicker for Ireland

It was a very controversial decision and, indeed, one that for years afterwards provoked a Ward-Campbell debate — perhaps one that did not always do justice to either of these great players. The tour manager refused requests from the press to interview Ward. That, in fact, went back on a pre-tour agreement. Requests that Ward be interviewed with the manager and coach present were also rejected. That management decision was a bad one and did no more than fan the flame of controversy. All sorts of reasons and speculation were flying about as to why Ward was dropped. People, especially at home, just could not understand that a player who had done so much to lift Ireland and played so well would be dropped. He must have misbehaved on tour was one theory. It was absolute nonsense. Quite simply the management decided that they would go with Campbell.

The Australian press was equally perplexed and there was speculation that the Irish management was playing a game of bluff to deceive the Wallabies and that Ward would play in the match. What some people found especially hard to understand was that, as Ireland had a problem in the centre where Paul McNaughton had clearly established his claims to one berth, but with Gibson's immense skills on the wane, why Ward and Campbell could not both be accommodated. Bearing in mind that, in fact, Ireland played a 10 man game in the two Tests and the great tackling skills of Campbell, debate on that issue lingered long after the tour. There was a view that Campbell was able to move the threequarter line into a more potent attacking unit than Ward. There was some substance in that view. But it would have been more readily understandable at that particular time had Ireland played an expansive game in the Test. That did not happen.

While no player in the history of Irish rugby can ever have been dropped after playing so well and scoring so freely as Ward did, the fact remains that Campbell, for all the pressure on him, rose to the challenge superbly. The Ireland pack was well on top from the outset, the diminutive Patterson at scrum-half sniped effectively at their heels, Campbell kicked brilliantly for position and it was the Australians who were under constant pressure at the Ballymore ground in Brisbane. Ireland won 27-12 with Patterson scoring two tries, and Campbell kicked four penalty goals, dropped a goal and converted both tries.

He put down a marker that afternoon, and from that point to the day injury forced his retirement in 1984, he was the first choice in the No. 10 jersey for Ireland and he filled it with immense distinction.

After the Test win, Ireland defeated New South Wales Country Districts, lost to Sydney when Campbell was chosen at full-back and Ward at outside half, and finished the tour with the second Test in Sydney when Ireland fielded an unchanged team. Ireland's win in that was nothing as convincing as their victory in the first Test, but they deserved their 9-3 victory achieved at the famous Sydney Cricket Ground with Campbell contributing the nine points with two dropped goals and a penalty goal. Ireland thus won the Test series and became the first of the home countries to do so in the southern hemisphere and to date the only one of the four home countries to do so. Three players won their first caps on the tour, full-back Rodney O'Donnell, hooker Ciaran Fitzgerald and full-back Frank Ennis, who had come on as a replacement for O'Donnell in the first Test. Fitzgerald had been preferred to Pat Whelan at hooker and that was the start of an international career for Fitzgerald that would see him lead Ireland to glory in the years ahead, but not in the immediate future.

In the aftermath of Ireland's Test wins, expectation was very high that the 1980 International Championship would see Ireland build on their great achievement. But expectation was not matched by realisation at the start of the second last decade of the twentieth century.

CHAPTER 21

DEVELOPMENT AND DISAPPOINTMENT

The appointment of George Spotswood as Game Development officer was to prove the prelude to changes of major consequence in this vital area of the game. There was now a new awareness that things were changing, that the old order was no longer enough.

It was in many respects a follow on to the attitude that now prevailed in relation to the essential nature of proper coaching. That had caused quite some debate in the late 1960s, when there was a reluctance to appoint a coach to the national team and a suspicion, so to speak, about the coaching concept. Now such an attitude was inconceivable.

On the issue of development, there was some concern, and it was very understandable, that many players were being lost to the game after they left school. There was also an acute awareness that not nearly enough was being done to encourage boys from non rugby-playing schools to play rugby and, equally, the desire was to see a greater proliferation of clubs in the rural areas. It all amounted to a challenge of considerable significance. Time, money, effort and alteration in structures were all required to bring about the essential changes in these areas and there was a willingness on the part of the IRFU and the Branches to take up the challenge embraced and the Game Development Committee under the chairmanship of Ewart Bell now had a central and crucial role in the future of Irish rugby.

One worry was the lack of competition at representative level that existed for young players leaving school. That gap was not being filled by junior interprovincials, and Under 19 representative matches were infrequent. Nor was there any structure at under age level that embraced an interprovincial series.

These were some of the areas that occupied the time and thoughts of the Game Development Committee. Reports were produced on various aspects of the game. One very quick development was the establishment of an Under 20 interprovincial championship series in 1980. It was believed, and rightly so, that this would provide a useful bridge for young players moving from the schools and under age club scene through to senior rugby.

The job specification of George Spotswood was also changed from game development officer to that of technical director, and early in the 1980s he was joined by John Murphy, a former Skerries player and, like Spotswood, a schoolteacher. He assumed the role of technical officer.

Those appointments were the by-product of an intensive study of the requirements, and before the decade was out others were brought in and appointed on a full-time basis as game development officers. Eventually each province had its own men in place to work in this aspect of the game. But that was in the future.

Meanwhile on the field, the splendid results on the Australian tour lifted hopes that Ireland would make a very strenuous bid for the Championship and Triple Crown in 1980. Noel Murphy was still in charge as coach and his fellow selectors for the 1980 series were former Ireland centre Kevin Flynn and former Leinster hooker Paddy Madigan, Joss Lapsley from Ulster and Brian O'Brien from Munster.

The days when Leinster and Ulster were guaranteed two selectors each and Munster one were gone, as were the days when the provinces actually named their own selectors for the national selection committee.

Now the system was different and the selection committee was chosen by a three man election subcommittee who made their choices from the names submitted from each province, with each province having the right to nominate three men from which the subcommittee chose five. While the provision was now there for Connacht to get a man on the selection five, as yet they had not been given representation and that was a contentious point in the west. The best they had ever managed was to get a man among the substitute selectors. That, too, was to change radically within a very short time.

Before the 1979–80 season started, the game was locked in debate and controversy centred on South Africa, where the Lions were due to undertake a tour in the summer of 1980. Opinion on the wisdom of that undertaking was very divided.

The political situation in South Africa and the lack of facilities and opportunities for non-white players allied to some repressive laws promoted many within and others outside rugby to the view that isolating South Africa in sporting terms was the only way to redress the balance in these areas of South African life. Furthermore, the disruption on some tours that had taken place with South African involvement in cricket as well as rugby, and indeed when South African teams visited these islands as well as New Zealand, was causing anxiety and adding to the tenor of the debate.

But there was a view that the way forward was to maintain contact and build bridges. That was the view that prevailed and the Home Unions duly agreed that the Lions would tour South Africa in the summer of 1980. One of the arguments used in favour of the tour was that much progress was being made in South African rugby towards bringing in the black and coloured players to the rugby family in that country. In reality, cricket in South Africa could argue a much more convincing case than rugby on that issue.

Before Ireland opened their championship campaign in 1980, there was a significant happening in October of 1979. For the first time Ireland fielded a team at Under 23 level. The match was against Holland in Hilversum. The Irish, in fact, played against the full Netherlands team. Ireland included four players who had been capped at senior level. They were Rodney O'Donnell, Jimmy Bowen, Moss Finn and Donal Spring. Spring, who had led the first Ireland schoolboys team to play in an international in 1975, now had the honour of leading the first Ireland Under 23 team.

The team included several players who had already worn the Ireland jersey at schools level and several more who would later wear the national jersey at senior level. Ireland won the match and played very well in doing so, 31-3. Moss Finn scored 15 points.

There was, too, the first visit to Ireland of the Italian national team. The Italians played two matches in Ireland, against Leinster on 30 December and Ulster at Ravenhill on 1 January. Leinster won 26-10 and Ulster won 15-6.

Ireland opened their championship campaign in 1980 against England at Twickenham on 19 January and it proved to be a chastening experience. Mike Gibson had retired but apart from him all the other players who had made the tour to Australia were available. Ireland played very badly in Twickenham and were comprehensively beaten 24-9, with Ollie Campbell kicking three penalty goals.

The next match was against Scotland in Dublin and Rodney O'Donnell was recalled at full-back, having very surprisingly been omitted against England, with the selectors favouring Kevin O'Brien who played his rugby with Broughton Park and Lancashire and who had Connacht qualifications and played subsequently for the province. John Moloney was restored to the left wing because of an injury to Alfred McLennan, Mick Fitzpatrick was preferred to Gerry McLoughlin at tight head prop, Donal Spring was brought in at No. 8 and the pack also included second row Jim Glennon from the Skerries club, who had made his debut against England.

Ireland won the match by 22-15 and were not flattered by the winning margin as Campbell scored 14 points. Ireland went to Paris and included a new cap in the centre, David Irwin. He had gone to Australia although he had not played in a Test, but his form for Ulster had been impressive. He came into the centre for Alistair McKibbin. McLennan was back on the left wing and Brendan Foley was recalled to the second row for Glennon. Ireland lost 19-18 but had every reason to feel aggrieved at the outcome. Everyone but the referee Alan Hosie believed that Ciaran Fitzgerald had scored a try for Ireland, but it was disallowed. However, while defeat was the portion, this was one occasion in which Ireland did indeed score a moral victory.

Wales came to Dublin on 15 March and came as reigning champions and warm favourites to add to their list of conquests, although they had lost to England in Twickenham by 9-8 in very controversial circumstances when they had a player sent off the field in the early stages of the match by Irish referee David Burnett. But Wales had beaten France and Scotland and still retained some hope that they might at least share the championship with England, who the same afternoon played Scotland in Murrayfield.

But Ireland gave their best display of the season in dismantling Wales, winning 21-7, a record victory for Ireland at the time over the Welsh. Moloney was again on the wing for McLennan, the only change from the side that had lost in Paris. Ireland scored three tries in the demolition of the Welsh and Campbell was again at his best with his kicking and splendid distribution and perception.

So Ireland ended the season with two wins from four matches and scored 70 points, a record for the championship, and Campbell created a personal bench-mark by scoring 46 points in the championship, the highest at that time by any player from any country in the series in a season.

Ireland's performances in the series found reward in the composition of the Lions squad. Rodney O'Donnell, Ollie Campbell, Colin Patterson, John O'Driscoll and Colm Tucker were all chosen for the tour. Ciaran Fitzgerald, at that time an officer in the Irish Army, was not available as the Irish government was against any Irish involvement in the tour. Syd Millar was named as manager and Noel Murphy as coach — so a very pronounced Irish influence.

Before the tour ended, no fewer than three more Irish players were called into the squad. Tony Ward, Philip Orr and John Robbie all joined the party as replacements during the tour.

The controversy about the morality of the tour continued right up to the day of the squad's departure, and quite apart from that element, the tour was to prove costly for the Irish. O'Donnell suffered a horrific neck injury playing against the Junior Springboks at the Wanderers ground in Johannesburg in the twelfth match of the tour. It was to end his highly promising career. Colin Patterson, who had played in the first, second and third Tests, sustained a very serious knee injury playing against Griquas West in Kimberly in the second last match of the tour. That injury ended his career despite a few brave attempts to return to the game.

The Lions lost the Test series 3-1, were unbeaten in all the provincial matches and would not have been flattered had they at least drawn the series. Ward, who had not featured at international level for well over a year, played in the first Test despite a badly bruised thigh. But with the two outside halves who had been in the original selection, Campbell and Gareth Davies, ruled out of the match, Ward played. He scored 18 points in the match, a figure that has not since been beaten for a Lions player in a Test, and equalled just once.

A bad lapse in concentration cost the Lions the crucial third Test in Port Elizabeth and enabled South Africa to score a crucial try and win 12-10. In the first Test in Cape Town, the Lions lost 26-22 in a match that was in the balance right to the end. The Springboks deservedly won the second Test in Bloemfontein 26-19 and then came the third Test in Port Elizabeth that enabled South Africa to win the series. That afternoon, in inclement weather, even Campbell's place-kicking was well below par. But allowing for that, the Lions had chances to win the Test.

In the fourth Test in Pretoria, the Lions gave a superb display to win 17-13 and Campbell, Robbie, O'Driscoll and Tucker all played in the match. O'Driscoll scored a crucial try. England's Bill Beaumont was captain of the Lions and he proved an excellent leader on and off the field.

Noel Murphy's tenure as Ireland coach ended with the 1980 championship and Tom Kiernan was chosen as his successor. He was not in fact a selector. In that regard there were two happenings of significance. For the first time Connacht had a selector and the man chosen was former Ireland prop P. J. Dwyer. The other unprecedented element was that Munster did not have a selector. The stipulation that Munster, Ulster and Leinster had all to be represented on the committee was now gone.

It was the selectors' prerogative to select their own chairman and the coach, with the coach being chosen from nominations submitted to the selectors. Paddy Madigan was named as chairman and Kiernan was made coach defeating one of the selectors, Kevin Flynn, for the position.

Ireland's first match under Kiernan was against Romania at Lansdowne Road on 18 October 1980. The Romanian side that came on a five match tour of Ireland and played one match in England was surely among the strongest and best to emerge from that country. They gave a demonstration of their ability when they defeated Munster with a display of power, pace and flair at Thomond Park and won 32-9. They lost to Leinster in the next match but then defeated Ulster at Ravenhill. The national selectors decided to select Ward and Campbell, naming Campbell in the centre. That combination produced the initiative for an excellent try for Ireland by wing Frank Quinn, but that was the only try the Romanians conceded in the match for which caps were not awarded, as the old routine of not awarding caps against countries who were not on the International Board was still operative.

Ireland led 7-3 at the interval and 13-3 going into the last quarter. But Romania scored a try and two penalty goals to set the scene for an exciting finish. Indeed, with time almost up, Irish hearts missed a beat when the Romanians were awarded a penalty, but the difficult kick was missed so Ireland got a draw, a rather fortuitous draw in many respects.

Despite that rather indifferent performance, Ireland had been rated favourites to win the International Championship. It was a rating that proved to be very flawed as Ireland ended up being whitewashed. Ireland lost to France by 13-19 at Lansdowne Road with a newcomer Hugo MacNeill at full-back and with Fergus Slattery still captain. Ward was recalled against Wales in Cardiff and Campbell moved to centre yet again. Ireland played some great rugby that afternoon and scored two tries, but had the galling experience of seeing Wales win by 9-8, with the Welsh points coming from two penalty goals and a dropped goal. Remarkably, with two place kickers of the calibre of Campbell and Ward on the team, Ireland did not have a successful kick at goal and, to add to the sense of frustration and disappointment, one of Ward's conversion attempts hit the outside of an upright.

But the performance was deemed good enough to go with a team that showed just one change for the visit of England. Donal Spring replaced Brendan Foley in the second row. Ireland lost the match 10-6 and so went to Murrayfield to avoid a whitewash. The selectors persisted with Ward and Campbell but for the visit to Scotland, John Cantrell was recalled at hooker for Pat Whelan, who had regained his place that season as Ciaran Fitzgerald was ruled out by injury. Once more Ireland suffered the frustration of losing by a point, going down 10-9, with the winning try being scored by Scotland wing Bruce Hay from an interception. It had been that kind of year for Ireland.

But the season was not yet over for Ireland. A tour to South Africa was scheduled for the summer and that caused uproar in Irish rugby circles as the pro and anti South African supporters took issue. The Irish government was adamant the tour should not go ahead and it proved a very divisive issue for Irish rugby. But the IRFU decided that they would honour the commitment.

No fewer than nine players informed the Union that they would not be available. Some took the decision on the grounds of principle; a few had no option but to decline as they were refused leave of absence by their employers. Three players gave up their jobs to go on the tour.

It was a depleted Irish party that set off for South Africa and the departure of the squad was shrouded in secrecy to avoid demonstrations at the airport. They assembled in London and flew out from there to South Africa. Paddy Madigan was manager, Tom Kiernan coach and Malcolm Little team doctor.

The itinerary was rather strange. There was a concerted attempt to give a multiracial aspect to the teams Ireland played, but quite candidly it was contrived opposition. Ireland played such teams as the South African Gazelles, the South African Mining XV, the President's Trophy XV, the Gold Cup XV and the South African Districts B side. It was an itinerary without precedent.

Ireland lost the first match to the Gazelles 18-15 in Pretoria, overwhelmed the Mining XV in Potchestrom 46-7 and then beat a very poor President's side 54-3 in East London. The District side edged Ireland out by a point in the match before the first Test. Ireland went into the Test as rank outsiders, and if the opposition in some of the provincial matches was contrived, not so the Springboks who fielded at full strength. Ireland played superbly in that match, revealing tremendous character and commitment. Nor did it help that Ollie Campbell, who was injured early in the tour, played in the Test

THE IRELAND PARTY THAT TOURED SOUTH AFRICA 1981

but did not last the match. Nor did full-back John Murphy. Both had to be replaced during the match. But while Ireland had a hard core of experience in their squad represented by such players as Fergus Slattery, Willie Duggan, John O'Driscoll, Alfred McLennan, Terry Kennedy, Campbell and Philip Orr, the squad included a host of young players who had not been capped. Several of those were later to leave a very profound impact on the scene and share in memorable triumphs.

South Africa won the Test in Newlands by 23-15, with Campbell in the centre and a newcomer, Paul Dean, at outside half. Campbell, unfortunately, broke a wrist and to compound that problem Murphy sustained a very badly pulled thigh muscle. It was level at the interval. Indeed, it was the kicking of the Springboks outside half Nass Botha that kept them in touch in the initial period. In the second half, South Africa got two tries on their route to victory, but it was a very close and exciting affair and Ireland surpassed all expectations by their performance.

The Springboks team included Errol Tobias who became the first non-white player to wear the Springboks jersey in a full international.

Ireland had to send for reinforcements because of the injuries with scrum-half Barry O'Connor, from Palmerston, being flown out because of an injury to John Robbie, and Mick Quinn was called out because of Campbell's problems.

Ireland defeated the Gold Cup team 51-10 in Oudsthoorn in the second last match of the tour and then faced South Africa in the second Test in Durban.

IRELAND NO. 8, WILLIE DUGGAN PREPARES TO PASS TO HOOKER PAT WHELAN. DONAL SPRING, JOHN O'DRISCOLL AND MOSS KEANE ARE ALSO READY TO LEND SUPPORT

Quinn did not have much time to acclimatise before he was chosen for the Test and Dean moved to centre. Kevin O'Brien was in at full-back for Murphy. The pack which had played so well in the first test was unchanged. Ireland lost by two points, 12-10, a result which contradicted the trend of the match. Had Ireland been able to avail of kicking chances, then the match would have been won, and deservedly so.

Ireland led 7-6 at the interval with a try from O'Brien and a penalty goal from Quinn to a penalty and a dropped goal by Botha. Quinn kicked a penalty early in the second half to leave Ireland ahead 10-6 and victory beckoned. But two dropped goals by Botha saw South Africa edge clear. Ireland lost a great scoring chance late in the game when Slattery, who had played so well in the match, was tackled in possession with support on hand had he sought to use it.

Scrum-half Robbie McGrath, who had won two caps four years previously, had a great tour. Three players won their first caps on the tour, John Murphy, Dean and second row Jerry Holland. Other players on the tour who got very useful experience, later to assert itself, included wing Keith Crossan, centre Michael Kiernan and prop Des Fitzgerald.

For two in the Irish party it was their last farewell to Irish rugby. McLennan stayed on in Cape Town and subsequently played for Western Province, and John Robbie returned to South Africa and played with distinction for Transvaal and indeed was also chosen as a bench reserve for the Springboks.

So the 1980–81 season ended for Ireland with the draw against Romania in an unofficial international the only tangible return. Ireland had played six internationals and lost six. But two of the six matches had been lost by a point against Wales and Scotland, and the second Test against South Africa by two points. The 23-15 loss in the first Test was the biggest defeat.

None the less, six consecutive defeats came as a great disappointment after the promise that had been so evident the previous season, especially after the demolition of the Welsh in 1980. Kiernan, as coach, faced into the 1981–82 season with the task of ending that losing sequence and getting the best out of a talented squad.

CHAPTER 22

RETURN TO GLORY

However unfortunate Ireland had been the previous season and however promising some of the young talent that was emerging on the scene, breaking a losing sequence imposes its own psychological problems. It was Tom Kiernan's task to help his players overcome that and to harness the young, the talented and uninhibited with the hard core of experience he had at his disposal.

Kevin Flynn had taken over as chairman of selectors from Paddy Madigan, and Roly Meates, the man who had coached Ireland for two years in the 1970s, was now a selector. He replaced Madigan, who had completed his three year tenure. Munster also had a selector as Brian O'Brien returned to the committee. He replaced Joss Lapsley, who had also completed three years of service.

When Ireland faced Australia at Lansdowne Road on 21 November, they did so against a background of six consecutive losses. Not since the early 1960s had Ireland endured such a losing sequence. Kiernan had been a player for Ireland in those days and knew better than most the thin dividing line that can separate the victor from the vanquished. He was not a man to be intimidated by reference to the past. But he was realistic enough to know the magnitude of the task Ireland faced.

Australia had opened their tour in Ireland on 14 November and defeated Ulster 12-6 at Ravenhill. Then on 17 November they faced Munster. Once more the Munstermen rose to the challenge against a touring side and yet again humbled the Australians, this time at Musgrave Park. Once more Tony Ward was centre stage in executing another famous win over a major touring team. He played superbly behind his excellent pack and contributed 11 points in Munster's 15-6 victory. Hooker Packie Derham marked his Munster debut by scoring a try and Ward did the rest with a conversion, two penalty goals and a dropped goal.

It was the ideal boost for Ireland as they prepared for the task against the Australians. Ireland included two new caps in Trevor Ringland on the right wing and Donal Lenihan from UCC in the second row. Lenihan had made the progression from the Ireland schools side through the Under 23 and Ireland B teams and now was on the big stage. Slattery again led Ireland, his seventeenth time to captain his country. He had considerable experience at his side in the pack to which John Cantrell had returned as hooker. Ward was at outside half and was partnered by McGrath. Dean and David Irwin were in the centre.

But it was not to be Ireland's day as a heroic Australian defence, allied to their ability to take a try-scoring opportunity, saw the Wallabies frustrate Ireland, whose 12 points came from four penalty goals kicked by Ward.

The Irish pack played well, but an inability to break down the Australian defence in the face of some first-rate tackling enabled Australia to prevail. So it was seven consecutive defeats for Ireland as the championship loomed.

Not since 1949 had Ireland won the Triple Crown, a spell of 33 years. In the Ireland trial on 19 December the Possibles defeated the Probables by 16-9 to complicate matters as the selectors contemplated the composition of the side to meet Wales in the opening of the championship scheduled for 16 January.

Ciaran Fitzgerald, the inspirational captain of the 1982 Triple Crown winning team

The team was chosen and showed two changes in the back line, with Campbell in at outside half for Ward and Moss Finn on the left wing for Terry Kennedy. Ciaran Fitzgerald, now fully recovered from the injury that had plagued him the previous season, was fit again and he was named as captain even though Slattery was still in the team. Gerry McLoughlin was recalled at tight head prop for Mick Fitzpatrick, and Moss Keane was back in the second row for Brendan Foley.

The match against Wales was postponed because of a heavy fall of snow in Dublin and refixed for the following Saturday, 23 January. Ireland did not go into the match burdened by the mantle of favourites and the general expectation was that Wales would win. They had beaten Australia in Cardiff and now it was anticipated that they would start their championship challenge with a victory.

But with the Ireland pack in full flow and Campbell at his brilliant best, it was Ireland who triumphed and did so by 20 points to 12, and they outscored Wales by three tries to one. Finn marked his return to the team by scoring two tries, with Campbell the creator. Ringland also scored a try and Campbell contributed a conversion and two penalty goals.

So the losing sequence of seven consecutive defeats had been broken and now hopes rose that Ireland would this time mount a really vigorous challenge for the Championship and Triple Crown. There were two casualties from that match. David Irwin broke an ankle and was replaced by Michael Kiernan, who thus won his first cap as a replacement and started on an international career during which he was to make an immense contribution. Dean was also injured and John Murphy took his place.

With Irwin ruled out for the season, Kiernan was chosen for the match against England. Dean recovered and was in the side. So Kiernan for Irwin was the only change in the team that went to Twickenham to play England on 6 February.

England still had many of those who had won the Championship two years earlier in their side and although no longer Triple Crown candidates, having drawn with Scotland at Murrayfield, still had championship ambitions. Those ambitions were effectively killed by Ireland who won the match 16-15. A one point win for Ireland flattered England as it was not until injury time that England got a try and conversion.

For most of the game the Ireland pack was in control and Campbell played one of his greatest matches. He was superb behind the pack. Ireland led 10-3 at half-time with penalty goals from Campbell and a fine try by Hugo MacNeill. England hit back early in the second half when Marcus Rose kicked his second penalty but then came the decisive score. Campbell had a drop goal attempt blocked down by the England scrum-half Steve Smith. But Ireland regained possession and Campbell was the instigator of a movement down the right-hand side. He was supported by Fergus Slattery and Willie Duggan and Ireland, with prop Gerry McLoughlin in the van, swept to the England line and McLoughlin got the try in the corner. Campbell kicked a magnificent conversion across a fitful wind. England's late surge, which yielded a penalty from Rose and a try from Mike Slemen converted by Rose, did no more than present a rather imbalanced aspect to the scoreboard.

Donal Lenihan passes to Robbie McGrath in the match against England in Twickenham

So now a Triple Crown beckoned for Ireland whose next assignment was against Scotland at Lansdowne Road on 20 February. Ireland had not won the Triple Crown since 1949 and had never won it at Lansdowne Road. To say anticipation hung in the air as the thousands flocked to Lansdowne Road was to understate the situation. Trevor Ringland was ruled out of the match through injury and he was replaced by Keith Crossan from Instonians.

Once more the Irish pack, with its collection of old hands and superbly led by Fitzgerald, paved the way for victory and Campbell, at their heels, gave another vintage performance. It was not a match that offered a lot in the way of fluid back movement. But that did not worry the crowd. Campbell kicked two penalty goals to give Ireland an early lead before Roy Laidlaw, the Scotland scrum-half, opened the way for his half-back partner John Rutherford to score a try for Scotland. Andy Irvine converted to bring the scores level. But Campbell, in excellent kicking form, scored two more penalties and dropped a goal to leave Ireland 15-6 up at the interval and in control.

Having established superiority, Ireland did not relinquish it and, in the second half, had much the better of the play. Campbell and Jim Renwick exchanged penalty goals with Renwick having taken over the kicking duties from Irvine who had missed four chances. As the match entered its final phase, Campbell and Renwick again kicked penalty goals, but it was Ireland's and Campbell's day as Ireland won 21-12.

The ground erupted as Ireland's triumph was confirmed. A 33 year gap had been bridged and the celebrations were in accordance with that protracted wait. Campbell was the hero of the hour. He scored all Ireland's points and his six penalty goals equalled the then world record for penalty goals kicked by an individual in an international. His personal contribution of 21 points set a new Ireland record. So Tom Kiernan had done it again as coach to add one more notch to the legend of his accomplishments.

Now Ireland's sights were on a Grand Slam and the last assignment was against France in Paris on 20 March. Ireland had not won in Paris for ten years but hopes were high especially as France had lost all three championship matches before going into the game. France rang the changes in a big way and brought back some of their old and tried campaigners to their pack.

Unfortunately Willie Duggan was ruled out of the side on the eve of the match and was replaced by Ronan Kearney. The French did not stand on ceremony and their forwards' rugged approach cost them penalties and Campbell kicked two to leave Ireland 6-3 ahead at the break.

But there were ominous signs as France got well on top and scored a try nine minutes after the interval, with Serge Blanco the man who finished the job. Then Ireland missed a fine chance to get a try when Slattery's pass to Campbell did not go to hand. No similar chance presented itself and France added three penalty goals to move 16-9 in front. Campbell kicked his third penalty but France finished with yet another try and that was the end of Ireland's Grand Slam ambitions.

If it was a disappointing end to the campaign, none the less Ireland had won the Triple Crown, won the Championship and Campbell had written himself into the record books. He had scored 46 points in the campaign, as he had done in 1980, his 13 penalty goals created a championship record and his 21 points against Scotland was a record for an Ireland player in an international.

A sad footnote to the season was that one of the men who had helped to do the Grand Slam in 1948 and win Triple Crown and Championship in 1949, Des McKee, died a week after Ireland had beaten Wales.

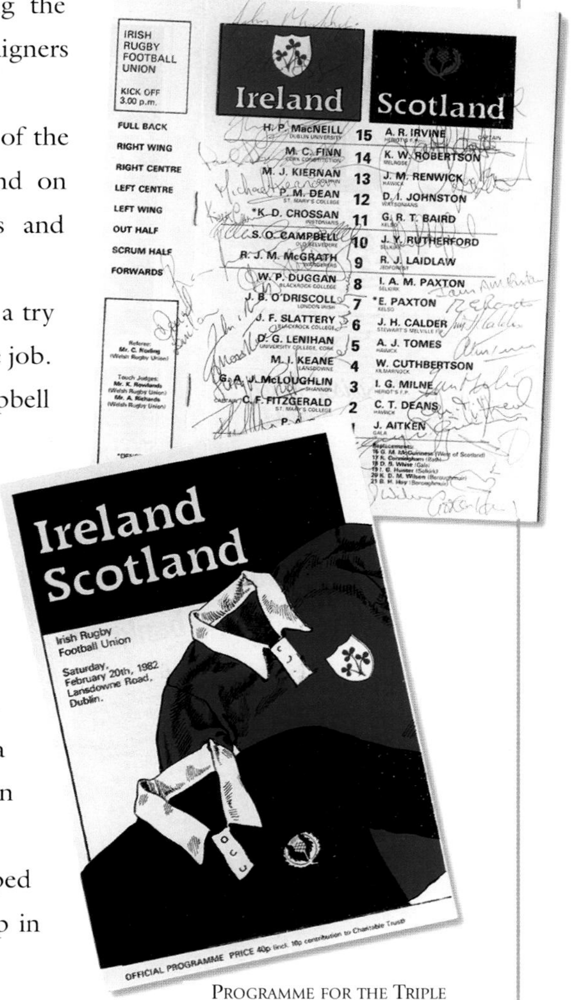

PROGRAMME FOR THE TRIPLE CROWN AND CHAMPIONSHIP WINNING MATCH V SCOTLAND AT LANSDOWNE 1982

The Triple Crown and Championship win saw the wheel of fortune turn full circle for Kiernan and his players. Ciaran Fitzgerald had proved a truly inspirational leader of his team in the front row of a pack at times labelled 'Dad's Army' because some of the forwards had been around a long time. But they were a vibrant force. The IRFU president in that glory year of 1982 was John Moore. A Dublinman by birth, but a Galwayman by adoption, he had played for UCG and Connacht and was a very effective Connacht representative on the IRFU. He was the first Connacht president to preside over a Triple Crown and Championship-winning season for Ireland. Unfortunately he died unexpectedly at a comparatively early age in the early 1990s.

The essential nature of coaching was now well established and in May of 1982 the IRFU held a coaching course and conference, the third such event that the union had organised. Roly Meates had been succeeded by Niall Brophy as chairman of the coaching committee.

Ireland faced into the 1982–83 season with Kiernan yet again coach to the national team and the only change on the selection committee was the advent of Mick Cuddy to the five in place of Kevin Flynn who had completed three years.

Cuddy had been chairman of the Leinster selection committee and a highly successful one at that, as Leinster had enjoyed a level of success in the Interprovincial Championship over the previous four

The Triple Crown and Championship winning squad 1982

seasons that was without precedent, with Cuddy as chairman and Mick Doyle as coach. Doyle was one of two substitute Ireland selectors with Jim Donaldson from Ulster.

Leinster lost to Munster in the interprovincial series in the autumn of 1982, the first defeat inflicted on the province in four years, and the interprovincial series was a three-way tie between Munster, Leinster and Ulster in a keenly fought and very exciting series. Connacht, who ended the series pointless, had, in fact, lost one match by a point and another by two points. It was all as close as that.

As preparations were made for the International Championship, Ireland had assumed the mantle of favourites after their exploits the previous season. The final trial ended in a 15-15 draw, but the Ireland team to meet Scotland in the opening assignment showed two changes from the side that had lost to France the previous March. Willie Duggan, an original selection for that match, returned in place of Ronan Kearney, and David Irwin, fit again, took over in the centre from Paul Dean.

Ireland made a fine start to the campaign defeating Scotland 15-13. Kiernan scored a try; Campbell contributed the rest of the points. It was once more an unchanged line-up that played against France at Lansdowne Road. Ireland had not beaten France since 1975. But they ended that sequence with a very worthy 22-16 win. Moss Finn scored two tries and Campbell made his usual invaluable contribution with four penalty goals and a conversion.

Now it was on to Cardiff and Wales on 5 March. The level of expectation was considerable, but Ireland carried a burden into that match. Ireland had not won in Cardiff for 20 years. Yet again the Arms

Park proved a bogey ground. Wales, inspired by scrum-half Terry Holmes behind a pack that proved a match for anything Ireland could produce, won 23-9 and scored three tries in attaining a well-deserved win.

That ended Triple Crown and Grand Slam hopes but championship ambitions still burned when England came to Lansdowne Road on 19 March. The defeat in Cardiff did not induce any panic among the selection committee, now under the chairmanship of P. J. Dwyer.

Ireland fielded an unchanged team and the selectors' faith was rewarded in the form of an excellent display that saw Ireland win 25-15 and Campbell yet again left his own indelible mark on the proceedings by scoring 21 points. He kicked five penalty goals, scored a try and converted it. Fergus Slattery also scored a try. Campbell, in fact, did not finish the match because of injury and he was replaced by Tony Ward. But while on the field Campbell had been at his perceptive best.

So Ireland ended with six out of a possible eight points in the championship and shared the title with France. The win over England was the last with Kiernan as coach. His players had brought down the curtain on his coaching career in a most fitting manner.

There was, too, another element to the Ireland-England match. It was the last played at Lansdowne Road with the old East Stand in operation. Immediately after the match the demolition of the stand started as the prelude to the building of a new two-tier structure.

In the summer, the Lions went to New Zealand. During the season there had been animated debate about who would captain the tourists. Ciaran Fitzgerald's credentials were, to say the least, impressive. But a concerted campaign was waged by sections of the British press against Fitzgerald. His leadership record was ignored. He had led Ireland to the Triple Crown and Championship in 1982, to a share in the Championship with France in 1983, but he was subjected to a series of negative comments in a section of the British press. He was not good enough as a player, it was alleged, to warrant a Test place; his throwing into the line-out was not good enough; he did not have the stature to lead the Lions.

But the Lions selectors ignored the negative comments and Fitzgerald was duly named as captain and thus joined a very distinguished band of Irishmen to be so honoured. Willie John McBride was named as Lions manager, a unique distinction for a man who had retired from playing only a matter of five years previously and from international rugby only eight years previously. Jim Telfer of Scotland was named as coach.

Ireland's very good record over two years was reflected in the Lions squad and eight Irishmen were chosen in the touring party. They were Ciaran Fitzgerald, Hugo MacNeill, Ollie Campbell, David Irwin, Michael Kiernan, Trevor Ringland, Donal Lenihan and John O'Driscoll.

On the night before the departure of the party from London, Lenihan was ruled out of the tour because the team doctor said it was necessary for him to have a hernia operation. It was a shattering blow to Lenihan, who instead of travelling on his first Lions tour, returned to his native Cork. But there was some element of compensation for the Corkman later on when he was called out as a replacement, and so too was Gerry McLoughlin.

On the field it was very far from being a successful tour. The Lions could and should have won the first Test in Christchurch, but lost the match and also lost one of their key players, Terry Holmes, for the rest of the tour. Unfortunately after that it was trouble and disappointment piled on trouble and disappointment.

The All Blacks won the series 4-0 with the third Test in Dunedin being played in appalling conditions and Ollie Campbell was among the victims of the bitter wind, pouring rain, freezing conditions and a flooded pitch.

Not surprisingly Ciaran Fitzgerald took a barrage of constant criticism during the tour. He was a handy fall guy for the many deficiencies in the Lions touring party. The tour was a bitter disappointment for Fitzgerald, yet he would again have his hour of glory upon the international stage, but not before Irish rugby on the field of international competition would have yet another season of trial and torment, and one of Ireland's greatest players, McBride, would have to endure the downside of celebrity totally at variance with what he had experienced as a player.

Michael Kiernan tackles John Carleton in the match against England at Twickenham 1982

Off the field a unique situation existed on the IRFU committee. The president of the union was Jimmy Nelson, a man who had been on the Grand Slam and Triple Crown teams of the late 1940s, as distinguished on the administrative side as he was as a player. He had been elected honorary treasurer of the union in succession to Tommy O'Reilly in 1976. He had discharged the responsibilities of that onerous office so well that his union colleagues requested that he retain it even during his year as president — thus a dual role for a man who was surely among the most respected figures of his generation. A self-effacing man, Jimmy Nelson never sought self-advancement but was ever ready to serve and he accepted the dual mandate, if somewhat reluctantly. True to his reputation, he filled both offices with immense distinction and effect. It was, too, during his year as president that the ten year ticket scheme to help finance the building of the new East Stand was launched and that added to the burden of his responsibilities. But that launch was a great success and during his stewardship the finances of the Union were handled in the most efficient and diligent manner.

CHAPTER 23

McBRIDE'S UNHAPPY TENURE

WITH TOM KIERNAN GONE AS COACH, the selectors had the task of electing a new coach and a new chairman. The selection committee itself underwent some changes and Willie John McBride and Jim Donaldson were both elected to the committee in place of Dion Glass and P. J. Dwyer, who had both served their three year tenure and had made considerable contributions during their period as selectors. Both were rightly regarded as men who knew the game, were good judges of players and as men of great integrity, not motivated by provincial considerations.

The task of the committee was to pick a coach and chairman, selecting the coach from the list submitted. The divisive nature of this process was again underlined. The two candidates for the coaching post were McBride and Mick Doyle. One was a selector, the other, Doyle, a sub-selector. The selection committee had to choose.

Doyle's credentials for the post were, to say the least, impressive. His record with Leinster had been excellent and no Leinster coach before or since equalled it. McBride, of course, had vast experience as a player, a very high profile, and he had taken over as coach to the Ulster team, but in that capacity had very limited experience. Ulster were, it is true, in the process of rebuilding their team when McBride took over, and part of that rebuilding process had been to take the team on a successful tour of Romania in 1982.

The Ireland selectors decided that McBride would be coach to the national side in 1983–84. Doyle had every reason to be disappointed. He had support from within the selection committee, but obviously not enough.

McBride's initial task was to coach the B team for a match against Scotland in Melrose in December 1983. It was a match Ireland lost 22-13 in which Scotland scored four tries to Ireland's one.

It did not favour Ireland that the first match in the International Championship was against France in Paris. Ireland went to France with a team that included one cap in the centre, Rory Moroney from Lansdowne. Keith Crossan, who had played in the Triple Crown-winning team against Scotland in 1982, was on the left wing.

The French were on top from the outset of the match and did not relinquish their grip. They won by 25 points to 12. Four penalty goals from Campbell was Ireland's response. There were hopes that Ireland would avenge the heavy defeat of the previous season against the Welsh, but it was not to be. Ireland brought in two new caps, tight head Jim McCoy, a former schools international, and Willie Duncan from Malone on the flank for Slattery. Slattery, in fact, was not to play international rugby again. His magnificent representative career had come to an end. His last farewell had been in Paris. The Welsh won readily 18-9, and yet again three penalty goals from Campbell accounted for Ireland's total. During the match Ciaran Fitzgerald was injured and replaced by Harry Harbison, another former schools international who had played for UCD and Bective Rangers.

The match against Wales was to prove very significant. It was Campbell's last international, but at the time neither he nor anyone else realised that. His contribution to Ireland had been truly immense, his scoring exploits of record proportions. Few have served Irish rugby better. On and off the field he was exemplary in his attitude.

He was actually selected for the third match in the series, against England in Twickenham on 18 February. Two days before the match he had to withdraw because of a hamstring injury and that injury in effect finished his career. It was much more serious than initially thought and he never again managed to regain full fitness.

THE SCOREBOARD TELLS ITS OWN STORY 1983, WHEN IRELAND SHARED THE CHAMPIONSHIP

Tony Ward was recalled to the side in Campbell's absence. Out too was Ciaran Fitzgerald, over whose fitness doubts lingered, so Harbison was retained. Moss Finn was recalled in the centre for Moroney and Michael Kiernan for Irwin. There was a new scrum-half, Tony Doyle from the Greystones club. Des Fitzgerald, who had toured South Africa in 1981, won his first cap at tight head prop.

So many of the players who had played crucial parts in the very good sequence of results over the previous two years were now gone. The captaincy of the team was taken over by Willie Duggan.

The result of the match was in the balance to the end in a contest singularly lacking much in the way of fluid movement or indeed excitement. England won the match 12-9. Neither team scored a try. Ward kicked three penalty goals for Ireland. Full-back Dusty Hare kicked three for England and outside half Les Cusworth dropped a goal, and that in the end was the decisive factor.

It was a difficult time for McBride. Tom Kiernan was a very hard act to follow and the departure of some of the experienced players added to the problems. It would be true to say, too, that some of the senior members of the team felt that McBride's inexperience as a coach was proving an inhibiting factor, however hard he worked.

Ireland's last match of the season was against Scotland at Lansdowne Road on 3 March. This time there was no Triple Crown or championship incentive for the Irish players. The task was to win and thus avoid a whitewash.

John Murphy, who had made his international debut in South Africa, was brought in at full-back for MacNeill in the only alteration behind the scrum. In the pack, John O'Driscoll was moved from the open to the blind side flank and Derek McGrath, a young veterinary student at UCD, won his first cap on the open side.

It was a day when the wind blew down Lansdowne Road with more than a refreshing vigour; in fact, it was gale force. Duggan actually won the toss, but decided that Ireland would play into that gale in the first half. It was to prove a very bad decision. The Scots took full advantage of the elements and some very poor play by Ireland. At the interval Scotland led 22-0. Their scrum-half Roy Laidlaw scored two tries and Ireland conceded a penalty try.

So Ireland faced the Scots with a 22 points deficit to make up after the interval and never remotely looked like making the wind advantage pay as the Scots had done. To compound their problems, Ireland lost Ward who was concussed after a very heavy tackle. Ireland did manage a try from Kiernan which Murphy converted, but the Scots finished as they had begun, with style. They added two more tries to decorate a great performance and victory.

The new East Stand at Lansdowne, built in 1983

Unlike two years previously, this time it was the Scots who invaded the pitch to acclaim their side who had won the Triple Crown for the first time in 42 years. They had done so with some real style.

Ireland and McBride were left to reflect on a season of frustration and disappointment. But, in reality, Ireland's performances were accurately reflected in the results.

That season marked the end of the international careers of some truly great players, Ollie Campbell, Robbie McGrath, Moss Keane, Fergus Slattery, Willie Duggan and John O'Driscoll. All but McGrath had played for the Lions. Between them that sextet had won nearly 200 caps, Slattery (61), Keane (51), Duggan (41), O'Driscoll (26), Campbell (22) and McGrath (16). All of them had helped Ireland to regain the Triple Crown after 33 years. It was unfortunate that their final season in the Ireland jersey should have ended with a whitewash. Unfortunately their experiences in their final season in the Ireland jersey had not been marked by the kind of glory they had savoured at times during their splendid careers.

CHAPTER 24

THE CUDDY-DOYLE ALLIANCE

THE TASK OF SELECTING the Ireland selectors for the 1984–85 season was entrusted to Ronnie Dawson, Noel Henderson and Gerald Reidy. The process of the provinces nominating their candidates was still in place. It was still the prerogative of the selection committee to select from their own ranks the chairman and to pick the coach from the names submitted by the coaching subcommittee of the union.

The selection committee showed two changes from the previous season and that was to prove crucial in subsequent events that gave rise to no little controversy.

The two newcomers to the selection committee were Mick Doyle, who had moved up from being a substitute selector and replaced Roly Meates, while Jim Kiernan, an older brother of Tom, father of Michael and a fine player who had represented Munster and had a distinguished club career for UCC, Cork Constitution and Dolphin, came in for Brian O'Brien, whose tenure, like that of Meates, was over.

In fact, when Munster submitted their three selectorial nominees, Kiernan was not among them. But Mick Molloy, who had been among the three, withdrew. As permitted by law, Munster had the right to nominate someone in his place and Kiernan got the nomination. It was to prove an important decision. Thus the selection committee consisted of Cuddy, Doyle, McBride, Jim Donaldson and Jim Kiernan.

There were distinct indications that McBride was under considerable pressure to hold off the challenge of Doyle for the coaching position before the selectors met. There was no doubt that Mick Cuddy, who had worked so closely and effectively with Doyle for Leinster, firmly and honestly believed that Doyle was the man to coach Ireland. Obviously when it came to a vote in selection, McBride and Doyle would both have a vote themselves. Donaldson opted for McBride. The key issue was who would Jim Kiernan support.

At the meeting of the selectors, Cuddy was elected chairman and when it came to the selection of a coach, it was Doyle who emerged victorious, getting the votes of Cuddy and Kiernan. One cannot doubt the sincerity of the five men involved; they supported the person they believed was best suited for the job. But the decision to dispense with McBride's services after just one season was seen by some as unjust, that he had not got a fair chance in just one season. No Ireland coach before him had been given just one season. Roly Meates, who had lost out in the seventies had served two years. All the others who had coached Ireland had a three year tenure.

McBride certainly felt he had not been given a reasonable time to make an imprint. But those who supported Doyle believed that, in fact, he should have been given the job the previous year and in view of Ireland's dismal results in 1984, he was the man to lead the Irish revival. As events transpired, Doyle fully justified the faith placed in him.

There was dissatisfaction in Ulster about McBride being defeated, but the very system itself by which the coach was appointed was divisive, as had been seen previously. There was a lot of speculation that McBride would resign as a selector and for about a week the rumour factory was in full production. There is no doubt McBride contemplated that course of action, but decided wisely not to resign. After all, he had gone into the situation knowing the system that operated. It had worked in his favour the previous season; now it had worked against him. But it did focus attention on what was a flawed system.

The appointments had to be ratified by the IRFU committee, and the man at the helm of that was Mick Carroll. He had been chairman of selectors in the 1970s, had been president of the Branch and was a man of considerable experience. His total integrity and his tact were rightly admired throughout Ireland.

Had the IRFU failed to ratify the selectors' choice, it would in essence have been a vote of no confidence in the selection committee and no man knew better than Mick Carroll the consequences of that. He knew, too, that if McBride resigned as a selector, it would further fan the flames of controversy. McBride wisely decided not to resign, and to his credit Doyle gave a warm welcome to that decision. He was in many respects in an awkward situation.

That controversy out of the way, Doyle set about making his plans for the season. He knew he had to build a side and in particular the loss of such experience from the pack from the previous season made the process far from easy.

He still had Philip Orr, Ciaran Fitzgerald and Donal Lenihan available to him among the forwards, and apart from Campbell and McGrath he also had all the backs from the previous season. Having assessed the situation, Doyle decided that the best chance of success lay in a running game. Paul Dean, who had played in the centre in the Triple Crown-winning side three years previously, had in fact gone out of favour even at interprovincial level. Dean was more at home as an outside half and in that position he had first made his mark at schools international level.

A charity match in Cork fairly early in the season brought about a situation where Dean was paired with scrum-half Michael Bradley. Bradley was another former schools international who had made his mark playing for Cork Constitution and who, in fact, had already sat on the bench for Ireland at senior level. Ironically, it was Tony Ward who had been due to partner Bradley that afternoon in Cork but, after Ward withdrew, Dean was called in. It was a very fortunate circumstance indeed. The Bradley-Dean combination worked extremely well and Doyle went away from the match believing he had the half-back pairing to replace Campbell and McGrath. Tactical kicking was not a strength in Dean's play, but he had pace, an excellent pair of hands and the ability to get the best out of a threequarter that had pace and flair.

Building a pack was not proving an easy task. A partner for Lenihan in the second row, for instance, was a problem. Here some improvisation proved beneficial. Willie Anderson, from the Dungannon club, primarily a back row forward, but big enough, astute enough and with the necessary attributes to play in the second row, was asked to play as a guest player in a match for Garryowen in the second row. Anderson played sufficiently well to convince Cuddy, Doyle and their colleagues that he could solve their problems.

Philip Matthews, a very good flank forward who had impressed with Ulster and Queen's University and now playing with the Ards club, was in the John O'Driscoll mould, and was the man earmarked for the blind side flank. Ireland needed pace in the back row and that was another priority for the selectors. It was some help that the Wallabies were touring Ireland and Britain that season and so the first test for the Ireland team came against the touring side at Lansdowne Road on 10 November. The only new cap behind the scrum was a young centre from Dublin University, Brendan Mullin. He had been an outstanding schoolboy just a matter of a few years previously and was a first-class athlete with great pace and an instinctive football brain. He was partnered in the centre by Moss Finn, with Michael Kiernan on the left wing and Trevor Ringland on the right. Dean and Bradley formed the half-back partnership, with Bradley winning his first cap. Ciaran Fitzgerald was back to lead the team, with Orr and Jim McCoy as his props. Anderson partnered Lenihan in the second row and Matthews won his first cap in a back row that included Ronan Kearney and another new cap from the Garryowen club, Willie Sexton, on the open side flank.

There was one worrying factor about the team: it did not include a recognised first-rate place kicker and that, as had been seen and so well demonstrated by both Campbell and Ward, was a very important consideration in international rugby.

Finn and Kiernan could both kick goals, but neither was recognised as a first-rank kicker as such. It was to Kiernan eventually that Doyle entrusted the task and the way he met that challenge was subsequently a revelation.

Australia at that time had a superb team splendidly coached by Alan Jones. They beat Ireland 16-9, but there had been encouraging elements in Ireland's performance. Doyle and Cuddy worked in close co-operation and had the support of the other selectors.

Ulster, with a team now arguably the best of the four provinces, scored a historic victory over the touring side at Ravenhill four days after the international. This was the first win by Ulster over a major touring team and was celebrated accordingly under the lights at Ravenhill. It was Munster's turn next and they met Australia at Thomond Park. That match went into the annals as one of the most bizarre ever played. Thick fog enveloped the ground and it was impossible to see across the pitch. Had it not been a touring team involved, stuck with a tight schedule, the match would not have been played. Australia won 31-19, but no one present could claim they had seen the match. Once the play moved across the field no one on the side away from the play could see what was happening.

On 1 December the Ireland B team met Scotland at the Sports ground in Galway. Here was a match the selectors hoped would help them put the remaining pieces of their side together before the International Championship. It was encouraging for them to see Ireland avenge the previous season's defeat as Ireland won 23-20. In that regard there was indeed a bonus. The open side flanker on the Ireland side was Nigel Carr, another of the young Ulster side. He, like Matthews, had been a student at Queen's University and was now also a member of the Ards club.

The first match on the championship schedule was due to be against England at Lansdowne Road on 19 January. But yet again the snow came down and Dublin had a decidedly white aspect on the day prior to the match. It was decided that the game could not go on, even if the pitch could be cleared, as the terraces would be dangerous. The match was, consequently, called off the day before it was scheduled. It was refixed for Lansdowne Road on 30 March. So, instead of starting the championship at home, Ireland had the task of travelling to Murrayfield for the first championship engagement on 2 February. (In fact, adverse weather caused the postponement of no fewer than three of the matches in the championship that year.)

THE IRELAND TEAM THAT DEFEATED WALES IN CARDIFF 1985

The Ireland team that went to Murrayfield showed three changes from the side that lost to Australia. Michael Kiernan reverted to centre for Moss Finn and Keith Crossan was restored to the left wing. The pack included two new caps. Carr came in on the open side flank and the No. 8 berth was filled by Brian Spillane. Spillane, a medical doctor who had played for UCC, was now with the Bohemians club. Possessing pace and quite a lot of football ability, he fitted nicely into the back row and had the attributes to play the kind of game Doyle wanted.

Ireland no longer had a pack endowed with great experience or physical strength. The object was to win the ball and get it out to a potent back line. But Ireland did have ball-winning ability in the pack, a formidable front row, a great leader in Fitzgerald, line-out ball winners, and a back row that had pace and strength in defence, as well as the ability to get to the loose ball quickly.

One has to bear in mind that in playing Scotland in the opening championship match Ireland had to face the reigning Grand Slam champions and the team that had overwhelmed Ireland the previous season. This was Scotland's opening defence of their titles.

In the first half of the match it looked as if Ireland could pay a heavy price for not having included a specialist place kicker as Michael Kiernan was off target with his kicking from three penalty attempts. But he did drop a goal and at the interval Scotland led 6-3. It was Ireland who played the more expansive game and it paid a dividend shortly after the interval. Michael Bradley broke from a scrum and took out the Scotland defence before giving a well-timed inside pass to Trevor Ringland and the wing scored in the right-hand corner. Kiernan then kicked a great conversion.

The Scotland pack revealed some of the attributes that had proved so effective in the previous season and full-back Dods kicked three penalty goals to add to the two he had kicked in the first half. With time running out, Scotland led 15-12. Then Ireland got a scrum deep inside Scotland territory as the Scots got ready to acclaim another win. Bradley transferred the ball to Paul Dean and Dean, after passing the ball, looped outside and a superb movement of pace and control outwitted the Scotland defence and Ringland finished off a move worthy to win any match. Kiernan converted the try, Ireland won 18-15 and ingenuity had its reward.

Next on the agenda came France who visited Lansdowne Road on 2 March. What was memorable about this match unfortunately was the unedifying spectacle into which it degenerated. Brendan Mullin was ruled out by injury and that earned a return to the centre for Rory Moroney.

In the end it was French indiscipline which cost them a match drawn 15-15, with Kiernan having kicked five penalties for Ireland. France conceded no fewer than 18 penalties and both Philip Matthews and Brian Spillane failed to finish the match through injuries.

A draw meant both countries stood unbeaten with two matches each to play. Ireland, in that match, had to rely on Kiernan's kicking accuracy and certainly practice made perfect in that discipline for Kiernan, who was now mastering the art as his responsibilities in that area grew. Despite having failed to score a try against France, it was now evident that Ireland's challenge for crown and championship was on course.

Any doubts that lingered in that direction were well and truly killed in Cardiff on 16 March. Ireland went into that match against a background of recurring failure at the Arms Park, not having won there since 1967. Doyle told his players to forget the past and not be inhibited by any suggestions of Cardiff as a bogey ground.

Mullin was fit again and back in the centre, and Matthews and Spillane had recovered from their injuries. The back row did especially well defending against early Welsh pressure which came as a result of the line-out and scrummaging superiority the Welsh managed to exercise.

It could be said that Wales did not use their forward superiority very well and their attempts to break Ireland down in defence by an expansive game proved futile. That, allied to the fact that full-back Mark Wyatt missed no fewer than six kicks at goal in the first half, frustrated the Welsh.

Despite the marked territorial superiority Wales enjoyed, it was Ireland who scored first, and yet again it was the Bradley-Ringland combination that produced a try when Bradley timed an inch-perfect chip into Ringland's flight path and the wing scored and Kiernan converted. Wales drew level with a try from centre Lewis which was converted by Gareth Davies.

Then Kiernan kicked three penalty goals and converted a try scored by Keith Crossan which was the culmination of a great back movement. Crossan, that afternoon, both in defence and attack, had a superb match. The only response Wales could offer was a dropped goal from Gareth Davies and so Ireland won 21-9. The Cardiff bogey had been well and truly laid.

The level of expectation and anticipation prior to Ireland's final match of the series against England on 30 March at Lansdowne Road was immense. This Irish team had really captured the imagination and had about it a real ring of excitement.

Not surprisingly, Ireland fielded unchanged against an England side still very much in contention for the championship and indeed the Triple Crown. England had drawn with France and defeated Scotland. A win over Ireland would mean that their match against Wales a fortnight later would be for the Triple Crown and championship. So every incentive for England no less than Ireland.

Three years previously Ireland had won the Triple Crown at Lansdowne Road for the first time in over 100 years. A chance to do it twice within a three year spell presented itself. Ireland sought to make the complete transition yet again in the space of twelve months from being whitewashed to being Triple Crown and Championship winners.

Once more the back row of Matthews, Spillane and Carr served Ireland superbly with their tremendous zeal and zest. Bradley, behind his pack, played with remarkable astuteness and maturity and his partner Dean read his brief very well. But England, too, had their incentive and their pack was ready to answer any questions asked. It was England who took an early lead when outside half Rob Andrew kicked a penalty goal.

Then Ireland enjoyed a stroke of luck. The England full-back Martin delayed a clearing kick and Brendan Mullin was up very quickly to charge Martin's kick down and then ran on to score a try. That was not converted but Kiernan stretched Ireland's advantage to 7-3 when he kicked a penalty.

As half-time approached, England laid siege to the Ireland line but failed to break the defence. Ireland had one great moment of anxiety when England back row Bob Hesford actually got over the Ireland line, but the referee, Jim Fleming of Scotland, had spotted a forward pass.

It was a nail-biting encounter and it was patently obvious that this England side was not in any mood to offer passive surrender to Ireland's vibrancy. England got a try when Rory Underwood capitalised on a well-placed kick from centre Paul Dodge, and then Andrew kicked a penalty to leave the score at 10-7 to England.

When Kiernan kicked a penalty that levelled the score, the atmosphere in the ground was electric. Yet as the match entered its final phase, it looked as if a 10-10 draw was going to be the outcome. It was at this point that Fitzgerald's leadership qualities were revealed. The image recurs of him calling on his players to make the final supreme effort and his exhortation to them, 'Where is your pride?', got the necessary response.

With just a matter of seconds remaining in the match, Ireland won a line-out inside their own half. Spillane was in the van as Ireland moved forward and Donal Lenihan then drove on. That had carried play into the England half and Lenihan laid the ball back. Bradley was on hand to send out an accurate pass to Michael Kiernan. Kiernan did not hesitate and his dropped goal sailed high between the posts to give Ireland a victory in the most dramatic and exciting circumstances. In that instant, the Triple Crown and the Championship had been won.

Michael Kiernan celebrates scoring the drop goal to win the Triple Crown for Ireland v England, Lansdowne Road, 1985. Michael Bradley also acclaims the effort

After Kiernan's great dropped goal, the crowd did not have long to wait to run on to the pitch to acclaim a famous victory. The wheel had turned full circle yet again for Ireland in the space of twleve months. Dublin was a happy and hospitable city that night. The Cuddy-Doyle alliance had done for Ireland what it had done for Leinster.

They both deserve immense credit for what was achieved and Cuddy's contribution as chairman of selectors was an important factor in the success. So a season that had started in the controversy of McBride's dismissal had ended in triumph. Unity of purpose had replaced doubts and suspicions and the IRFU president Mick Carroll had the great joy of presiding over the victory dinner in Dublin. He, too, had reason for reflecting with considerable satisfaction on a job well done. His tact and diplomacy had been significant in bringing out that crucial unity in what had been so contentious and fractious a situation.

CHAPTER 25

RECORDS SET AND NEW GROUND BROKEN

AS TALKS WENT ON ABOUT THE INAUGURATION of the Rugby World Cup in the mid-eighties, the focus in these islands still very much centred on the Five Nations series.

That was still the coin of highest value in this part of the world and its appeal grew ever stronger. Sponsorship was now, of course, very much a central part of the rugby scene. For years Rugby Union had stubbornly resisted any commercial involvement in the game; now all that had changed. Rugby had embraced the sponsors. And while initially a fairly tight reign was kept on this, eventually the barriers came down and the money flowed in.

At representative level the interprovincial series had taken sponsorship on board several years previously with the Northern Bank as the sponsors. Esso Teoranta sponsored the schoolboy internationals. Now the international team was also sponsored. All sorts of stringent laws about not displaying firms' logos on the team jerseys were put in place. Sponsorship by tobacco firms was outlawed, as was sponsorship by firms manufacturing alcoholic spirits. But many of the earlier barriers were dismantled and the laws relating to sponsorship underwent radical change as time went by.

The IRFU, in common with their brethren in Britain, accepted sponsorship for their home international matches from the Digital Equipment Company, a multinational computer concern. The IRFU found Digital generous and co-operative partners. That alliance lasted for a decade and was no doubt mutually beneficial.

Aware that inevitably in a physical contact sport such as rugby players would occasionally suffer very serious injury and that it could cause financial hardship, the IRFU had set up a Charitable Trust. The deed was put in place in May 1978, but as the eighties dawned, the trust was still in its infancy as far as building up a substantial capital sum was concerned.

With Bobby Deacy in the chair, an appeal was organised in 1981 to all affiliated clubs for contributions to the fund in two instalments, the first in April 1981, the second in April 1982.

What was especially heartening was the way some old internationals responded, as did other individuals and indeed some companies. Under the guidance of Bobby Deacy, by the mid-eighties the fund had reached £250,000, and during the 1984–85 season the Trust Fund paid out £16,000.

At this period, too, the structure of senior competitive rugby was very much exercising the minds of the Game Development committee under the chairmanship of Tom Kiernan. The possibility of a National League was high on the agenda, but it was not until the 1990s that this came to fruition.

In the international context, with Ireland now installed as Triple Crown and Five Nations champions, political issues again intervened to force the cancellation of a scheduled tour. Ireland had been due to travel to Argentina in the summer of 1985, but the tour was cancelled in the aftermath of the Falklands War a few years previously. Relations between Britain and Argentina had not been re-established on a sound footing and in those circumstances, with several of the Ireland squad holding British passports, it was deemed inadvisable for the tour to go ahead.

But the cancellation of that tour opened the door for another and Japan, who had been anxious for an Ireland visit, got their wish in May of 1985 when the Argentinian mission was called off. Thus it was that a 26-man playing squad set out for Japan in May. The team was managed by Des McKibbin, Mick Doyle was coach and Joe Gallagher was medical officer.

The players who had helped Ireland to win the Triple Crown were all chosen and the squad included seven uncapped players: Philip Rainey, Terry McMaster, Ralph Keyes, Rab Brady, Paul Kennedy, Paul Collins and Paddy Kenny.

Ireland played five matches on the tour and won all five. The itinerary included two Tests, but caps were not awarded for these. One casualty of the tour was Terry McMaster, the Ulster and Ballymena wing. He had suffered an ankle injury prior to the tour but came through a test on the eve of departure. But, unfortunately, the problem reasserted itself during training in Japan and after he had been selected to play in the second match of the tour against a Japan selected side in Sendai, he was forced out of the tour and had to return home. John Hewitt, the Ulster and NIFC centre, travelled out as a replacement.

The team that won the Triple Crown was named *en bloc* for the first Test. However, Nigel Carr had to withdraw because of a knee injury and Paddy Kenny replaced him. During the course of the second Test, the final match of the tour, both half-backs Paul Dean and Michael Bradley were injured. Ralph Keyes and Rab Brady came on for Dean and Bradley and thus, like Kenny, got their initial experience of senior international rugby, if not the reward of international caps. Kenny, in fact, had the distinction of playing in all five matches on the tour, having come on as a replacement in one match.

Ireland won the first and second matches easily beating Kanto (East Japan) 42-15 in Morioka; they followed that with a 34-10 win over Japan Selected in Sendai. Then came the first Test in Osaka. Watched by over 20,000 vociferous spectators, Ireland played extremely well and established a 29-3 lead, subsequently led 35-13, and eventually won 48-13. Several records were set in that match. Forty-eight points was the highest ever scored by Ireland in a Test and the winning margin of 35 points was also a record. Ireland scored eight tries, another first, and Michael Kiernan set two marks. He scored 20 points, the highest by an individual on an overseas tour in a match, and his five conversions was also a record. Unfortunately, those very notable achievements were diminished as the match did not have the status of a full international. Trevor Ringland scored three tries and that, too, equalled the individual try-scoring record for an Irish player in an international.

In the fourth tour match, Ireland defeated Kansai (West Japan) 44-13 in Nagoya and then came the final Test in Tokyo. This attracted a capacity crowd of 30,000 and Ireland finished, as they had started the tour, with a win.

But it was not by any means as easily attained as the victory in the first Test. The Japanese had certainly learned a lot from the initial match and duly applied it. Their forwards, in particular, did not lose possession as they had done in the first match and they cut down mistakes and tackled well. It was 12-12 at the interval and the crowd gave the home team tremendous support as they felt that they might be about to witness a historic win.

Ireland had to replace Dean and Bradley in the second half. Rab Brady and Ralph Keyes came into the team. They performed well behind a pack that gradually got on top and Ireland played with sensible application in the prevailing circumstances, rather than with flair, as they opted for a percentage approach. Kiernan emerged as the scoring hero once more, his points made up of two tries, four conversions and three penalty goals. That broke the individual scoring record for an Ireland player in a Test set by Ollie Campbell a few years previously. Brendan Mullin and Willie Anderson scored tries. Kiernan scored 65 points on the tour in four appearances, a truly excellent contribution.

So it was five wins out of five for Ireland and there was every reason to look forward to 1985–86 with great optimism. But that expectation was not matched by realisation. Mick Cuddy had served his three year term as a selector and he was replaced by Eddie Coleman. Jim Donaldson had taken over as chairman of selectors.

Ireland opened their campaign in 1985–86 with a match against Fiji on their first visit to these shores and whom Ireland had played in 1979 in Suva. The Fijians had a three match schedule in Ireland beginning with the international at Lansdowne Road on 19 October, a match played on a lovely autumn afternoon.

Ireland put in the best available side with Kiernan on the wing in place of the injured Trevor Ringland, and John Hewitt was in the centre for Kiernan. Nigel Carr was again ruled out by injury and that meant a return for Willie Sexton.

It was obvious from the outset that the Fijians had not come to offer token opposition. They played some really good rugby in the first half. While their forwards could not exercise any control, their backs were a constant threat. It was 6-6 at the interval and it was the Fijians who had scored a try and conversion, while Kiernan kicked two penalty goals for Ireland.

A big surprise looked on when Fiji went into a 12-6 lead after an interception. The Irish were struggling to assert any authority. Then, after Kiernan kicked another penalty and Michael Bradley scored a try, Ireland led rather fortunately 13-12. But the drama and anxiety were not over. The Fijians edged ahead with a penalty goal and again it was Kiernan who came to Ireland's rescue with his fourth penalty to leave Ireland 16-15 in front. In the closing minutes Ireland lived on the edge. The Fijians lost a great try-scoring chance when one of their players knocked on, with the Irish line open and, in injury time, a penalty attempt by the Fijians drifted inches wide — so a win, but by no means a convincing performance. Fiji then lost to Ulster but ended their tour by beating Connacht 7-6 in Galway.

As the Irish prepared for the Five Nations series, they could reflect on the fact that they had played eight matches under Mick Doyle, had won six, drawn one, and lost one to Australia. It was certainly an excellent record and the championship was awaited with eager anticipation.

There was a break in procedure in relation to the final trial. Instead of Whites versus Blues or Probables against Possibles, the selectors decided on a match between an Ireland XV against the Combined Provinces, a contest won by Ireland 21-12.

But the opening match in the championship series hoisted the danger cones for Ireland of difficulties ahead. These came in Paris on 1 February with a team that included twelve of the side that had won the Triple Crown. Ireland lost 29-9. David Morrow of Bangor won his first cap and Moss Finn and Ronan Kearney were back in the team.

That defeat unfortunately was to set the pattern for the season as Ireland went on to lose the next three matches against Wales, Scotland and England despite, in every instance, having led at the interval. Wales won in Dublin 19-12, and for that match Philip Orr was dropped and replaced by Paul Kennedy of London Irish. Out, too, went tight head prop Jim McCoy and he was replaced by Des Fitzgerald. Willie Anderson was another to lose out with Jerry Holland, who had played in the two Tests in South Africa, being recalled to partner Donal Lenihan. Philip Matthews was ruled out by injury, so Ronan Kearney continued to deputise for him in a back row that also included Brian Spillane and Nigel Carr.

For the match against England, Ralph Keyes was called in for his first cap as Dean was injured and Brian McCall partnered Lenihan in the second row with Morrow on the flank for Kearney. There was grave doubt that the match would be played because of a frozen surface at Twickenham. But the English Union got to work using burners to thaw out the ground, and it was eventually deemed playable.

Yet again Ireland led at the interval but lost 25-20 despite scoring three tries. But it was the power of the England pack that really told as they got two push-over tries, both scored by their No. 8 Dean Richards.

So Ireland went into the final match of the season against Scotland seeking not a Triple Crown but to avoid a whitewash. Tony Ward was recalled after two years in the international wilderness for this match as Keyes was out injured. And while Ward played very well on his return, Ireland lost a very tight and indeed good match by a point 9-10. Ireland actually led 9-0 at the interval, having played with the wind. Trevor Ringland scored a try — his third in three successive matches — and Kiernan kicked a penalty and a conversion. But the Scots cut the deficit with two penalty goals from Gavin Hastings and went ahead with a superb try from scrum-half Roy Laidlaw.

While this was Ireland's best display of the season, it was not marked by the much needed win and it added to the disappointment when, just before the end, Ireland got a penalty just to the right of the posts at the Lansdowne Road end of the ground. Unfortunately, Kiernan uncharacteristically kicked it wide. Thus it was a whitewash for Ireland. The wheel had turned full circle again in a twelve month period. That, in fact, was to be the last match Ciaran Fitzgerald played for Ireland. He did not get into the side the following year as Harry Harbison made the hooking berth his own. Fitzgerald had been a magnificent servant to his country and led the team to two Triple Crown and two Championship triumphs as another great hooker Karl Mullen had done in the late 1940s.

In April 1986, the International Board celebrated the centenary of its foundation. This very notable milestone was marked by a special centenary congress to which representatives from all rugby-playing nations were invited.

On the field, two matches were arranged with a Lions team playing against the Rest of the World in Cardiff and a Five Nations team against the Overseas Unions at Twickenham.

That year the Lions had been scheduled to travel to South Africa but the tour was called off and so those chosen for the Lions side in the centenary match were, in fact, given full Lions status. Donal Lenihan was given the honour of leading the team and Mick Doyle was appointed coach. In addition to Lenihan, Trevor Ringland, Brendan Mullin, Michael Kiernan, Des Fitzgerald and Nigel Carr were selected, with Ringland, Mullin, Fitzgerald, Lenihan and Carr all in the Lions team that lost 7-15 to the Rest in a match played in a downpour in Cardiff. Ringland, Kiernan and Lenihan played for the Five Nations team that lost 32-13 in Twickenham to the Overseas Unions.

A big dark cloud was cast over the International Board celebrations when it was discovered that arrangements were in hand for a rebel tour to South Africa by a New Zealand squad. By this time the IRFU had adopted a change in policy towards South Africa; nor would South African teams be able to play in Ireland. The news of that rebel tour was received by the International Board with dismay. The New Zealand Rugby Union officially washed its hands on the issue and the South African Rugby Board subsequently gave assurances that no such tour would take place again. It had a very hollow ring.

Bob FitzGerald, secretary/treasurer of the IRFU since 1964, retired after 22 years' service with the union on 30 June 1986. He was succeeded by Paddy Moss, a former Trinity and Wanderers player who, in fact, had had no involvement in rugby for many years when he was chosen to succeed Bob FitzGerald. FitzGerald, in contrast, had not alone played for Palmerston and indeed for Leinster, but also had considerable administrative experience on the Leinster executive and had been president of the Leinster Branch before he took over the secretarial job with the IRFU. There was, too, a sad occurrence when in March of 1986, Shiela MacSweeney, who had been on the staff at Lansdowne Road since 1963, died aged 43. She had served the IRFU very well and had been its longest serving member.

In September 1986 Canada sent a touring team to Ireland. It was part of their preparation for the inaugural World Cup scheduled for twelve months ahead. The Canadians opened their tour against Ulster who won by 32-13 and then Ireland put an Under 25 team into the field against the Canadian national team at Lansdowne Road on 27 September. Former Ireland back row Jimmy Davidson managed the Ireland side and he had gained considerable coaching experience at representative level with a very successful Ulster team. The Ireland team was captained by centre Paul Clinch (Lansdowne), who had also played for Trinity and is a member of a renowned Irish rugby family whose grandfather Jamie and great grandfather Andrew had played for Ireland. Ireland fielded a team that included only two capped players, centre John Hewitt and Ralph Keyes. The rest of the side was made up of young and emerging talent and many of those chosen went on to win full international honours. Ireland won the match 26-20 with Keyes the scorer-in-chief with a personal contribution of a try, two conversions and two penalty goals. Neil Francis, Michael Moylett and Ger O'Kelly, of Dolphin, also scored tries for Ireland. The Canadians also played Leinster and Connacht. They lost to Leinster 13-9 and drew 27 all with Connacht.

New ground was broken on 1 November 1986 when the Romanians played Ireland, now captained by Donal Lenihan, at Lansdowne Road and this time full caps were awarded for the match. It was a very disappointing and disjointed Romanian team that played Ireland and Ireland ran riot winning by 60-0.

That total equalled the world record score in a full international set by France in 1967 and the victory was a new world record. Michael Kiernan kicked seven conversions to set another record and Keith Crossan's three tries equalled the individual record for an Ireland player in an international. Brendan Mullin and Paul Dean scored two tries each with Hugo MacNeill and Willie Anderson also scoring tries. Ireland's try total of 10 was also a record. The Ireland team did not include any new caps but there was a return for No. 8 Michael Gibson, the Lansdowne No. 8 who had previously been capped in 1979.

Ireland opened the Five Nations campaign against England and the team showed one change from the side that beat Romania. Jim Glennon was recalled to the side after seven years and partnered Lenihan in the second row, and Willie Anderson moved from the second row to No. 8 for Gibson. Ireland won 17-0. They led 9-0 at the interval and were in total control in the second half and added another eight points.

That match took place on 2 February. Ireland should have opened their campaign against Wales on 17 January, but the match was postponed because of a heavy snowfall in Cardiff and was refixed for 4 April.

Phil Orr winning his fiftieth cap v Scotland 1986

Ireland's second match was against Scotland in Murrayfield and all hopes of another Triple Crown vanished when Ireland, with an unchanged team, lost 16-12.

Ireland had to wait a month for the next match, against France in Dublin. With the inaugural World Cup on the horizon, the selectors decided to hold a special trial match at Ravenhill. Following the trial Nigel Carr was dropped and Brian Spillane recalled with Philip Matthews switched to the open side flank and Spillane on the blind side. Ireland started brilliantly against the French and went into a 10-0 lead with tries from Trevor Ringland and Michael Bradley and a conversion from Michael Kiernan. At the interval Ireland led 10-3 after Philippe Berot kicked a penalty for France. In the second half the French flair asserted itself. Eric Champ scored two tries as France went into the lead and eventually won 19-12. This gave France the Grand Slam, their first since 1981 and they celebrated accordingly.

Nigel Carr was recalled for the match against Wales on 4 April and Anderson was switched to the second row for Glennon. Wales started in brilliant fashion on a wet surface. They scored two tries to go into an 8-0 lead. Then just before half-time Ireland struck a crucial blow. Philip Orr, now very much the veteran of the side, set up a ruck, the ball was moved out to Dean and he scored under the Welsh posts. Kiernan converted and Ireland trailed by only two points at the break.

It was cut and thrust in the second period before Ireland scored a fine try to take the lead. Michael Bradley broke from his own '25', got support from Carr and Matthews, and Brendan Mullin was put clear to score a try which Kiernan converted. Wales cut their deficit to a point with a penalty, but then Kiernan landed a long-range penalty to put Ireland ahead 15-11. The Irish held firm in the face of a tremendous Welsh assault and so won in Cardiff for the second successive occasion.

It was seen as a very important victory for Ireland not least because little more than a month later the countries were scheduled to meet again in the World Cup in Wellington. The win made Ireland favourites to win their World Cup group. That month another who had served the IRFU well, Harry Booker, retired. He had acted as baggage master for Ireland teams since 1967 and in 1975 joined the union as assistant secretary. He held that position until 1984 and then took over as Executive Officer for three years with special responsibility for the Lansdowne Road ground.

Now it was on to the World Cup and, with that pending, the Ireland players involved were asked not to play for their clubs in the closing stages of the provincial cup competitions. Two Irish referees, David Burnett and Stephen Hilditch, were also chosen to officiate in a competition which in reality would change the face of the game across the world within a few years.

CHAPTER 26

THE INAUGURAL WORLD CUP

THE CONCEPT OF A RUGBY UNION WORLD CUP had been on the table long before the competition became a reality in 1987. The French, for instance, had explored the possibility of such a competition several years previously but got little encouragement as there was no real enthusiasm for the competition.

It would not be untrue to say that what gave the competition the push, so to speak, towards becoming a reality was that a new mood was pervading the scene, mostly in the southern hemisphere, and it was to a large extent motivated by commercialism and money.

There was another factor, too, that had its roots in history. The International Championship or to give it its modern title, the Five Nations Championship, had always had a very special place in the hearts of the rugby fraternity in the home countries and France. It was looked upon with some envy by the southern hemisphere countries who had nothing comparable. Certainly the visits of such as the Springboks, the All Blacks and the Wallabies were always attractive; likewise the tours by the Lions and individual countries to the southern hemisphere had their appeal. But the Five Nations had an attraction and an aura that was and, indeed, is to this day very special.

There was a belief current in the home countries that, among other things, a World Cup would diminish the Five Nations series. But the anxieties about the World Cup concept went beyond that consideration.

At the annual general meetings of the IRFU in 1984 and 1985 the issue was raised and it was patently obvious that there was no enthusiasm for the competition.

During the centenary celebrations of the Connacht Branch in 1985–86, the IRFU held one of its meetings in Galway to mark the occasion. At the meeting men such as Ronnie Dawson and his International Board colleague, Harry McKibbin, very strenuously pointed out the dangers inherent in a World Cup, with particular emphasis on the commercial aspects and the danger to the amateur ethic. They made a point, too, of stressing that professionalism and all it embraced would be unsustainable in most unions of the International Rugby Football Board. They believed, and events were to prove them to be conclusively correct, that a World Cup would eventually lead to professionalism and the demise of the amateur ethic, a concept that had been sacrosanct for over a hundred years and one on which the game had survived, evolved and prospered.

New Zealand and Australia, in particular, were especially keen on the World Cup and set about doing a vast propagation job for the competition. One of the arguments used was that it would do an immense amount for the emerging nations and they pointed in particular to what it would do for the countries in the South Pacific such as Western Samoa, Fiji and Tonga. The South Africans, while still at that time members of the International Rugby Board, were effectively isolated from the world game and had no part to play in the World Cup.

Eventually it was decided by the IRFU and indeed the other home unions that they would enter for the competition, but reservations remained certainly in the IRFU about several aspects of it. Not least the decision to enter was promoted by the belief that, by being in the competition, Ireland would have an input into the scene and help exercise some element of control. Arrangements were put in hand for the inaugural competition which was scheduled to take place in New Zealand and Australia in May-June 1987. The cup for the competition was named the Webb Ellis trophy.

THE 1987 WORLD CUP SQUAD

The tournament was run by an organising committee appointed by the International Board. The committee was under the chairmanship of John Kendall Carpenter (England) and he, together with Ronnie Dawson (Ireland), Keith Rowlands (Wales), Bob Stuart (New Zealand) and Ross Turnbull (Australia), were charged with the effective running of the cup. Two executive directors from the two countries acting as hosts were also appointed. They were Sir Nicholas Shehadie (Australia) and Dick Littlejohn (New Zealand).

Sixteen nations were involved with four groups of four contesting the league stages. Each group had two seeded nations and two countries who were not members of the International Board. Two countries from each pool qualified for the quarter-finals.

Ireland was one of the two seeded nations in Pool 2 which also included Wales, the second seeded country, together with Canada and Tonga. Each country was allowed to bring a squad of 26 players. Syd Millar was appointed manager of the Ireland team, Mick Doyle coach and Donal Lenihan was captain.

Even before the team left these shores Ireland sustained a set-back. Three Irish players, Philip Rainey, David Irwin and Nigel Carr, were travelling from Belfast to Dublin for a training session when their car was caught in a bomb explosion near the border on the Northern Ireland side of Dundalk. That killed two people travelling from Dublin to Belfast, a senior judge and his wife who were the targets, and the Irish players' car was caught in the blast.

Both Irwin and Rainey escaped serious injury but Carr did not, and while happily he recovered from his injuries, not alone his World Cup but his career as a player was over.

Ireland went to the tournament with a squad that contained a fair leavening of experience and youth with six uncapped players in the squad. Ciaran Fitzgerald was not available for the trip and thus an uncapped hooker from the Dolphin club, Terry Kingston, was included. Carr's withdrawal meant that Derek McGrath, who had been capped while a veterinary student at UCD but now with Cork Constitution, was called into the squad.

All the backs who had done so much to fashion Ireland's Triple Crown triumph in 1985 were in the party and there was a recall for Tony Ward, who had not played at international level since the match against Scotland twelve months previously. All the forwards, too, who had helped win the Triple Crown and championship, with the exception of Carr and Mick Fitzpatrick, the Wanderers prop who had come on as a substitute against France in 1985, were in the party.

Ireland opened their campaign against Wales on a very windy day in Wellington. Ireland went into the match having beaten Wales in Cardiff on 4 April and so there was understandable confidence that they would repeat that win and so take a major step towards topping the pool. A few days before the first match, hooker Harry Harbison, the man who displaced Ciaran Fitzgerald during the 1986 championship series, was forced to withdraw from the squad because of a back injury. The Ireland management sent for John McDonald, the Malone and Ulster hooker, as a replacement. But it was to Kingston that the selectors turned to replace Harbison for the opening match.

On the management side there was also a casualty. On the day after their arrival in Wellington, Ireland underwent a vigorous training session under Mick Doyle. That night Doyle was taken ill and rushed to hospital. It was feared that he had suffered a heart attack. But fortunately it was nothing as serious as initially feared and he was released from hospital within a few days and was back with the squad and supervising training. In his absence Millar and George Spotswood, who travelled as assistant to the management, took the training sessions.

Ireland fielded a team that showed just two changes from the side that had beaten Wales the previous month for their first World Cup assignment. McGrath was on the flank for Carr and Kingston at hooker for Harbison. From the outset it was Wales who looked the more likely winners, and so it transpired. Their outside half Jonathan Davies kicked superbly and used the wind to tremendous effect. Wales scored the only try through Mark Ring, Paul Thorburn converted it and Davies dropped two goals. Michael Kiernan kicked two penalty goals for Ireland.

TONY WARD IN ACTION IN DUNEDIN AGAINST CANADA IN WORLD CUP, MARCH 1987

That result meant that Ireland had to beat both Canada and Tonga to make sure of finishing second and thus qualify for the quarter-final. But a second place pool finish meant assuredly that Ireland would run into Australia at the quarter-final stage, not an enticing prospect as at the time the Australians were especially strong and indeed rated with New Zealand as cup favourites.

Ireland's second assignment was against Canada at Carisbrook, Dunedin. Canada had opened their campaign with an impressive and convincing 37-4 demolition of Tonga. So unless the Irish were to make a premature departure from the World Cup, victory was essential in Dunedin. Ireland brought Tony Ward in at outside half in the only change in the back line. McDonald was named as hooker for Kingston, and Paul Collins was on the flank for Philip Matthews. So it meant first caps for McDonald and Collins.

Ireland eventually wore the Canadians down but had to endure some anxiety before putting the Canadians away. It was not until well into the second period that Ireland got well on top and made their superiority pay the dividend. Ireland eventually won the match 46-19, a win more convincing in statistical terms than it was in execution. But the primary objective had been attained. Keith Crossan scored two tries. Brian Spillane, Michael Bradley, Trevor Ringland and Hugo MacNeill also scored tries. Michael Kiernan converted five, kicked two penalty goals and Ward dropped a goal.

Now it was a journey across the Tasman Sea for Ireland whose third pool match was against Tonga at the Ballymore ground in Brisbane. Ireland's last appearance on that ground had been the great win over Australia in 1979 when Ollie Campbell was preferred to Ward and marked the occasion with such a telling performance.

The win against Canada was not attained without a price being paid and McDonald was ruled out of the remainder of the tour because of a leg injury. That meant Ireland had to send for yet another replacement hooker and Steve Smith from Ballymena joined the party.

Ireland met Tonga on 3 June in Brisbane and made one change in the back line (David Irwin replaced Michael Kiernan in the centre) but made five changes in the pack. The front row was recast. Job Langbroek from Blackrock College came in for Philip Orr, Kingston was back as hooker, Jim McCoy replaced Des Fitzgerald at tight head prop, Matthews returned to the blind side flank for Collins, and Neil Francis, ordinarily a second row and a player who had a very distinguished schools career with Blackrock College, was named at No. 8 for Spillane. Langbroek and Francis won their first caps.

On a warm afternoon and on a very hard ground, Ireland won without much difficulty, scoring five tries in the 32-9 victory. The match was notable for the fact that Crossan equalled the individual try-scoring record for an Ireland player in an international by scoring three. MacNeill scored two and Ward kicked three penalty goals and converted two tries.

So a quarter-final place had been secured by finishing in second place in the pool. Wales took the top spot and that put the Welsh in against England. Ireland's next task was against Australia, the venue, the Concorde Oval, in Sydney on 7 June.

Kiernan returned to the centre, Dean came in at outside half for Ward, Orr and Des Fitzgerald were back as props, and Francis was retained at No. 8 with Spillane on the bench. From the outset, the Australians stamped their authority on the match and by the interval it was over as a contest. The Wallabies won 33-15. Ireland did play with some resolution after the interval, but it was always no more than a damage limitation exercise. Australia lost their scrum-half Nick Farr Jones early on and he was replaced by Brian Smith. We did not know it then, but Smith would subsequently wear the green jersey of Ireland. That afternoon he scored two of Australia's four tries.

For Ireland the World Cup experience was now over and the journey home was made the day after the defeat by Australia. Australia subsequently lost to France in the semi-final in a marvellous match, played again at Concorde Oval; while Wales, having beaten England, were overwhelmed by New Zealand in the semi-final.

Thus it was the southern versus the northern hemisphere in the final as France faced the All Blacks at Eden Park, Auckland, on 20 June. The All Blacks won 29-9 and were crowned World champions.

Meanwhile in a bad-tempered match, Wales defeated Australia in the play-off for third place. Third place in the world was an exalted rating and few could have envisaged that afternoon in Rotorua that, in the years ahead, the Welsh would have to endure unprecedented difficulties.

The inaugural World Cup was consigned to history. It had been marked by some memorable matches, and worthy champions had emerged. It was not the financial success that had been predicted, but it set rugby on a course that within a few years was to change the game radically and herald the era of professionalism as rugby moved from being a sport to being a business.

Four years before the inaugural World Cup, attempts were made to form a professional rugby union circus and those attempts failed. But rugby and its long-cherished idealism were changing and the World Cup hastened the change. Money was now very much a central factor that in the end would see the amateur ethic and over a hundred years of tradition sacrificed on the altar of commercialism and greed. Sadly it has to be said that this was a by-product of the inaugural World Cup as television became a major factor and the nations in the South Pacific, far from gaining benefit, were left behind in the rush.

One central figure in the concerted attempts to professionalise the game was, remarkably, a man who had been a member of the 1987 World Cup Organising Committee, Ross Turnbull. There were those who very understandably greatly resented his activities and the part he played for personal gain. He was a leading figure in what has been termed 'The Rugby War'. A vital element in that was the battle between the two television moguls, Rupert Murdoch and Kerry Packer, who effectively sought control over the leading players by offering big financial inducements. Turnbull had been recruited by the Packer Organisation who had attempted to counter the fact that Murdoch's men had signed so many leading Rugby League players which had a very significant effect on the league structure and competitions in Australia and subsequently elsewhere and the consequent television audiences. A professional Rugby Union structure was seen as the counter to that and Turnbull set about the task of implementing that and using his contacts to bring it to fruition. That activity by a man who was a former Australian Rugby Union international and leading administrator in the union game was, to say the least of it, viewed by many not alone with utter distaste but with dismay.

There is no doubt that top Rugby Union players had always been targets for Rugby League. With more money than ever available in the league game, it was true that more Rugby Union players would be lured away. That was a greater problem in Australia and New Zealand than elsewhere, but it is not a defence for some of the activities that went on that made Rugby Union professional.

Turnbull was a man who was well aware of the consequences for the union game and one who knew from his own experience that the amateur ethic had been so crucial in its evolution. If he had been conscious of that, then his activity showed absolutely no appreciation of it. The same could be said for some others.

Certainly times had changed and there was a more liberal attitude in Rugby Union towards the right and ability of players to earn money from the game and their standing in it. But direct payment for playing the game was a path paved with major obstacles and pitfalls. Rugby Union was to learn that lesson in the years ahead when men with no background in or regard for the game and its true values gouged and gorged over control of the clubs and players. Long-standing alliances and friendships between unions, elements so vital to the propagation of rugby, were strained to breaking point. Those who had forecast chaos, disloyalty and the very survival of clubs were proved to be correct. The price for professionalism went well beyond the financial rewards that accrued to the top players, as subsequent events all too graphically revealed.

CHAPTER 27

JIMMY DAVIDSON TAKES OVER

After the inaugural World Cup had been consigned to history, there was now a realisation it would precipitate major changes in the years ahead. The next competition was set for four years hence in the home countries and France. But it was back to the 1988 International Championship on the home front for the World Cup runners-up France and the other four nations. France had kept the northern hemisphere flag flying by reaching the final of the World Cup.

Mick Doyle's term as coach was now over and he was, as anticipated, succeeded by Jimmy Davidson. Davidson was the logical choice. He had been a very good and honest player who had been honoured at international level. He had taken a profound interest and involvement in the coaching side of the game after his playing days had finished.

He came in as Ireland's coach, having served a good apprenticeship with the Ulster team, and during his tenure Ulster had achieved an unprecedented run of success.

He outlined his philosophy at a press conference prior to the first training session he took at Lansdowne Road. 'Leaner, meaner, fitter and faster' was his creed. Now he had the chance to put it into practice.

He had at his disposal some very experienced players, but two who had gone were Nigel Carr, the victim of that appalling incident prior to the World Cup, and Philip Orr, who decided to retire. Orr had won his 58th cap against Australia in the World Cup and retired as the world's most capped prop forward. His era in the Ireland team had been marked by disappointment but also considerable achievement. He had helped win two Triple Crowns, two Championships and had gone on two Lions tours.

The Interprovincial Championship, a competition now sponsored by Heineken and with a trophy at stake, the Heineken Bowl, was shared by Ulster and Munster. There was considerable interest in the final trial as some of those who had made their international debuts in the World Cup now sought to establish their places on the national side. But the Whites (Probables) had a very familiar ring, with the vast majority of the Triple Crown winners still in pole position. Ciaran Fitzgerald led the Possibles and Tony Ward was outside half in that team. The match ended in a 19-19 draw, with a late try from Brendan Mullin saving the Probables' blushes.

Ireland opened their campaign against Scotland at Lansdowne Road with a team that included a new cap at full-back, Philip Danaher. He had played for Ireland schools while a student at St Munchin's College and was now playing his club rugby with Lansdowne. Danaher displaced Hugo MacNeill. Young Munster loose head prop John Fitzgerald was also brought in, while Des Fitzgerald held off the challenge of Jim McCoy at tight head. No. 8, Michael Gibson, now with London Irish, was in the back row with Philip Matthews and Willie Sexton, who had been recalled yet again.

The match proved to be a very good start to Davidson's tenure as Ireland coach. Ireland won 22-18 and were not flattered to have done so. In fact MacNeill, who had come on as a replacement for the injured Ringland, scored a crucial try. It was not until injury time that Scotland scored a try, the reward for a lot of late pressure. The try was converted, but it still left the Scots four points adrift.

Davidson and Ireland experienced another side of the fickle international scene when Ireland travelled to Parc des Princes on 20 February with a team that saw the Ulster and Bangor flanker, Don Whittle, gain his first cap at the expense of Willie Sexton. With France having lost to Scotland, there was reason for some Irish optimism going to a venue where Ireland had never won. France that afternoon never looked likely to surrender their unbeaten record against Ireland and won 25-6, and just as comprehensively as that scoreline indicates.

Ireland's next assignment was against Wales in Dublin and the Welsh were going for the Triple Crown. Tom Clancy, the Lansdowne prop, won his first cap at the expense of John Fitzgerald, while another debutante was the Malone and Ulster flanker Denis McBride. Ireland led 9-3 at the break, but in the second half the Welsh drew level and with the match in injury time, it was nine points each when the Welsh were awarded a penalty out near the left touchline. Their full-back Paul Thorburn stepped up and duly kicked the goal to leave Wales victorious and Ireland to contemplate what was sure to be a difficult assignment, a visit to Twickenham on 19 March.

Just how difficult that was is illustrated by the scoreline as England won 35-3. That amounted to the heaviest defeat ever inflicted on Ireland in the championship by any country. Ireland, having played with a very strong wind, led three points to nil at the interval, but had failed to use the wind, a major factor on the day. The changes Ireland had made included the return of Hugo MacNeill and the selection of a new cap, former schools international Mick Moylett, in the second row, as well as Anderson reverting to No. 8 to the exclusion of Michael Gibson. The changes certainly did not bring any improvement in the overall level of Ireland's performance.

England overwhelmed Ireland in the second half and the match was a personal triumph for the England wing Chris Oti, who scored three tries and that against an opponent of Trevor Ringland's calibre. It was a dark and dismal day for Ireland. But there was a chance for Ireland to gain some measure of revenge. Due to the initiative of the IRFU president that year, Paddy Madigan, England agreed to play Ireland in a special match to mark the Dublin Millennium at Lansdowne Road on 23 April. It had the status of a full international and caps were accordingly awarded.

Some distinguished names were omitted from the Ireland team, namely Trevor Ringland, Keith Crossan and Michael Bradley. They were replaced by three news caps, John Sexton, the Dublin University wing, Vincent Cunningham, the St Mary's College centre, and Fergus Aherne, the Lansdowne scrum-half. There was another new cap at hooker in Steve Smith of Ballymena. Out too went Des Fitzgerald, and he was replaced at prop by Jim McCoy, and the back row was again revised.

It was a notable and unique occasion but by no means a memorable match as England won and, if not in the devastating manner of a few weeks previously, comprehensively enough. They led 12-0 at the interval and 15-0 shortly after the break, having played with the wind in the initial period. Smith marked his international debut for Ireland with a try which Kiernan converted, and then MacNeill got a try to bring Ireland very much in sight of their opponents. But England finished strongly, adding a try which was again converted and were not flattered by a 21-10 win. So Ireland finished with one win and four defeats in Jimmy Davidson's first season as coach.

The Millennium match did not end Ireland's campaign that season. It had been decided that Ireland would travel to France for a four match tour in May. This tour was, in part, a development process that would give experience to some young players, but the selectors did have an open brief as to whom they would select in the 25 man playing party. Several of the senior players opted not to go on the tour and that opened the way for some of the younger school.

The Irish party that toured France 1988

In fact 10 of the 25 man playing squad had been uncapped. The then Ireland captain, Donal Lenihan, was among those not available and Willie Anderson took over as captain, and a very fine leader he proved. Several of the young players who travelled in that party were later to leave a very profound mark on the international scene.

It was a tough enough schedule. Ireland opened the tour in Biarritz against a very strong Côté Basque side and lost 33-23. The centrepiece of the tour was the match against a French XV in Auch. That was the home base of the former French captain, coach and scrum-half, Jacques Fouroux. That evening Ireland faced a full-strength French side. This was an international in all but name and was treated accordingly by the French. It proved to be not alone a superb match but a wonderful triumph for Ireland, who won a great match 19-18. Ireland played brilliantly that evening, with the forwards giving the French pack a torrid time. Behind them Tony Ward, who had not been selected by Davidson and his selectors all season, was at his brilliant best. He teased and tormented the French with some superb kicking and went through the whole scoring range that evening. Neil Francis was the key figure in the line-out and won some great possession which was used most effectively.

The backs tackled with tremendous effect and none better than the two uncapped players in the back line, Paul Clinch and Peter Purcell. Anderson was an inspirational leader. It was unfortunate that caps were not awarded for this match as surely the occasion and the quality of the opposition deserved that distinction.

In the third match Ireland lost 12-7 to a French XV in Lorient, but it was by no means as strong as the team in Auch and the tour ended with a spectacular affair against the French Barbarians in La Rochelle which the Barbarians won 41-26.

Altogether the tour had been a very rewarding experience for the Irish players. It also signalled the end of Tony Ward's representative career. Shortly after the tour he announced his retirement. He had achieved an immense amount in a career too often marked by controversy. But he had won 19 caps, went on a Lions tour, set a new record points total for a Lions player in a Test in 1980, was on the Munster team that had beaten the All Blacks in 1978 and had also helped Munster to beat Australia. Being based in Dublin at this stage, he had declared for Leinster in the closing stages of his representative career and so had the distinction of having played for two provinces.

A sad footnote to that season was that in December Paddy Patterson of Ulster died. He had rendered outstanding service to the game and at the time of his death was a member of the Marketing subcommittee, a body that had now assumed considerable importance in the changing climate of the game.

At this time the existing regulations on amateurism were coming under increasing stress. The additional money accruing to the game from sponsorship and related activities gave added impetus to demands from players for some form of reimbursement. Tour allowances had gone up appreciably, but that was seen as little more than a small move forward.

While the IRFU reiterated its stand on the amateur principles, so also did the International Board. But the storm clouds were gathering apace, a fact acknowledged when the Board announced that they were submitting a paper on amateurism to all unions and asked for a response by 31 July 1989. But one good thing the Board did do in 1988 was to reinstate several players who had gone to Rugby League. Thus three former eminent Irish internationals who had followed that path, Paddy Reid, Ken Goodall and Robin Thompson, were reinstated.

As Jim Davidson prepared his side for the 1989 championship he had the advantage of two internationals prior to the series. The first was against Western Samoa at Lansdowne Road on 29 October. The team was captained by Philip Matthews and included a new cap in the Corinthians No. 8, Noel Mannion. That made it not alone a very special occasion for Mannion, who was also an inter-county Gaelic footballer, but for his club as he was the first Corinthians player to win a full cap. Another new cap made his advent during the game in Pat O'Hara, the Sunday's Well flanker who had been in France the previous summer with the Ireland squad.

Ireland won the match 49-22 and Matthews, the first man to captain Ireland at schools and senior levels, marked his leadership with a try. That was one of eight Ireland scored that afternoon. Western Samoa also played Ulster and lost 47-17 and then went on to play Connacht at the Sports Ground in Galway. Connacht won 25-19 and Mannion was also a member of that side, the first Connacht team to defeat a national touring side.

Tony Twomey of Lansdowne, a fine scrum-half in his day, had now taken over as chairman of selectors from Eddie Coleman and he, Neil Jackson (Ulster) and Davidson (Ulster) were joined by the Munster pair John Moroney and Jerry Murray. Moroney was, of course, a former international and former Munster coach, while Murray was a great player with Cork Constitution who was extremely unfortunate not to have played for his country, although he did have the consolation of having played for the Barbarians.

That quintet saw Ireland register yet another win when, for the first time, Ireland played Italy. That match was at Lansdowne Road on 31 December 1988 and Ireland won 31-15. The only change on the side from that which had defeated Western Samoa was Vincent Cunningham in the centre for Michael Kiernan, who had been injured in the final trial. It was by no means a vintage performance from Ireland but sufficient for the needs. Ireland, as a consequence of those wins, went into the Five Nations Championship on the back of two victories. Prior to the international Italy had played the Ireland Under 25 team at Ravenhill which Ireland won 21-16. That team was captained by Michael Bradley, who had now lost out at senior level to Fergus Aherne. The side also included Peter Clohessy, Terry Kingston, Nick Popplewell, Paddy Johns and Jim Staples of London Irish, a highly rated full-back who was chosen on the wing. All those players went on to have distinguished international careers and, remarkably, five of them, Bradley, Staples, Kingston, Popplewell and Johns were later to captain the Ireland side. Meanwhile the Italians completed their Irish visit by beating the Combined Provinces in Cork 15-14.

Nick Popplewell and Brian Robinson in action

Ireland's first match of the championship was against France at Lansdowne Road on 21 January and what a match that was! When Ireland at one stage built a 21-7 lead, it seemed that the French would perish yet again before the Irish onslaught. But it was not to be as the French came back and scored three second half tries, two of them superb efforts inspired by their great full-back Serge Blanco and outside half Franck Mesnel. Yet it was a match Ireland might have won. David Irwin had been recalled and Pat O'Hara was chosen on the flank and so won his second cap, having won the first as a replacement against Western Samoa. Michael Kiernan and Willie Anderson were also back for that encounter.

Next up was a trip to Cardiff and the match against Wales. Ireland brought in the Trinity College full-back Fergus Dunlea for his first cap with Philip Danaher losing out, and wing John Sexton also lost out when Michael Kiernan was moved to the right wing, with Keith Crossan being recalled on the left. Irwin and Brendan Mullin again formed the centre combination. Yet again Ireland found Cardiff fertile territory and for the third successive occasion won on Welsh soil. Ireland won 19-13. It was Wales who dominated in the first half, but two penalty goals from Paul Thorburn was all they had to show for their superiority.

Early in the second half Michael Kiernan kicked three penalties for Ireland, then in the 57th minute came a truly remarkable and memorable try. Wales tried to initiate an attack deep in Ireland's territory. As the Welsh outside half went to kick the ball, Mannion literally took it off his boot and set off down the right touchline. He outpaced the Welsh pursuit to score a famous try in the right corner after a superb run. Kiernan did not convert, however Ireland led 13-6. But Wales hit back with a penalty and a try to level matters as the match entered its final crucial stage. Then came the decisive score. David Irwin blocked an attempted Welsh clearance and Paul Dean gathered and scored under the Welsh posts. Kiernan converted. Ireland led 19-13 and held the Welsh out in the closing hectic minutes. It was a third successive win in Cardiff and no country had ever previously achieved that against the Welsh in the championship.

Ireland had just one change for the visit of England. Keith Crossan was ruled out through injury and he was replaced by Paul Haycock (Terenure College) who won his first cap, and that made up for his disappointment at not getting a match in the World Cup when he was a member of the squad.

It was not a productive afternoon for Ireland who lost 16-3 and it was a well-deserved win for England. Ireland's last engagement was against Scotland in Murrayfield. That was the centenary match between the countries. It was the Scots who had reason to celebrate as they won 37-21 and it was an especially memorable day for their wing, Iwan Tukalo, who scored three tries. Ireland had made three changes after the defeat by England. Crossan returned for Haycock, Neil Francis displaced Willie Anderson in the second row and made his Five Nations debut. Pat O'Hara was ruled out through injury and was replaced by Denis McBride, who had played against Western Samoa and Italy but not in the Five Nations series.

By this time there had been a very important development at Under 21 level. Ireland had been anxious to establish regular fixtures at this level to provide a bridge between the schools scene and the senior representative arena. So it was that Ireland met Italy in the Under 21 grade in September. Ireland won the match 22-13 and so had an encouraging start. What made the Under 21 grade even more important was the fact that B internationals were no longer on the schedule. They had been discontinued after the 1984–85 season. They were, in fact, revived the following year. Either way the Under 21 international area was seen as a vital part of development for Ireland.

Willie Anderson tackles Dewi Morris, the England scrum half 1989

Ireland's indifferent performances in the championship were reflected in the composition of the Lions team that toured Australia in the summer of 1989. Only four Ireland players were chosen for the Lions. They were Paul Dean, Donal Lenihan, Brendan Mullin and Steve Smith. This was the first tour by the Lions to Australia as a separate entity. Previously, all Lions' visits to Australia had been part of their tours to New Zealand. It was its own compliment to the status the Wallabies had now attained.

It was, too, a highly successful tour as the Lions won the series and won every provincial match. They won the series 2-1 coming from one down to do so. Paul Dean was most unfortunate to get injured in the first match of the tour against Western Australia in Perth and the knee injury he sustained not alone finished his tour but also his career. Brendan Mullin made the Lions team for the first Test but was the only Irish representative in the series. Donal Lenihan proved an outstanding captain on the unbeaten midweek side. It was a rather controversial series. The Lions had shown great character to come from behind to win the series, but some of their rather robust tactics subsequently did not endear them to the Australians. Finlay Calder of Scotland captained the team, Ian McGeechan of Scotland was coach, and Roger Uttley of England assistant coach, with Clive Rowlands of Wales the manager. Noel Murphy had been Ireland's representative on the Lions selection committee. That tour also broke new ground in that it was the first of the short tours by the Lions and lasted eight weeks and embraced twelve matches. The days of the long tours lasting three months and more and at times over 20 matches were gone.

Once more Jimmy Davidson had a chance to build and bond prior to the 1989–90 campaign when a four match tour to Canada and the United States was arranged for September 1989. The touring party was selected well in advance of the tour and it included a very controversial choice in Brian Smith, who had captained Oxford University the previous season. Smith had played for Australia against Ireland in the 1987 World Cup, but apparently had a falling out subsequently with the Wallabies after Bob Dwyer had supplanted Alan Jones as coach. Smith had offered his services to Scotland but was given no guarantees and was told to come into the system and see how things went. Ireland had no inhibitions. After he stated he had an Irish qualification through a grandmother born somewhere in County Wexford, he was duly chosen for the tour to Canada and the United States. He had never played for an Irish club or province or contributed anything to Irish rugby but was still given the reward of an overseas tour. Not surprisingly, the decision of the Ireland selectors was not greeted with unanimous approval.

He had played at scrum-half against Ireland but was more at home in the outside half position. David Irwin had been chosen to captain the side but was ruled out by injury and so it was to Willie Anderson that the selectors turned yet again to lead the team. Ken Reid was, once more, the manager.

The tour opened against British Colombia in Vancouver and Ireland won the match 21-18, but rather fortuitously. They had even more good fortune in the international against Canada in Victoria when it took an interception in injury time for Ireland to get the vital points and win 24-21 as a famous victory beckoned for the Canadians. It was an interception by Paul Clinch that enabled John Sexton to score the vital try. Ireland overwhelmed Mid West in Chicago 58-6 and then defeated the United States in Downing Island, New York, by 32-7 in a match played in almost 100 degrees of heat. Yet again no caps were awarded for this tour, an extraordinary decision bearing in mind that Ireland had played Canada in the World Cup two years previously when caps were awarded. The USA had also played in the 1987 World Cup finals and caps were awarded by all the countries who played in them. One element of that tour was that Philip Danaher had played well enough in the centre to suggest he had a very definite future in that position.

There was no soft prelude to the Five Nations Championship series as the visiting touring team was New Zealand, the reigning World champions, who had embellished that achievement with a succession of great wins against all opposition.

Ireland played New Zealand on 18 November and by then New Zealand had beaten Leinster, Munster and Connacht and had done so in a convincing manner. Nor did Ireland offer them any trouble.

Ireland included three new caps, Smith at outside half, Nick Popplewell at loose head prop and the Ulster full-back Philip Rainey. He had been in the World Cup squad but had not played, and so, like Haycock the previous season, got the much cherished cap. Ken Hooks, the Ulster wing, was recalled to the side after eight years, having won his only previous cap in 1981.

Having played with the wind, Ireland trailed 13-6 at the interval, by which stage Popplewell had to go off with a rib injury and was replaced by Des Fitzgerald. Hooks also failed to finish the match and was replaced by Danaher. But New Zealand certainly finished the job and won 23-6 in a match highlighted by a superb try from New Zealand full-back John Gallagher, a man with very strong Irish family connections. He subsequently, many years later, was to play for the Irish A team after he had returned to the union code, having played Rugby League in England. Ulster fared no better than the other Irish teams against that All Blacks side in the final match of their Irish itinerary.

The B internationals were resumed in December 1989 and Ireland played Scotland at Murrayfield in an exciting match that ended in a 22 all draw. Included in that Ireland team was Ken Murphy, the Cork Constitution full-back, whose father Noel A. and grandfather Noel F. had played for Ireland. Jim Staples was also in the team, but full internationals who had played in the Five Nations series were still not eligible and the only full cap in the Irish side was Paul Collins, who had played against Canada in the World Cup.

England did a demolition job on Ireland in the opening match of the Five Nations Championship at Twickenham in January. Ireland had a team that showed six alterations to the side that lost to New Zealand, and Ken Murphy was in the side and thus created history. By his selection it meant father, son and grandson had played for Ireland, the only such instance in the history of the game in Ireland. Murphy replaced Philip Rainey. Another new cap was the Wanderers prop Gary Halpin, like Murphy, a former schools international. Brian Smith was dropped and replaced by Peter Russell from Instonians, who had also played for Ireland at schools level. Donal Lenihan was ruled out by injury and Neil Francis came in for him, while Popplewell was omitted in a rearranged front row of Halpin, Smith and Des Fitzgerald. Michael Kiernan was back after injury.

England led 7-0 at the interval, but despite playing into the wind in the second half, once England began to open up the game, Ireland had no answer. Yet again the side was recast for the visit of Scotland to Lansdowne Road. Smith returned at outside half and Lenihan to the second row. Halpin lost out as John Fitzgerald returned to the side to win his third cap. John McDonald was at hooker for the injured Steve Smith, whom McDonald had replaced during the course of the England match.

The changes did not bring the required result and Scotland won 13-10. Now it was on to Paris for the third match and once more the Irish were comprehensively outplayed and lost 31-12. That win for France came after they had lost heavily to both England and Scotland. Ireland never looked like making it a hat-trick of losses for the French.

It was a much changed Ireland team. Ken Hooks returned on the wing, Kiernan moved to centre where Brendan Mullin was an absentee due to injury, and David Irwin was omitted, and so Ireland had a centre combination of Philip Danaher and Kiernan. Philip Matthews was ruled out through illness and Denis McBride was recalled to the back row. Neil Francis was chosen ahead of Willie Anderson and the captaincy reverted to Donal Lenihan. Terry Kingston was at hooker for John McDonald. Ireland did reasonably well in the first half and Crossan was unfortunate to have a try disallowed. But an interval deficit of 10-6 was soon turned into a deficit of much more intimidating proportions and Ireland lost 31-12.

The visit of Wales to Dublin saw Ireland attempting to avoid a whitewash and that was achieved when Ireland won 14-8. By the time this match took place the Scots had already won the Grand Slam, creating a major surprise by beating England at Murrayfield. Brendan Mullin was back for the match against Wales. Michael Bradley was recalled at scrum-half for Fergus Aherne. Ireland had named John McDonald at hooker but he cried off minutes before the match and Terry Kingston filled the No. 2 jersey.

Ireland started very well and soon led 10-0 with a try from Brian Smith, converted by Kiernan, and another from Denis McBride. Ireland lost Bradley through injury and Aherne came on as replacement. Now the task was to protect the 10 points interval advantage into the wind. Wales did cut the deficit with a try, but Ireland defended well, and when Kingston scored a try following a line-out won by Lenihan, Irish anxieties were considerably eased. Wales did get a late consolation try but Ireland had been worth their six points win and their back-to-back victories over Wales, the first time Ireland had achieved that against the Welsh for 20 years.

The American Eagles undertook a two match tour to Ireland in March and played the Irish Students at Anglesea Road and the Ireland Under 25 team at Thomond Park. For some of those who attended at Anglesea Road, it was their first glimpse of a young wing, Simon Geoghegan. He had been creating quite an impression with London Irish. That Students team was managed by Noel O'Mahony and coached by George Hook, a man who had been involved in the coaching area for some time and who had played for St Mary's College. The Under 25 side was managed by Noel Murphy, with former Ireland scrum-half John Moloney as coach and Ciaran Fitzgerald as his assistant. That same three man team was now also in charge of the Ireland Under 21 team.

Off the field there was considerable activity. The IRFU had set up a President's Review Committee with the brief of reporting on such matters as the Structure of the Union committee, the increasing pressure on players, the method of appointing the Ireland coach and selectors, and the IRFU coaching structure.

There was, too, another important development with regard to the Exiles. The IRFU had appointed Tom Kiernan chairman of the Irish Exiles committee and set up a structure in Britain with a view to getting players there with Irish qualifications to play for the Exiles and to come into the Irish system. In October 1989 an important meeting took place in London to progress these matters further. One of the objectives was to get an Exiles team to compete in the Interprovincial Championship, thus affording players a good opportunity to reveal their abilities. A match had been arranged against Ulster and the objective was to get an Exiles side into the interprovincial series within a matter of a few years.

Meanwhile, money matters were occupying the International Board. They held a special meeting in London in March. All member nations were represented. That meeting considered the responses of the unions to changes in the law relating to amateurism. In the natural order of things there were divergent options, but the necessary 75 per cent voting strength for amendments to the regulations was forthcoming on some issues. In that regard one very significant change was that payment was now allowed for what was deemed financial disadvantage resulting from the time spent in preparation for national representative matches. Each union had discretionary powers about payments. There was a stipulation that any payments must not exceed any money lost by a player or up to four nominated officials of a union's national team, the maximum payment not to exceed £20 per day.

Another item on the agenda was the vexed question of communication for reward. It was decided to establish a working party to study aspects of that and it was chaired by Sir Ewart Bell.

On the home front there was eager anticipation that a new national league was to start in 1990–91 and the special subcommittee to oversee that was in place. Roy Loughead of Ulster was in the chair of this important subcommittee. Things were changing at quite a rapid pace in several areas and even the IRFU Commercial subcommittee under the chairmanship of Mick Cuddy now had a commercial consultant to offer advice. He was the former Walker Cup golfer Roddy Carr.

Jimmy Davidson had completed three years as national coach and none of his predecessors had exceeded that tenure. So there was speculation about a successor. But Davidson had expressed a desire to carry on and coach Ireland for the next World Cup scheduled for the autumn of 1991.

A very important change had, however, taken place with regard to the Ireland Selection committee for the 1990–91 season. It was decided that in future Ireland would have a manager who would also be chairman of selectors. Well gone now the days when the selectors chose their own chairman and coach. The man chosen to manage the team was Ken Reid, who thus returned to the selection arena, an area in which he had served over a decade earlier.

CHAPTER 28

FITZGERALD AT THE HELM

JIMMY DAVIDSON WAS TO BE DISAPPOINTED and did not realise his ambition to stay on as a coach. His period in that capacity had not been marked by much success, however hard he tried. One championship win in each of his three years, allied to wins over Western Samoa and Italy did not offer strong recommendation for a protracted stay at the helm.

An extremely decent and honest man, some of the players found him too intense and at times his lengthy discourses prior to training sessions tended to have an adverse effect, so much so that some players complained that they were mentally tired before they had to go out and undertake hard training sessions. He had called in a fitness adviser and did all within his capacity to get the best out of his players. There was also a feeling that he had got three years as coach and none of his predecessors had exceeded that tenure. Two of them had not even lasted that long.

Three candidates were interviewed for the coaching position. They were Ciaran Fitzgerald, John Moloney and Pat Whelan. Fitzgerald, in fact, had been appointed as Connacht coach for the season and he and Moloney had formed a good team with the Under 21 side to which Moloney was coach and Fitzgerald his assistant. They had played together for St Mary's College and for Ireland, knew each other well and were very comfortable working together. Whelan carried the greatest level of coaching experience of the three. He had coached his club Garryowen, his province Munster and the Ireland B team.

But it was Fitzgerald who was chosen and he had Moloney as his assistant. That meant that Connacht had to look elsewhere for a coach. Kevin Flynn, who had been chairman of the selectors when Ireland won the Triple Crown in 1982, was invited to return to the selection committee and Jerry Murray and Harry McKibbin Junior completed the five man line-up. Moloney as assistant coach sat in on selection meetings.

So a brave new world, and one could say Fitzgerald's selection as coach was a brave decision. His leadership qualities had been well demonstrated as Ireland captain and, indeed, Moloney had also captained Ireland.

Off the field the International Board took some important decisions in relation to allowances, compensation and reimbursements and communication for reward. These came about following the review the Board had undertaken. Players were now able to receive payment for attendance at any social function or gathering organised by their union, club or supporters' club, provided that the benefits did not specifically relate to any actual playing activity. The maximum personal allowance payable on tours remained at £20 sterling a day, but there was a big increase in the compensation payable for financial disadvantage for those preparing for national representative matches. That was increased from £20 to £40 per day.

The climate was changing rapidly in the circumstances that now obtained. Broken time had been the very issue that had led to the formation of the Rugby League a century earlier. There was, too, in place in the IRFU an Amateur Status subcommittee. That was chaired by Roly Meates. Other members were Sir Ewart Bell, Don Crowley, Tom Kiernan and Billy Lavery.

Matters were moving forward in relation to the Exiles, too. An Exiles Under 21-Students team was formed as well as a senior side. The Under 21-Students team played four matches including one against the Irish Under 21 team, another against an English Students side, as well as against Leinster and an Anglo-Scots team. The senior side played against Ulster and the Welsh Exiles.

The formation of an Irish Colleges Rugby Union to cater for players attending third level institutions, apart from the established universities, had been another important development. A subcommittee had been set up the previous season under the chairmanship of Noel O'Mahony with representatives from the universities and colleges on the committee. The object was to establish proper communications between the IRFU, the universities and the colleges. The contribution of the universities to Irish rugby runs through the thread of this history. Now the third level colleges which had been established were also on board unquestionably to the benefit of the game in Ireland. Like the universities, they also provided a very important bridge from the schools scene.

The Irish Students, the by-product of universities and colleges, played two matches against Argentina in Cork in October 1990 and in Edinburgh on the eve of the senior international against Scotland. Another important development was the decision to play a Students World Cup in Italy in 1992. The Irish Students team was entered for that.

The desire to get youngsters into the game who did not attend rugby-playing schools prompted the establishment of a Youth subcommittee in September. Brendan O'Dowd was the man entrusted with the chairmanship of this committee and it embraced two representatives from each province, one from each province to act as selector.

The Youths played an Irish Schools B selection in March 1991 and the Youths won as they had won their inaugural meeting the previous season. With a provincial competition now in place for the Youths, the object was to organise international fixtures at this grade.

At senior level, Ciaran Fitzgerald and John Moloney had the opportunity to assess the talent at their disposal prior to the Five Nations series when Argentina came on a tour in October. The Argentinians had beaten the Irish Students in Cork and had lost to Ireland B in Limerick before they played the international in Dublin. The B side included Simon Geoghegan, who had declared for Connacht in the interprovincial series, as of course had Jim Staples two years previously. Another London Irish player now with Connacht was centre David Curtis whose father Brian had played for Ireland.

The Ireland Under 25 side had also played Spain early in September and Staples and Geoghegan also played in that encounter, won 36-17 by Ireland.

Donal Lenihan led the senior side against Argentina on 27 October and Ireland included three new caps. They were the Bective Rangers No. 8 Phil Lawlor, the Blackrock College scrum-half Alain Rolland

and Paddy Johns, a dental student from Trinity College.

It was a remarkable match and remembered for the inordinate amount of injury time played by the referee, Colin Hawke, of New Zealand. It was as well for Ireland that he did, for it took a long-range penalty deep into injury time from Michael Kiernan to win the match for Ireland 20-18. It was a very fortunate victory indeed after the visitors had looked as if they had clinched victory when they scored a try and it was converted by their brilliant outside half Hugo Porta with injury time looming. That left Argentina a point ahead. Then came Ireland's late late reprieve when Kiernan kicked the match-winning penalty goal for a two points win.

Ciaran Fitzgerald had made a winning start to his tenure as Ireland coach. And if fortune favoured Ireland that afternoon, the Irish were to enjoy a similar level of good luck in the Five Nations series.

A match that was to have a profound influence on the selectors' thinking was the B international against Scotland at Ravenhill on 22 December. Ireland played extremely well in that match and won 16-0. Meanwhile a decision had been taken that, just after Christmas, the Ireland squad would travel to Portugal for warm weather training and they duly made that trip.

Ireland's first match in the championship was against France at Lansdowne Road on 2 February. That Ireland team included only six players who had been in the side against Argentina. Donal Lenihan was ruled out by a shoulder/neck injury and did not play in the championship. The only forward in the side who had played against Argentina was prop Des Fitzgerald.

The side contained six new caps. They were Rob Saunders, the London Irish scrum-half, Simon Geoghegan, now playing with Connacht in the interprovincial series, Gordon Hamilton, the NIFC and Ulster flanker, Mick Galwey, the Shannon and Munster second row, Brian Rigney, the Greystones second row, and Brian Robinson, the Ballymena and Ulster No. 8.

Saunders was made captain of the side; so for the first time since 1956 when Jim Ritchie led Ireland, a man was made captain on his debut.

Ireland led 10-6 at the interval, but conceded a try after the break when Saunders's loose kick was gathered by Serge Blanco, who captained France that afternoon, and Blanco opened the way for a try. Michael Kiernan put Ireland back in the lead again with a penalty, but a penalty and a late converted try saw France prevail. But in many respects it had been an encouraging performance from Ireland.

Ireland went to Cardiff on 16 February and the team showed three changes. Ken Murphy, Ken Hooks and Kiernan were dropped. Three more new caps were enlisted, Jim Staples, Jack Clarke, the Dolphin wing, and David Curtis.

Ireland preserved their unbeaten record in Cardiff when the match was drawn 21-21 and Geoghegan scored a memorable try. Both Clarke and Staples also marked their international debuts by scoring tries. But Staples injured an elbow and was replaced by Ken Murphy during the course of the match.

England came to Dublin early in March and left with a 16-7 win. It was not until the closing stages that England copperfastened their victory. Ireland had missed scoring chances by exercising some poor options. Yet again Geoghegan scored a try. Keith Crossan had been restored to the side for Clarke and Neil Francis displaced Mick Galwey.

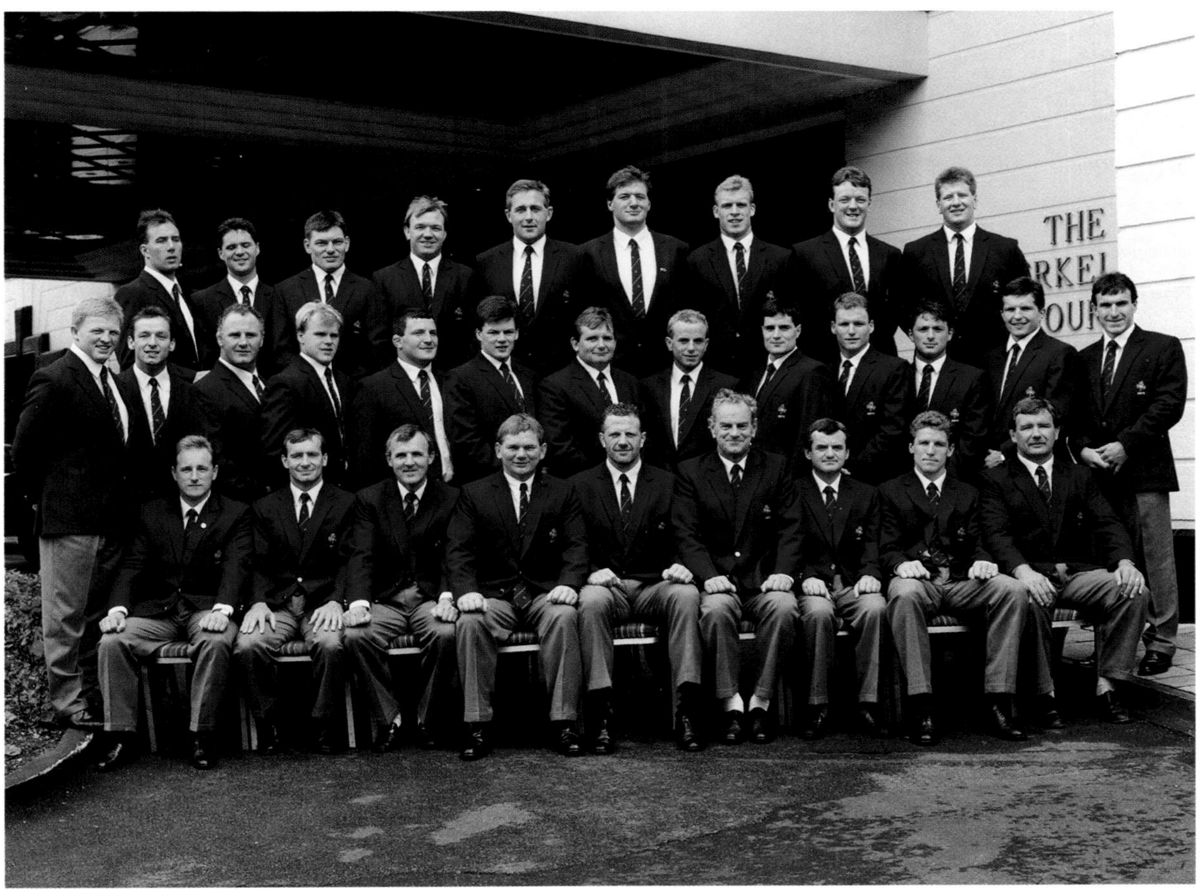

1991 World Cup squad

Ireland's last assignment was against Scotland in Murrayfield, a very exciting encounter which ended with Scotland winning 28-25. Ireland fielded unchanged, and for the third successive match Geoghegan scored a try. He had certainly made a great impact in his first season in the Ireland team. For Brendan Mullin it was an especially auspicious occasion. He scored his 15th try for Ireland and so broke George Stephenson's record of 14 tries. That record had stood for 61 years. Mullin became the highest try scorer in international rugby for Ireland that afternoon.

So Ireland ended the season with just one point from the championship. They had played some really good rugby but had paid a high price for going into three matches without a recognised place kicker. Brian Smith took over the role when Kiernan was dropped, but he was not a place kicker of the high quality that is required at this level.

Smith, who had joined the Ireland scene in controversial circumstances, left it in an even more dubious fashion. He was now with the Leicester club and some days prior to Ireland's match against Scotland there were strong suggestions that he was going to sign a Rugby League contract with a club in his native Australia as soon as Ireland's involvement in the championship was finished. He categorically denied this at a training session three days prior to the match in Murrayfield and gave assurances to the Ireland management that the reason he was travelling to Australia was to visit his family. He denied any suggestion that it had anything to do with playing Rugby League, an area in which his former mentor Alan Jones was now involved in Australia.

Four days after the match against Scotland, it was announced that Smith had indeed signed with a Rugby League club and the Irish were left to think again about the outside half berth for the forthcoming tour to Namibia and, of course, the World Cup scheduled for the autumn. What compounded their problems was that Ralph Keyes, who had been overlooked for Smith, was out injured and not available for the tour. Ciaran Fitzgerald and manager Ken Reid felt especially let down by Smith.

The tour to Namibia was arranged as a warm-up for the World Cup. Namibia had not been operating as a separate country when the World Cup draw was made, having previously played as South West Africa prior to independence and were part of the South Africa Rugby Board. But they had built a good side and had a good rugby tradition. Namibia had already defeated Italy twice and Zimbabwe, both of whom were in the World Cup finals.

A number of circumstances combined to make life difficult, infinitely more difficult, for Ireland than had been anticipated. The most important one was that Namibia were a very useful side and deserved their two Test wins. The tour took place in mid-July and at an altitude of over 5,000 feet. Some Irish players suffered in the altitude and stomach upsets, for one thing, hit more than a few of the players. In addition, Brian Rigney tore a cruciate knee ligament and was ruled out of the World Cup. Rigney was replaced on the tour by Donal Lenihan, now fit again and striving to make the World Cup squad.

Ireland won the opening tour match 45-16 against Namibia B in Windhoek, but lost the first Test 15-6 in the same venue. Keith Crossan missed the match because of a stomach upset and some of the players were less than 100 per cent when they took the field in that first Test. Ireland played Vincent Cunningham at outside half rather than opt for Nicky Barry, the Garryowen player, who had toured France in 1988 and Canada and the United States in 1989, but still awaited the breakthrough to a full cap.

Richard Wallace, the Garryowen wing, won his first cap when he came on as a replacement for Geoghegan in the second half, and Noel Mannion came in for Rigney. Lenihan played in the third match against Namibia South Sub Union in Keetmanschoop just 24 hours after he arrived in Namibia. Ireland won the match 35-4 and so went into the second Test, again in Windhoek, with two wins and a defeat.

Crossan was fit for the match but Geoghegan was ruled out and so too were Matthews and Pat O'Hara, both of whom were ill. Saunders regained the captaincy. But yet again Namibia won and did so comprehensively by 26-15. Lenihan was in the second row in Rigney's absence. Crossan had to leave the field after 40 minutes and was replaced by Barry, who thus got his first cap. Francis was injured and ruled out after 54 minutes and Mick Galwey replaced him.

So as Ireland prepared for the World Cup, Fitzgerald and his management colleagues had to reflect on one win and a draw from seven internationals. That was disappointing, to say the least, but Fitzgerald felt that his side was capable of much better than that, and he felt he still had the players to make an impression in the World Cup.

CHAPTER 29

THE SECOND WORLD CUP AND ITS AFTERMATH

THE PREPARATIONS AND ARRANGEMENTS for the 1991 World Cup presented some problems for the IRFU and indeed the other home unions and France. But some of the difficulties that had been encountered in 1987 were avoided.

The new chairman of RWC was Russ Thomas of New Zealand, who had succeeded John Kendal Carpenter, who unfortunately had died suddenly in 1990.

All the players in the tournament were required to sign a Participation Agreement and this caused some differences of opinion between the IRFU and the players. There were aspects of the agreement that the players wanted clarifying. The players now had an agent, a sign of the changing face of the game. Eventually the problems were overcome and so it was a case of getting on with preparations for the encounters on the field.

Ireland had been drawn in Pool 2 together with Zimbabwe, Japan and Scotland. Zimbabwe had topped the African qualifying group with full points, and Japan had finished runners-up in the Asian-Pacific Group. Philip Matthews was named as captain of the Ireland side, with Ken Reid as manager and Ciaran Fitzgerald coach assisted by John Moloney.

Ireland played some warm-up matches including a visit to Gloucester and also a match at the Cooke RFC ground in Belfast. No new caps were included in the 26 man squad. Several survivors remained from the 1987 tournament. These were Keith Crossan, Brendan Mullin, Des Fitzgerald, Terry Kingston, Steve Smith, who had joined the 1987 squad as a replacement, Neil Francis, Donal Lenihan and Philip Matthews.

There was a return to the international scene for Ralph Keyes and he and Vincent Cunningham were selected as the outside halves. Rob Saunders and Fergus Aherne were the scrum-halves.

Ireland's first assignment was against Zimbabwe at Lansdowne Road on Sunday, 6 October. It was a historic occasion on two grounds, the first international between Ireland and Zimbabwe and the first time that an international was played at Lansdowne Road on a Sunday.

Ireland made a very impressive opening and won 55-11. Ireland scored eight tries in the demolition and the superiority of the Ireland pack was illustrated by the fact that six of the tries were scored by forwards. It was a day of triumph for two Ireland players. No. 8 Brian Robinson scored four tries, a record for an Ireland player in an international. So also for Ralph Keyes, who marked his return to the international arena by kicking five penalty goals and four conversions for a total of 23 points. That broke the 22 points record held by Ollie Campbell.

Next for Ireland was the match against Japan at Lansdowne Road on 9 October. The Japanese, unable to match Ireland up front in the basic elements of scrummaging, rucking and mauling and the line-out, decided on a policy of running the ball from every position. It was entertaining but not effective as a means of achieving victory.

Ireland established an early 13 points advantage before Japan scored a try and conversion. But Ireland's response was rapid and effective. Jim Staples scored a try, Keyes converted and Ireland led 19-6 at the interval.

That was advanced to a lead of 28-6 in the second half and while Japan scored a spectacular try, Noel Mannion got Ireland's fourth try and Ireland eventually won 32-16.

Qualification for the quarter-finals was now assured but Ireland had to go to Murrayfield for the last match in the pool. A win would have meant playing Western Samoa in the quarter-final; a defeat meant a match against Australia at Lansdowne Road.

As events transpired, it was Scotland who won in Murrayfield, but rather fortunately. It was a match marred in part by a very late and dangerous tackle on Jim Staples by Finlay Calder. In the first half it was Ireland who had been on top and some great kicking by Ralph Keyes enabled Ireland to lead 12-9 at the interval. When Keyes added another three points 15 minutes into the second half, Ireland led 15-9. Keyes had kicked four penalty goals and also a dropped goal. Staples had clearly been injured in the incident with Calder and would have been well advised to have left the field. But he played on and his distress was evident in a crucial incident that turned the match Scotland's way.

The Scotland scrum-half Gary Armstrong kicked a high ball into Irish territory, but Staples allowed the ball to bounce from his chest and it went into the hands of Scotland's wing Tony Stanger, who passed to Graham Shiel and Shiel, who had come on as a replacement at outside half, scored a try which was converted by Gavin Hastings and the scores were level.

Simon Geoghegan in full flight against Australia in World Cup quarter final at Lansdowne Road 1991

The initiative had swung to Scotland and they underlined their superiority as Hastings kicked a penalty. Then Armstrong scored a late try which Hastings converted for a very flattering 24-15 win.

So it was Ireland to meet Australia in the quarter-final at Lansdowne Road and this will go down as one of the greatest internationals witnessed at the oldest international ground in the world. It will also be remembered as the match that got away from Ireland when a huge upset seemed imminent as the match entered the final three minutes and Ireland led by three points. But with the crowd ready to acclaim what would have been a famous Ireland win, the Australians struck back with a try.

The match had started with Australia scoring a great try through David Campese, which Mick Lynagh converted. But it did not induce any inferiority in the Ireland side who proceeded to take the Wallabies on up front. Keyes kicked two penalty goals to leave Ireland level at the interval and the Australians knew they were in for a tough fight.

Lynagh kicked a penalty for Australia early in the second half but Keyes, who had a truly outstanding tournament, dropped a goal to bring Ireland level again at 9-9.

Then Campese struck again for a try and Lynagh converted to leave Australia 15-9 in front and Keyes kicked yet another penalty to cut the deficit to 15-12. The Australians could not shake free from the Irish tenacity and dedication of purpose and, with six minutes remaining, the ground erupted. The Australians were attacking but Staples gathered the ball and kicked down the left-hand touchline. Campese was slow to react and failed to clear the danger and Jack Clarke was up to gather the ball. Clarke had Gordon Hamilton in support and passed to the flanker. Hamilton set off for the Australian line and the Australians were unable to catch him as he scored wide on the left. Keyes kicked a magnificent conversion and Ireland led 18-15.

Ireland scrum half Rob Saunders gets his pass away against Australia 1991

A major surprise was now very much on, but the drama was still not over. A ball kicked into Irish territory was fielded by Rob Saunders. Had he kicked to touch, then the likelihood was that Ireland would have won. But instead he kicked downfield. The ball was gathered by Australian wing David Egerton. He kicked back downfield. The ball rolled inside the Ireland '25' and Brian Robinson touched it with a hand and it went over the Ireland line and had to be touched down for a five yard scrum to Australia.

They won possession and while Lynagh had the chance to drop a goal and so level the match, instead he passed outside, looped behind his backs and took a pass after Campese had been tackled to score a try. It was a real heart-break for the Irish but a tribute to the Wallabies that they managed to come back when all seemed lost.

The Australian coach Bob Dwyer was effusive in his praise for Ireland after the match. 'What a match and what a performance from Ireland! Yes, I thought we had lost it when Ireland got that try. My knees are still knocking. Quite honestly I thought we were gone,' he said. So did most in the ground that memorable afternoon.

Australia went on to give a superb display in defeating the holders New Zealand in the semi-final at Lansdowne Road and then, in a disappointing final at Twickenham, defeated England to claim the Webb Ellis trophy.

So near and yet so far for Ireland, yet such had been the performances in the World Cup that there was great optimism about the prospects in the forthcoming Five Nations series.

But it was a case of optimism misplaced. Ireland's first match was against Wales in Dublin. Gordon Hamilton was injured and replaced by the Shannon flanker Mick Fitzgibbon, who won his first cap. Richard Wallace and Keith Crossan came in for Simon Geoghegan, who was unable to play because of a family illness, and Jack Clarke who was omitted.

Ireland dominated in the first half, but an interval lead of 9-6 was not compatible with the level of Ireland's territorial superiority. Ireland's points had come from Ralph Keyes through three penalty goals. When Richard Wallace scored a try and Keyes converted, Ireland led 15-6 and were in control of the match or so it seemed. Two penalty goals from Neil Jenkins enabled Wales to get to within three points of Ireland, and then, remarkably, it was Wales who took control of the match and they won it with a try after applying a lot of pressure on the Ireland line. It was a thoroughly disappointing finish to a match that had looked in safe keeping. Ireland never recovered that season from the defeat.

Ireland scrum half, Rob Saunders, gets the ball away against Wales at Lansdowne Road

That was the last match that Donal Lenihan played for Ireland and brought to an end a career that embraced 52 caps and which lasted from 1981 to 1992. He is still the most capped Munster forward to play for Ireland. He was dropped after the defeat by Wales for the visit to Twickenham, as were Keith Crossan and Rob Saunders, with Geoghegan returning and Mick Galwey and Fergus Aherne being recalled. Then on the evening prior to the match, Des Fitzgerald was forced to cry off because of illness and he was replaced by Gary Halpin.

England scored a try in the first minute of the match and it was converted, but Ireland hit back and Keyes got a fine try as he outwitted the England defence with a clever dummy and then added the conversion points. He and Jonathan Webb, the England full-back, exchanged penalties and it was 9-9 after half an hour. But it was England who got on top and two tries before the interval left them well in command of the match as they led 24-9. Ireland could make no inroads into their deficit and England added 14 points in the second period for a 38-9 win.

Inevitably Ireland made changes for the visit of Scotland and Kenny Murphy returned in place of the injured Jim Staples and Philip Danaher was also recalled. But the much needed win did not come. The Scots led at the interval 9-3, with Keyes having kicked a penalty for Ireland. Ireland had the wind in the second period but failed to use it. The Scottish forwards' superiority, notably in the line-out, saw them increase their advantage early in the second period and it was generally a poor performance from Ireland who faced the intimidating prospect of travelling to play France in Paris in the final match of the championship.

Prior to the announcement of the team, Brendan Mullin announced his retirement from international rugby. That was a blow as here was a quality centre who had served Ireland so well. New caps in the Ballymena outside half Derek McAleese and the Garryowen flanker Paul Hogan were brought into the team. Neil Francis was ruled out through injury and so Brian Rigney got a recall.

The French overwhelmed Ireland in Paris and scored a victory of record proportions, 44 points to 12. The French scored seven tries, Ireland's only reply coming from four penalty goals kicked by McAleese. So it was the wooden spoon for Ireland, a sad end to a season in which earlier Ireland had stood on the brink of reaching the World Cup semi-finals.

Ireland outside half Ralph Keyes gains possession against England at Twickenham 1992

There was one casualty of the poor performances and that was the Ireland assistant coach, John Moloney. The decision to dispense with his services was not unexpected as the rumblings and rumours were in full swing prior to the match in Paris. The problem was that no one spoke to Moloney. With Ireland due to travel to New Zealand in May, Moloney was not asked about his availability. Instead, an approach was made to Gerry Murphy. Murphy had a very good coaching pedigree. He had been involved at club and provincial level and, indeed, with the Ireland Under 21 team. One difficulty was that he and Ciaran Fitzgerald did not really know each other, a fact readily admitted by Fitzgerald.

Ciaran Fitzgerald did not have any enthusiasm for dismissing Moloney, but in effect did not really have any say in the decision which was finalised on the weekend the Irish side was in Paris.

With Ken Reid's tenure as manager due to end in June, Reid suggested that it would be in the best interests of the team if he were to step aside before the tour to New Zealand and allow Noel Murphy to take over as manager. Murphy was the man the IRFU had chosen to manage the team after Reid. It was a generous gesture from Reid and a highly practical one.

Meanwhile the IRFU Amateur Status subcommittee had a busy season and met eight times under the chairmanship of Roly Meates. The responsibility of the subcommittee was to ensure that the International Board regulations on amateurism were enforced. With this in mind, Sir Ewart Bell, one of Ireland's International Board's representatives who had succeeded Harry McKibbin in that capacity, was appointed as Regulations officer. A Code of Practice for players selected and invited to play for Ireland teams had been drawn up in consultation with representatives of the players and approved by the IRFU and was implemented. Central to this issue was the payment of compensation for financial disadvantage to the Irish players.

The Union had appointed Slattery Public Relations as their advisers and the Commercial subcommittee under the chairmanship of Mick Cuddy worked in close harmony with Slattery PR. Sponsorship and related matters were important items on the agenda. Slattery PR also advised on publicity related to the promotion of the game. In that regard one of the innovations was the publication of a newsletter produced by the firm for the dissemination of information on ongoing developments in Irish rugby.

There had, too, been a change in the important position of the IRFU secretary. Former Ireland prop Paddy O'Donoghue, who had done so splendid a job as Irish organiser for the World Cup, took over the secretarial role from Paddy Moss, who took early retirement.

There was a major development with regard to the Exiles. Arrangements were now in place for the Exiles to participate in the Interprovincial Championship in the 1992–93 season.

The squad to tour New Zealand was selected and Philip Danaher was named as tour captain. It marked the return to the international squad of Michael Bradley. But some players were not available including Philip Matthews, Phil Lawlor, Gordon Hamilton and Neil Francis. In fact Bradley was the only tangible link with the team that won the Triple Crown and Championship in 1985. He, Terry Kingston and Steve Smith were the only links left with the squad that had participated in the 1987 World Cup. So it was a relatively inexperienced 30 man squad that went to the most formidable of all rugby nations.

Ireland opened the tour with a win over South Canterbury in Timaru by 21-16, but lost 38-13 to Canterbury in Christchurch. A victim of this match was Richard Wallace, who sustained a broken jaw as a result of a punch and he took no further part in the tour. He was replaced by Dominic O'Brien, the Clontarf and Leinster wing. O'Brien is a New Zealander who had joined Clontarf.

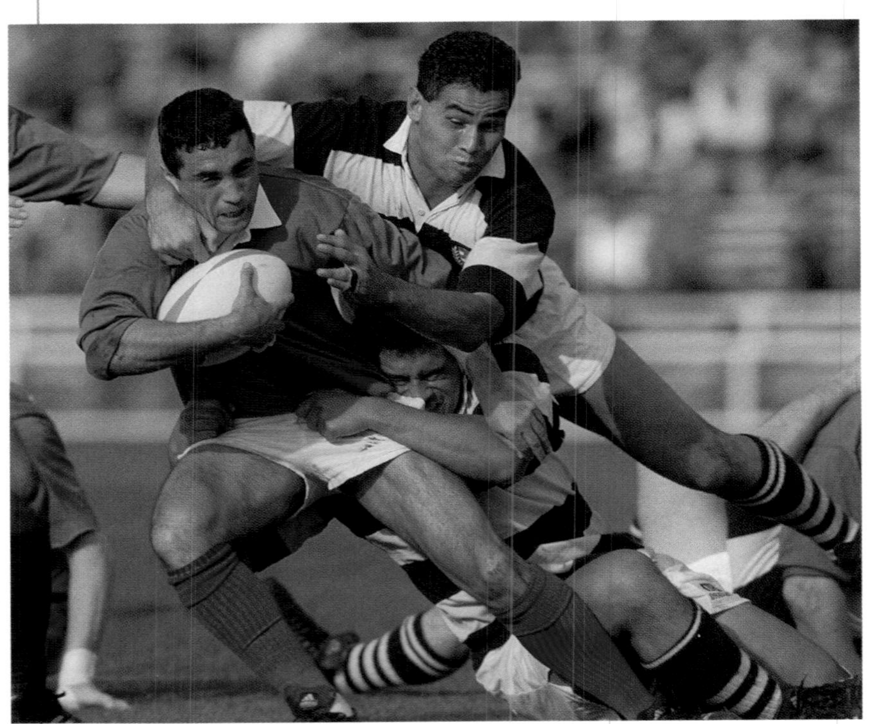

Auckland v Ireland at Eden Park 1992. Michael Bradley caught in possession

In the third match of the tour, Ireland scored a good win over Bay of Plenty in Rotorua by 39-23, but four days later were overwhelmed by Auckland 62-7. The fifth match was in Gisborne where Ireland defeated Poverty Bay-East Coast 22-7. The next assignment was the first Test in Dunedin.

It had been an unfortunate tour for Danaher, who was injured early in the first match. He was declared fit for the Test and so led an Ireland team that had new caps in wings Ronnie Carey from Dungannon and Neville Furlong from UCG, prop Paul McCarthy from Cork Constitution, and flanker Kelvin Leahy from Wanderers.

Ireland started brilliantly and led 12-0 after twelve minutes. In fact, the lead could have been even more but Peter Russell missed a fine dropped goal chance and Carey was unable to hold on after an interception.

Danaher had to leave the field and was replaced by Mark McCall, the Bangor and Ulster centre, who won his first cap. Then Leahy, who had played extremely well in a pack in which Nick Popplewell and

Brian Robinson were outstanding, broke an ankle and was replaced by Brian Rigney.

The All Blacks gradually clawed their way back into the game but one of their tries was very doubtful and the Australian referee Sandy McNeill certainly erred in his judgment. Two tries from Vincent Cunningham, one from Jim Staples and three conversions from Russell left Ireland trailing by just three points with the game entering its final phase. Then Ireland lost a great chance when they broke out of defence, but unfortunately Carey was unable to gather the ball and the opportunity was lost. New Zealand hung on, if only barely, for a three points win.

One can but speculate as to what the effect would have been had Ireland won that match, but they earned tremendous praise for their performance and the All Blacks captain, Sean Fitzpatrick, was the first to admit that his team had been very lucky to have won.

But such efforts could not be sustained and Ireland lost 58-24 to Manawatu in Palmerston North in the second last match of the tour. The second Test was in Wellington which lived up to its reputation for wind and rain. Ireland, in fact, made a dream start when Furlong scored a try and Russell converted. But it was a very depleted Ireland side. Danaher and Leahy were ruled out and Mick Fitzgibbon, who had played so bravely in the first Test, lasted no more than a quarter of an hour. Russell, too, took the field less than fully fit. Michael Bradley, who had regained the scrum-half berth in the first Test, captained Ireland in Danaher's absence.

Ireland's injury problems were compounded when, after Fitzgibbon's departure, Staples and Russell followed early in the second half. Paddy Kenny, the man who had toured Japan in 1985 and had joined the tour as the replacement for Leahy, won his first cap when he replaced Fitzgibbon. Ken Murphy came in for Staples and when Russell left the field, Jack Clarke, a wing, was the replacement with Mark McCall moving to the outside half position. That realigned force was swamped in the second half.

The All Blacks ran riot and scored 44 points for a total of 59 and a win by 53 points. That amounted to a record defeat for Ireland. It was a sad end to a season that had promised much and in the end yielded so very little.

Ciaran Fitzgerald was reappointed as coach for the 1992–93 season and Noel Murphy manager. But the selection committee underwent radical alteration. Kevin Flynn and Jerry Murray, who had completed his tenure, both stood down. They were replaced by Pat Whelan and Frank Sowman. Sowman had played for Wanderers and had been chairman of the Leinster selectors. But now national selectors could no longer sit on their provincial selection committee. This was a complete reversal to the order that obtained in the past when a man could not be a national selector unless he was also on his provincial selection committee. Harry McKibbin and Ciaran Fitzgerald were the only survivors on the selection committee from the previous season.

On 12 September 1992, the Exiles played their first match in the Interprovincial Championship. The match was against Munster. The Exiles, who had former international full-back Barry O'Driscoll as chairman of selectors and Dave Donovan as honorary secretary, with John O'Driscoll as coach, made a great start to the interprovincial series. They defeated Munster by 19-13 at the London Irish ground in Sunbury. The Exiles, of course, had Simon Geoghegan, Jim Staples and David Curtis in their ranks now, and they were a considerable loss to Connacht.

The Exiles' second assignment was against Leinster at Donnybrook and they lost by two points, with Leinster overcoming a deficit late in the game to win. The series was then interrupted and did not resume until December. This was due to the visit of the World champions, Australia.

The laws of the game, meanwhile, were undergoing radical alteration. Now, for instance, a temporary replacement could come on to the field for up to five minutes to enable a player to have a bleeding wound treated. On a broader base, it was decided that Rugby League players could now play Rugby Union provided they had not received material benefit from playing League. If that was the case, the player had to wait two years.

The upgrading of the Lansdowne Road ground was under constant review under the chairmanship of Ronnie Dawson and the design for new floodlighting at the ground was completed and all objections from local residents had been overcome. Work was started on this project in the summer of 1993.

The Australian tour was scheduled for Ireland and Wales and they came to Ireland in October 1992. They opened their tour with a 38-11 win over Leinster on 17 October. Then it was on to Cork and the match against Munster. This was to prove a torrid experience for the World champions. Yet again Munster rose to the challenge, as they had done so often in the past, and once more claimed a famous victory, winning by 22-19. The Munster team, led superbly by Terry Kingston and coached by Garret Fitzgerald, never allowed the Australians to settle. After the match the Australian coach Bob Dwyer was critical of Munster and suggested that some of his players had been deliberately targeted and that prop forward Peter Clohessy had been selected by Munster specifically to take out opponents. But this was dismissed by the Munster players, officials and coach, who resented what they considered to be a very unjust accusation that smacked of sour grapes. Two players were sent off during the match, Mick Galwey, and Garrick Morgan of Australia. Neither player was really guilty of a major transgression but rather paid the price for a general mêlée in the middle of the field. Minimum suspensions were imposed on both players and that was its own commentary.

The Wallabies soon resumed their winning ways after the defeat in Cork and beat Ulster 38-11 at Ravenhill and then had anything but a convincing 14-6 win over Connacht in Galway.

The Wallabies captain, Michael Lynagh, unfortunately had been injured against Leinster and took no further part in the tour. Even without Lynagh, the Wallabies played brilliantly to defeat Ireland 42-17 at Lansdowne Road on 31 October. Ireland had included one new cap in their side, John Murphy of Greystones and Leinster.

Within a few days of that defeat, Ciaran Fitzgerald announced that he was standing down as Ireland coach. He had taken his decision in what he considered to be the best interests of Irish rugby and also because of increased business commitments. He had worked assiduously during his period of office. Fortune had not smiled on him or Ireland in several of the crucial matches. His period as coach had not been blessed with the kind of success he had enjoyed as Ireland's captain.

CHAPTER 30

A BARREN SPELL IS BROKEN

When Ciaran Fitzgerald resigned, the IRFU faced a dilemma. In accordance with their own laws the coach to the national team had to come from those nominated at the end of the previous season.

There was immense speculation as to who would succeed Fitzgerald. Names from all quarters, notably the southern hemisphere, were being mentioned, but it was no more than idle speculation. One thing it did do was lead to a change in the IRFU laws in relation to the appointment of a coach. The lessons were learned and the options widened considerably so that in the event of a coach resigning in mid-season, as indeed happened twice subsequently, the union's hands would not be tied in relation to naming a successor.

But after Fitzgerald's resignation in fact justice was done. Initially, Gerry Murphy, Fitzgerald's assistant, was appointed on a temporary basis and then his appointment was confirmed for the season.

So it was a Murphy combination of Noel as manager and Gerry as coach at the helm of team affairs. Their first test came against Scotland in Murrayfield and Ireland that afternoon included three new caps. They were the Malone and Ulster full-back Roger Wilkinson, former schools international Niall Malone who went to London Irish initially and then to Leicester at outside half, and the Garryowen second row Richard Costello. Costello had toured New Zealand the previous summer and had played for the Whites (the Probables) in the final trial.

That came after the Interprovincial Championship had been resumed late in November and Ulster won it and did the Grand Slam in achieving their win. For the Exiles, their advent to the championship had been very encouraging. In addition to beating Munster, they also defeated Connacht, who that season scored their most emphatic win in the history of the series by beating Leinster, and in Dublin at that, by 28-9. It was a measure of the manner in which Ulster dominated the championship for almost a decade that this was their eighth outright win in nine seasons and they had also shared the title in the season they did not win it outright.

The Ireland selectors had made eight changes for the match against Scotland in Edinburgh from the team that had lost to Australia. Michael Bradley was back at scrum-half, Steve Smith returned as hooker, and Denis McBride and Noel Mannion were recalled to the back row, in addition to the advent of three new caps.

But the Scots took an early 10 points lead and never surrendered the initiative. By the interval, Scotland led 15-0 and the only inroad Ireland made was a penalty from Malone. It was a singularly unimpressive performance from Ireland and an inauspicious start to the reign of the two Murphys.

Ireland's next match was against France in Dublin and while France won the match the Irish put up a great fight and it was not until the very last minute that France really sealed their win, being victorious by 21-6. Yet again Ireland rang the changes and brought in new caps in the Terenure College full-back Ciaran Clarke and the young Munster prop Peter Clohessy. Out went Wilkinson and Paul McCarthy to make way for the newcomers. Neil Francis returned to the side as did Pat O'Hara and Mick Galwey. In all Ireland made six changes.

The Irish fought tenaciously in the first half and were not flattered to be level at the interval 6-6, with Malone having kicked two penalty goals. Indeed, Ireland actually led 6-0 until a few minutes before the interval. France took the lead for the first time with a penalty early in the second half, and it was still 9-6 with just seven minutes to go as Ireland defended with tremendous resolution and bravery. The crucial try came after a kick ahead and a kind bounce and Phillipe Saint Andre got a try which was converted. Then, in the last minute, France got another try and conversion for a very flattering 21-6 win.

Ireland's next match was away to Wales in Cardiff and the background to that was an ongoing chapter of defeats. Ireland went into that match not having won in the Five Nations series since the win over Wales in Dublin in 1990. The best result they had achieved in the interim was the draw against Wales in 1991 in Cardiff. Ireland's last international win had been achieved in the World Cup against Japan.

On the night prior to the championship match, the Ireland A team beat the Wales A team in Newport 29-28. Earlier in the season the Ireland Under 21 team had beaten Wales 22-11 in Donnybrook, and in April the Ireland Schools side defeated Wales in Ebbw Vale by 8-0.

Ireland brought in just one new cap for the visit to Cardiff. He was Eric Elwood, the Connacht and Lansdowne outside half who replaced Niall Malone. Brian Robinson, now recovered from injury, was back in the side at No. 8 and Mick Galwey reverted to the second row.

Although Wales took an early lead with a penalty, Clarke dropped a goal to bring Ireland level. There were some good signs for Ireland early in the match and their determination and concentration were evident. Elwood, too, was cool and composed in the outside half berth. Then Ireland scored a great try, with Robinson marking his return by getting it. Elwood converted and Ireland led 10-3 with the try now worth five points.

At the interval Ireland led 13-6 with Elwood having kicked another penalty for Ireland and Neil Jenkins one for Wales. Elwood and Jenkins both kicked penalty goals early in the second half and so Ireland led 16-9 as the midway point of the half approached. But Wales struck with a try when Ieuan Evans produced a great run down the touchline and, while Jenkins missed the conversion, Ireland's lead was a tenuous two points at 16-14. Ireland held the vigorous Welsh assaults that followed with some excellent tackling and then Elwood kicked another penalty to leave his side 19-14 in front. It was Ireland on the attack at the final whistle, and so a run of eight consecutive championship defeats had ended at last. The celebrations that night by the Irish were in accordance with the significance of the occasion. It had been a great debut for Elwood who scored 11 points. So at that point of the season it was Ireland played three and won three against the Welsh, and the schools then made it a clean sweep at every level against the Welsh.

One shrewd move by the Ireland management was bringing in Willie Anderson to help coach the forwards. Anderson was at that time a game development officer with the IRFU.

Again, on the eve of the championship match against England, Ireland A met England A at Donnybrook. This time Ireland lost a fine contest 22-18. It was a match that could so easily have gone the other way.

Then the following afternoon came the big one, the final match of the Five Nations series, against England at Lansdowne Road. Now fortified by that win over Wales, the Irish were not in the mood to allow England to follow pre-match predictions of a win without undue difficulty.

There followed one of the great Irish displays of the modern era. From the kick-off the Irish carried the match to England. They tackled superbly, the pack chased, hunted and harassed the opposition, and the English were clearly rattled. The dangerous England back line was readily held in check as their forwards struggled to match the controlled Irish ferocity.

It was 3-3 at the interval, each team scoring a penalty, Elwood for Ireland and Jonathan Webb for England. But if the Irish display was good and effective in the first period, it was positively awesome in the second half. Elwood set the pattern early in the period with a penalty and then scored a superb dropped goal and Ireland led 9-3. England had one very good chance to score a try but a knock-on saw the opportunity lost. As the match entered its final phase, England lost their composure and were clearly unsettled. Michael Bradley at scrum-half was in his element, and his tactical play and superb defence were complemented by a great Ireland back row.

Five Nations Championships 1993. Mick Galwey of Ireland scores a try despite the efforts of England's Tony Underwood, in Ireland's 17-3 victory

With five minutes remaining, Ireland stretched their lead to 12-3 when Elwood dropped his second goal after Ireland won a ruck and he was fed by Bradley. Now it was desperation stakes for England and they tried to initiate an attack through their backs. A poor pass by their captain, Will Carling, as he was hit by a tremendous tackle was to prove costly. The Irish were on to the loose ball and Elwood picked up and passed to Mick Galwey. The Shannon man drove for the line and scored a try to leave Ireland 17-3 in front and now assured of victory.

The cheer that greeted that try could be heard miles away. Ireland had truly now come back from the wilderness and at the final whistle it was a ragged England outfit that left the field. The Irish players were given a tremendous reception by the capacity crowd. The Murphy alliance had seen Ireland win two matches back to back in the championship. Had Ireland played anyway near as well against the Scots as they had against Wales and England, then they would have won the Triple Crown. But the win over England was a huge boost to Irish morale and Bradley's leadership had been superbly demonstrated.

The Lions were due to tour New Zealand in the summer and the squad was announced a few days after the Ireland-England match. There is no doubt it had already in effect been chosen before Ireland played England. The Irish representation was, to say the least, disappointing. Only two Irish players were chosen, prop Nick Popplewell and the versatile Mick Galwey. The team was captained by Gavin Hastings and managed by England's Geoff Cooke. Ken Reid had represented Ireland on the selection committee.

The Lions lost the Tests by two matches to one, but should have won the series. They were cruelly unfortunate to lose the first Test in Christchurch to an injury time penalty goal awarded in the most doubtful of circumstances. Furthermore, a try that New Zealand got in the first half was, to say the least, controversial. In the second Test the Lions played brilliantly to win in Wellington, and Popplewell, who played in all three Tests, was outstanding in the match. In the final Test New Zealand won comprehensively in Auckland. Galwey did not make the Test side but had a good tour and his versatility was demonstrated as a back and second row forward. Two Irishmen joined the tour as replacements, Vincent Cunningham and Richard Wallace.

Ireland competed in the inaugural World Seven-a-side Championship which was played in Murrayfield in April and reached the semi-final before losing in the last minute to Australia.

The laws on amateurism were again under review and a major alteration was made in relation to the qualification for the World Cup. It was decided that, following the 1995 World Cup, only the two finalists, the winners of third place and the nation acting as official hosts would not have to qualify.

Tom Kiernan was now chairman of the IRFU Amateur Status subcommittee in succession to Roly Meates, who was no longer on the union. His departure came in controversial circumstances after some injudicious public comments precipitated severe disagreements with fellow union members. He was, in fact, defeated from the floor of the annual general meeting of the Council of the IRFU.

The Irish Students had reached the quarter-final of the Students World Cup in Italy the previous summer and a fixture of some significance took place in December 1992 when the Colleges met the Universities. The Colleges won the inaugural fixture.

It was also decided that Ireland would send a Development team on a tour to Zimbabwe, Namibia and South Africa in July 1993. Noel Murphy was appointed as manager with Gerry Murphy as coach. It was also decided that Dave Haslett and Harry Williams would also be in the party. Williams had been a very successful coach of the Ulster side and he had also coached the Ireland A team, while David Haslett's contribution to schools and Under 21 rugby was immense.

The Development team included several players who were later to leave a profound mark on the senior side. The squad included some players who had played at senior international level. Kevin Potts of St Mary's College was captain.

Ireland did extremely well on the tour and lost only one of the seven matches played. That was against Namibia A who won 33-19.

CHAPTER 31

AUSTRALIA REVISITED

THE WINS OVER WALES AND ENGLAND the previous season had raised the level of optimism that Ireland would do well in the championship in 1994 and there was an added incentive for the players as a tour to Australia was scheduled for the summer.

With the World Cup scheduled for South Africa in 1995, obviously team managements were seeking to build their teams with that in view. It was now an Irishman, Sir Ewart Bell, at the helm of RWC (Rugby World Cup). Sir Ewart had succeeded Russ Thomas in the onerous position of chairman.

The sponsorship of the national team by Digital Equipment had now come to an end after ten very fruitful years of mutual co-operation between sponsor and union. Sponsorship was taken over by the Irish Permanent Building Society.

The Interprovincial series proved to be extremely competitive as Ulster sought to maintain their dominant position. They opened the defence of their title with a 21-3 win over the Exiles at Ravenhill and played well enough to suggest a bold bid to retain their title. The Exiles also lost to Leinster and Munster but defeated Connacht. Munster had scored an exciting 21-19 win over Leinster, but then came a very severe shock for Ulster. Leinster not alone ended Ulster's dominance, but did it to the extent of a win by 25 points to nil. That brought to an end a sequence of 32 unbeaten matches for Ulster in the series. But Ulster did manage to defeat Munster 24-21. Had Munster won or drawn that match at Ravenhill, then they would have taken the title. Munster led in the match until a few minutes before the end when a dropped goal and then a penalty goal, kicked in injury time, gave Ulster the win. On the same afternoon, Leinster defeated Connacht, and so the championship ended in a three-way tie between Leinster, Ulster and Munster.

Romania came to Dublin and played Ireland at Lansdowne Road on 13 November and Ireland won the match 25-3 with Elwood, whose contribution the previous season had been so important, again emphasising his value by scoring 20 points. That win meant Ireland had now won three internationals in a row, a sharp contrast to what had been endured prior to that win in Cardiff the previous season. Ireland included one new cap against Romania, Conor O'Shea, the Lansdowne full-back, who replaced Ciaran Clarke. Gary Halpin had replaced Peter Clohessy at prop. Clohessy had been suspended because of an incident in an AIL match the previous season.

It was a controversial decision after a video of the match had been submitted to the IRFU. The laws relating to such submissions were subsequently changed, but Clohessy had to serve a 10 weeks ban and that had carried over until December 1993, thus ruling him out of the match against Romania. Neil Francis, who had not played since the match against France the previous season, returned to the side, but Pat O'Hara was ruled out through injury.

Ireland played Scotland in an A international in Ayr on 28 December and Clohessy, who had now finished his suspension, played in the match and proved his fitness. He played for the Whites in the final trial, a match won by the Whites 25-14. Following that, the team to play France in Paris on 15 January was selected. One new cap was included in the team, the Sunday's Well flank forward, Ken O'Connell, a former schools international.

Ireland put up a creditable performance in the match, but the French had the depth and the flair that Ireland just could not match. France led 16-12 at the break after Elwood had kicked four penalty goals for Ireland. With eight minutes remaining the score stood at 23-15 to France and indeed it might have been closer as Elwood was inches wide with two penalty attempts.

With three minutes to go, France put the issue beyond all doubt with a try, but a win by 30 points to 15 was rather flattering.

Vincent Cunningham sustained a very bad leg injury playing in a league match and was ruled out for the season. Mark McCall was brought into the centre to partner Philip Danaher for the visit of Wales to Dublin. Paddy Johns was named at No. 8, Brian Robinson on the blind side flank and Mick Galwey in the second row.

The Welsh came into the match with rather indifferent form and it was expected that Ireland would win. Midway through the first half Ireland led 9-3 with Elwood having kicked three penalty goals. Wales did score a try prior to the interval, but Ireland led 12-8 at the break, Elwood having added a fourth penalty.

Ireland lost a great chance to stretch their lead early in the second half, but a knock-on saw the opportunity lost and, with fifteen minutes remaining, Ireland led 15-14 despite not having made the most productive use of possession. Wales took the lead ten minutes from time when Jenkins kicked yet another penalty, and then Elwood saw a penalty attempt come back off an upright. No similar chance presented itself and Ireland had to endure a very disappointing 17-15 defeat.

Prior to the next match against England at Twickenham, events at Lansdowne Road the previous season when Ireland had inflicted so severe a defeat on England were very much to the forefront. This would be England's opportunity to put matters right. Ireland went into the match with just one change from the team that lost to Wales. Maurice Field, the Malone and Ulster centre, displaced his provincial colleague Mark McCall.

Yet again the Ireland team revealed tremendous resilience and the Irish pack once more harassed their opponents. They disrupted their line-out possession and were very quick on to the loose ball. The scrum was rock solid. England enjoyed a 6-3 lead after two penalty goals and Elwood kicked one for Ireland. Three times the Irish were penalised near the England line, but then came a crucial score.

Ireland won possession on the right, the ball was fed outside by Elwood to Danaher, Richard Wallace came in off the blind side wing, he made ground and his intervention disrupted the England defence. Wallace passed outside to Simon Geoghegan. He went into full flight and beat an attempted tackle to score a superb try wide on the left. Elwood kicked the conversion and Ireland led 10-6.

England exerted tremendous pressure early in the second half, but the tackling was iron clad. England reduced their deficit with a penalty and then Geoghegan relieved pressure on the Ireland line with a good run and a kick deep into English territory. He was up quickly and the England outside half

Rob Andrew was penalised for not releasing the ball after being tackled. This gave Elwood the chance to kick another penalty and he duly obliged to leave Ireland 13-9 in front.

England v Ireland 1994 (Twickenham). Simon Geoghegan after scoring a famous try. Phil Danaher also celebrates

England did add a fourth penalty with just over a quarter of an hour remaining, but that was all Ireland surrendered. They defended superbly in a very exciting finish, but England could not make the breakthrough. So Ireland had done it again, defying the odds and the predictions. Not alone had Ireland won, but for the second year in succession England had failed to score a try against Ireland. Michael Bradley, who had led the team superbly, mounted the rostrum in Twickenham to be presented with the Millennium trophy, the prize at stake annually between the two countries since the Millennium match in 1988.

It was a confident Ireland side that went into the final match of the championship against Scotland at Lansdowne Road on 5 March. But on a day when the wind blew with a disconcerting vigour making kicking difficult, the match ended in a disappointing 6-6 draw. Both teams scored two penalties, Elwood for Ireland and Gavin Hastings for Scotland. Ireland did not really strike a rhythm until the closing quarter and exerted concerted pressure on the Scots, but they did not manage to get the try that would have proved decisive.

So Ireland ended the season with a 50 per cent record, two wins, against Romania and England, a draw, and two defeats by Wales and France.

The Ireland party to tour Australia in May was announced and contained several young players such as Jeremy Davidson and Jonathan Bell, Victor Costello, the Cork Constitution flanker, David Corkery, and the Blackrock College wing Niall Woods, all of whom had been capped at under 21 level and all but Woods at schools level. Michael Bradley was the tour captain. But Ireland manager Noel Murphy was unable to travel and so his fellow selector Frank Sowman took over that role, and a fine job he made of the task. Former Ireland hooker, Locky Butler from Blackrock College, was named as assistant manager. Gerry Murphy was coach and Willie Anderson was in the party as technical adviser but was, in effect, the coach to the pack.

Ireland opened their itinerary with a very big win over Western Australia at the famous Western Australia Cricket Ground, the 'WACCA' in Perth. Ireland won 64-8. The next assignment was of an altogether different dimension, the powerful New South Wales side. That match was played at the Concord Oval and Ireland lost 55-18. In the third match Ireland lost 22-9 to ACT in Canberra. The fourth match was against Queensland in Brisbane. That afternoon Ireland gave a performance in total contrast to the displays against New South Wales and ACT. It took an injury time penalty from Michael Lynagh, the Queensland outside half, to see off the Irish challenge.

That match was to have a considerable influence on the composition of the team for the first Test a week later in Brisbane. Prior to that, Ireland went to Mount Isa, a mining town in Northern Queensland, to play a very powerful Australian A side. Ireland lost 57-9 fielding a team that bore little comparison with the side that lined out in the first Test.

That Test took place on 5 June in Ballymore, Brisbane. Ireland included four new caps in the team. They were Jonathan Bell, Niall Woods, Keith Wood and David Corkery. The Australians were very short odds-on favourites to win the Test. Remarkably, the Australians had never beaten Ireland in a Test in Australia. In the three previous internationals played in Australia, in 1967 and twice in 1979, Ireland had won.

This time the Australians justified the odds. They were 13-3 up at the interval. Ireland contested well, especially initially, but the Australians' pace and flair behind the scrum was demonstrated by the fact that they scored four tries in the second half. Ireland's try was scored by Paddy Johns, Elwood converted and he and Conor O'Shea both kicked penalty goals.

By the last week of the tour, Ireland had had to call out no fewer than four replacements. They were the Terenure College scrum-half Niall Hogan, a replacement for Alain Rolland, back row forwards Ben Cronin (Garryowen) and Ken O'Connell (Sunday's Well) and the Blackrock College hooker Shane Byrne.

The Australians went into the second Test and the final match of Ireland's tour as even firmer favourites than they were prior to the first Test. In the interim Ireland had played the second last match of the tour against New South Wales Country in Lismore and won 20-18.

In the Test Ireland gave a heartening and spirited performance and one that drew considerable praise from the Australian coach Bob Dwyer. He readily admitted in a very gracious manner that the Australians were flattered to win 32-18.

The Australians looked to have the match tied up when they led at the interval 21-6. But Ireland fought back and scored two tries in the second half through Peter Clohessy and Neil Francis. But Ireland paid the price for conceding penalties and Lynagh kicked five for Australia. His 17 points in the match meant that he brought his total in international rugby past the 800 mark, a truly astonishing record for a superb player.

So Ireland returned from Australia in good heart. Some of the young players on the tour such as Keith Wood, who was outstanding, Jonathan Bell and David Corkery looked to have really bright futures. Overall, the tour was seen as a very important part of the development of the younger players in the squad.

There was an added dimension to the 1994–95 season with the World Cup due to take place in May and June. Meanwhile the IRFU had decided on some changes in the game development area. There were now eight development officers placed around the country and it was also decided to appoint a Director of Rugby Development. This meant, in effect, a change in the job specification of George Spotswood who was now Rugby Administrator. The new Director of Rugby was Ray Southam, who came to the IRFU from Canterbury, New Zealand. Southam was a Welshman who had emigrated to New Zealand.

An important change came in a key position when Paddy O'Donoghue retired as secretary of the union in 1995. He was succeeded by Philip Browne, who had joined the union staff some years earlier as Administrative officer. Paddy O'Donoghue, who had been RWC Director in Ireland from 1989 to 1991, had done a splendid job in his relatively short time as secretary, taking over in difficult circumstances.

Ulster's great run in the Interprovincial Championship came to an end when they surrendered the title to Munster. Munster had won their opening match by beating Ulster 17-16 and went from strength to strength. The Exiles, after beating Connacht 35-9, lost a very exciting match to Leinster 20-18. But Munster's potential was realised in full measure when they went to London and overwhelmed the Exiles by 46-8, giving a superb performance. The match was a personal triumph for Munster's Kenny Smith, the versatile Garryowen back who contributed 31 points, a record for a player in an interprovincial.

Connacht again edged Leinster out, winning 20-19 in Galway, and the Munster team went to Donnybrook and beat Leinster 36-14 and scored five tries in the process. Now a Grand Slam beckoned for Munster whose last match was against Connacht at Thomond Park. Munster scored a win of record proportions over Connacht (60-20) and they scored eight tries and a penalty try in the demolition. On the same afternoon, Leinster again defeated Ulster, this time at Ravenhill, by 12-6. So it was Munster Grand Slam champions. Kenny Smith ended the championship by setting a new individual mark for a player in the series with a total of 68 points.

A very familiar figure was now no longer on the IRFU committee. Ronnie Dawson retired at the end of the 1993–94 season. He had served Irish rugby superbly as a player and official. He had captained his country and the Lions and then served on the Leinster Branch as Wanderers' representative, had been president of the branch and was president of the IRFU in 1989–90. He had been one of Ireland's representatives on the International Board for 20 years. His contribution to the development of the Lansdowne Road ground was immense. He was succeeded on the International Board by Tom Kiernan, who thus joined with Syd Millar, who had succeeded Sir Ewart Bell a few years previously.

The United States came to Ireland in November and Ireland won the International at Lansdowne Road 26-15. The Blackrock College outside half Alan McGowan won his first cap in the match, having been chosen when Eric Elwood was ruled out through injury. The four players who had been capped in Australia, Keith Wood, David Corkery, Gabriel Fulcher and Jonathan Bell, were all in the Ireland team. The USA played with great courage and determination, but the Irish were always in control of a match they won with 11 points to spare. Simon Geoghegan and Michael Bradley both scored tries. McGowan marked his debut by scoring 16 points through four penalty goals and two conversions.

There had been a significant development prior to that match when Brendan Mullin decided to make himself available again for representative rugby. He had been playing very well for Blackrock College and he was prevailed upon to return to the international scene.

There was a novel pairing in the final trial at Lansdowne Road on 30 December. Indeed, there were two trials that afternoon. In the main event the Irish XV played the Combined Universities Past and Present and won 48-16. Prior to that match what was termed an Ireland A team played against the Irish Students on the back pitch at Lansdowne Road. The Ireland A team won the match 40-17. It was indeed a very powerful A team that included full internationals in Jim Staples, Richard Wallace, Maurice Field, Eric Elwood, Fergus Aherne, Gary Halpin, Richard Costello and Philip Lawlor.

Ireland's first match in the International Championship was against England at Lansdowne Road on 21 January. Unfortunately the Ireland team was disrupted because of injuries and then a few days prior to the match the Ireland captain Michael Bradley had to withdraw in the most unfortunate of circumstances, the death of his infant son. Bradley's withdrawal meant that the Terenure College scrum-half Niall Hogan, a medical student, won his first cap and Brendan Mullin took over the captaincy.

Ireland included a new cap at outside half in Paul Burke. He had come to the Irish scene by a rather circuitous route. Born in London of Irish parents, he had been an outstanding player for England Schools while a student at Epsom College and had also played for England at Under 21 level. A member of the London Irish club, he decided to declare for Ireland. He had the unique distinction of playing for the Ireland Under 21 team against England, having the previous season played for England Under 21 against Ireland. Now he had gained the ultimate distinction at senior level. He subsequently joined Cork Constitution after taking up a teaching post in Cork. Another newcomer to the Ireland side was the Shannon No. 8 Anthony Foley, the son of the former Ireland and Shannon second row Brendan.

Niall Woods, who had been capped in Australia, returned for the match against England, who played into the wind in the first half on a very inclement afternoon of high wind and heavy rain. From the outset the England forwards exerted their authority on the match. They scored an early try, and led at the interval by 12-3, having scored two tries to Ireland's solitary penalty kicked by Burke.

Armed with that lead, England never looked likely to surrender it and won readily by 20-8, with Foley marking his debut by scoring a try for Ireland.

Bradley returned to lead the side against the Scots and his return was one of several changes, with Jonathan Bell being named on the wing in place of Woods. Gabriel Fulcher replaced Neil Francis, who had been injured against England, in the second row. Denis McBride returned in the back row and Paddy Johns moved from No. 8 to the second row for Mick Galwey.

Scotland took an early lead with a penalty, but after Burke equalised, Ireland went ahead with a try from Mullin and Ireland led 8-3. Unfortunately, Burke was below par with his kicking, while Gavin Hastings was in top form in this respect for the Scots. At the interval Scotland led 9-8.

Ireland scored a great try early in the second half when Bell finished off a splendid movement. So Ireland led 13-9. Then Scotland enjoyed a great stroke of good fortune that effectively turned the match. A kick ahead by Hastings seemed to present no danger, but the ball bounced off the outside of Craig Joiner's right foot and went across the Ireland line and Joiner was able to accept the gift. Hastings converted and Scotland led 16-13. From this point Scotland took over and ran out 26-13 winners.

Yet again the Ireland side was badly disrupted by injuries prior to the visit of France. Paddy Johns and Ben Cronin were both ruled out two days before the match. So the Ballymena and Ulster veteran second row David Tweed got an unexpected call-up. Foley moved to No. 8 and his Shannon clubmate Eddie Halvey won his first cap on the flank. Jim Staples returned at full-back, displacing Conor O'Shea, and Elwood was back to replace Burke.

Ireland did a useful containment job in the initial period and France led 3-0 at the break with a penalty being the only score. But immediately after the interval France scored a try. From this point on, France took control of the game and subsequently ran in three more tries, with a try from Simon Geoghegan and a penalty from Elwood being Ireland's response.

Ireland went to Cardiff seeking to avoid a whitewash and preserve their great unbeaten record stretching back a decade in Cardiff. Ireland succeeded admirably in achieving both objectives.

Hogan was preferred to Bradley at scrum-half, and Terry Kingston took over the captaincy. Richard Wallace returned to the side on the right wing with Geoghegan switching to the left. Johns moved back to No. 8 with Foley replacing McBride on the flank.

It was Wales who scored first with a penalty from Neil Jenkins and the Welsh were on top initially. Then Elwood had to leave the field after being the recipient of a very dangerous tackle from the Welsh back row forward Richie Collins. He was replaced by Burke who made an immediate impact and dropped a goal to level matters and then put Ireland ahead with a penalty that was followed by a splendid try from Brendan Mullin after Wallace played a vital part in its execution. Burke converted and Ireland led 13-6 at the break.

The Welsh increased the tempo of their play in the early stages of the second half, but Ireland held firm. But two penalty goals kicked by Jenkins cut Ireland's advantage to a very tenuous one point, 13-12. With twelve minutes remaining, Burke kicked a penalty for Ireland to lead 16-12 and Ireland protected that advantage readily enough to win by a four points margin and embellished that great record in Cardiff and avoid a whitewash.

Meanwhile there was disquieting news emanating from the meeting of the International Board in March 1995. The Board recognised that there were problems enforcing the laws on amateurism in most of the major unions. There was recognition that it was not, however, realistic to return to the pre-1990 revision of the laws. The Trust schemes which had been put in place so that players could be compensated for their efforts, time and profile, were now seen in many respects as a disguised method of paying players to play the game. It was recognised that further measures were required if the progression to a professional game, certainly at the top levels, was to be avoided. The regulations were now being disregarded in some countries. A copy of the report of the Board's working party was circulated to member unions for comment. The working party was scheduled to meet again in Paris in August 1995. By now membership of the Board had increased to 67 nations.

An application had been made for admission to the Olympic Movement for rugby as a non-participation sport. An acknowledgment of admission had been signed in November 1994 by Vernon Pugh, the chairman of the Board, and Juan Samaranch, the president of the International Olympic Committee. By now, too, the Lansdowne Road floodlights were in operation, not just for rugby but indeed for international soccer. The ground was being constantly upgraded. There was, however, an awareness that the time was at hand to have an all-seater stadium. That presented obvious difficulties if the capacity of the ground was not to be greatly reduced. Talk about moving elsewhere was also on the agenda and indeed 90 acres of land had been purchased on the west side of Dublin near Clondalkin. Tom Kiernan was now chairman of the Lansdowne Road Development subcommittee.

Another option that was being explored was the possibility of playing internationals at a new stadium proposed for a site on the old Phoenix Park racecourse as part of a major complex. But that project did not materialise.

South Africa came on a tour during the season and while they did not play an international against Ireland, they did play and comprehensively beat the Combined Provinces in Ravenhill 54-19. However, in a memorable match at Lansdowne Road, the Barbarians, who included Simon Geoghegan and an all-Irish front row of Nick Popplewell, Keith Wood and Peter Clohessy, scored a splendid 23-15 victory.

CHAPTER 32

THE THIRD WORLD CUP

AS THE COUNTRIES PREPARED TO TRAVEL to South Africa for the third World Cup, there was a total awareness that amateurism was now under the most severe strain.

On 16 May, the IRFU called a press conference at which the union's attitude to amateurism was made explicitly clear. Billy Lavery, the chairman of the IRFU Amateurism subcommittee, and Ken Reid, the IRFU president, stated the case with some clarity and the IRFU issued a paper outlining their attitude. What they saw as inherent dangers were pointed out, as were what they perceived to be inconsistencies in the interpretation of the laws relating to amateurism.

They were in essence fighting the good fight to try and preserve the game from what was described as a degeneration into chaos. Later happenings were to prove those fears to be well founded.

As a preparation for the World Cup, the Ireland team travelled to Treviso to play Italy in a warm-up match. That took place on 6 May and it proved to be less than a satisfactory outing for the Ireland side. The Ireland World Cup squad travelled to Italy with three exceptions. Both scrum-halves Niall Hogan and Michael Bradley were unavailable. So David O'Mahony (Cork Constitution) and Alain Rolland travelled as the scrum-halves. Out too was Simon Geoghegan, again hit by injury. His place went to a new cap, the UCD wing Darragh O'Mahony. David O'Mahony was given the scrum-half berth in the Test.

Other changes from the side that beat Wales were Jonathan Bell in the centre for Philip Danaher, who was not available for business reasons for the World Cup, nor was Peter Clohessy, also because of business commitments. That meant a return for Gary Halpin.

Ireland took an early 6-0 lead against Italy but that was soon cancelled out by two penalties from the Italian outside half Diego Dominguez, the Argentinian who was now playing for Italy and doing so with telling effect. By the interval Ireland led 12-9 with Burke and Dominguez having done all the scoring.

In the second half, the Italians, coached by a Frenchman and playing rugby that bore very much the stamp of the French connection, got on top and made it pay on the scoreboard. They were more controlled up front and much more dangerous behind the scrum. Ireland failed to score in the second half and the Italians thoroughly deserved their win by 22-12. So Ireland had fallen to a country from outside the big eight — shades of the visit to Namibia in 1991. It was not the kind of background that Ireland wanted to bring into the South African adventure.

The Ireland squad in 1995 World Cup, South Africa

One man who had departed from the Ireland management team was Willie Anderson. He had also resigned as an IRFU Game Development officer for what he described as family reasons. Pat Whelan, a selector, had in fact been supervising some of the scrummaging sessions during the championship and Anderson may have seen this as something of an intrusion into his area.

The Ireland World Cup squad included four players who had been in the squad for the inaugural competition eight years earlier. They were Brendan Mullin, Michael Bradley, Terry Kingston, now the captain, and Neil Francis. The Ireland pre-cup training on the home front took place in Kilkenny.

A few days into training John Fitzgerald, the Young Munster prop, was ruled out of the tournament because he damaged a calf muscle which did not respond to intensive treatment. So instead of flying to South Africa and to the World stage, he had to return to his native Limerick. The man called in to replace him was the Old Wesley and Leinster prop forward, Henry Hurley. He had toured Australia the previous season but had been unable to make the Test team.

The Ireland side was drawn in Pool C with New Zealand, Wales and Japan and had the unenviable task of facing New Zealand, the cup favourites, in their opening match. That was played under lights at the newly refurbished Ellis Park in Johannesburg on 27 May.

Ireland had been drawn in the same pool as Wales in the inaugural World Cup and in the same pool as Japan in the second World Cup. Now New Zealand was added to the list.

There was a tremendous air of excitement in South Africa. Their isolation from world rugby had whetted their appetite. Now, not alone were they back, but they were the focus of the rugby world. 'Support the rainbow nation', was the battlecry led by their president Nelson Mandela, who asked that the whole nation get behind the Springboks.

The same day that Ireland played New Zealand, Wales opened their challenge by playing Japan in Bloemfontein. Wales, who had to go through the qualifying tournament having failed to make the last eight in 1991, won 57-10.

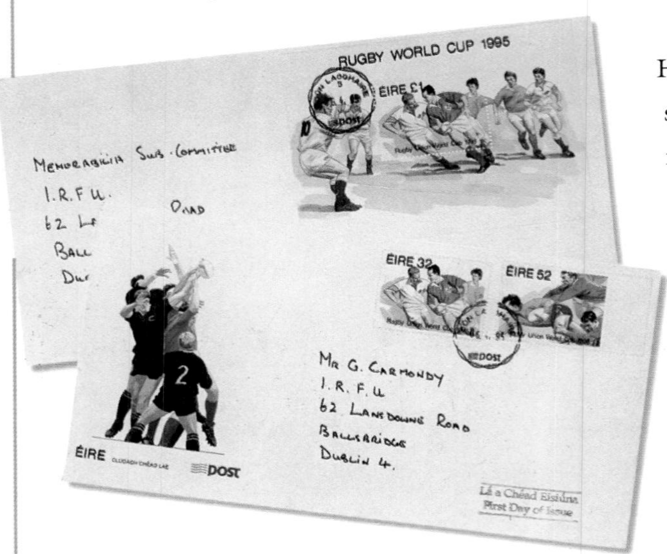

Ireland started brilliantly against New Zealand when Gary Halpin got an early try, but the quality of the All Blacks was soon evident and they carried too much power and expertise up front and pace and flair behind the scrum. They had in wing Jonah Lomu a huge man who would not have been out of place in the second or back rows of the scrum. But Ireland battled to the end of the match before going down 43-19. Ireland scored three tries against the All Blacks, who scored five, and Lomu got two of them.

Ireland's second match was against Japan in Bloemfontein and a victory in this encounter was essential if the Irish were to go into the final pool match against Wales with a quarter-final berth at stake.

The match took place on 31 May and that evening Wales lost to New Zealand by 34-9. Ireland duly defeated Japan, but at something of a cost. Keith Wood, who had had severe trouble with a shoulder injury earlier in the season, lasted no more than nine minutes when yet again he suffered a shoulder injury. He was replaced by Kingston. Popplewell had been named as captain of the team in Kingston's initial absence. For the Wallace brothers, wing Richard and prop Paul, it was a very auspicious occasion as they were both chosen to play against Japan, with Paul gaining his first cap. Not since the Doyle brothers, Mick and Tom, had played together for Ireland in the late 1960s had two brothers played together on the Ireland side.

Ireland duly defeated Japan 50-28, gradually wearing down the opposition, who fought tenaciously but did not have the depth or the forward power required. Ireland's scrummaging superiority was emphasised by the concession of two penalty tries by Japan. In addition David Corkery, Neil Francis, Simon Geoghegan, Eddie Halvey and Niall Hogan all scored tries. Paul Burke converted six of the tries and kicked a penalty goal.

The match between Wales and Ireland at Ellis Park on the evening of 4 June was in fact a quarter-final qualifier. That win by Ireland over Wales some weeks earlier in Cardiff helped instil confidence, but in 1987 Ireland had also beaten Wales shortly before Wales reversed that decision in Wellington. Now it was a must-win match for both sides, in fact a knock-out situation. The winners would go on to the quarter-final a week later; the losers would be on the way home the following day.

Jim Staples was ruled out of the match because of injury and he and Keith Wood were now out of the competition and returned home. Shane Byrne, the Blackrock hooker, flew out for Wood, and Philip Danaher was able to make business arrangements that enabled him to join the squad for the remainder of Ireland's involvement in the cup.

Ireland prepared assiduously for the match with Wales. Compared to the side that had beaten Japan, Jonathan Bell came into the centre for Maurice Field. Eric Elwood was at outside half, Kingston was at hooker for Wood, Halpin at tight head for Paul Wallace, Gabriel Fulcher in the second row for David Tweed and Denis McBride on the open side flank for Halvey.

It was Ireland who made the initial running in the match and a particularly cheeky try by McBride really gave Ireland the initiative and they did not surrender it. Nick Popplewell and Eddie Halvey, who had come on as a temporary replacement for McBride, also scored tries. Elwood converted all three and kicked a penalty goal. Wales did come with a late rally to cut their deficit, but a one point win for Ireland, 24-23 sufficed for the urgent need, but did not really reflect the level of Ireland's overall superiority as Wales got those points late in the game. It was a very happy Ireland party that returned to the team hotel in Sandton that night to celebrate their achievement in reaching the quarter-final of the cup.

While the tournament was in progress, there was a significant happening off the field. The then president of the South African Rugby Union, Luis Luyt, had travelled to London to meet with executives of the Rupert Murdoch controlled Sky television. It emerged that New Zealand, South Africa and Australia had signed a ten year television contract that gave Sky the primary rights to the internationals played in the three main southern hemisphere countries. Not alone that, but arrangements had also been put in place for a Super 12 series between provincial teams in the three countries to be played on an annual basis, as well as an annual tri-nations tournament.

Countries such as Fiji, Western Samoa and Tonga were left out in the cold and out of the Super 12. Bearing in mind the sentiments that had been uttered by New Zealand in particular when the 1987 World Cup was proposed, when they argued a strenuous case as to how helpful it would be to the South Seas countries, such sentiments now had a very hollow ring.

Those arrangements were to have a profound bearing on events a few months hence when the International Board met in Paris in August.

Back on the field of play, South Africa, to the delight of the new 'Rainbow Nation', were making progress in the tournament. Ireland, meanwhile, as runners-up in Pool C, were preparing for their quarter-final match against France, the winners of Pool D. France had edged Scotland out of first place in the decisive match in Pool D, coming with a late rally to win 22-19 after it looked as if the Scots were going to prevail in what was a really great match in Pretoria.

Ireland's quarter-final was scheduled for King's Park, Durban, and so the Irish travelled down to sea level for this crucial engagement which took place on 10 June.

Ireland brought in Darragh O'Mahony on the wing for Richard Wallace in the only change from the team that had beaten Wales. However strong the determination in the Ireland squad, on the hard dry ground and humid atmosphere that obtained in Durban, Ireland just did not manage to stoke the fires of passion. They hung in for a long time, but it was the superb kicking of the French outside half Thierry Lacroix which enabled France to build a formidable lead. He kicked eight penalty goals. Elwood kicked four penalty goals for Ireland, but the French, as so often in the past, finished with a flourish and scored two late tries to embellish their victory by 36-12.

So the World Cup adventure was over for Ireland, but the level of expectation was rising by the day as the South Africans had advanced to the semi-final, as had England, New Zealand and France.

Durban was also the venue for the semi-final between France and South Africa and, in appalling conditions of torrential rain and with pools of water on a saturated surface, South Africa got through but in very fortunate and controversial circumstances against a French team that deserved to win and a team that felt, with considerable justification, that they had got the wrong end of several decisions.

New Zealand overwhelmed England in the other semi-final and so what was termed the 'dream final' between South Africa and the All Blacks had become a reality. Ellis Park was an emotional arena as South Africa won the title. France beat England to finish third.

Now the carnival was over, but as the supporters went their diverse ways home across the seas, they did not realise that they had witnessed the last hurrah for international rugby as an amateur game. The vultures were hovering to get their hands on money from whatever source it came and however doubtful the morality. Very soon it was no longer to be the greatest good for the greatest number.

CIGARETTE CARDS FROM THE 90S

CHAPTER 33

THE PROFESSIONAL ERA

THE AFTERNOON OF SUNDAY, 27 AUGUST 1995, will go down as one of the most significant days in the history of the great game. The International Board had, over the previous two days in Paris, been discussing the whole concept of amateurism and the changes that had been made in that area in the recent past. It had been anticipated that amendments would occur and further concessions made in relation to what players could earn from the game as well as a relaxation with regard to the direct appointment of professional coaches.

But the announcement, when it came from Paris on that Sunday afternoon, went much further than most had anticipated. In effect amateurism, a central plank of the game since rugby went its own defined way as a specific and separate art form of football and for 120 years so sacred a tradition in rugby, was swept away.

It was a momentous decision and it is no exaggeration to say that the announcement was received with utter dismay by the majority of people involved in the game. Likewise, it should be stressed it was greeted with enthusiasm by the top representative players who now saw, or thought they saw, the road open to untold riches. Amateurism had given the game so many of its most appealing aspects. Rugby as a healthy, manly sporting pursuit had evolved and prospered on the dedication, hard work and goodwill of successive generations through the years. Now it had gone from being a game to being a business overnight and all that so critical a movement would embrace.

The phraseology used by the Board was not that the game was going professional; the term used was 'open'. That in many respects did no more than add insult to injury for so many who cherished the amateur ethic.

Amateurism had been under constant pressure and virulent attack for quite some time and the signs had been ominous that, in fact, some unions were doing no more than circumventing the amateur laws by various means. None the less it was felt prior to the fateful meeting in Paris that, while there would be changes perhaps of major consequence in relation to amateurism, it was not anticipated that so revolutionary a decision would be taken to sweep away the amateur ethic.

The reaction in Ireland to the Board's announcement was surprise, even dismay, as it was elsewhere, and grave concern about the future administration and management of rugby. Several IRFU officials went on the record that Sunday evening to express their profound reservations.

Some were in no doubt that loyalty to club and country would no longer obtain; that it would put intolerable pressure on clubs and unions and that it would take several years for rugby to come to terms with the new order and that we would see much chaos before order was restored. Those forecasts were made by such men as Ken Reid, Syd Millar, Noel Murphy, Bobby Deacy, Tom Kiernan and Billy Lavery, all of whom had given a lifetime of service to rugby as players and administrators. Their forecasts were to prove prophetic as subsequent events so graphically illustrated.

Dr Syd Millar, President IRFU, 1995–96, with Tommy Wallis, Ireland's oldest surviving international

Ireland's two representatives on the International Board, Syd Millar and Tom Kiernan, had fought the good fight in Paris, but to no real avail. The winds that originated in the southern hemisphere had now become a hurricane. The home unions, for so long steadfastly working in unison for what was best for rugby in these islands, had effectively been sundered and the consequences of that fracture were also to have a profound effect in subsequent dealings on several vital issues.

There was recognition in this country that things were changing and that rugby had to keep abreast of those changes — though not by revolution, but by evolution, careful planning and strategy and prudent financial management. A headlong rush into so radical a change was bound to bring problems of a major dimension, and so it proved. The game was not ready to embrace professionalism on so broad a scale.

It is true that the International Board left it open to each country to legislate for its own needs within the parameters laid down. But for the established rugby nations the only realistic option open was to move forward with the new order or be left lagging badly behind. The IRFU realised that, if Irish rugby was to stay at the top table and continue to play the leading nations on a regular basis as they had for over a century, then it was unrealistic not to embrace the new order and try to meet the challenges contained in it. The intention was to try to manage the changes in an ordered and structured manner. That policy was, of course, criticised by some who saw such a policy not as prudence but as a reluctance to come to terms with the changes. Events were to prove the caution and the prudence to have been wise.

On the day after the announcement from Paris, the IRFU held a press conference in Dublin. Syd Millar, who was now president of the IRFU, presided and Tom Kiernan and other union officials attended.

The decisions taken in Paris were dealt with in some detail and Millar answered questions that came from the floor. He admitted that Ireland had not supported the move to professionalism but equally stressed that, in the prevailing circumstances, Ireland had no alternative but to go down the new route.

He cautioned players not to rush headlong into signing contracts that inevitably would now be offered by the bigger British clubs. 'As things stand, were I a player I would be very cautious about giving up the day job in the present circumstances to move into what I would see as an uncertain future. The game and all strands of it now needs a period of reflection. People should now stand back and carefully assess all this new situation contains. The IRFU must do that and try and keep pace with this new and challenging situation.' It was good advice but it was not, unfortunately, heeded as several players did, indeed, decide that their future was in England, most notably with the London Irish club. It was a trickle in the first year of professionalism that later grew, if not to a flood, then to a substantial stream, as players departed.

Lucrative contracts and other inducements were offered and accepted by Irish players and indeed players from around the world ranging from Italy to the southern hemisphere. The financial outlay was immense and bitter experience was to prove there was infinitely more money going out of than into the clubs.

The IRFU decided to call a meeting of representatives from all the senior clubs in the country and that took place in the reception area under the West Stand at Lansdowne Road. It was in essence a meeting to decide the clubs' attitude to professionalism. Not surprisingly, attitudes varied appreciably. The end product, however, was that there was little point in putting in place laws that could not be effectively policed. So in essence the way was now open officially for Irish clubs to pay their players, their coaches and, if they so desired or had the resources, their administrators.

It all amounted to a huge challenge and however hard clubs tried to keep their players, as did the union and the provinces, the outward flow had started and was to continue for some time. It was inevitable in the new situation that mistakes would be made, as they were initially by the IRFU and its constituent elements. It was akin to trial and error, a learning curve for all concerned.

The IRFU Amateur Status subcommittee now, as such, no longer had a function with that brief. That committee in effect became the Game Participation subcommittee. They carried a heavy responsibility. The committee was chaired by Billy Lavery and also included Tom Kiernan, Don Crowley, Eddie Coleman and Dan Daly. Their task was to work on aspects of the changes that had now come about in the move to professionalism and all they embraced and, in particular, the changes in the laws that were the inevitable consequence of the game going 'open'. That committee, in effect, spawned the establishment subsequently of the Contracts subcommittee.

Meanwhile the advent of professionalism meant that another function had to be undertaken as a matter of urgency. That was to negotiate with the players' committee about payments and other related matters, including insurance, and the insurance issue was one of considerable importance and of course also related to players who were now full-time professionals with English clubs. That task was entrusted to Billy Lavery, Bobby Deacy and Eddie Coleman. The scale of payments was eventually agreed, as well as payments for travelling to Ireland for squad sessions. The players subsequently also appointed agents to act on their behalf. That was not greeted with much enthusiasm. Rugby had always prided itself on addressing its problems within its own house free from outside involvement. That, like much else, was now gone.

Match fees and win bonuses were now on offer to the Irish players, as were other subsidiary benefits. So, too, interprovincial players had the facility to earn money of consequence, if not to the same extent, by roughly the same means of appearance and bonus. The amateur citadel had now truly fallen. The IRFU had to change its laws to meet the demands of the new situation. Law change is something that must be made by the Council, not the executive of the Union. It was in the circumstances necessary for the Council to give the authority to the executive to continue to work pro tem and administer the union on

THE IRISH XV AND THE BARBARIANS TEAM WHO PLAYED IN A SPECIAL PEACE MATCH ON 18 MAY 1996, ARRANGED BY TWO FORMER INTERNATIONALS, HUGO MACNEILL AND TREVOR RINGLAND

a day-to-day basis within the terms of the new professional era until the laws were changed. The task of rewriting the laws was entrusted to Billy Lavery, an onerous and tedious task that he performed so well that his work is now taken as the model from which other unions have worked. That season of 1995–96 was, to say the least, traumatic. Where previously rugby had been men at play, now it was men at work. The age of amateurism had gone and was irretrievably lost.

People who did not have any background in rugby and in some instances any real understanding of it came into the game and purchased clubs in England. Exaggerated ambition, allied to underinvestment and the very slow growth of productivity, soon asserted themselves. It did not take too long to bring the inevitable economic chill wind. As it blew it brought with it the breaching of promises, the fracturing of long-held friendships, mistrust and controversy. Elements that had been the very bedrock of the game were now shattered.

One cannot understate or in any way diminish the crucial importance in what happened in the three years that immediately followed the consequences of the game going open. As the money dried up across the channel, so also the leading English clubs' attempts to fashion matters to suit themselves became more and more pronounced. The demands were fuelled by money. It all had its origins in Paris on an August afternoon in 1995. Twelve months after that decision, the game was hit by a crisis in the aftermath of what can only be described as a price-fixing conspiracy in relation to the television rights for the Five Nations Championship.

What was happening on the field of play was constantly being submerged by the ongoing happenings off it. Money and controversy dominated the headlines. A very dark shadow had descended and those who tried to lift it were too often stifled and castigated as belonging to another era, lacking reality and trying to hinder initiative. That was grossly untrue and, even more so, unfair. They had seen and continued to see that what was happening was that the game was being forced down a path that was leading to nothing but trouble and economic bankruptcy. A plague of distrust and divisiveness was afflicting rugby. It was not a case of trying to defend a holy and now lost cause; it was an attempt to bring some semblance of reality to bear on a situation that was rapidly going out of control.

Club owners in England, some of whom never had any involvement whatsoever with rugby, tried to take control of the game. Some offered offence as their weapons against those who were not prepared to stand aside and allow them that control or see the rich being subsidised by the rest. There came the hour when the forecasts and the warnings of the so called conservative block came true and there was an urgent need to try and stem the extremes that were operating. There also came the hour when the time for tremulous talk ceased and had to be replaced by concerted action. That came in the summer of 1996 when a clandestine television deal was struck between the RFU and Sky television.

In the depth of all the worry, anxiety and, one could say, tumult that followed the decision taken in Paris, a new and very exciting dimension was being added to the game in Europe.

Arrangements had been put in place for a European Cup with Tom Kiernan and Vernon Pugh of Wales central figures in the initiative. The concept was to embrace clubs from England, Wales, France, Italy and Romania, provinces from Ireland and district teams from Scotland. Just as the RWC was established to run the World Cup, so ERC (European Rugby Cup) was formed to oversee the running of the new competition.

The RFU and the SRU decided that they would not be in a position to enter teams for the inaugural European Cup because of their domestic arrangements. That was accepted, but in fact English clubs were not happy with their parent union's decision as the competition got under way in the autumn of 1995.

Ireland had three provinces in the inaugural competition, Munster, Leinster and Ulster, who had filled the first three places in the interprovincial series the previous season. Twelve teams split into four pools of three contested the inaugural competition. France was represented by Toulouse, Begles-Bordeaux, and Castres; Wales by Cardiff, Swansea and Pontypridd; Italy by Milan and Benetton Treviso; and Romania by Farul Constanta. On 1 November 1995 Munster met Swansea at Thomond Park and Leinster travelled to Italy to play Milan. It was winning debuts for both Irish provinces. Munster defeated Swansea 17-13 and Leinster overcame Milan 24-21. Ulster made their debut in the competition against Cardiff in Cardiff on 28 November, but it proved to be a difficult and unrewarding experience, losing 46-6 to a Cardiff team that included practically a whole team of internationals. Ulster also played Begles-Bordeaux on 13 December at Ravenhill but lost 29-11.

Munster's second assignment was a visit to France to play Castres. Munster found the home following at their most volatile and vociferous. It was a tremendous match and, with the game in injury time, Munster looked set for the draw that could have given them a place in the semi-final, Castres scored a try in very controversial circumstances after a blatant knock-on. No advantage accrued to Munster, but the referee ignored that and Castres scored the try and converted it to win 19-12. Swansea, who had lost to Munster, were now back in contention and they defeated Castres 22-10 to win the group on points difference from Munster.

But Leinster kept the Irish flag flying high. Their win in Milan was followed by a fine victory over Pontypridd under the lights at Lansdowne Road with Leinster winning by 23-22. That meant a place in the semi-final against Cardiff and that was fixed for Lansdowne Road on 30 December.

It was a very inclement day but it was Cardiff who adapted better to the conditions and they proved to be very worthy winners by 30-14. The same afternoon Toulouse defeated Swansea in the other semi-final by 30-3 and so it was a Wales-France final in Cardiff on 7 January. That proved a fitting climax to what had been a very successful competition. Toulouse won in extra time by 21-18. Leinster, meanwhile, did have the consolation of winning the Interprovincial Championship and of doing the Grand Slam in the process. But the changed circumstances that professionalism brought to the scene in England inevitably meant that the Exiles' participation in the interprovincial series was effectively doomed. The situation, ironically, had now arisen whereby more Irish players played their rugby in England. But the demands of their clubs imposed their own restrictions.

The decision to make the game open now also meant professional coaches could be employed by the unions for their national teams. Pending the outcome of events in Paris the IRFU Election subcommittee had kept their options open with regard to the appointment of a coach to succeed Gerry Murphy. Ordinarily the appointments were announced at the annual general meeting of the Council, but Council had given the authority the previous June to defer the selection of a coach, although in compliance with the laws three names had been submitted for consideration as coach. They were those of the outgoing coach Gerry Murphy, Harry Williams of Ulster and the Exiles' coach John O'Driscoll. Pat Whelan had been appointed manager of the team in succession to Noel Murphy. Whoever was appointed had of necessity to have a good working relationship with Whelan.

The decision in Paris effectively prompted the IRFU to go for a full-time professional coach. Both Williams and O'Driscoll withdrew their names from contention amid some element of controversy. The name of Willie Anderson was now also in the ring under the new order. Now director of rugby with Dungannon, he, however, decided to withdraw.

The three members of the Election subcommittee, Tom Kiernan, Syd Millar and Eddie Coleman, did not rush into a hasty decision. They had discussions with the Queensland coach John Connolly, who at that time was coaching Old Belvedere in between his commitments in Australia. Another with whom discussions took place was Bob Dwyer. He had taken up an appointment with Racing Club in Paris. But Dwyer, like Connolly, was not available.

It was, however, to a New Zealander that the committee turned and Murray Kidd was appointed. He thus became the first foreigner to coach the Ireland national team. This was yet another clear illustration of the ongoing changes in the game. Administratively, too, in other respects, there were changes made by the union to move forward and streamline administration. The former Blackrock

College and Garryowen scrum-half Stephen Aboud, who had been a Game Development officer, was now National Player Development officer. The union also decided to appoint a National Referee Development officer and the man chosen was former international referee Owen Doyle.

The appointment of Murray Kidd meant that he worked with Whelan, Frank Sowman, Joe Miles and Donal Lenihan on the National Selection committee. Kidd had been a successful coach with Garryowen for three years and had guided the club to win the All Ireland League and subsequently the Munster Senior Cup. He then moved to the Sunday's Well club and, under his guidance, they won promotion from the second to the first division of the AIL and to Munster Senior Cup success.

Neil Francis, Ireland's second row forward, about to pass to his backs in the match against Fiji at Lansdowne Road in 1995

He then decided to return to his native New Zealand and was appointed coach of provincial side King Country. But his tenure there did not last very long, a matter of months, and he returned to Sunday's Well as coach for the 1995–96 season. Then came the call from the IRFU and he was on the international stage.

His first assignment was to prepare the team for the match against Fiji at Lansdowne Road on 18 November 1995. Ireland, captained by Jim Staples, included two new caps, the Dungannon second row Jeremy Davidson and the Sale scrum-half Christian Saverimutto. His brother Robin had played for Ireland at Under 21 level. They were qualified for Ireland through their mother. In fact three other players earned their first caps that afternoon as replacements when Ireland won 44-8. They were the Northampton hooker Allan Clarke, the old Wesley prop Henry Hurley and the Sunday's Well utility back Sean McCahill, who was from New Zealand and whose brother Bernie had been a member of the 1987 New Zealand World Cup winning squad. The McCahills' parents were Irish and Sean, who had been playing in Ireland for several years, had played for Munster.

So a winning start for Kidd and he was to be successful in his second match as well. That took place against the United States in Atlanta on 5 January 1996. It was decided that, as part of the preparation for the Five Nations Championship, Ireland would travel for warm weather training to Atlanta. Unfortunately the weather was appalling. Torrential rain greeted the Irish initially. That cleared up, but on the day of the match the rain poured down relentlessly and the playing surface quite candidly was not really playable. But Ireland won 25-18 with a team that included two new caps. One was the Bective Rangers centre Kurt McQuilkin, a New Zealand provincial player whose father Noel was Bective Rangers coach. Kurt subsequently became an IRFU Game Development officer and moved to the Lansdowne club. The second new cap was Victor Costello, the St Mary's College No. 8. Costello thus emulated the achievement of his father Paddy who had been capped for Ireland in the 1950s. Victor was also an Olympic athlete and had represented Ireland in the shot putt in the Barcelona Olympics.

There was, too, an addition to the Ireland management team for that visit to Atlanta. The former Waikato and All Black forward John Mitchell was brought in as forwards coach. Mitchell had played for a season for Garryowen and that gave him some insight into the game in Ireland. He had returned to New Zealand after his term with Garryowen and he captained Waikato to a famous win over the 1993 Lions. He now saw his future role in the coaching sphere.

Ireland's first match in the championship was against Scotland at Lansdowne Road, but Ireland gave an indifferent performance in that and lost 16-10. That was to be the last international appearance for Neil Francis, who was dropped for the visit to Paris and the second match in the championship.

Against France, Niall Woods came in on the wing for Geoghegan, who was injured. Paddy Johns moved from No. 8 to the second row for Francis. The pack was recast with Costello being restored to the No. 8 berth and Paddy Johns moved into the second row. Niall Hogan was recalled at scrum-half and David Humphreys, the former Ballymena outside half now with London Irish, was in at outside half for Elwood. It was a tough introduction to senior international rugby for Humphreys.

France overwhelmed Ireland that afternoon by 45-10. There was, too, an unfortunate sequel to the match. Ireland prop Peter Clohessy was cited on video evidence for having stamped on an opponent. The incident had not been seen by the referee, but the video evidence was clear cut. Clohessy was given a suspension of 26 playing weeks, which in effect had him out of the game for almost a year. While the offence was blatant, it was a very severe punishment, especially bearing in mind that far more lenient sentences had been imposed on others for similar offences. Clohessy contemplated retirement but decided to accept his punishment, learn from his indiscretion and subsequently came back to the international scene.

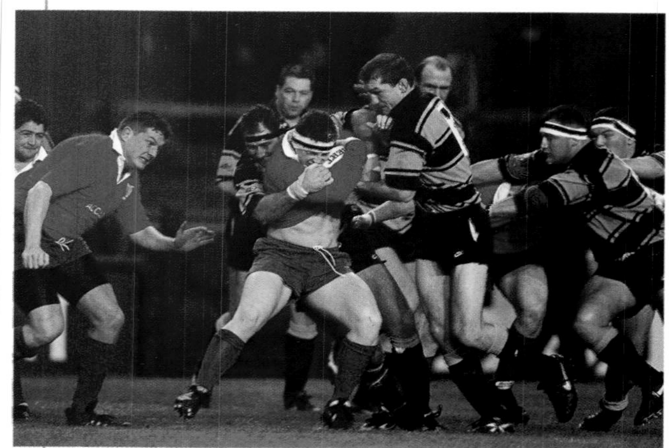

International prop forward, Paul Wallace, battles against the Cardiff pack in the European Cup semi-final at Lansdowne Road in December 1995. Cardiff won the match.

The Ireland team that played against Wales in the third championship match was much changed from the line-up in Paris. Simon Mason, the former Ireland Under 21 full-back, replaced Staples. Geoghegan returned and Niall Hogan was given the captaincy. Paul Wallace was in the front row for Clohessy, Denis McBride was back on the flank, Allan Clarke was at hooker for Kingston and Gabriel Fulcher and Davidson formed the second row.

Ireland scored a record 30-17 win over Wales at Lansdowne Road and got four tries in the process. It was a very welcome victory. The last match was against England at Twickenham and Ireland fielded an unchanged team. Ireland played quite well that afternoon although in the end England won 28-15. A try by England wing John Sleightholme was to prove the crucial score as England eventually broke the Irish challenge.

So Ireland ended the first season of the professional era with three wins and three defeats from six matches, with the three defeats coming in the championship.

But while the initial season of professionalism was now part of history, the problems, unrest, controversy and some of the unethical activity that was to follow gave absolute credence to those who had forecast disharmony and major problems ahead.

CHAPTER 34

CONTRACTS AND CONTROVERSIES

EVEN BEFORE A BALL WAS KICKED at the outset of the 1996–97 season, the game in these islands was thrown into controversy by the action of the RFU in agreeing a television deal with Sky for all of England's home internationals.

These crucially included the Five Nations Championship matches and, understandably, this incensed the other home unions, the IRFU, the SRU and the WRU.

With just a year to run of the home unions' contract with the BBC for the championship, negotiations on a new contract were due to start. But the RFU declared what was akin to a unilateral declaration of independence and agreed an £87.5 million deal with Sky.

The other unions totally rejected not alone the deal, but the RFU's right to enter such a deal. They felt that England had sold what did not belong to them in relation to the championship. They also felt that it was a total breach of faith and a break with long-established precedent, that was, that television deals were a collective effort of the four nations. It was not alone what the RFU had done, but the way they did it that added to the sense of annoyance. It was seen as a clandestine deal motivated by self-interest and the other unions would have nothing to do with it.

The summer of 1996 was, consequently, what one might justly describe as fractious and friendships and trust that had been established for over 100 years were strained to breaking point. An attempt by Sky to buy off the other home unions with offers for the rights to the televising of their home matches was rejected out of hand.

Initially the RFU would not budge and, as a consequence, the other three unions made it clear that, if the RFU continued with their obdurate stand, then England would be dismissed from the championship in 1997–98. The French had their own deal with French television but essentially supported the three unions. The offers that were made by Sky, and the manner in which they were made, were such that it was never even remotely possible they would be accepted.

England's argument was that, as they had the largest television audience, they were, consequently, entitled to the largest proportion of the money. That argument made absolutely no impression. The championship was a competition that embraced five nations, no one more or less important than the others. They were all an integral part of the same body. Furthermore, Lions teams were the pick of the four home unions who had always acted in unison. Obviously the future of the Lions was also at stake.

Ongoing discussions failed to break the impasse and, in the end, the RFU was given an ultimatum. Finally the message got home that the other unions would not back off. They knew the gravity of the situation and had no desire to see a championship that had run for over a century being sundered. But neither could they stand back and tolerate being effectively relegated to second-class citizenship to suit the RFU.

It was at a meeting in Cardiff on 4 August 1996 that the issue was finally resolved. That meeting was attended by representatives from all four unions, not just the members of the television committees of the unions. Ireland was represented at the meeting by union president Bobby Deacy, Syd Millar and Tom Kiernan, Ireland's two representatives on the International Board, and the IRFU honorary treasurer John Lyons.

The breakthrough eventually came and that saved England's place in the championship. They could not break the deal they had signed with Sky and so all their home matches were the exclusive preserve of that channel for primary rights to live television of the matches at Twickenham. But it was agreed that the RFU would have to put some of the money they had received into the kitty for distribution to the other unions, the sum to be agreed by an independent arbitrator.

Following the crucial meeting in Cardiff, the announcement that agreement had been reached was made at a press conference held in Dublin at which all the unions were represented. In the wake of that, negotiations took place between the unions and the BBC and a new deal was signed. It was, too, a very good deal that brought in a considerable sum of money greater than that offered to the IRFU, WRU and SRU by Sky. They had offered the IRFU £27.5 million, made the same offer to the Scots, and about £10 million more to the WRU. The Celtic nations had stood firm and won the day.

Meanwhile on the home front, the IRFU had other matters of immense importance to deal with. English clubs were offering lucrative contracts to Irish players and the exodus began in earnest. A few had gone the previous year; now the number was well into double figures. Internationals Keith Wood, Paul Wallace, Paddy Johns, Richard Wallace, Jeremy Davidson, David Corkery, Paul Burke, Victor Costello, Gabriel Fulcher, Niall Woods, Ken O'Connell, Malcolm O'Kelly, Jonathan Bell, Henry Hurley and Darragh O'Mahony, among others, all went to play in England. Wood went to Harlequins, Johns and the Wallace brothers to Saracens, Corkery and Burke to Bristol, Fulcher, Woods, O'Connell, O'Kelly and Costello all to London Irish, Bell to Northampton, and Hurley and O'Mahony to Moseley.

With Nick Popplewell having already moved from Wasps to Newcastle, Allan Clarke playing with Northampton, Conor O'Shea with London Irish, Simon Geoghegan with Bath and Jim Staples with Harlequins, the majority of players in the Ireland squad were now playing in England and all that such a situation embraced. Eric Miller had gone to Leicester where Niall Malone was also based after moving from London Irish. Subsequently, some more Irish players followed the route across the Irish sea, among them Ben Cronin, Mark McCall and Brian Walsh.

That exodus obviously ruled a host of players out of the interprovincial championship, but some had insisted as part of their contracts that they be free to play for the Irish provinces in the European Cup. That proved to be a very contentious issue, most especially with London Irish. It all represented a huge challenge to the IRFU. The Game Participation subcommittee which had done its job in relation to the changes in law after the game went professional now no longer had a function. The task of dealing with players' contracts was entrusted to the IRFU Contracts subcommittee. That committee was chaired by Billy Lavery and the other members were Bobby Deacy, Eddie Coleman, John Lyons, Noel Murphy, now

Ireland team that played Australia, 23 November 1996

the junior vice president of the Union, the IRFU secretary Philip Browne and Padraig Slattery from the union PR consultants, Slattery Public Relations.

The Ireland Selection committee remained unaltered with Pat Whelan manager and Murray Kidd as coach. Late in August the management found themselves in confrontation with the members of the national squad. A training weekend had been arranged in Kildare. The players' agents travelled to Kildare and, with the agreement of the Irish management, held a meeting with the players on Saturday night.

The following morning the Ireland management was informed by the agents that the players would not train on the Sunday as they were unhappy about the insurance element of the contracts. It was a *fait accompli* and it was less than well received by the IRFU. The players did not train and went home, but the issue was subsequently resolved. It was, in fact, a very poor demonstration of player power, or agent power, that backfired. But that was indicative of the climate that now obtained in the game. An apology from the players for their precipitous and ill-advised action was later made to the IRFU.

The European Cup, now sponsored by Heineken, had been extended to 20 teams, split into four groups of five teams each. Yet again Munster, Leinster and Ulster represented Ireland. There was also a subsidiary competition, the European Conference, and Connacht represented Ireland in that. The English clubs and Scottish Districts were now in Europe and that added to the significance of what was now truly a European competition.

While the Irish provinces scored some excellent victories in the competition, none managed a quarter-final place. Leinster were drawn in a group that included Leicester, Llanelli, Paul and Scottish

Borders. Leinster won two of their five matches but lost out on a quarter-final place on points difference to Llanelli. Ulster managed only one win in a group that included Harlequins, Neath, Caledonia and Brive. Munster were drawn with Cardiff, Toulouse, Wasps and Milan. Munster recorded a famous win over Wasps at Thomond Park, but that was one of only two wins and Munster went to Toulouse seeking a quarter-final berth but were comprehensively defeated. Connacht managed two wins out of five matches in Pool C of the Conference, with Northampton winning the group which also included Toulon, Orrell, Padova and Dunvant.

The release of players by the English clubs proved to be a major bone of contention, most notably with the London Irish club. They initially refused to release the players, but some of them insisted on the release agreement they had with the club being honoured. David Corkery, too, insisted on Bristol releasing him to play for Munster. But the presence of so many players in England was detrimental to the Irish provinces' cause.

The Exiles were, in the new situation that existed, no longer in a position to field a team in the interprovincial championship. That was won by Munster who won all three matches with Leinster as runners-up.

Ireland had a three match schedule prior to the Five Nations Championship with Western Samoa, Australia and Italy as visitors to Lansdowne Road. The Ireland forwards were now, being coached by former All Black Mike Brewer, who was player coach with Blackrock College.

The match against Western Samoa was held under the floodlights at Lansdowne Road and in midweek. This was the first occasion that an entire international was played under lights in Ireland. Ireland included three new caps. They were Victor Costello, Rob Henderson, the London Irish centre, and James Topping, the Ballymena wing. Ireland gave a very poor performance and paid the penalty for it, losing 40-25. They were, too, outscored by five tries to one, its own commentary on the manner in which they were outplayed.

Next up was the match against Australia at Lansdowne Road on 25 November. Not surprisingly, the team underwent radical alteration from the side that lost to Western Samoa and two new caps were brought into the much altered team. They were the Garryowen scrum-half Stephen McIvor and the Garryowen and former UCC player Dominic Crotty. Crotty, perhaps more comfortable at full-back, was chosen on the wing. Niall Hogan, now also playing his club rugby in England with Oxford University and who had led the team against Western Samoa, was one of those dropped and the captaincy passed to Keith Wood.

In what was basically a disappointing match, Australia won 22-12 with all Ireland's points coming from outside half Paul Burke, who had come into the team for David Humphreys.

Now it was not just the players who were under pressure. The coach Murray Kidd was also feeling the chill wind. Among his problems was that he seemed unable to motivate the players and confidence in his methods and training was ebbing away. The match against Italy at Lansdowne Road on 4 January was as important for his future as Ireland coach as it was for some of the players' international future. Yet again Ireland failed to deliver and lost 37-29. Ireland scored one try to Italy's four. In fact it was the superb penalty kicking of Paul Burke that kept the score within respectable proportions. Burke kicked eight penalties for a personal contribution of 24 points, a new Ireland record in an international. The match marked the international debut of Eric Miller, who had played for Ireland at schools and Under 21 level and was now making a very good impression with Leicester. However, he was injured at an early stage and had to be replaced.

The day after that match IRFU officials met with Pat Whelan for a meeting that had been scheduled prior to the match against Italy to discuss Ireland's performances and related matters. The position of the coach was discussed, but no statement was issued. A few days later the IRFU did issue a statement announcing that Kidd had been summoned to Dublin to discuss all matters in relation to the Ireland team with IRFU officials, led by union president Bobby Deacy. Kidd, obviously sensing that the end of his tenure as Ireland coach was at hand, brought his legal adviser with him. Severance terms were agreed at a protracted meeting and Kidd's resignation was announced.

Now the task was to appoint a successor to Kidd. The man who emerged was yet another from outside Ireland, Englishman Brian Ashton. He had been very successful with the Bath club in England and had recently severed connection with that club in controversial circumstances. He was appointed as coach initially in a caretaker capacity and he it was who prepared the team for the first match in the Five Nations Championship, against France at Lansdowne Road on 18 January. Wood led a side that saw the return of Eric Elwood at outside half, and Conor O'Shea at full-back. Maurice Field was in the centre. Hogan was back at scrum-half and Denis McBride was restored on the flank.

Brian Ashton who took over as coach from Murray Kidd for the International Championship 1997. His tenure was not of long duration

Ireland started well in the match, but yet another shoulder injury meant an early departure from the field for Keith Wood. The French had the flair and the depth to see off the Irish challenge and won 32-15. Elwood got Ireland's 15 points from five penalties.

Ireland's next assignment was against Wales in Cardiff, that happy hunting ground for Irish rugby over the previous decade. It proved so yet again as Ireland won 26-25. It was a fourth successive victory over Wales including the World Cup win, and that was a record run for Ireland against the Welsh. Ireland scored three tries through Jonathan Bell, Eric Miller and a newcomer in the St Mary's College wing Denis Hickie, who made an auspicious debut that afternoon. He is a member of a distinguished Irish rugby family. His uncle Denis had played for Ireland 25 years previously and his father Tony had been a final trialist. Ireland also had a new hooker in Roiss Nesdale of Newcastle. A New Zealander of Irish extraction, Nesdale came in for Keith Wood, whose season was over after the injury he sustained against France.

During the course of the weekend in Cardiff, discussions were held with Brian Ashton and his agent about his future with the Ireland team. The indications were very firm that Ashton was about to commit himself to Ireland for the foreseeable future.

He and many others were bitterly disappointed by Ireland's performance in the third Five Nations Championship encounter against England at Lansdowne Road. The match marked the international

Eric Elwood tackled in possession against France at Lansdowne Road 1997

debut of scrum-half Brian O'Meara from Cork Constitution. An outstanding player at under age level, O'Meara came on as a replacement during the match for Niall Hogan. Ireland, after a reasonably promising start, gave a very poor display and were overrun by England, notably in the second half, as England cruised to a record 46-6 victory and scored six tries in the demolition.

The last match of the campaign was against Scotland at Murrayfield. O'Meara was preferred to Hogan in that match in a much changed Ireland team. But happenings off the field before that match was played were of immense significance. Prior to the departure of the Ireland side for Murrayfield on Thursday, 27 March, the IRFU held a press conference at Dublin Airport. Eddie Coleman, the chairman of the IRFU Elections subcommittee, presided at the conference.

He announced that Brian Ashton had signed a six year contract with the IRFU as coach to the national side. It was a vote of confidence without precedent. Not alone that, but another major change was made in the selection process. Pat Whelan was confirmed as manager of the team up to and including the 1999 World Cup and it was also announced that the Selection committee would be reduced to three, Ashton, Whelan and a selector yet to be named.

Ireland wing, Denis Hickie, scores a try against Wales in Cardiff 1997

Ashton certainly did not get the psychological boost he had hoped for from events at Murrayfield. In addition to the inclusion of O'Meara, Ben Cronin was recalled at No. 8 to win his second cap. Kurt McQuilkin was recalled in the centre with Bell moved from centre to wing for James Topping. Paul Flavin (Blackrock College) came in at loose head prop for the injured Nick Popplewell and Cronin came in for Eric Miller, who was injured against England.

It all started well for Ireland and Hickie got a superb try after a great run by Staples, who unfortunately pulled a hamstring and had to be replaced by Conor O'Shea. O'Meara was another casualty and was replaced by Stephen McIvor. It was in some respects a repetition of what happened against England as Ireland got swamped in the second half and lost 38-10, another record defeat.

Eddie Coleman, in his capacity as chairman of the IRFU Tours subcommittee, had travelled to New Zealand earlier in the season and had arranged a tour to that country for the summer. It was what was termed an A-development tour aimed at giving experience to Irish players. Unfortunately, prior to departure there were quite a few defections from the Irish party and it was thin in some positions, especially bearing in mind the quality of the opposition that would be encountered. That proved to be the case as Ireland managed to win only one of the seven matches played.

Ireland had a back-up team of eight on the tour: manager Pat Whelan, Brian Ashton as coach, David Haslett as assistant coach, Denis Fanagan as physiotherapist, Donal O'Shaughnessy as doctor, Willie Bennett as masseur, Paddy O'Reilly as baggage master and a special fitness adviser in Andy Clarke, who had come into that position some time previously. So large a back-up team was an illustration of the changes that professionalism had brought about.

Ireland wing, James Topping, is tackled by England's Tim Rodber and Lawrence Dallaglio in the Championship match at Lansdowne Road in 1997

The Lions toured South Africa in the summer of 1997 and four Irish players were chosen for the tour. Donal Lenihan was Ireland's representative on the Lions selection committee. Four Irish players were chosen for the tour. They were Keith Wood, who had proved his fitness with his club Harlequins after his shoulder injury, Jeremy Davidson, Eric Miller and Peter Clohessy. Clohessy had gone to Australia to play for Queensland at the end of his 26 playing weeks' suspension. His form was monitored while he was with Queensland and he was chosen for the tour. The Lions were coached yet again by Ian McGeechan, who had acted in a similar capacity to the 1989 Lions in Australia and the 1993 Lions in New Zealand. His assistant was Scotland's Jim Telfer and the manager was Fran Cotton, the former England and Lions prop.

After the players assembled for training just outside London prior to departure, Clohessy failed to come through a fitness test, being troubled by a back injury. With his tenure with Queensland over, Clohessy returned to Limerick instead of travelling to South Africa with the Lions. It was a bitter disappointment for a player who had overcome his disciplinary problems and fought back to the top representative scene showing courage and character in doing so. Meanwhile it was another Irishman who was called in to replace Clohessy and the choice was Paul Wallace. He had been training with the Ireland Development squad in Limerick in preparation for the tour to New Zealand when he got the call to join the Lions.

It was a memorable tour as the Lions won the series 2-1. Wallace's chances of making the Test team were not deemed bright before the tour, but he played splendidly in South Africa and was chosen for the first Test. Indeed all four Irishmen were chosen for that Test. Miller, however, had to withdraw because of an attack of influenza. The Lions won the Test in Cape Town and all three Irishmen played their part in a famous win. Davidson was named man of the match.

Ireland forward, Jeremy Davidson, wins a line out against Scotland at Murrayfield in 1997. Ireland lost the match, but Davidson went on to star for the Lions in South Africa later that year.

Wood, Wallace and Davidson were all chosen for the second Test in Durban and Miller was a replacement. The Lions won the match and with it the series, through a late dropped goal from England centre Jeremy Guscott. When the final whistle blew, all four Irishmen were on the field as Miller had come on as a replacement. The Lions lost the third and the final fourth Test playing with a very depleted team and Wood missed the match because of an injury sustained in the second Test. Miller had been ruled out of contention because of an injury sustained in a provincial match — so a historic tour, the first by a professional Lions team and a famous series win for the Lions. Now the often stated view that rugby in these islands was far behind that in the southern hemisphere did not quite carry the same level of weight as prior to that series win. The Lions had, after all, beaten the reigning world champions.

The second season of professionalism had now been consigned to history, but some unexpected problems of major dimension lay ahead in Ireland and elsewhere and, from an Irish perspective, Ashton and Whelan were to be centre stage in controversy.

CHAPTER 35

RESIGNATIONS AND ACCUSATIONS

ULSTER HAD LED THE WAY with the appointment of a full-time coach to their provincial side when Tony Russ, a former Leicester coach, had been appointed to the job. His domestic circumstances were such, however, that he only stayed a year.

But with the demands of professionalism and, of course, the advent of the European Cup, the IRFU decided that all four Irish provinces would have full-time coaches, or to give them their official title, directors of coaching.

Two Welshmen had been offered those positions in Ulster and Munster but both, after initially accepting the positions, decided not to take up the option.

Leinster, however, had appointed the former Swansea and Welsh A team coach Mike Ruddock as their coach. Former international Jim Glennon was manager. It was home-based men in charge of the other provinces at the start of the 1997–98 season. Munster had the Shannon coach Niall O'Donovan and the former Ireland schools and Dolphin coach Declan Kidney as their coaching duo, with former international Gerry Holland as manager. David Haslett coached Ulster and Eddie O'Sullivan was coach to Connacht. However, as the season got under way, O'Sullivan resigned after failing to agree terms with Connacht on some issues in relation to his contract. Connacht sent what amounted to an SOS to New Zealand for Warren Gatland, the former All Black who had spent several years as player coach with Galwegians. He accepted the position and a splendid job he made of it.

Meanwhile, the IRFU contracted 37 players at international level on a graded basis. Prior to the start of the season the contracts were awarded to players nominated by the Ireland management. The players based outside the country were not available to the provinces, but they got paid for attending training sessions and there were ancillary benefits available to all. Now some Ireland players had the facility to earn very substantial sums of money as well as win bonuses and other benefits; some also were supplied with cars. It was another very concerted move towards getting the contract structure right and to give players based in England the incentive to return home.

The European Cup was on the agenda again and Leinster, Munster and Ulster represented Ireland, while Connacht played in the European Conference. Twenty teams contested the five pools in the Cup with each pool consisting of four teams with the pools played on a home and away basis, a new departure. Once more both Munster and Leinster recorded some notable victories, but the Irish provinces failed to make it to the knock-out stages. Leinster scored a great win over Leicester, the finalists the previous season, in a great match at Donnybrook, while Munster yet again rose to the challenge at Thomond Park and defeated a multinational Harlequins team. Munster had lost to Harlequins in London but had played

Pat Whelan resigned as Irish Manager May 1998

well, and while they defeated Bourgoin in Limerick, those two wins were not enough. They had also been extremely unlucky to lose to Cardiff at Musgrave Park. Ulster's one win saw the province score a very worthy victory over Swansea. The championship was won by Bath who defeated Brive in the final.

Connacht, under Gatland's prudent and perceptive guidance, performed with immense distinction in the Conference. They scored a great win over Northampton 45-13 in Galway, they beat Begles-Bordeaux away 15-9 and defeated Nice 28-25 in Galway after losing the away match. They completed the double, a 22-15 win over Begles-Bordeaux in Galway, and in a crucial match, went to Northampton and won 20-15 to top Pool D with five wins from six matches.

That gave Connacht a place in the quarter-finals and they put up a tremendous fight before going down away to Agen, the eventual finalists, by 40-27.

It was Leinster who emerged as interprovincial champions with wins over Ulster and Connacht and they won the title on points difference from Munster, who had beaten Leinster 15-12, Connacht 29-9, but lost to Ulster 22-12.

New Zealand, who had won the Tri-Nations Championship, came on a short tour in November to Ireland, Wales and England but played just the one match in Ireland, an international at Lansdowne Road on 15 November.

Ireland Manager Pat Whelan (left) and coach Brian Ashton at a training session at the Suttonians ground in January 1998. It followed a controversial press conference. Both had resigned by the end of the season

Influenced by what they had seen in the European competitions and the interprovincial series, the Ireland management decided to field a team that included five new caps. Three came from St Mary's College, full-back Keith Nowlan, wing John McWeeney and scrum-half Conor McGuinness. Two newcomers in the pack were the London Irish second row Malcolm O'Kelly and the London Irish flanker Kieron Dawson. Before the match was over, two other players had won caps as replacements. They were the Sale and Ulster back row forward David Erskine and the Bristol centre Kevin Maggs. An Englishman with Irish qualifications, he had gone on the Development tour to New Zealand.

It was not a combination that troubled New Zealand, who scored a record 63 points to 15 victory. Ireland's two tries were scored by captain Keith Wood.

Ireland had two other matches scheduled prior to the Five Nations Championship. Canada came to Lansdowne Road on 30 November and Ireland maintained their 100 per cent record against the Canadians with a 33-11 win. Nick Popplewell led the Ireland team in Wood's enforced absence and Nesdale replaced Wood. Maggs was chosen on the wing instead of McWeeney and only Dawson remained from the back row that lined out against New Zealand. Erskine and Victor Costello came in for the injured Eric Miller and Eddie Halvey who was dropped. Ireland won readily enough against moderate opposition. It was a Canadian team with a tangible Irish connection. The Canadian coach was Pat Parfrey who had been capped for Ireland over twenty years previously while a student at UCC.

Ireland went to Bologna to play Italy on 20 December and the Italians were now on a hat-trick against the Irish, having won in Treviso in 1995 and at Lansdowne Road in 1996. The Italians duly accomplished the three in a row and thoroughly deserved to do so. Darragh O'Mahony was back on the left wing, Niall Hogan was restored to the scrum-half berth, David Humphreys was at outside half and Reggie Corrigan of Greystones was at loose head prop for the injured Popplewell and so won his second cap, having come on as a replacement against the Canadians. Dylan O'Grady, of Sale, who had played several times for the Exiles in the interprovincial series, won his first cap on the flank.

Ireland had a reasonable first half, but thereafter it was the Italians who dictated the play, and with their outside half Diego Dominguez at his best, they outplayed Ireland and won 37-22. The match marked the return to the international arena of Peter Clohessy, who was now back with Young Munster after his stay in Australia.

The match in Bologna was scarcely an inspiring preface to the opening encounter in the Five Nations against Scotland at Lansdowne Road on 7 February. Prior to that match it was reported that all was not well between Brian Ashton and Pat Whelan. They had been joined in selection by Donal Lenihan, who had been named as the third man earlier in the season. The suggestion was that Ashton was finding it difficult to work with Whelan. Ashton was not quoted as saying that, but the implication was clear. Whelan was very surprised at the suggestions, as was the IRFU, as Ashton had not at any time given any indication to the IRFU that he had a problem in that area. He had ample opportunity to do so.

A press conference took place at a training session in the Suttonians ground prior to the match against the Scots, and while Ashton was not full hearted in denials of a problem with the manager, neither was he specific in denying them. 'Pat is an Irishman and I am an Englishman. He is an amateur and I am a professional.' It was a rather ambiguous comment, but at any rate it seemed that if he did feel he had problems, he also apparently felt they had been resolved sufficiently for the pair to work together.

Ireland yet again failed to beat the Scots, who won 17-16 and by so doing maintained an unbeaten record against Ireland that now stretched to 11 matches. The Scots went into that match in the immediate aftermath of problems in relation to their coach. Like Ireland, Scotland had lost to Italy. The consequences of that was the resignation of coach Richie Dixon, and his assistant David Johnson was dismissed. Scotland turned to an old reliable in the person of Jim Telfer. Ireland failed to capitalise on opportunities but none the less led 16-11 going into the last 20 minutes. Ireland then failed to take advantage of an overlap and had six scrums almost on the Scots line but could not make the breakthrough. Two penalties by Craig Chalmers saw Ireland off and a match that was there to be won had been cast away.

Immediately after the match, Ashton's frustration was apparent when he said, 'I do not know whose game plan that was, but it most certainly was not mine.'

A fortnight later Ashton had resigned. He got an attack of shingles and informed the IRFU that he had decided to resign. In his resignation letter he made no mention of any disagreement with Whelan, but in all the circumstances said that he no longer felt that he could continue as coach. So the man who

DONAL LENIHAN, WHO SUCCEEDED PAT WHELAN AS MANAGER AND WARREN GATLAND WHO SUCCEEDED BRIAN ASHTON AS COACH

had been given the longest contract in the history of the game by any country, ended up having the shortest tenure of any Ireland coach.

Ashton subsequently stated that he had made a mistake in taking the Irish coaching position. He also intimated that he did not understand the Irish character and had probably made an error in not attending All Ireland League matches. He was probably right on all three counts. But it would have been better had he stated that earlier and it would have avoided an unpleasant situation. He had been given a very lucrative contract, was supplied with a car and an apartment in Dun Laoghaire just outside Dublin. Some months after he left the Ireland post, he took up a coaching position with the RFFU.

Ireland was now a team without a coach and had the daunting task of a visit to Paris to play France less than a fortnight away. Ireland turned to Warren Gatland to stand in. His work with Connacht had been excellent and this was recognition of that. The former Ireland centre and captain Philip Danaher, the Garryowen coach, was brought in to help coach the backs.

Never has an Ireland team left the country rated as such long-odds outsiders. The French were rated at 33-1 on and the newspapers in France were full of speculation that France would not alone record the biggest win in the history of the Five Nations Championship, but could even break the world record of 145 points scored by New Zealand against Japan in the World Cup in 1995.

But it was not a meek and mild Irish side that the French faced in the superb new stadium in Paris, Stade de France, but an Ireland team at their unpredictable best. Gatland had done his homework and had the Irish worked up to fever pitch. He had also asked the Irish public to get behind the team and they received over 2,000 fax messages prior to the match. It all worked and Ireland came within an ace of scoring what would have been the most sensational win in the history of the championship. The Irish tackled superbly, their forwards matched the French in some facets and outplayed them in others. The French flair was stifled as effectively as it had ever been.

Ireland led 13-6 at the interval and were worth the lead. Eric Elwood kicked two penalty goals and Denis Hickie scored a try after he ran from halfway, having intercepted a pass. Elwood converted. The French reply had been two penalty goals kicked by Christophe Lamaison. France eventually broke the Irish defence when Philippe Bernat-Salles got a try, but Elwood kicked a third penalty for Ireland and, as the match entered its closing stages, a huge upset looked on. With seven minutes to go, the French got a second try when, from a maul near the Irish line, Raphael Ibanex managed to score a try and so France led 18-16. That was how it ended. But in the closing minutes, Ireland broke away and Victor Costello was in full flight. He elected to kick ahead rather than more prudently take the tackle and enable Ireland to win the ensuing ruck, and France cleared the danger. They will never have a more fortunate victory. Ireland included just one new cap in the match, the Ballynahinch flanker Andy Ward. A New Zealander, playing with a third division club in the AIB League, he made a magnificent debut.

Wales came to Lansdowne Road on 21 March and after the performance given by Ireland in Paris expectation was high. But Ireland turned in a very moderate performance, most notably the backs, who failed to turn even good possession to meaningful account. It was, in fact, Neil Jenkins' match. The Welsh outside half scored 20 points and he was the central figure in a 30-17 win. What was especially frustrating from an Irish viewpoint was that they scored two tries within 24 minutes of the start through Andy Ward and Victor Costello. But then after Ciaran Clarke, recalled at full-back, failed to hold a high kick under his posts, Alan Bateman, the Welsh centre, was able to gather and cross for a try under the Irish posts. It was Wales on top from this point on, adding two tries to Bateman's early effort.

Former All Black hooker, Warren Gatland, during an Ireland coaching session

The last match of the campaign was a visit to Twickenham, scarcely an enticing prospect bearing in mind that England had earlier in the championship scored 60 points against the Welsh. It was England who started well in the match with a try after just over two minutes, and they added a second from hooker Richard Cockerill. But Ireland were never less than competitive and Denis Hickie yet again revealed his facility for the interception when he scored a try in the 35th minute. But England struck again just before the interval when Mike Catt got a try. Ireland kept fighting on and Hickie scored a second try after a well-worked move with Eric Elwood. But it was really catch-up for Ireland in a match that included something of a private duel between the England captain Lawrence Dallaglio and David Corkery. Mark McCall, who was back in the side at centre, was badly injured in a clash of heads with Elwood and McCall had to be carried from the field. He was replaced by the Garryowen back Killian Keane, who thus won his first cap. In the end, England's 35-17 win was a reasonable enough reflection of the trend of the match and it gave England the Triple Crown for the fourth successive year.

Away from the playing field, the IRFU set up the IRFU Academy. This was aimed at a development programme for youngsters of exceptional talent and potential. It is in effect an extension of the Rugby Foundation set up four years earlier, but it embraces a much more elaborate programme. A very significant change was that the Foundation was aimed at boys a year after they left school; the Academy is aimed at players earlier in their careers.

It is an elite player development programme which identifies and develops potential international players. Screening for the elite players begins at Under 16 level and the final stage starts at the beginning of the Under 18 season. But there is also provision to bring in older players who meet the criteria of the Academy. The schools and youths selectors work with the provincial directors of coaching and propose candidates to the national screening panel. Contracts of between one and three years are offered to the successful candidates. These cover remuneration and other conditions. Contracts are tailored to meet individual needs so that non-rugby aspects of the Academy members' life can be developed.

With the Five Nations Championship over, Ireland had a scheduled tour to South Africa in the summer of 1998. But sometime before that was due, Pat Whelan resigned as Ireland manager. So, in the space of a few months, Ireland had lost both coach and manager. Whelan, in his resignation letter to the

IRFU, stated that he was standing aside for family and business reasons.

A few days before his resignation was announced, he had been accused of hitting the Irish rugby correspondent of *The Sunday Times* in a Limerick hostelry. Whelan never admitted that he had been involved in any incident and said that the accusation had nothing to do with his decision to resign. 'I had made my mind up some weeks previously and the IRFU knew that for the reasons I had stated that I was contemplating resignation', said Whelan.

The IRFU appointed Donal Lenihan as manager to succeed Whelan, and he, Warren Gatland and Philip Danaher made up the Ireland management team for the seven match tour to South Africa in May and June.

Jeremy Davidson, Eric Miller and Keith Wood, all of whom had toured with the Lions the previous season, were not considered for the tour. But Wood subsequently joined the squad after the tour had got under way. His decision was particularly welcome as Ross Nesdale had been unable to tour due to injury. The management handed the captaincy of the tour to Paddy Johns, the senior member of the side who had enjoyed, not alone a very good season in the Ireland jersey, but also with his club Saracens.

Ireland outside half, David Humphreys, is tackled by Scotland's Craig Chalmers in the championship match against Scotland at Lansdowne Road in 1998. Ireland lost the match when Chalmers kicked a penalty in injury time

Ireland brought several uncapped players on the tour including the Terenure College scrum-half Derek Hegarty, the Clontarf hooker Bernard Jackman, prop John Hayes from Shannon, prop Justin Fitzpatrick from London Irish, and the St Mary's College flanker Trevor Brennan. Dion O'Cuinneagain, a back row forward from the Sale club and a South African of Irish parentage, was another included. Ironically he was at one stage a candidate to make the Springboks team when he played for Western Province.

Ireland opened the tour with a 48-35 win over Boland, but no fewer than three players were injured in that match and took no further part in the tour. They were James Topping, Jonathan Bell and Reggie Corrigan. What made those injuries more worrying for the Ireland management was that Keith Wood, Malcolm O'Kelly and Paul Wallace were not available in the initial stages with O'Kelly and Wallace both injured. The injuries sustained in that opening assignment meant that reinforcements had to be brought in and Peter Clohessy's younger brother Des, a prop, joined the tour, as did wing Justin Bishop. Peter Clohessy and Mick Galwey were two of the senior players in the squad and they discharged their responsibilities admirably in every respect. Peter Clohessy's rehabilitation was now complete.

Ireland lost the second match to South West Districts in George 27-20 and were especially unfortunate to go down to Western Province in Cape Town, where a bad decision by the referee was a crucial element in the defeat. He subsequently apologised for his error, but it was too late to change anything. The fourth match was against Griquas West in Kimberley which Ireland lost 52-13 with a team that bore little resemblance to the side fielded in the first Test four days later. Ireland lost the Test 37-13, but that scoreline did not reflect the overall trend of the match. A notable feature of the game was that the Springboks' wing Stefan Terblanche scored four tries. The Ireland pack did well, but there was a lack of penetration behind the scrum. It was in the closing stages that the South Africans really emphasised their authority and superiority, and Ireland paid for some poor defending.

Ireland hooker, Keith Wood, is tackled by Christophe Dominici in the match against France at Stade Français, Paris, in the championship match in 1998

Ireland won the second last match against North West by 26-18 in Potchestrom and then, in the final Test, lost 33-0. That was a bad-tempered affair in the initial stages. And while the Ireland forwards again did quite well, the lack of depth was exposed in an Ireland team that looked tired and weary. A seven match tour including two Tests was really a bridge too far for a depleted Ireland squad. But there were positive elements from the tour which saw Justin Bishop, Justin Fitzpatrick, Dion O'Cuinneagain and Trevor Brennan all capped during the course of the Test series.

Two wins from seven matches was not a good return; neither did it quite reflect some of the better elements in the Irish performances.

So Ireland ended the 1997–98 season with one Test win from nine matches, that attained against Canada. That represents a bleak statistic, yet the season had not been without its positive aspects and Warren Gatland had seen some young players emerge as very credible Test players. Nor had good fortune attended Ireland in some of those matches, most notably against France. Gatland, Lenihan and Danaher were far from being despondent as Ireland prepared for the World Cup qualifying matches against Romania and Georgia scheduled for November and a match against South Africa also at Lansdowne Road in November.

There was, too, some remarkable success for Ireland teams at under age level in 1997–98 to offer further encouragement about the days and the years ahead.

CHAPTER 36

FAITH IN THE FUTURE

A MAJOR CONCERN FOR THE IRFU when the game went professional was the departure of so many prominent players to English clubs. The lure was lucrative contracts and one heard talk of players wanting to play in the English League as it was alleged this would improve their standard of performance.

No one blamed players for doing what they considered to be in their own best interest, but the IRFU had gone on record stating that players should exercise caution and prudence before giving up their jobs, leaving home and family and committing themselves to what could be an uncertain future.

English clubs were spending vast sums of money to sign players from all over the world. It was not long before it became obvious that many of the clubs just could not sustain the level of expenditure that their actions embraced.

The money coming into the club game in England went nowhere near meeting the outlay and the inevitable consequence was that, sadly, clubs found themselves going bankrupt and had to call in the receivers. That factor, allied to quite a lot of disillusionment in other respects, prompted many players to realise that all the hopes and the promises they had entertained and been given were not being realised.

Nor was there any evidence to suggest that standards of performance were getting better as a result of playing in the English League. Furthermore, those players based in England could not play in European competition for their Irish provinces and many of them were with clubs in England that had not qualified for the European Cup.

The IRFU watched and monitored the situation with great care. The objective was to get as many players as possible back to Ireland, and a crucial factor, to stop young and talented players from going to England.

With those worthy objectives in mind, the IRFU set about putting in place a financial structure that would meet their dual objective, getting the players home and stopping the departure of the younger element. That was their stated policy and they set about implementing it.

So a decision of the utmost importance was taken in the summer of 1998. When the game went professional the contracts issue was something akin to trial and error. It was unknown and uncharted waters in rugby. Inevitably mistakes were made, but so also lessons were learned. With increased revenue now coming from television, the IRFU had the money available to make radical alterations in the contracts.

Thus a crucial decision was taken. It was decided that 21 full-time contracts would be offered to players in all four provinces, together with 10 part-time contracts. All four provinces now had full-time professional coaches in place and a back-up team to oversee fitness. In addition, each province had the right to bring in two overseas players. It was a radical change and it paid a dividend.

The majority of the Irish players in England whose contracts were due for renewal or who had the right to exercise the option of coming home, exercised that option, and so it was that in the summer of 1998 the trend in player movement was now reversed.

Ireland full back, Conor O'Shea, is stopped in his tracks by the Springboks at Lansdowne Road in 1998

Internationals David Humphreys, Jonathan Bell, Allan Clarke, Gabriel Fulcher, David Corkery, Mark McCall, Henry Hurley and Ben Cronin all came 'home'. So too did Ireland A players Brian Walsh and Martin Ridge. Subsequently, Eric Miller also returned after his contract with Leicester was bought out by Terenure College. He declared for Ulster. International Simon Mason, who had played all his club rugby in England, also saw the opportunity to play in Ireland and he declared for Ulster and signed for Ballymena. Another in the same category, Justin Fitzpatrick, who had also played all his club rugby in England, followed a similar path to that of Mason. Niall Hogan, who had played for London Irish as well as Oxford University, was yet another international who returned to the home scene and his former club Terenure College.

When one bears in mind that two other internationals, Eddie Halvey and Victor Costello, had earlier been disillusioned with the game in England and had returned home, the IRFU had every reason to feel that their policy had reversed the trend to the benefit of clubs and provinces in Ireland.

The English clubs, meanwhile, decided that they would not enter the European Cup or Shield — the Shield replaced what had previously been termed the Conference as they were not satisfied with the structure or financial rewards from the competitions. The RFU had signed an agreement during the summer with the clubs, termed 'The Mayfair Agreement'. It was an extraordinary document in many ways, the terms of which did little or nothing to ease the ongoing bickering about structures and leagues.

Proposals were put for an Anglo-French League, but they fell through, and then came a proposal for a British and Irish League. The IRFU sent representatives for discussions on that, but completely rejected the idea when it was proposed that the Irish provinces would play in what was effectively a second division, as all the top English clubs, together with Cardiff and Swansea, would play in division one. The English left-overs, together with the Irish provinces, the Scottish Districts and some Welsh clubs would make up the second division. It would have involved 22 matches in a 12 team division played on a home and away basis.

A meeting in England in December 1998 on the proposed British and Irish League was attended by

IRFU president Noel Murphy, IRFU Rugby Administrator George Spotswood and IRFU Director of Rugby Eddie Wigglesworth. Wigglesworth had been Chief Executive of the Leinster Branch and in October succeeded Ray Southam as the IRFU Director of Rugby after Southam had returned to New Zealand. Following that meeting the IRFU announced that the Irish provinces would not participate in the league.

Ireland saw the way forward through the interprovincial championship and the European competitions. The interprovincial championship format had been changed for the 1998–99 season with a double programme of matches with each province meeting each other twice. The new format was a huge success and the climax came in Donnybrook on 23 October when Munster beat Leinster to win the title.

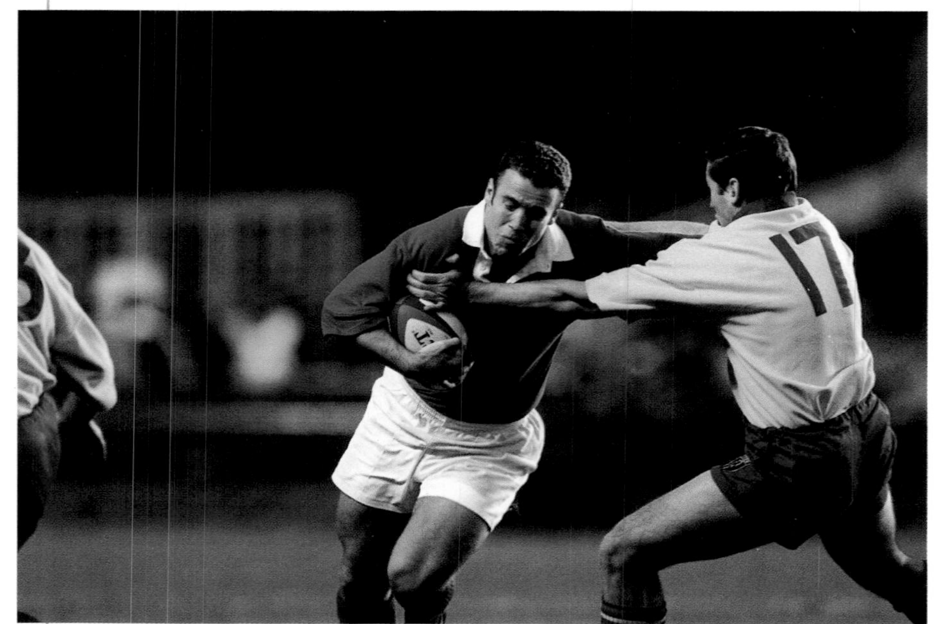

Ireland centre, Kevin Maggs, takes on the Romanian defence in the World Cup qualifier at Lansdowne Road in November 1998

The competitive nature of the championship was emphasised by the fact that the only double recorded in the series was by Munster who defeated Connacht twice.

In the European competitions both Ulster and Munster came out of their groups to reach the quarter-finals of the European Cup. Leinster failed narrowly losing the crucial match to Llanelli after building a very big lead within 20 minutes at Donnybrook before seeing the advantage wiped out and turned into a deficit.

Ulster had not made an auspicious start but put in a tremendous surge to make the knock-out stages. They had drawn with Edinburgh Reivers in their opening match at Ravenhill, lost to Toulouse 39-3 in Toulouse, and then came the fight back. Ulster defeated Ebbw Vale home and away, then scored a great 24-22 win over Toulouse at Ravenhill and went to Edinburgh requiring a victory over Edinburgh Reivers to reach the quarter-final. In a thrilling encounter Ulster came from behind to win 23-21.

That put Ulster into the quarter-final and they were drawn against Toulouse at Ravenhill. Watched by a capacity crowd under the floodlights at Ravenhill, Ulster scored a historic win over Toulouse, the winners of the inaugural European Cup, to earn a semi-final place and match at Ravenhill against Stade Français on 9 January 1999.

Munster, meanwhile, had got to the quarter-finals with home and away wins over Padova, a home win over Neath and a draw away from home against the Welsh side. They lost to Perpignan 24-42 in Perpignan but then at Musgrave Park defeated the French side 13-5 on 31 October. In the quarter-final Munster were drawn away to Colomiers and, after conceding early points, were unable to overcome the deficit and, although they held Colomiers pointless in the second half, Munster went out of the competition.

In the Shield, Connacht, now under the coaching of New Zealander Glenn Ross, who had succeeded Warren Gatland, had made a good start as they attempted to emulate their fine achievements of the previous season. But they were unable to sustain their efforts and failed to make the knock-out stages.

The new World Cup qualifying system meant that Ireland had to play Georgia and Romania to be sure of making it to the finals in October of 1999. Ireland achieved that objective with two wins. They defeated Georgia by 70-0 at Lansdowne Road on 14 November, and a week later beat Romania at Lansdowne Road 53-35.

The win over Georgia was the biggest ever recorded by an Ireland side, beating the 60 points scored against Romania in 1986. Ireland scored ten tries in the match and a feature was that Girvan Dempsey, the young Terenure College back who came on as a replacement, scored two. Another youngster who came on as a replacement, the UCD scrum-half Ciaran Scally, also marked his debut with a try, as did another new cap, the Connacht and Galwegians centre Pat Duignan. Eric Elwood also put another entry into the record books when he converted all ten.

The win over Romania was attained with equal facility, but an unsatisfactory aspect was that the Romanians scored five tries, two of them coming in the closing minutes. But the performance was sufficient for the needs thereof.

A week after the match against Romania, Ireland faced the world champions South Africa at Lansdowne Road. Keith Wood, who had refused to sign his international contract because he said it infringed his intellectual property rights, was ruled out of the match against Georgia on those grounds. He either signed the contract or would not be considered for Ireland and that was made clear to him. He then had a rapid change of mind and signed the contract. He was on the bench and came on against Romania. He was subsequently selected in his own right for the match against South Africa at Lansdowne Road on 28 November.

Ireland played very well in the first half against the world champions and a 7-6 interval lead for the Springboks was imbalanced to the trend of the match. Ireland had conceded a try through a defensive error. Then twice early in the second half the Springboks scored tries and that left Ireland with a mountain to climb. They played with tremendous heart and commitment and Wood, who had an outstanding match, scored a try for Ireland to bring the score to 13-24. They laid siege to the Springboks' line subsequently but could get no return for the pressure and the effort, and South Africa won 27-13.

In October former Ireland player Neil Francis made an allegation in a newspaper column that, during his time on the Ireland side which ran between 1987 and 1996, he knew that some players were taking performance-enhancing drugs. The allegation incensed the players with whom Francis had played and the IRFU.

The IRFU asked that any evidence available to substantiate so serious and damaging an allegation be made available to them. No such evidence was produced. However, there was major controversy shortly after the article appeared when it was announced that three Irish players had tested positive the

SCRUM HALF, CIARAN SCALLY, WON HIS FIRST CAP WHEN HE CAME ON AS A REPLACEMENT AGAINST GEORGIA IN THE WORLD CUP QUALIFIER AT LANSDOWNE ROAD IN NOVEMBER 1998. HE MARKED THE OCCASION BY SCORING A TRY

previous season. Remarkably, the British Sports Council, which was responsible for testing in Britain and Ireland, failed to notify the union of one of the cases until October 1998, even though the test had taken place over seven months previously.

The IRFU had, well before October of 1998, set up a drugs tribunal to investigate any allegations of drugs offences and make recommendations on any positive test. It emerged in one of the three cases that there was no breach of the regulations and in another the matter did not even have to go to an independent tribunal, which had also been set up by the IRFU, as there was no case to answer. The third case concerned an Under 21 player who unadvisedly had taken an illegal substance and he was severely reprimanded.

Shortly before Christmas 1998 the IRFU announced that 41 youth development officers and contracted players would set out and be available to encourage and help youngsters to play rugby with the personnel spread throughout the country. This initiative was aimed in particular at the youngsters who did not attend rugby-playing schools. It was an investment in the future and a worthy attempt to propagate the game. Every facility and help would be available to bring rugby to the young who had not previously played the game.

So Irish rugby faced into the final year of the final decade of the turbulent twentieth century. The IRFU knew the challenges were many, as indeed they had been through the years, most notably since the game went open. More development officers were in place; more schools were playing the game than at any time in history. The structures were in place from the IRFU Academy, schools and youth levels through to the Under 19 and Under 21 and A teams to offer every incentive and encouragement to those with the will and the ability to get the best out of their talents.

CHAPTER 37

THE REFEREES

AMBITION IS A NECESSARY ELEMENT for any participant in sport if the person aspires to reach the top echelon. That applies to referees as well as to those who actually play the games.

Refereeing has often been described as a thankless task but that is not an assessment to which those who officiate in matches would subscribe. They perform a crucial role, but like players they are involved because they enjoy it and have a love of the game.

Physical fitness is required, along with a deep knowledge of the laws, a feeling for the game, the ability to have a good relationship with the players and to establish a mutual understanding with them without surrendering any authority.

The professional era has, of course, increased the demands and the responsibilities. Now in this era of blanket television coverage of the big matches, the action replay will also reveal any mistakes and consequent embarrassment.

It is all very far removed from the early days. Indeed, when the first international took place between England and Scotland in 1871, there was no referee. Then in 1875–76 the referees for the internationals were from the country where the matches were being played. That arrangement did not last very long as, understandably, it was not deemed satisfactory as disputes inevitably arose. From 1885–86 onwards, neutral officials were appointed for the internationals played in the northern hemisphere. But, remarkably, until the 1970s when touring teams from these islands went to the southern hemisphere, the home nations were still appointing their own officials. That brought many a contentious decision and it was rightly changed and now every international is refereed by a neutral official.

From the outset Ireland provided its quota of international referees and through the years established a worthy reputation in this field. Great attention is now paid to the whole area of refereeing. For quite some time courses have been run for officials. Assessors operate to judge performances. As the years have gone by, so the greater the attention has become. Special committees at branch and union level are in place.

The level of importance placed in refereeing was recognised in 1995 when the IRFU decided to appoint a full-time National Referee Development officer. That task was entrusted to Owen Doyle, a man with a very distinguished record, having refereed sixteen internationals. The IRFU has for quite some time had a Referees Advisory panel in place and the elaborate structure is its own declaration of intent to get the best possible officials and to give the back-up support that is necessary.

All four provinces have long-established Referees Associations and these do a very good job within their own areas of operation. They hold regular meetings, regular discussions on different aspects of the game, and their role in it.

There is an interchange policy in place between different countries so that referees can get experience outside their own areas and in different environments. There are, too, financial rewards for officials at representative level and a few countries have actually appointed some full-time officials. In a word, like players, they are now full-time professionals.

What those who refereed back in the Victorian era would make of it all can be but a matter for conjecture. But in fact it was an Irishman who was the first official referee appointed at international level. He was appointed for the first international played on Irish soil, the first time that one man was put in charge. The distinction goes to Abram Coombe, who officiated at the Leinster Cricket Ground, Rathmines, when Ireland played England on 13 December 1875.

Coombe had actually played for Ireland the previous February when Ireland played at international level for the first time in the match against England at Kennington Oval. So he became the first man to do the double, play and referee, at international level. G. P. Nugent was the second Irishman to referee an international when he took charge of an Ireland-England match in 1880, and then came Hugh Kelly who, like Coombe, had played for Ireland.

William Goulding, later Sir William and another former international, was referee for the Ireland-Wales match in 1882 — the first time the countries met. Then later that season Dr William Neville was referee for Ireland's match against England.

In 1882, H. L. Robinson, of Ireland, was a neutral official when England played Scotland and the following season Hugh Kelly was referee for Scotland against England. Now the practice of appointing neutral officials was becoming more prevalent, but as such, not yet totally in place. Then in 1884, George Scriven created his place in rugby history. He refereed the England-Scotland match. There was a vigorous dispute about the legality of England's winning try and that led to the cancellation of the match between England and Scotland the following season. That was a key element in the subsequent formation of the International Board.

Scriven is unique. He was president of the IRFU in 1882–83 and he also played for Ireland against England and Scotland that season. Not alone that, he captained the side in both matches. As president of the IRFU, he was also, as it were, chairman of the selectors as the union committee selected the Ireland team in those days. Then in 1885–86 Scriven was again president of the IRFU and he is the only man in history to have occupied that office twice. There was an interval of several years between his two terms in the presidential chair.

When, by the mid-1800s, neutral referees were the common practice at international level, the appointments carried more merit, as it were. D. F. Moore, a former Ireland captain, Thomas Lyle, another former international and later Sir Thomas, Joseph Chambers, also later knighted, and Ed McAllister, who with Sir Thomas Lyle became Ireland's first representatives on the International Board, were all honoured.

As the task of refereeing became more specialised after the establishment of the International Board but still in no way comparable to what now obtains, Irishmen were appointed with great regularity. Many of them were former internationals such as R. G. Warren, an influential man in Irish rugby history. Then came J. T. Magee from a famous Irish rugby family, J. Dodds, M. G. Delaney, and R. W. Jeffares, later to become secretary of the IRFU. The list goes on. F. M. Hamilton, Ed Martelli, who had played for the Combined British and Irish side on tour but never for Ireland, Sam Lee, C. Lefevre, G. H. Kennedy, W. Kennedy, J. W. Allen, H. H. Corley, G. A. Harris, I. G. Davidson, J. J. Coffey, who emulated his father in becoming IRFU president, Fred Gardiner, Sam Crawford and V. Drennan. They had all been international referees when war called a halt to international rugby activity in 1914.

When internationals were resumed in 1919, Irish appointments were again made with regularity. Sam Crawford was still in action and he was the first Irishman to referee at international level in the post First World War era. Others were J. C. Crawford, Dickie Lloyd, among the greatest of Irish players, R. W. Harland, a famous figure in the world of refereeing who was in regular demand, J. B. McGowan, Dr E. de C. Wheeler, W. H. Acton, N. M. Purcell, Dr J. R. Wheeler, Rupert Jeffares, who emulated his father by being honoured and who succeeded his father as secretary of the IRFU, and Dickie Magrath, another former international and former president of the IRFU. In the 1930s Tom Bell was chosen several times and among others W.L. Freeman, F.W. Haslett and S. Donaldson were selected in the period up to 1939 when war again called a halt.

When internationals resumed in 1946–47, the first Irishman to be chosen was Michael Dowling from Cork. He was widely regarded as the best referee in the game during his very distinguished tenure. In 1948 former Ireland centre Ham Lambert officiated at the Scotland-Australia match at Murrayfield. This outstanding sportsman, who also played cricket for Ireland, was another highly regarded official. His involvement with the Association of Referees (Leinster Branch) spans well in excess of 50 years and his contribution was truly immense.

Ham Lambert and Michael Dowling were the two Irish referees who were chosen between 1947 and 1952. Then O. B. Glasgow was honoured in 1953. But Michael Dowling's international career continued until 1956. By then another fine and widely respected official, Bobby Mitchell, joined the distinguished array. Ray Williams made his debut in 1956–57.

The system of appointing referees at international level had by now changed appreciably and, unlike the pre-war era, the list was very much more confined and the task more specialised. For instance, in 1957–58 Ray Williams refereed four internationals and was the only Irishman to officiate that season. Indeed in 1957–58 and again the following season he was the only Irish referee appointed. In that two year spell he officiated in seven internationals.

A new figure emerged on the scene in 1959 in the person of Kevin Kelleher. His impact was considerable and he was to referee no fewer than 23 matches between his debut and his last appointment in 1971. That stood as a world record until beaten in 1991 by Clive Norling of Wales. Kelleher made headlines across the rugby world in 1967 when he sent the New Zealand second row Colin Meads off the field in Murrayfield against Scotland. That was only the second time in history that a player had been sent off during an international and the first since the 1920s. Another outstanding Irish referee who came on the international scene in 1966–67 was Paddy D'Arcy. He took charge of 17 internationals. R. W.

Gilliland and G. A. Jamison were two others from Ireland who were deemed worthy of a task that was becoming increasingly demanding as the game got more publicity and live television coverage. In 1973 K. H. Clarke took charge of his first international, and then in the England-Wales match in 1974, John West made his debut.

John West holds a unique place in the records as he was the first Irishman to referee an international in the southern hemisphere when he refereed the match between New Zealand and France in Auckland in 1979. That was one of 18 international matches at which he officiated in a splendid career.

In 1978–79 another Irishman Michael Rea joined the international fraternity, and in 1980 David Burnett made his debut in what was to be a career of immense distinction. Through the years the system of making appointments was altered and in the modern era referees were chosen from panels submitted by their own unions. One method of appointment that obtained for a while, and which was seen to be flawed in some respects, was that visiting countries were able to nominate the officials for matches. The variations in the system of appointments meant at one point that the best officials were not always called upon.

Owen Doyle made his debut in 1984 and then came another Irishman who made a considerable impact, Stephen Hilditch. David Burnett and Stephen Hilditch were chosen to officiate at the inaugural World Cup in New Zealand and Australia in 1987. David Burnett was given a quarter-final, but the panel who had the task of choosing the referees for the semi-finals and finals surprisingly overlooked Burnett and Hilditch. David Burnett refereed 15 internationals and Stephen Hilditch 17.

Hilditch and Owen Doyle were both chosen for the 1991 World Cup and Hilditch refereed one of the quarter-finals. Brian Stirling took charge of his first international when Fiji played England in 1989. David McHugh emerged on the international scene in 1994 and he and Stephen Hilditch both officiated at the World Cup in 1995 in South Africa. Hilditch thus had the singular distinction of having been involved in all three World Cups. McHugh sent three players off in the World Cup match between South Africa and Canada in 1995.

Gordon Black made the breakthrough to the international scene when he took charge of the Wales-Italy match in 1996, and former Ireland B international, Bertie Smith, and Leo Mayne joined the illustrious band in 1997.

Ireland's contribution to international refereeing has been considerable. Those who have been honoured at international level are, of course, a select band. They are, so to speak, the cream of the crop. But let us not forget the many who, while never elevated to the international arena, have made such an important contribution to the game at all levels.

CHAPTER 38

THE ALL IRELAND LEAGUE

FROM AN EARLY STAGE IN THE HISTORY of the IRFU the concept of competitive rugby had taken root. The clubs gave the impetus and the four branches and the IRFU gave the necessary support.

Much of the season in the early days was devoted to friendly fixtures and those expanded appreciably through the years as clubs from the various provinces travelled to meet each other. Those fixtures were competitive, but it was pride and prestige that were at stake.

As in other areas it was Trinity College who set the trend with their fixture in 1874 against NIFC. Clubs grew ambitious through the years and visits to Britain to play fixtures became popular, with the British clubs equally enthusiastic about visiting Ireland. Actual competitive rugby, however, was confined to the interprovincials and, of course, the internationals.

The medical profession has long been closely associated with rugby and that connection was given substance when, in 1882, the Dublin hospitals made the historic decision to have an annual competition for the Dublin Hospitals Cup which is still contested annually. The distinction of having won the inaugural competition goes to the Meath Hospital.

But the hospitals were not alone in seeking and seeing the advantages of a cup campaign. As early as October 1881 the Leinster Branch had decided to inaugurate a Leinster Senior Cup. The crucial meeting took place on 31 October 1881. The branch appointed a subcommittee of six to make the necessary arrangements and the clubs represented were Dublin University, Wanderers, Lansdowne, Phoenix, Dundalk and Kingstown.

Entries closed on 30 November 1881 and the draw for the cup took place on 1 December. Each participating club had to contribute £5 towards the cost of purchasing a cup and also pay an entry fee of 10 shillings (50 pence). All matches were scheduled for Lansdowne Road and the gate receipts were added to the cup funds. The winning team would receive medals or, as they were described in those days, crosses.

Five clubs entered, Dublin University, Phoenix, Wanderers, Lansdowne and Kingstown. Dublin University were drawn against Phoenix, Wanderers against Kingstown and Lansdowne received a bye into the semi-finals.

Trinity won the inaugural competition, defeating Kingstown by one goal to nil in the final played on 18 March. But while the medals were presented the cup was not, as it had not yet been purchased.

Trinity's severe criticism of the cup subcommittee was expressed at a meeting of the branch in October 1882. The subcommittee had only managed to collect just over £36. Two clubs, Wanderers and

Phoenix, had not paid the necessary £5 10*s*. Phoenix had, in fact, disbanded and Wanderers stated that their members had not come forward with the necessary money to enable the club to discharge its liability.

But all's well that ends well, and both Phoenix and Wanderers settled their debts. In November 1882 the cup was bought at a cost of £50 from the manufacturers Edmund Johnson of Grafton Street. Phoenix disappeared from the scene, Kingstown followed within a few years, and Monkstown and Bective Rangers duly entered the competition. Thus it can be claimed that Ireland led the way in establishing competitive rugby at club level.

Where Leinster led, the other provinces soon followed. Ulster established a senior cup competition in 1885 and, appropriately, it was won by NIFC, the club who with Trinity had done so much to bring organisation to the game in Ireland. The Munster Branch started their senior cup competition in 1886, with Bandon the inaugural winners. By 1896 Connacht had also inaugurated a senior cup and Galway Town, the club one could term the precursors to Galwegians, captured the trophy.

The competitive element was given further impetus when, in 1891, the Ulster Branch also started a senior league and this time it was Queen's University who proved the inaugural winners. Munster started a senior league in 1903 and Connacht in 1926. In Leinster there was both reluctance and resistance to the concept of a senior league. This was an extraordinary attitude, bearing in mind the fact that leagues operated in the province from second teams down through the structure.

Eventually, after much soul searching, the province did start a league, but it was not until 1971–72 that the competition took place. In fact, it was more of a league cup than a league, with three sections of four clubs and one of three. The opposition to a league was based on the premise that it would disrupt long-established friendly fixtures. That had been no deterrent to the clubs in the other provinces from having meaningful leagues and they valued their long-established fixtures as much as the Leinster clubs.

The concept of a national competition had exercised the minds of some rugby officials well over half a century earlier and in 1922 it was decided to inaugurate the Bateman Cup. That competition was for the four winners of the provincial cups. It was played in a weekend. Enthusiasm for it was greater in some places than in others. It went on from 1922 to 1932, with Lansdowne, the inaugural winners, winning it three times in a row between 1929 and 1931, a period during which they dominated Leinster rugby with five successive Leinster Cup triumphs.

The Bateman Cup did not take place for three years between 1933 and 1935 but was resumed in 1936 when UCC became the second Munster club to win the title. Young Munster had caused something of a sensation by winning it in 1928, just a few years after gaining senior status in Munster. UCD won the cup in 1938 and Blackrock College in 1939. The competition was halted during the 1939–45 war and sadly did not take place subsequently, although some attempts were made to revive it.

In 1975 the Munster Branch did arrange an All Ireland Cup based on the Bateman formula to mark the centenary of the union. The competition was a resounding success, but it did not prompt the authorities to revive the Bateman Cup. The Garryowen club also held a very successful competition in 1986 to mark their centenary, but those events were as near as Irish rugby got to having a national club competition.

However, there was an awareness in the IRFU that the competitive structure of the game in Ireland needed to be revised, an idea given added urgency by the fact that leagues had been established in the other home countries with beneficial consequences. The appointment by the IRFU of George Spotswood as Game Development officer was the first tangible step taken towards this revision.

Under 20 interprovincials were added to the annual calendar, a wise decision, and the Game Development committee of the union undertook an intensive study of the scene in Ireland. Men such as Sir Ewart Bell, Tom Kiernan and Ken Reid chaired this committee, which embraced people from a cross-section of the game in Ireland, including several former eminent players.

It was highly significant, too, that in England, Wales and Scotland the need for a well-structured national league had now been realised and came to fruition in those countries. In the early 1980s the union presented a paper to the clubs asking for their observations on a national competition, outlining several alternatives from a national league to a national cup competition. It met with a mixed response; but the feedback was sufficiently encouraging to prompt the Game Development committee to outline specific proposals for a league embracing all the senior clubs.

The response initially suggested that this would happen, but when the time came for a specific vote on the issue among the forty-eight senior clubs, there was, to say the least, some well-organised and well-orchestrated opposition to the proposal. Quite candidly there was a fear factor in some clubs that their long-held senior status and place at the top table could be threatened. It was a false fear. A league based on merit was the least the game in this country deserved.

There was, in fact, nothing new in the defensive attitude some clubs adopted. The Leinster Branch, for instance, had decided to form a two division senior league based on merit. Yet within weeks of an official announcement to that effect, the presidents of the senior clubs, at a meeting held in the Bective Rangers clubhouse effectively overthrew the decision taken by the executive committee of the branch.

Now with a national league on the horizon, the opposition of some clubs, and indeed individuals, intensified and some of the activity aimed at stopping the league was not what one could have reasonably called democratic. The union decided to have a vote on the issue. Twenty-three clubs voted for a league, twenty-three against, and two clubs, remarkably, did not vote at all, although one of those had intimated that it would support a league concept.

Thus it was that Des McKibbin, the president of the union in 1985-86, announced that, taking the outcome of the vote into consideration, the union did not have a strong enough mandate to start a national league competition, the only realistic decision that could be taken. But there was immense disappointment among the more progressive and forward-thinking clubs and, one could say, some relief amongst those who had opposed it. They had not, in fact, rendered Irish rugby any service by such an attitude.

The other countries in the championship had by now well-established national competitions, but Ireland plodded along under the old regime. However, there were men of sufficient vision in the IRFU and also in some clubs who refused to be deterred from putting in place a competition that was essential for the game in Ireland.

The debate and discussions went on for a further two years after which the IRFU decided that they would start a national league and that it would be a matter for each individual club as to whether or not it wished to participate. That was, in effect, throwing the issue back very firmly at those who had hindered the initial concept. The union announced that there would be two divisions and that entry would be based on merit — the results of the provincial leagues in each branch. By now Leinster had a meaningful league. The IRFU decision was taken in 1988 under the presidency of Paddy Madigan.

So the formula was drawn up, with the All Ireland League due to start in the 1990–91 season. The invitations to compete were sent on the basis of finishing positions in the provincial leagues over a two year period. It was decided that three clubs from each of the provinces of Leinster, Munster and Ulster would be in the first division. The second division comprised ten clubs. Leinster had three representatives, as did Ulster and Munster and Connacht had two each.

The clubs playing in Division 1 in the inaugural All Ireland League were Lansdowne, St Mary's College and Wanderers from Leinster; Ballymena, Instonians and Malone from Ulster; and Cork Constitution, Garryowen and Shannon from Munster.

The first competitors in Division 2 were Greystones, Terenure College and Old Wesley from Leinster; Bangor, CIYMS and NIFC from Ulster; Athlone and Corinthians from Connacht; and Young Munster and Sunday's Well from Munster. It was decided that relegation would operate from both divisions and, of course, promotion from the second to the first. The bottom two clubs in Division 1 would be relegated to Division 2 and three clubs would be relegated from the second division. Promotion would be gained to the second division through the provincial senior leagues, with the winners of the leagues in the four provinces taking part in a round robin play-off series to determine the three who would go forward to the second division.

The IRFU League subcommittee comprising Roy Loughead as chairman, Adam McKinley (Ulster), Ralph Murphy (Munster), Peter Squire (Leinster) and Eoin Hosty (Connacht) oversaw the competition. While obviously the league matches would draw gate receipts of consequence at many of the venues, there was an awareness that travel and hotel expenses would impose a financial strain on the clubs. To help alleviate difficulties in this area, the Union agreed to subsidise travel and hotel expenses for all the clubs in the league.

The inaugural championship started on 6 October 1990. The first division title was won by Cork Constitution, who in the last series of matches on 26 January 1991 defeated Garryowen 9-3 in the deciding match at Dooradoyle. It was a memorable encounter played before a capacity crowd. Ireland international scrum-half Michael Bradley led Cork Constitution to victory. The IRFU could not have asked for a more fitting finale to the inaugural national league. Meanwhile Old Wesley captured the second division title, with Young Munster as runners-up, and those two clubs were promoted. Malone and Wanderers finished last and second last respectively in the first division and were relegated. NIFC, Athlone and Corinthians filled the last three places in Division 2 and consequently reverted to their provincial leagues.

The round robin play-offs for the provincial league winners saw Blackrock College, Dolphin and Dungannon promoted to the second division of the league. Connacht champions Galwegians lost out in this series which was contested with all the vigour, enthusiasm and commitment of the league itself.

The first season of the league had exceeded expectations of even the most enthusiastic advocates. It was absolute justification for starting the competition. Now several of the clubs who had so vigorously opposed the league and voted down the concept five years previously began to realise just what they were missing. Suddenly the clamour came for a four division league, as every senior club wanted to be part of the action.

The Cork Constitution team that won the inaugural All Ireland League title in 1990-91

No sponsor had come forward to support the competition in its inaugural season, but such had been its success and the consequent huge public interest that several firms expressed more than a passing interest in sponsoring the competition. It was the Insurance Corporation of Ireland which came in as sponsor and agreed a three year sponsorship deal. In fact that alliance was mutually beneficial for a six year period until the 1997–98 season when Allied Irish Banks took over as sponsor.

Two major issues in relation to the league were the subject of considerable debate in the early years of the competition: one was the question of overseas players being brought in by clubs; and the second was the future format of the league. After consultation with the clubs it became clear that an overwhelming majority now favoured a four division format with every senior club being given the opportunity to play in the league. Initially it was thought that a five division format might evolve. There was anxiety that Ireland would become a haven for overseas players in pursuit of fortune, if not fame. The official view was that if clubs brought in too many overseas players it would inevitably hinder opportunity and consequently the development of Irish players, which was one of the primary reasons for starting the league in the first instance. Consequently clubs were limited to one overseas player.

The format for the second season of the league remained unchanged and Garryowen succeeded where they had failed the previous year by winning the title. Dungannon won the second division, with Greystones filling the second spot. Lansdowne and Instonians were relegated from the first division and Malone, Sunday's Well and CIYMS were relegated from the second. They were replaced by Clontarf, Galwegians and Old Crescent, with NIFC losing out in the round robin play-off series.

It was Young Munster who emerged as champions in the third year of the league. They won the title by beating St Mary's College in the crucial and final match at Lansdowne Road before a crowd in the region of 20,000. It was a wonderful occasion and a truly memorable match. Lansdowne won the second division with a 100 per cent record. Wanderers and Blackrock College were also promoted, while Ballymena lost their status in the first division. With the league due to be extended to four divisions in the 1993–94 season, the format had changed with three clubs promoted from Division 2 to Division 1. Only one, Ballymena, was relegated, while there was also just one relegated club from Division 2, with Clontarf losing out.

So, for the first time, in the 1993–94 season every senior club in the country was involved in a national competition. The first division now comprised eleven clubs, the second also included eleven clubs, while there were thirteen clubs in Division 3 and eleven in Division 4.

Yet again it was a Munster club that triumphed in the first division. Garryowen took the title for a second time, with Cork Constitution as runners-up. Greystones and Wanderers were both relegated. Instonians won the second division and they were promoted along with Sunday's Well, while Galwegians and Ballina were relegated. UCD had the distinction of becoming the first third division title winners and Bective Rangers also gained promotion. Portadown, Collegians and Sligo were relegated. Monkstown won Division 4 and were promoted along with Waterpark. While there was no relegation from Division 4, the Westport-Mayo club decided they would not again participate in the league.

There was constant examination of the rules of the league with eligibility of players under constant review. In that context players were not allowed to move from one club to another in the same area, but could join clubs in other areas if their work commitments were such that they took up residence in those areas.

Shannon won their initial title in 1994–95 and did so with a 100 per cent record, the first club to attain that feat in the top division. It was to be the beginning of a superb run of success for the Shannon club. Blackrock College finished runners-up, but Sunday's Well and Dungannon were both relegated. Old Belvedere won the second division title and thus competed in the top division for the first time in 1995–96. Ballymena finished second to regain first division status. UCD and Bangor were relegated. NIFC won Division 3 with Clontarf second. Two Connacht clubs, Corinthians and Ballina, had to endure relegation. Bohemians won the fourth division, with Skerries second.

The decision of the International Board at a meeting in Paris in autumn 1995 to declare rugby 'open', thus in effect making it professional, had far-reaching repercussions on the game and obviously the All Ireland League clubs were not immune. The placing of the league matches on the calendar became an issue with a gap left to accommodate the representative programme. With a European Cup now on the itinerary the calendar was more crowded.

Shannon became the first club to retain the first division title, and with the league due to be restructured numerically in 1996–97, there was no relegation from the first division. Three clubs won promotion from Division 2, Old Crescent, Dungannon and Terenure College. Thus Old Crescent and Terenure joined the top division for the first time. Monkstown won Division 3 and Portadown Division 4.

The first division comprised fourteen clubs in 1996–97, as did the second. The third division was made up of eleven clubs and the fourth of ten. By now a very significant element had been added to the league which allowed promotion for junior clubs to the fourth division. The winners of the provincial junior leagues played off for the right to enter the national league, with two of the four going forward. So when the 1996–97 league started, Ballynahinch from Ulster and Suttonians from Leinster were now in the league.

In Connacht, too, there had been a significant development the previous season when Athlone and Ballinasloe decided to amalgamate for the purposes of the league and the new amalgam entitled Buccaneers finished eighth in Division 3.

Shannon again took the title in the top division for a third successive season, with Lansdowne in second place. Instonians and Old Wesley were relegated. Clontarf and Dolphin finished first and second respectively in Division 2, with Highfield and NIFC being relegated. Buccaneers proved the wisdom of the amalgamation when they won Division 3, with Galwegians runners-up, thus bringing two Connacht clubs back into Division 2. Bangor and Waterpark were relegated.

A remarkable feature of Division 4 was that Suttonians won it and Ballynahinch finished runners-up, a major impact from these two clubs so soon after they had joined the national competition. Sadly Armagh and UCD finished at the bottom of the division and so were out of the league.

In the course of the season the clubs were brought together to discuss in detail the format of the league, with particular reference to the numerical strength of the top division. Proposals were put at what was a protracted meeting presided over by IRFU president Bobby Deacy. There were strenuous arguments from the floor for and against reducing the size of the first division for the 1997–98 season. But after a vote the *status quo* was maintained. Likewise, representatives from the first division clubs who had formed an alliance met with the president and other officials earlier in the season.

There was also a school of thought that clubs and not provinces should represent Ireland in the European Cup, but that suggestion did not get a positive response, the firm belief being that no Irish club could hope to compete in Europe and have any chance of success.

While the numerical strength of the first division remained at fourteen for the 1997–98 season, it had been decided that the division would be reduced to twelve for 1998–99. With the advent of the European Cup and the decision to move the interprovincial series forward to the start of the season, this meant that the league in 1996–97 did not start until December. This imposed hardship on clubs in terms of revenue from gate receipts as provincial development leagues did not carry the same attraction. To alleviate the financial hardship in clubs the IRFU gave special grants to all the clubs participating, with first division clubs getting £20,000 each and pro rata assistance to clubs in the other divisions.

The 1997–98 campaign saw another innovation that provoked great debate and division of opinion. It was decided that the top four clubs in the first division would play off for the title. That decision was not received with unanimous agreement. Some believed it was asking a club to win the title twice and it could, of course, mean that the club finishing top of the league might not in fact end up winning it.

As events transpired, that did not happen. Shannon finished top of the league with 24 points, followed by Garryowen and Young Munster both five points adrift, with St Mary's College in fourth place. In the semi-finals Shannon beat St Mary's College at Thomond Park and Garryowen defeated Young Munster at Dooradoyle. Shannon and Garryowen therefore met in the final at Lansdowne Road. Shannon won, capturing the title for a fourth successive season, a magnificent achievement. The union's view was that deciding the first division title by playing a knock-out series between the top clubs gave added incentive to clubs who, while they could not finish at the top of the league, now had an incentive to get into the top four. This ensured that interest was maintained to the very end of the league.

There was prize money, too, for the clubs in each division and another innovation was a series of play-offs in relation to promotion and relegation. The first division was reduced from fourteen to twelve clubs for 1998–99. This meant the bottom three clubs in Division 1 were automatically relegated, but the side that finished fourth from bottom had to play home and away against the team that finished second in Division 2. That resulted in Buccaneers meeting Dungannon home and away. After losing the first match on their home ground, Buccaneers won the second in Dungannon and gained promotion on the better points difference.

With Galwegians winning the second division title, it meant there were two Connacht clubs in the top division in 1998–99. No Connacht club had previously been in the top flight; now the province had two clubs among the elite. That was a major lift for the game in the west.

Play-offs for promotion and relegation in the other divisions likewise took place, but there was no top four competition to decree each divisional winner. Portadown won the third division and Ballynahinch, who finished in second place, were also promoted. County Carlow won Division 4 and Richmond, competing in the league for only the second season, won a place in Division 3 when they defeated Collegians who had finished third from the bottom in the third division in the play-off.

There was unfortunately a hitch in relation to the play-offs regarding the bottom clubs in Division 2. This came about because of a postponed match involving Wanderers and Buccaneers. The match, scheduled for the Wanderers ground at Merrion Road, had been called off in controversial circumstances. It was initially ruled that Wanderers would lose the points, but following legal action taken by the Wanderers club it was decided that only the bottom two clubs in Division 2 would be relegated. Thus Malone and Wanderers, who had finished third and fourth last respectively, maintained their status and two clubs were promoted from Division 3. That killed the plan to reduce the division numerically as had been envisaged.

The first division comprised twelve clubs in 1998–99, with fourteen in the second division. It was decided that the third division should be split into two sections of five clubs each, with eleven clubs contesting the fourth division.

For Buccaneers and Galwegians it was especially auspicious. They were the first Connacht clubs to contest the first division.

Shannon set out to try and record a fifth consecutive win in the top division but, in fact, made an uncharacteristically poor start by losing comprehensively to Ballymena at Eaton Park. That result increased speculation that an Ulster club might win the title for the first time. But it was a case of flattering to deceive in the Ballymena context. While Shannon put that adverse result behind them, they could not emulate the consistency that had been so profound a part of their ongoing success.

With the same format as the previous season — the top four to qualify for a play-off series — the position as to who would finish in the top four remained in doubt right to the last series of matches. Six clubs were in contention: Cork Constitution, Garryowen, Shannon, Lansdowne, Buccaneers and St Mary's College.

In the final series of matches, Cork Constitution defeated Shannon, Buccaneers defeated Lansdowne, Garryowen defeated Young Munster and St Mary's College defeated Galwegians. That meant that Garryowen, Cork Constitution, Buccaneers and St Mary's College qualified for the semi-finals. Garryowen finished on top on points difference from Cork Constitution, with Buccaneers third and St Mary's College, who finished on 14 points with Lansdowne but got through on superior points difference.

In the semi-finals Garryowen came from 17 down to defeat St Mary's College 18-17 and Cork Constitution defeated Buccaneers in a very good semi-final at Temple Hill winning 33-20. Buccaneers' achievement in finishing third in the league was outstanding bearing in mind that they were contesting the top division for the first time, having been promoted the previous season.

The final between Cork Constitution and Garryowen at Lansdowne Road produced a tremendous contest, won after extra time by Cork Constitution 14-11. So the club that won the inaugural title had now regained it and entered the new millennium as All Ireland champions.

At the other end of the table, Blackrock College and Galwegians were relegated, with Blackrock going down because of inferior points difference to Clontarf.

Dungannon won the second division. DLSP finished second and so will savour first division status for the first time, an appropriate way to celebrate the centenary of the foundation of the Palmerston club, who amalgamated with De La Salle to form DLSP in the 1980s. Skerries, Old Wesley and Ballynahinch were relegated. Three clubs were relegated from Division 2 and two promoted from Division 3 to reduce the number of clubs contesting Division 2 by one.

The Shannon squad that won the All Ireland League, the Munster Senior Cup and the Munster Junior Cup in 1995-96. Shannon won the League in four successive seasons from 1994-95 to 1997-98

UCD won Division 3 and gained promotion along with NIFC, while Dublin University and Highfield were relegated. Midleton, contesting the league for the first time, won Division 4, with Ballina as runners-up. CIYMS and Collegians were relegated. So two old established clubs made their exit from the senior sphere. Barnhall won the Leinster Junior League and then the round robin series between the junior league winners in the four provinces. Thomond, who finished second in that series, beat Collegians, who had finished second last in Division 4 in a play-off to determine which would play in the league next season. Thomond won and so became the seventh Limerick club in the league.

In fact, after their demotion Collegians announced that they would be amalgamating with NIFC — an alliance between two very old and highly respected clubs with great traditions. As circumstances should have it, NIFC had decided to move from their traditional home at Ormeau. So a happy alliance was promised.

Yet again the format of the league came under review, but it was decided that there would not be any change as Irish rugby enters the new millennium.

CHAPTER 39

THE UNDER AGE SCENE

WHEN IT WAS DECIDED that there would be an Under 20 interprovincial series in 1980, it was recognition that there was a gap after players left school that needed to be bridged at representative level.

There was also an awareness now, too, that not enough was being done to encourage youngsters who did not go to rugby-playing schools to play the game. In some areas, most notably Limerick, and at junior level, particularly in rural areas, clubs did work hard at providing facilities and encouragement to entice youngsters into the game. The under age scene was potentially a very fertile area that now needed to be developed.

Competitively, outside of the schools, there was not nearly enough on offer. There were some under age competitions at club level in some areas, but not very many, and certainly what was on offer was not enough.

In Leinster the McCorry Cup was inaugurated in the early 1970s and that was a help and very much a step in the right direction. However, the vast majority of those who played in the McCorry Cup had played the game at school. Indeed, there was anxiety, and it was well founded, that some clubs were offering inducements to youngsters to enlist and using rather unethical methods to do so.

When it was decided to introduce Youths interprovincials (Under 18) in the late 1980s, it was a major move forward. Then in 1991–92 came another very important initiative and that was Ireland's entry into the realm of Youths internationals. The first such match took place on 11 April 1992 between Ireland and Scotland at the Sports Ground in Galway. That followed trial matches and a match against the Ireland Schools B side. Brendan O'Dowd was the man at the helm as chairman of the IRFU Youths subcommittee. He had both the depth of knowledge and the intense interest in this area of development to make him the ideal choice.

That was the start of the Youths international involvement; now, happily, that has been extended considerably. Further up the scale, there was no international rugby of any consequence between the schools and the international B scene other than the universities internationals and that was also deemed to be unsatisfactory. Ireland had played one match at Under 23 level against Holland in 1979 and Ireland had played a few under 25 matches, but there was a definite desire for Ireland to play at Under 21 level on an annual basis.

Initially, finding opponents was difficult, but perseverance got its reward when Ireland played an Under 21 match for the first time on 28 September 1988. The opponents were Italy who had come on tour and played a few matches prior to the international. Ireland won the international 22-13. It is

The Irish Under 19 Rugby Team – World Youth Championship 1998

interesting to reflect on the fact that four of that Ireland team went on to win full senior caps. They were outside half Nicky Barry, hooker Allen Clarke, second row Paddy Johns and back row Paul Hogan. Several more of the side won senior interprovincial honours.

Then in September–October 1989 the Ireland Under 21 squad undertook a two match tour to Italy that included an international against the Italians in Treviso. The depth of experience in the Ireland management was a tremendous tribute to those concerned. The manager was Noel Murphy. Here was a man who had captained his country, coached his country, coached the Lions, but was now prepared to step down the ladder with a desire to help the youngsters. The coach to the team was former Ireland captain and scrum-half John Moloney and his assistant was Ciaran Fitzgerald, twice a Triple Crown-winning captain and a Lions captain.

Ireland won both matches in Italy, beating an Italian selection 21-6 in Arezzo and then winning the international 21-9 in Treviso. Five members of that team went on to senior caps. In November the Under 21 side was in action yet again when they played the New Zealand Rugby News Under 21 side in Donnybrook on 19 November. That was a great match that ended in a thrilling 13-13 draw. In September 1990 the Under 21 side travelled to Leiden to play Holland but lost to much more mature opposition. In October came a major breakthrough when Ireland played England at this level for the first time. That match was in the Moseley ground, Birmingham, and Ireland won a tremendous match 22-16. That Ireland team included Conor O'Shea, Niall Malone and Gabriel Fulcher, all later to play for Ireland at senior level. By now, too, Fitzgerald and Moloney were no longer coaching the side as they had taken over at senior level, with Fitzgerald coach to the national team and Moloney his assistant. Ian Bremner and Gerry Murphy had taken over the coaching roles.

The Welsh were added to the Ireland itinerary the following season when Ireland also played England. Ireland beat England but lost to Wales. But by now the annual Under 21 matches were on a regular schedule. And if not yet secure, then that was to come.

In addition to those matches and the long-standing Universities internationals, the Ireland Students were also now in the field, as were the Irish Colleges — students from third level institutions other than the universities — and that, together with the Youths, saw an elaborate structure in place towards the development of the young players.

In 1992–93 Ireland played the other three home countries, so in effect a Triple Crown series was now on the agenda. Ireland lost to England in Gateshead and then became the first country to beat Wales at this level when Ireland won 22-11 at Donnybrook. They followed that win with a very convincing 18-3 victory over the Scots at Murrayfield. The Ireland manager at this period was yet another man of vast experience, former international Brian O'Brien, who had been an Ireland senior selector. Dave Haslett was coach and his assistant was Ray Coughlan. Both men subsequently gave tremendous service to the Ireland A side.

Ireland's Des Dillon goes highest in the line out in the semi-final of the IRB-FIRA Under 19 World Cup 1999

The Ireland Students had competed in the inaugural Students World Cup in Italy in July 1992. Ireland beat Germany and CIS but lost to Italy and New Zealand. In January the Students travelled to Edinburgh and beat Scotland and then beat England 19-3 at Anglesea Road.

The following season the Under 21 side lost to England and Wales but had a 24-6 win over Scotland. The Youths side meanwhile played twice that year beating Wales 12-6 and Scotland 10-5.

The Under 21 team narrowly missed the Triple Crown in 1994-95. After beating England and Scotland, Ireland lost to the Welsh in a Triple Crown decider, going down 16-9. The Youths beat Scotland and lost to Wales. The Students lost heavily to England but then went down by just two points in the inaugural match against the French in Longford.

The 1995–96 season was a year of glory for the Under 21 side when they captured the Triple Crown for the first time. They beat England 23-10, scored a 21-9 win over Scotland at Stradbrook, and then on 1 March in Wicklow defeated Wales 20-12. As the Schools also won the Triple Crown that season, it was a tremendous double at under age level. Eddie O'Sullivan as coach and David Irwin as manager formed a very fine management team.

There is a remarkable statistic from that Under 21 side. No fewer than eight of the players who helped in that historic achievement are now full internationals. They are Dominic Crotty, James Topping, Justin Bishop, Conor McGuinness, Malcolm O'Kelly, Eric Miller, Kieron Dawson and Brian O'Meara.

That season the Ireland Youths team played Spain in Valladoid, Scotland and Wales, while the Students also broke new ground by playing against Natal Duikers in the Mardyke, Cork, as well as the French and English.

The scene had certainly changed dramatically over a period of less than a decade with regard to under age rugby in the international context, and now the structure was in place and the facilities there for the youngsters to take full advantage.

In 1997, Ireland once more beat England at Under 21 level and also beat Scotland, but the Welsh beat Ireland readily in Bridgend. Ireland lost to France but scored a fine 12-6 win over New Zealand Rugby News side at Thomond Park.

In March, Ireland contested the World Youths Cup (Under 19) for the first time. The championship was played in Argentina. The team was managed by Jim Glennon, Don Crowley was tour manager, Declan Kidney coach and Bart Fannin assistant coach. Ireland beat Portugal 39-20, beat Scotland 22-8 but then lost to a more mature and experienced Argentinian team 42-0. They ended their participation by losing to Wales 35-17.

Meanwhile, for the second time, Ireland also played in the Students World Cup which was played in South Africa. Andy Crawford managed the team which was coached by Bobby Byrne, with Tommy Connelly as technical assistant.

Ireland lost the opening match to Wales 27-34 and 37-53 to Argentina. They beat Uruguay 36-10 to finish in ninth place. The Youths Under 18 team once more had a fine campaign, winning their two matches against Scotland and Wales, while the Schools beat Wales and Scotland but lost to England.

There is no doubt that events in France in April 1998 represented not alone an achievement of immense significance, but was the highlight of the season in the Ireland rugby context. The Ireland team that went to France to contest the Under 19 World Championship was now under the jurisdiction of the IRB as well as the FIRA. Harry McKibbin managed the team, Declan Kidney was coach, assisted by Bart Fannin. The rest of the back-up team was former Ireland and Lions forward Bill Mulcahy as medical officer, with Mary Costello and Maeve Mitchell as the physiotherapists.

It was anticipated that Ireland would do well, for the squad was a highly talented one. But the players truly excelled as they captured the title. The opening match against the United States presented no problems as Ireland won 47-13. Ireland's next match was against a very strongly fancied South Africa and that ended in a 17-17 draw. The match went to a penalty shoot-out which South Africa won 4-3. But they violated the rules in regard to the shoot-out by using a player who was not qualified to participate as he had not played in the match. The South Africans were consequently ruled out of the competition after Ireland had rightly appealed. That meant a place for Ireland in the semi-final. Ireland beat Argentina 18-3 with a tremendous display, and it was an Ireland-France final. It was played in Stade Toulousain on 12 April.

With home advantage, and that for a French side means playing before a vociferous crowd, the

French fancied their chances. But the Ireland side was excellently prepared and totally focused. They played some quality rugby and stamped their authority on the game. The Ireland pack, with Damien Bourghall excellent out of touch and with the pack driving, rucking and mauling effectively, laid the foundations for a famous victory. At their heels half-backs Kieran Campbell and Paddy Wallace played with great perception. The inspirational captain Shane Moore and his centre partner Brian O'Driscoll were iron clad in defence.

Ireland scored two tries through Wallace and Darragh Holt, O'Driscoll kicked a penalty and conversion, and Wallace dropped a goal. Toulouse belonged to the Irish that night. The decision to participate in this championship was a splendid initiative and former IRFU Director of Rugby Development Ray Southam deserves a lot of credit for that. It was a splendid way for him to end his tenure in that office before he returned to New Zealand in the summer of 1998. Prior to participating in that championship, the Under 19 side had played two matches, beating Italy 26-19 and Spain 63-0.

That great triumph in France followed on the achievements of the Under 21 team who had lost to France but then went on to win the Triple Crown. The Irish Universities also won the Triple Crown. The Youths Under 18 team won all three matches they played, defeating Italy, Wales and Scotland.

When one looks at the level of success achieved at under age levels in a period of a decade, it is a telling illustration of the wisdom of devoting so much time, finance and expertise in this crucial aera of development.

One other competition that also came on the scene, as the decade neared its end, was the Students European Cup. This was contested by four Irish universities, Queen's, UCD, UCC and Dublin University. It is yet another worthy initiative that gives the university players added experience. The universities had been vital to the game in Ireland through the years. Circumstances have changed appreciably in the modern era, with increased academic demands and the fact that university teams are invariably very young. However, like the under age teams, the universities have a crucial role to play in the ongoing evolution, development and propagation of Irish rugby.

CHAPTER 40

THE SCHOOLS

THE CONTRIBUTION THAT THE SCHOOLS have made to Irish rugby, its development and progress, has been absolutely vital to the game in this country.

Successive generations of dedicated teachers, religious and lay, have sustained the game in the schools with a long and distinguished tradition. What is especially pleasing as we face into the next millennium is that more schools are playing the game now than at any time in the last 125 years.

There is not a doubt that but for the schools and the players they sent out, rugby would not have progressed as it has. Indeed for a long time not nearly enough was done to encourage youngsters who did not play rugby at school to take up the game. That meant the schools represented the only real area of development for players.

Now that has, of course, changed quite dramatically, yet the importance of the schools as a nursery and a crucial area of development remains no less important today than it was over 100 years ago.

When the first administrative body for the game in Ireland was founded, it was on the initiative of young men who had been influenced by the games they had played at school. The Trinity College duo Barrington and Wall were especially influential and their formative years and experience at school was central to what they subsequently put in place.

It is not a false claim to say that in the early days the propagation of the game owed more to what was happening in schools than in clubs, and how significant it is that so many clubs were subsequently founded by the boys who had come out of school and then gave the impetus for the clubs' foundation. Many of those clubs bear the names of the old schools these boys attended.

It is also of immense significance in the context of Irish rugby history that the first competitive rugby in this country was played between schools. Here Ulster has the distinction of leading the way, with the Ulster Schools Senior Cup being first contested in 1876.

The Leinster Schools Senior Cup was inaugurated in 1887, Munster followed in 1909 and Connacht in 1913. It should, however, be stressed that, while it was not until this century that the provincial schools competitions started in Munster and Connacht, rugby had been played in schools in those provinces prior to that. For instance, the two great Cork rugby schools, Presentation Brothers College and Christian Brothers College, were contesting a competition in Cork in the last century.

By long-standing tradition the finals of the senior cups in Ulster, Leinster and Munster are usually played on St Patrick's Day. Apart from the senior internationals, no area of the game in Ireland has the same appeal as the schools. Even in the early rounds of the cup competitions matches, especially in Leinster and Munster, draw big attendances. It is not unusual for crowds in the region of 50,000 to

IRISH SCHOOLS TO AUSTRALIA 1996

attend the three finals. That is its own ready testimony to the appeal of the game at schools level. Schools rugby in Connacht was never as strong as in the other provinces, but major strides have been made in the west in recent years.

The beginnings of the schools competitive scene were humble enough, with just four schools contesting the first Ulster Senior Cup. They were Methodist College Belfast, Royal Belfast Academical Institute, Armagh Royal and the Royal School Dungannon. Now over 120 years later, all four schools still compete in the competition. It is significant, too, within the context of game development and the contribution of the schools, that two of those schools, Methodist and RBAI, both had clubs formed from former pupils. Collegians were formed from the old boys of Methody and Instonians from RBAI. The Dungannon club, too, owed its origins to boys from Dungannon Royal. It is worth noting also that Dungannon Royal was in at the foundation of the Irish Football Union in 1874.

The Ulster Schools Senior Cup is not alone the oldest competition in Irish rugby, but the second oldest in the world, being pre-dated only by the London Hospitals Cup.

To Armagh Royal goes the distinction of being the first club or school in Ireland to win a competition. They won the inaugural Ulster Cup, beating RBAI in the final. But the competitive nature of schools rugby was emphasised by the fact that it took three matches before Armagh Royal prevailed. Armagh retained the trophy the following season before Methodist took the title in 1878. It was the first of many successes for Methodist, truly a great rugby school.

Armagh won the title seven times in the first decade of competition but had to wait until 1977 for their next success. Remarkably, Dungannon Royal's only success was recorded in 1907. But many schools have long and very distinguished involvement in the competition. These include Campbell, Coleraine AI, Foyle College and Portora. In a more recent era schools such as Ballymena Academy, Rainey Endowed, Bangor Grammar, Grosvenor High School, Ballyclare High School, Regent House, Annadale and Belfast Model, Belfast High School and Carrickfergus GS have all enhanced the competition. In 1910 the Schools Medallion for boys Under 16 was inaugurated and Methodist had the distinction of being the first inaugural winners.

Where Ulster led, Leinster followed in 1887 and the schools cups in Leinster have the biggest entry of any schools competitions in the country. It is not in any way unusual for the Donnybrook ground to have capacity attendances even for first round senior cup matches.

In terms of success, one school stands apart from all others in any province and that is Blackrock College. Perhaps appropriately they were, too, the winners of the inaugural competition. The trophy was bought by the Branch, with the schools contributing £5 each, and they paid an entry fee of two shillings (10 pence). The Branch contributed £10 and the honorary treasurer of the Branch, Harry Shepherd, contributed £10, a typical gesture from a man whose wisdom and foresight were so important in Lansdowne Road being the property of the IRFU.

The unique trophy, a composite of an old hunting trophy and another trophy, the foot of the cup was 50 years older than the bowl. Regrettably the trophy was stolen some years ago from Blackrock College together with other trophies and was never recovered. A replacement trophy was immediately purchased by the Branch.

Seven schools contested the inaugural competition, Blackrock, the High School Farra, Santry School, Rathmines School, Corrig and Wesley College. Blackrock won and thus established a tradition that has seen the school win the cup on over 60 occasions, a truly astonishing record and a great tribute to successive generations of priests and lay teachers who have coached the teams through the years.

Blackrock, Wesley and the High School survive from the original entrants, and in the intervening years several other schools have emerged to make their mark and a huge contribution: St Mary's College, Castleknock, Mountjoy, St Columba's, St Andrew's, Clongowes Wood College. Terenure College, CBC Monkstown, PBC Bray, Belvedere College, Newbridge College, Roscrea, the King's Hospital, De La Salle Churchtown and Kilkenny College made very significant contributions. Other schools such as St Michael's College, Templeogue College, St Paul's Raheny and Gonzaga have emerged in recent times, and St Michael's, a sister college of Blackrock, have actually contested a final.

De La Salle Churchtown won the cup twice in the 1980s and Clongowes Wood, Terenure College and St Mary's College invariably send out excellent teams. Clongowes, who first played in the cup in 1923, have become a major force over the last decade and won the trophy with a superb team in 1998.

It has long been necessary to have two sections in both the senior and junior cups with the weaker schools contesting section A which is a qualifying competition for section B. Just as at senior level, Blackrock College has been the dominant force at junior level, but it was St Andrew's who won the inaugural competition in 1933 when they beat Belvedere in the final.

The inaugural Munster Schools Senior Cup was in 1909 and it was won by Christian Brothers College Cork. Now, as then, they are still a major force on the scene, as are Presentation Brothers College Cork. Rockwell College has a great record in the competition but they have had to endure leaner times more recently. Crescent Comprehensive Limerick and St Munchin's have both emerged to challenge the superiority of PBC and CBC, but the two Cork colleges have been the most successful over the last 30 years. PBC led the way with wins both at senior and junior levels and, like so many of the schools, PBC has provided Ireland with a host of international players.

Schools such as Mungret College Limerick and Abbey are no longer on the scene but both made significant contributions, as did CBS Limerick. In more recent times St Enda's, St Clement's and Ard Scoil Rís are able to challenge the longer established academies. Midleton College, Waterpark and Glenstal Abbey are also schools who can reflect on contributions of significance. PBC Cobh actually won the Senior Cup back in the late 1930s but were never subsequently able to make such an impact.

The game in Connacht has had a long struggle. Ironically, it was a school, the now defunct Galway Grammar School, which played a major role in the establishment of the Connacht Branch. Galway Grammar and another school that no longer exists, Ranelagh, were driving forces for the schools game in the west. Indeed, with no competition available to them, at one stage Galway Grammar School competed in the Leinster Cup.

The most potent force in the schools game in Connacht has long been St Joseph's College, Garbally Park, Ballinasloe. They were the winners of the inaugural senior cup in 1913 and through the years have maintained their traditional strength. They have produced some superb players and many Irish internationals including two men who later captained Ireland, Ray McLoughlin and Ciaran Fitzgerald. St Joseph's College Galway and St Ignatius College Galway are two other colleges who have known success. But at times in the west rugby was banned in some colleges. All that has now changed and in 1998 no fewer than 25 schools were affiliated to the branch.

Clifden Community School won the senior cup in 1975 and more recently schools such as St Sarnan's Ferbane and Portumna Community College have made considerable impact, as indeed have such as St Muirdeach's Ballina. Tremendous work has been done in the west at schools level and that is reflected in the current growth.

All the branches have committees now to run the schools game and the IRFU Schools Standing Committee oversees schools rugby in Ireland. Remarkably, it was not until 1975 that Ireland first played at schools international level. That match against England on 29 March was arranged to mark the centenary of the IRFU. There was opposition to schools internationals on several grounds, most notably that giving schoolboys caps was not in their best interest. Other arguments were about possible disruption to studies and other such opposition. It was hard to understand it.

Bearing in mind that schools interprovincials date back to 1887 when Leinster and Ulster first met, and that Munster subsequently joined in as indeed did Connacht, representative rugby at schools level in Ireland has a long history. Connacht struggled to match the other provinces in the interprovincial series but now there is also an A series at schools interprovincial level in which Connacht competes annually.

Once the first schools international had been played in 1975 there was no going back. The following season Ireland played Wales and Scotland and for some years two matches were played annually. Now all four home countries meet annually and indeed the French too play at schools level, but as yet Ireland has not played French Schools.

There was an event of major significance in 1980 when Ireland Schools toured Australia. Now how dramatically the scene had changed in five years. The man chosen to manage the Ireland team was Roy Loughead of Ulster. He was a most appropriate choice for he has made and continues to make a huge contribution to the game in the schools. The coach was Caleb Powell and his assistant Brother Philip O'Reilly. Here are two more who have given tremendous service to schools rugby. Ireland and the schools have been singularly blessed in having so many people who have contributed so much.

One such is Kevin Kelleher. An international referee of world repute, he has been honorary secretary of the schools section of the Leinster Branch for over 40 years. Former internationals Ken Armstrong and Noel Turley are two others who have made huge contributions and have coached the Ireland Schools side, as has Dave Haslett, Declan Kidney and Keith Patton. Brian Cotter and John McClean have both given great service towards coaching schools sides. Connacht too have contributed with men of the calibre of Noel Carpenter and Gerry Kelly. Gerry was manager of the most successful Ireland Schools team of all in 1996. Ireland won the Schools Triple Crown that season and then went to Australia and won every match, a magnificent achievement. That team was coached by Keith Patton and his assistant John McClean, who had been a very successful coach to Terenure College. But these are but a few of the men who have left an indelible imprint on the schools scene.

Ireland has won the Triple Crown at schools level three times, in 1990 for the first time, again in 1993 and most recently in 1996. There have been three tours to Australia and one to New Zealand, while Ireland has also met Zimbabwe who toured in Ireland, as have both Australia and New Zealand, Australia as recently as December 1998.

The wisdom of playing schools international rugby is underlined and indeed emphasised by the number who, having played for Ireland schools, then went on to play for Ireland at the other levels. Indeed, no fewer than eight of the first Ireland team that played at schools level were subsequently capped at senior level. The progression has been very good ever since and more former Ireland Schools internationals have gone on to play at senior international level than has been the case in any other country.

CHAPTER 41

LANSDOWNE ROAD

LANSDOWNE ROAD HAS ALWAYS BEEN CONSIDERED among the most attractive of the international rugby grounds. Its location, situated so near to the city centre, is one of its attractions. It has about it, too, an old world charm.

The early development of the ground has already been outlined. There was a major refurbishment of the lower tier of the West Stand in 1974. And one man who deserves immense credit for the amount of time and effort he put into the ongoing development and improvement of the ground is Ronnie Dawson. An architect by profession, the former Ireland and Lions captain was subsequently an outstanding Irish representative on the International Board for a 20 year period from 1974 and was also president of the union.

LANSDOWNE ROAD

In 1983 it was decided to demolish the old East Stand and build a modern structure. That was financed by the sale of 10 year tickets, just as the refurbishment of the West Stand had been a decade earlier. But as time went by and the game changed, so did the needs in relation to international rugby stadia. The modern concept is very much geared towards all-seater stadia and the IRFU has recognised that need. A splendid set of floodlights was installed in the mid-1990s to meet another modern demand.

A major study has been made over the last four years by a special subcommittee under the chairmanship of Tom Kiernan on ground development and providing a stadium to serve the game in the new millennium with an increased capacity from the current one of just under 50,000.

The union purchased 90 acres of ground in west Dublin and development of that represents one option. Another project that was considered was playing internationals at another venue which had been proposed for development in the Phoenix Park. But that project did not materialise.

The redevelopment of the Lansdowne Road ground has been the subject of exhaustive study as to how best that could be accomplished. Increasing the capacity of the ground as an all-seater stadium and putting in all the modern amenities is still exercising the minds of the committee. The location of the ground with the railway line running behind the West Stand and other factors have all to be weighed. The cost factor of redevelopment is another. But these are all decisions to be taken in the future. In the interim the oldest international rugby ground in the game will yet again be a venue for the World Cup in the autumn of 1999.

Whatever the future holds, when dawn breaks over the twenty-first century, Lansdowne Road will still be the Mecca for Ireland's rugby followers as it was in the nineteenth and the twentieth centuries. It has served Irish rugby well, as indeed it served other sporting pursuits, most notably soccer, and has been the venue for major concerts. It holds a very special place in the hearts of the countless thousands from Ireland and much further afield who have, through the years, been part of the tumult and the shouting as the drama unfolded in a great sporting theatre.

CHAPTER 42

A DUAL TRIUMPH

THERE WERE FEW BETTER DAYS in the history of Irish rugby than 30 January 1999. That was the day that two Ireland teams were crowned champions of Europe.

Nature bestowed its bounty in the form of a lovely winter's day, as around 30,000 people made the journey to Dublin from diverse locations in Ulster to cheer on the provincial team in their quest to become European champions with the French side Colomiers standing between Ulster and triumph. No one could realistically have envisaged such a situation when Ulster set out on the long and arduous European road five months previously by drawing with Edinburgh Reivers at Ravenhill.

Sport has inspired many a writer to go into raptures about the agony and the ecstasy of wonderful triumphs and agonising defeats. Ulster's European Cup campaign had about it the ring of romance to prompt rhapsodic acclaim as few other happenings in Irish rugby.

ULSTER FULL BACK, SIMON MASON, WHOSE PLACE-KICKING WAS CRUCIAL IN ULSTER'S EUROPEAN CUP CAMPAIGN, RAISES THE TROPHY ALOFT AFTER ULSTER HAD DEFEATED COLOMIERS IN THE FINAL

But before Ulster took the field against Colomiers, University College Cork had an appointment of major consequence at Donnybrook on the morning of 30 January. They had reached the final of the Students European Cup with the French side Grenoble as opponents. The prize for the winners was The Times Trophy, presented by the tournament sponsors. But that was in essence the aperitif to the main event in the afternoon.

Ulster's European Cup crusade captured the imagination of the province and indeed the whole of Ireland. Ulster had travelled what one might term a rocky road to the final. A victory over Toulouse in the group stages set up a quarter-final against the same opposition, as both had qualified for the knock-out stages from the pool. The quarter-final was scheduled for Ravenhill with Ulster getting home advantage as pool winners.

Under the lights of Ravenhill, a capacity 12,000 crowd cheered Ulster on to a great victory by 15–13. That earned a semi-final place and a home match against the French champions, Stade Français. Temporary stands were erected at Ravenhill to bring the capacity of the ground to 20,000. The enthusiasm and excitement Ulster had generated was without precedent. Long queues formed outside the Ulster Branch offices at Ravenhill as thousands sought the much prized match tickets. People who had not previously seen a rugby match and who came from across the divide in Ulster, sporting and political, were united in a common cause.

Gary Longwell wins a line out for Ulster in the European Cup final

In a magnificent match, Ulster won 33–27 and the scenes that followed will live for ever in the memory of those who were at the match. Ulster had defied the improbable with the win, highlighted by a superb try from Ulster outside-half David Humphreys. The place kicking of full-back Simon Mason had also been a crucial element in Ulster's successful campaign.

Colomiers, who had defeated Munster in the quarter-final, then caused something of a surprise by beating a highly rated Perpignan team in the semi-final, and so the stage was set for an occasion that brought colour and celebrity to Lansdowne Road and unprecedented glory to Irish and Ulster rugby.

Lansdowne Road was packed to its capacity of over 48,000 for the final, with over 30,000 people travelling from Ulster. Politicians and people of the most diverse persuasions journeyed to Dublin to support Ulster and the whole country was united in its support. The famous old ground presented the most colourful aspect, with the red and white of Ulster everywhere. Not even an international occasion could match the scene for colour and enthusiasm. Rugby had succeeded where so much else had failed in the Ulster context. This was an occasion when the whole of Ulster said yes with a united voice.

The French must have felt that they were playing against a nation rather than a provincial team and the cheer of acclamation that greeted the Ulster side's arrival on the field was itself a declaration of intent.

Harry Williams, the Ulster coach, had done his homework well and had prepared his team superbly — tactically, physically and psychologically. It was not by any means a great match as the great kicking skills of Simon Mason were brought to bear on the proceedings. But as an occasion it was unmatched in the annals of the game of rugby in Ireland.

The French team took an early three points lead with a penalty, but as the Ulster forwards dominated and the half-backs Andrew Matchett and David Humphreys played to that strength, the French were forced on the defensive and into the concession of penalties. Mason kicked four to leave his side 12–3 up at the break and now glory beckoned and the crowd sensed it.

The French attacked after the interval, but the Ulster defence stood firm. Humphreys dropped an opportunist goal to put Ulster 15–3 ahead early in the second half and then Mason added a fifth penalty to leave Ulster 18–3 clear with just over 30 minutes to go. The French cut the deficit with a penalty but that was the only inroad they made and a try-scoring chance was wasted by the French because of a forward pass.

A scene that tells its own tale. Ulster supporters celebrate after Ulster's triumph in the European Cup at Lansdowne Road

As the match entered the closing stages Mason kicked a sixth penalty and Ulster led 21–6 and now there was no doubt about the result. The final minutes were marked by non-stop cheering in expectation as the crowd awaited the final whistle of Welsh referee Clayton Thomas.

The scenes at the end will for ever be etched in the memories of all present and the countless millions who watched the match across Europe on television. David Humphreys who led Ulster in the absence of the original team captain Mark McCall, who was ruled out of much of the campaign by a neck injury, was carried shoulder high from the playing area, as were his team colleagues. Tom Kiernan, chairman of ERC, and IRFU president Noel Murphy were on hand at the victory rostrum to make the presentations. The crowd lingered on well after the players had left the field after doing a lap of honour. It was a golden hour that people wanted to prolong for as long as possible. It was that kind of an occasion, unforgettable in every way.

It is right that the names of the 17 Ulster players who played that afternoon and whose names will be enshrined in the annals of the game in the province be recorded. They were: Simon Mason, Sheldon Coulter, Jan Cunningham, Jonathan Bell, Andrew Park, David Humphreys, Andrew Matchett, Justin Fitzpatrick, Allen Clarke, Rab Irwin, Mark Blaire, Gary Longwell, Stephen McKinty, Tony McWhirter and Andrew Ward. Gary Leslie came on as a replacement for Irwin in the seventy-second minute and Stuart Duncan for McWhirter in the seventy-fifth. Ulster's remarkable triumph was, in fact, the culmination of a day of glory for Irish rugby as UCC had set the scene earlier in the day. Sixteen teams had entered for the inaugural Students European Cup in 1997–98. UCC, where the traditions of rugby run so deep with a club at the college that predates the establishment of the first administrative body for Irish rugby in 1874, had reached the semi-final of the cup the previous season, but lost to the eventual winners, Toulouse.

The second Students European Cup attracted an increased entry of 21 teams. UCD, UCC, Dublin

University and Queen's University represented Ireland. UCD and UCC both reached the knock-out stages and UCD claimed a very notable win in Belfield over the holders UPS Toulouse. However, UCD's interest was terminated in the quarter-final by Brunel. UCC, meanwhile, accounted for Bristol and Barcelona in the pool matches to claim a quarter-final berth against Northumbria. That was duly won 23–13 and next up was English side, Harper Adams. UCC overwhelmed that opposition to win 64–7 with a superb performance that earned a standing ovation from the attendance at the Mardyke in Cork. UCC scored 10 tries with eight players sharing in the try feast and outside-half Brian O'Mahony converted seven. Such was the quality of the UCC performance that the visiting coach acclaimed the display as the best he had seen from any university team in many years.

Grenoble, meanwhile, had kept the French flag flying and qualified for the final. So it was UCC versus Grenoble in the decider and that was a joyous day for the SERC Tournament Director Dr Len Harty. He is a man who has contributed immensely to UCC and to university rugby in Ireland.

Grenoble did not want to play the match on Saturday, 30 January, as a few of their players were required by club side, Burgoin, for a match the following day. But the final had been fixed to coincide with the European Cup decider and the fixture stood. UCC had a great following at the match as students and former students came to support the team and it was estimated that UCC had about 2,000 supporters to cheer them on.

Ulster's trail of triumph brought all sections of the community together. Northern Ireland's First Mininster, David Trimble, and his Deputy, Seamus Mallon, support Ulster at Lansdowne Road

Grenoble, although short a few players because of the demands of Burgoin, fielded a very experienced side and were favourites to win the match. But the UCC coaches Peter Melia and Brian Hyland, like Harry Williams, had imbued a great spirit and tactical awareness into their team.

Grenoble started the match full of confidence and when they took a 10 points lead after 20 minutes, things looked ominous for UCC as Grenoble scored two tries. UCC took time to settle. They were making mistakes, most unforced — passes were not going to hand, the line-out was not tidy and compact, and the scrum was under pressure. But they maintained their composure and as the match progressed, so confidence and efficiency increased. They had tackled very well in the face of the Grenoble onslaught and when full-back Colin Healy kicked a penalty UCC had cut the deficit to seven points.

In the second half, UCC were a team transformed. Obviously conscious that they had the capacity to win this huge prize, and with tremendous support coming from the stand and terraces, the UCC pack played with renewed vigour and application. Line-out possession was now coming in quality and quantity from their excellent forwards Michael O'Driscoll and John Fitzgerald. Peter Stringer at scrum-half was outstanding and his passing and perception were key elements as UCC put their opponents under pressure.

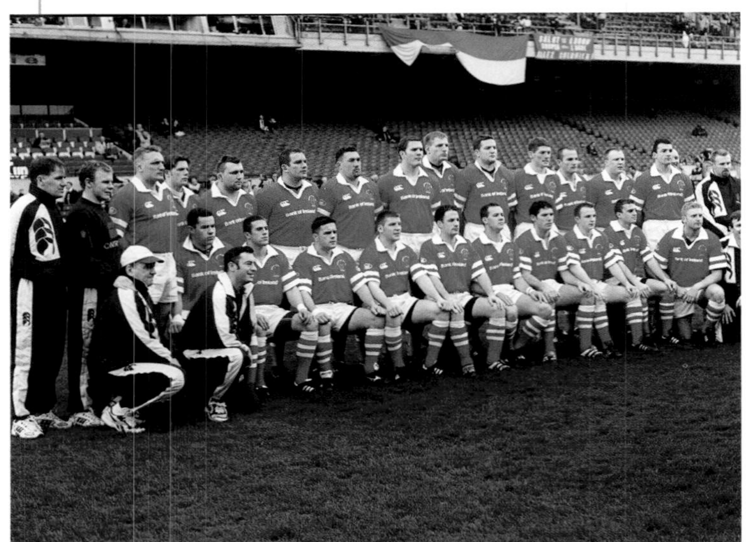

THE ULSTER TEAM THAT WON THE EUROPEAN CUP IN JANUARY 1999. COACH HARRY WILLIAMS IS ON THE EXTREME LEFT IN THE FRONT ROW

Within eight minutes of the restart, UCC scored a try after they had won a line-out and the pack drove over the line, with Niall Kennedy getting his hand to the ball to ground it. Now it was 10–8, and Grenoble were clearly unsettled by the play and commitment of the Irish side.

The ground erupted when Aidan O'Shea dropped a goal and UCC led for the first time in the match with 20 minutes remaining. Although Grenoble did not wilt, they could not break the resistance of the opposition. With five minutes to go Brian O'Mahony kicked a penalty to stretch his side's lead to 14–10 and the final minutes were tense and played out as spectators anxiously looked at watches and wished time away. Then came the final whistle and the celebrations began.

The trophy was presented to UCC's admirable captain Aidan O'Shea by Marcus Williams, Sports News Editor of *The Irish Times*. During the half-time interval at the European Cup final in the afternoon the teams were presented to the crowd at Lansdowne Road and UCC got a tremendous reception in keeping with the magnitude of their achievement. For the UCC club president Dr Peter Kenefick it was especially memorable. His club had been crowned European Student champions on his birthday.

THE UNIVERSITY COLLEGE CORK TEAM THAT WON THE EUROPEAN STUDENTS' CUP ON THE SAME DAY THAT ULSTER WON THE EUROPEAN CUP. TEAM CAPTAIN ADIAN O'SHEA IS HOLDING THE TROPHY. ALSO INCLUDED ARE TEAM COACHES, PETER MELIA, SECOND FROM LEFT, BACK ROW AND BRIAN HYLAND, SECOND FROM LEFT, FRONT ROW. UCC PRESIDENT, PETER KENEFICK AND TOURNAMENT CHAIRMAN LEN HARTY ARE ON THE RIGHT, BACK ROW

CHAPTER 43

THE LAST FIVE NATIONS CHAMPIONSHIP

AS THE MILLENNIUM WAS DRAWING to a close, so too was the Five Nations Championship. The final year of the final decade of the twentieth century also marked the last season of the Five Nations series.

It had graced the international calendar since early in the century when the French entered the fray and got annual fixtures against all four home countries. There had been a break between 1932 and 1946. The French were dismissed from the series in 1932 for violation of the laws on amateurism and that meant it became a four nations series until 1939. The Second World War called a halt and the championship was not resumed until 1947, when happily the French rejoined; and so it has gone on for the last 52 years. There was the brief hiccup when in 1972 Wales and Scotland refused to travel to Dublin, but normality was resumed in 1973.

The decision to admit Italy to the series in the year 2000 means that it will now be a six nations series. That should enhance a championship that has truly been the jewel in the crown of the game in the northern hemisphere. The advent of the World Cup, the European Cup, the Tri Nations and the Super 12 competitions have not detracted in any way from the appeal of the oldest of all international competitions.

Ireland went into the last Five Nations series with hopes relatively high of doing well, to the extent of winning at least two matches in the series. That was the stated objective of coach Warren Gatland before the competition started.

Ireland opened their challenge against France at Lansdowne Road on 6 February. Ulster's win in the European Cup a week earlier was a tremendous boost for Ireland, especially as Ulster had beaten French opposition in the European Cup final and indeed three French teams in the knock-out stages.

Paddy Johns led an Ireland team to which David Humphreys had been restored at outside-half following his exploits with Ulster. Malcolm O'Kelly was an absentee from the second row after sustaining a bad injury at club level and Jeremy Davidson partnered Paddy Johns in the second row. Ireland led in the match from the twenty-fifth minute when Humphreys kicked a penalty — he added two more penalties to leave Ireland nine points clear. The Ireland forwards won a lot of possession and while the attacking limitations in the Ireland back line were such that it was not turned to account, Ireland held France extremely well. It was not until 14 minutes from the end that France broke through for a try which came after a needlessly conceded penalty that set up the attacking position for the French. The try was converted. So Ireland led by two points as the match entered the last minute.

Then once more Ireland conceded a penalty when Paul Wallace was penalised and the French outside-half, Castaignede, kicked the goal. It was heart breaking for the Irish. But a chance came in injury time when the French were penalised 30 yards to the left of their posts. Humphreys stepped up to take the kick, but it floated inches wide on the wind and so a golden opportunity to end the long barren spell against France had been lost. Humphreys had not been kicking for Ulster and so went into the match cold, as it were, in respect of place kicking. His form in that regard was to improve appreciably as the championship progressed.

On the eve of the international both the Ireland Under 21 and A teams beat France; so it was not a barren weekend.

A visit to Wembley to play Wales was next on the schedule for Ireland. Wembley was the temporary Welsh home while the Arms Park was being rebuilt for the World Cup. So it was a visit to the famous London ground for Ireland. It was to prove extremely profitable in the form of an exciting victory 29–23 for Ireland. Thus Ireland's superb away record against Wales, which started in 1985, was yet again maintained.

Ireland built a 26–6 lead by the fiftieth minute and seemed set fair to win well. Then came a rather indifferent spell by the Irish with the winning post in sight. The Welsh fought back and, with 11 minutes to go, stood only three points adrift at 23–26. But Ireland steadied the ship in the stormy waters and Humphreys dropped a goal to leave his side six points clear with five minutes remaining. The Irish held out readily for a well merited and very welcome win. Ireland scored two tries through Kevin Maggs and Keith Wood and Humphreys kicked the rest of the points for a personal contribution of 19.

Girvan Dempsey, who had missed the match against Wales because of injury and was replaced by Niall Woods, returned for the visit of England. There was huge expectation prior to this visit to Lansdowne Road. One could say added spice was given to the fixture by the activities of English representatives who had met some French officials and produced an alleged blueprint for a revised European Cup. It was an extremely insensitive document that among other elements cast doubts on the integrity of ERC. Even members of the RFU committee were embarrassed by what it contained.

That apart, the Ireland side was unable to halt the onward march of England who won 27–13 and deserved to do so. The Irish were in the match until the last few minutes. Indeed, Ireland came within a few inches of scoring a try with a few minutes remaining when the score stood at 13–20. But England scored an injury time try and conversion, and there was no doubt about the merit of their win.

Ireland prepared to go to Murrayfield for their last match in the Five Nations series. In the interim, agreement was reached that brought the England clubs back into the European Cup and Ireland had been guaranteed three representatives, Munster, Leinster, and Ulster as the defending champions, in an expanded European Cup that now embraces 24 teams.

Yet again Murrayfield proved no field of dreams for Ireland and, once more, the Scots won to keep their great unbeaten record against the Irish that stretches back to 1989. Ireland got a dream start with a try in the first minute. But far from proving to be inspirational, Ireland made countless unforced errors and an eager and speedy Scotland back line capitalised for a very comprehensive win by 30 points to 13.

So one win from four matches was once more a poor return for Ireland. But such was the sequence of events in the competition that Ireland at least avoided the indignity of the wooden spoon. That, remarkably, went to France, the previous season's Grand Slam champions, who lost to Wales, England and Scotland. And it was Scotland who took the title when Wales dramatically beat England in Wembley with an injury time try and conversion for a glorious win that underlined once more just how unpredictable the championship can be. Scotland won the championship on superior points difference from England.

Italy travelled to play Ireland in Dublin on 10 April. This was, at it were, a prelude to a more important encounter between the countries which will come in the Six Nations Championship in 1999–2000. With a four match tour to Australia in June in mind, the Ireland management made seven changes in the side to meet Italy. Two players had been ruled out through injury. David Humphreys, who had to have an operation on a damaged finger, and Eric Miller, who underwent surgery for a troublesome ankle problem. Young Ciaran Scally was recalled at scrum-half and Keith Wood and Paul Wallace were rested.

It was to be a traumatic enough occasion for Ireland before the Italians were subdued; but Ireland ended a three match losing sequence against Italy by winning in the end 39–30. At the interval Italy led 23–8 as the Irish made several errors and paid the price, notably a series of handling errors near their own line. But the Irish gradually wore the Italians down in the second half when Ireland had the wind at their backs and Eric Elwood kicked shrewdly for position. Both Keith Wood and Paul Wallace were brought on to add experience to the Ireland side. It was a welcome win achieved in a rather unimpressive performance.

Once more Ireland's best performances came from the under age and schools teams. The Under 21 team beat France, England, Scotland and Italy, and were foiled of a Grand Slam because they had lost to Wales in very difficult conditions in Caerphilly by 24–18. The Under 21 side scored a record 57 points against Italy at Ravenhill on the eve of the senior international. One thing that did not help the Under 21 side was the fact that players such as full-back Gordon D'Arcy, scrum-half Ciaran Scally and centre Shane Horgan, all of whom were eligible, were required by the senior selectors for duty at A team level in the case of D'Arcy and Horgan, and Scally with the senior side.

On the evening prior to the senior match against Italy, the Ireland A side, who had lost to England, Wales and Scotland after beating France, scored 73 points in the demolition of Italy at Donnybrook. That was the highest score attained by any Ireland team in an international at any level. A feature of that match was that Jeremy Staunton, who played at outside-half for Ireland, created his own record. In the space of three weeks Staunton represented Ireland at three levels — A, Under 21 and Under 19.

The Ireland Under 19 team went to Wales to defend the IRB-FIRA World Cup at the end of March. And defend it well the team did despite being without the services of a few players unavailable due to injury, including Gordon D'Arcy.

Ireland beat Georgia and Italy to reach the semi-finals and at that stage lost 21–15 to New Zealand. Ireland laid siege to the New Zealand line in the closing stages, but New Zealand held on for victory. The effort took its tool on the Irish who, three days later, lost to South Africa in the play-off for third place, surrendering a good lead in the closing stages before going down 27–20. But by finishing in the top four Ireland had been guaranteed a seeded place for next year's championship, a very important consideration.

Dion O'Cuinneagain on the break against Scotland at Murrayfield in the last Five Nations Championship in 1999. O'Cuinneagain was subsequently named as Ireland captain for the tour to Australia in the summer of 1999

The Irish youngsters defended their title with great courage and honour. And it is a measure of how close they came to glory that New Zealand, who had escaped against Ireland, went on to beat Wales 25–0 in the final.

The Youths Under 18 team lost to Italy by a point in a match in Treviso in February and then participated in the Triple Crown series in Scotland in April. Ireland lost 10–15 to Wales, beat Scotland 19–5 and lost 15–12 to England.

The fact that Scotland decided not to play Ireland and Wales at schools level for financial reasons — apparently the finance was not available to the Scottish Schools from the parent union — very probably deprived Ireland of yet another Triple Crown at this level. Ireland defeated England 8 – 6 at Musgrave Park on 3 April 1999 and a week later went to Ebbw Vale and hammered Wales 41–0 to record the most comprehensive win by an Ireland Schools side in an international since Ireland first played at that level in 1975.

As the AIB All-Ireland League reached its climax with an exciting battle for the top four places in the first division, the IRFU announced what it termed 'The Clubs of Ireland Scheme'. This is, in effect, an incentive scheme based on clubs' input into the game in terms of teams, referees, youth development teams and facilities. It was produced by Eddie Wigglesworth, the IRFU Director of Rugby Development. A standardised programme of development was outlined to the clubs. The Development template focused on what it termed key areas of achievement. It centred on the number of teams a club is requested to field at adult-youth-mini levels throughout the season, the number of active referees a club should possess, the number of coaches recommended for each team in various categories, and the quality-qualification of the coaches.

The subventions which had been paid to clubs in the All-Ireland League over the last three years had been conditional. The Clubs of Ireland Scheme starting in 1999–2000 replaces this subvention and will be the mechanism whereby the IRFU can continue to support progressive structural and rugby developments within the club.

This was a plan for the new millennium to help greater development at every level of the game and to help bring more players into the game as well as to improve standards.

Meanwhile as the 1998–99 season drew to a close the IRFU was able to announce that more players were returning to Ireland from English clubs. Paddy Johns and Malcolm O'Kelly, two current internationals, are included among those who will be playing their rugby in Ireland next season. Such happenings are welcome in every respect and, of course, help to strengthen not alone Irish clubs, but the Irish provinces in Europe.

The visit of the Ireland senior squad to Australia was only one tour in the Irish schedule for the summer of 1999. The Ireland Under 21 squad also travelled abroad in quest of glory and experience to participate in a tournament in Argentina in July.

During the summer of 1999 the IRFU announced changes in the AIB League for the new millennium that embraces a bonus points system on similar lines to that which operates in the Interprovincial Championship. But there will be even more radical alteration in the 2000-2001 season. The structure of the three divisions will be altered and all will consist of sixteen teams split into two sections in each division, with matches played on a home-and-away basis. There will then be semi-finals and finals in each division.

Under the management of Donal Lenihan, Warren Gatland and Philip Danaher, the Ireland senior squad set off for Australia in May on a four match tour. The back-up team on the squad was in sharp constrast to earlier tours, with every area catered for from medical officer to baggage master.

Ireland brought a squad that embraced the experienced and youthful promise. Mike Mullins, the West Hartlepool centre, and Matt Mostyn, the Begles Bordeaux wing, were included, both from the Antipodes. These two players had been brought into the Ireland A side against Italy. They also declared that their rugby would be played in Ireland in 1999-2000. The Cork Constitution scrum-half, Brian O'Meara was chosen but had to withdraw because of a fractured thumb and Tom Tierney of Garryowen was called in. The captaincy of the team passed from Paddy Johns to Dion O'Cuinneagain, obviously with a view to the World Cup.

The youths in the side were: centre Brian O'Driscoll (UCD), an Ireland Under 21 player, the Ireland Under 19 outside half, Jeremy Staunton, and the Blackrock College Under 21 international,

Robert Casey. In all, the squad included six uncapped players.

Ireland won the opening match against New South Wales Country Districts by 43-6, but then suffered a setback when they lost in Sydney to a New South Wales team that was as formidable as the New South Wales teams of the recent past. In the first test in Ballymore, Brisbane, Ireland included three new caps in Mostyn, O'Driscoll and Tierney, but went down to a record 46-10 defeat. Conor O'Shea broke his jaw in the match and was ruled out of the second test in Perth a week later.

Ireland faced an awesome task in the second test, but rose to the occasion splendidly and put up a very good performance before going down 32-26. Ireland, in fact, outscored Australia by 3-2 in tries. A few mistakes in the midway period of the second half allowed Australia in for two crucial tries that saw Ireland's interval lead turn into a deficit. But there was no capitulation and Ireland finished very well.

So Ireland returned from Australia with much to contemplate and a lot of hard work to do, but very encouraged by the performance in the second test. They had one more international before the World Cup, a visit from Argentina to Dublin in August.

With the World Cup on the schedule for October 1999, rugby football was saying farewell to the twentieth century in some style. Much had changed in 100 years, but the grand old game is now, in every respect, truly a world game that has spread its net to embrace countries from all over the world. Let us be grateful for that.

Professionalism has brought immense changes that could not have been envisaged as the century entered its last quarter, even its last decade. Changes have also brought huge challenges to every area of the game that started, if legend is to be believed, with an act of disobedience on a stretch of ground at a school that gave the game its name. It went its own way as a separate and specific art form of football and was perfected by the evolutionary process, spread through the vision and wisdom of the many, and survived and prospered in this country on the love and dedication of successive generations.

It is about the thrill the youngster gets when he holds the rugby ball for the first time, seeking to emulate his heroes; and as he grows old, still delights in watching from the touchline and talking of days when he first came to terms with the intricacies of an odd-shaped ball. The fascination has never left any of us, whether we are distinguished former internationals or never more than extras in the cast. To many, rugby football is something very special, it is and has been an essential part of the fabric of the way of life of so many in Ireland. They are all players in the story of Irish rugby. This book, in essence, is about them.

APPENDIX 1

THE LAWS OF RUGBY

The laws of rugby adopted by the annual general meeting of the Dublin University Football Club in October 1868:

1. The Kick-off from the middle must be a place kick.
2. Kick-out must be 25 yards out of goal, not a place kick.
3. Charging is fair in case of a place kick, as soon as the ball has touched the ground: In case of a kick from a catch, as soon as the player offers to kick, but he may always draw back unless he has touched the ball with his foot.
4. If a player makes a Fair Catch he shall be entitled to a free kick, provided he claims it by making a mark with his heel at once, and in order to take such kick he may go back as far as he pleases and no player on the opposite side shall advance beyond his mark until he has kicked.
5. A Fair Catch cannot be made from touch.
6. A player is offside when the ball has been kicked or thrown or knocked on, or is being run with by one of his own behind him.
7. A player offside may impede the game by standing close to the ball; but he may not, in any case, kick or touch it, charge or put over.
8. A player is onside when the ball has been kicked or thrown or knocked on, or when it has rebounded from the body of any player of the opposite side.
9. It is not lawful to take up the ball when not in touch, except in an evident hop. Lifting the ball is strictly prohibited.
10. Running in is allowed to any player onside provided he does not run through touch.
11. In case of a run-in, the ball is held in a maul, it shall not be lawful for any other player on his own side to take it from the runner and run with it.
12. It shall be lawful for any player to call upon any other player, holding the ball in a maul, to put it down when evidently unable to get away.
13. A player, if he wishes to enter a maul, must do so onside.
14. No player, out of a maul, may be held or pulled over, unless he himself is holding the ball.
15. No hacking, as distinct from tripping, is fair.
16. Try at goal. A ball touched between the goal posts, may be brought up to either of them but not between.
17. When the ball has been touched down behind the goal, the player who touched it down is entitled to walk out straight 25 yards, and any of his side may take a place kick but as soon as the ball has been placed the opposite side may charge.
18. It shall be a goal if the ball be dropped, but not if punted, hit or thrown, between the posts or posts produced at any height over the horizontal bar, whether it touch it or not.
19. No goal may be kicked from touch.
20. A ball in touch is dead. Consequently, the first player on his side must, in any case, touch it down, bring it to the side of touch and throw it straight out.
21. Holding or throttling is disallowed.
22. Sneaking in opponents' goal is discountenanced.
23. The captains of sides, or any two deputed by them, shall be the sole arbiters of all disputes.

APPENDIX 2

PRESIDENTS OF THE IRFU

1874–76	Duke of Abercorn
1876–79	Duke of Marlborough
1879–80	W.C. Neville MD
1880–81	Rt Hon. Sir William Goulding PC, MA, JP, DL
1881–82	R.B. Walkington
1882–83	G. Scriven MD
1883–84	A.R. McMullen
1884–85	R.E. McLean
1885–86	G. Scriven MD
1886–87	W.L Stokes
1887–88	J. Chambers KC, MP
1888–89	R. Biggs LLD
1889–90	Sir F.W. Moore FLS
1890–91	M.H. Turnbull
1891–92	H. Hook
1892–93	J.R. Blood
1893–94	R. Garratt MD
1894–95	J. Macaulay
1895–96	R.G. Warren
1896–97	J. Dodds
1897–98	J.F. Maguire
1898–99	J.B. Moore
1899–1900	S. Lee
1900–1901	J. O'Sullivan
1901–02	T. Thornhill
1902–03	J. Johnston
1903–04	V.J. Murray
1904–05	A.D. Clinch MD
1905–06	F.M. Hamilton
1906–07	J. Flynn
1907–08	G.H.B. Kenny
1908–09	A. Barr
1909–10	Prof. C.W.L. Alexander
1910–11	F.C. Purer MD
1911–12	J.H. O'Conor
1912–13	Major R. Stevenson
1913–16	F.H. Browning BL
1916–19	Office not filled
1919–20	A. Tedford
1920–21	W.P. Hinton
1921-22	R.M Magrath
1922-23	G.G. McRea
1923-24	H. Thrift SF, TCD
1924-25	J.J. Coffey
1925-26	F.J. Strain
1926-27	G.T. Hamlet
1927-28	Judge Sealy KC
1928-29	H.J. Millar
1929-30	T.J. Greeves
1930–31	J.G. Musgrave
1931–32	W.A. Clarke
1932–33	C.S Neill
1933–34	S.E. Polden
1934–35	J. Wallace MB
1935–36	Sir S.T. Irwin CBE, MCh, FRCS, MP
1936–37	The Hon. Mr Justice Davitt
1937–38	H.E. Emerson MB, OBE, MC
1938–45	J.J. Warren
1945–46	H.J. Anderson LDSI
1946–47	W.A.B. Douglas JP, FRGS
1947–48	T.M. McGrath MB
1948–49	GPS Hogan BL, PC
1949–50	W.G. Fallon BL
1950–51	Air Vice Marshall Sir W. Tyrrell KBE, DSO, MC, MB, LLD
1951–52	D.F. O'Connell
1952–53	V.E. Kirwan
1953–54	J.B. O'Callaghan
1954–55	C.J. Hanrahan
1955–56	H.M. Read
1956–57	Capt. J. Ramsey PC
1957–58	W.E. Crawford BL
1958–59	J.J. Glynn
1959–60	J.R. Wheeler MB, FRCS
1960–61	N.F. Murphy
1961–62	L.B. McMahon
1962–63	J.A.E. Siggins
1963–64	T.A. O'Reilly
1964–65	C.C. Harte
1965–66	P.E. Murray FFA
1966–67	D.G. O'Donovan
1967–68	E. O'D. Davy
1968–69	C.P. Crowley
1969–70	J.W.S. Irwin MB, FRCS
1970–71	E. Patterson
1971–72	D.A. Dineen
1972–73	The Hon. Mr Justice J.C. Conroy
1973–74	I.F. Mahony
1974–75	H.R. McKibbin CBE, LLB
1975–76	J.J. Keane LRCP & SI
1976–77	J.A.D. Higgins
1977–78	J.F. Coffey
1978–79	K.J. Quilligan
1979–80	J. Montgomery MC
1980–81	R. Ganly MIAVI
1981–82	J.J. Moore BSc
1982–83	J.E. Nelson OBE, FCA
1983–84	G.F. Reidy
1984–85	M.H. Carroll
1985–86	D. McKibbin BSc, CEng, MICE
1986–87	Sir Ewart Bell KCB
1987–88	P.F. Madigan
1988–89	T.J. Kiernan, BComm, FCA
1989–90	A.R. Dawson FRIAI, FASI
1990–91	N.J. Henderson BSc
1991–92	Dr A.D. Browne BDS
1992–93	C.A. Quaid PhD
1993–94	M. Cuddy
1994–95	K.E. Reid MA, HDipEd
1995–96	Dr S. Millar MBE, DSc
1996–97	R.M. Deacy FCA
1997–98	N.H. Brophy BComm, FCA
1998–99	N.A. Murphy
1999–2000	W.H. Lavery LLB

APPENDIX 3

UNION OFFICIALS

Honorary Secretaries of Union

1874–76	H.D. Walsh
1876–78	W. Wilson
1878–79	W.C. Neville
1879–82	R.M. Peter
1882–86	H.G. Cook
1886–97	E. McAlister
1897–1925	C.F. Ruxton

Secretaries

1925–47	R.W. Jeffares Sr

Honorary Treasurers

1875–79	R.M. Peter
1879–80	E. Hughes
1880–81	C.B. Croker
1881–82	J. Atkinson
1882–86	W.J. Goulding
1888–92	J.R. Blood
1892–94	E.L. Maunsell
1895–1906	H.C. Shepperd
1907–16	F.H. Browning
1920–45	W.A. Clarke
1945–47	J.R. Ramsey
*1964–76	T.A. O'Reilly
1976–87	J.E. Nelson
1987–96	R.M. Deacy
1996	J.P. Lyons

*Honorary treasurer of the union restored as a separate office from that of treasurer in 1964.

Joint Secretary-Treasurers

1947–51	R.W. Jeffares Sr
1951–64	R.W. Jeffares Jr
1964–86	R. FitzGerald
1986–92	P. Moss
1992–95	P.J. O'Donoghue
1995	P. Browne*

*The office of joint secretary-treasurer held by Philip Browne has been discontinued and replaced by the office of chief executive.

Chief Executive

1999	P. Browne

Irish International Board Representatives

1886–92	T.R. Lyle
1886–97	E.A. McAlister
1887	W. Hogg*
1887	Kirkpatrick*
1887–1938	R.G. Warren
1888–91	J. Chambers
1889	Asher*
1892–1927	J.B. Moore
1893	J. Stewart*
1896	W. Ayres*
1897–1906	H.C. Shepperd
1898	J. Dodds*
1899	C.F. Ruxton*
1928–36	Dr A.D. Clinch
1931–56	H. Thrift
1932–46	F. Strain
1945	Judge C. Davitt
1946–71	G.P.S. Hogan
1948	J.R. Ramsey*
1957–71	J.A.E. Siggins
1967–87	H.R. McKibbin
1971–73	J.W.S. Irwin
1973–75	D.A. Dineen
1974	A.R. Dawson*
1975–94	A.R. Dawson
1987–93	Sir E. Bell
1993	S. Millar
1994	T.K. Kiernan

*Substituted for elected member

PRESIDENTS OF THE IRFU 1874–98

Duke of Abercorn
1874–76

Duke of Marlboro
1876–79

W.C. Neville
1879–80

Rt. Hon. Sir Wm. Goulding
1880–81

R.B. Walkington
1881–82

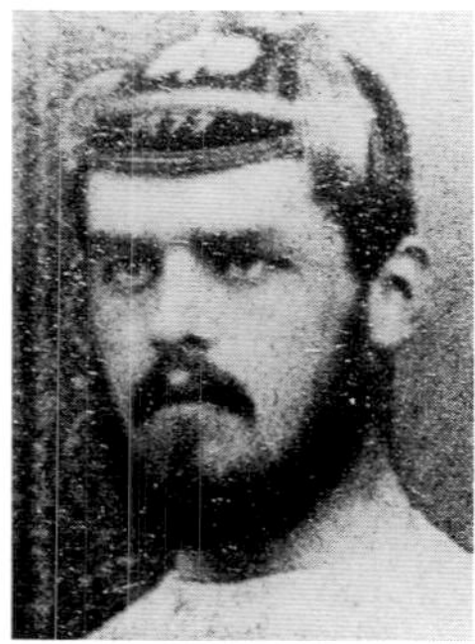
G. Scriven
1882–83 1885–86

A.R. McMullen
1883–84

R.E. McLean
1884–85

W.L. Stokes
1886–87

J. Chambers
1887–88

R. Biggs
1888–89

Sir F.W. Moore
1889–90

M.H. Turnbull
1890–91

H. Hook
1891–92

J.R. Blood
1892–93

R. Garratt M.D.
1893–94

J. Macaulay
1894–95

R.G. Warren
1895–96

J. Dodds
1896–97

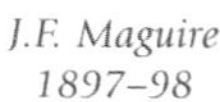
J.F. Maguire
1897–98

CAPTAINS OF IRELAND TEAMS 1874–92

G. H. Stack
1874–75

R. Bell
1875–76

W.H. Wilson
1876–77

R. Galbriath
1876–77

R.B. Walkington
1877–78

C.W. Neville
1878–79

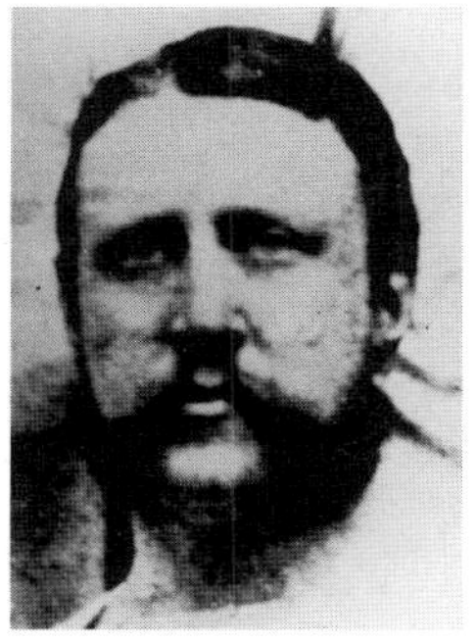

H.C. Kelly
1879–80

A.J. Forrest
1880–81

J.W. Taylor
1881–82

G. Scriven
1882–83

J.A. MacDonald
1883–84

D.F. Moore
1883–84

W.G. Rutherford
1884–85

M. Johnston
1885–86

J.P. Ross
1885–86

R.G. Warren
1886–87

H.J. Neill
1887–88

R. Stevenson
1890–91

D.B. Walkington
1890–91

V.C. le Fanu
1891–92

APPENDIX 4

IRISH SELECTION COMMITTEES

1893–94	J.R. Blood, R.G. Warren, R. Garret, R. Stevenson, J. Hook, H. McOstrich
1894–95	W. O'Conor, R.G. Warren, R. Garret, J. Dodds, J. Hook
1895–96	T. Thornhill, R.G. Warren, R. Garret, J. Chambers, J. Macaulay
1896–97	T. Thornhill, R.G. Warren, J. Dodds, C. le Fanu, J. Macaulay
1897–98	T. Thornhill, R.G. Warren, J. Dodds, C. le Fanu, J. Maguire
1898–99	T. Thornhill, L.H. Gwynn, R. Stevenson, S. Lee, J. Macaulay
1899–1900	T. Thornhill, L.H. Gwynn, C.S. Harden, S. Lee, J. Macaulay
1900–1901	T. Thornhill, J. Sealy, C.S. Harden, J.J. Ferris, G.D. Bateman
1901–02	T. Thornhill, C.V. Rooke, C.S. Harden, F.M. Hamilton, J. Macaulay
1902–03	H.W. Jones, J. Sealy, C.S. Harden, A. Barr, J. Macaulay
1903–04	A.D. Clinch, J. Sealy, C.D. Neill, W.G. Macome, J. Macaulay
1904–05	A.D. Clinch, J. Sealy, J. Fulton, A. Barr, J. Macauley
1905–06	A.D. Clinch, J. Sealy, A.F. Clarke, S.T. Irwin, J. Macaulay
1906–07	A.D. Clinch, C.B. Cullinan, A.F. Clarke, F. Gardiner, J. Macaulay
1907–08	A.D. Clinch, F.C. Purcer, A. Barr, F. Gardiner, J. Macaulay
1908–09	A.D. Clinch, J.J. Rowland, A. Barr, J. Fulton, J. Macaulay
1909–10	A.D. Clinch, F.C. Purcer, A. Barr, F. Gardiner, J. Macaulay
1910–11	A.D. Clinch, F.C. Purcer, T.N. Heron, F. Gardiner, J. Macaulay
1911–12	A.D. Clinch, B. Solomons, T.N. Heron, A. Tedford, J. Macaulay
1912- 13	A.D. Clinch, J.J. Coffey, S. Lee, F.G. Strain, J. Macaulay
1913–14	A.D. Clinch, J.J. Coffey, C.S. Neill, F.G. Strain, J. Macaulay
1915–18	No Selection committees appointed
1919–20	B.R. Doran, B. Solomons, S.B. Campbell, F.G. Strain, J. Macaulay
1920–21	B.R. Doran, W.A. Daish, S.B. Campbell, F.G. Strain, J. Macauley
1921–22	H. Thrift, W.A. Daish, Dr H. Emerson, F.G. Strain, M.F. Landers
1922–23	S.E. Polden, J. Warren, A.R. Foster, A. Tedford, M.F. Landers
1923–24	S.E. Polden, J. Warren, A.R. Foster, A. Tedford, J. Macaulay
1924–25	S.E. Polden, J. Warren, A.R. Foster, Dr H. Emerson, J. Macaulay
1925–30	S.E. Polden, J. Warren, T.J. Greeves, Dr H. Emerson, J. Macaulay
1930–31	S.E. Polden, J. Warren, T.J. Greeves, Dr H. Emerson, J.G. Musgrave
1931–32	A.D. Clinch, J. Warren, T.J. Greeves, J. Gillespie, J.G. Musgrave
1932–33	S.E. Polden, J. Warren, T.J. Greeves, J. Gillespie, J.G. Musgrave
1933–34	S.E. Polden, J. Warren, T.J. Greeves, Dr F.P. Montgomery, J.G. Musgrave
1934–36	Dr P.F. Murray, G.P.S. Hogan, T.J. Greeves, Dr F.P. Montgomery, J.G. Musgrave
1936–37	W.P. Collopy, G.P.S. Hogan, F.J. Greeves, R. Hamilton, J.G. Musgrave
1937–38	W.P. Collopy, Comdt J. Gleeson, T.J. Greeves, R. Hamilton, J. Quilligan
1938–40	N.M. Purcell, G.P.S. Hogan, T.J. Greeves, R. Hamilton, J. Quilligan
1940–41	N.M. Purcell, Dr H. Michael, T.J. Greeves, R. Hamilton, J. Quilligan
1941–42	E.C.G. Mulhern, G.P.S. Hogan, T.J. Greeves, R. Hamilton, J. Quilligan
1942–43	Dr H. Michael, L.B. McMahon, T.J. Greeves, R. Hamilton, C. Hanrahan
1943–44	G.P.S. Hogan, L.B. McMahon, T.J. Greeves, W.E. Crawford, C. Hanrahan
1944–46	G.J. Morgan, E.C.G. Mulhern, W.E. Crawford, E.B.I. Goldsborough, C. Hanrahan
1946–47	G.J. Morgan, L.B. McMahon, W.E. Crawford, E.B.I. Goldsborough, C. Hanrahan
1947–49	E.J. Lightfoot, L.B. McMahon, W.E. Crawford, J.A.E. Siggins, C.J. Hanrahan

1949–50 E.J. Lightfoot, C.R. Graves, W.E. Crawford, J.B. O'Callaghan, D.B. O'Loughlin
1950–51 J.J. Winters, G.R. Graves, W.E. Crawford, J.B. O'Callaghan, D.B. O'Loughlin
1951–52 J.J. Winters, C.R. Graves, C.C. Harte, J.B. O'Callaghan, N. Murphy
1952–53 J.J. Winters, P. Tighe, C.C. Harte, J.B. O'Callaghan, N. Murphy
1953–54 G.J. Quinn, P. Tighe, C.C. Harte, J.W.S. Irwin, N. Murphy
1954–55 G.J. Quinn, P. Tighe, C.C. Harte, J.A.D. Higgins, D.B. O'Loughlin
1955–56 G.J. Quinn, C.A. Boyle, W.E. Crawford, O.B. Glasgow, D.B. O'Loughlin
1956–57 M.P. Crowe, C.A. Boyle, W.E. Crawford, O.B. Glasgow, D.B. O'Loughlin
1957–58 M.P. Crowe, C.A. Boyle, J.A.D. Higgins, O.B. Glasgow, D. Barry
1958–59 L. Lysaght, C.A. Boyle, J.A.D. Higgins, O.B. Glasgow, D. Barry
1959–60 L. Lysaght, C.R. Graves, J.A.D. Higgins, O.B. Glasgow, D. Barry
1960–61 C.R. Graves, D.P. Smyth, O.B. Glasgow, H.R. McKibbin, C. St George
1961–62 Dr K.D. Mullen, Dr G. O'Reilly, J.A.D. Siggins, H.R. McKibbin, C. St George
1962–63 Dr K.D. Mullen, Dr G. O'Reilly, H.R. McKibbin, J.E. Nelson, C. St George
1963–64 Dr K.D. Mullen, Dr G. O'Reilly, D. McKibbin, J.E. Nelson, M. Powell
1964–65 J.F. Coffey, Dr G. O'Reilly, D. McKibbin, J.E. Nelson, M. Powell
1965–66 J.F. Coffey, D.P. Smyth, D. McKibbin, J.E. Nelson, M. Powell
1966–67 J.F. Coffey, D.P. Smyth, D. McKibbin, W.E. Bell, J. Roche
1967–68 D. O'Leary, D.P. Smyth, W.E. Bell, D. McKibbin, J. Roche
1968–69 D. O'Leary, N. McConnell, W.E. Bell, N.J. Henderson, J. Roche
1969–70 D. O'Leary, A.R. Dawson, W.E. Bell, N.J. Henderson, Dr D. Gleeson
1970–72 A.R. Dawson, M. Carroll, N.J. Henderson, J. Hewitt, Dr D. Gleeson
1972–73 M. Carroll, F. McMullen, J. Hewitt, S. Millar, P. O'Callaghan
1973–74 J.P. Fanagan, F. McMullen, W.J. Hewitt, S. Millar, P. O'Callaghan
1974–75 J.P. Fanagan, F. McMullen, S. Millar, R. Saunders, P. O'Callaghan
1975–76 J.P. Fanagan, N.H. Brophy, K.E. Reid, S. Millar, N.A. Murphy
1976–77 N.H. Brophy, R. Carroll, K.E. Reid, R. Saunders, N.A. Murphy
1977–78 N.H. Brophy, R. Carroll, K.E. Reid, R. Saunders, N.A. Murphy
1978–79 R. Carroll, P.F. Madigan, K.E. Reid, J.C. Lapsley, N.A. Murphy
1979–80 P.F. Madigan, M.K. Flynn, J.C. Lapsley, N.A. Murphy, B.P. O'Brien
1980–81 P.F. Madigan, M.K. Flynn, J.C. Lapsley, D.C. Glass, P.J. Dwyer
1981–82 M.K. Flynn, T.W.R. Meates, D.C. Glass, P.J. Dwyer, B.A. O'Brien
1982–83 T.W.R. Meates, M. Cuddy, D.C. Glass, P.J. Dwyer, B.A. O'Brien
1983–84 T.W.R. Meates, M. Cuddy, B.A. O'Brien, J. Donaldson, W.J. McBride
1984–85 M. Cuddy, M.G. Doyle, J.A. Donaldson, W.J. McBride, J. Kiernan
1985–86 M.G. Doyle, E. Coleman, W.J. McBride, J.A. Donaldson, J. Kiernan
1986–87 E. Coleman, M.G. Doyle, T.H.N. Jackson, J.A. Kiernan, J.C.M. Moroney
1987–88 E.J. Coleman, J.C. Davidson, T.H.N. Jackson, A. Twomey, J.C.M. Moroney
1988–89 A. Twomey, J.C. Davidson, T.H.N. Jackson, J.C.M. Moroney, J.E. Murray
1989–90 A. Twomey, J.C. Davidson, J.C.M. Moroney, J.E. Murray, C.H. McKibbin
1990–91 K.E. Reid, C.F. Fitzgerald, J.E. Murray, M.K. Flynn, C.H. McKibbin
1991–92 K.E. Reid, C.F. Fitzgerald, J.E. Murray, M.K. Flynn, C.H. McKibbin
1992–93 N.A. Murphy, F.E. Sowman, C.H. McKibbin, C.F. Fitzgerald (replaced by G.F. Murphy, Nov. 1992), P.C. Whelan
1993–94 N.A. Murphy, F.E. Sowman, G.F. Murphy, J. Miles, P.C. Whelan
1994–95 N.A. Murphy, G.F. Murphy, F.E. Sowman, J. Miles, P.C. Whelan
1995–96 P.C. Whelan, M. Kidd, F.E. Sowman, J. Miles, D.G. Lenihan
1996–97 P.C. Whelan, M. Kidd (replaced by B. Ashton, Jan. 1997), J. Miles, F.E. Sowman, D.G. Lenihan
1997–98 P.C. Whelan, D.G. Lenihan, B. Ashton (replaced by W.D. Gatland, Feb. 1998)
1998–99 D.G. Lenihan, W. Gatland, P.P.A. Danaher

N.B. The selection committee was reduced to three from the 1997–98 season.

APPENDIX 5

COACHES TO THE IRELAND TEAM

(First appointed 1969–70)

1969–70 to 1971–72 A.R. Dawson
1972–73 to 1974–75 S. Millar
1975–76 to 1976–77 T.W.R. Meates
1977–78 to 1979–80 N.A. Murphy
1980–81 to 1982–83 T.J. Kiernan
1983–84 W.J. McBride
1984–85 to 1986–87 M.G. Doyle
1987–88 to 1989–90 J.C. Davidson
1990–91 to 1992–93 C.F. Fitzgerald
C.F. Fitzgerald resigned Nov. 92, replaced by G.F. Murphy
1992–93 to 1994–95 G.F. Murphy
1995–96 to 1996–97 M. Kidd
M. Kidd resigned Jan. 97, replaced by B. Ashton
1996–97 to 1997–98 B. Ashton
B. Ashton resigned Feb. 98, replaced by W.D. Gatland
1997–98 W.D. Gatland

APPENDIX 6

MANAGERS TO THE IRELAND TEAM

The appointment of a manager to the national team was first made in 1990–91.
1990–91 to 1991–92 K.E. Reid
1992–93 to 1994–95 N.A. Murphy
1995–96 to 1997–98 P.C. Whelan
P.C. Whelan resigned in April 1998, replaced by D.G. Lenihan
1998–99 D.G. Lenihan

APPENDIX 7

SENIOR CUP AND LEAGUE WINNERS IN FOUR PROVINCES

Leinster Senior Cup Winners

1882 Dublin U
1883 Dublin U
1884 Dublin U
1885 Wanderers
1886 Dublin U
1887 Dublin U
1888 Wanderers
1889 Bective Rangers
1890 Dublin U
1891 Lansdowne
1892 Bective Rangers
1893 Dublin U
1894 Wanderers
1895 Dublin U
1896 Dublin U
1897 Dublin U
1898 Dublin U
1899 Monkstown
1900 Dublin U
1901 Lansdowne
1902 Monkstown
1903 Lansdowne
1904 Lansdowne
1905 Dublin U
1906 Wanderers
1907 Dublin U
1908 Dublin U
1909 Old Wesley
1910 Bective Rangers
1911 Wanderers
1912 Dublin U
1913 Dublin U
1914 Bective Rangers
1915–1919 No competition
1920 Dublin U
1921 Dublin U
1922 Lansdowne
1923 Bective Rangers
1924 UCD
1925 Bective Rangers
1926 Dublin U
1927 Lansdowne
1928 Lansdowne
1929 Lansdowne
1930 Lansdowne
1931 Lansdowne
1932 Bective Rangers
1933 Lansdowne
1934 Bective Rangers
1935 Bective Rangers
1936 Clontarf
1937 Blackrock Coll
1938 UCD
1939 Blackrock Coll
1940 Old Belvedere
1941 Old Belvedere
1942 Old Belvedere
1943 Old Belvedere
1944 Old Belvedere
1945 Old Belvedere
1946 Old Belvedere
1947 Wanderers
1948 UCD
1949 Lansdowne
1950 Lansdowne
1951 Old Belvedere
1952 Old Belvedere
1953 Lansdowne
1954 Wanderers
1955 Bective Rangers
1956 Bective Rangers
1957 Blackrock Coll
1958 St Mary's Coll
1959 Wanderers
1960 Dublin U
1961 Blackrock Coll
1962 Bective Rangers
1963 UCD
1964 UCD
1965 Lansdowne
1966 Terenure
1967 Terenure
1968 Old Belvedere
1969 St Mary's Coll
1970 UCD
1971 St Mary's Coll
1972 Lansdowne
1973 Wanderers
1974 St Mary's Coll
1975 St Mary's Coll
1976 Dublin U
1977 UCD
1978 Wanderers
1979 Lansdowne
1980 Lansdowne
1981 Lansdowne
1982 Wanderers
1983 Blackrock Coll
1984 Wanderers
1985 Old Wesley
1986 Lansdowne
1987 St Mary's Coll
1988 Blackrock Coll
1989 Lansdowne
1990 Wanderers
1991 Lansdowne
1992 Blackrock Coll
1993 St Mary's Coll
1994 Terenure Coll
1995 St Mary's Coll
1996 Terenure Coll
1997 Lansdowne
1998 Lansdowne
1999 Clontarf

Leinster Senior League Winners

1971–72 St Mary's Coll
1972–73 Wanderers
1973–74 Lansdowne
1974–75 Blackrock Coll
1975–76 Wanderers
1976–77 Lansdowne
1977–78 St Mary's Coll
1978–79 Wanderers
1979–80 St Mary's Coll
1980–81 Lansdowne
1981–82 Blackrock Coll
1982–83 Blackrock Coll
1983–84 Terenure
1984–85 Wanderers
1985–86 Lansdowne
1986–87 Lansdowne
1987–88 Lansdowne
1988–89 St Mary's Coll
1989–90 Wanderers
1990–91 Blackrock Coll
1991–92 Clontarf
1992–93 Old Belvedere
1993–94 No competition
1994–95 No competition
1995–96 Terenure Coll
1996–97 St Mary's Coll
1997–98 Lansdowne
1998–99 Terenure Coll

Ulster Senior Cup Winners

1885 NIFC
1886 Queen's U
1887 Queen's U
1888 Lisburn
1889 Albion
1890 Queen's U
1891 Queen's U
1892 Queen's U
1893 NIFC
1894 NIFC
1895 NIFC
1896 NIFC
1897 NIFC
1898 NIFC
1899 NIFC
1900 Queen's U
1901 NIFC
1902 NIFC
1903 Queen's U
1904 Malone
1905 Malone
1906 Collegians
1907 Malone
1908 NIFC
1909 Queen's U
1910 Collegians
1911 Knock
1912 Queen's U
1913 Collegians
1914–1919 No competition
1920 NIFC
1921 Queen's U
1922 Instonians
1923 Instonians
1924 Queen's U
1925 Queen's U
1926 Collegians
1927 Instonians
1928 Instonians
1929 Instonians
1930 NIFC
1931 Instonians
1932 Queen's U
1933 Queen's U
1934 Instonians
1935 NIFC
1936 Queen's U
1937 Queen's U
1938 Instonians
1939 NIFC
1940–1945 No competition
1946 Instonians
1947 Queen's U
1948 Instonians
1949 Instonians
1950 Instonians
1951 Queen's U
1952 Collegians
1953 CIYMS
1954 Instonians
1955 NIFC
1956 Instonians
1957 Instonians
1958 Instonians
1959 Queen's U
1960 Queen's U
1961 Collegians
1962 Collegians
1963 Ballymena
1964 Dungannon
1965 Instonians
1966 CIYMS
1967 CIYMS
1968 Dungannon
1969 NIFC
1970 Ballymena
1971 Malone
1972 CIYMS
1973 NIFC
1974 CIYMS
1975 Ballymena
1976 Dungannon
1977 Ballymena
1978 CIYMS
1979 Instonians
1980 Bangor
1981 Queen's U
1982 Bangor
1983 Collegians
1984 Malone
1985 Ards
1986 Bangor
1987 Ards
1988 Malone
1989 Ballymena
1990 Ballymena
1991 Ballymena
1992 Malone
1993 Dungannon
1994 Dungannon
1995 Dungannon
1996 Dungannon
1997 Ballymena
1998 Dungannon
1999 Instonians

Ulster Senior League Winners

1890–91 Queen's U
1891–92 NIFC
1892–93 NIFC
1893–94 NIFC
1894–95 NIFC
1895–96 NIFC
1896–97 NIFC
1897–98 NIFC
1898–99 NIFC

1899–1900 Queen's U
1900–01 NIFC
1901–02 NIFC
1902–03 Collegians
1903–04 Malone
1904–05 Malone
1905–06 Malone
1906–07 Malone
1907–08 Collegians
1908–09 NIFC
1909–10 No competition
1910–11 Collegians
1911–12 Queen's U
1912–13 Collegians
1913–19 No competition
1919–1920 Queen's U
1920–21 NIFC
1921–22 Queen's U
1922–23 Queen's U
1923–24 Queen's U
1924–25 Instonians
1925–26 Instonians
1926–27 NIFC/Instonians (shared)
1927–28 Instonians
1928–29 Civil Service
1929–30 Bangor
1930–45 No League competition
1945–46 NIFC
1946–47 Queen's U
1947–48 Queen's U
1948–49 Queen's U
1949–50 Queen's U
1950–51 Collegians/Instonians (shared)
1951–52 Collegians
1952–53 Instonians/Queen's U (shared)
1953–54 Collegians/Queen's U (shared)
1954–55 NIFC
1955–56 Collegians
1956–57 Instonians/Queen's U (shared)
1957–58 Instonians
1958–59 NIFC
1959–60 Instonians
1960–61 Dungannon
1961–62 Collegians
1962–63 CIYMS
1963–64 Queen's U
1964–65 Dungannon
1965–66 NIFC
1966–67 Queen's U
1967–68 Dungannon
1968–69 Malone
1969–70 Civil Service
1970–71 CIYMS
1971–72 CIYMS
1972–73 Ballymena/CIYMS (shared)
1973–74 CIYMS
1974–75 Bangor
1975–76 Ballymena
1976–77 Bangor
1977–78 Ballymena
1978–79 Ballymena
1979–80 Queen's U
1980–81 Bangor
1981–82 Bangor
1982–83 Bangor
1983–84 Ards
1984–85 Instonians
1985–86 Ballymena
1986–87 Instonians
1987–88 Bangor
1988–89 Ballymena
1989–90 Ballymena
1990–91 Dungannon
1991–92 NIFC
1992–93 Malone
1993–94 No competition
1994–95 No competition
1995–96 Portadown
1996–97 Ballymena
1997–98 Ballymena
1998–99 Ballymena

Munster Senior Cup Winners

1886 Bandon
1887 Queen's Coll
1888 Queen's Coll
1889 Garryowen
1890 Garryowen
1891 Garryowen
1892 Not awarded
1893 Garryowen
1894 Garryowen
1895 Garryowen
1896 Garryowen
1897 Queen's Coll
1898 Garryowen
1899 Garryowen
1900 Queen's Coll
1901 Queen's Coll
1902 Garryowen
1903 Garryowen
1904 Garryowen
1905 Constitution
1906 Constitution
1907 Constitution
1908 Garryowen
1909 Garryowen
1910 Constitution
1911 Garryowen
1912 UCC
1913 UCC
1914 Garryowen
1915–1919 No competition
1920 Garryowen
1921 Dolphin
1922 Constitution
1923 Constitution
1924 Garryowen
1925 Garryowen
1926 Garryowen
1927 Bohemians
1928 Young Munster
1929 Constitution
1930 Young Munster
1931 Dolphin
1932 Garryowen
1933 Constitution
1934 Garryowen
1935 UCC
1936 UCC
1937 UCC
1938 Young Munster
1939 UCC
1940 Garryowen
1941 UCC
1942 Constitution
1943 Constitution
1944 Dolphin
1945 Dolphin
1946 Constitution
1947 Garryowen
1948 Dolphin
1949 Sunday's Well
1950 UCC
1951 UCC
1952 Garryowen
1953 Sunday's Well

1954 Garryowen
1955 UCC
1956 Dolphin
1957 Constitution
1958 Bohemians
1959 Bohemians
1960 Shannon
1961 Constitution
1962 Bohemians
1963 UCC
1964 Constitution
1965 Constitution
1966 Highfield
1967 Constitution
1968 Highfield
1969 Garryowen
1970 Constitution
1971 Garryowen
1972 Constitution
1973 Constitution
1974 Garryowen
1975 Garryowen
1976 UCC
1977 Shannon
1978 Shannon
1979 Garryowen
1980 Young Munster
1981 UCC
1982 Shannon
1983 Constitution
1984 Young Munster
1985 Constitution
1986 Shannon
1987 Shannon
1988 Shannon
1989 Constitution
1990 Young Munster
1991 Shannon
1992 Shannon
1993 Garryowen
1994 Sunday's Well
1995 Garryowen
1996 Shannon
1997 Garryowen
1998 Shannon
1999 Garryowen

Munster Senior League Winners

1902–03 Garryowen
1903–04 Garryowen
1904–05 Garryowen
1905–06 Garryowen
1906–07 Garryowen
1907–08 Garryowen
1908–09 Garryowen
1909–10 Garryowen
1910–11 Garryowen/Constitution (shared)
1911–12 Garryowen/Constitution (shared)
1912–13 UCC
1913–14 UCC/Constitution (shared)
1914–15 to 1920–21 No competition
1921–22 Constitution
1922–23 Constitution
1923–24 Dolphin
1924–25 Garryowen
1925–26 Dolphin
1926–27 Constitution
1927–28 Sunday's Well
1928–29 Dolphin
1929–30 Young Munster
1930–31 Bohemians/UCC (shared)
1932–33 UCC
1933–34 UCC
1934–35 Sunday's Well
1935–36 Garryowen/UCC (shared)
1936–37 Unfinished
1937–38 Unfinished
1938–39 Constitution
1939–40 Unfinished
1940–41 Unfinished
1941–42 UCC
1942–43 UCC
1943–44 Young Munster
1944–45 Unfinished
1945–46 Garryowen
1946–47 Unfinished
1947–48 Sunday's Well
1948–49 Dolphin
1949–50 UCC
1950–51 Sunday's Well
1951–52 Young Munster
1952–53 Constitution
1953–54 Garryowen
1954–55 Dolphin
1955–56 Dolphin
1956–57 Constitution
1957–58 UCC
1958–59 Bohemians
1959–60 Sunday's Well
1960–61 UCC
1961–62 UCC
1962–63 UCC
1963–64 Constitution
1964–65 Constitution
1965–66 Constitution
1966–67 Constitution
1967–68 Constitution
1968–69 Constitution
1969–70 Constitution
1970–71 Constitution
1971–72 Constitution
1972–73 Dolphin
1973–74 UCC
1974–75 Constitution
1975–76 Constitution
1976–77 Constitution
1977–78 UCC
1978–79 Constitution
1979–80 UCC
1980–81 Shannon
1981–82 Garryowen
1982–83 Garryowen
1983–84 Constitution
1984–85 UCC
1985–86 Shannon
1986–87 Constitution
1987–88 Constitution
1988–89 Shannon
1989–90 Highfield
1990–91 Dolphin
1991–92 Old Crescent
1992–93 Sunday's Well
1993–94 No competition
1994–95 No competition
1995–96 Young Munster
1996–97 Old Crescent
1997–98 Cork Constitution N.B.

N.B. Now officially known as Cork Constitution

Connacht Senior Cup Winners

1896 Galway Town
1897 Queen's Coll

1898 Galway GS
1899 Queen's Coll
1900 No competition
1901 No competition
1902 No competition
1903 Queen's Coll
1904 Queen's Coll
1905 Queen's Coll
1906 Galway Town
1907 Queen's Coll
1908 Queen's Coll
1909 UCG‡
1910 UCG
1911 Galway Town
1912 UCG
1913 Galway Town
1914 Sligo Town
1915–1921 No competition
1923 UCG
1924 UCG
1925 UCG
1926 Galwegians
1927 Galwegians
1928 Galwegians
1929 Galwegians
1930 UCG
1931 Loughrea
1932 UCG
1933 Corinthians
1934 Corinthians
1935 UCG
1936 UCG
1937 UCG
1938 Galwegians
1939 UCG
1940 UCG
1941 Corinthians
1942 UCG
1943 Galwegians
1944 UCG
1945 UCG
1946 UCG
1947 Corinthians
1948 Ballinasloe
1949 Corinthians
1950 Ballinasloe
1951 Ballina
1952 Galwegians
1953 UCG
1954 Corinthians
1955 Athlone
1956 Galwegians
1957 Galwegians
1958 Galwegians
1959 Galwegians
1960 Galwegians
1961 UCG
1962 UCG
1963 Galwegians
1964 UCG
1965 Galwegians
1966 UCG
1967 UCG
1968 Galwegians
1969 Galwegians
1970 UCG
1971 Galwegians
1972 Corinthians
1973 Galwegians
1974 UCG
1975 Galwegians
1976 Athlone
1977 Athlone
1978 Corinthians
1979 Ballina
1980 Galwegians
1981 Galwegians
1982 Corinthians
1983 Galwegians
1984 Corinthians
1985 Corinthians
1986 Galwegians
1987 UCG
1988 Corinthians
1989 UCG
1990 Athlone
1991 Athlone
1992 Ballinasloe
1993 Corinthians
1994 Corinthians
1995 Buccaneers N.B.
1996 Galwegians
1997 Galwegians
1998 Corinthians
1999 Buccaneers

N.B. Amalgamation of Athlone and Ballinasloe

‡Queen's College Galway renamed University College Galway (UCG)

Connacht Senior League Winners

1925–26 Galwegians
1926–27 Loughrea
1927–28 Ballinasloe
1928–29 Ballina
1929–30 Ballina
1930–31 UCG
1931–32 UCG
1932–33 UCG
1933–34 Corinthians
1934–35 UCG
1935–36 Corinthians
1936–37 UCG
1937–38 UCG
1938–39 Corinthians
1939–40 Corinthians
1940–41 Corinthians
1941–42 UCG
1942–43 Corinthians
1943–44 Corinthians
1944–45 Ballinasloe
1945–46 Ballinasloe
1946–47 Galwegians
1947–48 UCG
1948–49 Ballinasloe
1949–50 Corinthians
1950–51 Corinthians/Ballina (shared)
1951–52 Corinthians
1952–53 Ballina
1953–54 Corinthians
1954–55 UCG
1955–56 Athlone
1956–57 Galwegians
1957–58 Galwegians
1958–59 Galwegians
1959–60 Galwegians
1960–61 Galwegians
1961–62 UCG
1962–63 UCG
1963–64 Galwegians
1964–65 Corinthians
1965–66 UCG/Galwegians (shared)
1966–67 UCG
1967–68 UCG
1968–69 UCG
1969–70 Galwegians
1970–71 Galwegians
1971–72 Galwegians

1972–73 UCG
1973–74 UCG
1974–75 UCG
1975–76 Corinthians
1976–77 Athlone
1977–78 Corinthians
1978–79 Corinthians
1979–80 Corinthians
1980–81 Corinthians
1981–82 Corinthians
1982–83 Corinthians
1983–84 Galwegians
1984–85 Galwegians
1985–86 Corinthians
1986–87 Athlone
1987–88 Athlone
1988–89 Corinthians
1989–90 Galwegians
1990–91 Galwegians
1991–92 Galwegians
1992–93 Ballina
1993–94 No competition
1994–95 No competition
1995–96 Corinthians
1996–97 Galwegians
1997–98 Buccaneers

APPENDIX 8

IRELAND INTERNATIONAL PLAYERS (UP TO JUNE 1999)

Legend:
A, Australia; Arg, Argentina; C, Canada; E, England; F, France; Fj, Fiji;
Ga, Georgia; It, Italy; J, Japan; M, Maoris; Nm, Namibia; NZ, New Zealand;
R, Romania; S, Scotland; SA, South Africa; Tg, Tonga; US, United States;
W, Wales; WS Western Samoa; Z, Zimbabwe
Square brackets denote World Cup games
P, President's XV
(R) replacement
(t) temporary replacement

Abraham, M. (Bective Rangers) 1912 E,S,W,SA, 1914 W
Adams, C. (Old Wesley) 1908 E, 1909 E,F, 1910 F, 1911 E,S,W,F, 1912 S,W,SA, 1913 W,F, 1914 F,E,S
Agar, R.D. (Malone) 1947 F,E,S,W, 1948 F, 1949 S,W, 1950 F,E,W
Agnew, P.J. (CIYMS) 1974 F(R), 1976 A
Ahearne, T. (Queen's Coll Cork) 1899 E
Aherne, L.F.P. (Dolphin, Lansdowne) 1988 E2,WS,It, 1989 F,W,E,S,NZ, 1990 E,S,F,W(R), 1992 E,S,F,A
Alexander, R. (NIFC, Police Union) 1936 E,S,W, 1937 E,S,W, 1938 E,S, 1939 E,S,W
Allen, C.E. (Derry, Liverpool) 1900 E,S,W, 1901 E,S,W, 1903 S,W, 1904 E,S,W, 1905 E,S,W,NZ, 1906 E,S,W,SA, 1907 S,W
Allen, G.G. (Derry, Liverpool) 1896 E,S,W, 1897 E,S, 1898 E,S, 1899 E,W
Allen, T.C. (NIFC) 1855 E,S1
Allen, W.S. (Wanderers) 1875 E
Allison, J.B. (Edinburgh U) 1899 E,S, 1900 E,S,W, 1901 E,S,W, 1902 E,S,W, 1903 S
Anderson, F.E. (QUB, NIFC) 1953 F,E,S,W, 1954 NZ,F,E,S,W, 1955 F,E,S,W
Anderson, H.J. (Old Wesley) 1903 E,S, 1906 E,S
Anderson, W.A. (Dungannon) 1984 A, 1985 S,F,W,E, 1986 F,S,R, 1987 E,S,F,W,[W,C,Tg,A], 1988 S,F,W,E1,2, 1989 F,W,E,NZ, 1990 E,S
Andrews, G. (NIFC) 1875 E, 1876 E
Andrews, H.W. (NIFC) 1888 M, 1889 S,W
Archer, A.M. (Dublin U, NIFC) 1879 S
Arigho, J.E. (Lansdowne) 1928 F,E,W, 1929 F,E,S,W, 1930 F,E,S,W, 1931 F,E,S,W,SA
Armstrong, W.K. (NIFC) 1960 SA, 1961 E
Arnott, D.T. (Lansdowne) 1876 E
Ash, W.H. (NIFC) 1875 E, 1876 E, 1877 S
Aston, H.R. (Dublin U) 1908 E,W
Atkins, A.P. (Bective Rangers) 1924 F
Atkinson, J.M. (NIFC) 1927 F,A
Atkinson, J.R. (Dublin U) 1882 W,S

Bagot, J.C. (Dublin U, Lansdowne) 1879 S,E, 1880 E,S, 1881 S
Bailey, A.H. (UCD, Lansdowne) 1934 W, 1935 E,S,W,NZ, 1936 E,S,W, 1937 E,S,W, 1938 E,S
Bailey, N. (Northampton) 1952 E
Bardon, M.E. (Bohemians) 1934 E
Barlow, M. (Wanderers) 1875 E
Barnes, R.J. (Dublin U, Armagh) 1933 W
Barr, A. (Methodist Coll) 1898 W, 1899 S, 1901 E,S
Barry, N.J. (Garryowen) 1991 Nm2(R)
Beamish, C.E. St J. (RAF, Leicester) 1933 W,S, 1934 S,W, 1935 E,S,W,NZ, 1936 E,S,W, 1938 W
Beamish, G.R. (RAF, Leicester) 1925 E,S,W, 1928 F,E,S,W, 1929 F,E,S,W, 1930 F,S,W, 1931 F,E,S,W,SA, 1932 E,S,W, 1933 E,W,S
Beatty, W.J. (NIFC, Richmond) 1910 F, 1912 F,W
Becker, V.A (Lansdowne) 1974 F,W
Beckett, G.G.P. (Dublin U) 1908 E,S,W
Bell, J.C. (Ballymena, Northampton, Dungannon) 1994 A1,2,US, 1995 S,It,[NZ,W,F],Fj, 1996 US,S,F,W,E,WS,A, 1997 It,F,W,E,S, 1998 [Ga,R],SA, 1999 F,W,S,It(R),A2
Bell, R.J. (NIFC) 1875 E, 1876 E
Bell, W.E. (Belfast Collegians) 1953 F,E,S,W
Bennett, F. (Belfast Collegians) 1913 S
Bent, G.C. (Dublin U) 1882 W,E
Berkery, P.J. (Lansdowne) 1954 W, 1955 W, 1956 S,W, 1957 F,E,S,W, 1958 A,E,S
Bermingham, J.J.C. (Blackrock Coll) 1921 E,S,W,F
Bishop, J.P. (London Irish) 1998 SA1,2,[Ga,R],SA, 1999 F,W,E,S,It,A1,2
Blackham, J.C. (Queen's Coll Cork) 1909 S,W,F, 1910 E,S,W
Blake-Knox, S.E.F. (NIFC) 1976 E,S, 1977 F(R)
Blayney, J.J. (Wanderers) 1950 S
Bond, A.T.W. (Derry) 1894 S,W
Bornemann, W.W. (Wanderers) 1960 E,S,W,SA
Bowen, D. St J. (Cork Con) 1977 W,E,S
Boyd, C.A. (Dublin U) 1900 S, 1901 S,W
Boyle, C.V. (Dublin U) 1935 NZ, 1936 E,S,W, 1937 E,S,W, 1938 W, 1939 W
Brabazon, H.M. (Dublin U) 1884 E, 1885 S1, 1886 E
Bradley, M.J. (Cork Con) 1984 A, 1985 S,F,W,E, 1986 F,W,E,S,R, 1987 E,S,F,W,[W,C,Tg,A], 1988 S,F,W,E1, 1990 W, 1992 NZ1,2, 1993 S,F,W,E,R, 1994 F,W,E,S,A1,2,US, 1995 S,F,[NZ]
Bradshaw, G. (Belfast Collegians) 1903 W
Bradshaw, R.M. (Wanderers) 1885 E,S1,2
Brady, A.M. (UCD, Malone) 1966 S, 1968 E,S,W
Brady, J.A. (Wanderers) 1976 E,S
Brady, J.R. (CIYMS) 1951 S,W, 1953 F,E,S,W, 1954 W, 1956 W, 1957 F,E,S,W
Bramwell, T. (NIFC) 1928 F
Brand, T.N. (NIFC) 1924 NZ
Brennan, J.I. (CIYMS) 1957 S,W
Brennan, T. (St Mary's Coll) 1998 SA1(R),SA2(R), 1999 F(R),S(R),It,A2
Bresnihan, F.P.K. (UCD, Lansdowne, London Irish) 1966 E,W, 1967 A1,E,S,W,F, 1968 F,E,S,W,A, 1969 F,E,S,W, 1970 SA,F,E,S,W, 1971 F,E,S,W
Brett, J.T. (Monkstown) 1914 W
Bristow, J.R. (NIFC) 1879 E
Brophy, N.H. (Blackrock Coll, UCD, London Irish) 1957 F,E, 1959 E,S,W,F, 1960 F,SA, 1961 S,W, 1962 E,S,W, 1963 E,W, 1967 E,S,W,F,A2
Brown, E.L. (Instonians) 1958 F
Brown, G.S. (Monkstown, United Services) 1912 S,W,SA
Brown, H. (Windsor) 1877 E
Brown, T. (Windsor) 1877 E,S
Brown, W.H. (Dublin U) 1899 E
Brown, W.J. (Malone) 1970 SA,F,S,W
Brown, W.S. (Dublin U) 1893 S,W, 1894 E,S,W
Browne, A.W. (Dublin U) 1951 SA
Browne, D. (Blackrock Coll) 1920 F
Browne, H.C. (United Services, RN) 1929 E,S,W
Browne, W.F. (United Services, Army) 1925 E,S,W, 1926 S,W, 1927 F,E,S,W,A, 1928 E,S
Browning, D.R. (Wanderers) 1881 E,S
Bruce, S.A.M. (NIFC) 1883 E,S, 1884 E
Brunker, A.A. (Lansdowne) 1895 E,W
Bryant, C.H. (Cardiff) 1920 E,S
Buchanan, A. McM. (Dublin U) 1926 E,S,W, 1927 S,W,A
Buchanan, J.W.B. (Dublin U) 1882 S, 1884 E,S
Buckley, J.H. (Sunday's Well) 1973 E,S
Bulger, L.Q. (Lansdowne) 1896 E,S,W, 1897 E,S, 1898 E,S,W
Bulger, M.J. (Dublin U) 1888 M
Burges, J.H. (Rosslyn Park) 1950 F,E
Burgess, R.B. (Dublin U) 1912 SA
Burke, P.A. (Cork Con, Bristol) 1995 E,S,W(R),It,[J], Fj, 1996 US(R),A, 1997 It,S(R)
Burkitt, J.C.S. (Queen's Coll Cork) 1881 E
Burns, I.J. (Wanderers) 1980 E(R)
Butler, L.G. (Blackrock Coll) 1960 W
Butler, N. (Bective Rangers) 1920 E
Byers, R.M. (NIFC) 1928 S,W, 1929 E,S,W
Byrne, E.M.J. (Blackrock Coll) 1977 S,F, 1978 F,W,E,NZ
Byrne, N.F. (UCD) 1962 F
Byrne, S.J. (UCD, Lansdowne) 1953 S,W, 1955 F
Byron, W.G. (NIFC) 1896 E,S,W, 1897 E,S, 1898 E,S,W, 1899 E,S,W

Caddell, E.D. (Dublin U, Wanderers) 1904 S, 1905 E,S,W,NZ, 1906 E,S,W,SA, 1907 E,S, 1908 S,W
Cagney, S.J. (London Irish) 1925 W, 1926 F,E,S,W, 1927 F, 1928 E,S,W, 1929 F,E,S,W
Callan, C.P. (Lansdowne) 1947 F,E,S,W, 1948 F,E,S,W, 1949 F,E
Cameron, E.D. (Bective Rangers) 1891 S,W
Campbell, C.E. (Old Wesley) 1970 SA
Campbell, E.F. (Monkstown) 1899 S,W, 1900 E,W
Campbell, S.B.B. (Derry) 1911 E,S,W,F, 1912 F,E,S,W,SA, 1913 E,S,F
Campbell, S.O. (Old Belvedere) 1976 A, 1979 A1,2, 1980 E,S,F,W, 1981 F,W,E,S,SA1, 1982 W,E,S,F, 1983 S,F,W,E, 1984 F,W
Canniffe, D.M. (Lansdowne) 1976 W,E
Cantrell, J.L. (UCD, Blackrock Coll) 1976 A,F,W,E,S, 1981 S,SA1,2,A
Carey, R.W. (Dungannon) 1992 NZ1,2
Carpendale, M.J. (Monkstown) 1886 S, 1887 W, 1888 W,S
Carr, N.J. (Ards) 1985 S,F,W,E, 1986 W,E,S,R, 1987 E,S,W
Carroll, C. (Bective Rangers) 1930 F
Carroll, R. (Lansdowne) 1947 F, 1950 S,W
Casement, B.N. (Dublin U) 1875 E, 1876 E, 1879 E
Casement, F. (Dublin U) 1906 E,S,W
Casey, J.C. (Young Munster) 1930 S, 1932 E
Casey, P.J. (UCD, Lansdowne) 1963 F,E,S,W,NZ, 1964 E,S,W,F, 1965 F,E,S
Chambers, J. (Dublin U) 1886 E,S, 1887 E,S,W
Chambers, R.R. (Instonians) 1951, F,E,S,W, 1952 F,W
Clancy, T.P.J. (Lansdowne) 1988 W,E1,2,WS,It, 1989 F,W,E,S
Clarke, A.T.H. (Northampton) 1995 Fj(R), 1996 W,E,WS, 1997 F(R),It(R)
Clarke, C.P. (Terenure Coll) 1993 F,W,E, 1998 W,E
Clarke, D.J. (Dolphin) 1991 W,Nm1,2,[J,A], 1992 NZ2(R)
Clarke, J.A.B. (Bective Rangers) 1922 S,W,F, 1923 F, 1924 E,S,W
Clegg, R.J. (Bangor) 1973 F, 1975 E,S,F,W
Clifford, J.T. (Young Munster) 1949 F,E,S,W, 1950 F,E,S,W, 1951 F,E,SA, 1952 F,S,W
Clinch, A.D. (Dublin U, Wanderers) 1892 S, 1893 W, 1895 E,S,W, 1896 E,S,W, 1897 E,S
Clinch, J.D. (Wanderers, Dublin U) 1923 W, 1924 F,E,S,W,NZ, 1925 F,E,S, 1926 E,S,W, 1927 F, 1928 F,E,S,W, 1929 F,E,S,W, 1930 F,E,S,W, 1931 F,E,S,W,SA
Clohessy, P.M. (Young Munster) 1993 F,W,E, 1994 F,W,E,S,A1,A2,US 1995 E,S,F,W, 1996 S,F, 1997 It, 1998 F(R),W(R),SA2(R),[Ga,R],SA, 1999 F,W,E,S,It,A1,2
Clune, J.J. (Blackrock Coll) 1912 SA, 1913 W,F, 1914 F,E,W
Coffey, J.J. (Lansdowne) 1900 E, 1901 W, 1902 E,S,W, 1903 E,S,W, 1905 E,S,W,NZ, 1906 E,S,W,SA, 1907 E, 1908 W, 1910 F
Cogan, W. St J. (Queen's Coll Cork) 1907 E,S
Collier, S.R. (Queen's Coll Belfast) 1883 S
Collins, P.C. (Lansdowne, London Irish) 1987 [C], 1990 S(R)
Collis, W.R.F. (KCH, Harlequins) 1924, F,W,NZ, 1925 F,E,S, 1926 F
Collis, W.S. (Wanderers) 1884 W
Collopy, G. (Bective Rangers) 1891 S, 1892 S
Collopy, R. (Bective Rangers) 1923 E,S,W,F, 1924 F,E,S,W,NZ, 1925 F,E,S,W
Collopy, W.P. (Bective Rangers) 1914, F,E,S,W, 1921 E,S,W,F, 1922 E,S,W,F, 1923 S,W,F, 1924 F,E,S,W
Combe, A. (NIFC) 1875 E
Condon, H.C. (London Irish) 1984 S(R)
Cook, H.G. (Lansdowne) 1884 W
Coote, P.B. (RAF, Leicester) 1933 S
Corcoran, J.C. (London Irish) 1947 A, 1948 F
Corken, T.S. (Belfast Collegians) 1937 E,S,W
Corkery, D.S. (Cork Con, Terenure Coll, Bristol) 1994 A1,2,US, 1995 E,[NZ,J,W,F],Fj, 1996 US,S,F,W,E,WS,A, 1997 It,F,W,E,S, 1998 S,F,W,E, 1999 A1(R),A2(R)
Corley, H.H. (Dublin U, Wanderers) 1902 E,S,W, 1903 E,S,W, 1904 E,S
Cormac, H.S.T. (Clontarf) 1921 E,S,W
Corrigan, R. (Greystones, Lansdowne) 1997 C(R),It, 1998 S,F,W,E, 1999 A1(R), A2(R)
Costello, P. (Bective Rangers) 1960 F
Costello, R.A. (Garryowen) 1993 S
Costello, V.C.P. (London Irish, St Mary's Coll) 1996 US,F,W,E,WS(R), 1997 C,It(R), 1998 S(R),F,W,E,SA1,2,[Ga,R],SA, 1999 F,W(R),E,S(R),It,A1
Cotton, J. (Wanderers) 1889 W
Coulter, H.H. (QUB) 1920 E,S,W
Courtney, A.W. (UCD) 1920 S,W,F, 1921 E,S,W,F
Cox, H.L. (Dublin U) 1875 E, 1876 E, 1877 E,S
Craig, R.G. (QUB) 1938 S,W
Crawford, E.C. (Dublin U) 1885 E,S1
Crawford, W.E. (Lansdowne) 1920 E,S,W,F, 1921 E,S,W,F, 1922 E,S, 1923 E,S,W,F, 1924 F,E,W,NZ, 1925 F,E,S,W, 1926 F,E,S,W, 1927 F,E,S,W
Crean, T.J. (Wanderers) 1894 E,S,W, 1895 E,S,W, 1896 E,S,W
Crichton, R.Y. (Dublin U) 1920 E,S,W,F, 1921 F, 1922 E, 1923 W,F, 1924 F,E,S,W,NZ, 1925 E,S
Croker, E.W.D. (Limerick) 1878 E
Cromey, G.E. (QUB) 1937 E,S,W, 1938 E,S,W, 1939 E,S,W
Cronin, B.M. (Garryowen) 1995 S, 1997 S
Cronyn, A.P. (Dublin U, Lansdowne) 1875 E, 1876 E, 1880 S

Crossan, K.D. (Instonians) 1982 S, 1984 F,W,E,S, 1985 S,F,W,E, 1986 E,S,R, 1987 E,S,F,W,[W,C,Tg,A], 1988 S,F,W,E1,WS,It, 1989 W,S,NZ, 1990 E,S,F,W,Arg, 1991 E,S,Nm2,[Z,J,S], 1992 W
Crotty, D.J. (Garryowen) 1996 A, 1997 It,F,W
Crowe, J.F. (UCD) 1974 NZ
Crowe, L. (Old Belvedere) 1950 E,S,W
Crowe, M.P. (Lansdowne) 1929 W, 1930 E,S,W, 1931 F,S,W,SA, 1932 S,W, 1933 W,S, 1934 E
Crowe, P.M. (Blackrock Coll) 1935 E, 1938 E
Cullen, T.J. (UCD) 1949 F
Cullen, W.J. (Monkstown, Manchester) 1920 E
Culliton, M.G. (Wanderers) 1959 E,S,W,F, 1960 E,S,W,F,SA, 1961 E,S,W,F, 1962 S,F, 1964 E,S,W,F
Cummins, W.E.A. (Queen's Coll Cork) 1879 S, 1881 E, 1882 E
Cunningham, D. McC. (NIFC) 1923 E,S,W, 1925 F,E,W
Cunningham, M.J. (UCC) 1955 F,E,S,W, 1956 F,S,W
Cunningham, V.J.G. (St Mary's Coll) 1988 E2,It, 1990 Arg(R), 1991 Nm1,2,[Z,J(R)], 1992 NZ1,2,A, 1993 S,F,W,E,R, 1994 F
Cunningham, W.A. (Lansdowne) 1920 W, 1921 E,S,W,F, 1922 E, 1923 S,W
Cuppaige, J.L. (Dublin U) 1879 E, 1880 E,S
Currell, J. (NIFC) 1877 S
Curtis, A.B. (Oxford U) 1950 F,E,S
Curtis, D.M. (London Irish) 1991 W,E,S,Nm1,2,[Z,J,S,A], 1992 W,E,S(R),F
Cuscaden, W.A. (Dublin U, Bray) 1876 E
Cussen, D.J. (Dublin U) 1921 E,S,W,F, 1922 E, 1923 E,S,W,F, 1926 F,E,S,W, 1927 F,E

Daly, J.C (London Irish) 1947 F,E,S,W, 1948 E,S,W
Daly, M.J. (Harlequins) 1938 E
Danaher, P.P.A. (Lansdowne, Garryowen) 1988 S,F,W,WS,It, 1989 F,NZ(R), 1990 F, 1992 S,F,NZ1,A, 1993 S,F,W,E,R, 1994 F,W,E,S,A1,2,US, 1995 E,S,F,W
Dargan, M.J. (Old Belvedere) 1952 S,W
Davidson, C.T. (NIFC) 1921 F
Davidson, I.G. (NIFC) 1899 E, 1900 S,W, 1901 E,S,W, 1902 E,S,W
Davidson, J.C. (Dungannon) 1969 F,E,S,W, 1973 NZ, 1976 NZ
Davidson, J.W. (Dungannon, Castres) 1995 Fj, 1996 S,F,W,E,WS,A, 1997 It,F,W,E,S, 1998 [GA(R), R(R)],SA(R), 1999 F,W,E,S,It,A1,A2(R)
Davies, F.E. (Lansdowne) 1892 S,W, 1893 E,S,W
Davis, J.L. (Monkstown) 1898 E,S
Davis, W.J.N. (Edinburgh U, Bessbrook) 1890 S,W,E, 1891 E,S,W, 1892 E,S, 1895 S
Davison, W. (Belfast Academy) 1887 W
Davy, E. O'D. (UCD, Lansdowne) 1925 W, 1926 F,E,S,W, 1927 F,E,S,W,A, 1928 F,E,S,W, 1929 F,E,S,W, 1930 F,E,S,W, 1931 F,E,S,W,SA, 1932 E,S,W, 1933 E,W,S, 1934 E
Dawson, A.R. (Wanderers) 1958 A,E,S,W,F, 1959 E,S,W,F, 1960 F,SA, 1961 E,S,W,F,SA, 1962 S,F,W, 1963 F,E,S,W,NZ, 1964 E,S,F
Dawson, K. (London Irish) 1997 NZ,C, 1998 S
Dean, P.M. (St Mary's Coll) 1981 SA1,2,A, 1982 W,E,S,F, 1984 A, 1985 S,F,W,E, 1986 F,W,R, 1987 E,S,F,W,[W,A], 1988 S,F,W,E,1,2,WS,It, 1989 F,W,E,S
Deane, E.C. (Monkstown) 1909 E
Deering, M.J. (Bective Rangers) 1929 W
Deering, S.J. (Bective Rangers) 1935 E,S,W,NZ, 1936 E,S,W, 1937 E,S
Deering, S.M. (Garryowen, St Mary's Coll) 1974 W, 1976 F,W,E,S, 1977 W,E, 1978 NZ
de Lacy, H. (Harlequins) 1948 E,S
Delany, M.G. (Bective Rangers) 1895 W
Dempsey, G. (Terenure Coll) [Ga(R)],SA, 1999 F,E,S,A2
Dennison, S.P. (Garryowen) 1973 F, 1975 E,S
Dick, C.J. (Ballymena) 1961 W,F,SA, 1962 W, 1963 F,E,S,W
Dick, J.S. (QUB) 1962 E
Dick, J.S. (Queen's U Cork) 1887 E,S,W
Dickson, J.A.N. (Dublin U) 1920 E,W,F
Doherty, A.E. (Old Wesley) 1974 P(R)
Doherty, W.D. (Guy's Hospital) 1920 E,S,W, 1921 E,S,W,F
Donaldson, J.A. (Belfast Collegians) 1958 A,E,S,W
Donovan, T.M. (Queen's Coll Cork) 1889 S
Dooley, J.F. (Galwegians) 1959 E,S,W
Doran, B.R.W. (Lansdowne) 1900 S,W, 1901 E,S,W, 1902 E,S,W
Doran, E.F. (Lansdowne) 1890 S,W
Doran, G.P. (Lansdowne) 1899 S,W, 1900 E,S, 1902 S,W, 1903 W, 1904 E
Douglas, A.C. (Instonians) 1923 F, 1924 E,S, 1927 A, 1928 S
Downing, A.J. (Dublin U) 1882 W
Dowse, J.C.A. (Monkstown) 1914 F,S,W
Doyle, J.A.P. (Greystones) 1984 E,S
Doyle, J.T. (Bective Rangers) 1935 W
Doyle, M.G. (Blackrock Coll, UCD, Cambridge U, Edinburgh Wands) 1965 F,E,S,W,SA, 1966 F,E,S,W, 1967 A1,E,S,W,F,A2, 1968 F,E,S,W,A
Doyle, T.J. (Wanderers) 1968 E,S,W
Duggan, A.T.A. (Lansdowne) 1963 NZ, 1964 F, 1966 W, 1967 A1,S,W,A2, 1968 F,E,S,W, 1969 F,E,S,W, 1970 SA,F,E,S,W, 1971 F,E,S,W, 1972 F2
Duggan, W. (UCC) 1920 S,W
Duggan, W.P. (Blackrock Coll) 1975 E,S,F,W, 1976

A,F,W,S,NZ, 1977 W,E,S,F, 1978 S,F,W,E,NZ, 1979 E,S,A1,2, 1980 E, 1981 F,W,E,S,SA1,2,A, 1982 W,E,S, 1983 S,F,W,E, 1984 F,W,E,S
Duignan, P. (Galwegians) 1998 [Ga(R)]
Duncan, W.R. (Malone) 1984 W,E
Dunlea, F.J. (Lansdowne) 1989 W,E,S
Dunlop, R. (Dublin U) 1889 W, 1890 S,W,E, 1891 E,S,W, 1892 E,S, 1893 W, 1894 W
Dunn, P.E.F. (Bective Rangers) 1923 S
Dunn, T.B. (NIFC) 1935 NZ
Dunne, M.J. (Lansdowne) 1929 F,E,S, 1930 F,E,S,W, 1932 E,S,W, 1933 E,W,S, 1934 E,S,W
Dwyer, P.J. (UCD) 1962 W, 1963 F,NZ, 1964 S,W

Edwards, H.G. (Dublin U) 1877 E, 1878 E
Edwards, R.W. (Malone) 1904 W
Edwards, T. (Lansdowne) 1888 M, 1890 S,W,E, 1892 W, 1893 E
Edwards, W.V. (Malone) 1912 F,E
Egan, J.D. (Bective Rangers) 1922 S
Egan, J.T. (Cork Con) 1931 F,E,SA
Egan, M.S. (Garryowen) 1893 E, 1895 S
Ekin, W. (Queen's Coll Belfast) 1888 W,S
Elliott, W.R.J. (Bangor) 1979 S
Elwood, E.P. (Lansdowne, Galwegians) 1993 W,E,R, 1994 F,W,S,A1,2 1995 F,W,[NZ,W,F], 1996 US,S, 1997 F,W,E,NZ,C,It(R), 1998 F,W,E,SA1,2,[Ga(R)],SA, 1999 It
English, M.A.F. (Lansdowne, Limerick Bohemians) 1958 W,F, 1959 E,S,F, 1960 E,S, 1961 S,W,F, 1962 F,W, 1963 E,S,W,NZ
Ennis, F.N.G. (Wanderers) 1979 A1(R)
Ensor, A.H. (Wanderers) 1973 W,F, 1974 F,W,E,S,P,NZ, 1975 E,S,F,W, 1976 A,F,W,E,NZ, 1977 E, 1978 S,F,W,E
Entrican, J.C. (QUB) 1931 S
Erskine, D.J. (Sale) 1997 NZ(R),C,It

Fagan, G.L. (Kingstown School) 1878 E
Fagan, W.B.C. (Wanderers) 1956 F,E,S
Farrell, J.L. (Bective Rangers) 1926 F,E,S,W, 1927 F,E,S,W,A, 1928 F,E,S,W, 1929 F,E,S,W, 1930 F,E,S,W, 1931 F,E,S,W,SA, 1932 E,S,W
Feddis, N. (Lansdowne) 1956 E
Feighery, C.F.P. (Lansdowne) 1972 F1,E,F2
Feighery, T.A.O. (St Mary's Coll) 1977 W,E
Ferris, H.H. (Queen's Coll Belfast) 1901 W
Ferris J.H. (Queen's Coll Belfast) 1900 E,S,W
Field, M.J. (Malone) 1994 E,S,A1(R), 1995 F(R),W(t),It(R),[NZ(t+R),J],Fj, 1996 F(R),W,E,A(R), 1997 F,W,E,S
Finlay, J.E. (Queen's Coll Belfast) 1913 E,S,W, 1920 E,S,W
Finlay, W. (NIFC) 1876 E, 1877 E,S, 1878 E, 1879 S,E, 1880 S, 1882 S
Finn, M.C. (UCC, Cork Con) 1979 E, 1982 W,E,S,F, 1983 S,F,W,E, 1984 E,S,A, 1986 F,W
Finn, R.G.A. (UCD) 1977 F
Fitzgerald, C.C. (Glasgow U, Dungannon) 1902 E, 1903 E,S
Fitzgerald, C.F. (St Mary's Coll) 1979 A1,2, 1980 E,S,F,W, 1982 W,E,S,F, 1983 S,F,W,E, 1984 F,W,A, 1985 S,F,W,E, 1986 F,W,E,S
Fitzgerald, D.C. (Lansdowne, De La Salle Palmerston) 1984 E,S, 1986 W,E,S,R, 1987 E,S,F,W,[W,C,A], 1988 S,F,W,E1, 1989 NZ(R), 1990 E,S,F,W,Arg, 1991 F,W,E,S,Nm1,2,[Z,S,A], 1992 W,S(R)
Fitzgerald, J. (Wanderers) 1884 W
Fitzgerald, J.J. (Young Munster) 1988 S,F, 1990 S,F,W, 1991 F,W,E,S,[J], 1994 A1,2
Fitzgibbon, M.J.J. (Shannon) 1992 W,E,S,F,NZ1,2
Fitzpatrick, J.M. (London Irish, Dungannon) 1998 SA1,2[Ga(R),R(R)],SA, 1999 F(t)(R),W(R),E(R),It,A1(R)
Fitzpatrick, M.P. (Wanderers) 1978 S, 1980 S,F,W, 1981 F,W,E,S,A, 1985 F(R)
Flavin, P. (Blackrock Coll) 1997 F(R),S
Fletcher, W.W. (Kingstown) 1882 W,S, 1883 E
Flood, R.S. (Dublin U) 1925 W
Flynn, M.K. (Wanderers) 1959 F, 1960 F, 1962 E,S,F,W, 1964 E,S,W,F, 1965 F,E,S,W,SA, 1966 F,E,S, 1972 F1,E,F2, 1973 NZ
Fogarty, T. (Garryowen) 1891 W
Foley, A.G. (Shannon) 1995 E,S,F,W,It,[J(t+R)], 1996 A, 1997 It,E(R)
Foley, B.O. (Shannon) 1976 F,E, 1977 W(R), 1980 F,W, 1981 F,E,S,SA1,2,A
Forbes, R.E. (Malone) 1907 E
Forrest, A.J. (Wanderers) 1880 E,S, 1881 E,S, 1882 W,E, 1883 E, 1885 S2
Forrest, E.G. (Wanderers) 1888 M, 1889 S,W, 1890 S,E, 1891 E, 1893 S, 1894 E,S,W, 1895 W, 1897 E,S
Forrest, H. (Wanderers) 1893 S,W
Fortune, J.J. (Clontarf) 1963 NZ, 1964 E
Foster, A.R. (Derry) 1910 E,S,F, 1911 E,S,W,F, 1912 F,E,S,W, 1914 E,S,W, 1921 E,S,W
Francis, N.P.J. (Blackrock Coll, London Irish, Old Belvedere) 1987 [Tg,A], 1988 WS,It, 1989 S, 1990 E,F,W, 1991 E,S,Nm1,2,[Z,J,S,A], 1992 W,E,S, 1993 F,R, 1994 F,W,E,S,A1,2,US, 1995 E,[NZ,J,W,F],Fj, 1996 US,S
Franks, J.G. (Dublin U) 1898 E,S,W
Frazer, E.F. (Bective Rangers) 1891 S, 1892 S
Freer, A.E. (Lansdowne) 1901 E,S,W

Fulcher, G.M. (Cork Con, London Irish) 1994 A2,US, 1995 S,W,F,It[NZ,W,F],Fj, 1996 Us,S,F,W,E,A, 1997 It,W(R), 1998 SA1(R)
Fulton, J. (NIFC) 1895 S,W, 1896 E, 1897 E, 1898 W, 1899 E, 1900 W, 1901 E, 1902 E,S,W, 1903 E,S,W, 1904 E,S
Furlong, J.N. (UCG) 1992 NZ1,2

Gaffikin, W. (Windsor) 1875 E
Gage, J.H. (QUB) 1926 S,W, 1927 S,W
Galbraith, E. (Dublin U) 1875 E
Galbraith, H.T. (Belfast Acad) 1890 W
Galbraith, R. (Dublin U) 1875 E, 1876 E, 1877 E
Galwey, M.J. (Shannon) 1991, F,W,Nm2(R),[J], 1992 E,S,F,NZ1,2,A, 1993 F,W,E,R, 1994 F,W,E,S,A1,US(R), 1995 E, 1996 WS, 1998 F(R), 1999 W(R)
Ganly, J.B. (Monkstown) 1927 F,E,S,W,A, 1928 F,E,S,W, 1929 F,S, 1930 F
Gardiner, F. (NIFC) 1900 E,S, 1901 E,W, 1902 E,S,W, 1903 E,W, 1904 E,S,W, 1906 E,S,W, 1907 S,W, 1908 S,W, 1909 E,S,F
Gardiner, J.B. (NIFC) 1923 E,S,W,F, 1924 F,E,S,W,NZ, 1925 F,E,S,W
Gardiner, S. (Belfast Albion) 1893 E,S
Gardiner, W. (NIFC) 1892 E,S, 1893 E,S,W, 1894 E,S,W, 1895 E,S,W, 1896 E,S,W, 1897 E,S, 1898 W
Garry, M.G. (Bective Rangers) 1909 E,S,W,F, 1911 E,S,W
Gaston, J.T. (Dublin U) 1954 NZ,F,E,S,W, 1955 W, 1956 F,E
Gavin, T.J. (Moseley, London Irish) 1949 F,E
Geoghegan, S.P. (London Irish, Bath) 1991 F,W,E,S,Nm1,[Z,S,A], 1992 E,S,F,A, 1993 S,F,W,E,R, 1994 F,W,E,S,A1,2,US, 1995 E,S,F,W,[NZ,J,W,F],Fj, 1996 US,S,W,E
Gibson, C.M.H. (Cambridge U, NIFC) 1964 E,S,W,F, 1965 F,E,S,W,SA, 1966 F,E,S,W, 1967 A1,E,S,W,F,A2, 1968 E,S,W,A, 1969 E,S,W, 1970 SA,F,E,S,W, 1971 F,E,S,W, 1972 F1,E,F2, 1973 NZ,E,S,W,F, 1974 F,W,E,S,P, 1975 E,S,F,W, 1976 A,F,W,E,S,NZ, 1977 W,E,S,F, 1978 F,W,E,NZ, 1979 S,A1,2
Gibson, M.E. (Lansdowne, London Irish) 1979 F,W,E,S, 1981 W(R), 1986 R, 1988 S,F,W,E2
Gifford, H.P. (Wanderers) 1890 S
Gillespie, J.C. (Dublin U) 1922 W,F
Gilpin, F.G. (QUB) 1962 E,S,F
Glass, D.C. (Belfast Collegians) 1958 F, 1960 W, 1961 W,SA
Glennon, B.T. (Lansdowne) 1993 F(R)
Glennon, J.J. (Skerries) 1980 E,S, 1987 E,S,F,[W(R)]
Godfrey, R.P. (UCD) 1954 S,W
Goodall, K.G. (City of Derry, Newcastle U) 1967 A1,E,S,W,F,A2, 1968 F,E,S,W,A, 1969 F,E,S, 1970 SA,F,E,S,W
Gordon, A. (Dublin U) 1884 S
Gordon, T.G. (NIFC) 1877 E,S, 1878 E
Gotto, R.P.C. (NIFC) 1906 SA
Goulding, W.J. (Cork) 1879 S
Grace, T.O. (UCD, St Mary's Coll) 1972 F1,E, 1973 NZ,E,S,W, 1974 E,S,P,NZ, 1975 E,S,F,W, 1976 A,F,W,E,S,NZ, 1977 W,E,S,F, 1978 S
Graham, R.I. (Dublin U) 1911 F
Grant, E.L. (CIYMS) 1971, F,E,S,W
Grant P.J. (Bective Rangers) 1894 S,W
Graves, C.R.A. (Wanderers) 1934 E,S,W, 1935 E,S,W,NZ, 1936 E,S,W, 1937 E,S, 1938 E,S,W
Gray, R.D. (Old Wesley) 1923 E,S, 1925 F, 1926 F
Greene, E.H. (Dublin U, Kingstown) 1882 W, 1885 E,S2, 1886 E
Greer, R. (Kingstown) 1876 E
Greeves, T.J. (NIFC) 1907 E,S,W, 1909 W,F
Gregg, R.J. (QUB) 1953 F,E,S,W, 1954 F,E,S
Griffin, C.S. (London Irish) 1951 F,E
Griffin, J.L. (Wanderers) 1949 S,W
Griffiths, W. (Limerick) 1878 E
Grimshaw, C. (QUB) 1969 E(R)
Guerin, B.N. (Galwegians) 1956 S
Gwynn, A.P. (Dublin U) 1895 W
Gwynn, L.H. (Dublin U) 1893 S, 1894 E,S,W, 1897 S, 1898 E,S

Hakin, R.F. (CIYMS) 1976 W,S,NZ, 1977 W,E,F
Hall, R.O.N. (Dublin U) 1884 W
Hall, W.H. (Instonians) 1923 E,S,W,F, 1924 F,S
Hallaran, C.F.G.T. (Royal Navy) 1921 E,S,W, 1922 E,S,W, 1923 E,F, 1924 F,E,S,W, 1925 F, 1926 F,E
Halpin, G.F. (Wanderers, London Irish) 1990 E, 1991 [J], 1992 E,S,F, 1993 R, 1994 F(R), 1995 It,[NZ,W,F]
Halpin, T. (Garryowen) 1909 S,W,F, 1910 E,S,W, 1911 E,S,W,F, 1912 F,E,S
Halvey, E.O. (Shannon) 1995 F,W,It,[J,W(t),F(R)], 1997 NZ,C(R)
Hamilton, A.J. (Lansdowne) 1884 W
Hamilton, G.F. (NIFC) 1991 F,W,E,S,Nm2,[Z,J,S,A], 1992 A
Hamilton, R.L. (NIFC) 1926 F
Hamilton, R.W. (Wanderers) 1893 W
Hamilton, W.J. (Dublin U) 1877 E
Hamlet, G.T. (Old Wesley) 1902 E,S,W, 1903 E,S,W, 1904 S,W, 1905 E,S,W,NZ, 1906 SA, 1907 E,S,W, 1908 E,S,W, 1909 E,S,W,F, 1910 E,S,F, 1911 E,S,W,F
Hanrahan, C.J. (Dolphin) 1926 S,W, 1927 E,S,W,A, 1928 F,E,S, 1929 F,E,S,W, 1930 F,E,S,W, 1931 F, 1932 S,W

Harbison, H.T. (Bective Rangers) 1984 W(R),E,S, 1986 R, 1987 E,S,F,W
Hardy, G.G. (Bective Rangers) 1962 S
Harman, G.R.A. (Dublin U) 1899 E,W
Harper, J. (Instonians) 1947 F,E,S
Harpur, T.G. (Dublin U) 1908 E,S,W
Harrison, T. (Cork) 1879 S, 1880 S, 1881 E
Harvey, F.M.W. (Wanderers) 1907 W, 1911 F
Harvey, G.A.D. (Wanderers) 1903 E,S, 1904 W, 1905 E,S
Harvey, T.A. (Dublin U) 1900 W, 1901 S,W, 1902 E,S,W, 1903 E,W
Haycock, P.P. (Terenure Coll) 1989 E
Headon, T.A. (UCD) 1939 S,W
Healey, P. (Limerick) 1901 E,S,W, 1902 E,S,W, 1903 E,S,W, 1904 S
Heffernan, M.R. (Cork Con) 1911 E,S,W,F
Hemphill, R. (Dublin U) 1912 F,E,S,W
Henderson, N.J. (QUB, NIFC) 1949 S,W, 1950 F, 1951 F,E,S,W,SA, 1952 F,S,W,E, 1953 F,E,S,W, 1954 NZ,F,E,S,W, 1955 F,E,S,W, 1956 S,W, 1957 F,E,S,W, 1958 A,E,S,W,F, 1959 E,S,W,F
Henderson, R.A.J. (London Irish, Wasps) 1996 WS, 1997 NZ,C, 1998 F,W,SA1(R),2(R) 1999 F(R),E,S(R),It
Henebrey, G.J. (Garryowen) 1906 E,S,W,SA, 1909 W,F
Heron, A.G. (Queen's Coll Belfast) 1901 E
Heron, J. (NIFC) 1877 S, 1879 E
Heron, W.T. (NIFC) 1880 E,S
Herrick, R.W. (Dublin U) 1886 S
Heuston, F.S. (Kingstown) 1882 W, 1883 E,S
Hewitt, D. (QUB, Instonians) 1958 A,E,S,F, 1959 S,W,F, 1960 E,S,W,F, 1961 E,S,W,F, 1962 S,F, 1965 W
Hewitt, F.S. (Instonians) 1924 W,NZ, 1925 F,E,S, 1926 E, 1927 E,S,W
Hewitt, J.A. (NIFC) 1981 SA1(R),2(R)
Hewitt, T.R. (QUB) 1924 W,NZ, 1925 F,E,S, 1926 F,E,S,W
Hewitt, V.A. (Instonians) 1935 S,W,NZ, 1936 E,S,W
Hewitt, W.J. (Instonians) 1954 E, 1956 S, 1959 W, 1961 SA
Hewson, F.T. (Wanderers) 1875 E
Hickie, D.A. (St Mary's Coll) 1997 W,E,S,NZ,C,It, 1998 S,W,F,E,SA1,2
Hickie, D.J. (St Mary's Coll) 1971 F,E,S,W, 1972 F1,E
Higgins, J.A.D. (Civil Service) 1947 S,W,A, 1948 F,S,W
Higgins, W.W. (NIFC) 1884 E,S
Hillary, M.F. (UCD) 1952 E
Hingerty, D.J. (UCD) 1947 F,E,S,W
Hinton, W.P. (Old Wesley) 1907 W, 1908 E,S,W, 1909 E,S, 1910 E,S,W,F, 1911 E,S,W, 1912 F,E,W
Hipwell, M.L. (Terenure Coll) 1962 E,S, 1968 F,A, 1969 F(R),S(R),W, 1971 F,E,S,W, 1972 F2
Hobbs, T.H.M. (Dublin U) 1884 S, 1885 E
Hobson, E.W. (Dublin U) 1876 E
Hogan, N.A. (Terenure Coll, London Irish) 1995 E,W,[J,W,F], 1996 F,W,E,WS, 1997 F,W,E,It
Hogan, P. (Garryowen) 1992 F
Hogg, W. (Dublin U) 1885 S2
Holland, J.J. (Wanderers) 1981 SA1,2, 1986 W
Holmes, G.W. (Dublin U) 1912 SA, 1913 E,S
Holmes, L.J. (Lisburn) 1889 S,W
Hooks, K.J. (QUB, Ards, Bangor) 1981 S, 1989 NZ, 1990 F,W,Arg, 1991 F
Horan, A.K. (Blackheath) 1920 E,W
Houston, K.J. (Oxford U, London Irish) 1961 SA, 1964 S,W, 1965 F,E,SA
Hughes, R.W. (NIFC) 1878 E, 1880 E,S, 1881 S, 1882 E,S, 1883 E,S, 1884 E,S, 1885 E, 1886 E
Humphreys, D.G. (London Irish, Dungannon) 1996 F,W,E,WS, 1997 E(R),S,It, 1998 S,E(R),SA(2)(R), 1999 F,W,E,S,A1,2
Hunt, E.W.F. de Vere (Army, Rosslyn Park) 1930 F, 1932 E,S,W, 1933 E
Hunter, D.V. (Dublin U) 1885 S2
Hunter, L. (Civil Service) 1968 W,A
Hunter, W.R. (CIYMS) 1962 E,S,W,F, 1963 F,E,S, 1966 F,E,S
Hurley, H.D. (Old Wesley, Moseley) 1995 Fj(t), 1996 WS
Hutton, S.A. (Malone) 1967 S,W,F,A2

Ireland, J. (Windsor) 1876 E, 1877 E
Irvine, H.A.S. (Collegians) 1901 S
Irwin, D.G. (QUB, Instonians) 1980 F,W, 1981 F,W,E,S,SA1,2,A, 1982 W, 1983 S,F,W,E, 1984 F,W, 1987 [Tg,A(R)], 1989 F,W,E,S,NZ, 1990 E,S
Irwin, J.W.S. (NIFC) 1938 E,S, 1939 E,S,W
Irwin, S.T. (Queen's Coll Belfast) 1900 E,S,W, 1901 E,W, 1902 E,S,W, 1903 S

Jack, H.W. (UCC) 1914 S,W, 1921 W
Jackson, A.R.V. (Wanderers) 1911 E,S,W,F, 1913 W,F, 1914 F,E,S,W
Jackson, F. (NIFC) 1923 E
Jackson, H.W. (Dublin U) 1877 E
Jameson, J.S. (Lansdowne) 1888 M, 1889 S,W, 1891 W, 1892 E,W, 1893 S
Jeffares, E.W. (Wanderers) 1913 E,S
Johns, P.S. (Dublin U, Dungannon, Saracens) 1990 Arg, 1992 NZ1,2,A, 1993 S,F,W,E,R, 1994 F,W,E,S,A1,2,US, 1995 E,S,W,It,[NZ,J,W,F],Fj, 1996 US,S,F,WS, 1997 F,W,E,S,NZ,C,It, 1998 S,F,W,E,SA1,2,[Ga,R],SA, 1999 F,W,E,S,It,A1,2
Johnston, J. (Belfast Acad) 1881 S, 1882 S, 1884 S, 1885

S1,2 1886 E, 1887 E,S,W
Johnston, M. (Dublin U) 1880 E,S, 1881 E,S, 1882 E, 1884 E,S, 1886 E
Johnston, R. (Wanderers) 1893 E,W
Johnston, R.W. (Dublin U) 1890 S,W,E
Johnston, T.J. (Queen's Coll Belfast) 1892 E,S,W, 1893 E,S, 1895 E
Johnstone, W.E. (Dublin U) 1884 W
Johnstone-Smyth, T.R. (Lansdowne) 1882 E
Jordan, H.M. (Newport) 1884 W

Kavanagh, J.R. (UCD, Wanderers) 1953 F,E,S,W, 1954 NZ,S,W, 1955 F,E, 1956 E,S,W, 1957 F,E,S,W, 1958 A,E,S,W, 1959 E,S,W,F, 1960 E,S,W,F,SA, 1961 E,S,W,F,SA, 1962 F
Kavanagh, P.J. (UCD, Wanderers) 1952 E, 1955 W
Keane, K.P. (Garryowen) 1998 E(R)
Keane, M.I. (Lansdowne) 1974 F,W,E,S,P,NZ, 1975 E,S,F,W, 1976 A,F,W,E,S,NZ, 1977 W,E,S,F, 1978 S,F,W,E,NZ, 1979 F,W,E,S,A1,2, 1980 E,S,F,W, 1981 F,W,E,S, 1982 W,E,S,F, 1983 S,F,W,E, 1984 F,W,E,S
Kearney, R.K. (Wanderers) 1982 F, 1984 A, 1986 F,W
Keeffe, E. (Sunday's Well) 1947 F,E,S,W,A, 1948 F
Kelly, H.C. (NIFC) 1877 E,S, 1878 E, 1879 S, 1880 E,S
Kelly, J.C. (UCD) 1962 F,W, 1963 F,E,S,W,NZ, 1964 E,S,W,F
Kelly, S. (Lansdowne) 1954 S,W, 1955 S, 1960 W,F
Kelly, W. (Wanderers) 1884 S
Kennedy, A.G. (Belfast Collegians) 1956 F
Kennedy, A.P. (London Irish) 1986 W,E
Kennedy, F. (Wanderers) 1880 E, 1881 E, 1882 W
Kennedy, F.A. (Wanderers) 1904 E,W
Kennedy H. (Bradford) 1938 S,W
Kennedy, J.M. (Wanderers) 1882 W, 1884 W
Kennedy, K.W. (QUB, London Irish) 1965 F,E,S,W,SA, 1966 F,E,W, 1967 A1,E,S,W,F,A2, 1968 F,A, 1969 F,E,S,W, 1970 SA,F,E,S,W, 1971 F,E,S,W, 1972 F1,E,F2, 1973 NZ,E,S,W,F, 1974 F,W,E,S,P,NZ, 1975 F,W
Kennedy, T.J. (St Mary's Coll) 1978 NZ, 1979 F,W,E(R),A1,2, 1980 E,S,F,W, 1981 SA1,2,A
Kenny, P. (Wanderers) 1992 NZ2(R)
Keogh, F.S. (Bective Rangers) 1964 W,F
Keon, J.J. (Limerick) 1879 E
Keyes, R.P. (Cork Con) 1986 E, 1991 [Z,J,S,A], 1992 W,E,S
Kidd, F.W. (Dublin U, Lansdowne) 1877 E,S, 1878 E
Kiely, M.D. (Lansdowne) 1962 W, 1963 F,E,S,W
Kiernan, M.J. (Dolphin, Lansdowne) 1982 W(R),E,S,F, 1983 S,F,W,E, 1984 E,S,A, 1985 S,F,W,E, 1986 F,W,E,S,R, 1987 E,S,F,W,[W,C,A], 1988 S,F,W,E1,2,WS, 1989 F,W,E,S, 1990 E,S,F,W,Arg, 1991 F
Kiernan, T.J. (UCC, Cork Con) 1960 E,S,W,F,SA, 1961 E,S,W,F,SA, 1962 E,W, 1963 F,S,W,NZ, 1964 E,S, 1965 F,E,S,W,SA, 1966 F,E,S,W, 1967 A1,E,S,W,F,A2, 1968 F,E,S,W,A, 1969 F,E,S,W, 1970 SA,F,E,S,W, 1971 F, 1972 F1,E,F2, 1973 NZ,E,S
Killeen, G.V. (Garryowen) 1912 E,S,W, 1913 E,S,W,F, 1914 E,S,W
King, H. (Dublin U) 1883 E,S
Kingston, T.J. (Dolphin) 1987 [W,Tg,A], 1988 S,F,W,E1, 1990 F,W, 1991 [J], 1993 F,W,E,R, 1994 F,W,E,S, 1995 F,W,It,[NZ,J(R),W,F],Fj, 1996 US,S,F
Knox, J.H. (Dublin U, Lansdowne) 1904 W, 1905 E,S,W,NZ, 1906 E,S,W, 1907 W, 1908 S
Kyle, J.W. (QUB, NIFC) 1947 F,E,S,W,A, 1948 F,E,S,W, 1949 F,E,S,W, 1950 F,E,S,W, 1951 F,E,S,W,SA, 1952 F,S,W,E, 1953 F,E,S,W, 1954 NZ,F, 1955 F,E,W, 1956 F,E,S,W, 1957 F,E,S,W, 1958 A,E,S

Lambert, N.H. (Lansdowne) 1934 S,W
Lamont, R.A. (Instonians) 1965 F,E,SA, 1966 F,E,S,W, 1970 SA,F,E,S,W
Landers, M.F. (Cork Con) 1904 W, 1905 E,S,W,NZ
Lane, D. (UCC) 1934 S,W, 1935 E,S
Lane, M.F. (UCC) 1947 W, 1949 F,E,S,W, 1950 F,E,S,W, 1951 F,S,W,SA, 1952 F,S, 1953 F,E
Lane, P. (Old Crescent) 1964 W
Langan, D.J. (Clontarf) 1934 W
Langbroek, J.A. (Blackrock Coll) 1987 [Tg]
Lavery, P. (London Irish) 1974 W, 1976 W
Lawlor, P.J. (Clontarf) 1951 S,SA, 1952 F,S,W,E, 1953 F, 1954 NZ,E,S, 1956 F,E
Lawlor, P.J. (Bective Rangers) 1935 E,S,W, 1937 E,S,W
Lawlor, P.J. (Bective Rangers) 1990 Arg, 1992 A, 1993 S
Leahy, K.T. (Wanderers) 1992 NZ1
Leahy, M.W. (UCC) 1964 W
Lee, S. (NIFC) 1891 E,S,W, 1892 E,S,W, 1893 E,S,W, 1894 E,S,W, 1895 E,W, 1896 E,S,W, 1897 E, 1898 E
Le Fanu, V.C. (Cambridge U, Lansdowne) 1886 E,S, 1887 E,W, 1888 S, 1889 W, 1890 E, 1891 E, 1892 E,S,W
Lenihan, D.G. (UCC, Cork Con) 1981 A, 1982 W,E,S,F, 1983 S,F,W,E, 1984 F,W,E,S,A, 1985 S,F,W,E, 1986 F,W,E,S,R, 1987 E,S,F,W,[W,C,Tg,A], 1988 S,F,W,E1,2,WS,It, 1989 F,W,E,S,NZ, 1990 S,F,W,Arg, 1991 Nm2,[Z,S,A], 1992 W
L'Estrange, L.P.F. (Dublin U) 1962 E
Levis, F.H. (Wanderers) 1884 E
Lightfoot, E.J. (Lansdowne) 1931 F,E,S,W,SA, 1932 E,S,W, 1933 E,W,S
Lindsay, H. (Dublin U, Armagh) 1893 E,S,W, 1894 E,S,W, 1895 E, 1896 E,S,W, 1898 E,S,W
Little, T.J. (Bective Rangers) 1898 W, 1899 S,W, 1900 S,W,

1901 E,S
Lloyd, R.A. (Dublin U, Liverpool) 1910 E,S, 1911 E,S,W,F, 1912 F,E,S,W,SA, 1913 E,S,W,F, 1914 F,E, 1920 E,F
Lydon, C.T.J. (Galwegians) 1956 S
Lyle, R.K. (Dublin U) 1910 W,F
Lyle, T.R. (Dublin U) 1885 E,S1,2, 1886 E, 1887 E,S
Lynch, J.F. (St Mary's Coll) 1971 F,E,S,W, 1972 F1,E,F2, 1973 NZ,E,S,W, 1974 F,W,E,S,P,NZ
Lynch, L. (Lansdowne) 1956 S
Lytle, J.H. (NIFC) 1894 E,S,W, 1895 W, 1896 E,S,W, 1897 E,S, 1898 E,S, 1899 S
Lytle, J.N. (NIFC) 1888 M, 1889 W, 1890 E, 1891 E,S, 1894 E,S,W
Lyttle, V.J. (Collegians, Bedford) 1938 E, 1939 E,S

McAleese, D.R. (Ballymena) 1992 F
McAllan, G.H. (Dungannon) 1896 S,W
Macauley, J. (Limerick) 1887 E,S
McBride, W.D. (Malone) 1988 W,E1,WS,It, 1989 S, 1990 F,W,Arg, 1993 S,F,W,E,R, 1994 W,E,S,A1(R), 1995 S,F,[NZ,W,F],Fj(R), 1996 W,E,WS,A, 1997 It(R),F,W,E,S
McBride, W.J. (Ballymena) 1962 E,S,F,W, 1963 F,E,S,W,NZ, 1964 E,S,F, 1965 F,E,S,W,SA, 1966 F,E,S,W, 1967 A1,E,S,W,F,A2, 1968 F,E,S,W,A, 1969 F,E,S,W, 1970 SA,F,E,S,W, 1971 F,E,S,W, 1972 F1,E,F2, 1973 NZ,E,S,W,F, 1974 F,W,E,S,P,NZ, 1975 E,S,F,W
McCahill, S.A. (Sunday's Well) 1995 Fj(t)
McCall, B.W. (London Irish) 1985 F(R), 1986 E,S
McCall, M.C. (Bangor, Dungannon, London Irish) 1992 NZ1(R),2, 1994 W, 1996 E(R),A, 1997 It,NZ,C,It, 1998 S,E,SA1,2
McCallan, B. (Ballymena) 1960 E,S
McCarten, R.J. (London Irish) 1961 E,W,F
McCarthy, E.A. (Kingstown) 1882 W
McCarthy, J.S. (Dolphin) 1948 F,E,S,W, 1949 F,E,S,W, 1950 W, 1951 F,E,S,W,SA, 1952 F,S,W,E, 1953 F,E,S, 1954 NZ,F,E,S,W, 1955 F,E
McCarthy, P.D. (Cork Con) 1992 NZ1,2,A, 1993 S,R(R)
MacCarthy, St G. (Dublin U) 1882 W
McCarthy, T. (Cork) 1898 W
McClelland, T.A. (QUB) 1921 E,S,W,F, 1922 E,W,F, 1923 E,S,W,F, 1924 F,E,S,W,NZ
McClenahan, R.O. (Instonians) 1923 E,S,W
McClinton, A.N. (NIFC) 1910 W,F
McCombe, W. McM. (Dublin U, Bangor) 1968 F, 1975 E,S,F,W
McConnell, A.A. (Collegians) 1947 A, 1948 F,E,S,W, 1949 F,E
McConnell, G. (Derry, Edinburgh U) 1912 F,E, 1913 W,F
McConnell, J.W. (Lansdowne) 1913 S
McCormac, F.M. (Wanderers) 1909 W, 1910 W,F
McCormick, W.J. (Wanderers) 1930 E
McCoull, H.C. (Belfast Albion) 1895 E,S,W, 1899 E
McCourt, D. (QUB) 1947 A
McCoy, J.J. (Dungannon, Bangor, Ballymena) 1984 W,A, 1985 S,F,W,E, 1986 F, 1987 [Tg], 1988 E2,WS,It, 1989 F,W,E,S,NZ
McCracken, H. (NIFC) 1954 W
McDaniel, J. (Newport) 1884 W
McDermott, S.J. (London Irish) 1955 S,W
Macdonald, J.A. (Methodist Coll Belfast) 1875 E, 1876 E, 1877 S, 1878 E, 1879 S, 1880 E, 1881 S, 1882 E,S, 1883 E,S, 1884 E,S
McDonald, J.P. (Malone) 1987 [C], 1990 E(R),S,Arg
McDonnell, A.C. (Dublin U) 1889 W, 1890 S,W, 1891 E
McDowell, J.C. (Instonians) 1924 F,NZ
McFarland, B.A.T. (Derry) 1920 S,W,F, 1922 W
McGann, B.J. (Lansdowne) 1969 F,E,S,W, 1970 SA,F,E,S,W, 1971 F,E,S,W, 1972 F1,E,F2, 1973 NZ,E,S,W, 1976 F,W,E,S,NZ
McGowan, A.N. (Blackrock Coll) 1994 US
McGown, T.M.W. (NIFC) 1899 E,S, 1901 S
McGrath, D.G. (UCD, Cork Con) 1984 S, 1987 [W,C,Tg,A]
McGrath, N.F. (Oxford U, London Irish) 1934 W
McGrath, P.J. (UCC) 1965 E,S,W,SA, 1966 F,E,S,W, 1967 A1,2
McGrath, R.J.M. (Wanderers) 1977 W,E,F(R), 1981 SA1,2,A, 1982 W,E,S,F, 1983 S,F,W,E, 1984 F,W
McGrath, T. (Garryowen) 1956 W, 1958 F, 1960 E,S,W,F, 1961 SA
McGuinness, C.D. (St Mary's Coll) 1997 NZ,C, 1998 F,W,E,SA1,2,[Ga,R(R)],SA, 1999 F,W,E,S
McGuire, E.P. (UCG) 1963 E,S,W,NZ, 1964 E,S,W,F
MacHale, S. (Lansdowne) 1965 F,E,S,W,SA, 1966 F,E,S,W, 1967 S,W,F
McIldowie, G. (Malone) 1906 SA, 1910 E,S,W
McIlrath, J.A. (Ballymena) 1976 A,F,NZ, 1977 W,E
McIlwaine, E.H. (NIFC) 1895 S,W
McIlwaine, E.N. (NIFC) 1875 E, 1876 E
McIlwaine, J.E. (NIFC) 1897 E,S, 1898 E,S,W, 1899 E,W
McIntosh, L.M. (Dublin U) 1884 S
MacIvor, C.V. (Dublin U) 1910 F, 1912 F,E,S,W, 1913 E,S,F
McIvor, S.C. (Garryowen) 1996 A, 1997 It,S(R)
McKay, J.W. (QUB) 1947 F,E,S,W,A, 1948 F,E,S,W, 1949 F,E,S,W, 1950 F,E,S,W, 1951 F,E,S,W,SA, 1952 F
McKee, W.D. (NIFC) 1947 A, 1948 F,E,S,W, 1949 F,E,S,W, 1950 F,E, 1951 SA
McKelvey, J.M. (QUB) 1956 F,E
McKibbin, A.R. (Instonians, London Irish) 1977 W,E,S,

1978 S,F,W,E,NZ, 1979 F,W,E,S, 1980 E,S
McKibbin, C.H. (Instonians) 1976 S(R)
McKibbin, D. (Instonians) 1950 F,E,S,W, 1951 F,E,S,W
McKibbin, H.R. (QUB) 1938 W, 1939 E,S,W
McKinney, S.A. (Dungannon) 1972 F1,E,F2, 1973 W,F, 1974 F,E,S,P,NZ, 1975 E,S, 1976 A,F,W,E,S,NZ, 1977 W,E,S, 1978 S(R),F,W,E
McLaughlin, J.H. (Derry) 1887 E,S, 1888 W,S
McLean, R.E. (Dublin U) 1881 S, 1882 W,E,S, 1883 E,S, 1884 E,S, 1885 E,S1
MacLear, B. (Cork County, Monkstown) 1905 E,S,W,NZ, 1906 E,S,W,SA, 1907 E,S,W
McLennan, A.C. (Wanderers) 1977 F, 1978 S,F,W,E,NZ, 1979 F,W,E,S, 1980 E,F, 1981 F,W,E,S,SA1,2
McLoughlin, F.M. (Northern) 1976 A
McLoughlin, G.A.J. (Shannon) 1979 F,W,E,S,A1,2, 1980 E, 1981 SA1,2, 1982 W,E,S,F, 1983 S,F,W,E, 1984 F
McLoughlin, R.J. (UCD, Blackrock Coll, Gosforth) 1962 E,S,F, 1963 E,S,W,NZ, 1964 E,S, 1965 F,E,S,W,SA, 1966 F,E,S,W, 1971 F,E,S,W, 1972 F1,E,F2, 1973 NZ,E,S,W,F, 1974 F,W,E,S,P,NZ, 1975 E,S,F,W
McMahon, L.B. (Blackrock Coll, UCD) 1931 E,SA, 1933 E, 1934 E, 1936 E,S,W, 1937 E,S,W, 1938 E,S
McMaster, A.W. (Ballymena) 1972 F1,E,F2, 1973 NZ,E,S,W,F, 1974 F,E,S,P, 1975 F,W, 1976 A,F,W,NZ
McMordie, J. (Queen's Coll Belfast) 1886 S
McMorrow, A. (Garryowen) 1951 W
McMullen, A.R. (Cork) 1881 E,S
McNamara, V. (UCC) 1914 E,S,W
McNaughton, P.P. (Greystones) 1978 S,F,W,E, 1979 F,W,E,S,A1,2, 1980 E,S,F,W, 1981 F
MacNeill, H.P. (Dublin U, Oxford U, Blackrock Coll, London Irish) 1981 F,W,E,S,A, 1982 W,E,S,F, 1983 S,F,W,E, 1984 F,W,E,A, 1985 S,F,W,E, 1986 F,W,E,S,R, 1987 E,S,F,W,[W,C,Tg,A], 1988 S(R),E1,2
McQuilkin, K.P. (Bective Rangers, Lansdowne) 1996 US,S,F, 1997 F(t&R),S
MacSweeney, D.A. (Blackrock Coll) 1955 S
McVicker, H. (Army, Richmond) 1927 E,S,W,A, 1928 F
McVicker, J. (Collegians) 1924 F,E,S,W,NZ, 1925 F,E,S,W, 1926 F,E,S,W, 1927 F,E,S,W,A, 1928 W, 1930 F
McVicker, S. (QUB) 1922 E,S,W,F
McWeeney, J.P.J. (St Mary's Coll) 1997 NZ
Madden, M.N. (Sunday's Well) 1955 E,S,W
Magee, J.T. (Bective Rangers) 1895 E,S
Magee, A.M. (Louis) (Bective Rangers, London Irish) 1895 E,S,W, 1896 E,S,W, 1897 E,S, 1898 E,S,W, 1899 E,S,W, 1900 E,S,W, 1901 E,S,W, 1902 E,S,W, 1903 E,S,W, 1904 W
Maggs, K.M. (Bristol, Bath) 1998 SA1,2,[Ga,R],SA, 1999 F,W,E,S,It,A1,2
Maginiss, R.M. (Dublin U) 1875 E, 1876 E
Magrath, R.M. (Cork Con) 1909 S
Maguire, J.F. (Cork) 1884 S
Mahoney, J. (Dolphin) 1923 E
Malcolmson, G.L. (RAF, NIFC) 1935 NZ, 1936 E,S,W, 1937 E,S,W
Malone, N.G. (Oxford U, Leicester) 1993 S,F, 1994 US(R)
Mannion, N.P. (Corinthians, Lansdowne, Wanderers) 1988 WS,It, 1989 F,W,E,S,NZ, 1990 E,S,F,W,Arg, 1991 Nm1(R),2,[J], 1993 S
Marshall, B.D.E. (QUB) 1963 E
Mason, S.J.P. (Orrell, Richmond) 1996 W,E,WS
Massey-Westropp, R.H. (Limerick, Monkstown) 1886 E
Matier, R.N. (NIFC) 1878 E, 1879 S
Matthews, P.M. (Ards, Wanderers) 1984 A, 1985 S,F,W,E, 1986 R, 1987 E,S,F,W,[W,Tg,A], 1988 S,F,W,E1,2, WS,It, 1989 F,W,E,S,NZ, 1990 E,S, 1991 F,W,E,S,Nm1[Z,S,A], 1992 W,E,S
Mattsson, J. (Wanderers) 1948 E
Mayne, R.B. (QUB) 1937 W, 1938 E,W, 1939 E,S,W
Mayne, R.H. (Belfast Academy) 1888 W,S
Mayne, T. (NIFC) 1921 E,S,F
Mays, K.M.A. (UCD) 1973 NZ,E,S,W
Meares, A.W.D. (Dublin U) 1899 S,W, 1900 E,W
Megaw, J. (Richmond, Instonians) 1934 W, 1938 E
Millar, A. (Kingstown) 1880 E,S, 1883 E
Millar, H.J. (Monkstown) 1904 W, 1905 E,S,W
Millar, S. (Ballymena) 1958 F, 1959 E,S,W,F, 1960 E,S,W,F,SA, 1961 E,S,W,F,SA, 1962 E,S,F, 1963 F,E,S,W, 1964 F, 1968 F,E,S,W,A, 1969 F,E,S,W, 1970 SA,F,E,S,W
Millar, W.H.J. (QUB) 1951 E,S,W, 1952 S,W
Miller, E.R.P. (Leicester, Terenure Coll) 1997 It,F,W,E,NZ,It, 1998 S,W(R)[Ga,R], 1999 F,W,E(R),S
Miller, F.H. (Wanderers) 1886 S
Milliken, R.A. (Bangor) 1973 E,S,W,F, 1974 F,W,E,S,P,NZ, 1975 E,S,F,W
Millin, T.J. (Dublin U) 1925 W
Minch, J.B. (Bective Rangers) 1912 SA, 1913 E,S, 1914 E,S
Moffat, J. (Belfast Academy) 1888 W,S,M, 1889 S, 1890 S,W, 1891 S
Moffatt, J.E. (Old Wesley) 1904 S, 1905 E,S,W
Moffett, J.W. (Ballymena) 1961 E,S
Molloy, M.G. (UCG, London Irish) 1966 F,E, 1967 A1,E,S,W,F,A2, 1968 F,E,S,W,A, 1969 F,E,S,W, 1970 F,E,S,W, 1971 F,E,S,W, 1973 F, 1976 A
Moloney, J.J. (St Mary's Coll) 1972 F1,E,F2, 1973 NZ,E,S,W,F, 1974 F,W,E,S,P,NZ, 1975 E,S,F,W, 1976 S, 1978 S,F,W,E, 1979 A1,2 1980 S,W
Moloney, L.A. (Garryowen) 1976 W(R),S, 1978 S(R),NZ
Molony, J.U. (UCD) 1950 S

Monteith, J.D.E. (QUB) 1947 E,S,W
Montgomery, A. (NIFC) 1895 S
Montgomery, F.P. (QUB) 1914 E,S,W
Montgomery, R. (Cambridge U) 1887 E,S,W, 1891 E, 1892 W
Moore, C.M. (Dublin U) 1887 S, 1888 W,S
Moore, D.F. (Wanderers) 1883 E,S, 1884 E,W
Moore, F.W. (Wanderers) 1884 W, 1885 E,S2, 1886 S
Moore, H. (Windsor) 1876 E, 1877 S
Moore, H. (QUB) 1910 S, 1911 W,F, 1912 F,E,S,W,SA
Moore, T.A.P. (Highfield) 1967 A2, 1973 NZ,E,S,W,F, 1974 F,W,E,S,P,NZ
Moore, W.D. (Queen's Coll Belfast) 1878 E
Moran, F.G. (Clontarf) 1936 E, 1937 E,S,W, 1938 S,W, 1939 E,S,W
Morell, H.B. (Dublin U) 1881 E,S, 1882 W,E
Morgan, G.J. (Clontarf) 1934 E,S,W, 1935 E,S,W,NZ, 1936 E,S,W, 1937 E,S,W, 1938 E,S,W, 1939 E,S,W
Moriarty, C.C.H. (Monkstown) 1899 W
Moroney, J.C.M. (Garryowen) 1968 W,A, 1969 F,E,S,W
Moroney, R.J.M. (Lansdowne) 1984 F,W, 1985 F
Moroney, T.A. (UCD) 1964 W, 1967 A1,E
Morphy, E. McG. (Dublin U) 1908 E
Morris, D.P. (Bective Rangers) 1931 W, 1932 E, 1935 E,S,W,NZ
Morrow, J.W.R. (Queen's Coll Belfast) 1882 S, 1883 E,S, 1884 E,W, 1885 S1,2, 1886 E,S, 1888 S
Morrow, R.D. (Bangor) 1986 F,E,S
Mortell, M. (Bective Rangers, Dolphin) 1953 F,E,S,W, 1954 NZ,F,E,S,W
Morton, W.A. (Dublin U) 1888 S
Mostyn, M. (Begles-Bordeaux) 1999 A1
Moyers, L.W. (Dublin U) 1884 W
Moylett, M.M.F. (Shannon) 1988 E1
Mulcahy, W.A. (UCD, Bective Rangers, Bohemians) 1958 A,E,S,W,F, 1959 E,S,W,F, 1960 E,S,W,SA, 1961 E,S,W,SA, 1962 E,S,F,W, 1963 F,E,S,W,NZ, 1964 E,S,W,F, 1965 F,E,S,W,SA
Mullan, B. (Clontarf) 1947 F,E,S,W, 1948 F,E,S,W
Mullane, J.P. (Limerick Bohemians) 1928 W, 1929 F
Mullen, K.D. (Old Belvedere) 1947 F,E,S,W,A, 1948 F,E,S,W, 1949 F,E,S,W, 1950 F,E,S,W, 1951 F,E,S,W,SA, 1952 F,S,W
Mulligan, A.A. (Wanderers) 1956 F,E, 1957 F,E,S,W, 1958 A,E,S,F, 1959 E,S,W,F, 1960 E,S,W,F,SA, 1961 W,F,SA
Mullin, B.J. (Dublin U, Oxford U, Blackrock Coll, London Irish) 1984 A, 1985 S,W,E, 1986 F,W,E,S,R, 1987 E,S,F,W,[W,C,Tg,A], 1988 S,F,W,E1,2,WS,It, 1989 F,W,E,S,NZ, 1990 E,S,W,Arg, 1991 F,W,E,S,Nm1,2,[J,S,A], 1992 W,E,S, 1994 US, 1995 E,S,F,W,It,[NZ,J,W,F]

Murphy, C.J. (Lansdowne) 1939 E,S,W, 1947 F,E
Murphy, J.G.M.W. (London Irish) 1951 SA, 1952 S,W,E, 1954 NZ, 1958 W
Murphy, J.J. (Greystones) 1981 SA1, 1982 W(R), 1984 S
Murphy, J.N. (Greystones) 1992 A
Murphy, K.J. (Cork Con) 1990 E,S,F,W,Arg, 1991 F,W(R),S(R), 1992 S,F,NZ2(R)
Murphy, N.A.A. (Cork Con) 1958 A,E,S,W,F, 1959 E,S,W,F, 1960 E,S,W,F,SA, 1961 E,S,W, 1962 E, 1963 NZ, 1964 E,S,W,F, 1965 F,E,S,W,SA, 1966 F,E,S,W, 1967 A1,E,S,W,F, 1969 F,E,S,W
Murphy, N.F. (Cork Con) 1930 E,W, 1931 F,E,S,W,SA, 1932 E,S,W, 1933 E
Murphy-O'Connor, J. (Bective Rangers) 1954 E
Murray, H.W. (Dublin U) 1877 S, 1878 E, 1879 E
Murray, J.B. (UCD) 1963 F
Murray, P.F. (Wanderers) 1927 F, 1929 F,E,S, 1930 F,E,S,W, 1931 F,E,S,W,SA, 1932 E,S,W, 1933 E,W,S
Murtagh, C.W. (Portadown) 1977 S
Myles, J. (Dublin U) 1875 E

Nash, L.C. (Queen's Coll Cork) 1889 S, 1890 W,E, 1891 E,S,W
Neely, M.R. (Collegians) 1947 F,E,S,W
Neill, H.J. (NIFC) 1885 E,S1,2, 1886 S, 1887 E,S,W, 1888 W,S
Neill, J. McF. (Instonians) 1926 F
Nelson, J.E. (Malone) 1947 A, 1948 E,S,W, 1949 F,E,S,W, 1950 F,E,S,W, 1951 F,E,W, 1954 F
Nelson, R. (Queen's Coll Belfast) 1882 E,S, 1883 S, 1886 S
Nesdale, R.P. (Newcastle) 1997 W,E,S,NZ(R),C, 1998 F(R),W(R),[Ga],SA(R),A2(R)
Nesdale, T.J. (Garryowen) 1961 F
Neville, W.C. (Dublin U) 1879 S,E
Nicholson, P.C. (Dublin U) 1900 E,S,W
Norton, G.W. (Bective Rangers) 1949 F,E,S,W, 1950 F,E,S,W, 1951 F,E,S
Notley, J.R. (Wanderers) 1952 F,S
Nowlan, K.W. (St Mary's Coll) 1997 NZ,C,It

O'Brien, B. (Derry) 1893 S,W
O'Brien, B.A.P. (Shannon) 1968 F,E,S
O'Brien, D.J. (London Irish, Cardiff, Old Belvedere) 1948 E,S,W, 1949 F,E,S,W, 1950 F,E,S,W, 1951 F,E,S,W,SA, 1952 F,S,W,E
O'Brien, K.A. (Broughton Park) 1980 E, 1981 SA1(R),2
O'Brien-Butler, P.E. (Monkstown) 1897 S, 1898 E,S, 1899 S,W, 1900 E
O'Callaghan, C.T. (Carlow) 1910 W, 1911 E,S,W,F, 1912 F
O'Callaghan, M.P. (Sunday's Well) 1962 W, 1964 E,F
O'Callaghan, P. (Dolphin) 1967 A1,E,A2, 1968 F,E,S,W,

1969 F,E,S,W, 1970 SA,F,E,S,W, 1976 F,W,E,S,NZ
O'Connell, K.D. (Sunday's Well) 1994 F,E(t)
O'Connell, P. (Bective Rangers) 1913 W,F, 1914 F,E,S,W
O'Connell, W.J. (Lansdowne) 1955 F
O'Connor, H.S. (Dublin U) 1957 F,E,S,W
O'Connor, J. (Garryowen) 1895 S
O'Connor, J.J. (Garryowen) 1909 F
O'Connor, J.J. (UCC) 1933 S, 1934 E,S,W, 1935 E,S,W,NZ, 1936 S,W, 1938 S
O'Connor, P.J. (Lansdowne) 1887 W
O'Conor, J.H. (Bective Rangers) 1888 M, 1890 S,W,E, 1891 E,S, 1892 E,W, 1893 E,S, 1894 E,S,W, 1895 E, 1896 E,S,W
O'Cuinneagain, D. (Sale) 1998 SA1,2,[Ga(R),R(R)],SA, 1999 F,W,E,S,It,A1,2
Odbert, R.V.M. (RAF) 1928 W
O'Donnell, R.C. (St Mary's Coll) 1979 A1,2, 1980 S,F,W
O'Donoghue, P.J. (Bective Rangers) 1955 F,E,S,W, 1956 W, 1957 F,E, 1958 A,E,S,W
O'Driscoll, B.G. (UCD) 1999 A1,2
O'Driscoll, B.J. (Manchester) 1971 F(R),E,S,W
O'Driscoll, J.B. (London Irish, Manchester) 1978 S, 1979 A1,2, 1980 E,S,F,W, 1981 F,W,E,S,SA1,2,A, 1982 W,E,S,F, 1983 S,F,W,E, 1984 F,W,E,S
O'Flanagan, K.P. (London Irish) 1947 A
O'Flanagan, M. (Lansdowne) 1948 S
O'Grady, D. (Sale) 1997 It
O'Hanlon, B. (Dolphin) 1947 E,S,W, 1948 F,E,S,W, 1949 F,E,S,W, 1950 F
O'Hara, P.T.J. (Sunday's Well, Cork Con) 1988 WS(R), 1989 F,W,E,NZ, 1990 E,S,F,W, 1991 Nm1,[J], 1993 F,W,E, 1994 US
O'Kelly, M.E. (London Irish) 1997 NZ,C,It, 1998 S,F,W,E,SA1,2,[Ga,R],SA, 1999 SA1(R),SA2
O'Leary, A. (Cork Con) 1952 S,W,E
O'Loughlin, D.B. (UCC) 1938 E,S,W, 1939 E,S,W
O'Mahony, Darragh (UCD, Moseley, Bedford) 1995 It,[F], 1997 It, 1998 [R]
O'Mahony, David (Cork Con) 1995 It
O'Meara, B.T. (Cork Con) 1997 E(R),S,NZ(R), 1998 S
O'Meara, J.A. (UCC, Dolphin) 1951 F,E,S,W,SA, 1952 F,S,W,E, 1953 F,E,S,W, 1954 NZ,F,E,S, 1955 F,E, 1956 S,W, 1958 W
O'Neill, H. O'H. (QUB, UCC) 1930 E,S,W, 1933 E,S,W
O'Neill, J.B. (QUB) 1920 S
O'Neill, W.A. (UCD, Wanderers) 1952 E, 1953 F,E,S,W, 1954 NZ
O'Reilly, A.J.F. (Old Belvedere, Leicester) 1955 F,E,S,W, 1956 F,E,S,W, 1957 F,E,S,W, 1958 A,E,S,W,F, 1959 E,S,W,F, 1960 E, 1961 E,F,SA, 1963 F,S,W, 1970 E
Orr, P.A. (Old Wesley) 1976 F,W,E,S,NZ, 1977 W,E,S,F, 1978 S,F,W,E,NZ, 1979 F,W,E,S,A1,2, 1980 E,S,F,W, 1981 F,W,E,S,SA1,2,A, 1982 W,E,S,F, 1983 S,F,W,E, 1984 F,W,E,S,A, 1985 S,F,W,E, 1986 F,S,R, 1987 E,S,F,W,[W,C,A]
O'Shea, C.M.P. (Lansdowne, London Irish) 1993 R, 1994 F,W,E,S,A1,2, 1995 E,S,[J,W,F], 1997 It,F,S(R), 1998 S,F,SA1,2,[Ga,R],SA, 1999 F,W,E,S,It,A1
O'Sullivan, A.C. (Dublin U) 1882 S
O'Sullivan, J.M. (Limerick) 1884 S, 1887 S
O'Sullivan, P.J.A. (Galwegians) 1957 F,E,S,W, 1959 E,S,W,F, 1960 SA, 1961 E,S, 1962 F,W, 1963 F,NZ
O'Sullivan, W. (Queen's Coll Cork) 1895 S
Owens, R.H. (Dublin U) 1922 E,S

Parfrey, P. (UCC) 1974 NZ
Parke, J.C. (Monkstown) 1903 W, 1904 E,S,W, 1905 W,NZ, 1906 E,S,W,SA, 1907 E,S,W, 1908 E,S,W, 1909 E,S,W,F
Parr, J.S. (Wanderers) 1914 F,E,S,W
Patterson, C.S. (Instonians) 1978 NZ, 1979 F,W,E,S,A1,2 1980 E,S,F,W
Patterson, R. d'A. (Wanderers) 1912 F,S,W,SA, 1913 E,S,W,F
Payne, C.T. (NIFC) 1926 E, 1927 F,E,S,A, 1928 F,E,S,W, 1929 F,E,W, 1930 F,E,S,W
Pedlow, A.C. (CIYMS) 1953 W, 1954 NZ,F,E, 1955 F,E,S,W, 1956 F,E,S,W, 1957 F,E,S,W, 1958 A,E,S,W,F, 1959 E, 1960 E,S,W,F,SA, 1961 S, 1962 W, 1963 F
Pedlow, J. (Bessbrook) 1882 S, 1884 W
Pedlow, R. (Bessbrook) 1891 W
Pedlow, T.B. (Queen's Coll Belfast) 1889 S,W
Peel, T. (Limerick) 1892 E,S,W
Peirce, W. (Cork) 1881 E
Phipps, G.C. (Army) 1950 E,W, 1952 F,W,E
Pike, T.O. (Lansdowne) 1927 E,S,W,A, 1928 F,E,S,W
Pike, V.J. (Lansdowne) 1931 E,S,W,SA, 1932 E,S,W, 1933 E,W,S, 1934 E,S,W
Pike, W.W. (Kingstown) 1879 E, 1881 E,S, 1882 E, 1883 S
Pinion, G. (Belfast Collegians) 1909 E,S,W,F
Piper, O.J.S. (Cork Con) 1909 E,S,W,F, 1910 E,S,W,F
Polden, S.E. (Clontarf) 1913 W,F, 1914 F, 1920 F
Popham, I. (Cork Con) 1922 S,W,F, 1923 F
Popplewell, N.J. (Greystones, Wasps, Newcastle) 1989 NZ, 1990 Arg, 1991 Nm1,2,[Z,S,A], 1992 W,E,S,F,NZ1,2,A, 1993 S,F,W,E,R, 1994 F,W,E,S,US, 1995 E,S,F,W,It,[NZ,J,W,F],Fj, 1996 US,S,F,W,E,A, 1997 It,F,W,E,NZ,C, 1998 S(t),F(R)
Potterton, H.N. (Wanderers) 1920 W
Pratt, R.H. (Dublin U) 1933 E,W,S, 1934 E,S
Price, A.H. (Dublin U) 1920 S,F
Pringle, J.C. (NIFC) 1902 S,W
Purcell, N.M. (Lansdowne) 1921 E,S,W,F

Purdon, H. (NIFC) 1879 S,E, 1880 E, 1881 E,S
Purdon, W.B. (Queen's Coll Belfast) 1906 E,S,W
Purser, F.C. (Dublin U) 1898 E,S,W

Quinlan, S.V.J. (Blackrock Coll) 1956 F,E,W, 1958 W
Quinn, B. (Old Belvedere) 1947 F
Quinn, F.P. (Old Belvedere) 1981 F,W,E
Quinn, J.P. (Dublin U) 1910 E,S, 1911 E,S,W,F, 1912 E,S,W, 1913 E,W,F, 1914 F,E,S
Quinn, K. (Old Belvedere) 1947 F,A, 1953 F,E,S
Quinn, M.A.M. (Lansdowne) 1973 F, 1974 F,W,E,S,P,NZ, 1977 S,F, 1981 SA2
Quirke, J.M.T. (Blackrock Coll) 1962 E,S, 1968 S

Rainey, P.I. (Ballymena) 1989 NZ
Rambaut, D.F. (Dublin U) 1887 E,S,W, 1888 W
Rea, H.H. (Edinburgh U) 1967 A1, 1969 F
Read, H.M. (Dublin U) 1910 E,S, 1911 E,S,W,F, 1912 F,E,S,W,SA, 1913 E,S
Reardon, J.V. (Cork Con) 1934 E,S
Reid, C. (NIFC) 1899 S,W, 1900 E, 1903 W
Reid, J.L. (Richmond) 1934 S,W
Reid, P.J. (Garryowen) 1947 A, 1948 F,E,W
Reid, T.E. (Garryowen) 1953 E,S,W, 1954 NZ,F, 1955 E,S, 1956 F,E, 1957 F,E,S,W
Reidy, C.J. (London Irish) 1937 W
Reidy, G.F. (Dolphin, Lansdowne) 1953 W, 1954 F,E,S,W
Richey, H.A. (Dublin U) 1889 W, 1890 S
Ridgeway, E.C. (Wanderers) 1932 S,W, 1935 E,S,W
Rigney, B.J. (Greystones) 1991 F,W,E,S,Nm1, 1992 F,NZ1(R),2
Ringland, T.M. (QUB, Ballymena) 1981 A, 1982 W,E,F, 1983 S,F,W,E, 1984 F,W,E,S,A, 1985 S,F,W,E, 1986 F,W,E,S,R, 1987 E,S,F,W,[W,C,Tg,A], 1988 S,F,W,E1
Riordan, W.F. (Cork Con) 1910 E
Ritchie, J.S. (London Irish) 1956 F,E
Robb, C.G. (Queen's Coll Belfast) 1904 E,S,W, 1905 NZ, 1906 S
Robbie, J.C. (Dublin U, Greystones) 1976 A,F,NZ, 1977 S,F, 1981 F,W,E,S
Robinson, B.F. (Ballymena, London Irish) 1991 F,W,E,S,Nm1,2,[Z,S,A], 1992 W,E,S,F,NZ1,2,A, 1993 W,E,R, 1994 F,W,E,S,A1,2
Robinson, T.T.H. (Wanderers) 1904 E,S, 1905 E,S,W,NZ, 1906 SA, 1907 E,S,W
Roche, J. (Wanderers) 1890 S,W,E, 1891 E,S,W, 1892 W
Roche, R.E. (UCG) 1955 E,S, 1957 S,W
Roche, W.J. (UCC) 1920 E,S,F
Roddy, P.J. (Bective Rangers) 1920 S,F
Roe, R. (Lansdowne) 1952 E, 1953 F,E,S,W, 1954 F,E,S,W, 1955 F,E,S,W, 1956 F,E,S,W, 1957 F,E,S,W

Rolland, A.C. (Blackrock Coll) 1990 Arg, 1994 US(R), 1995 It(R)
Rooke, C.V. (Dublin U) 1891 E,W, 1892 E,S,W, 1893 E,S,W, 1894 E,S,W, 1895 E,S,W, 1896 E,S,W, 1897 E,S
Ross, D.J. (Belfast Acad) 1884 E, 1885 S1,2, 1886 E,S
Ross, G.R.P. (CIYMS) 1955 W
Ross, J.F. (NIFC) 1886 S
Ross, J.P. (Lansdowne) 1885 E,S1,2, 1886 E,S
Ross, N.G. (Malone) 1927 F,E
Ross, W. McC. (QUB) 1932 E,S,W, 1933 E,W,S, 1934 E,S, 1935 NZ
Russell, J. (UCC) 1931 F,E,S,W,SA, 1933 E,W,S, 1934 E,S,W, 1935 E,S,W, 1936 E,S,W, 1937 E,S
Russell, P. (Instonians) 1990 E, 1992 NZ1,2,A
Rutherford, W.G. (Tipperary) 1884 E,S, 1885 E,S1, 1886 E, 1888 W
Ryan, E. (Dolphin) 1937 W, 1938 E,S
Ryan, J. (Rockwell Coll) 1897 E, 1898 E,S,W, 1899 E,S,W, 1900 S,W, 1901 E,S,W, 1902 E, 1904 E
Ryan, J.G. (UCD) 1939 E,S,W
Ryan, M. (Rockwell Coll) 1897 E,S, 1898 E,S,W, 1899 E,S,W, 1900 E,S,W, 1901 E,S,W, 1903 E, 1904 E,S

Saunders, R. (London Irish) 1991 F,W,E,S,Nm1,2,[Z,J,S,A], 1992 W, 1994 F(t)
Saverimutto, C. (Sale) 1995 Fj, 1996 US,S
Sayers, H.J.M. (Lansdowne) 1935 E,S,W, 1936 E,S,W, 1938 W, 1939 E,S,W
Scally, C.J. (UCD) 1998 [GA(R),R],S(R),It
Schute, F. (Wanderers) 1878 E, 1879 E
Schute, F.G. (Dublin U) 1912 SA, 1913 E,S
Scott, D. (Malone) 1961 F,SA, 1962 S
Scott, R.D. (QUB) 1967 E,F, 1968 F,E,S
Scovell, R.H. (Kingstown) 1883 E, 1884 E
Scriven, G. (Dublin U) 1879 S,E, 1880 E,S, 1881 E, 1882 S, 1883 E,S,
Sealy, J. (Dublin U) 1896 E,S,W, 1897 S, 1899 E,S,W, 1900 E,S
Sexton, J.F. (Dublin U, Lansdowne) 1988 E2,WS,It, 1989 F
Sexton, W.J. (Garryowen) 1984 A, 1988 S,E2
Shanahan, T. (Lansdowne) 1885 E,S1,2, 1886 E, 1888 S,W
Shaw, G.M. (Windsor) 1877 S
Sheehan, M.D. (London Irish) 1932 E
Sherry, B.F. (Terenure Coll) 1967 A1,E,S,A2, 1968 F,E
Sherry, M.J.A. (Lansdowne) 1975 F,W
Siggins, J.A.E. (Belfast Collegians) 1931 F,E,S,W,SA, 1932 E,S,W, 1933 E,W,S, 1934 E,S,W, 1935 E,S,W,NZ, 1936 E,S,W, 1937 E,S,W
Slattery, J.F. (UCD, Blackrock Coll) 1970 SA,F,E,S,W, 1971 F,E,S,W, 1972 F1,E,F2, 1973 NZ,E,S,W,F, 1974 F,W,E,S,P,NZ, 1975 E,S,F,W, 1976 A, 1977 S,F, 1978

S,F,W,E,NZ, 1979 F,W,E,S,A1,2, 1980 E,S,F,W, 1981 F,W,E,S,SA1,2,A, 1982 W,E,S,F, 1983 S,F,W,E, 1984 F
Smartt, F.N.B. (Dublin U) 1908 E,S, 1909 E
Smith, B.A. (Oxford U, Leicester) 1989 NZ, 1990 S,F,W,Arg, 1991 F,W,E,S
Smith, J.H. (London Irish) 1951 F,E,S,W,SA, 1952 F,S,W,E, 1954 NZ,W,F
Smith, R.E. (Lansdowne) 1892 E
Smith, S.J. (Ballymena) 1988 E2,WS,It, 1989 F,W,E,S,NZ, 1990 E, 1991 F,W,E,S,Nm1,2,[Z,S,A], 1992 W,E,S,F,NZ1,2, 1993 S
Smithwick, F.F.S. (Monkstown) 1898 S,W
Smyth, J.T. (QUB) 1920 F
Smyth, P.J. (Belfast Collegians) 1911 E,S,F
Smyth, R.S. (Dublin U) 1903 E,S, 1904 E
Smyth, T. (Malone, Newport) 1908 E,S,W, 1909 E,S,W, 1910 E,S,W,F, 1911 E,S,W, 1912 E
Smyth, W.S. (Belfast Collegians) 1910 W,F, 1920 E
Solomons, B.A.H. (Dublin U) 1908 E,S,W, 1909 E,S,W,F, 1910 E,S,W
Spain, A.W. (UCD) 1924 NZ
Sparrow, W. (Dublin U) 1893 W, 1894 E
Spillane, B.J. (Bohemians) 1985 S,F,W,E, 1986 F,W,E, 1987 F,W,[W,C,A(R)], 1989 E(R)
Spring, D.E. (Dublin U) 1978 S,NZ, 1979 S, 1980 S,F,W, 1981 W
Spring, R.M. (Lansdowne) 1979 F,W,E
Spunner, H.F. (Wanderers) 1881 E,S, 1884 W
Stack, C.R.R. (Dublin U) 1889 S
Stack, G.H. (Dublin U) 1875 E
Staples, J.E. (London Irish, Harlequins) 1991 W,E,S,Nm1,2,[Z,J,S,A], 1992 W,E,NZ1,2,A, 1995 F,W,It,[NZ],Fj, 1996 US,S,F,A, 1997 W,E,S
Steele, H.W. (Ballymena) 1976 E, 1977 F, 1978 F,W,E, 1979 F,W,E,A1,2
Stephenson, G.V. (QUB, London Hosp) 1920 F, 1921 E,S,W,F, 1922 E,S,W,F, 1923 E,S,W,F, 1924 F,E,S,W,NZ, 1925 F,E,S,W, 1926 F,E,S,W, 1927 F,E,S,W,A, 1928 F,E,S,W, 1929 F,E,W, 1930 F,E,S,W
Stephenson, H.W.V. (United Services) 1922 S,W,F, 1924 F,E,S,W,NZ, 1925 F,E,S,W, 1927 A, 1928 E
Stevenson, J. (Dungannon) 1888 M, 1889 S
Stevenson, J.B. (Instonians) 1958 A,E,S,W,F
Stevenson, R. (Dungannon) 1887 E,S,W, 1888 M, 1889 S,W, 1890 S,W,E, 1891 W, 1892 W, 1893 E,S,W
Stevenson, T.H. (Belfast Acad) 1895 E,W, 1896 E,S,W, 1897 E,S
Stewart, A.L. (NIFC) 1913 W,F, 1914 F
Stewart, W.J. (QUB, NIFC) 1922 F, 1924 S, 1928 F,E,S,W, 1929 F,E,S,W
Stoker, E.W. (Wanderers) 1888 W,S
Stoker, F.O. (Wanderers) 1886 S, 1888 W,M, 1889 S, 1891 W
Stokes, O.S. (Cork Bankers) 1882 E, 1884 E
Stokes, P. (Garryowen) 1913 E,S, 1914 F, 1920 E,S,W,F, 1921 E,S,F, 1922 W,F
Stokes, R.D. (Queen's Coll Cork) 1891 S,W
Strathdee, E. (QUB) 1947 E,S,W,A, 1948 W,F, 1949 E,S,W
Stuart, C.P. (Clontarf) 1912 SA
Stuart, I.M.B. (Dublin U) 1924 E,S
Sugars, H.S. (Dublin U) 1905 NZ, 1906 SA, 1907 S
Sugden, M. (Wanderers) 1925 F,E,S,W, 1926 F,E,S,W, 1927 E,S,W,A, 1928 F,E,S,W, 1929 F,E,S,W, 1930 F,E,S,W, 1931 F,E,S,W
Sullivan, D.B. (UCD) 1922 E,S,W,F
Sweeney, J.A. (Blackrock Coll) 1907 E,S,W
Symes, G.R. (Monkstown) 1895 E
Synge, J.S. (Lansdowne) 1929 S

Taggart, T. (Dublin U) 1887 W
Taylor, A.S. (Queen's Coll Belfast) 1910 E,S,W, 1912 F
Taylor, D.R. (Queen's Coll Belfast) 1903 E
Taylor, J. (Belfast Collegians) 1914 E,S,W
Taylor, J.W. (NIFC) 1879 S, 1880 E,S, 1881 S, 1882 E,S, 1883 E,S
Tector, W.R. (Wanderers) 1955 F,E,S
Tedford, A. (Malone) 1902 E,S,W, 1903 E,S,W, 1904 E,S,W, 1905 E,S,W,NZ, 1906 E,S,W,SA, 1907 E,S,W, 1908 E,S,W
Teehan, C. (UCC) 1939 E,S,W
Thompson, C. (Belfast Collegians) 1907 E,S, 1908 E,S,W, 1909 E,S,W,F, 1910 E,S,W,F
Thompson, J.A. (Queen's Coll Belfast) 1885 S1,2
Thompson, J.K.S. (Dublin U) 1921 W, 1922 E,S,F, 1923 E,S,W,F
Thompson, R.G. (Lansdowne) 1882 W
Thompson, R.H. (Instonians) 1951 SA, 1952 F, 1954 NZ,F,E,S,W, 1955 F,S,W, 1956 W
Thornhill, T. (Wanderers) 1892 E,S,W, 1893 E
Thrift, H. (Dublin U) 1904 W, 1905 E,S,W,NZ, 1906 E,W,SA, 1907 E,S,W, 1908 E,S,W, 1909 E,S,W,F
Tierney, D. (UCC) 1938 S,W, 1939 E
Tierney, T. (Garryowne) 1999 A1,2
Tillie, C.R. (Dublin U) 1887 E,S, 1888 W,S
Todd, A.W.P. (Dublin U) 1913 W,F, 1914 F
Topping, J.A. (Ballymena) 1996 WS,A, 1997 It,F,E
Torrens, J.D. (Bohemians) 1938 W, 1939 E,S,W
Tucker, C.C. (Shannon) 1979 F,W, 1980 F(R)
Tuke, B.B. (Bective Rangers) 1890 E, 1891 E,S, 1892 E, 1894 E,S,W, 1895 E,S
Turley, N. (Blackrock Coll) 1962 E
Tweed, D.A. (Ballymena) 1995 F,W,It,[J]

Tydings, J.J. (Young Munster) 1968 A
Tyrrell, W. (QUB) 1910 F, 1913 E,S,W,F, 1914 F,E,S,W

Uprichard, R.J.H. (Harlequins, RAF) 1950 S,W

Waide, S.L. (Oxford U, NIFC) 1932 E,S,W, 1933 E,W
Waites, J. (Bective Rangers) 1886 S, 1888 M, 1889 W, 1890 S,W,E, 1891 E
Waldron, O.C. (Oxford U, London Irish) 1966 S,W, 1968 A
Walker, S. (Instonians) 1934 E,S, 1935 E,S,W,NZ, 1936 E,S,W, 1937 E,S,W, 1938 E,S,W
Walkington, D.B. (NIFC) 1887 E,W, 1888 W, 1890 W,E, 1891 E,S,W
Walkington, R.B. (NIFC) 1875 E, 1876 E, 1877 E,S, 1878 E, 1879 S, 1880 E,S, 1882 E,S
Wall, H. (Dolphin) 1965 S,W
Wallace, Jas (Wanderers) 1904 E,S
Wallace, Jos (Wanderers) 1903 S,W, 1904 E,S,W, 1905 E,S,W,NZ, 1906 W
Wallace, P.S. (Blackrock Coll, Saracens) 1995 [J],Fj, 1996 US,W,E,WS,A, 1997 It,F,W,E,S,NZ,C, 1998 S,F,W,E,SA1,2[Ga,R], 1999 F,W,E,S,It(R),A1,2
Wallace, R.M. (Garryowen, Saracens) 1991 Nm1(R), 1992 W,E,S,F,A, 1993 S,F,W,E,R, 1994 F,W,E,S, 1995 W,It,[NZ,J,W],Fj, 1996 US,S,F,WS, 1998 S,F,W,E
Wallace, T.H. (Cardiff) 1920 E,S,W
Wallis, A.K. (Wanderers) 1892 E,S,W, 1893 E,W
Wallis, C. O'N. (Old Cranleighans, Wanderers) 1935 NZ
Wallis, T.G. (Wanderers) 1921 F, 1922 E,S,W,F
Wallis, W.A. (Wanderers) 1880 S, 1881 E,S, 1882 W, 1883 S
Walmsley, G. (Bective Rangers) 1894 E
Walpole, A. (Dublin U) 1888 S,M
Walsh, E.J. (Lansdowne) 1887 E,S,W, 1892 E,S,W, 1893 E
Walsh, H.D. (Dublin U) 1875 E, 1876 E
Walsh, J.C. (UCC, Sunday's Well) 1960 S,SA, 1961 E,S,F,SA, 1963 E,S,W,NZ, 1964 E,S,W,F, 1965 F,S,W,SA, 1966 F,S,W, 1967 E,S,W,F,A2
Ward, A.J. (Ballynahinch) 1998 F,W,E,SA1,2,[Ga,R],SA, 1999 W,E,S,It(R),A1,2
Ward, A.J.P. (Garryowen, St Mary's Coll, Greystones) 1978 S,F,W,E,NZ, 1979 F,W,E,S, 1981 W,E,S,A, 1983 E(R), 1984 E,S, 1986 S, 1987 [C,Tg]
Warren, J.P. (Kingstown) 1883 E
Warren, R.G. (Lansdowne) 1884 W, 1885 E,S1,2, 1886 E, 1887 E,S,W, 1888 W,S,M, 1889 S,W, 1890 S,W,E
Watson, R. (Wanderers) 1912 SA
Wells, H.G. (Bective Rangers) 1891 S,W, 1894 E,S
Westby, A.J. (Dublin U) 1876 E
Wheeler, G.H. (Queen's Coll Belfast) 1884 S, 1885 E
Wheeler, J.R. (QUB) 1922 E,S,W,F, 1924 E
Whelan, P.C. (Garryowen) 1975 E,S, 1976 NZ, 1977 W,E,S,F, 1978 S,F,W,E,NZ, 1979 F,W,E,S, 1981 F,W,E
White, M. (Queen's Coll Cork) 1906 E,S,W,SA, 1907 E,W
Whitestone, A.M. (Dublin U) 1877 E, 1879 S,E, 1880 E, 1883 S
Whittle, D. (Bangor) 1988 F
Wilkinson, C.R. (Malone) 1993 S
Wilkinson, R.W. (Wanderers) 1947 A
Williamson, F.W. (Dolphin) 1930 E,S,W
Willis, W.J. (Lansdowne) 1879 E
Wilson, F. (CIYMS) 1977 W,E,S
Wilson, H.G. (Glasgow U, Malone) 1905 E,S,W,NZ, 1906 E,S,W,SA, 1907 E,S,W, 1908 E,S,W, 1909 E,S,W, 1910 W
Wilson, W.H. (Bray) 1877 E,S
Withers, H.H.C. (Army, Blackheath) 1931 F,E,S,W,SA
Wolfe, E.J. (Armagh) 1882 E
Wood, G.H. (Dublin U) 1913 W, 1914 F
Wood, B.G.M. (Garryowen) 1954 E,S, 1956 F,E,S,W, 1957 F,E,S,W, 1958 A,E,S,W,F, 1959 E,S,W,F, 1960 E,S,W,F,SA, 1961 E,S,W,F,SA
Wood, K.G.M. (Garryowen, Harlequins), 1994 A1,2,US, 1995 E,S,[J], 1996 A, 1997 It,F,NZ,It, 1998 S,F,W,E,SA1,2,[R(R)],SA, 1999 F,W,E,S,It(R),A1,2
Woods, D.C. (Bessbrook) 1888 M, 1889 S
Woods, N.K.P.J. (Blackrock Coll) 1994 A1,2, 1995 E,F, 1996 F,W,E
Wright, R.A. (Monkstown) 1912 S

Yeates, R.A. (Dublin U) 1889 S,W
Young, G. (UCC) 1913 E
Young, R.M. (Collegians) 1965 F,E,S,W,SA, 1966 F,E,S,W, 1967 W,F, 1968 W,A, 1969 F,E,S,W, 1970 SA,F,E,S,W, 1971 F,E,S,W

APPENDIX 9

FATHERS, SONS AND BROTHERS

Fathers, sons and brothers who have played for Ireland. In each instance the year of first cap is given.

Father, Son and Grandson

N.F. Murphy (Cork Constitution) 1930
N.A. Murphy (Cork Constitution) 1958
K.J. Murphy (Cork Constitution) 1990

Father and Two Sons

G. Collopy (Bective Rangers) 1891
W.P. Collopy (Bective Rangers) 1914
R. Collopy (Bective Rangers) 1923
H.R. McKibbin (Queen's U and Instonians) 1938
C.H. McKibbin (Instonians) 1976
A.R. McKibbin (Instonians and London Irish) 1977

Father and Son

W. Hallaran (Dublin University) 1884
C.F. Hallaran (United Services) 1921

A.D. Clinch (Dublin U and Wanderers) 1885
J.D. Clinch (Dublin U and Wanderers) 1924

W. Collis (Wanderers) 1884
W.R. Collis (Harlequins and KCH) 1924

S. Deering (Bective Rangers) 1935
S.M. Deering (Garryowen and St Mary's College) 1974

B.O. Foley (Shannon) 1976
A.G. Foley (Shannon) 1995

T.R. Hewitt (Queen's U) 1925
D. Hewitt (Queen's U and Instonians) 1958

S.T. Irwin (Queen's U) 1900
J.W.S. Irwin (NIFC) 1938

N.F. Murphy (Cork Constitution) 1930
N.A. Murphy (Cork Constitution) 1958

N.A. Murphy (Cork Constitution) 1958
K.J. Murphy (Cork Constitution) 1990

P.F. Murray (Wanderers) 1927
J.B. Murray (UCD) 1963

F. Schute (Wanderers) 1978
F.G. Schute (Dublin U) 1913

B.G.M. Wood (Garryowen and Lansdowne) 1954
K.G.M. Wood (Garryowen and Harlequins) 1994

Three Brothers

E. Doran (Lansdowne) 1890
G.P. Doran (Lansdowne) 1899
B.R. Doran (Lansdowne) 1900

A.J. Forrest (Wanderers) 1880
E.G. Forrest (Wanderers) 1889
H. Forrest (Wanderers) 1893

T.A. Harvey (Dublin U) 1900
A.D. Harvey (Wanderers) 1903
F.M.W. Harvey (Wanderers) 1907

T.R. Hewitt (Queen's U) 1924
F.S. Hewitt (Instonians) 1926
V.A. Hewitt (Instonians) 1935

W.E. Johnstone (Dublin U) 1884
R.W. Johnstone (Dublin U) 1890
R. Johnstone (Wanderers) 1893

S. McVicker (Queen's U) 1922
J. McVicker (Collegians) 1924
H. McVicker (Army) 1927

D.F. Moore (Wanderers) 1883
F.W. Moore (Wanderers) 1884
C.M. Moore (Dublin U) 1887

J. Pedlow (Bessbrook) 1882
T.B. Pedlow (Queen's U) 1889
R. Pedlow (Bessbrook) 1891

D.J. Ross (Belfast Albion) 1884
J.P. Ross (Lansdowne) 1885
J.F. Ross (NIFC) 1886

T. Smyth (Malone) 1908
W.S. Smyth (Collegians) 1910
P.J. Smyth (Collegians) 1911

Two Brothers

C. Glynn Allen (Derry, Liverpool) 1896
C. Elliott Allen (Derry, Liverpool) 1900

George R. Beamish (Coleraine, RAF) 1925
Charles E. Beamish (Coleraine, RAF) 1935

H. Brown (Windsor) 1877
T. Brown (Windsor) 1877

L.Q. Bulger (Dublin U, Lansdowne) 1896
M.J. Bulger (Dublin U, Lansdowne) 1899

S.J. Byrne (Lansdowne, UCD) 1953
F. Byrne (UCD) 1962

W.P. Collopy (Bective Rangers) 1914
R. Collopy (Bective Rangers) 1923

M.P. Crowe (Lansdowne) 1929
P. Crowe (Blackrock Coll) 1935

M. Deering (Bective Rangers) 1929
S.J. Deering (Bective Rangers) 1935

C.J. Dick (Ballymena) 1961
J.S. Dick (Queen's U) 1962

M. Doyle (Cambridge U, Blackrock Coll) 1965
T. Doyle (Wanderers) 1968

C. Feighery (Lansdowne) 1972
T. Feighery (St Mary's Coll) 1977

E. Galbraith (Dublin U) 1875
R. Galbraith (Dublin U) 1875

W. Gardiner (NIFC) 1892
F.T. Gardiner (NIFC) 1900

L.H. Gwynn (Dublin U) 1894
A.P. Gwynn (Dublin U) 1895

J. Heron (NIFC) 1877
W.T. Heron (NIFC) 1880

W.R. Hunter (CIYMS) 1962
L. Hunter (Civil Service) 1968

P. Kavanagh (UCD) 1952
R. Kavanagh (UCD, Wanderers) 1953

F. Kennedy (Wanderers) 1880
J.M. Kennedy (Wanderers) 1882

J. Lyttle (NIFC) 1889
J.H. Lyttle (NIFC) 1894

L.M. Magee (Bective Rangers, London Irish) 1895
J.T. Magee (Bective Rangers) 1895

E.H. McIlwaine (NIFC) 1895
J.E. McIlwaine (NIFC) 1897

H.R. McKibbin (Queen's U, Instonians) 1938
D.E. McKibbin (Instonians) 1950

C.H. McKibbon (Instonians) 1976
A.R. McKibbin (Instonians, London Irish) 1977

R.J. McLoughlin (Gosforth, Blackrock Coll) 1962
F. McLoughlin (Northern) 1976

R.B. Montgomery (Queen's U, Cambridge U) 1887
A. Montgomery (NIFC) 1895

H. Moore (Windsor) 1876
W. Moore (Queen's U) 1878

Jack O'Connor (Garryowen) 1895
Joe O'Connor (Garryowen) 1910

B. O'Driscoll (Manchester) 1971
J. O'Driscoll (London Irish) 1978

K.P. O'Flanagan (London Irish) 1947
M. O'Flanagan (Lansdowne) 1949

T.O. Pike (Lansdowne) 1927
V.J. Pike (Lansdowne) 1931

M. Ryan (Rockwell Coll) 1897
J. Ryan (Rockwell Coll) 1897

D. Scott (Malone) 1961
R.D. Scott (Queen's U) 1967

Donal Spring (Dublin U, Lansdowne) 1978
Dick Spring (Lansdowne) 1979

G.V. Stephenson (Queen's U, United Services) 1920
H.W. Stephenson (United Services) 1922

R. Stevenson (Lisburn, NIFC, Dungannon) 1887
J. Stevenson (Lisburn, NIFC, Dungannon) 1888

F.O. Stoker (Wanderers) 1886
E.W. Stoker (Wanderers) 1888

R.B. Walkington (NIFC) 1875
D.B. Walkington (Dublin U) 1887

Joseph Wallace (Wanderers) 1902
James Wallace (Wanderers) 1904

R.M. Wallace (Garryowen and Saracens) 1991
P.S. Wallace (Blackrock Coll and Saracens) 1995

W.A. Wallis (Wanderers) 1881
A.K. Wallis (Wanderers) 1892

APPENDIX 10

IRISH UNIVERSITIES OVERSEAS TOURS

Tour to New Zealand

2–29 JULY 1978

Playing Party (25 + 1)

Backs

J.P.K. Barry (UCC)
P.A.M. Shaffrey (UCD)
M.C. Finn (UCC)
C. Gardiner (QUB)
M.P. McIlpatrick (QUB)
A.W. Irwin (QUB)
R.G.A. Finn (UCD)
P.A. Joyce (UCD)
D.J.B. Coakley (UCD)
P. Rolls (UCC)
J.C. Robbie (DU) Capt.
R.H. Stewart (QUB)

Forwards

J.G. Langbroek (DU)
T.F. Kavanagh (UCD)
H.A.M. McGuire (UCG)
J.L. Cantrell (UCD)
N.J. Ardiss (QUB)
J.J. Holland (UCC)
D.E.J. Spring (DU)
B.A.S. Mays (UCD)
S.R. Hall (UCD)
A.F. O'Leary (UCC)
C.D. Cantillon (UCC)
R.K. Kearney (UCD)
M.E. Gibson (DU)

Rep. on Tour W.J.M. Ryan (DU for Rolls)
Hon. Manager Dr Malcolm Little (UCG)
Coach T.W.R. (Roly) Meates (DU)
Played 9; won 6, lost 3
Points for 110
Points against 67

Tour to Japan and South Korea

17 SEPTEMBER–3 OCTOBER 1987

Playing Party 26

Backs

F.J. Dunlea (DU)
J.M. Fanagan (UCD)
J.F. Sexton (DU)
E.M. Howlett (UCD)
J.C. Riordan (UCC)
J.P. Mulhall (UCD) Capt.
R.P. Hernan (UCD)
D.B.M. Hyland (UCC)
P. Bell (DU)
E. Crotty (UCC)
S.M.K. O'Beirne (UCD)
C.J.F. McCarthy (UCG)

Forwards

R.A. Ward (UCD)
J. Feehan (DU)
R. Murray (DU)
P.J. Kenny (DU)
J.A. O'Riordan (UCG)
J.P.P. Colclough (UCD)
J.J. O'Callaghan (UCG)
J.C. Collins (DU)
B. Murray (QUB)
D.P.S. Sheehan (DU)
D. Caughey (QUB)
P.J. Swan (UCD)
K. Byrne (UCC)
M.S. Egan (DU)

Hon. Manager Dr Jim McKelvey (QUB)
Hon. Ass. Manager Trevor West (DU)
Coach T.W.R. (Roly) Meates (DU)
Played 6; won 5, lost 1
Points for 167
Points against 75

Tour to South Africa

29 JUNE–19 JULY 1994

Playing Party 30

Backs

D.J. Crotty (UCC)
P.T.J. Barr (UCD)
R.T. McIlreavy (DU)
R. Browne (DU)
B. Kenny (UCG)
K. Jess (QUB)
S.R. Tynan (DU)
K.M. McCarthy (UCD)
D.J. Blewitt (QUB)
D.G. Humphreys (QUB) Capt.
K.P. Keane (UCD)
J. Kenefick (UCC)
K.E.C. Hilman (QUB)

Forwards

D.E. Cole (DU)
J. O'Driscoll (UCC)
M. Cox (DU)
P.A. Walsh (UCD)
B. Heffernan (UCC)
K.A. Synnott (DU)
H.J. Kos (UCD)
G.W. Longwell (QUB)
H. Farrelly (UCC)
A.G. Dick (QUB)
G. Tuohy (UCC)
C. McCarthy (DU)
J. Canning (UCC)
N. Ryan (DU)
G.S. McConkey (UCD)
G. Heaslip (UCG)
K. Spicer (UCD)

Hon. Manager Dr Len Harty (UCC)
Hon. Ass. Manager John West (DU)
Coach Finbar Dennehy (UCC)
Physiotherapist Brian Sommerville (QUB)
Press Officer Darragh O'Mahony (UCD)
On field co-ordinator David Hurley (UCD)

Played 7; won 4, lost 3
Points for 207
Points against 129

Tour to Australia

11 JULY–9 AUGUST 1997

Playing Party 30

BACKS
R. Morrow (QUB) Capt.
C. Kilroy (UCG)
J. Kelly (UCC)
A. Hood (QUB)
D. McElligott (DU)
A. Turtle (DU)
A. Clarke (QUB)
A.D. O'Shea (UCC)
P. Stewart (QUB)
J. O'Mahony (UCC)
R. Wallace (DU)
P. Spence (QUB)
P.A. Stringer (UCC)

FORWARDS
A.C. McSweeney (UCC)
R. Laffin (UCC)
J.W.L. McKee (DU)
B. Hall (QUB)
R. Weir (QUB)
H.W. O'Neill (UCC)
J.K. Ryan (UCD)
M.R. O'Driscoll (UCC)
W.J. Fitzgerald (UCC)
R.J. Powell (UCD)
F. Twomey (UCC)
P. Lynch (UCG)
W.B. Robb (DU)
R. Dunlop (QUB)
G.B. Cantrell (UCD)
C. Kehelly (UCC)
D. Finn (UCD)

Hon. Manager John West (DU)
Management Assistant Bruce St J. Blake (UCG)
Coaches Ray Pattison (QUB), Phil Lawlor (IRFU)
Medical Officer Dr William O'Flynn (UCG)
Physiotherapist Dick O'Hanlon (UCG)
Press Officer/Bagman Diarmuid Murphy (UCC)

Played 7; won 4, lost 3
Points for 265
Points against 124

APPENDIX 11

IRISH UNIVERSITIES INTERNATIONAL RESULTS

(UP TO AND INCLUDING 1997–98)

Date	Venue
Sat. 6.3.54	Ravenhill, Irish U 3 Scottish U 5
Sat. 7.5.55	Parc des Princes, French U* 22 Irish U 11
Sat. 7.1.56	Sale, Cheshire, English U 6 Irish U 16
Wed. 2.1.57	Ravenhill, Irish U 12 South African U 0
Sat. 15.1.57	Donnybrook, Irish U 17 English U 9
Sat. 3.5.58	Stade Jean Bouin, Paris, French U 25 Irish U 14
Thur. 1.1.59	Gosforth, English U 3 Irish U 17
Sat. 2.1.60	Donnybrook, Irish U 19 English U 5
Sat. 9.4.60	Donnybrook, Irish U 12 Welsh U 3
Wed. 10.1.62	Ravenhill, Irish U 9 Scottish U 3
Wed. 17.10.62	Ravenhill, Irish U 32 Canada 8
Wed. 13.1.65	Craiglochart, Edinburgh, Scottish U 6 Irish U 14
Tues. 6.4.65	Thomond Park, Irish U 12 South Africa 10
Wed. 5.1.66	Donnybrook, Irish U 14 Scottish U 10
Wed. 23.10.68	Musgrave Park, Irish U 3 Australia 11
Sun. 11.5.69	Stade Jean Bouin, Paris, French U* 19 Irish U 11
Wed. 6.11.74	Mardyke, Irish U 3 New Zealand 10
Sat. 13.3.76	Mardyke, Irish U 18 New Zealand U 16
Sun. 5.2.78	Donnybrook, Irish U 24 Scottish U 6
Sun. 16.7.78	Athletic Pk, Wellington, New Zealand U 15 Irish U 10
Sat. 22.7.78	Carisbrook, Dunedin, New Zealand U 4 Irish U 18
Fri. 2.3.79	Stirling U, Scottish U 9 Irish U 39
Thur. 17.1.80	Motspur Pk, Surrey, English U 8 Irish U 10
Fri. 6.3.81	Belfield Bowl, Irish U 12 English U 0
Wed. 24.2.82	Birkenhead Pk, English U 15 Irish U 25
Wed. 28.4.82	Nice, French U 33 Irish U 15
Fri. 18.2.83	College Pk, Irish U 12 French U 7
Fri. 18.3.83	Donnybrook, Irish U 14 English U 3
Sat. 21.1.84	Stade Jean Bouin, Paris, French U 20 Irish U 8
Mon. 12.3.84	Wyncote, Liverpool, English U 10 Irish U 28
Sat. 9.2.85	College Pk, Irish U 9 New Zealand U 33
Fri. 1.3.85	Anglesea Rd, Irish U 6 French U 23
Thur. 26.9.85	Ravenhill, Irish U 37 Tunisia 8
Fri. 31.1.86	Stade de Begles, Bordeaux, French U 18 Irish U 3
Fri. 14.2.86	College Pk, Irish U 20 Welsh U 7
Fri. 28.2.86	Southampton, English U 10 Irish U 8
Fri. 14.3.86	Belfield, Irish U 40 Scottish U 6
Thur. 8.1.87	Mardyke, Irish U 30 English U 6
Wed. 18.2.87	Penarth, Welsh U 27 Irish U 12
Fri. 20.3.87	College Pk, Irish U 9 French U 11

Thur. 17.9.87	Seoul, South Korea 12 Irish U 15
Wed. 30.9.87	Kobe, West Japan, Japanese U 9 Irish U 29
Sat. 3.10.87	Olympic Stadium, Tokyo, Japan U 12 Irish U 24
Wed. 13.1.88	Mardyke, Irish U 12 Welsh U 9
Fri. 19.2.88	Le Havre, French U 29 Irish U 15
Fri. 20.1.89	Mardyke, Irish U 7 French U 22
Fri. 10.2.89	Pandy Pk, Cross Keys, Welsh U 23 Irish U 27
Wed. 1.3.89	Preston Grasshoppers, English U 3 Irish U 22
Fri. 19.1.90	Sunbury, English U 18 Irish U 34
Fri. 2.3.90	Reims, French U 19 Irish U 13
Fri. 23.3.90	College Pk, Irish U 25 Welsh U 4
Fri. 1.2.91	Mardyke, Irish U 9 French U 7
Fri. 15.2.91	St Julians, Newport, Welsh U 3 Irish U 27
Fri. 1.3.91	College Pk, Irish U 17 English U 16
Fri. 8.3.91	Ravenhill, Irish U 3 Japanese U 22
Fri. 17.1.92	College Pk, Irish U 43 Welsh U 10
Fri. 31.1.92	Richmond, English U 26 Irish U 11
Fri. 21.3.92	Nancy, French U 42 Irish U 9
Fri. 19.2.93	Thomond Pk, Irish U 16 French U 25
Fri. 5.3.93	Pandy Pk, Cross Keys, Welsh U 20 Irish U 18
Sun. 21.3.93	Donnybrook, Irish U 8 English U 44
Fri. 14.1.94	Rennes, French U 50 Irish U 6
Sun. 6.2.94	Anglesea Rd, Irish U 39 Welsh U 0
Tues. 19.7.94	Auckland Pk, Jo'burg, South African Studs+ 24 Irish U 19
Wed. 9.11.94	Mardyke, Irish U 11 USA 9
Fri. 4.2.95	Peffer Mill, Edinburgh, Scottish U 17 Irish U 22
Fri. 17.3.95	Llan Wern, Welsh U 5 Irish U 12
Fri. 5.1.96	Sale, Cheshire, English U 23 Irish U 30
Fri. 19.1.96	College Pk, Irish U 43 Scottish U 9
Fri. 1.3.96	College Pk, Irish U 21 Welsh U 22
Fri. 31.1.97	Cyn Coed, Cardiff, Welsh U 11 Irish U 19
Fri. 14.2.97	College Pk, Irish U 40 English U 14
Fri. 28.2.97	Peffer Mill, Edinburgh, Scottish U 5 Irish U 27
Wed. 6.8.97	Sydney No. 1 Oval, Australian U 31 Irish U 17
Fri. 6.2.98	Anglesea Rd, Irish U 25 Scottish U 11
Fri. 6.3.98	Chalons-sur-Marne, French U 35 Irish U 11
Fri. 20.3.98	College Pk, Irish U 44 Welsh U 24
Fri. 3.4.98	Rosslyn Pk, English U 30 Irish U 80
Fri. 5.2.99	Crowley Park, Irish U 29 French U 38
Fri. 19.2.99	Llanrumney, Welsh U 26 Irish U 8
Fri. 5.3.99	College Park, Irish U 8 English U 22
Fri. 19.3.99	Peppermill, Scottish U 14 Irish Un 24

* French student players doing military service *en route* to universities and teacher training colleges.
+ South African Technical Colleges

	P	W	D	L	F	A	±	
v A	1	0	0	1	3	11	–8	15
v AU	1	0	0	1	17	31	–14	16
v CAN	1	1	0	0	32	8	+24	15
v EU	19	16	0	3	438	249	+189	307
v FU	17	2	0	15	175	407	–232	273
v J	1	1	0	0	24	12	+12	16
v JU	2	1	0	1	32	31	+1	33
v NZ	1	0	0	1	3	10	–7	15
v NZU	4	2	0	2	55	68	–13	91
v SA	1	1	0	0	12	10	+2	15
v SAU	2	1	0	1	31	24	+7	32
v SK	1	1	0	0	15	12	+3	15
v SU	11	10	0	1	260	87	+173	175
v T	1	1	0	0	37	8	+29	16
v US	1	1	0	0	11	9	+2	16
v WU	14	11	0	3	331	168	+163	227
	78	49	0	29	1,476	1,145	+331	

APPENDIX 12

IRISH UNIVERSITIES PLAYERS

+ Denotes International

AHERNE D.M. (UCC) E79/80, E81/82, F81/82
AHERNE J.F. (UCG) W88/89, E 88/89
+AHERNE L.F.P. (UCC) F84/85, F85/86, W85/86, E85/86, S85/86
+ANDERSON F.E. (QUB) S53/54
ARCHIBOLD P. (QUB) F97/98(R), W97/98, E97/98
ARDISS N.J. (QUB) S77/78, NZU 77/78, 2(R)
ARMSTRONG C.J. (QUB) E86/87, W86/87, F86/87
ARGYLE C.M.R. (DU) SA64/65

BAINBRIDGE A.M. (UCD) E98/99(R), S98/99(R)
BARLOW P. (DU) W90/91
BARR P.T.J. (UCD) W93/94
BARRY J.P.K. (UCC) W77/78, NZU77/78, 1,2, E81/82, F81/82
BARRY P.J. (UCC) F97/98(R), W97/98(R), E97/98
BEAMISH S.H. (QUB) F68/69
BELL P. (DU) K,J87/88
BENNER N. (UCC) S94/95
BEVAN R. (UCC) F82/83, E82/83
BEVERLAND S. (UCD) E81/82
BIELENBERG C.A. (DU) CAN62/63
BLACK B. (QUB) E81/82, F81/82
BLAIR A.C. (DU) E80/81, E81/82
BLAKE I.P. (DU) W94/95
BLEWITT D.J. (QUB) E92/93
BOURKE A. de V. (DU) S64/65
BOYLE J. (QUB) E59/60, W59/60
+BRADY A.M. (UCD) S65/66

BRADY R.C. (QUB) F82/83, E82/83, F83/84, E83/84
BREDIN P.J. (UCD) E98/99, S98/99(R)
+BRENNAN J.I. (TCD) S53/54, SAU56/57
+BRESNIHAN F.P.K. (UCD) S64/65, S65/66
+BROPHY N.H. (UCD) E55/56, SAU56/57, E56/57, F57/58, E58/59
BROUGHALL D. (UCD) S98/99
BROWNE M. (UCG) A68/69, F68/69
BROWNE R. (DU) SAU93/94, S94/95, W94/95
BUCKLEY D. (UCC) W76/77
BURNS W.P.J. (UCD) F82/83, E82/83, F83/84, E83/84, NZU84/85, F84/85
BYRNE R.M. (UCD) E83/84, F84/85, T85/86, F85/86, W85/86, E85/86, S85/86
+BYRNE N.F. (UCD) W59/60
BYRNE K. (UCC) F85/86, W85/86, E85/86, E86/87, W86/87, F86/87 K87/88

CAHILL B.A. (UCC) S98/99(R)
CAHILL T.J. (UCC) F98/99, W98/99, E98/99(R)
CAMPBELL C.P. (QUB) E86/87
CANNING J. (UCC) F92/93, W92/93, E92/93, F93/94(R), SAU93/94(R), W94/95(R)
CANTILLON C.D. (UCC) NZ74/75, S77/78, NZU77/78 1,2
+CANTRELL J.L. (UCD) NZ74/75, NZU75/76, W76/77, NZU77/78 1,2
CANTWELL G.B. (UCD) W96/97, S96/97, AU96/97, E97/98
CAREY B. (UCD) W94/95, E95/96
CAREY M.A. (UCD) S64/65, SA64/65
CARNEY V.M. (UCD) W77/78, F88/89, E88/89
+CARR N.J. (QUB) E79/80, E80/81, E81/82, F81/82, F82/83, E82/83
CARROLL J.W. (UCC) W87/88, F87/88
CARROLL R.N. (UCD) W59/60
CASSIDY P.J. (UCG) CAN62/63
CATERS W.N. (QUB) E55/56, E56/57
CAUGHEY D. (QUB) T85/86, K,J87/88
CLANCY J.A. (UCG/UCD) SAU56/57, E56/57, F57/58, E58/59
CLARKE A. (QUB) W96/97, E96/97, S96/97, AU96/97
CLINCH P.D. (DU) F81/82, F83/84, E83/84, NZU84/85, F84/85, T85/86, F85/86, W85/86, E85/86, S85/86
COAKLEY D.J.B. (UCD) NZU75/76, W76/77, S77/78, W77/78, NZU77/78, 1,2, S78/79, E79/80, E80/81
CODY W. (DU) F84/85
COEN D. (UCD) F91/92
COLCLOUGH J.P.P. (UCD) F83/84, E83/84, NZU84/85, F85/86, E85/86, E86/87, W86/87, F86/87, J,K87/88
COLE D.E. (DU) E92/93, F93/94, W93/94, SAU93/94, US94/95, S94/95, W94/95
COLEMAN P.L.R. (UCC) F88/89, W88/89(R)
COLLINS J.C. (DU) W85/86, E86/87, W86/87, F86/87, J87/88, F87/88
+COLLINS P.C. (UCC) S78/79, E79/80, E80/81, E81/82, F82/83, E82/83
COLLINS R. (UCC) S97/98
CONNOLLY M.J.S. (UCD) F83/84, E83/84, T85/86, E85/86(R), S85/86
CORLEY M.A. (UCG) A68/69
COUGHLAN N.C. (UCD) W98/99(R)
COULTER J.E.M. (QUB) T85/86
COVENEY R.G. (UCC) W93/94, S94/95
CRAWFORD R.C. (QUB) A68/69
CROMIE T.A. (QUB) F92/93, W92/93
CROSS G.B. (UCD) F57/58
+CROTTY D.J. (UCC) F92/93, SAU93/94, US94/95, E95/96
CROTTY E. (UCC) E86/87, F86/87, JU87/88, W87/88, F88/89, W88/89, E88/89
CROTTY J.M. (UCC) F82/83, E82/83, F83/84, E83/84, NZU84/85, F84/85, T85/86, F85/86, S85/86
+CROWE J.F. (UCD) NZ74/75
CROWE P.H. (UCD) S53/54
CROWTHER S.M. (QUB) F89/90(R), JU90/91(R)
CULHANE P. (UCC) NZU84/85, F84/85, T85/86, F85/86, W85/86, S85/86
CULLEN R.N. (QUB) W86/87
CULLITON M.W.B. (UCC) F85/86, S85/86, W86/87, W87/88, F87/88
+CUNNINGHAM J.L. (DU) E96/97, S96/97
CUNNINGHAM M.J. (UCC) F54/55
CURNEEN C.P. (DU) F98/99(R), W98/99(R), E98/99, S98/99(R

DALY D. (UCC) E79/80
DARRAGH C. (QUB) T85/86(R), E85/86
+DAVIDSON J.C. (QUB) S64/65, SA64/65, NZ74/75
DAVIES R. (DU) F68/69
DEE P.F. (DU) NZ74/75
DEERING K.J. (UCC) S78/79(R), F83/84, E83/84
+DEERING S.M. (UCD) A68/69, F68/69
DENNEHY F. (UCC) E81/82, F81/82
DERHAM P.D. (UCC) S78/79(R), E79/80, E81/82, F81/82
DICK A.G. (QUB) E92/93
DICK C. (QUB) W86/87, F87/88(R)
+DICK C.J. (QUB) F57/58, E58/59, E59/60, W59/60
+DICK J. (QUB) S61/62

DIXON A.J. (DU) W85/86, E85/86, S85/86
DOGGETT S.R. (UCD) F97/98, W97/98
DONEGAN M.J. (UCC) E55/56
DONEGAN P.J. (UCC) E55/56
DONNELLY G. (UCC) F90/91, W90/91, E90/91, JU90/91, W91/92, E91/92
DONNELLY V. (UCC) W87/88, F87/88(R)
DONOVAN A. (UCD) F92/93, W92/93, E92/93, W93/94, US94/95, S94/95
DONOVAN D.P. (DU) A68/69
DORRITY M. (QUB) F89/90, W89/90
DOWSE P.R.C. (DU) F54/55, SAU56/57, E56/57, F57/58, E58/59
DOYLE G. (UCC) NZU84/85, F84/85
+DOYLE M.G.M. (UCD) S61/62, CAN62/63, S64/65
DUFFY G. (DU) F90/91, W90/91, E90/91, JU90/91, W91/92, E91/92, F91/92
DUFFY J. (UCD) E81/82, F81/82, F82/83, E82/83
+DUNLEA F.J. (DU) F83/84, E83/84, NZU84/85, F84/85, T85/86, F85/86, W85/86, E85/86, S85/86, E86/87, F86/87, J87/88, F87/88
DUNLOP R. (QUB) E96/97, F97/98(R), W97/98(R)
DUNNE C.C. (UCD) T85/86, F85/86, W85/86, E85/86, S86/87
DWYER M.J.M. (UCD) F87/88

ENDALL A.C. (DU) E58/59
EDWARDS M. (DU) W96/97, E96/97, S96/97
EGAN M.S. (DU) S85/86, E86/87, F86/87, JU,J87/88, F87/88
ELLIOTT D. (QUB) F82/83, E82/83, F83/84

FAHY T.J. (UCD) E55/56, SAU56/57, E56/57
FANAGAN J.M. (UCD) F86/87(R), K,JU87/88
FARRELLY H. (UCC) SA93/94(R)
FEDDIS P. (UCD) T85/86
FEEHAN J. (DU) E86/87, F86/87, K,JU,J87/88, F87/88
+FEIGHERY T.A.D. (UCD) A68/69, F68/69
FINEGAN R.A.J. (UCD) E89/90, F89/90, W89/90, F91/92
FINN D. (UCD) W96/97, E96/97, S96/97, AU96/97
+FINN M.C. (UCC) W77/78, NZU77/78 1,2
+FINN R.G.A. (UCD) NZ74/75, NZU75/76, W76/77, NZU77/78 1,2
FITZGERALD D.C. (DU) E79/80, E80/81
FITZGERALD G. (UCC) W77/78
FITZGERALD J. (UCC) NZU75/76
FITZGERALD W.J. (UCC) S95/96(R), E96/97, S96/97, AU96/97, S97/98, F97/98, W97/98, E97/98
+FITZGIBBON M.J.J. (DU) NZU84/85, E86/87, W86/87, F86/87, F87/88

FITZPATRICK D.J. (DU) W59/60
+FITZPATRICK M.P. (DU) NZ74/75, NZU75/76
FITZSIMONS M.J. (UCD) E56/57, F57/58
FLANNERY J.P. (UCC) S97/98(R), F97/98, W97/98, E97/98
FORTUNE J.M. (UCD) NZU75/76, W76/77
+FULCHER G.M. (UCD) W91/92, E91/92
FULLERTON J.R. (DU) SAU56/57
+FURLONG J.N. (UCG) W91/92

GAHAN P.J. (UCD) NZ74/75
GALLICK K. (QUB) W88/89, E88/89, E89/90, F89/90
GARDINER C. (QUB) NZU77/78 1,2
GARDINER J.L. (UCD) E82/83
+GASTON J.T. (DU) S53/54, F54/55
GIBNEY E.E. (UCD) E56/57
+GIBSON M.E. (DU) NZU75/76, W76/77, S77/78, W77/78, NZU77/78 1,2
GILL G.P. (UCD) S65/66
GILLESPIE S. (QUB) W91/92, E91/92, F91/92
+GILPIN F.G. (QUB) CAN62/63
+GLASS D.C. (QUB) F54/55, E55/56
GLEESON T.M. (UCC) F54/55
+GLENNON B.T. (UCD) E89/90, W89/90
GLYNN W.G. (UCG) SA64/65
+GODFREY R.P. (UCD) F54/55
+GRACE T.D. (UCD) F68/69
GRAY I.R.H. (QUB) F92/93, E92/93
GREALLY J. (UCG) E59/60, W59/60
+GREGG R.J. (QUB) S53/54, F54/55
GRIFFIN J.F. (UCD) F88/89, W88/89
GRIMSHAW M.N. (QUB) S64/65, SA64/65, A68/69, F68/69

HALDANE J.B. (QUB) F57/58, E58/59
HALL B. (QUB) S96/97
HALL S.R. (UCD) NZU75/76, W76/77, W77/78, NZU77/78 1,2
HALY C.M. (UCC) F88/89, W88/89, E89/90, W89/90, W91/92
HAMILTON N.G. (QUB) F57/58, E58/59
HAMPTON D. (QUB) E90/91(R), JU90/91
HANNA C. (DU) E80/81
+HARBISON T.H. (UCD) S78/79, E80/81
HARLEY J.R. (QUB) W87/88, F87/88, F88/89, W88/89, E88/89, E89/90, F89/90, W89/90, F90/91, W90/91, E90/91, JU90/91
HARRISON T.D. (QUB) W76/77
HARVEY G.O. (UCD) F91/92, W92/93, E92/93
HAWKESWORTH C.J. (DU) A68/69
HAYES B. (UCD) S96/97(R)

HEALY C.H. (UCC) S97/98, F97/98, E97/98
HEASLIP G. (UCG) US94/95
HEASLIP R. (DU) E95/96, S95/96
HEFFERNAN B. (UCC) F93/94, SAU93/94
+HENDERSON N.J. (QUB) SAU56/57
HERNAN D.C.S. (UCD) F90/91, E90/91
HERNAN R.P. (UCD) F85/86, J,K87/88
HERNAN R.M. (UCD) W88/89, E88/89
HEWITT A.D. (QUB) F89/90, F90/91, W91/92, E91/92, F91/92
HEWITT A. (QUB) E59/60, W59/60
+HEWITT D. (QUB) F57/58, E58/59, E59/60
HEYWOOD D.S. (DU) S65/66
HICKIE A.J. (UCD) S64/65, SA64/65, S65/66
+HICKIE D.A. (UCD) US94/95(R)
HIGGINS A.J. (UCG) F88/89, W88/89, E88/89
HILL J.J. (UCC) W59/60
HILMAN K.E.C. (QUB) W93/94
HINKSON P.A. (UCD) F82/83
HITCHCOCK C.T. (UCG) S78/79, E79/80, E80/81, E81/82
+HOLLAND J.J. (UCC) NZU75/76, W76/77, S77/78, W77/78, NZU77/78 1,2, S78/79, E79/80
HOLT D. (UCC) S97/98, F97/98, W97/98
HOOD A. (QUB) E95/96, S95/96, W95/96, W96/97, E96/97(R), AU96/97
+HOOKS K.J. (QUB) E80/81, E81/82, F81/82, E82/83
HOSTY C.J.M. (UCG) T85/86, F85/86, W85/86, E85/86, S85/86
+HOUSTON K.J. (QUB) S61/62
HOWARD D. (UCC) E82/83, F83/84, E83/84
HOWARD W.T.J. (QUB) W76/77, S78/79
HOWLETT E.M. (UCD) F86/87, J87/88
+HUMPHREYS D.G. (QUB) F92/93, F93/94, W93/94, SAU93/94
HURLEY J.G. (UCC) W77/78
HUTCHINSON R.C. (DU) F68/69
HYLAND B.M.T. (UCC) E89/90
HYLAND D.B.M. (UCC) E86/87, W86/87, S86/87, JU87/88
HYLAND D.F. (UCD) W87/88

IRWIN A.W. (QUB) W77/78, NZU77/78 1,2, E80/81
+IRWIN D.G. (QUB) S78/79, E79/80
IVESTON W.B. (QUB) E79/80

+JOHNS P.S.C. (DU) E89/90, F89/90, W89/90, F90/91 W90/91, JU90/91
JONES J.N. (QUB) S65/66
JOHNSTON C.J. (UCD) E92/93
JOYCE C. (QUB) F97/98(R), W97/98(R), E97/98(R)
JOYCE P.A. (UCD) W77/78

KAHN J. (UCC) W91/92, E91/92
+KAVANAGH J.R. (UCD) SAU 56/57
KAVANAGH T.F. (UCD) W77/78
KEANE C.G. (UCD) S97/98, F97/98, W97/98, E97/98
KEANE F.B.V. (DU) F68/69
+KEANE K.P. (UCD) F92/93, W92/93, F93/94(R), W93/94(R)
KEARNEY A.F. (UCD) F98/99(R), W98/99(R), E98/99(R), S98/99
+KEARNEY R.K. (UCD) S78/79
KEEPE J.W. (QUB) E59/60
KEHELLY C. (UCC) AU96/97(R)
+KELLY J.C. (UCD) S61/62, CAN62/63
KELLY J. (UCC) US94/95, S94/95, W94/95, E95/96, S95/96, W95/96, W96/97, E96/97, S96/97, AU96/97
+KENNEDY K.W. (QUB) S64/65
KENNY B. (UCG) W93/94
KENNY J. (UCD) E88/89
KENNY P. (UCD) E82/83
KENNY P.J. (DU) E86/87, W86/87, F86/87, J87/88, W87/88, F87/88, F88/89, W88/89, E88/89, E89/90
KENEFICK J. (UCC) F93/94, SAU93/94, US94/95, S94/95, W94/95
+KENNEDY I.G. (QUB) F54/55
KIELY E.M. (UCC) A68/69, F68/69
+KIELY M.D. (UCC) E56/57
+KIERNAN T.J. (UCC) E58/59, E59/60, S61/62
KOS H.J. (UCC/UCD) F92/93, W92/93, E92/93, F93/94, W93/94, SAU93/94, US94/95, S94/95, W94/95
KYLE J.W. (QUB) SAU56/57

LAFFIN R. (UCC) E95/96, S95/96, W95/96, W96/97, E96/97, S96/97, AU96/97
LANE D.T. (UCC) S97/98, F97/98, W97/98, E97/98
LANE J. (UCD) E98/99
+LANGBROEK J.G. (DU) W76/77, S77/78, NZ77/78 1,2, S78/79
LAVELLE R.C. (UCD) S78/79
+LEAHY M.W. (UCC) S64/65, SA64/65, A68/69
+LENIHAN D.G. (UCC) E79/80, E80/81
LESLIE G.S. (QUB) F90/91, W90/91, E90/91, JU90/91
+L'ESTRANGE L.P.F. (DU) S61/62
LIDDY D. (UCD) E89/90, E89/90, W89/90, W90/91, E90/91, JU90/91, F91/92
LIGHTBODY M. (QUB) E95/96, S95/96, W95/96
LINDSAY E.D. (QUB) E55/56
LIVESEY J. (UCC) NZU84/85, F84/85, F85/86,

W85/86, E85/86
LONGWELL G.W. (QUB) F91/92, F92/93, W92/93, F93/94, W93/94, SAU93/94
LUCY M.H.A. (UCC) S61/62, SA64/65
LYNAGH D.J.J. (DU) E89/90, F89/90, W89/90
LYNCH M. (UCG) S61/62, CAN62/63, S65/66
LYONS J. (UCC) F92/93, W92/93, E92/93
LYONS S.M.T. (UCD) E79/80
LYSAGHT E. (UCG) S77/78

McARDLE M.F. (DU) W86/87(R), W87/88, F87/88
McCALL B.W. (QUB) S78/79
McCARTHY C.M. (UCC) NZU75/76
McCARTHY C. (DU) F93/94, W93/94, S94/95(R), W94/95
McCARTHY C.J.F. (UCG) T85/86, W86/87, K87/88
McCARTHY K.M. (UCD) F93/94, W93/94, SAU93/94, W94/95
McCLELLAND H.R. (QUB) W76/77, S77/78
McCLUSKEY N. (QUB) S95/96(R), W95/96
+McCOMBE W. McM. (DU) A68/69
McCONKEY G.S. (UCD) W93/94, SAU93/94, US94/95, E95/96, S95/96, W95/96
McCORMACK R. (UCD) S97/98, F97/98, W97/98, E97/98
McCORMACK S. (UCC) E95/96, W95/96
McCOURT M. (DU) W92/93, E92/93(R)
McDONOUGH M.D. (DU) W90/91(R), W92/93
McELLIGOTT D. (DU) E96/97(R)
McFARLAND J. (QUB) E56/57, F57/58, E58/59
McGARRY K. (QUB) F90/91, W90/91, E90/91, JU90/91
+McGRATH D.G. (UCD) F81/82, F82/83, F83/84, E83/84, NZU84/85, F84/85
+McGRATH P.J. (UCC) CAN62/63, S64/65, S65/66
+McGUIRE E.P. (UCG) S61/62, CAN62/63, SA64/65
McGUIRE H.A.M. (UCG) S77/78, NZU77/78 1,2
McHUGH M.R.J. (DU) S97/98, F97/98, W97/98, E97/98
McILREAVY R.T. (DU) SAU93/94, US94/95, S94/95, E95/96
+McIVOR S.C. (UCD) F90/91, W90/91, E90/91, JU90/91
McKEE J.W.L. (DU) S96/97, E96/97(R)
+McKELVEY J.M. (QUB) E95/96
MCKENNA F. (UCC) S98/99
+McKIBBIN C.H. (TCD) A68/69, F68/69
McLAUGHLIN S.O. (DU) E97/98
+McLOUGHLIN R.J. (UCD) S61/62
McMAHON G.P. (DU) F81/82
McMULLEN R.M. (DU) E58/59, W59/60

+MacNEILL H.P. (DU) S78/79, F81/82
McSWEENEY A.C. (UCC) AU96/97, S97/98, F97/98, W97/98, E97/98

MACKEN L.F. (DU) F82/83(R)
MADDEN P. (UCC) F84/85
MADIGAN D.G.G. (UCD) W87/88, F87/88
MAGUIRE K.G. (QUB) S53/54, F54/55
MARMION D. (QUB) S97/98(R)
+MARSHALL B.D.E. (QUB) CAN62/63
MATHEWS N.E. (QUB) E86/87
+MATTHEWS P.M. (QUB) E79/80, E81/82, F82/83, E82/83, F83/84, E83/84
MAYS B.A.S. (UCD) W77/78, E80/81
+MAYS K.M.A. (UCD) NZ74/75
MESCAL D. (UCG) F98/99, W98/99
MILLAR D.C. (QUB) JU90/91
MILLAR J. (QUB) CAN62/63
MOLONEY R.J. (UCC) F88/89, E89/90, F89/90, W89/90
MOLLOY D.M. (UCD) NZ74/75
MOLLOY J.E.M. (UCC) A68/69
+MOLLOY M.G. (UCG) S65/66
MOORE C. (UCD) E92/93, F93/94(R)
MOORE D.P. (UCD) S77/78, S78/79, E79/80
MOORE J.J. (UCG) S53/54
MOORE S. (UCD) F98/99(R), W98/99(R), E98/99
MORAN S. (UCG) W90/91, E90/91, JU90/91
MORGAN C. (DU) S94/95, W94/95(R), E95/96, S95/96, W95/96
MORGAN I.F. (DU) E88/89(R), E90/91(R)
MORONEY M.F. (UCD) E59/60, W59/60
MORONEY J. (UCD) W97/98(R)
+MORONEY T.A. (UCD) S64/65, SA64/65, S65/66, M66/67
MORROW R. (QUB) W94/95, S95/96, W95/96, W96/97, E96/97, S96/97, AU96/97
+MULCAHY W.A. (UCD) F54/55, E55/56, SAU56/57, E56/57, F57/58, E59/60
MULHALL J.P. (UCD) F81/82(R), F82/83, E82/83, F83/84, E83/84, F85/86, W85/86, E85/86, S85/86, E86/87, W86/87, S86/87, K,JU,J87/88
+MULLIN B.J. (DU) F82/83, E82/83, F83/84, E83/84, NZU84/85
MULLINS M.F. (UCC) E58/59
MURRAY B. (QUB) JU,J87/88(R), W87/88
+MURRAY J.B. (UCD) SA64/65, R65/66, S65/66
MURRAY R. (DU) K87/88, W87/88
MURPHY B. (UCG) E55/56
MURPHY B. (UCG) F93/94

MURPHY D.C. (UCC) S97/98, F97/98, W97/98, E97/98
MURPHY H.R. (UCD) A68/69
MURPHY K. (UCC) F88/89(R), W88/89
MURPHY K.F. (DU) F98/99(R), E98/99(R), S98/99(R)
MURPHY L.F. (UCC) F90/91, W90/91, E90/91, W91/92, E91/92, F91/92
MURRAY G.D. (UCC) F98/99(R), E98/99(R), S98/99(R)

NISBET M.A. (DU) F57/58

O'BEIRN F. (UCG) E88/89(R), E89/90(R), F89/90
O'BEIRNE F.T. (UCD) F88/89, W89/90
O'BEIRNE S.M.K. (UCD) E86/87, F86/87, JU,J87/88
O'BRIEN C.P.K. (DU) E88/89, E89/90, F89/90, W89/90
O'BYRNE P. (UCG) S77/78
O'CALLAGHAN J.J. (UCG) NZU84/85, F84/85, T85/86, W85/86, E85/86, S85/86, K,JU87/88
+O'CONNOR H.S. (DU) E55/56, SAU56/57, E56/57, F57/58, E58/59
O'DONNELL R. (UCG) JU90/91, E91/92
O'DONNELL S. (DU) S96/97(R)
O'DONOVAN R. (UCC) S98/99
O'DRISCOLL F.C. (UCD) F68/69
O'DRISCOLL J. (UCC) W93/94, SAU93/94, US94/95, S94/95, W94/95, W96/97, E96/97
O'DRISCOLL M.E. (UCC) E89/90, F89/90, W89/90
O'DRISCOLL M.R. (UCC) W96/97, E96/97(R), S96/97
O'DRISCOLL N. (UCD) F97/98(R), W97/98(R), E97/98(R)
ODUMERU O. (UCD) W91/92, E91/92, F91/92, F93/94
O'FARRELL A.P.L. (UCD) F88/89, W88/89, E88/89
O'FLAHERTY M. McD. (UCD) F88/89, E89/90, F89/90, W89/90, F90/91, W90/91, E90/91, JU90/91
O'GORMAN W. (UCD) F54/55, E55/56
O'GRADY P.J. (UCD) S53/54
O'HAGAN J.W. (UCD) F68/69
O'HALLORAN B.R. (UCD) S61/62
O'KELLY C.J. (DU) F81/82
O'LEARY A.F. (UCC) NZU75/76, W76/77, S77/78, W77/78
O'MAHONY B.G. (UCC) F90/91, E90/91, W91/92, E91/92
O'MAHONY B.N. (UCC) S98/99(R)
O'MAHONY W.F. (UCC) S65/66, F68/69
+O'MAHONY D.W. (UCC/UCD) F92/93, W92/93, E92/93, F93/94, W93/94, US94/95
+O'MAHONY D.P. (UCC) W91/92, E91/92
O'MAHONY J. (UCC) E96/97, AU96/97
+O'MEARA J.A. (UCC) SAU56/57
O'NEILL B. (UCC) F90/91, W90/91, E90/91, JU90/91, E91/92, F91/92
O'NEILL H.W. (UCC) S97/98
O'REGAN K.A. (UCC) E81/82, F81/82
O'RIORDAN J.A. (UCG) K,JU87/88
ORMOND R.J. (UCD) W96/97, S96/97
+ORR P.A. (DU) NZ74/75
O'SHEA A.D. (UCC) S97/98, F97/98, W97/98, E97/98
O'SULLIVAN F. (UCC) NZU84/85

+PARFREY P.S. (UCC) NZU75/76
PARKER S. (QUB) E95/96, S95/96, W95/96
PATRIKIOS G. (DU) E59/60, W59/60
+PEDLOW A.C. (QUB) S53/54, E55/56, SAU56/57, E56/57
POLLARD C.G. (UCD) S78/79
PORTER D. (UCD) F93/94, W93/94(R)
POWELL C.C. (DU) S61/62
POWER I.A. (DU) W87/88(R)
PRENDERGAST M. (UCD) W97/98(R), E97/98(R)

+RAINEY P.I. (QUB) E80/81, E81/82, F82/83
READ R.F. (DU) S61/62, CAN62/63
REES M.S. (DU) E59/60, W59/60
REID J.H. (DU) NZU75/76
REILLY M.P.A. (DU) US94/95, S94/95
+RINGLAND T.M. (QUB) E80/81
RIORDAN J.C. (UCC) W86/87, F86/87, K,JU87/88, W87/88
RITCHIE S. (QUB) F90/91, W90/91, E90/91, JU90/91, W91/92, E91/92, F91/92
ROBB W.B. (DU) F97/98(R), W97/98(R), E97/98(R)
+ROBBIE J.C. (DU) NZU75/76, W76/77, W77/78, NZU77/78 1,2
+ROCHE R.E. (UCG) S53/54, F54/55, SAU56/57
+ROE R. (DU) S53/54, SAU56/57
ROLLS P. (UCC) S77/78, W77/78
ROONEY S.V.J. (UCD) F92/93, W92/93
ROSS M. (UCC) F98/99(R
RYAN J.K. (UCD) W94/95, W95/96, W96/97, E96/97, AU96/97
RYAN N. (DU) F93/94, S94/95, W94/95
RYAN W.J.M. (DU) W77/78

+SAUNDERS R. (QUB) W87/88, F87/88, F88/89, W88/89, E88/89, E89/90, F89/90, W89/90
SCALLY B. (UCD) S95/96

+SCOTT R.D. (QUB) S64/65, S65/66
+SEXTON J.F. (DU) F83/84, E83/84, NZU84/85, F84/85, T85/86, W85/86, E85/86, W86/87, K,JU,J87/88, F87/88
SHALLOE J. (UCC) W88/89, E88/89, F90/91, W90/91, E90/91
SHEAHAN F. (UCC) S95/96, W95/96
SHEEHAN D.P.S. (DU) K,JU,J87/88, W87/88, F88/89, W88/89, E88/89
SHEEHAN J. (UCC) S77/78
SHINE J. (UCD) S97/98, F97/98, W97/98
SLOAN W.G. (QUB) W76/77
SMITH J. (UCD) W98/99, E98/99
SMITH R.A.F. (QUB) E59/60, W59/60
SMYTH T.P. (DU) E56/57
SPARKS C.G. (UCD) NZ74/75
SPENCE P. (QUB) S95/96, W95/96, E96/97(R), AU96/97, S97/98, E97/98(R)
SPICER K. (UCD) SAU93/94
SPICER P. (DU) S95/96
+SPILLANE B.J. (UCC) E81/82(R), F81/82, F82/83
SPILLARD B.C. (QUB) S53/54, F54/55
+SPRING R.M. (DU) NZ74/75
+SPRING D.E.J. (DU) NZU77/78 1,2
+STEELE H.W. (QUB) NZ74/75
STEWART A.J.A. (QUB) W91/92, E91/92, F92/93
STEWART P. (QUB) S97/98(R)
STEWART R.H. (QUB) S77/78, S78/79, E80/81
STRINGER P.A. (UCC) F97/98, W97/98, E97/98
STYLES B. (QUB) US94/95, S95/96, W95/96
SWAN P.F. (UCD) E58/59
SWAN P.J. (UCD) E86/87(R), W86/87, JU87/88
SYNNOTT K.A. (DU) F93/94(R)

TAYLOR W.G. (DU) E55/56, E56/57
THOMPSON H.W.K. (QUB) S53/54
THORNE M.C. (UCD) F91/92
TIMLIN R. (UCD) E97/98(R)
TINMAN M. (QUB) F84/85
TOLAND B.E. (UCD) E91/92(R), F91/92
TORMEY W.G. (UCD) S61/62
TRACEY S.F. (DU) F92/93, W92/93, E92/93
TUOHY G. (UCC) F92/93, W92/93, E92/93, F93/94, W93/94(R), SAU93/94, US94/95, S94/95, W94/95
TURNER J.A.N. (QUB) F54/55, E55/56, E56/57
TURTLE A. (DU) W96/97, E96/97, S96/97, AU96/97
TWOMEY F. (UCC) E95/96, S95/96, W95/96, W96/97, E96/97, S96/97, AU96/97
TWOMEY L.J. (UCC) E97/98(R)
TYNAN S.R. (DU) F93/94, W93/94, SAU93/94, US94/95, S94/95, W94/95

UNDERWOOD B.M.T. (DU) A68/69

WAIN H.B. (UCD) F57/58
+WALDRON O.C. (UCC/DU) SA64/65, NZU75/76
+WALL H. (UCD) E59/60, W59/60, SA64/65
+WALLACE P.S. (UCC) F92/93, W92/93
WALLACE R. (DU) S97/98, F97/98, W97/98
WALSH J.C. (UCC) F57/58, E59/60, CAN62/63, S64/65, SA64/65
WALSHE G. (DU) E95/96, F97/98(R)
WARD M. (UCG) F91/92
WARD R.A. (UCD/DU) W86/87(R), JU,J87/88, F87/88, F88/89, W88/89, E88/89, F89/90, W89/90
WATSON T.F. (UCD) E59/60, W59/60, CAN62/63
WEBB D.W.M. (UCD) T85/86, F85/86, W85/86, E85/86, S85/86
WEIR R. (QUB) E95/96, W96/97, E96/97, AU96/97
WHITE J. (UCC) JU90/91(R)
WHITESIDE W.G. (QUB) S64/65, SA64/65
WILSON J. (QUB) S53/54
WILSON K. (QUB) S61/62
WILSON R. McC. (QUB) E58/59
WOODS J. (DU) JU90/91(R), W91/92, E91/92

+YOUNG R.M. (QUB) S65/66

PRESIDENTS OF THE IRFU 1898–1923

J.B. Moore
1898–99

S. Lee
1899–1900

J. O'Sullivan
1900–01

T. Thornhill
1901–02

J. Johnston
1902–03

V.J. Murray
1903–04

A.D. Clinch
1904–05

F.M. Hamilton
1905–06

J. Flynn
1906–07

G.N.B. Kennedy
1907–08

A. Barr
1908–09

Prof. C.W.L. Alexander
1909–10

F.C. Purser
1910–11

J.H. O'Conor
1911–12

Major R. Stevenson
1912–13

F. H. Browning
1913–16

A. Tedford
1919–20

W.P. Hinton
1920–21

R.M. Magrath
1921–22

G.G. McRea
1922–23

CAPTAINS OF IRELAND TEAMS 1892–1920

S. Lee
1892–93

C.G. Forrest
1893–94

J.H. O'Conor
1894–95

C.V. Rooke
1894–95

C.G. Allen
1897–98

W. Gardiner
1897–98

L.M. Magee
1898–99

J. Fulton
1901–02

H.H. Corley
1902–03

C.E. Allen
1903–04

A. Tedford
1906–07

H. Trift
1907–08

J.C. Parke
1907–08

F. Gardiner
1908–09

G. Hamlet
1909–10

T. Smith
1909–10

R.A. Lloyd
1911–12

A.R. Foster
1912–13

J.P. Quinn
1913–14

T. Wallace
1919–20

APPENDIX 13

IRISH PLAYERS, MANAGERS, CAPTAINS AND COACHES ON LIONS TOURS

Irish Players on Combined British and Irish Tours

Ireland has been represented on all British and Irish sides that have toured Australia, New Zealand and South Africa since 1896. The number of each player's Test match appearances is given in brackets after each tour entry.

Legend: A, Australia; NZ, New Zealand; SA, South Africa

Where a player joined the tour as a replacement it is indicated by an asterisk (*) and where a player came on as a replacement for a Test match it is indicated by 'S' with the number of substitutions in brackets.

R. Alexander (North of Ireland) SA 1938 (3)
W. Ashby (UCC) SA 1910 (0)

G. Beamish (Leicester) A, NZ 1930 (5: 1 v A, 4 v NZ)
C.A. Boyd (Dublin U) SA 1896 (1)
C.V. Boyle (Dublin U) SA 1938 (3)
M.J. Bradley (Dolphin) SA 1924 (0)
T.N. Brand (North of Ireland) SA 1924 (2)
F.P.K. Bresnihan (UCD, Blackrock Coll) A, NZ 1966, SA 1968 (3 v SA)
N.H. Brophy (UCD) A, NZ 1959, SA 1962 (2: 2 v SA)
L.Q. Bulger (Dublin U, Lansdowne) SA 1896 (4)

T. Clifford (Young Munster) A, NZ 1950 (5: 2 v A, 3 v NZ)
S.O. Campbell (Old Belvedere) SA 1980 (3) (1S), NZ 1983 (4)
A.D. Clinch (Dublin U) SA 1896 (4)
J.D. Clinch (Dublin U) SA 1924 (0)
T.J. Crean (Wanderers) SA 1896 (4)
G.E. Cromey (Queen's U) SA 1938 (1)
W.A. Cunningham (Lansdowne) SA 1924 (1)
V.J. Cunningham (St Mary's Coll) NZ 1993 (0)*

J.W. Davidson (London Irish) SA 1997 (3)
I.G. Davidson (North of Ireland) SA 1903 (1)
A.R. Dawson (Wanderers) A, NZ 1959 (6: 2 v A, 4 v NZ)
P.M. Dean (St Mary's Coll) A 1989 (0)
G.P. Doran (Lansdowne) A 1899 (2)
M.G. Doyle (Blackrock Coll) SA 1968 (1)
W.P. Duggan (Blackrock Coll) NZ 1977 (4)
M.J. Dunne (Lansdowne) A, NZ 1930 (0)

R.W. Edwards (Malone) A, NZ 1904 (3: 2 v A, 1 v NZ)
M.F. English (Bohemians) A, NZ 1959 (0)

J.L. Farrell (Bective Rangers) A, NZ 1930 (5: 1 v A, 4 v NZ)
C. Fitzgerald (St Mary's Coll) NZ 1983 (4)
A.R. Foster (Derry) SA 1910 (2)

M.J. Galwey (Shannon) NZ 1993 (0)
C.M.H. Gibson (Cambridge U, NIFC) NZ 1966, SA 1968, A, NZ 1971 (12: 4 v NZ 1966, 4 v SA 1968, 4 v NZ 1971), SA 1974 (0), NZ 1977 (0)
K. Goodall (City of Derry) SA 1968 (0)
T.O. Grace (St Mary's Coll) SA 1974 (0)
C.R.A. Graves (Wanderers) SA 1938 (2)

N.J. Henderson (Queen's U) A, NZ 1950 (2: 2 v NZ)
D. Hewitt (Queen's U) A, NZ 1959, SA 1962 (6: 3 v NZ, 2 v A, 1 v SA)
M.L. Hipwell (Terenure Coll) A, NZ 1971 (0)
W.R. Hunter (CIYMS) SA 1962 (0)

D. Irwin (Queen's U, Instonians) NZ 1983 (3)

R. Johnston (Wanderers) SA 1896 (3)

M.I. Keane (Lansdowne) NZ 1977 (1)
K.W. Kennedy (CIYMS, London Irish) A, NZ 1966 (4: 2 v A, 2 v NZ), SA 1974 (0)
M. Kiernan (Dolphin, Lansdowne) NZ 1983 (3)

T.J. Kiernan (UCC, Cork Con) SA 1962 (1), SA 1968 (4)
J.W. Kyle (Queen's U) A, NZ 1950 (6: 2 v A, 4 v NZ)

R.A. Lamont (Instonians) A, NZ 1966 (6: 4 v NZ)
M.F. Lane (UCC) A, NZ 1950 (1 v A)
D. Lenihan (UCC, Cork Con) NZ 1983 (0),* A 1989 (0)
J.F. Lynch (St Mary's Coll) A, NZ 1971 (4 v NZ)

W.J. McBride (Ballymena) SA 1962 (2), A, NZ 1966 (3 v NZ), SA 1968 (4), A, NZ 1971 (4 v NZ), SA 1974 (4)
H. MacNeill (Dublin U, Oxford U, London Irish) NZ 1983 (3) (1S)
J.S. McCarthy (Dolphin) A, NZ 1950 (0)
A.N. McClinton (NIFC) SA 1910 (0)
T.M.W. McGown (NIFC) A 1899 (4)
J.W. McKay (Queen's U) A, NZ 1950 (6: 2 v A, 4 v NZ)
H.R. McKibbin (Queen's U) SA 1938 (3)
S. McKinney (Dungannon) SA 1974 (0)
G. McLoughlin (Shannon) NZ 1983 (0)*
R.J. McLoughlin (Gosforth, Blackrock Coll) A, NZ 1966, A, NZ 1971 (3: 2 v A 1966, 1 v NZ 1966)
J. McVicker (Collegians) SA 1924 (3)
J.T. Magee (Bective Rangers) SA 1896 (2)
L.M. Magee (Bective Rangers) SA 1896 (4)
B.S. Massey (Hull, ER, Ulster) A, NZ 1904 (1 v A)
E. Martelli (Dublin U) A 1899 (1)
R.B. Mayne (Queen's U) SA 1938 (3)
A.D. Meares (Dublin U) SA 1896 (2)
S. Millar (Ballymena) A, NZ 1959, SA 1962, SA 1968 (9: 2 v A 1959, 1 v NZ 1959, 4 v SA 1962, 2 v SA 1968)
E.R.P. Miller (Leicester) SA 1997 (1)(S)
R. Milliken (Bangor) SA 1974 (4)
J.J. Moloney (St Mary's Coll) SA 1974 (0)
G.P. Morgan (Clontarf) SA 1938 (1)
W.A. Mulcahy (UCD, Bohemians) A, NZ 1959, SA 1962 (7: 1 v A 1959, 2 v NZ 1959, 4 v SA 1962)
K.D. Mullen (Old Belvedere) A, NZ 1950 (Capt.) (3: 1 v A, 2 v NZ)
A.A. Mulligan (Cambridge U) A, NZ 1959 (1 v NZ)
B.J. Mullin (Blackrock Coll) A 1989 (1)
N.A.A. Murphy (Cork Con) A, NZ 1959, A, NZ 1966 (8:1 v A 1959, 3 v NZ 1959, 2 v A 1966, 2 v NZ 1966)
P.F. Murray (Wanderers) A, NZ 1930 (4: 1 v A, 3 v NZ)

J.E. Nelson (Malone) A, NZ 1950 (4: 2 v A, 2 v NZ)
G.W. Norton (Bective Rangers) A, NZ 1950 (0)

R. O'Donnell (St Mary's Coll) SA 1980 (1)
J. O'Driscoll (London Irish, Manchester) SA 1980 (4), NZ 1983 (2)
H. O'Neill (Queen's U) A, NZ 1930 (5: 1 v A, 4 v NZ)
A.J.F. O'Reilly (Old Belvedere, Leicester) SA 1955 (4), A, NZ 1959 (2 v A, 4 v NZ)
P. Orr (Old Wesley) NZ 1977 (1) SA 1980 (0)

C. Patterson (Instonians) SA 1980 (3)
C.D. Patterson (Malone) A, NZ 1904 (0)
A.C. Pedlow (Queen's U) SA 1955 (2)
O.S. Piper (Cork Con) SA 1910 (1)
N.J. Popplewell (Greystones) NZ 1993 (3)

T. Reid (Garryowen) SA 1955 (2)
J.C. Robbie (Dublin U, Cambridge U, Greystones) SA 1980 (1)
W.J. Roche (UCC, Newport) SA 1924 (0)
T. Ringland (Ballymena) NZ 1983 (1)
R. Roe (Lansdowne) SA 1955 (0)

J. Sealy (Dublin U) SA 1896 (4)
F. Slattery (UCD) A, NZ 1971 (0), SA 1974 (4)
S.J. Smith (Ballymena) A 1989 (0)
R.S. Smyth (Dublin U) SA 1903 (3)
T. Smyth (Malone) SA 1910 (2)

A. Tedford (Malone) SA 1903 (3)
R.H. Thompson (Instonians, London Irish) SA 1955 (3)
C.C. Tucker (Shannon) SA 1980 (2)
W. Tyrrell (Queen's U) SA 1910 (0)

James Wallace (Wanderers) SA 1903 (0)
Joseph Wallace (Wanderers) SA 1903 (3)
P.S. Wallace (Saracens) SA 1997 (3)
R.M. Wallace (Garryowen) NZ 1993 (0)*
S. Walker (Instonians) SA 1938 (3)
J.C. Walsh (Sunday's Well) A 1966 (0)
A.J. Ward (Garryowen) SA 1980 (1)
B.G.M. Wood (Garryowen) A, NZ 1959 (2 v NZ)
K.G.M. Wood (Harlequins) SA 1997 (2)
R.M. Young (Queen's U) A, NZ 1966, SA 1968 (4: 1 v NZ, 2 v A, 1 v SA)

In April 1986 a special match to mark the centenary of the International Board was played in Cardiff between the Lions and the Rest of the World. Full Lions honours were awarded to the 21 players chosen. The six Irishmen so honoured were: T. Ringland (Ballymena), B. Mullin (Dublin U), M. Kiernan (Dolphin), D. Fitzgerald (Lansdowne), D. Lenihan (Constitution) and N. Carr (Ards)

Irish Captains (Lions)

The following Irishmen have captained Lions teams:

T. Smyth (Malone) South Africa 1910
S. Walker (Instonians) South Africa 1938
K. Mullen (Old Belvedere) Australia and New Zealand 1950
R.H. Thompson (Instonians, London Irish) South Africa 1955
A.R. Dawson (Wanderers) Australia and New Zealand 1959
T.J. Kiernan (Cork Con) South Africa 1968
W.J. McBride (Ballymena) South Africa 1974
C. Fitzgerald (St Mary's Coll) New Zealand 1983
D.G. Lenihan (Cork Con) in International Board Centenary Match 1986

Lions Irish Managers, Assistant Managers and Coaches:

J. Siggins Manager 1955 South Africa
O.B. Glasgow Assistant Manager 1959 Australia and New Zealand
H.R. McKibbin Assistant Manager 1962 South Africa
D. O'Brien Manager 1966 Australia and New Zealand
A.R. Dawson Coach 1968 South Africa.
S. Millar Coach 1974 South Africa
S. Millar Manager 1980 South Africa
N.A. Murphy Coach 1980 South Africa.
W.J. McBride Manager 1983 New Zealand

APPENDIX 14

UNOFFICIAL MATCHES 1942–1946: RESULTS AND TEAMS

IRISH XV V BRITISH ARMY

7 February 1942 (Ravenhill): lost 1 try, 1 penalty goal (6) to 2 tries, 1 penalty goal (9)
30 January 1943 (Ravenhill): lost 1 goal, 2 tries (11) to 1 goal, 1 try, 1 dropped goal (12)
12 February 1944 (Ravenhill): lost 0 to 3 tries, 2 penalty goals (15)
10 February 1945 (Ravenhill): lost 1 goal (5) to 1 try, 2 penalty goals (9)
15 December 1945 (Ravenhill): won 2 goals, 2 tries, 1 penalty goal (19) to 1 penalty goal (3)

The following were the Irish XVs that played against the British Army:

7 FEBRUARY 1942
M.R. Williams (Clontarf)
K.P. O'Flanagan (UCD)
S.D. Walsh (Dublin U)
J.D. Torrens (Bohemians)
T. Chamberlain (Blackrock Coll)
H. Greer (NIFC)
H. de Lacy (Dublin U)
D. Riordan (UCC)
M.R. Neely (Queen's U)
D. Ryan (UCD)
T. Headon (UCD)
E. Keeffe (Sunday's Well)
R. Alexander (NIFC)
J.J. Guiney (Clontarf)
K. O'Brien (Bective Rangers)

30 JANUARY 1943
C. Murphy (Lansdowne)
W.J. Higson (Queen's U)
S.D. Walsh (Dublin U)
H. Greer (NIFC)
T. Chamberlain (Blackrock Coll)
E.A. Carry (Old Wesley)
S.J. McComb (Malone)
F. Cromey (Collegians)
E.G. Ryan (Blackrock Coll)
J. Griffin (Corinthians)
J. Joyce (Galwegians)
E. Keeffe (Sunday's Well)
K. O'Brien (Bective Rangers)
D.B. O'Loughlin (Dolphin)
J.J. Guiney (Clontarf)

12 FEBRUARY 1944
C.C. Murphy (Lansdowne)
F.G. Moran (Clontarf)
G.J. Quinn (Old Belvedere)
L. O'Brien (UCC)
N. Burke (Lansdowne)
H. Greer (NIFC)
J.W. Adrain (NIFC)
W.J. Moynan (Dublin U)
F. Cromey (Collegians)
J. Corcoran (UCC)
E. Keeffe (Sunday's Well)
J.E. Nelson (Malone)
K. O'Brien (Bective Rangers)
D.B. O'Loughlin (Dolphin)
T. Halpenny (UCD)

10 FEBRUARY 1945
C. Murphy (Lansdowne)
F.G. Moran (Clontarf)
G. Quinn (Old Belvedere)
K. Quinn (Old Belvedere)
W.H. Miller (Queen's U)
E.A. Carry (Old Wesley)
E. O'Mullane (UCC)
J. Belton (Old Belvedere)
H. Dudgeon (Collegians)
C. Callan (Lansdowne)

J.E. Nelson (Malone)
J. Guiney (Bective Rangers)
D.B. O'Loughlin (Dolphin)
D. Hingerty (Lansdowne)

15 DECEMBER 1945
C. Murphy (Lansdowne)
F.G. Moran (Clontarf)
H. Greer (NIFC)
K. Quinn (Old Bevedere)
B. Quinn (Old Belvedere)
J. Kyle (Queen's U)
D. Thorpe (Old Belvedere)
J. Belton (Old Bevedere)
K.D. Mullen (Old Belvedere)
J. Corcoran (UCC)
C. Callan (Lansdowne)
R.D. Agar (Malone)
J. Guiney (Bective Rangers)
H. Dudgeon (Collegians)
D. McCourt (Instonians)

Unofficial Internationals 1946

IRISH XV v FRENCH XV
26 January 1946 (Lansdowne Road): lost 1 penalty goal (3) to 1 dropped goal (4).

IRISH XV v ENGLISH XV
6 February 1946 (Lansdowne Road): lost 2 tries (6) to 1 goal, 1 try, 2 penalty goals (14).

IRISH XV v WELSH XV
9 March 1946 (Cardiff): lost 1 dropped goal (4) to 2 tries (6).

IRISH XV v SCOTTISH XV
23 March 1946 (Murrayfield): lost 0 to 1 goal, 1 dropped goal (9).

The following players represented Ireland in the unofficial internationals of 1946:

J. Belton (Old Belvedere) (F,E)
C. Callan (Lansdowne) (F,E,S,W)
E.A. Carry (Old Wesley) (S,W)
J. Corcoran (UCC) (S,W)
R.E. Coolican (Dublin U) (W)
T. Coveney (St Mary's Coll) (S)
H. Dolan (UCD) (F)
H.G. Dudgeon (Collegians) (S,W)
H. Greer (NIFC) (F)
J.J. Guiney (Bective Rangers) (F,E)
D. Hingerty (Lansdowne) (E,S,W)
E. Keeffe (Sunday's Well) (E,S,W)
J.W. Kyle (Queen's U) (F,E,)
D. McCourt (Instonians) (F,E)
F.G. Moran (Clontarf) (F,E,S)
K.D. Mullen (Old Belvedere) (F,E,S,W)
C. Murphy (Lansdowne) (F,E,S,W)
M.R. Neely (Royal Navy, Queen's U) (F,E,S,W)
K.P. O'Flanagan (London Irish) (F)
D.B. O'Loughlin (Dolphin) (F,E)
B.T. Quinn (Old Belvedere) (E,S,W)
G.T. Quinn (Old Belvedere) (E,W)
K. Quinn (Old Belvedere) (E,S,W)
P. Reid (Garryowen) (F,W)
E. Strathdee (Queen's U) (S,W)
D. Thorpe (Old Belvedere) (F,E)

APPENDIX 15

IRELAND INTERNATIONAL TEAMS
Results, Scorers, Dates and Venues
1874 to June 1999

+ denotes new cap

* denotes team captain

1874–75	1875–76	1876–77		1877–78
v ENGLAND	v ENGLAND	v ENGLAND	v SCOTLAND	v ENGLAND
+R.B. Walkington	R.B. Walkington	R.B. Walkington	+G.M. Shaw	*R.B. Walkington
+H.L. Cox	+H. Moore	*R. Galbraith	H. Moore	
				+R.N. Matier
+R.J. Bell	+E.W. Hobson	+H. Brown	R.B. Walkington	F.W. Kidd
+A.P. Cronyn	B.N. Casement	+F.W. Kidd	F.W. Kidd	
				+G.L. Fagan
+J. Myles	*R.J. Bell	+A.M. Whitestone	+J. Heron	T.G. Gordon
+R. Galbraith	A.P. Cronyn	+T.G. Gordon	T.G. Gordon	
+E.N. McIlwaine				+E.W.D. Croker
	R. Galbraith	+H.W. Jackson	+J. Currell	+W.D. Moore
+W.S. Allen	H.L. Cox	H.L. Cox	H.L. Cox	+F. Schute
+R.M. Maginness	R.M. Maginness	W. Finlay	W. Finlay	H.W. Murray
+A. Combe	+J. Ireland	J. Ireland	J.A. McDonald	W. Finlay
+F.T. Hewson	+W.A. Cuscaden	+W.H. Wilson	*W.H. Wilson	J.A. McDonald
+G. Andrews	G. Andrews	+H.G. Edwards	+H.W. Murray	H.G. Edwards
+E. Galbraith	+R. Greer	+H.C. Kelly	H.C. Kelly	H.C. Kelly
*+G.H. Stack	+A.J. Westby	+T. Brown	T. Brown	+R.W. Hughes
+W.H. Ash	W.H. Ash	+W.J. Hamilton	W.H. Ash	+W. Griffiths
+J.A. McDonald	J.A. McDonald	Kennington Oval	Belfast	Lansdowne Road
+M. Barlow	+W. Finlay	lost	lost	lost
+H.D. Walsh	H.D. Walsh	Eng. 2G, 2T	Ire. Nil	Ire. Nil
+W. Gaffikin	+D.T. Arnott	Ire. Nil	Scot. 4G, 2DG, 2T	Eng. 1T, 2G
+B.N. Casement	E.N. McIlwaine	5 February 1877	19 February 1877	11 March 1878
Kennington Oval	Leinster C.G.			
lost	lost			
Eng. 1G, 1DG, 1T	Ire. Nil			
Ire. Nil	Eng. 1G, 1T			
15 February 1875	13 December 1875			

1878–79		1879–80	
v SCOTLAND	v ENGLAND	v ENGLAND	v SCOTLAND
R.B. Walkington	+W.W. Pike	R.B. Walkington	R.B. Walkington
+T. Harrison			
	+W.J. Willis	A.M. Whitestone	T. Harrison
+J.C. Bagot	J.C. Bagot	J.C. Bagot	J.C. Bagot
R.N. Matier			
	A.M. Whitestone	+W.T. Heron	W.T. Heron
A.M. Whitestone	J. Heron	+M. Johnston	M. Johnston
+W.J. Goulding			
	B.N. Casement	+A.J. Forrest	A.J. Forrest
+W.E.A. Cummins	+J.R. Bristow	+F. Kennedy	A.P. Cronyn
+A.M. Archer	F. Schute	+A. Millar	A. Millar
H.C. Kelly	H.W. Murray	*H.C. Kelly	*H.C. Kelly
W. Finlay	W. Finlay	J.W. Taylor	J.W. Taylor
J.A. McDonald	+J.J. Keon	J.A. McDonald	W. Finlay
+J.W. Taylor	+J.L. Cuppaidge	J.L. Cuppaidge 1T	J.L. Cuppaidge
*+W.C. Neville	*W.C. Neville	R.W. Hughes	R.W. Hughes
+G. Scriven	G. Scriven	G. Scriven	G. Scriven
+H. Purdon	H. Purdon	H. Purdon	+W.A. Wallis
Belfast	Kennington Oval	Lansdowne Road	Glasgow
lost	lost	lost	lost
Ire. Nil Scot. 1G, 1DG, 1T	Eng. 2G, 1DG, 2T Ire. Nil	Ire. 1T Eng. 1G, 1T	Scot. 1G, 2DG, 2T Ire. Nil
17 February 1879	24 March 1879	30 January 1880	14 February 1880

1880–81		1881–82		
v ENGLAND	v SCOTLAND	v WALES	v ENGLAND	v SCOTLAND
T. Harrison	+R.E. McLean	R.E. McLean	R.B. Walkington	R.B. Walkington
+W. Peirce	W.W. Pike	+J.R. Atkinson	R.E. McLean	R.E. McLean
W.W. Pike	J.C. Bagot 1DG	+T. St G. McCarthy	+E.J. Wolfe	J.R. Atkinson
		+W.W. Fletcher	W.W. Pike	+R.W. Morrow
+H.F. Spunner	H.F. Spunner			
M. Johnston	M. Johnston	+E.H. Greene	M. Johnston 1T	W.W. Fletcher
		+G.C. Bent	G.C. Bent	+J. Pedlow
*A.J. Forrest	*A.J. Forrest			
+D.R. Browning	D.R. Browning	*A.J. Forrest	A.J. Forrest	+A.C. O'Sullivan
+J.C.S. Burkitt	J.W. Taylor	+J.M. Kennedy	*J.W. Taylor	*J.W. Taylor
F. Kennedy	+J. Johnston	F. Kennedy	+R. Nelson	R. Nelson
+H.B. Morell	H.B. Morell	H.B. Morell	H.B. Morell	+J.B.W. Buchanan
W.E.A. Cummins	J.A. McDonald	+E.A. McCarthy	W.E.A. Cummins	W. Finlay
W.A. Wallis	W.A. Wallis	W.A. Wallis	J.A. McDonald	J.A. McDonald
+A.R. McMullen	A.R. McMullen	+A.J. Downing	R.W. Hughes	R.W. Hughes
G. Scriven	R.W. Hughes	+F.S. Heuston	+T.R. Johnson-Smyth	G. Scriven
H. Purdon	H. Purdon	+R.G. Thompson	+O.S. Stokes 1T	J. Johnston
Manchester	Belfast	Lansdowne Road	Lansdowne Road	Glasgow
lost	won	lost	drawn	lost
Eng. 2G, 2T Ire. Nil	Ire. 1DG Scot. 1T	Ire. Nil Wales 2G, 2T	Ire. 2T Eng. 2T	Scot. 2T Ire. Nil
5 February 1881	19 February 1881	28 January 1882	6 February 1882	18 February 1882

1882–83

v ENGLAND	v SCOTLAND
R.W. Morrow	R.W. Morrow
R.E. McLean	R.E. McLean
+R.H. Scovell	W.W. Pike
W.W. Fletcher	A.M. Whitestone
+J.P. Warren	+S.R. Collier
+S.A.M. Bruce	S.A.M. Bruce
A.J. Forrest 1T	*G. Scriven
J.W. Taylor	J.W. Taylor
A. Millar	W.A. Wallis
+D.F. Moore	D.F. Moore
+H. King	H. King
J.A. McDonald	J.A. McDonald
R.W. Hughes	R.W. Hughes
F.S. Heuston	F.S. Heuston
*G. Scriven	R. Nelson
Manchester lost	Belfast lost
Eng. 1G, 3T Ire. 1T	Ire. Nil Scot. 1G, 1T
5 February 1883	17 February 1883

1883–84

v ENGLAND	v SCOTLAND	v WALES
R.W. Morrow	+J.M. O'Sullivan	R.W. Morrow
R.E. McLean	R.E. McLean	E.H. Greene
R.H. Scovell	+G.H. Wheeler	J. Pedlow
+D.J. Ross	+L.M. MacIntosh 1T	H.F. Spunner
		+R.G. Warren
M. Johnston	M. Johnston	
+W.W. Higgins	W.W. Higgins	+W. Hallaran
		+A.J. Hamilton
S.A.M. Bruce	+W. Kelly	
+F.H. Levis	+T.H.M. Hobbs	J.M. Kennedy
+H.M. Brabazon	+A. Gordon	J.M. Cook
D.F. Moore	+J.F. Maguire	*D.F. Moore
J.B.W. Buchanan	J.B.W. Buchanan	+F.W. Moore
*J.A. McDonald	*J.A. McDonald	+W.S. Collis
R.W. Hughes	R.W. Hughes	+L. Moyers
+W.G. Rutherford	W.G. Rutherford	+W.E. Johnstone
O.S. Stokes	J. Johnston	+J. Fitzgerald
Lansdowne Road lost	Raeburn Place lost	NB: H.M. Joredan (Newport) and J. McDaniel (Newport) both played for Ireland in this match, but the team above is the one officially listed.
Ire. Nil Eng. 1G	Scot. 2G, 2T Ire. 1T	Cardiff Arms Park lost
4 February 1884	16 February 1884	Wales 1DG, 2T Ire. nil
		12 April 1884

1884–85

v ENGLAND	v SCOTLAND
G.H. Wheeler	R.W. Morrow
R.E. McLean	D.J. Ross
+J.P. Ross	J.P. Ross
E.H. Greene 1T	E.H. Greene
+E.C. Crawford	+D.V. Hunter
+R.G. Warren	R.G. Warren
+H.J. Neill	H.J. Neill
+T. Shanahan	T. Shanahan
T.H.M. Hobbs	+J. Thompson
+T.R. Lyle	T.R. Lyle
F.W. Moore	F.W. Moore
+R.M. Bradshaw	R.M. Bradshaw
R.W. Hughes	J. Johnston
*W.G. Rutherford	+W. Hogg
+T.C. Allen	*A.J. Forrest
Manchester lost	Raeburn Place lost
Eng. 2T Ire. 1T	Scot. 1G, 2T Ire. Nil
7 February 1885	7 March 1885

1885–86

v ENGLAND	v SCOTLAND
R.W. Morrow	R.W. Morrow
D.J. Ross	D.J. Ross
J.P. Ross	*J.P. Ross
E.H. Greene	+M.J. Carpendale
*M. Johnston	+J.F. Ross
R.G. Warren	+R.W. Herrick
+J. Chambers	J. Chambers
T. Shanahan	F.W. Moore
+V.C. Le Fanu	V.C. Le Fanu
T.R. Lyle	+J. McMordie
H.M. Brabazon	+F.H. Miller
J. Johnston	+J. Waites
R.W. Hughes	R. Nelson
W.G. Rutherford	H.J. Neill
+R.H. Massy-Westropp	+F.O. Stoker
Lansdowne Road lost	Raeburn Place lost
Ire. Nil Eng. 1T	Scot. 3G, 1DG, 2T Ire. Nil
6 February 1886	20 February 1886

1886–87			1887–88	
v ENGLAND	v SCOTLAND	v WALES	v WALES	v SCOTLAND
+D.B. Walkington	J.M. O'Sullivan	D.B. Walkington	D.B. Walkington	R.W. Morrow
+C.R. Tillie 1T	C.R. Tillie	M.J. Carpendale	C.R. Tillie	C.R. Tillie
+D.F. Rambaut 2C	D.F. Rambaut	D.F. Rambaut	D.F. Rambaut 1C	+A. Walpole
+R. Montgomery 1T	R. Montgomery	R. Montgomery 3T	M.J. Carpendale 1DG	M.J. Carpendale
+J.H. McLaughlin	J.H. McLaughlin	+P.J. O'Connor	J.H. McLaughlin	J.H. McLaughlin
*R.G. Warren	*R.G. Warren	*R.G. Warren	R.G. Warren 1T	R.G. Warren
			+R.H. Mayne	
J. Chambers	J. Chambers	J. Chambers	T. Shanahan 1T	R.H. Mayne
+J.S. Dick	J.S. Dick	J.S. Dick		T. Shanahan
V.C. Le Fanu	+C.M. Moore	V.C. Le Fanu	+W. Ekin	W. Ekin
T.R. Lyle	T.R. Lyle	+T. Taggart	+J. Moffatt	J. Moffatt
+E.J. Walsh	E.J. Walsh	E.J. Walsh	C.M. Moore	C.M. Moore
J. Johnston	J. Johnston	J. Johnston	+E.W. Stoker	E.W. Stoker
+R. Stevenson	R. Stevenson	R. Stevenson	W.G. Rutherford	V.C. Le Fanu
H.J. Neill	H.J. Neill	H.J. Neill	*H.J. Neill	*H.J. Neill
+J. Macauley	J. Macauley	+W. Davison	F.O. Stoker	+W.A. Morton
Lansdowne Road	Belfast	Birkenhead	Lansdowne Road	Raeburn Place
won	lost	lost	won	lost
Ire. 2G	Ire. Nil	Wales 1DG, 1T	Ire. 1G, 1DG, 1T	Scot. 1G
Eng. Nil	Scot. 1G, 1GM, 2T	Ire. 3T	Wales Nil	Ire. Nil
5 February 1887	19 February 1887	12 March 1887	3 March 1888	10 March 1888

1888–89		
v MAORIS	v SCOTLAND	v WALES
+T. Edwards	+L.J. Holmes	L.J. Holmes
+D.C. Woods 1T	D.C. Woods	R.A. Yeates
A. Walpole	+R.A. Yeates	+R. Dunlop
+M.J. Bulger	+B.T. Pedlow	B.T. Pedlow
+J. Stevenson 1C	J. Stevenson	+A.C. McDonnell 1T
*R.G. Warren	*R.G. Warren	*R.G. Warren
+H.W. Andrews	H.W. Andrews	H.W. Andrews
+E.G. Forrest	E.G. Forrest	E.G. Forrest
+J.H. O'Conor	+L.C. Nash	V.C. Le Fanu
J. Moffatt	J. Moffatt	+J. Cotton 1T
+J.N. Lytle	+C.R.R. Stack	J.N. Lytle
J. Waites 1T	+T.M. Donovan	J. Waites
R. Stevenson	R. Stevenson	R. Stevenson
+J.S. Jameson	J.S. Jameson	J.S. Jameson
F.O. Stoker	F.O. Stoker	+H.A. Richey
Lansdowne Road	Belfast	St Helen's
lost	lost	won
Ire. 1G, 1T	Ire. Nil	Wales Nil
Maoris 4G, 1T	Scot. 1DG	Ire. 2T
1 December 1888	16 February 1889	2 March 1889

1889–90

v SCOTLAND	v WALES	v ENGLAND
+H.P. Gifford	D.B. Walkington	D.B. Walkington
R. Dunlop	R. Dunlop 1T	R. Dunlop
+R.W. Johnston	R.W. Johnston	R.W. Johnston
T. Edwards	T. Edwards	T. Edwards
A.C. McDonnell	A.C. McDonnell	+B.B. Tuke
*R.G. Warren	*R.G. Warren	*R.G. Warren
J. Moffatt	J. Moffatt	J.N. Lytle
E.G. Forrest	+H.T. Galbraith	E.G. Forrest
J. Waites	J. Waites	J. Waites
J.H. O'Conor	J.H. O'Conor	J.H. O'Conor
R. Stevenson	R. Stevenson	R. Stevenson
+J. Roche	J. Roche 1C	J. Roche
+E.F. Doran	E.F. Doran	V.C. Le Fanu
H.A. Richey	L.C. Nash	L.C. Nash
+W.J.N. Davis	W.J.N. Davis	W.J.N. Davis
Raeburn Place	Lansdowne Road	Blackheath
lost 0-5	drawn 3-3	lost 0-3
Scot. 1DG, 1T	Ire. 1G	Eng. 3T
Ire. Nil	Wales 1G	Ire. Nil
22 February 1890	1 March 1890	15 March 1890

1890–91

v ENGLAND	v SCOTLAND	v WALES
*D.B. Walkington	*D.B. Walkington	D.B. Walkington 1DG
R. Dunlop	R. Dunlop	R. Dunlop
+S. Lee	S. Lee	S. Lee 1T
R. Montgomery	+H.G. Wells	H.G. Wells
A.C. McDonnell	+E.D. Cameron	E.D. Cameron
B.B. Tuke	B.B. Tuke	+R. Pedlow
J.N. Lytle	J.N. Lytle	+T. Fogarty
E.G. Forrest	+R.D. Stokes	R.D. Stokes
J. Waites	J. Moffatt	F.O. Stoker
J.H. O'Conor	J.H. O'Conor	J.S. Jameson
+C.V. Rooke	+G. Collopy	*R. Stevenson
J. Roche	J. Roche	J. Roche
V.C. Le Fanu	+E.F. Frazer	C.V. Rooke
L.C. Nash	L.C. Nash	L.C. Nash
W.J.N. Davis	W.J.N. Davis	W.J.N. Davis
Lansdowne Road	Belfast	Stradey Park
lost 0-9	lost 0-14	lost 4-6
Ire. Nil	Ire. Nil	Wales 1G, 1DG
Eng. 2G, 3T	Scot. 3G, 1DG, 2T	Ire. 1DG, 1T
7 February 1891	21 February 1891	7 March 1891

1891–92

v ENGLAND	v SCOTLAND	v WALES
+T. Peel	T. Peel	T. Peel
R. Dunlop	R. Dunlop	T. Edwards
S. Lee	S. Lee	S. Lee
+W. Gardiner	W. Gardiner	R. Montgomery
+T. Thornhill	T. Thornhill	T. Thornhill
B.B. Tuke	+F.E. Davies	F.E. Davies 1T
*V.C. Le Fanu	*V.C. Le Fanu	*V.C. Le Fanu
+T.J. Johnston	T.J. Johnston	T.J. Johnston
E.J. Walsh	E.J. Walsh	E.J. Walsh 2T
+A.K. Wallis	A.K. Wallis	A.K. Wallis
J.S. Jameson	G. Collopy	J.S. Jameson
+R.E. Smith	+A.D. Clinch	J. Roche 1C
J.H. O'Conor	E.F. Frazer	J.H. O'Conor
W.J.N. Davis	W.J.N. Davis	R. Stevenson
C.V. Rooke	C.V. Rooke	C.V. Rooke
Manchester	Raeburn Place	Lansdowne Road
lost 0-7	lost 0-2	won 9-0
Eng. 1G, 1T	Scot. 1T	Ire. 1G, 2T
Ire. Nil	Ire. Nil	Wales Nil
6 February 1892	20 February 1892	5 March 1892

1892–93

v ENGLAND	v SCOTLAND	v WALES
+S. Gardiner	S. Gardiner	+W. Sparrow
T. Edwards	+L.H. Gwynn	R. Dunlop
*S. Lee	*S. Lee	*S. Lee
W. Gardiner	W. Gardiner	W. Gardiner
T. Thornhill	+W.S. Brown	W.S. Brown
F.E. Davies	F.E. Davies	F.E. Davies
+R. Johnston	+B. O'Brien	B. O'Brien
T.J. Johnston	T.J. Johnston	R. Johnston
E.J. Walsh	E.G. Forrest	E.G. Forrest
A.K. Wallis	+H. Forrest	A.K. Wallis
+H. Lindsay	H. Lindsay	H. Lindsay
+M.S. Egan	J.S. Jameson	+R.W. Hamilton
J.H. O'Conor	J.H. O'Conor	A.D. Clinch
R. Stevenson	R. Stevenson	R. Stevenson
C.V. Rooke	C.V. Rooke	C.V. Rooke
Lansdowne Road	Belfast	Stradey Park
lost 0-4	drawn 0-0	lost 0-2
Ire. Nil	Ire. Nil	Wales 1T
Eng. 2T	Scot. Nil	Ire. Nil
4 February 1893	18 February 1893	11 March 1893

1893–94

v ENGLAND	v SCOTLAND	v WALES
W. Sparrow	+P.J. Grant	P.J. Grant
H.G. Wells	H.G. Wells 1T	R. Dunlop
S. Lee	S. Lee	S. Lee
W. Gardiner	W. Gardiner	W. Gardiner
L.H. Gwynn	L.H. Gwynn	L.H. Gwynn
W.S. Brown	W.S. Brown	W.S. Brown
B.B. Tuke	B.B. Tuke	B.B. Tuke
J.N. Lytle 1T	J.N. Lytle 1C	J.N. Lytle 1PG
+J.H. Lytle	J.H. Lytle	J.H. Lytle
+G. Walmsley	+A.T.W. Bond	A.T.W. Bond
J.H. O'Conor	J.H. O'Conor	J.H. O'Conor
H. Lindsay	H. Lindsay	H. Lindsay
*E.G. Forrest 1DG	*E.G. Forrest	*E.G. Forrest
+T.J. Crean	T.J. Crean	T.J. Crean
C.V. Rooke	C.V. Rooke	C.V. Rooke
Blackheath	Lansdowne Road	Belfast
won 7-5	won 5-0	won 3-0
Eng. 1G	Ire. 1G	Ire. 1PG
Ire. 1DG, 1T	Scot. Nil	Wales Nil
3 February 1894	24 February 1894	10 March 1894

1894–95

v ENGLAND	v SCOTLAND	v WALES
+G.R. Symes	+J. Fulton	J. Fulton
W. Gardiner	W. Gardiner	W. Gardiner
S. Lee	+A. Montgomery	S. Lee
+T.H. Stevenson	J.T. Magee	T.H. Stevenson
+J.T. Magee	+J. O'Conor	+A.P. Gwynn
+A.M. Magee 1T	A.M. Magee	A.M. Magee
B.B. Tuke	B.B. Tuke	+M.G. Delany
T.J. Johnston	+E.H. McIlwaine	E.H. McIlwaine
H. Lindsay	+W. O'Sullivan	J.H. Lytle
+A.A. Brunker	W.J.N. Davis	A.A. Brunker
*J.H. O'Conor	M.S. Egan	*E.G. Forrest
+H.C. McCoull	H.C. McCoull	H.C. McCoull
A.D. Clinch	A.D. Clinch	A.D. Clinch
T.J. Crean	T.J. Crean	T.J. Crean 1T
C.V. Rooke	*C.V. Rooke	C.V. Rooke
Lansdowne Road	Raeburn Place	Cardiff Arms Park
lost 3-6	lost 0-6	lost 3-5
Ire. 1T	Scot. 2T	Wales 1G
Eng. 2T	Ire. Nil	Ire. 1T
2 February 1895	2 March 1895	16 March 1895

1895–96			1896–97	
v ENGLAND	v SCOTLAND	v WALES	v ENGLAND	v SCOTLAND
J. Fulton	+G.H. McAllan	G.H. McAllan	J. Fulton	+P.E. O'Brien-Butler
W. Gardiner	W. Gardiner	W. Gardiner	W. Gardiner 2T	W. Gardiner
*S. Lee	*S. Lee	*S. Lee	S. Lee	L.H. Gwynn
T.H. Stevenson 1T	T.H. Stevenson	T.H. Stevenson	T.H. Stevenson	T.H. Stevenson
+L.Q. Bulger 2C	L.Q. Bulger	L.Q. Bulger 1C	L.Q. Bulger 1GM, 1T	L.Q. Bulger 1T
A.M. Magee	A.M. Magee	A.M. Magee	A.M. Magee	A.M. Magee
+G.G. Allen	G.G. Allen	G.G. Allen	G.G. Allen	G.G Allen
J.H. O'Conor	J.H. O'Conor	J.H. O'Conor	+J.E. McIlwaine	J.E. McIlwaine
J.H. Lytle	J.H. Lytle	J.H. Lytle 1T	J.H. Lytle	J.H. Lytle
+W.G. Byron	W.G. Byron	W.G. Byron	W.G. Byron	W.G. Byron
H. Lindsay	H. Lindsay	H. Lindsay	+M. Ryan	M. Ryan
+J. Sealy 1T	J. Sealy	J. Sealy	+J. Ryan	J. Sealy
A.D. Clinch	A.D. Clinch	A.D. Clinch	A.D. Clinch	A.D. Clinch
T.J. Crean	T.J. Crean	T.J. Crean 1T	*E.G. Forrest	*E.G. Forrest
C.V. Rooke	C.V. Rooke	C.V. Rooke	C.V. Rooke	C.V. Rooke
Leeds	Lansdowne Road	Lansdowne Road	Lansdowne Road	Powderhall
won 10-4	drawn 0-0	won 8-4	won 13-9	lost 3-8
Eng. 1DG	Ire. Nil	Ire. 1G, 1T	Ire. 1GM, 3T	Scot. 1G, 1PG
Ire. 2G	Scot. Nil	Wales 1DG	Eng. 2PG, 1T	Ire. 1T
1 February 1896	15 February 1896	14 March 1896	6 February 1897	20 February 1897

1897–98		
v ENGLAND	v SCOTLAND	v WALES
P.E. O'Brien-Butler	P.E. O'Brien-Butler	J. Fulton
+F.C. Purser	F.C. Purser	F.C. Purser
*S. Lee	+F.F.S. Smithwick	F.F.S. Smithwick
L.H. Gwynn	L.H. Gwynn	*W. Gardiner
L.Q. Bulger 1PG	L.Q. Bulger	L.Q. Bulger 1PG
A.M. Magee 1T	A.M. Magee	A.M. Magee
G.G. Allen	*G.G. Allen	+A. Barr
W.G. Byron	W.G. Byron	W.G. Byron
J.E. McIlwaine	J.E. McIlwaine	J.E. McIlwaine
+J.G. Franks	J.G. Franks	J.G. Franks
M. Ryan	M. Ryan	M. Ryan
J. Ryan	J. Ryan	J. Ryan
J.H. Lytle	J.H. Lytle	+T.J. Little
H. Lindsay 1T	H. Lindsay	H. Lindsay
+J.L. Davis	J.L. Davis	+T. McCarthy
Richmond	Belfast	Limerick
won 9-6	lost 0-8	lost 3-11
Eng. 1PG, 1T	Ire. Nil	Ire. 1PG
Ire. 1PG, 2T	Scot. 1G, 1T	Wales 1G, 1PG, 1T
5 February 1898	19 February 1898	19 March 1898

1898–99

v ENGLAND	v SCOTLAND	v WALES
J. Fulton	P.E. O'Brien-Butler	P.E. O'Brien-Butler
+I.G. Davidson	+G.P. Doran 1T	G.P. Doran 1T
+G.R.A. Harman	+C. Reid 1T	G.R.A. Harman
+J.B. Allison	J.B. Allison	C. Reid
+W.H. Brown	+E.F. Campbell 1T	E.F. Campbell
*A.M. Magee 1PG	*A.M. Magee	*A.M. Magee
G.G. Allen 1T	A. Barr	G.G. Allen
W.G. Byron	W.G. Byron	W.G. Byron
J.E. McIlwaine	J.H. Lytle	J.E. McIlwaine
+T. Ahearne	+A.W.D. Meares	A.W.D. Meares
M. Ryan	M. Ryan	M. Ryan
J. Ryan	J. Ryan	J. Ryan
H.C. McCoull	T.J. Little	T.J. Little
J. Sealy	J. Sealy 1T	J. Sealy
+T.M.W. McGown	T.M.W. McGown	+C.C.H. Moriarty
Lansdowne Road	Inverleith	Cardiff Arms Park
won 6-0	won 9-3	won 3-0
Ire. 1PG, 1T	Scot. 1PG	Wales Nil
Eng. Nil	Ire. 3T	Ire. 1T
4 February 1899	18 February 1899	18 March 1899

1899–1900

v ENGLAND	v SCOTLAND	v WALES
P.E. O'Brien-Butler	+C.A. Boyd	J. Fulton
G.P. Doran	I.G. Davidson	I.G. Davidson
J.B. Allison 1DG	J.B. Allison	J.B. Allison
C. Reid	+B.R.W. Doran	B.R.W. Doran
E.F. Campbell	G.P. Doran	E.F. Campbell
*A.M. Magee	*A.M. Magee	*A.M. Magee
+J.H. Ferris	J.H. Ferris	J.H. Ferris
+S.T. Irwin	S.T. Irwin	S.T. Irwin
+C.E. Allen	C.E. Allen	C.E. Allen
J. Sealy	J. Sealy	+T.A. Harvey
+P.C. Nicholson	P.C. Nicholson	P.C. Nicholson
M. Ryan	M. Ryan	M. Ryan
+J.J. Coffey	J. Ryan	J. Ryan
A.W.D. Meares	T.J. Little	A.W.D. Meares
+F. Gardiner	F. Gardiner	T.J. Little
Richmond	Lansdowne Road	Belfast
lost 4-15	drawn 0-0	lost 0-3
Eng. 1G, 1DG, 2T	Ire. Nil	Ire. Nil
Ire. 1DG	Scot. Nil	Wales 1T
3 February 1900	24 February 1900	17 March 1900

1900–01

v ENGLAND	v SCOTLAND	v WALES
J. Fulton	C.A. Boyd	C.A. Boyd
I.G. Davidson 1T	I.G. Davidson	I.G. Davidson 1T
J.B. Allison	J.B. Allison	J.B. Allison
B.R.W. Doran	B.R.W. Doran 1T	B.R.W. Doran
+A.E. Freear	A.E. Freear	A.E. Freear 1T
*A.M. Magee	*A.M. Magee	*A.M. Magee
A. Barr	A. Barr	+H.H. Ferris
S.T. Irwin 2C	+H.A.S. Irvine 1C	S.T. Irwin
C.E. Allen	C.E. Allen	C.E. Allen
+A.G. Heron	T.A. Harvey	T.A. Harvey
+P. Healey	P. Healey	P. Healey
M. Ryan	M. Ryan	M. Ryan
J. Ryan	J. Ryan	J. Ryan 1T
T.J. Little	T.J. Little	J.J. Coffey
F. Gardiner 1T	T.M.W. McGown	F. Gardiner
Lansdowne Road	Inverleith	St Helen's
won 10-6	lost 5-9	lost 9-10
Ire. 2G	Scot. 3T	Wales 2G
Eng. 1PG, 1T	Ire. 1G	Ire. 3T
9 February 1901	23 February 1901	16 March 1901

1901–02

v ENGLAND	v SCOTLAND	v WALES
*J. Fulton	*J. Fulton	J. Fulton
I.G. Davidson	I.G. Davidson	I.G. Davidson
J.B. Allison	J.B. Allison	J.B. Allison
B.R.W. Doran	B.R.W. Doran	B.R.W. Doran
+C.C. Fitzgerald	G.P. Doran 1T	G.P. Doran
A.M. Magee	A.M. Magee	*A.M. Magee
+H.H. Corley	H.H. Corley 1C	H.H. Corley
S.T. Irwin	S.T. Irwin	S.T. Irwin
+A. Tedford	A. Tedford	A. Tedford
T.A. Harvey	T.A. Harvey	T.A. Harvey
P. Healey	P. Healey	P. Healey
+G.T. Hamlet	G.T. Hamlet	G.T. Hamlet
J. Ryan	+J.C. Pringle	J.C. Pringle
J.J. Coffey	J.J. Coffey	J.J. Coffey
F. Gardiner 1T	F. Gardiner	F. Gardiner
Leicester	Belfast	Lansdowne Road
lost 3-6	won 5-0	lost 0-15
Eng. 2T	Ire. 1G	Ire. Nil
Ire. 1T	Scot. Nil	Wales 1G, 1DG, 2T
8 February 1902	22 February 1902	8 March 1902

1902–03

v ENGLAND	v SCOTLAND	v WALES
J. Fulton	J. Fulton	J. Fulton
+H.J. Anderson	H.J. Anderson	+G. Bradshaw
+D.R. Taylor	J.B. Allison	+J.C. Parke
+G.A.D. Harvey	G.A.D. Harvey	C. Reid
C.C. Fitzgerald	C.C. Fitzgerald	G.P. Doran
A.M. Magee	A.M. Magee	A.M. Magee
*H.H. Corley 1PG	*H.H. Corley	*H.H. Corley
M. Ryan 1T	C.E. Allen	C.E. Allen
A. Tedford	A. Tedford	A. Tedford
T.A. Harvey	+Jos. Wallace	Jos. Wallace
P. Healey	P. Healey	P. Healey
G.T. Hamlet	G.T. Hamlet	G.T. Hamlet
+R.S. Smyth	R.S. Smyth	T.A. Harvey
J.J. Coffey	J.J. Coffey	J.J. Coffey
F. Gardiner	S.T. Irwin	F. Gardiner
Lansdowne Road	Inverleith	Cardiff Arms Park
won 6-0	lost 0-3	lost 0-18
Ire. 1PG, 1T	Scot. 1T	Wales 6T
Eng. Nil	Ire. Nil	Ire. Nil
14 February 1903	28 February 1903	14 March 1903

1903–04

v ENGLAND	v SCOTLAND	v WALES
J. Fulton	J. Fulton	+M.F. Landers
+C.G. Robb	C.G. Robb	C.G. Robb
J.C. Parke	J.C. Parke	J.C. Parke 1C
*H.H. Corley	*H.H. Corley	G.A.D. Harvey
G.P. Doran	+J.E. Moffatt 1T	+H.B. Thrift 1T
+T.T.H. Robinson	T.T.H. Robinson	A.M. Magee
+F.A. Kennedy	+E.D. Caddell	F.A. Kennedy
A. Tedford	A. Tedford	A. Tedford 2T
C.E. Allen	C.E. Allen	*C.E. Allen
Jos. Wallace	Jos. Wallace	Jos. Wallace 1T
+Jas Wallace	Jas Wallace	+H.J. Millar
R.S. Smyth	G.T. Hamlet	G.T. Hamlet
M. Ryan	M. Ryan	+R.W. Edwards
J. Ryan	P. Healey	+H.J. Knox
F. Gardiner	F. Gardiner	F. Gardiner
Blackheath	Lansdowne Road	Belfast
lost 0-19	lost 3-19	won 14-12
Eng. 2G, 3T	Ire. 1T	Ire. 1G, 3T
Ire. Nil	Scot. 2G, 3T	Wales 4T
13 February 1904	27 February 1904	12 March 1904

1904–05

v ENGLAND	v SCOTLAND	v WALES
M.F. Landers	M.F. Landers	M.F. Landers
H.B. Thrift	H.B. Thrift	H.B. Thrift
+B. Maclear 1T, 1C	B. Maclear 1C	B. Maclear
G.A.D. Harvey	G.A.D. Harvey	J.C. Parke
J.E. Moffatt 2T	J.E. Moffatt 1T	J.E. Moffatt
T.T.H. Robinson	T.T.H. Robinson	T.T.H. Robinson 1T
E.D. Caddell	E.D. Caddell	E.D. Caddell
A. Tedford	A. Tedford 1T	A. Tedford
*C.E. Allen 1T	*C.E. Allen	*C.E. Allen
Jos. Wallace 1T	Jos. Wallace 1T	Jos. Wallace
H.J. Millar	H.J. Millar	H.J. Millar
G.T. Hamlet	G.T. Hamlet	G.T. Hamlet
+H.G. Wilson	H.G. Wilson	H.G. Wilson
H.J. Knox	H.J. Knox	H.J. Knox
J.J. Coffey	J.J. Coffey	J.J. Coffey
Cork	Inverleith	St Helen's
won 17-3	won 11-5	lost 3-10
Ire. 1G, 4T	Scot. 1G	Wales 2G
Eng. 1T	Ire. 1G, 2T	Ire. 1T
11 February 1905	25 February 1905	11 March 1905

1905–06

v NZ	v ENGLAND	v SCOTLAND	v WALES
M.F. Landers	+G.J. Henebrey	G.J. Henebrey	G.J. Henebrey
H.B. Thrift	H.B. Thrift	C.G. Robb 1T	H.B. Thrift 1T
B. Maclear	+F. Casement	F. Casement	F. Casement
J.C. Parke	J.C. Parke	J.C. Parke 1T	J.C. Parke
C.G. Robb	H.J. Anderson	H.J. Anderson	B. Maclear 1T
T.T.H. Robinson	B. Maclear 1C, 1T	B. Maclear	E.D. Caddell
E.D. Caddell	E.D. Caddell	E.D. Caddell	W.B. Purdon
Jos. Wallace	+W.B. Purdon 1T	W.B. Purdon	
			A. Tedford
A. Tedford	A. Tedford 2T	A. Tedford	*C.E. Allen
*C.E. Allen	*C.E. Allen	*C.E. Allen	Jos. Wallace 1T
+H.S. Sugars	F. Gardiner 1C	F. Gardiner	F. Gardiner 1C
G.T. Hamlet	+M. White	M. White	M. White
H.G. Wilson	H.G. Wilson	H.G. Wilson	H.G. Wilson
H.J. Knox	H.J. Knox	H.J. Knox	H.J. Knox
J.J. Coffey	J.J. Coffey	J.J. Coffey	J.J. Coffey
Lansdowne Road	Leicester	Lansdowne Road	Belfast
lost 0-15	won 16-6	lost 6-13	won 11-6
Ire. Nil	Eng. 2T	Ire. 2T	Ire. 1G, 2T
NZ 3G	Ire. 2G, 2T	Scot. 2G, 1GM	Wales 2T
25 November 1905	10 February 1906	24 February 1906	10 March 1906

1906–07

v S. AFRICA	v ENGLAND	v SCOTLAND	v WALES
G.J. Henebrey	+C. Thompson	C. Thompson	+W.P. Hinton
H.B. Thrift	H.B. Thrift 1T	H.B. Thrift	H.B. Thrift
+R.P.C. Gotto	B. Maclear	T.J. Greeves	T.J. Greeves
J.C. Parke 1PG	J.C. Parke 1C, 1GM	J.C. Parke 1PG	J.C. Parke
B. Maclear 1T	+T.J. Greeves	B. Maclear	B. Maclear
T.T.H. Robinson	T.T.H. Robinson	T.T.H. Robinson	T.T.H. Robinson
E.D. Caddell	E.D. Caddell 2T	E.D. Caddell	+F.M.W. Harvey
A. Tedford	*A. Tedford 1T	A. Tedford	A. Tedford
*C.E. Allen	+R.E. Forbes	*C.E. Allen	*C.E. Allen
H.S. Sugars 2T	+W. St J. Cogan	W. St J. Cogan	H.J. Knox
G.T. Hamlet	G.T. Hamlet	G.T. Hamlet	G.T. Hamlet
M. White	M. White	H.S. Sugars	M. White
+G. McIldowie	+J.A. Sweeney	J.A. Sweeney	J.A. Sweeney
H.G. Wilson	H.G. Wilson	H.G. Wilson	H.G. Wilson
J.J. Coffey	J.J. Coffey	F. Gardiner	F. Gardiner
Belfast lost 12-15	Lansdowne Road won 17-9	Inverleith lost 3-15	Cardiff Arms Park lost 0-29
Ire. 1PG, 3T SA 1PG, 4T	Ire. 1G, 1GM, 3T Eng. 1PG, 2T	Scot. 3G Ire. 1PG	Wales 2G, 1PG, 1DG, 4T Ire. Nil
24 November 1906	9 February 1907	23 February 1907	9 March 1907

1907–08

v ENGLAND	v SCOTLAND	v WALES
W.P. Hinton	W.P. Hinton 1C	W.P. Hinton
*H.B. Thrift	H.B. Thrift 2T	H.B. Thrift
+G.C.P. Beckett	G.C.P. Beckett 1T	G.C.P. Beckett
J.C. Parke 1PG	*J.C. Parke 1C	*J.C. Parke 1C
C. Thompson	C. Thompson 1T	C. Thompson
+H.R. Aston	E.D. Caddell	E.D. Caddell
+F.N.B. Smartt	F.N.B. Smartt	H.R. Aston 1T
A. Tedford	A. Tedford	A. Tedford
+T. Smyth	T. Smyth	T. Smyth
+B.A. Solomons	B.A. Solomons	B.A. Solomons
+T.G. Harpur	T.G. Harpur	T.G. Harpur
G.T. Hamlet	G.T. Hamlet	G.T. Hamlet
H.G. Wilson	H.G. Wilson	H.G. Wilson
+E. McG. Morphy	H.J. Knox	J.J. Coffey
+C. Adams	F. Gardiner	F. Gardiner
Richmond lost 3-13	Lansdowne Road won 16-11	Belfast lost 5-11
Eng. 2G, 1T Ire. 1PG	Ire. 2G, 2T Scot. 1G, 1PG, 1T	Ire. 1G Wales 1G, 2T
8 February 1908	29 February 1908	14 March 1908

1908–09

v ENGLAND	v SCOTLAND	v WALES	v FRANCE
W.P. Hinton	W.P. Hinton	G.J. Henebrey	G.J. Henebrey
H.B. Thrift	H.B. Thrift	H.B. Thrift	H.B. Thrift
J.C. Parke 1T	J.C. Parke 1PG	J.C. Parke 1C	J.C. Parke 1PG, 1C
C. Thompson	C. Thompson	T.J. Greeves	C. Thompson 2T
+E.C. Deane	+R.M. Magrath	C. Thompson 1T	T.J. Greeves
+G. Pinion 1C	G. Pinion	G. Pinion	G. Pinion
F.N.B. Smartt	*F. Gardiner	+F.M. McCormac	+J.J. O'Connor 1T
+M.G. Garry	M.G. Garry	M.G. Garry	M.G. Garry
T. Smyth	T. Smyth	T. Smyth	C. Adams
B.A. Solomons	B.A. Solomons	B.A. Solomons	B.A. Solomons
+O.J.S. Piper	O.J.S. Piper	O.J.S. Piper	O.J.S. Piper
G.T. Hamlet	G.T. Hamlet	*G.T. Hamlet	G.T. Hamlet
H.G. Wilson	H.G. Wilson	H.G. Wilson	*F. Gardiner 1C, 1T
C. Adams	+J.C. Blackham	J.C. Blackham	J.C. Blackham
*F. Gardiner	+T. Halpin	T. Halpin	T. Halpin
Lansdowne Road	Inverleith	St Helen's	Lansdowne Road
lost 5-11	lost 3-9	lost 5-18	won 19-8
Ire. 1G	Scot. 3T	Wales 3G, 1T	Ire. 2G, 1PG, 2T
Eng. 1G, 2T	Ire. 1PG	Ire. 1G	Fr. 1G, 1T
13 February 1909	27 February 1909	13 March 1909	20 March 1909

1909–10

v ENGLAND	v SCOTLAND	v WALES	v FRANCE
W.P. Hinton	W.P. Hinton	W.P. Hinton	W.P. Hinton
+J.P. Quinn	J.P. Quinn	+C.T. O'Callaghan	+ C.V. MacIvor
+A.R. Foster	A.R. Foster	A.S. Taylor	A.R. Foster
+A.S. Taylor	A.S. Taylor	+R.K. Lyle	R.K. Lyle
C. Thompson	C. Thompson	C. Thompson	C. Thompson 1T
+R.A. Lloyd	R.A. Lloyd	+A.N. McClinton	A.N. McClinton 1C
+H.M. Read	H.M. Read	F.M. McCormac	F.M. McCormac
G. McIldowie	G. McIldowie	G. McIldowie 1T	+W.J. Beatty
T. Smyth	T. Smyth	*T. Smyth	T. Smyth 1T
B.A. Solomons	B.A. Solomons	B.A. Solomons	*G.T. Hamlet
O.J.S. Piper	O.J.S. Piper	O.J.S. Piper	O.J.S. Piper
*G.T. Hamlet	*G.T. Hamlet	+W.S. Smyth	W.S. Smyth
+W.F. Riordan	+H. Moore	H.G. Wilson	C. Adams
J.C. Blackham	J.C. Blackham	J.C. Blackham	J.J. Coffey
T. Halpin	T. Halpin	T. Halpin	+W. Tyrrell
Twickenham	Belfast	Lansdowne Road	Parc des Princes
drawn 0-0	lost 0-14	lost 3-19	won 8-3
Eng. Nil	Ire. Nil	Ire. 1T	Fr. 1T
Ire. Nil	Scot. 1G, 3T	Wales 1DG, 5T	Ire. 1G, 1T
12 February 1910	26 February 1910	12 March 1910	28 March 1910

1910–11

v ENGLAND	v SCOTLAND	v WALES	v FRANCE
W.P. Hinton	W.P. Hinton 1C	W.P. Hinton	F.M.W. Harvey
C.T. O'Callaghan	C.T. O'Callaghan 1T	C.T. O'Callaghan	C.T. O'Callaghan 1T
A.R. Foster	A.R. Foster 1T	A.R. Foster	A.R. Foster
+A.R.V. Jackson	A.R.V. Jackson	A.R.V. Jackson	A.R.V. Jackson 2T
J.P. Quinn	J.P. Quinn 1T	J.P. Quinn	J.P. Quinn 1T
R.A. Lloyd	R.A. Lloyd 1C	R.A. Lloyd	R.A. Lloyd 1DG, 3C
H.M. Read	H.M. Read	H.M. Read	H.M. Read
M.G. Garry	M.G. Garry	M.G. Garry	+R.I. Graham
T. Smyth 1T	T. Smyth	T. Smyth	P.J. Smyth
+S.B.B. Campbell	S.B.B. Campbell	S.B.B. Campbell	S.B.B. Campbell
+P.J. Smyth	P.J. Smyth	H. Moore	H. Moore
*G.T. Hamlet	*G.T. Hamlet	*G.T. Hamlet	*G.T. Hamlet
C. Adams	C. Adams 1T	C. Adams	C. Adams
+M.R. Heffernan	M.R. Heffernan	M.R. Heffernan	M.R. Heffernan 1T
T. Halpin	T. Halpin	T. Halpin	T. Halpin
Lansdowne Road	Inverleith	Cardiff Arms Park	Cork
won 3-0	won 16-10	lost 0-16	won 25-5
Ire. 1T	Scot. 1DG, 2T	Wales 2G, 1PG, 1T	Ire. 3G, 1DG, 2T
Eng. Nil	Ire. 2G, 2T	Ire. Nil	Fr. 1G
11 February 1911	25 February 1911	11 March 1911	25 March 1911

1911–12

v FRANCE	v ENGLAND	v SCOTLAND	v WALES
W.P. Hinton	W.P. Hinton	+R.A. Wright	W.P. Hinton
C.V. MacIvor	C.V. MacIvor	C.V. MacIvor	C.V. MacIvor 1T
A.S. Taylor 1T	+M. Abraham	M. Abraham	M. Abraham
A.R. Foster 1T	*A.R. Foster	A.R. Foster 1T	A.R. Foster
C.T. O'Callaghan	J.P. Quinn	J.P. Quinn	J.P. Quinn
*R.A. Lloyd 1T, 1C	R.A. Lloyd	*R.A. Lloyd 1DG, 1PG	*R.A. Lloyd 1DG, 1C
H.M. Read	H.M. Read	H.M. Read	H.M. Read
W.J. Beatty	T. Smyth	+G.S. Brown	G.S. Brown 1T
+R. Hemphill	R. Hemphill	R. Hemphill	R. Hemphill
S.B.B. Campbell	S.B.B. Campbell	S.B.B. Campbell	S.B.B. Campbell
H. Moore	H. Moore	H. Moore	H. Moore
+G. McConnell	G. McConnell	C. Adams	C. Adams
+W.V. Edwards	W.V. Edwards	R. d'A. Patterson	R. d'A. Patterson
+R. d'A. Patterson	+G.V. Killeen	G.V. Killeen	G.V. Killeen
T. Halpin	T. Halpin	T. Halpin	W.J. Beatty
Parc des Princes	Twickenham	Lansdowne Road	Belfast
won 11-6	lost 0-15	won 10-8	won 12-5
Fr. 2T	Eng. 5T	Ire. 1DG, 1PG, 1T	Ire. 1G, 1DG, 1T
Ire. 1G, 2T	Ire. Nil	Scot. 1G, 1T	Wales 1G
1 January 1912	10 February 1912	24 February 1912	9 March 1912

1912–13

v S. AFRICA	v ENGLAND	v SCOTLAND	v WALES	v FRANCE
+C.P. Stuart	+G. Young	+J.W. McConnell	+A.W.P. Todd	A.W.P. Todd
+R. Watson	C.V. MacIvor	C.V. MacIvor	+G.H. Wood	C.V. MacIvor
+G.W. Holmes	G.W. Holmes	G.W. Holmes	A.R.V. Jackson	A.R.V. Jackson
+J.B. Minch	J.B. Minch	J.B. Minch	+A.L. Stewart 1T	A.L. Stewart
M. Abraham	J.B. Quinn	+F. Bennett	J.P. Quinn 1T	J.P. Quinn 3T
*R.A. Lloyd	*R.A. Lloyd 1DG	*R.A. Lloyd 1DG, 2C	*R.A. Lloyd 2C, 1PG	*R.A. Lloyd 3C
H.M. Read	H.M. Read	H.M. Read	+S.E. Polden	S.E. Polden
G.S. Brown	+J.E. Finlay	J.E. Finlay	J.E. Finlay	G. McConnell
+R.B. Burgess	W. Tyrrell	W. Tyrrell	W. Tyrrell	W. Tyrrell 2T
S.B.B. Campbell	S.B.B. Campbell	S.B.B. Campbell	G. McConnell	S.B.B. Campbell
H. Moore	+E.W. Jeffares	E.W. Jeffares	+P. O'Connell	P. O'Connell
C. Adams	G.V. Killeen	G.V. Killeen	G.V. Killeen	G.V. Killeen
R. d'A. Patterson	R. d'A. Patterson	R. d'A. Patterson	R. d'A. Patterson	R. d'A. Patterson 1T
+F.G. Schute	F.G. Schute	F.G. Schute 1T	C. Adams	C. Adams
+J.J. Clune	+P. Stokes	P. Stokes 1T	J.J. Clune	J.J. Clune
Lansdowne Road	Lansdowne Road	Inverleith	St Helen's	Cork
lost 0-38	lost 4–15	lost 14-29	lost 13-16	won 24-0
Ire. Nil	Ire. 1DG	Scot. 4G, 3T	Wales 2G, 1PG, 1T	Ire. 3G, 3T
SA 4G, 6T	Eng. 1PG, 4T	Ire. 2G, 1DG	Ire. 2G, 1PG	Fr. Nil
30 November 1912	8 February 1913	22 February 1913	8 March 1913	24 March 1913

1913–14

v FRANCE	v ENGLAND	v SCOTLAND	v WALES
A.W.P. Todd	+F.P. Montgomery	F.P. Montgomery	F.P. Montgomery
G.H. Wood	A.R. Foster	*A.R. Foster	*A.R. Foster 1T
A.R.V. Jackson	A.R.V. Jackson 1T	A.R.V. Jackson	A.R.V. Jackson
A.L. Stewart	J.B. Minch	J.B. Minch	M. Abraham
J.P. Quinn 1T	J.P. Quinn 1T	J.P. Quinn 1T	+J.T. Brett
*R.A. Lloyd 1C	*R.A. Lloyd 1DG, 1C	+H.W. Jack	H.W. Jack
S.E. Polden	+V. McNamara	V. McNamara 1T	V. McNamara
+J.C.A. Dowse	+J. Taylor	J. Taylor	J. Taylor
W. Tyrrell 1T	W. Tyrrell	W. Tyrrell	W. Tyrrell
+J.S. Parr	J.S. Parr	J.S. Parr	J.S. Parr
P. O'Connell	P. O'Connell	P. O'Connell	P. O'Connell
C. Adams	C. Adams	C. Adams	J.J. Clune
J.J. Clune	J.J. Clune	J.C.A. Dowse	J.C.A. Dowse
+W.P. Collopy	W.P. Collopy	W.P. Collopy	W.P. Collopy
P. Stokes	G.V. Killeen	G.V. Killeen	G.V. Killeen
Parc des Princes	Twickenham	Lansdowne Road	Belfast
won 8–6	lost 12-17	won 6-0	lost 3-11
Fr. 2T	Eng. 1G, 4T	Ire. 2T	Ire. 1T
Ire. 1G, 1T	Ire. 1G, 1DG, 1T	Scot. Nil	Wales 1G, 2T
1 January 1914	14 February 1914	28 February 1914	14 March 1914

1919–20

v ENGLAND	v SCOTLAND	v WALES	v FRANCE
+W.E. Crawford	W.E. Crawford	W.E. Crawford	W.E. Crawford
+J.A.N. Dickson 1T	C.H. Bryant	J.A.N. Dickson	J.A.N. Dickson
+T. Wallace	*T. Wallace	*T. Wallace	+G.V. Stephenson
+W.J. Cullen	+P.J. Roddy	W. Duggan	P.J. Roddy
+C.H. Bryant	+B.A.T. McFarland	B.A.T. McFarland 1DG	B.A.T. McFarland
*R.A. Lloyd 1T, 1C, 1PG	+W. Duggan		*R.A. Lloyd 1DG
+A.K. Horan	+J.B. O'Neill	+W. Cunningham	S.E. Polden
		A.K. Horan	
	+A.H. Price		M.J. Bradley
+N. Butler	H.H. Coulter	+M.J. Bradley	A.H. Price 1T
+H.H. Coulter	+A.W. Courtney	H.H. Coulter	A.W. Courtney
W.S. Smyth	J.E. Finlay	A.W. Courtney	+J.T. Smyth
J.E. Finlay	R.Y. Crichton	J.E. Finlay	R.Y. Crichton
+R.Y. Crichton	W.D. Doherty	R.Y. Crichton	+D. Browne
+W.D. Doherty	W.J. Roche	W.D. Doherty	W.J. Roche
+W.J. Roche	P. Stokes	+H.N. Potterton	P. Stokes
P. Stokes		P. Stokes	
Lansdowne Road	Inverleith	Cardiff Arms Park	Lansdowne Road
lost 11-14	lost 0-19	lost 4-28	lost 7-15
Ire. 1G, 1PG, 1T	Scot. 2G, 1PG, 2T	Wales 3G, 1DG, 3T	Ire. 1DG, 1T
Eng. 1G, 3T	Ire. Nil	Ire. 1DG	Fr. 5T
14 February 1920	28 February 1920	13 March 1920	3 April 1920

1920–21

v ENGLAND	v SCOTLAND	v WALES	v FRANCE
W.E. Crawford	W.E. Crawford	W.E. Crawford	W.E. Crawford
+D.J. Cussen	D.J. Cussen 1T	D.J. Cussen	D.J. Cussen
G.V. Stephenson	G.V. Stephenson 1T	G.V. Stephenson	G.V. Stephenson
A.R. Foster	A.R. Foster	A.R. Foster	+T.G. Wallis 2C
+H.S.T. Cormac	H.S.T. Cormac	H.S.T. Cormac	+C.T. Davidson
W. Cunningham	W. Cunningham 1T	W. Cunningham	W. Cunningham
+T. Mayne	T. Mayne	H.W. Jack	T. Mayne
*W.D. Doherty	*W.D. Doherty	*W.D. Doherty	*W.D. Doherty
+T.A. McClelland	T.A. McClelland	T.A. McClelland	T.A. McClelland
A.W. Courtney	A.W. Courtney	A.W. Courtney	A.W. Courtney
+J.J. Bermingham	J.J. Bermingham	J.J. Bermingham	J.J. Bermingham
+C.F.G.T. Hallaran	C.F.G.T. Hallaran	C.F.G.T. Hallaran	R.Y. Crichton
W.P. Collopy	W.P. Collopy	W.P. Collopy	W.P. Collopy
+N.M. Purcell	N.M. Purcell	N.M. Purcell	N.M. Purcell
P. Stokes	P. Stokes	+J.K.S. Thompson	P. Stokes 2T
Twickenham	Lansdowne Road	Balmoral	Stade Colombes
lost 0-15	won 9-8	lost 0-6	lost 10-20
Eng. 1G, 1DG, 2T	Ire. 3T	Ire. Nil	Fr. 4G
Ire. Nil	Scot. 1G, 1T	Wales 1PG, 1T	Ire. 2G
12 February 1921	26 February 1921	12 March 1921	9 April 1921

1921–22

v ENGLAND	v SCOTLAND	v WALES	v FRANCE
W.E. Crawford	W.E. Crawford	B.A.T. McFarland	+J.W. Stewart
T.G. Wallis 1T	T.G. Wallis	T.G. Wallis 1C	T.G. Wallis 1C, 1PG
+D.B. Sullivan	D.B. Sullivan	D.B. Sullivan	D.B. Sullivan
G.V. Stephenson	G.V. Stephenson	G.V. Stephenson	G.V. Stephenson 1T
D.J. Cussen	+H.W.V. Stephenson	H.W.V. Stephenson	H.W.V. Stephenson
+J.R. Wheeler	J.R. Wheeler	J.R. Wheeler	J.R. Wheeler
W. Cunningham	+J.A.B. Clarke 1T	J.A.B. Clarke	J.A.B. Clarke
M.J. Bradley	M.J. Bradley	M.J. Bradley	M.J. Bradley
T.A. McClelland	+J.D. Egan	T.A. McClelland	T.A. McClelland
+S. McVicker	S. McVicker	S. McVicker	S. McVicker
C.F.G.T. Hallaran	C.F.G.T. Hallaran	C.F.G.T. Hallaran	J.C. Gillespie
R.Y. Crichton	+I. Popham	I. Popham	I. Popham
*W.P. Collopy	*W.P. Collopy	*W.P. Collopy	*W.P. Collopy
+R.H. Owens	R.H. Owens	P. Stokes 1T	P. Stokes
J.K.S. Thompson	J.K.S. Thompson	+J.C. Gillespie	J.K.S. Thompson
Lansdowne Road	Inverleith	St Helen's	Lansdowne Road
lost 3-12	lost 3-6	lost 5-11	won 8-3
Ire. 1T	Scot. 2T	Wales 1G, 2T	Ire. 1G, 1PG
Eng. 4T	Ire. 1T	Ire. 1G	Fr. 1T
11 February 1922	25 February 1922	11 March 1922	8 April 1922

1922–23

v ENGLAND	v SCOTLAND	v WALES	v FRANCE
W.E. Crawford 1C	W.E. Crawford	W.E. Crawford 1C	W.E. Crawford 1C
+R.O. McClenahan	R.O. McClenahan	R.O. McClenahan	D.J. Cussen
+F. Jackson	G.V. Stephenson	G.V. Stephenson	G.V. Stephenson
G.V. Stephenson	J.B. Gardiner	J.B. Gardiner	J.B. Gardiner
D.J. Cussen	D.J. Cussen 1T	D.J. Cussen IT	+A.C. Douglas 1T
+W.H. Hall	W.H. Hall	W.H. Hall	W.H. Hall
+J.B. Gardiner	W. Cunningham	W. Cunningham	J.A.B. Clarke
M.J. Bradley	M.J. Bradley	M.J. Bradley	M.J. Bradley
T.A. McClelland 1T	T.A. McClelland	T.A. McClelland	T.A. McClelland 1T
+R. Collopy	R. Collopy	R. Collopy	R. Collopy
C.F.G.T. Hallaran	+P.E.F. Dunn	+J.D. Clinch	C.F.G.T. Hallaran
+D.M. Cunningham	D.M. Cunningham	D.M. Cunningham	I. Popham
+J. Mahony	W.P. Collopy	W.P. Collopy	W.P. Collopy
+R.D. Gray	R.D. Gray	R.Y. Crichton	R.Y. Crichton
*J.K.S. Thompson	*J.K.S. Thompson	*J.K.S. Thompson	*J.K.S. Thompson
Leicester	Lansdowne Road	Lansdowne Road	Stade Colombes
lost 5-23	lost 3-13	won 5-4	lost 8-14
Eng. 2G, 1DG, 3T	Ire. 1T	Ire. 1G	Fr. 1G, 3T
Ire. 1G	Scot. 2G, 1T	Wales 1DG	Ire. 1G, 1T
10 February 1923	24 February 1923	10 March 1923	14 April 1923

1923–24

v FRANCE	v ENGLAND	v SCOTLAND	v WALES
*W.E. Crawford	*W.E. Crawford	J.W. Stewart	*W.E. Crawford 2C
H.W.V. Stephenson	H.W.V. Stephenson	H.W.V. Stephenson	H.W.V. Stephenson 1T
G.V. Stephenson 1T	G.V. Stephenson	G.V. Stephenson 1C,	G.V. Stephenson
J.B. Gardiner	J.B. Gardiner	2T	J.B. Gardiner
+A.P. Atkins 1T	A.C. Douglas 1T	J.B. Gardiner	+T.R. Hewitt 1T
		A.C. Douglas	
W.H. Hall	J.R. Wheeler		+F.S. Hewitt 1T
+J.C. McDowell	J.A.B. Clarke	W.H. Hall	J.A.B. Clarke
		J.A.B. Clarke	
+J. McVicker	J. McVicker	J. McVicker	J. McVicker
T.A. McClelland	T.A. McClelland	T.A. McClelland	T.A. McClelland
R. Collopy	R. Collopy	R. Collopy	R. Collopy
C.F.G.T. Hallaran	C.F.G.T. Hallaran	C.F.G.T. Hallaran	C.F.G.T. Hallaran
+W.R.F. Collis	+I.M.B. Stuart	I.M.B. Stuart	W.R.F. Collis
W.P. Collopy	W.P. Collopy	*W.P. Collopy	W.P. Collopy
R.Y. Crichton	R.Y. Crichton	R.Y. Crichton	R.Y. Crichton
J.D. Clinch	J.D. Clinch	J.D. Clinch	J.D. Clinch
Lansdowne Road	Ravenhill	Inverleith	Cardiff Arms Park
won 6-0	lost 3-14	lost 8-13	won 13-10
Ire. 2T	Ire. 1T	Scot. 2G, 1T	Wales 1DG, 2T
Fr. Nil	Eng. 1G, 3T	Ire. 1G, 1T	Ire. 2G, 1T
26 January 1924	9 February 1924	23 February 1924	8 March 1924

1924–25

v NZ	v FRANCE	v ENGLAND	v SCOTLAND	v WALES
W.E. Crawford	*W.E. Crawford 1PG	*W.E. Crawford	*W.E. Crawford 1PG,	*W.E. Crawford
			1C	
H.W.V. Stephenson	H.W.V. Stephenson	H.W.V. Stephenson 1T		H.W.V. Stephenson 1T
*G.V. Stephenson	G.V. Stephenson 1T	J.B. Gardiner	H.W.V. Stephenson 1T	+T.J. Millin 1T
J.B. Gardiner	J.B. Gardiner 1T	T.R. Hewitt 1T	G.V. Stephenson	J.B. Gardiner
T.R. Hewitt	T.R. Hewitt	G.V. Stephenson	J.B. Gardiner	G.V. Stephenson 1PG,
			T.R. Hewitt	2C, 1T
F.S. Hewitt	F.S. Hewitt	F.S. Hewitt		
J.C. McDowell	+M. Sugden	M. Sugden	F.S. Hewitt	+E. O'D. Davy
			M. Sugden	M. Sugden
J. McVicker	J. McVicker	J. McVicker	J. McVicker	
T.A. McClelland	M.J. Bradley	D.M. Cunningham	M.J. Bradley	J. McVicker
R. Collopy	R. Collopy	R. Collopy	R. Collopy	M.J. Bradley
+A.W. Spain	C.F.G.T. Hallaran	R.Y. Crichton	R.Y. Crichton	R. Collopy
W.R.F. Collis	W.R.F. Collis	W.R.F. Collis	W.R.F. Collis	+S.J. Cagney
+T.N. Brand	D.M. Cunningham	+W.F. Browne	W.F. Browne	+R.S. Flood
R.Y. Crichton	R.D. Gray	+G.R. Beamish	G.R. Beamish	W.F. Browne 1T
J.D. Clinch	J.D. Clinch	J.D. Clinch	J.D. Clinch	G.R. Beamish
Lansdowne Road	Stade Colombes	Twickenham	Lansdowne Road	D.M. Cunningham
lost 0-6	won 9–3	drawn 6-6	lost 8-14	Ravenhill
Ire. Nil	Fr. 1T	Eng. 2T	Ire. 1G, 1PG	won 19-3
NZ 1PG, 1T	Ire. 1PG, 2T	Ire. 2T	Scot. 2G, 1DG	Ire. 2G, 1PG, 2T
1 November 1924	1 January 1925	14 February 1925	28 February 1925	Wales IT
				14 March 1925

1925–26

v FRANCE	v ENGLAND	v SCOTLAND	v WALES
*W.E. Crawford	*W.E. Crawford	*W.E. Crawford	*W.E. Crawford
D.J. Cussen	D.J. Cussen 2T	D.J. Cussen	D.J. Cussen
G.V. Stephenson 2T, 1PG	G.V. Stephenson 1T, 1PG, 2C	G.V. Stephenson	G.V. Stephenson 1PG, 1C
T.R. Hewitt 1C	F.S. Hewitt 1T	T.R. Hewitt	T.R. Hewitt
+R.L. Hamilton	T.R. Hewitt	+J.H. Gage 1T	J.H. Gage
E. O'D. Davy	E. O'D. Davy	E. O'D. Davy	E. O'D. Davy
M. Sugden	M. Sugden	M. Sugden	M. Sugden
R.D. Gray	S.J. Cagney	M.J. Bradley	M.J. Bradley
M.J. Bradley	M.J. Bradley	A.M. Buchanan	A.M. Buchanan
+J. McF. Neill	+A.M. Buchanan	W.F. Browne	W.F. Browne
S.J. Cagney	C.F.G.T. Hallaran	S.J. Cagney	S.J. Cagney
W.R.F. Collis	J.L. Farrell	J. McVicker	J. McVicker
C.F.G.T. Hallaran	J.D. Clinch	J.D. Clinch	J.D. Clinch
J. McVicker	J. McVicker	+C.J. Hanrahan	C.J. Hanrahan 1T
+J.L. Farrell	+C.T. Payne	J.L. Farrell	J.L. Farrell
Belfast	Lansdowne Road	Murrayfield	St Helen's
won 11-0	won 19-15	won 3-0	lost 8-11
Ire. 1G, 1PG, 1T Fr. Nil	Ire. 2G, 1PG, 2T Eng. 3G	Scot. Nil Ire. 1T	Wales 1G, 2T Ire. 1G, 1PG
23 January 1926	13 February 1926	27 February 1926	13 March 1926

1926–27

v FRANCE	v ENGLAND	v SCOTLAND	v WALES
*W.E. Crawford	*W.E. Crawford	*W.E. Crawford	*W.E. Crawford
D.J. Cussen	D.J. Cussen	J.B. Ganly 1T	J.B. Ganly 2T
G.V. Stephenson 1PG, 1C	G.V. Stephenson 1PG	G.V. Stephenson	G.V. Stephenson 1PG, 2C, 2T
+J.M. Atkinson	F.S. Hewitt	F.S. Hewitt	F.S. Hewitt
+J.B. Ganly	J.B. Ganly	J.H. Gage	J.H. Gage
E. O'D. Davy 1T	E. O'D. Davy	E. O'D. Davy	E. O'D. Davy
+P.F. Murray	M. Sugden	M. Sugden	M. Sugden
M.J. Bradley	C.J. Hanrahan	C.J. Hanrahan	C.J. Hanrahan
J.L. Farrell	C.T. Payne	C.T. Payne	M.J. Bradley
J. McVicker	J. McVicker	J. McVicker	J. McVicker
C.T. Payne	J.L. Farrell	J.L. Farrell	J.L. Farrell
S.J. Cagney	+H. McVicker 1T	H. McVicker	H. McVicker
J.D. Clinch	+T.O. Pike	T.O. Pike 1T	T.O. Pike
+N.G. Ross	N.G. Ross	A.M. Buchanan	A.M. Buchanan
W.F. Browne	W.F. Browne	W.F. Browne	W.F. Browne
Stade Colombes	Twickenham	Lansdowne Road	Lansdowne Road
won 8-3	lost 6-8	won 6-0	won 19-9
Fr. 1T Ire. 1G, 1PG	Eng. 1G, 1T Ire. 1PG, 1T	Ire. 2T Scot. Nil	Ire. 2G, 1PG, 2T Wales 1G, 1DG
1 January 1927	12 February 1927	26 February 1927	12 March 1927

1927–28

v NSW	v FRANCE	v ENGLAND	v SCOTLAND	v WALES
A.C. Douglas	J.W. Stewart	J.W. Stewart	J.W. Stewart	J.W. Stewart
J.B. Ganly 1PG	J.B. Ganly 2T	H.W.V. Stephenson	+R.M. Byers	R.M. Byres
J.M. Atkinson	+R.V.M. Odbert	J.B. Ganly	J.B. Ganly 1T	J.B. Ganly 1T
*G.V. Stephenson	*G.V. Stephenson	*G.V. Stephenson	*G.V. Stephenson 1T, 2C	*G.V. Stephenson 2C
H.W.V. Stephenson	+J.E. Arigho 2T	J.E. Arigho 1T	A.C. Douglas	J.E. Arigho 2T
E. O'D. Davy	E. O'D. Davy	E. O'D. Davy	E. O'D. Davy 1T	E. O'D. Davy
M. Sugden	M. Sugden	M. Sugden 1T	M. Sugden	M. Sugden
C.J. Hanrahan	C.J. Hanrahan	C.J. Hanrahan	C.J. Hanrahan	J. McVicker
J.L. Farrell	J.L. Farrell	C.T. Payne	C.T. Payne	C.T. Payne
J. McVicker	T.O. Pike	T.O. Pike	T.O. Pike	T.O. Pike
C.T. Payne	C.T. Payne	J.L. Farrell	J.L. Farrell	J.L. Farrell
H. McVicker	H. McVicker	S.J. Cagney	S.J. Cagney	S.J. Cagney
T.O. Pike	+T. Bramwell	W.F. Browne	W.F. Browne	+J.P. Mullane
A.M. Buchanan	G.R. Beamish	G.R. Beamish	G.R. Beamish	G.R. Beamish
W.F. Browne	J.D. Clinch	J.D. Clinch	J.D. Clinch	J.D. Clinch
Lansdowne Road	Belfast	Lansdowne Road	Murrayfield	Cardiff Arms Park
lost 3-5	won 12-8	lost 6-7	won 13-5	won 13-10
Ire. 1PG	Ire. 4T	Ire. 2T	Scot. 1G	Wales 2G
NSW 1G	Fr. 1G, 1T	Eng. 1DG, 1T	Ire. 2G, 1T	Ire. 2G, 1T
12 November 1927	28 January 1928	11 February 1928	25 February 1928	10 March 1928

1928–29

v FRANCE	v ENGLAND	v SCOTLAND	v WALES
J.W. Stewart	J.W. Stewart	J.W. Stewart	J.W. Stewart
J.B. Ganly	R.M. Byers	R.M. Byers	R.M. Byers
*G.V. Stephenson 1T	*G.V. Stephenson	J.B. Ganly	*G.V. Stephenson
P.F. Murray	P.F. Murray	P.F. Murray	+M.P. Crowe
J.E. Arigho	J.E. Arigho	J.E. Arigho 1T	J.E. Arigho
E. O'D. Davy 1T	E. O'D. Davy 1T	*E. O'D. Davy 1DG	E. O'D. Davy 1T
M. Sugden	M. Sugden 1T	M. Sugden	M. Sugden
C.J. Hanrahan	C.J. Hanrahan	C.J. Hanrahan	J.L. Farrell
J.P. Mullane	+H.C. Browne	H.C. Browne	C.T. Payne
C.T. Payne	S.J. Cagney	+J.S. Synge	H.C. Browne 1C
J.L. Farrell	J.L. Farrell	J.L. Farrell	C.J. Hanrahan
+M.J. Dunne	M.J. Dunne	M.J. Dunne	+M. Deering
J.D. Clinch	J.D. Clinch	J.D. Clinch	J.D. Clinch
G.R. Beamish	G.R. Beamish	G.R. Beamish	G.R. Beamish
S.J. Cagney	C.T. Payne	S.J. Cagney	S.J. Cagney
Stade Colombes	Twickenham	Lansdowne Road	Belfast
won 6-0	won 6-5	lost 7-16	drawn 5-5
Fr. Nil	Eng. 1G	Ire. 1DG, 1T	Ire. 1G
Ire. 2T	Ire. 2T	Scot. 2G, 2T	Wales 1G
31 December 1928	9 February 1929	23 February 1929	9 March 1929

1929–30

v FRANCE	v ENGLAND	v SCOTLAND	v WALES
+E.W.F. de Vere Hunt	+F.W. Williamson	F.W. Williamson	F.W. Williamson
J.B. Ganly	*G.V. Stephenson	*G.V. Stephenson	*G.V. Stephenson
*G.V. Stephenson	E. O'D. Davy	E. O'D. Davy 3T	E. O'D. Davy 1DG
P.F. Murray	M.P. Crowe	M.P. Crowe 1T	M.P. Crowe
J.E. Arigho	J.E. Arigho	J.E. Arigho	J.E. Arigho
E. O'D. Davy	P.F. Murray 1DG	P.F. Murray 1C	P.F. Murray 1PG
M. Sugden	M. Sugden	M. Sugden	M. Sugden
C.J. Hanrahan	C.J. Hanrahan	C.J. Hanrahan	C.J. Hanrahan
M.J. Dunne	M.J. Dunne	M.J. Dunne	M.J. Dunne
C.T. Payne	+H. O'H. O'Neill	H. O'H. O'Neill	H. O'H. O'Neill
+C. Carroll	C.T. Payne	C.T. Payne	C.T. Payne
J.L. Farrell	J.L. Farrell	J.L. Farrell	J.L. Farrell
J. McVicker	+N.F. Murphy	+T.C. Casey	N.F. Murphy
G.R. Beamish	+W.J. McCormick	G.R. Beamish	G.R. Beamish
J.D. Clinch	J.D. Clinch	J.D. Clinch	J.D. Clinch
Ravenhill	Lansdowne Road	Murrayfield	St Helen's
lost 0--5	won 4-3	won 14-11	lost 7-12
Ire. Nil	Ire. 1DG	Scot. 1G, 2T	Wales 1PG, 3T
Fr. 1G	Eng. 1T	Ire. 1G, 3T	Ire. 1DG, 1PG
25 January 1930	8 February 1930	22 February 1930	8 March 1930

1930–31

v FRANCE	v ENGLAND	v SCOTLAND	v WALES
+J.T. Egan	J.T. Egan	+J.C. Entrican	+D.P. Morris
+E.J. Lightfoot	E.J. Lightfoot	E.J. Lightfoot	E.J. Lightfoot
P.F. Murray	E. O'D. Davy	E. O'D. Davy	E. O'D. Davy
M.P. Crowe	+L.B. McMahon 1T	M.P. Crowe	M.P. Crowe
J.E. Arigho	J.E. Arigho	J.E. Arigho	J.E. Arigho
E. O'D. Davy	P.F. Murray 1PG	P.F. Murray 1C	P.F. Murray
*M. Sugden	*M. Sugden	*M. Sugden 1T	*M. Sugden
C.J. Hanrahan	+V.J. Pike	V.J. Pike 1T	V.J. Pike
+H.H.C. Withers	H.H.C. Withers	H.H.C. Withers	H.H.C. Withers
J.L. Farrell	J.L. Farrell	J.L. Farrell	J.L. Farrell
+J.A.E. Siggins	J.A.E. Siggins	J.A.E. Siggins	J.A.E. Siggins 1T
+J. Russell	J. Russell	J. Russell	J. Russell
N.F. Murphy	N.F. Murphy	N.F. Murphy	N.F. Murphy
G.R. Beamish	G.R. Beamish	G.R. Beamish	G.R. Beamish
J.D. Clinch	J.D. Clinch	J.D. Clinch	J.D. Clinch
Stade Colombes	Twickenham	Lansdowne Road	Ravenhill
lost 0-3	won 6-5	won 8-5	lost 3-15
Fr. 1T	Eng. 1G	Ire. 1G, 1T	Ire. 1T
Ire. Nil	Ire. 1PG, 1T	Scot. 1G	Wales 1G, 1DG, 2T
1 January 1931	14 February 1931	28 February 1931	14 March 1931

1931–32

v S. AFRICA	v ENGLAND	v SCOTLAND	v WALES
J.T. Egan	D.P. Morris	+E.C. Ridgeway	E.C. Ridgeway
E.J. Lightfoot	E.J. Lightfoot	E.J. Lightfoot 2T	E.J. Lightfoot 1T
E. O'D. Davy	P.F. Murray 1PG, 1C	M.P. Crowe	M.P. Crowe
M.P. Crowe	E.W.F. de Vere Hunt	E.W.F. de Vere Hunt 1T	E.W.F. de Vere Hunt
J.E. Arigho	+S.L. Waide 1T	S.L. Waide 1T	S.L. Waide 1T
L.B. McMahon 1PG	E. O'D. Davy	E. O'D. Davy	E.O'D. Davy
P.F. Murray	+M.D. Sheehan	P.F. Murray 4C	P.F. Murray
H.H.C. Withers	T.C. Casey	C.J. Hanrahan	C.J. Hanrahan
V.J. Pike	V.J. Pike	V.J. Pike	V.J. Pike
J.L. Farrell	J.L. Farrell	J.L. Farrell	J.L. Farrell
J. Russell	M.J. Dunne	M.J. Dunne	M.J. Dunne
J.A.E. Siggins	J.A.E. Siggins	J.A.E. Siggins	J.A.E. Siggins
N.F. Murphy	N.F. Murphy	N.F. Murphy	N.F. Murphy
*G.R. Beamish	*G.R. Beamish	*G.R. Beamish	*G.R. Beamish
J.D. Clinch	+W. McC. Ross	W. McC. Ross	W. McC. Ross 2T
Lansdowne Road	Lansdowne Road	Murrayfield	Cardiff Arms Park
lost 3-8	lost 8-11	won 20-8	won 12-10
Ire. 1PG	Ire. 1G, 1PG	Scot. 1G, 1T	Wales 1DG, 2T
SA 1G, 1T	Eng. 1G, 2PG	Ire. 4G	Ire. 4T
19 December 1931	13 February 1932	27 February 1932	12 March 1932

1932–33

v ENGLAND	v WALES	v SCOTLAND
+R.H. Pratt	R.H. Pratt	R.H. Pratt
E.J. Lightfoot	E.J. Lightfoot	E.J. Lightfoot
L.B. McMahon	M.P. Crowe	M.P. Crowe 1T
E.W.F. de Vere Hunt 1T	+R.J. Barnes 1T	+P.B. Coote
S.L. Waide	S.L. Waide	+J.J. O'Connor
*E. O'D. Davy	*E. O'D. Davy 1DG	*E. O'D. Davy
P.F. Murray 1PG	P.F. Murray	P.F. Murray 1T
G.R. Beamish	G.R. Beamish	G.R. Beamish
M.J. Dunne	M.J. Dunne	M.J. Dunne
H. O'H. O'Neill	H. O'H. O'Neill	H. O'H. O'Neill
J.A.E. Siggins	J.A.E. Siggins 1PG	J.A.E. Siggins
J. Russell	J. Russell	J. Russell
N.F. Murphy	+C.E. Beamish	C.E. Beamish
V.J. Pike	V.J. Pike	V.J. Pike
W. McC. Ross	W. McC. Ross	W. McC. Ross
Twickenham	Ravenhill	Lansdowne Road
lost 6-17	won 10-5	lost 6-8
Eng. 1G, 4T	Ire. 1DG, 1PG, 1T	Ire. 2T
Ire. 1PG, 1T	Wales 1G	Scot. 2DG
11 February 1933	11 March 1933	1 April 1933

1933–34

v ENGLAND	v SCOTLAND	v WALES
R.H. Pratt	R.H. Pratt	+D.J. Langan
J.J. O'Connor	+D.J. Lane	D.J. Lane
M.P. Crowe	+N.H. Lambert	N.H. Lambert
+J.V. Reardon	J.V. Reardon	+A.H. Bailey
L.B. McMahon	J.J. O'Connor 1T	J.J. O'Connor
E. O'D. Davy	+J.L. Reid	J.L. Reid
+G.J. Morgan 1T	G.J. Morgan	G.J. Morgan
+S. Walker	S. Walker	+N.F. McGrath
V.J. Pike	V.J. Pike	V.J. Pike
+M.E. Bardon	C.E. Beamish	+J. Megaw
J. Russell	J. Russell 2T	J. Russell
*J.A.E. Siggins	*J.A.E. Siggins	*J.A.E. Siggins
+C.R.A. Graves	C.R.A. Graves	C.R.A. Graves
M.J. Dunne	M.J. Dunne	M.J. Dunne
W. McC. Ross	W. McC. Ross	C.E. Beamish
Lansdowne Road lost 3-13	Murrayfield lost 9-16	St Helen's lost 0-13
Ire. 1T Eng. 2G, 1T	Scot. 2G, 1PG, 1T Ire. 3T	Wales 2G, 1T Ire. Nil
10 February 1934	24 February 1934	10 March 1934

1934–35

v ENGLAND	v SCOTLAND	v WALES
D.P. Morris	D.P. Morris	D.P. Morris
D.J. Lane	D.J. Lane	+J.I. Doyle 1T
+P.M. Crowe	A.H. Bailey 1T	A.H. Bailey 1PG
E.C. Ridgeway	E.C. Ridgeway 1T	E.C. Ridgeway
J.J. O'Connor 1T	J.J. O'Connor 1T	J.J. O'Connor
A.H. Bailey	+V.A. Hewitt	V.A. Hewitt
G.J. Morgan	G.J. Morgan	G.J. Morgan
C.E. Beamish	C.E. Beamish	C.E. Beamish
C.R.A. Graves	C.R.A. Graves	C.R.A. Graves
S. Walker	S. Walker	S. Walker
J. Russell	J. Russell	J. Russell
+S.J. Deering	S.J. Deering	S.J. Deering
+H.J.M. Sayers	H.J.M. Sayers	H.J.M. Sayers
*J.A.E. Siggins	*J.A.E. Siggins	*J.A.E. Siggins 1PG
+P.J. Lawlor	P.J. Lawlor 1T	P.J. Lawlor
Twickenham lost 3-14	Lansdowne Road won 12-5	Ravenhill won 9–3
Eng. 1G, 3PG Ire. 1T	Ire. 4T Scot. 1G	Ire. 2PG, 1T Wales 1PG
9 February 1935	23 February 1935	9 March 1935

1935–36

v NZ	v ENGLAND	v SCOTLAND	v WALES
D.P. Morris	G.L. Malcolmson	G.L. Malcolmson	G.L. Malcolmson
+C.V. Boyle	C.V. Boyle 1T	C.V. Boyle	C.V. Boyle
A.H. Bailey 1PG	L.B. McMahon	L.B. McMahon 1T	A.H. Bailey
+G.L. Malcolmson	A.H. Bailey 1T	A.H. Bailey	L.B. McMahon
J.J. O'Connor	+F.G. Moran	J.J. O'Connor	J.J. O'Connor
V.A. Hewitt	V.A. Hewitt	V.A. Hewitt 1DG	V.A. Hewitt
G.J. Morgan	G.J. Morgan	G.J. Morgan	G.J. Morgan
+T.B. Dunn	S. Walker	S. Walker 1T	S. Walker
C.R.A. Graves	C.R.A. Graves	C.R.A. Graves	C.R.A. Graves
+C. O'N. Wallis	C.E. Beamish	C.E. Beamish	C.E. Beamish
S. Walker	J. Russell	J. Russell	J. Russell
S.J. Deering	S.J. Deering	S.J. Deering	S.J. Deering
C.E. Beamish 1T	+R. Alexander	R. Alexander	R. Alexander
*J.A.E. Siggins 1PG	*J.A.E. Siggins	*J.A.E. Siggins	*J.A.E. Siggins
W. McC. Ross	H.J.M. Sayers	H.J.M. Sayers	H.J.M. Sayers
Lansdowne Road	Lansdowne Road	Murrayfield	Cardiff Arms Park
lost 9-17	won 6-3	won 10-4	lost 0-3
Ire. 2PG, 1T	Ire. 2T	Scot. 1DG	Wales 1PG
NZ 1G, 2PG, 2T	Eng. 1T	Ire. 1DG, 2T	Ire. Nil
7 December 1935	8 February 1936	22 February 1936	14 March 1936

1936–37

v ENGLAND	v SCOTLAND	v WALES
G.L. Malcolmson	G.L. Malcolmson	G.L. Malcolmson
F.G. Moran 2T	F.G. Moran 1T	F.G. Moran
L.B. McMahon	L.B. McMahon 1T	L.B. McMahon
A.H. Bailey 1C	A.H. Bailey 1C	A.H. Bailey 1T
C.V. Boyle	C.V. Boyle	C.V. Boyle
+G.E. Cromey	G.E. Cromey	G.E. Cromey
*G.J. Morgan	*G.J. Morgan	*G.J. Morgan
S. Walker	S. Walker	S. Walker 1C
+T.S. Corken	T.S. Corken	T.S. Corken
C.R.A. Graves	C.R.A. Graves	+E. Ryan
J. Russell	J. Russell	+C.J. Reidy
S.J. Deering	S.J. Deering	+R.B. Mayne
R. Alexander	R. Alexander 1T	R. Alexander
J.A.E. Siggins	J.A.E. Siggins	J.A.E. Siggins
P.J. Lawlor	P.J. Lawlor	P.J. Lawlor
Twickenham	Lansdowne Road	Ravenhill
lost 8-9	won 11-4	won 5-3
Eng. 1PG, 2T	Ire. 1G, 2T	Ire. 1G
Ire. 1G, 1T	Scot. 1DG	Wales 1PG
13 February 1937	27 February 1937	3 April 1937

1937–38

v ENGLAND	v SCOTLAND	v WALES
P.M. Crowe 1C	+R.G. Craig	R.G. Craig
+M.J. Daly 1T	F.G. Moran 1T	F.G. Moran 1T
A.H. Bailey 1T	A.H. Bailey	+H.R. McKibbin 1C
L.B. McMahon	L.B. McMahon	+J.D. Torrens
+V.J. Lyttle	J.J. O'Connor	C.V. Boyle
G.E. Cromey 1T	G.E. Cromey 1T	G.E. Cromey
*G.J. Morgan	*G.J. Morgan 1T	G.J. Morgan
E. Ryan	E. Ryan	C.E. Beamish
C.R.A. Graves	C.R.A. Graves	C.R.A. Graves
+D.B. O'Loughlin	+H. Kennedy	H. Kennedy
S. Walker	+D. Tierney	D. Tierney
R.B. Mayne 1T	D.B. O'Loughlin 1T	R.B. Mayne
R. Alexander	R. Alexander	D.B. O'Loughlin
+J.W.S. Irwin	S. Walker 1C	*S. Walker
J. Megaw	J.W.S. Irwin	H.J.M. Sayers
Lansdowne Road	Murrayfield	St Helen's
lost 14-36	lost 14-23	lost 5-11
Ire. 1G, 3T	Scot. 2G, 1DG, 1PG, 2T	Wales 1G, 1PG, 1T
Eng. 6G, 1PG, 1T	Ire. 1G, 3T	Ire. 1G
12 February 1938	26 February 1938	12 March 1938

1938–39

v ENGLAND	v SCOTLAND	v WALES
+C.J. Murphy	C.J. Murphy	C.J. Murphy
F.G. Moran	F.G. Moran 1T	F.G. Moran
H.R. McKibbin 1C	H.R. McKibbin 1PG	H.R. McKibbin
J.D. Torrens	J.D. Torrens 1T	J.D. Torrens
V.J. Lyttle	V.J. Lyttle	C.V. Boyle
G.E. Cromey	G.E. Cromey	G.E. Cromey
*G.J. Morgan	*G.J. Morgan	*G.J. Morgan
D. Tierney	+T.A. Headon	T.A. Headon
+C. Teehan	C. Teehan	C. Teehan
+J.G. Ryan	J.G. Ryan	J.G. Ryan
D.B. O'Loughlin	D.B. O'Loughlin	D.B. O'Loughlin
R.B. Mayne	R.B. Mayne	R.B. Mayne
R. Alexander	R. Alexander	R. Alexander
J.W.S. Irwin 1T	J.W.S. Irwin	J.W.S. Irwin
H.J.M. Sayers	H.J.M. Sayers 1GM	H.J.M. Sayers
Twickenham	Lansdowne Road	Ravenhill
won 5-0	won 12-3	lost 0-7
Eng. Nil	Ire. 1PG, 1GM, 2T	Ire. Nil
Ire. 1G	Scot. 1T	Wales 1DG, 1T
11 February 1939	25 February 1939	11 March 1939

1946–47

v FRANCE	v ENGLAND	v SCOTLAND	v WALES
*C.J. Murphy	*C.J. Murphy	+J.A.D. Higgins	J.A.D. Higgins
+B.T. Quinn	+B.R. O'Hanlon 2T	B.R. O'Hanlon	B.R. O'Hanlon
+K.N. Quinn	+J.D.E. Monteith	*J.D.E. Monteith	*J.D.E. Monteith
+J. Harper	J. Harper	J. Harper	+M.F. Lane
+B. Mullan 1PG, 1C	B. Mullan 2C, 1PG, 2T	B. Mullan 1T	B. Mullan
+J.W. Kyle	J.W. Kyle	J.W. Kyle	J.W. Kyle
+R. Carroll	+E. Strathdee	E. Strathdee	E. Strathdee
+M.R. Neely	M.R. Neely	M.R. Neely	M.R. Neely
+K.D. Mullen	K.D. Mullen	K.D. Mullen	K.D. Mullen
+J.C. Daly	J.C. Daly	J.C. Daly	J.C. Daly
+C.P. Callan	C.P. Callan	C.P. Callan	C.P. Callan
+E. Keeffe	E. Keeffe	E. Keeffe	E. Keeffe
+J.W. McKay 1T	J.W. McKay 1T	J.W. McKay	J.W. McKay
+R.D. Agar	R.D. Agar	R.D. Agar	R.D. Agar
+D.J. Hingerty	D.J. Hingerty	D.J. Hingerty	D.J. Hingerty
Lansdowne Road	Lansdowne Road	Murrayfield	St Helen's
lost 8-12	won 22-0	won 3-0	lost 0-6
Ire. 1G, 1PG	Ire. 2G, 1PG, 3T	Scot. Nil	Wales. 1PG, 1T
Fr. 4T	Eng. Nil	Ire. 1T	Ire. Nil
25 January 1947	8 February 1947	22 February 1947	29 March 1947

1947–48

v AUSTRALIA	v FRANCE	v ENGLAND	v SCOTLAND	v WALES
J.A.D. Higgins	J.A.D. Higgins	+J.A. Mattsson	J.A.D. Higgins	J.A.D. Higgins
+W.D. McKee	B.R. O'Hanlon	B.R. O'Hanlon	B.R. O'Hanlon	B.R. O'Hanlon
K.N. Quinn 1PG	W.D. McKee	W.D. McKee 1T	W.D. McKee	W.D. McKee
+P.J. Reid	P.J. Reid 1T	P.J. Reid	+M. O'Flanagan	P.J. Reid
+K.P. O'Flanagan	B. Mullan 2C, 1T	B. Mullan 1C	B. Mullan 1T	B. Mullan 1T
J.W. Kyle	J.W. Kyle	J.W. Kyle 1T	J.W. Kyle 1T	J.W. Kyle
*E. Strathdee	*E. Strathdee	+H. de Lacy	H. de Lacy	E. Strathdee
+J.C. Corcoran	J.C. Corcoran	J.C. Daly	J.C. Daly	J.C. Daly 1T
K.D. Mullen	K.D. Mullen	*K.D. Mullen	*K.D. Mullen	*K.D. Mullen
+A.A. McConnell	A.A. McConnell	A.A. McConnell	A.A. McConnell	A.A. McConnell
+R.W. Wilkinson	C.P. Callan	C.P. Callan	C.P. Callan	C.P. Callan
+J.E. Nelson	E. Keeffe	J.E. Nelson	J.E. Nelson	J.E. Nelson
J.W. McKay	J.W. McKay	J.W. McKay 1T	J.W. McKay	J.W. McKay
E. Keeffe	R.D. Agar	+D.J. O'Brien	D.J. O'Brien	D.J. O'Brien
+D. McCourt	+J.S. McCarthy 1T	J.S. McCarthy	J.S. McCarthy	J.S. McCarthy
Lansdowne Road	Stade Colombes	Twickenham	Lansdowne Road	Ravenhill
lost 3-16	won 13-6	won 11-10	won 6-0	won 6-3
Ire. 1PG	Fr. 2T	Eng. 2G	Ire. 2T	Ire. 2T
Aust. 2G, 2T	Ire. 2G, 1T	Ire. 1G, 2T	Scot. Nil	Wales 1T
6 December 1947	1 January 1948	14 February 1948	28 February 1948	13 March 1948

1948–49

v FRANCE	v ENGLAND	v SCOTLAND	v WALES
+G.W. Norton 3PG	G.W. Norton 2PG, 1C	G.W. Norton 1PG, 2C	G.W. Norton 1C
M.F. Lane	M.F. Lane	M.F. Lane	M.F. Lane
W.D. McKee	W.D. McKee 1T	W.D. McKee	W.D. McKee
+T.J. Gavin	T.J. Gavin	+N.J. Henderson	N.J. Henderson
B.R. O'Hanlon	B.R. O'Hanlon 1T	B.R. O'Hanlon	B.R. O'Hanlon
J.W. Kyle	J.W. Kyle	J.W. Kyle	J.W. Kyle
+T.J. Cullen	E. Strathdee	E. Strathdee	E. Strathdee
+T. Clifford	T. Clifford	T. Clifford	T. Clifford
*K.D. Mullen	*K.D. Mullen	*K.D. Mullen	*K.D. Mullen
A.A. McConnell	A.A. McConnell	+J.L. Griffin	J.L. Griffin
C.P. Callan	C.P. Callan	R.D. Agar	R.D. Agar
J.E. Nelson	J.E. Nelson	J.E. Nelson	J.E. Nelson
J.W. McKay	J.W. McKay	J.W. McKay	J.W. McKay
D.J. O'Brien	D.J. O'Brien	D.J. O'Brien	D.J. O'Brien
J.S. McCarthy	J.S. McCarthy	J.S. McCarthy 2T	J.S. McCarthy 1T
Lansdowne Road	Lansdowne Road	Murrayfield	St Helen's
lost 9-16	won 14-5	won 13-3	won 5-0
Ire. 3PG	Ire. 1G, 2PG, 1T	Scot. 1PG	Wales Nil
Fr. 2G, 2PG	Eng. 1G	Ire. 2G, 1PG	Ire. 1G
29 January 1949	12 February 1949	26 February 1949	12 March 1949

1949–50

v FRANCE	v ENGLAND	v SCOTLAND	v WALES
G.W. Norton	G.W. Norton	G.W. Norton 2PG, 3C	G.W. Norton 1PG
M.F. Lane	M.F. Lane	M.F. Lane	M.F. Lane
W.D. McKee	W.D. McKee	+R.J.H. Uprichard	R.J.H. Uprichard
N.J. Henderson	+G.C. Phipps	J.J. Blayney 1T	G.C. Phipps
B.R. O'Hanlon	+L. Crowe	L. Crowe 1T	L. Crowe
J.W. Kyle	J.W. Kyle	J.W. Kyle	J.W. Kyle
+J.H. Burges 1PG	J.H. Burges	R. Carroll	R. Carroll
T. Clifford	T. Clifford	T. Clifford	T. Clifford
*K.D. Mullen	*K.D. Mullen	*K.D. Mullen	*K.D. Mullen
+D. McKibbin	D. McKibbin	D. McKibbin	D. McKibbin
J.E. Nelson	J.E. Nelson	J.E. Nelson	J.E. Nelson
R.D. Agar	R.D. Agar	+J.U. Molony	R.D. Agar
J.W. McKay	J.W. McKay	J.W. McKay	J.W. McKay
D.J. O'Brien	D.J. O'Brien	D.J. O'Brien	D.J. O'Brien
+A.B. Curtis	A.B. Curtis	A.B. Curtis 1T	J.S. McCarthy
Stade Colombes	Twickenham	Lansdowne Road	Ravenhill
drawn 3-3	lost 0-3	won 21–0	lost 3-6
Fr. 1DG	Eng. 1T	Ire. 3G, 2PG	Ire. 1PG
Ire. 1PG	Ire. Nil	Scot. Nil	Wales 2T
28 January 1950	11 February 1950	25 February 1950	11 March 1950

1950–51

v FRANCE	v ENGLAND	v SCOTLAND	v WALES
G.W. Norton	G.W. Norton	G.W. Norton	+A. McMorrow
+C.S. Griffin	C.S. Griffin	W.H.J. Millar	W.H.J. Millar
N.J. Henderson 1PG	N.J. Henderson	N.J. Henderson 1DG	N.J. Henderson
+R.R. Chambers	R.R. Chambers	R.R. Chambers	R.R. Chambers
M.F. Lane	+W.H.J. Millar	M.F. Lane	M.F. Lane
J.W. Kyle	J.W. Kyle	J.W. Kyle	J.W. Kyle 1T
+J.A. O'Meara	J.A. O'Meara	J.A. O'Meara	J.A. O'Meara
T. Clifford 1T	T. Clifford	D. McKibbin	D. McKibbin
*K.D. Mullen	*K.D. Mullen	*K.D. Mullen	*K.D. Mullen
+J.H. Smith	J.H. Smith	J.H. Smith	J.H. Smith
J.E. Nelson 1T	J.E. Nelson	+P.J. Lawler	J.E. Nelson
D. McKibbin	D. McKibbin 1PG	+J.R. Brady	J.R. Brady
J.W. McKay	J.W. McKay	J.W. McKay	J.W. McKay
D.J. O'Brien	D.J. O'Brien	D.J. O'Brien 1T	D.J. O'Brien
J.S. McCarthy	J.S. McCarthy	J.S. McCarthy	J.S. McCarthy
Lansdowne Road	Lansdowne Road	Murrayfield	Cardiff Arms Park
won 9-8	won 3-0	won 6-5	drawn 3-3
Ire. 1PG, 2T	Ire. 1PG	Scot. 1G	Wales 1PG
Fr. 1G, 1T	Eng. Nil	Ire. 1DG, 1T	Ire. 1T
27 January 1951	10 February 1951	24 February 1951	10 March 1951

1951–52

v S. AFRICA	v FRANCE	v SCOTLAND	v WALES	v ENGLAND
+J.G.M.W. Murphy 1C	+J.R. Notley 1C	J.G.M.W. Murphy	J.G.M.W. Murphy 1PG	J.G.M.W. Murphy
W.D. McKee	G.C. Phipps	W.H.J. Millar	W.H.J. Millar	+M.F. Hillary
N.J. Henderson	N.J. Henderson 1T,	N.J. Henderson 1PG,	N.J. Henderson	N.J. Henderson
+A.W. Browne 1T	1PG	1T	R.R. Chambers	G.C. Phipps
M.F. Lane	R.R. Chambers	J.R. Notley	G.C. Phipps	+N. Bailey
	M.F. Lane	M.F. Lane 1T		
J.W. Kyle			J.W. Kyle	J.W. Kyle
J.A. O'Meara	J.W. Kyle	J.W. Kyle 1T	J.A. O'Meara	J.A. O'Meara
	J.A. O'Meara	J.A. O'Meara		
T. Clifford			T. Clifford	+W.A. O'Neill
K.D. Mullen	T. Clifford	T. Clifford	K.D. Mullen	+R. Roe
J.H. Smith	K.D. Mullen	K.D. Mullen	J.H. Smith	J.H. Smith
P.J. Lawler	J.H. Smith	J.H. Smith	P.J. Lawler	P.J. Lawler
+R.H. Thompson	P.J. Lawler	P.J. Lawler	A.F. O'Leary	A.F. O'Leary
J.W. KcKay	R.H. Thompson	+A.F. O'Leary	M.J. Dargan	+P.J. Kavanagh
*D.J. O'Brien	J.W. McKay	+M.J. Dargan	*D.J. O'Brien	*D.J. O'Brien
J.S. McCarthy	*D.J. O'Brien	*D.J. O'Brien	J.S. McCarthy	J.S. McCarthy
Lansdowne Road	J.S. McCarthy 1T	J.S. McCarthy	Lansdowne Road	Twickenham
lost 5-17	Stade Colombes	Lansdowne Road	lost 3-14	lost 0-3
Ire. 1G	won 11–8	won 12-8	Ire. 1PG	Eng. 1T
SA 1G, 1DG, 3T	Fr. 1G, 1PG	Ire. 1PG, 3T	Wales 1G, 1PG, 2T	Ire. Nil
8 December 1951	Ire. 1G, 1PG, 1T	Scot. 1G, 1PG	8 March 1952	29 March 1952
	26 January 1952	23 February 1952		

1952–53

v FRANCE	v ENGLAND	v SCOTLAND	v WALES
+R.J. Gregg 2C	R.J. Gregg	R.J. Gregg 4C	R.J. Gregg
M.F. Lane	M.F. Lane	+S.J. Byrne 3T	S.J. Byrne 1T
N.J. Henderson	N.J. Henderson 2PG	N.J. Henderson	N.J. Henderson
K.N. Quinn	K.N. Quinn	K.N. Quinn	+A.C. Pedlow
+M. Mortell 1T	M. Mortell 1T	M. Mortell 1T	M. Mortell
*J.W. Kyle 1T	*J.W. Kyle	*J.W. Kyle	*J.W. Kyle
J.A. O'Meara	J.A. O'Meara	J.A. O'Meara	J.A. O'Meara
W.A. O'Neill	W.A. O'Neill	W.A. O'Neill	W.A. O'Neill
R. Roe	R. Roe	R. Roe	R. Roe
+F.E. Anderson	F.E. Anderson	F.E. Anderson	F.E. Anderson
P.J. Lawler 1T	+T.E. Reid	T.E. Reid	T.E. Reid
J.R. Brady	J.R. Brady	J.R. Brady	J.R. Brady
+W.E. Bell	W.E. Bell	W.E. Bell	W.E. Bell
+J.R. Kavanagh	J.R. Kavanagh	J.R. Kavanagh 1T	J.R. Kavanagh
J.S. McCarthy 1T	J.S. McCarthy	J.S. McCarthy 1T	+G.F. Reidy
Ravenhill	Lansdowne Road	Murrayfield	St Helen's
won 16-3	drawn 9-9	won 26-8	lost 3-5
Ire. 2G, 2T	Ire. 2PG, 1T	Scot. 1G, 1PG	Wales 1G
Fr. 1DG	Eng. 2PG, 1T	Ire. 4G, 2T	Ire. 1T
24 January 1953	14 February 1953	28 February 1953	14 March 1953

1953–54

v NZ	v FRANCE	v ENGLAND	v SCOTLAND	v WALES
J.G.M.W. Murphy	R.J. Gregg	R.J. Gregg	R.J. Gregg	+P.J. Berkery
M. Mortell	M. Mortell	M. Mortell	M. Mortell 2T	M. Mortell
N.J. Henderson 1PG	N.J. Henderson	N.J. Henderson	N.J. Henderson	N.J. Henderson 1PG
A.C. Pedlow	A.C. Pedlow	A.C. Pedlow	+R.P. Godfrey	R.P. Godfrey
+J.T. Gaston	J.T. Gaston	J.T. Gaston	J.T. Gaston	J.T. Gaston 1T
*J.W. Kyle	*J.W. Kyle	+W.J. Hewitt	+S. Kelly	S. Kelly 1PG
J.A. O'Meara	J.A. O'Meara	J.A. O'Meara	J.A. O'Meara	+H. McCracken
W.A. O'Neill	F.E. Anderson	F.E. Anderson	F.E. Anderson	F.E. Anderson
F.E. Anderson	R. Roe	R. Roe	R. Roe	R. Roe
J.H. Smith	J.H. Smith	+B.G.M. Wood	B.G.M. Wood	J.H. Smith
P.J. Lawler	T.E. Reid	P.J. Lawler	P.J. Lawler	J.R. Brady
R.H. Thompson	R.H. Thompson	R.H. Thompson	R.H. Thompson	R.H. Thompson
J.R. Kavanagh	G.F. Reidy	G.F. Reidy	G.F. Reidy	G.F. Reidy
T.E. Reid	J.E. Nelson	+J. Murphy-O'Connor 1PG	J.R. Kavanagh	J.R. Kavanagh
J.S. McCarthy	J.S. McCarthy	*J.S. McCarthy	*J.S. McCarthy	*J.S. McCarthy
Lansdowne Road	Stade Colombes	Twickenham	Ravenhill	Lansdowne Road
lost 3-14	lost 0-8	lost 3-14	won 6-0	lost 9-12
Ire. 1PG	Fr. 1G, 1T	Eng. 1G, 1PG, 2T	Ire. 2T	Ire. 2PG, 1T
NZ 1G, 1DG, 1PG, 1T	Ire. Nil	Ire. 1PG	Scot. Nil	Wales 1DG, 3PG
9 January 1954	23 January 1954	13 February 1954	27 February 1954	13 March 1954

1954–55

v FRANCE	v ENGLAND	v SCOTLAND	v WALES
+W.R. Tector	W.R. Tector	W.R. Tector	P.J. Berkery
S.J. Byrne	+R.E. Roche	R.E. Roche	A.C. Pedlow
N.J. Henderson 1PG	N.J. Henderson 1PG	N.J. Henderson	N.J. Henderson 1PG
+A.J.F. O'Reilly	A.J.F. O'Reilly	A.J.F. O'Reilly	A.J.F. O'Reilly
A.C. Pedlow	A.C. Pedlow 1T	A.C. Pedlow	J.T. Gaston
J.W. Kyle	J.W. Kyle	S. Kelly 1PG	J.W. Kyle
J.A. O'Meara	J.A. O'Meara	+S.J. McDermott	S.J. McDermott
F.E. Anderson	F.E. Anderson	F.E. Anderson	F.E. Anderson
R. Roe	R. Roe	R. Roe	R. Roe
+P.J. O'Donoghue	P.J. O'Donoghue	P.J. O'Donoghue	P.J. O'Donoghue
*R.H. Thompson	T.E. Reid	T.E. Reid	*R.H. Thompson
+W.J. O'Connell	+M.N. Madden	M.N. Madden	M.N. Madden
+M.J. Cunningham	M.J. Cunningham	M.J. Cunningham	M.J. Cunningham
J.R. Kavanagh	J.R. Kavanagh	*R.H. Thompson	+G.R.P. Ross
J.S. McCarthy	*J.S. McCarthy	+D.A. MacSweeney	P.J. Kavanagh
Lansdowne Road lost 3-5	Lansdowne Road drawn 6–6	Murrayfield lost 3-12	Cardiff Arms Park lost 3-21
Ire. 1PG Fr. 1G	Ire. 1PG, 1T Eng. 2T	Scot. 2PG, 1DG, 1T Ire. 1PG	Wales 3G, 1PG, 1T Ire. 1PG
22 January 1955	12 February 1955	26 February 1955	12 March 1955

1955–56

v FRANCE	v ENGLAND	v SCOTLAND	v WALES
+J.M. McKelvey	J.M. McKelvey	P.J. Berkery	P.J. Berkery
+S.V.J. Quinlan	S.V.J. Quinlan	W.J. Hewitt	S.V.J. Quinlan
A.J.F. O'Reilly 1T	A.J.F. O'Reilly	*N.J. Henderson 1T	*N.J. Henderson
A.C. Pedlow 1PG, 1C	A.C. Pedlow	A.J.F. O'Reilly 1T	A.J.F. O'Reilly
J.T. Gaston	J.T. Gaston	A.C. Pedlow 1C	A.C. Pedlow 1PG, 1C
J.W. Kyle	J.W. Kyle	J.W. Kyle 1T	J.W. Kyle 1DG
+A.A. Mulligan	A.A. Mulligan	J.A. O'Meara 1T	J.A. O'Meara
+W.B.C. Fagan	W.B.C. Fagan	W.B.C. Fagan	P.J. O'Donoghue
R. Roe	R. Roe	R. Roe	R. Roe
B.G.M. Wood	B.G.M. Wood	B.G.M. Wood	B.G.M. Wood
P.J. Lawler	P.J. Lawler	+B.N. Guerin	R.H. Thompson
T.E. Reid	T.E. Reid	+L.M. Lynch	J.R. Brady
M.J. Cuningham	+N. Feddis	M.J. Cunningham	M.J. Cunningham 1T
+A.G. Kennedy	J.R. Kavanagh	J.R. Kavanagh	+T. McGrath
*+J.S. Ritchie	*J.S. Ritchie	+C.T.J. Lydon	J.R. Kavanagh
Stade Colombes lost 8-14	Twickenham lost 0-20	Lansdowne Road won 14-10	Lansdowne Road won 11-3
Fr. 1G, 2PG, 1T Ire. 1G, 1PG	Eng. 1G, 3PG, 2T Ire. Nil	Ire. 1G, 3T Scot. 2G	Ire. 1G, 1DG, 1PG Wales 1PG
28 January 1956	11 February 1956	25 February 1956	10 March 1956

1956–57

v FRANCE	v ENGLAND	v SCOTLAND	v WALES
P.J. Berkery	P.J. Berkery	P.J. Berkery 1C	P.J. Berkery
A.J.F. O'Reilly	A.J.F. O'Reilly	R.E. Roche	R.E. Roche
*N.J. Henderson	*N.J. Henderson	A.J.F. O'Reilly	A.J.F. O'Reilly
A.C. Pedlow 1C, 1PG	A.C. Pedlow	*N.J. Henderson	*N.J. Henderson
+N.H. Brophy 1T	N.H. Brophy	A.C. Pedlow	A.C. Pedlow 1C
J.W. Kyle 1T	J.W. Kyle	J.W. Kyle	J.W. Kyle
A.A. Mulligan	A.A. Mulligan	A.A. Mulligan	A.A. Mulligan
P.J. O'Donoghue	P.J. O'Donoghue	+J.I. Brennan	J.I. Brennan
R. Roe	R. Roe	R. Roe	R. Roe
B.G.M. Wood	B.G.M. Wood	B.G.M. Wood	B.G.M. Wood
T.E. Reid	T.E. Reid	T.E. Reid	T.E. Reid
J.R. Brady	J.R. Brady	J.R. Brady	J.R. Brady
+H.S. O'Connor	H.S. O'Connor	H.S. O'Connor	H.S. O'Connor
+P.J.A. O'Sullivan	P.J.A. O'Sullivan	P.J.A. O'Sullivan 1T	P.J.A. O'Sullivan
J.R. Kavanagh	J.R. Kavanagh	J.R. Kavanagh	J.R. Kavanagh 1T
Lansdowne Road	Lansdowne Road	Murrayfield	Cardiff Arms Park
won 11-6	lost 0-6	won 5-3	lost 5-6
Ire. 1G, 1PG, 1T	Ire. Nil	Scot. 1PG	Wales 2PG
Fr. 2PG	Eng. 1PG, 1T	Ire. 1G	Ire. 1G
26 January 1957	9 February 1957	23 February 1957	9 March 1957

1957–58

v AUSTRALIA	v ENGLAND	v SCOTLAND	v WALES	v FRANCE
P.J. Berkery	P.J. Berkery	P.J. Berkery 1PG	J.G.M.W. Murphy	*N.J. Henderson 2PG
A.J.F. O'Reilly	A.J.F. O'Reilly	A.J.F. O'Reilly	S.V.J. Quinlan	A.J.F. O'Reilly
*N.J. Henderson 1T	*N.J. Henderson	*N.J. Henderson 1PG	*N.J. Henderson 1PG	+D.C. Glass
+D. Hewitt	D. Hewitt	D. Hewitt	A.J.F. O'Reilly	D. Hewitt
A.C. Pedlow 1PG	A.C. Pedlow	A.C. Pedlow 2T	A.C. Pedlow	A.C. Pedlow
J.W. Kyle	J.W. Kyle	J.W. Kyle	+M.A.F. English	M.A.F. English
A.A. Mulligan	A.A. Mulligan	A.A. Mulligan	J.A. O'Meara 1T	A.A. Mulligan
P.J. O'Donoghue	P.J. O'Donoghue	P.J. O'Donoghue	P.J. O'Donoghue	+S. Millar
+A.R. Dawson 1T	A.R. Dawson	A.R. Dawson	A.R. Dawson	A.R. Dawson
B.G.M. Wood	B.G.M. Wood	B.G.M. Wood	B.G.M. Wood	B.G.M. Wood
+J.B. Stevenson	J.B. Stevenson	J.B. Stevenson	J.B. Stevenson	J.B. Stevenson
+W.A. Mulcahy	W.A. Mulcahy	W.A. Mulcahy	W.A. Mulcahy	W.A. Mulcahy
+J.A. Donaldson	J.A. Donaldson	J.A. Donaldson	J.A. Donaldson	+E.L. Brown
J.R. Kavanagh	J.R. Kavanagh	J.R. Kavanagh	J.R. Kavanagh	T. McGrath
+N.A.A. Murphy	N.A.A. Murphy	N.A.A. Murphy	N.A.A. Murphy	N.A.A. Murphy
Lansdowne Road	Twickenham	Lansdowne Road	Lansdowne Road	Stade Colombes
won 9-6	lost 0-6	won 12-6	lost 6-9	lost 6-11
Ire. 1PG, 2T	Eng. 1PG, 1T	Ire. 2PG, 2T	Ire. 1PG, 1T	Fr. 1G, 1DG, 1PG
Aust. 2T	Ire. Nil	Scot. 2T	Wales 3T	Ire. 2PG
18 January 1958	8 February 1958	1 March 1958	15 March 1958	19 April 1958

1958–59

v ENGLAND	v SCOTLAND	v WALES	v FRANCE
N.J. Henderson	N.J. Henderson	N.J. Henderson	N.J. Henderson
A.C. Pedlow	A.J.F. O'Reilly	A.J.F. O'Reilly 1T	A.J.F. O'Reilly
+J.F. Dooley	J.F. Dooley 1T	J.F. Dooley	+M.K. Flynn
A.J.F. O'Reilly	D. Hewitt 1PG, 1C	D. Hewitt 1PG	D. Hewitt 1PG
N.H. Brophy	N.H. Brophy	N.H. Brophy	N.H. Brophy 1T
M.A.F. English	M.A.F. English	W.J. Hewitt	M.A.F. English 1DG
A.A. Mulligan	A.A. Mulligan	A.A. Mulligan	A.A. Mulligan
B.G.M. Wood	B.G.M. Wood	B.G.M. Wood	B.G.M. Wood
*A.R. Dawson	*A.R. Dawson	*A.R. Dawson	*A.R. Dawson
S. Millar	S. Millar	S. Millar	S. Millar
W.A. Mulcahy	W.A. Mulcahy	W.A. Mulcahy	W.A. Mulcahy
+M.G. Culliton	M.G. Culliton	M.G. Culliton	M.G. Culliton
N.A.A. Murphy	N.A.A. Murphy	N.A.A. Murphy	N.A.A. Murphy
P.J.A. O'Sullivan	P.J.A. O'Sullivan	P.J.A. O'Sullivan	P.J.A. O'Sullivan
J.R. Kavanagh	J.R. Kavanagh	J.R. Kavanagh	J.R. Kavanagh
Lansdowne Road	Murrayfield	Cardiff Arms Park	Lansdowne Road
lost 0-3	won 8-3	lost 6–8	won 9-5
Ire. Nil	Scot. 1PG	Wales 1G, 1T	Ire. 1DG, 1PG, 1T
Eng. 1PG	Ire. 1G, 1PG	Ire. 1PG, 1T	Fr. 1G
14 February 1959	28 February 1959	14 March 1959	18 April 1959

1959–60

v ENGLAND	v SCOTLAND	v WALES	v FRANCE
+T.J. Kiernan 1C	T.J. Kiernan	T.J. Kiernan	T.J. Kiernan
+W.W. Bornemann	W.W. Bornemann	W.W. Bornemann	A.C. Pedlow
A.C. Pedlow	+J.C. Walsh	A.C. Pedlow	M.K. Flynn
D. Hewitt	D. Hewitt 1C	D. Hewitt	D. Hewitt
A.J.F. O'Reilly	A.C. Pedlow	D.C. Glass	N.H. Brophy 2T
M.A.F. English	M.A.F. English	S. Kelly 2PG	S. Kelly
*A.A. Mulligan	*A.A. Mulligan	*A.A. Mulligan	A.A. Mulligan
B.G.M. Wood	B.G.M. Wood 1T	B.G.M. Wood	B.G.M. Wood
+B. McCallan	B. McCallan	+L.G. Butler	*A.R. Dawson
S. Millar	S. Millar	S. Millar	S. Millar
W.A. Mulcahy	W.A. Mulcahy	W.A. Mulcahy	+P.J. Costello
M.G. Culliton 1T	M.G. Culliton	M.G. Culliton	M.G. Culliton
N.A.A. Murphy	N.A.A. Murphy	N.A.A. Murphy 1T	N.A.A. Murphy
T. McGrath	T. McGrath	T. McGrath	T. McGrath
J.R. Kavanagh	J.R. Kavanagh	J.R. Kavanagh	J.R. Kavanagh
Twickenham	Lansdowne Road	Lansdowne Road	Stade Colombes
lost 5-8	lost 5--6	lost 9-10	lost 6-23
Eng. 1G, 1DG	Ire. 1G	Ire. 2PG, 1T	Fr. 1G, 3DG, 3T
Ire. 1G	Scot. 1DG, 1T	Wales 2G	Ire. 2T
13 February 1960	27 February 1960	12 March 1960	9 April 1960

1960–61

v S. AFRICA	v ENGLAND	v SCOTLAND	v WALES	v FRANCE
T.J. Kiernan 1PG	T.J. Kiernan	T.J. Kiernan	T.J. Kiernan	T.J. Kiernan 1PG
W.W. Bornemann	+R.J. McCarten	A.C. Pedlow	N.H. Brophy	A.J.F. O'Reilly
J.C. Walsh	D. Hewitt	D. Hewitt 1T	D. Hewitt	D. Hewitt
A.C. Pedlow	J.C. Walsh	J.C. Walsh	D.C. Glass	J.C. Walsh
N.H. Brophy	A.J.F. O'Reilly	N.H. Brophy	R.J. McCarten	R.J. McCarten
+W.K. Armstrong	W.K. Armstrong	M.A.F. English	M.A.F. English	M.A.F. English
A.A. Mulligan	+J.W. Moffett 2PG, 1C	J.W. Moffett 1C	A.A. Mulligan	A.A. Mulligan
S. Millar	S. Millar	S. Millar	S. Millar	S. Millar
*A.R. Dawson	*A.R. Dawson	*A.R. Dawson	*A.R. Dawson	*A.R. Dawson
B.G.M. Wood	B.G.M. Wood	B.G.M. Wood	B.G.M. Wood	B.G.M. Wood
W.A. Mulcahy	W.A. Mulcahy	W.A. Mulcahy	W.A. Mulcahy	+J.T. Nesdale
M.G. Culliton	M.G. Culliton	M.G. Culliton	+C.J. Dick	C.J. Dick
N.A.A. Murphy	N.A.A. Murphy	N.A.A. Murphy	N.A.A. Murphy	+D. Scott
P.J.A. O'Sullivan	P.J.A. O'Sullivan	P.J.A. O'Sullivan	J.R. Kavanagh	J.R. Kavanagh
J.R. Kavanagh	J.R. Kavanagh 1T	J.R. Kavanagh 1T	M.G. Culliton	M.G. Culliton
Lansdowne Road	Lansdowne Road	Murrayfield	Cardiff Arms Park	Lansdowne Road
lost 3-8	won 11-8	lost 8-16	lost 0-9	lost 3-15
Ire. 1PG	Ire. 1G, 2PG	Scot. 2G, 1PG, 1T	Wales 2PG, 1T	Ire. 1PG
SA 1G, 1T	Eng. 1G, 1T	Ire. 1G, 1T	Ire. Nil	Fr. 2DG, 2PG, 1T
17 December 1960	11 February 1961	25 February 1961	11 March 1961	15 April 1961

1961–62

v S. AFRICA	v ENGLAND	v SCOTLAND	v FRANCE	v WALES
T.J. Kiernan 1C, 1T, 1PG	T.J. Kiernan	F.G. Gilpin	F.G. Gilpin	T.J. Kiernan
A.J.F. O'Reilly	+L.P.F. L'Estrange	W.R. Hunter 1PG, 1T	W.R. Hunter	W.R. Hunter
J.C. Walsh	M.K. Flynn	M.K. Flynn	D. Hewitt	A.C. Pedlow
+K.J. Houston	+W.R. Hunter	D. Hewitt	M.K. Flynn	M.K. Flynn
W.J. Hewitt	N.H. Brophy	N.H. Brophy	+N.F. Byrne	N.H. Brophy
D.C. Glass	+F.G. Gilpin	+G.G. Hardy	M.A.F. English	M.A.F. English 1DG
A.A. Mulligan	+J.T.M. Quirke	J.T.M. Quirke	+J.C. Kelly	J.C. Kelly
S. Millar	S. Millar	S. Millar	S. Millar	+M.P. O'Callaghan
*A.R. Dawson	+J.S. Dick	A.R. Dawson	A.R. Dawson	A.R. Dawson
B.G.M. Wood	+R.J. McLoughlin	R.J. McLoughlin	R.J. McLoughlin	+P.J. Dwyer
W.A. Mulcahy	*W.A. Mulcahy	*W.A. Mulcahy	*W.A. Mulcahy	*W.A. Mulcahy
C.J. Dick	+W.J. McBride	W.J. McBride	W.J. McBride	W.J. McBride
D. Scott	+P.N. Turley	D. Scott	J.R. Kavanagh	P.J.A. O'Sullivan
T. McGrath	+M.L. Hipwell	M.L. Hipwell	P.J.A. O'Sullivan	C.J. Dick
J.R. Kavanagh	N.A.A. Murphy	M.G. Culliton	M.G. Culliton	+M.D. Kiely
Cape Town	Twickenham	Lansdowne Road	Stade Colombes	Lansdowne Road
lost 8-24	lost 0-16	lost 6-20	lost 0-11	drawn 3-3
SA 3G, 1PG, 2T	Eng. 2G, 1PG, 1T	Ire. 1PG, 1T	Fr. 1G, 2T	Ire. 1DG
Ire. 1G, 1PG	Ire. Nil	Scot. 1G, 1DG, 2PG, 2T	Ire. Nil	Wales 1PG
13 May 1961	10 February 1962	24 February 1962	14 April 1962	17 November 1962

1962–63

v FRANCE	v ENGLAND	v SCOTLAND	v WALES
*T.J. Kiernan 1C	+B.D.E. Marshall	T.J. Kiernan	T.J. Kiernan 2PG, 1C
W.R. Hunter	W.R. Hunter	W.R. Hunter	A.J.F. O'Reilly
A.C. Pedlow	J.C. Walsh	J.C. Walsh	J.C. Walsh
A.J.F. O'Reilly 1T	P.J. Casey	P.J. Casey	P.J. Casey 1T
+P.J. Casey	N.H. Brophy	A.J.F. O'Reilly	N.H. Brophy
+J.B. Murray	M.A.F. English	M.A.F. English	M.A.F. English 1DG
J.C. Kelly	J.C. Kelly	J.C. Kelly	J.C. Kelly
S. Millar	S. Millar	S. Millar	S. Millar
A.R. Dawson	A.R. Dawson	A.R. Dawson	A.R. Dawson
P.J. Dwyer	R.J. McLoughlin	R.J. McLoughlin	R.J. McLoughlin
W.A. Mulcahy	*W.A. Mulcahy	*W.A. Mulcahy	*W.A. Mulcahy
W.J. McBride	W.J. McBride	W.J. McBride	W.J. McBride
P.J.A. O'Sullivan	+E.P. McGuire	E.P. McGuire	E.P. McGuire
C.J. Dick	C.J. Dick	C.J. Dick	C.J. Dick
M.D. Kiely	M.D. Kiely	M.D. Kiely	M.D. Kiely
Lansdowne Road	Lansdowne Road	Murrayfield	Cardiff Arms Park
lost 5-24	drawn 0-0	lost 0-3	won 14-6
Fr. 3G, 2DG, 1T	Ire. Nil	Scot. 1PG	Wales 1DG, 1T
Ire. 1G	Eng. Nil	Ire. Nil	Ire. 1G, 1DG, 2PG
26 January 1963	9 February 1963	23 February 1963	9 March 1963

1963–64

v NZ	v ENGLAND	v SCOTLAND	v WALES	v FRANCE
T.J. Kiernan 1C	T.J. Kiernan 3C	T.J. Kiernan 1PG	+F.S. Keogh 2PG	F.S. Keogh
+J.J. Fortune 1T	P.J. Casey 1T	P.J. Casey	P.J. Casey	P.J. Casey 1T
P.J. Casey	J.C. Walsh	M.K. Flynn	M.K. Flynn	M.K. Flynn
J.C. Walsh	M.K. Flynn 2T	J.C. Walsh	J.C. Walsh	J.C. Walsh
+A.T.A. Duggan	J.J. Fortune	K.J. Houston	K.J. Houston	A.T.A. Duggan
M.A.F. English	+C.M.H. Gibson	C.M.H. Gibson	C.M.H. Gibson	C.M.H. Gibson 1DG
*J.C. Kelly	J.C. Kelly	J.C. Kelly	J.C. Kelly	J.C. Kelly
P.J. Dwyer	M.P. O'Callaghan	P.J. Dwyer	P.J. Dwyer	S. Millar
A.R. Dawson	A.R. Dawson	A.R. Dawson	+P. Lane	A.R. Dawson
R.J. McLoughlin	R.J. McLoughlin	R.J. McLoughlin	+T.A. Moroney	M.P. O'Callaghan
W.J. McBride	W.J. McBride	W.J. McBride	+M.W. Leahy	W.J. McBride
W.A. Mulcahy	*W.A. Mulcahy	*W.A. Mulcahy	*W.A. Mulcahy	*W.A. Mulcahy
E.P. McGuire	E.P. McGuire	E.P. McGuire	E.P. McGuire	E.P. McGuire
P.J.A. O'Sullivan	M.G. Culliton	M.G. Culliton	M.G. Culliton	M.G. Culliton
N.A.A. Murphy	N.A.A. Murphy 1T	N.A.A. Murphy	N.A.A. Murphy	N.A.A. Murphy
Lansdowne Road	Twickenham	Lansdowne Road	Lansdowne Road	Stade Colombes
lost 5-6	won 18-5	lost 3-6	lost 6-15	lost 6-27
Ire. 1G	Eng. 1G	Ire. 1PG	Ire. 2PG	Fr. 3G, 1DG, 3T
NZ 1PG, 1T	Ire. 3G, 1T	Scot. 2PG	Wales 3G	Ire. 1DG, 1T
7 December 1963	8 February 1964	22 February 1964	7 March 1964	11 April 1964

1964–65

v FRANCE	v ENGLAND	v SCOTLAND	v WALES	v S. AFRICA
T.J. Kiernan	T.J. Kiernan 1C	T.J. Kiernan 2C	T.J. Kiernan 1PG, 1C	T.J. Kiernan 2PG
P.J. Casey	P.J. Casey	P.J. Casey	D. Hewitt	K.J. Houston
J.C. Walsh	M.K. Flynn	J.C. Walsh	J.C. Walsh	J.C. Walsh
M.K. Flynn	K.J. Houston	M.K. Flynn	M.K. Flynn 1T	M.K. Flynn
K.J. Houston	+P.J. McGrath	P.J. McGrath 1T	P.J. McGrath	P.J. McGrath 1T
C.M.H. Gibson	C.M.H. Gibson	C.M.H. Gibson 1DG	C.M.H. Gibson	C.M.H. Gibson
+R.M. Young	R.M. Young	R.M. Young 1T	R.M. Young	R.M. Young
+S. MacHale	S. MacHale	S. MacHale	S. MacHale	S. MacHale
+K.W. Kennedy	K.W. Kennedy	K.W. Kennedy	K.W. Kennedy	K.W. Kennedy
*R.J. McLoughlin	*R.J. McLoughlin	*R.J. McLoughlin	*R.J. McLoughlin	*R.J. McLoughlin
W.J. McBride	W.J. McBride	W.J. McBride	W.J. McBride	W.J. McBride
W.A. Mulcahy	W.A. Mulcahy	W.A. Mulcahy	W.A. Mulcahy	W.A. Mulcahy
+M.G. Doyle 1T	M.G. Doyle	M.G. Doyle	M.G. Doyle	M.G. Doyle
+R.A. Lamont	R.A. Lamont 1T	+C.H. Wall	C.H. Wall	R.A. Lamont
N.A.A. Murphy	N.A.A. Murphy	N.A.A. Murphy 1T	N.A.A. Murphy	N.A.A. Murphy
Lansdowne Road drawn 3-3	Lansdowne Road won 5-0	Murrayfield won 16-6	Cardiff Arms Park lost 8-14	Lansdowne Road won 9-6
Ire. 1T Fr. 1T	Ire. 1G Eng. Nil	Scot. 1PG, 1DG Ire. 2G, 1DG, 1T	Wales 1G, 1DG, 1PG, 1T Ire. 1G, 1PG	Ire. 2PG, 1T SA 1PG, 1T
23 January 1965	13 February 1965	27 February 1965	13 March 1965	10 April 1965

1965–66

v FRANCE	v ENGLAND	v SCOTLAND	v WALES
T.J. Kiernan 1DG	T.J. Kiernan 1PG	T.J. Kiernan 1PG	*T.J. Kiernan
W.R. Hunter	W.R. Hunter	W.R. Hunter	A.T.A. Duggan
J.C. Walsh	M.K. Flynn	M.K. Flynn	F.P.K. Bresnihan 1T
M.K. Flynn	+F.P.K. Bresnihan	J.C. Walsh	J.C. Walsh
P.J. McGrath	P.J. McGrath 1T	P.J. McGrath	P.J. McGrath
C.M.H. Gibson 1PG	C.M.H. Gibson	C.M.H. Gibson	C.M.H. Gibson 1PG 1DG
R.M. Young	R.M. Young	R.M. Young	R.M. Young
S. MacHale	S. MacHale	S. MacHale	S. MacHale
K.W. Kennedy	K.W. Kennedy	+A.M. Brady	K.W. Kennedy
*R.J. McLoughlin	*R.J. McLoughlin	*R.J. McLoughlin	R.J. McLoughlin
+M.G. Molloy	M.G. Molloy	+O.C. Waldron	O.C. Waldron
W.J. McBride	W.J. McBride	W.J. McBride	W.J. McBride
M.G. Doyle	M.G. Doyle	M.G. Doyle	M.G. Doyle
R.A. Lamont	R.A. Lamont	R.A. Lamont	R.A. Lamont
N.A.A. Murphy	N.A.A. Murphy	N.A.A. Murphy	N.A.A. Murphy
Stade Colombes lost 6-11	Twickenham drawn 6-6	Lansdowne Road lost 3-11	Lansdowne Road won 9-6
Fr. 1G, 1PG, 1T Ire. 1PG, 1DG	Eng. 1PG, 1T Ire. 1PG, 1T	Ire. 1PG Scot. 1G, 2T	Ire. 1DG, 1PG, 1T Wales 1PG, 1T
29 January 1966	12 February 1966	26 February 1966	12 March 1966

1966–67

v AUSTRALIA	v ENGLAND	v SCOTLAND	v WALES	v FRANCE
T.J. Kiernan 1PG	T.J. Kiernan 1PG	T.J. Kiernan 1C	T.J. Kiernan	T.J. Kiernan 1PG
A.T.A. Duggan 1T	+R.D. Scott	A.T.A. Duggan	A.T.A. Duggan 1T	R.D. Scott
F.P.K. Bresnihan	F.P.K. Bresnihan	F.P.K. Bresnihan	F.P.K. Bresnihan	F.P.K. Bresnihan
+H.H. Rea	J.C. Walsh	J.C. Walsh	J.C. Walsh	J.C. Walsh
P.J. McGrath	N.H. Brophy	N.H. Brophy	N.H. Brophy	N.H. Brophy
C.M.H. Gibson 2DG, 1T	C.M.H. Gibson	C.M.H. Gibson	C.M.H. Gibson	C.M.H. Gibson
+B.F. Sherry	B.F. Sherry	B.F. Sherry	R.M. Young	R.M. Young
+P. O'Callaghan	P. O'Callaghan	S. MacHale	S. MacHale	S. MacHale
K.W. Kennedy	K.W. Kennedy	K.W. Kennedy	K.W. Kennedy	K.W. Kennedy
T.A. Moroney	T.A. Moroney	+S.A. Hutton	S.A. Hutton	S.A. Hutton
W.J. McBride	W.J. McBride	W.J. McBride	W.J. McBride	W.J. McBride
M.G. Molloy	M.G. Molloy	M.G. Molloy	M.G. Molloy	M.G. Molloy 1T
M.G. Doyle	M.G. Doyle	M.G. Doyle	M.G. Doyle	M.G. Doyle
+K.G. Goodall	K.G. Goodall	K.G. Goodall	K.G. Goodall	K.G. Goodall
*N.A.A. Murphy	*N.A.A. Murphy	*N.A.A. Murphy 1T	*N.A.A. Murphy	*N.A.A. Murphy
Lansdowne Road won 15–8	Lansdowne Road lost 3-8	Murrayfield won 5-3	Cardiff Arms Park won 3-0	Lansdowne Road lost 6-11
Ire. 2DG, 1PG, 2T Aust. 1G, 1DG	Ire. 1PG Eng. 1G, 1PG	Scot. 1PG Ire. 1G	Wales Nil Ire. 1T	Ire. 1PG, 1T Fr. 1G, 2DG
21 January 1967	11 February 1967	25 February 1967	11 March 1967	15 April 1967

1967–68

v AUSTRALIA	v FRANCE	v ENGLAND	v SCOTLAND	v WALES
*T.J. Kiernan 1DG, 1C	*T.J. Kiernan	*T.J. Kiernan 3PG	*T.J. Kiernan 1PG, 1C	*T.J. Kiernan 1PG
A.T.A. Duggan	A.T.A. Duggan	A.T.A. Duggan	A.T.A. Duggan 2T	A.T.A. Duggan
J.C. Walsh 1T	+B.A.P. O'Brien	B.A.P. O'Brien	B.A.P. O'Brien	F.P.K. Bresnihan
P.J. McGrath 1T	F.P.K. Bresnihan	F.P.K. Bresnihan	F.P.K. Bresnihan 1T	+L.M. Hunter
N.H. Brophy	R.D. Scott	R.D. Scott	R.D. Scott	+J.C.M. Moroney
C.M.H. Gibson	+W.M. McCombe 2PG	C.M.H. Gibson	C.M.H. Gibson	C.M.H. Gibson 1DG
B.F. Sherry	B.F. Sherry	B.F. Sherry	J.T.M. Quirke	R.M. Young
P.O'Callaghan	P. O'Callaghan	P. O'Callaghan	P. O'Callaghan	P. O'Callaghan
K.W. Kennedy	K.W. Kennedy	A.M. Brady	A.M. Brady	A.M. Brady
S.A. Hutton	S. Millar	S. Millar	S. Millar	S. Millar
W.J. McBride	W.J. McBride	W.J. McBride	W.J. McBride	W.J. McBride
M.G. Molloy	M.G. Molloy	M.G. Molloy	M.G. Molloy	M.G. Molloy
M.G. Doyle	M.G. Doyle	M.G. Doyle	M.G. Doyle	M.G. Doyle 1T
+T.A.P. Moore	M.L. Hipwell	K.G. Goodall	K.G. Goodall	K.G. Goodall
K.G. Goodall	K.G. Goodall	+T.J. Doyle	T.J. Doyle	T.J. Doyle
Sydney won 11-5	Stade Colombes lost 6-16	Twickenham drawn 9-9	Lansdowne Road won 14-6	Lansdowne Road won 9-6
Aust. 1G Ire. 1G, 1DG, 1T	Fr. 2G, 1DG, 1PG Ire. 2PG	Eng. 2PG, 1DG Ire. 3PG	Ire. 1G, 1PG, 2T Scot. 2PG	Ire. 1DG, 1PG, 1T Wales 1DG, 1PG
13 May 1967	27 January 1968	10 February 1968	24 February 1968	9 March 1968

1968–69

v AUSTRALIA	v FRANCE	v ENGLAND	v SCOTLAND	v WALES
*T.J. Kiernan 1C	*T.J. Kiernan	*T.J. Kiernan 2PG, 1C	*T.J. Kiernan	*T.J. Kiernan 2PG, 1C
J.C.M. Moroney 1C	A.T.A. Duggan	A.T.A. Duggan	A.T.A. Duggan 1T	A.T.A. Duggan
F.P.K. Bresnihan 1T	F.P.K. Bresnihan	F.P.K. Bresnihan 1T	F.P.K. Bresnihan 1T	F.P.K. Bresnihan
L.M. Hunter	H.H. Rea	C.M.H. Gibson	C.M.H. Gibson 1T	C.M.H. Gibson 1T
+J.J. Tydings	J.C.M. Moroney 1T, 1C, 3PG	J.C.M. Moroney	J.C.M. Moroney 2C	J.C.M. Moroney
C.M.H. Gibson	+B.J. McGann 1DG	B.J. McGann 1DG	B.J. McGann 1T	B.J. McGann
R.M. Young	R.M. Young	R.M. Young[1]	R.M. Young	R.M. Young
S. Millar	S. Millar	S. Millar	S. Millar	S. Millar
K.W. Kennedy	K.W. Kennedy	K.W. Kennedy	K.W. Kennedy	K.W. Kennedy
O.C. Waldron	P. O'Callaghan	P. O'Callaghan	P. O'Callaghan	P. O'Callaghan
W.J. McBride	W.J. McBride	W.J. McBride	W.J. McBride	W.J. McBride
M.G. Molloy	M.G. Molloy	M.G. Molloy	M.G. Molloy	M.G. Molloy
M.G. Doyle	+J.C. Davidson	J.C. Davidson	J.C. Davidson	J.C. Davidson
M.L. Hipwell	K.G. Goodall	K.G. Goodall	K.G. Goodall[1]	M.L. Hipwell
K.G. Goodall 1T	N.A.A. Murphy[1]	N.A.A. Murphy 1T	N.A.A. Murphy	N.A.A. Murphy
Lansdowne Road won 10-3	Lansdowne Road won 17–9	Lansdowne Road won 17-15	Murrayfield won 16-0	Cardiff Arms Park lost 11-24
Ire. 2G Aust. 1T	Ire. 1G, 1DG, 3PG Fr. 2PG, 1T	Ire. 1G, 2PG, 1DG, 1T Eng. 4PG, 1T	Scot. Nil Ire. 2G, 2T	Wales 3G, 1DG, 1PG, 1T Ire. 1G, 2PG
26 October 1968	25 January 1969	8 February 1969	22 February 1969	8 March 1969
	[1]Rep. by M.L. Hipwell	[1]Rep. by +C. Grimshaw	[1]Rep. by M.L. Hipwell	

1969–70

v S. AFRICA	v FRANCE	v ENGLAND	v SCOTLAND	v WALES
*T.J. Kiernan 1C, 1PG	*T.J. Kiernan	*T.J. Kiernan 1PG	*T.J. Kiernan 2C	*T.J. Kiernan 1PG, 1C
A.T.A. Duggan 1T	A.T.A. Duggan	A.T.A. Duggan	A.T.A. Duggan	A.T.A. Duggan 1T
F.P.K. Bresnihan	F.P.K. Bresnihan	F.P.K. Bresnihan	F.P.K. Bresnihan	F.P.K. Bresnihan
C.M.H. Gibson	C.M.H. Gibson	C.M.H. Gibson	C.M.H. Gibson 1T	C.M.H. Gibson
+W.J. Brown	W.J. Brown	A.J.F. O'Reilly	W.J. Brown 1T	W.J. Brown
B.J. McGann	B.J. McGann	B.J. McGann	B.J. McGann	B.J. McGann 1DG
R.M. Young	R.M. Young	R.M. Young	R.M. Young	R.M. Young
S. Millar	S. Millar	S. Millar	S. Millar	S. Millar
K.W. Kennedy	K.W. Kennedy	K.W. Kennedy	K.W. Kennedy	K.W. Kennedy
P. O'Callaghan	P. O'Callaghan	P. O'Callaghan	P. O'Callaghan	P. O'Callaghan
+C.E. Campbell	M.G. Molloy	M.G. Molloy	M.G. Molloy 1T	M.G. Molloy
W.J. McBride	W.J. McBride	W.J. McBride	W.J. McBride	W.J. McBride
R.A. Lamont	R.A. Lamont	R.A. Lamont	R.A. Lamont	R.A. Lamont
K.G. Goodall	K.G. Goodall	K.G. Goodall	K.G. Goodall 1T	K.G. Goodall 1T
+J.F. Slattery	J.F. Slattery	J.F. Slattery	J.F. Slattery	J.F. Slattery
Lansdowne Road drawn 8-8	Stade Colombes lost 0-8	Twickenham lost 3-9	Lansdowne Road won 16-11	Lansdowne Road won 14-0
Ire. 1G, 1PG SA 1G, 1PG	Fr. 1G, 1DG Ire. Nil	Eng. 2DG, 1T Ire. 1PG	Ire. 2G, 2T Scot. 1G, 1DG, 1T	Ire. 1G, 1DG, 1PG, 1T Wales Nil
10 January 1970	24 January 1970	14 February 1970	28 February 1970	14 March 1970

1970–71

v FRANCE	v ENGLAND	v SCOTLAND	v WALES
*T.J. Kiernan[1]	B.J. O'Driscoll	B.J. O'Driscoll	B.J. O'Driscoll
A.T.A. Duggan	A.T.A. Duggan 1T	A.T.A. Duggan 2T	A.T.A. Duggan
F.P.K. Bresnihan	F.P.K. Bresnihan	F.P.K. Bresnihan	F.P.K. Bresnihan
C.M.H. Gibson	*C.M.H. Gibson	*C.M.H. Gibson 2PG, 1C	*C.M.H. Gibson 3PG
+E.L. Grant 1T	E.L. Grant 1T	E.L. Grant 1T	E.L. Grant
B.J. McGann	B.J. McGann	B.J. McGann	B.J. McGann
R.M. Young	R.M. Young	R.M. Young	R.M. Young
R.J. McLoughlin	R.J. McLoughlin	R.J. McLoughlin	R.J. McLoughlin
K.W. Kennedy	K.W. Kennedy	K.W. Kennedy	K.W. Kennedy
+J.F. Lynch	J.F. Lynch	J.F. Lynch	J.F. Lynch
W.J. McBride	W.J. McBride	W.J. McBride	W.J. McBride
M.G. Molloy	M.G. Molloy	M.G. Molloy	M.G. Molloy
M.L. Hipwell	M.L. Hipwell	M.L. Hipwell	M.L. Hipwell
+D.J. Hickie	D.J. Hickie	D.J. Hickie	D.J. Hickie
J.F. Slattery	D.J. Slattery	J.F. Slattery	J.F. Slattery
Lansdowne Road drawn 9-9	Lansdowne Road lost 6-9	Murrayfield won 17-5	Cardiff Arms Park lost 9-23
Ire. 2PG, 1T Fr. 2PG, 1DG	Ire. 2T Eng. 3PG	Scot. 1G Ire. 1G, 2PG, 2T	Wales 1G, 2PG, 1DG, 3T Ire. 3PG
30 January 1971	13 February 1971	27 February 1971	13 March 1971

[1]Rep. by +B.J. O'Driscoll 2PG

1971–72

1ST v FRANCE	v ENGLAND	2ND v FRANCE
*T.J. Kiernan 2PG	*T.J. Kiernan 1PG, 1C	*T.J. Kiernan 3C, 2PG
+T.O. Grace	T.O. Grace 1T	A.T.A. Duggan 1T
C.M.H. Gibson	C.M.H. Gibson	C.M.H. Gibson
M.K. Flynn	M.K. Flynn 1T	M.K. Flynn 1T
+A.W. McMaster	A.W. McMaster	A.W. McMaster
B.J. McGann	B.J. McGann 1DG	B.J. McGann
+J.J. Moloney 1T	J.J. Moloney	J.J. Moloney 1T
R.J. McLoughlin 1T	R.J. McLoughlin	R.J. McLoughlin
K.W. Kennedy	K.W. Kennedy	K.W. Kennedy
J.F. Lynch	J.F. Lynch	J.F. Lynch
W.J. McBride	W.J. McBride	W.J. McBride
+C.F.P. Feighery	C.F.P. Feighery	C.F.P. Feighery
+S.A. McKinney	S.A. McKinney	S.A. McKinney
D.J. Hickie	D.J. Hickie	M.L. Hipwell
J.F. Slattery	J.F. Slattery	J.F. Slattery
Stade Colombes won 14–9	Twickenham won 16-12	Lansdowne Road won 24-14
Fr. 1G, 1PG Ire. 2PG, 2T	Eng. 1G, 2PG Ire. 1G, 1DG, 1PG, 1T	Ire. 3G, 2PG Fr. 1G, 2T
29 January 1972	12 February 1972	29 April 1972

1972–73

v NZ	v ENGLAND	v SCOTLAND	v WALES	v FRANCE
*T.J. Kiernan	*T.J. Kiernan	*T.J. Kiernan 1T	+A.H. Ensor	A.H. Ensor 1PG
T.O. Grace 1T	T.O. Grace 1T	T.O. Grace	T.O. Grace	+S.P. Dennison
M.K. Flynn	+R.A. Milliken 1T	R.A. Milliken	R.A. Milliken	R.A. Milliken
C.M.H. Gibson	C.M.H. Gibson	C.M.H. Gibson	C.M.H. Gibson 1T	C.M.H. Gibson 1PG
A.W. McMaster	A.W. McMaster	A.W. McMaster 1T	A.W. McMaster	A.W. McMaster
B.J. McGann 2PG	B.J. McGann 1PG, 1DG, 2C	B.J. McGann 2PG	B.J. McGann 2PG, 1C	+M.A.M. Quinn
J.J. Moloney	J.J. Moloney	J.J. Moloney	J.J. Moloney	J.J. Moloney
R.J. McLoughlin	R.J. McLoughlin	R.J. McLoughlin	R.J. McLoughlin	R.J. McLoughlin
K.W. Kennedy	K.W. Kennedy	K.W. Kennedy	K.W. Kennedy	K.W. Kennedy
J.F. Lynch	J.F. Lynch	J.F. Lynch	J.F. Lynch	+R.J. Clegg
W.J. McBride	W.J. McBride	W.J. McBride	*W.J. McBride	*W.J. McBride
+K.M.A. Mays	K.M.A. Mays	K.M.A. Mays	K.M.A. Mays	M.G. Molloy
J.C. Davidson	+J.H. Buckley	J.H. Buckley	S.A. McKinney	S.A. McKinney
T.A.P. Moore	T.A.P. Moore	T.A.P. Moore	T.A.P. Moore	T.A.P. Moore
J.F. Slattery	J.F. Slattery	J.F. Slattery	J.F. Slattery	J.F. Slattery
Lansdowne Road drawn 10-10	Lansdowne Road won 18-9	Murrayfield lost 14-19	Cardiff Arms Park lost 12-16	Lansdowne Road won 6-4
Ire. 2PG, 1T NZ 1G, 1T	Ire. 2G, 1PG, 1DG Eng. 1G, 1PG	Scot. 3DG, 2PG, 1T Ire. 2PG, 2T	Wales 1G, 2PG, 1T Ire. 1G, 2PG	Ire. 2PG Fr. 1T
20 January 1973	10 February 1973	24 February 1973	10 March 1973	14 April 1973

1973–74

v FRANCE	v WALES	v ENGLAND	v SCOTLAND
A.H. Ensor 2PG	A.H. Ensor 3PG	A.H. Ensor 1PG	A.H. Ensor
+V.A. Becker	V.A. Becker	T.O. Grace	T.O. Grace
C.M.H. Gibson	C.M.H. Gibson	C.M.H. Gibson 2T, 2C	C.M.H. Gibson 1C
R.A. Milliken	R.A. Milliken	R.A. Milliken	R.A. Milliken 1T
A.W. McMaster	+P.J. Lavery	A.W. McMaster	A.W. McMaster
M.A.M. Quinn	M.A.M. Quinn	M.A.M. Quinn 1DG	M.A.M. Quinn
J.J. Moloney	J.J. Moloney	J.J. Moloney 1T	J.J. Moloney
R.J. McLoughlin[1]	R.J. McLoughlin	R.J. McLoughlin	R.J. McLoughlin
K.W. Kennedy	K.W. Kennedy	K.W. Kennedy	K.W. Kennedy
J.F. Lynch	J.F. Lynch	J.F. Lynch	J.F. Lynch
*W.J. McBride	*W.J. McBride	*W.J. McBride	*W.J. McBride
+M.I. Keane	M.I. Keane	M.I. Keane	M.I. Keane
S.A. McKinney	+S.M. Deering	S.A. McKinney	S.A. McKinney 1PG
T.A.P. Moore	T.A.P. Moore	T.A.P. Moore 1T	T.A.P. Moore
J.F. Slattery	J.F. Slattery	J.F. Slattery	J.F. Slattery
Parc des Princes lost 6–9	Lansdowne Road drawn 9-9	Twickenham won 26–21	Lansdowne Road won 9-6
Fr. 1G, 1PG Ire. 2PG	Ire. 3PG Wales 1G, 1PG	Eng. 1G, 5PG Ire. 2G, 1PG, 1DG, 2T	Ire. 1G, 1PG Scot. 2PG
19 January 1974	2 February 1974	16 February 1974	2 March 1974

[1]Rep. by +P.J. Agnew

1974–75

v OVERSEAS XV	v NZ	v ENGLAND	v SCOTLAND	v WALES	v FRANCE
A.H Ensor	A.H. Ensor 2PG	A.H. Ensor 2PG	A.H. Ensor	A.H. Ensor 1T	A.H. Ensor
T.O. Grace	T.O. Grace	T.O. Grace	T.O. Grace 1T	T.O. Grace 1T	T.O. Grace
C.M.H. Gibson[1]	R.A. Milliken	R.A. Milliken	R.A. Milliken	R.A. Milliken	R.A. Milliken
2PG, 2C	+J.F. Crowe	C.M.H. Gibson 1T	C.M.H. Gibson	C.M.H. Gibson	C.M.H. Gibson
R.A. Milliken	+P. Parfrey	S.P. Dennison	S.P. Dennison 1T	A.W. McMaster	A.W. McMaster
A.W. McMaster					
	M.A. Quinn	W.M. McCombe	W.M. McCombe	W.M. McCombe	W.M. McCombe
M.A.M. Quinn	J.J. Maloney	1T, 2C	1PG, 1C	2C, 1PG, 2DG	J.J. Maloney
J.J. Moloney		J.J. Maloney	J.J. Maloney	J.J. Maloney	
	R.J. McLoughlin				R.J. McLoughlin
R.J. McLoughlin	K.W. Kennedy	R.J. McLoughlin	R.J. McLoughlin	R.J. McLoughlin	K.W. Kennedy
K.W. Kennedy	J.F. Lynch	+P.C. Whelan	P.C. Whelan	R.W. Kennedy	R.J. Clegg
J.F. Lynch	*W.J. McBride	R.J. Clegg	R.J. Clegg	R.J. Clegg	*W.J. McBride
*W.J. McBride	M.I. Keane	*W.J. McBride	*W.J. McBride	*W.J. McBride 1T	M.I. Keane
M.I. Keane	S.A. McKinney	M.I. Keane	M.I. Keane	M.I. Keane	M.J.A. Sherry
S.A. McKinney 1T	T.A.P. Moore	S.A. McKinney	S.A. McKinney	+M.J.A. Sherry	W.P. Duggan 1T
T.A.P. Moore	J.F. Slattery	+W.P. Duggan	W.P. Duggan	W.P. Duggan	J.F. Slattery
J.F. Slattery 1T		J.F. Slattery	J.F. Slattery	J.F. Slattery	
Lansdowne Road	Lansdowne Road	Lansdowne Road	Murrayfield	Lansdowne Road	Cardiff Arms Park
drawn 18-18	lost 6-15	won 12-9	lost 13-20	won 25-6	lost 4-32
Ire. 2G, 2PG	Ire. 2PG	Ire. 2G	Scot. 2PG, 2DG, 2T	Ire. 2G, 1PG, 2DG, 1T	Wales 3G, 2PG, 2T
O/SXV 2G, 2PG	NZ 1G, 3PG	Eng. 1G, 1DG	Ire. 1G, 1PG, 1T	Fr. 1PG, 1DG	Ire. 1T
7 September 1974	23 November 1974	18 January 1975	1 February 1975	1 March 1975	15 March 1975

[1]Rep. By +A. Doherty

1975–76

v AUSTRALIA	v FRANCE	v WALES	v ENGLAND	v SCOTLAND
A.H. Ensor	A.H. Ensor	A.H. Ensor	A.H. Ensor	L.A. Moloney
T.O. Grace	T.O. Grace	*T.O. Grace	*T.O. Grace 1T	*T.O. Grace
+J.A. McIlrath	J.A. McIlrath	P.J. Lavery[1]	+J.A. Brady	J.A. Brady
*C.M.H. Gibson	*C.M.H. Gibson	C.M.H. Gibson	C.M.H. Gibson	C.M.H. Gibson[1]
A.W. McMaster 1T	A.W. McMaster	A.W. McMaster	+S.E.F. Blake-Knox	S.E.F. Blake-Knox
+S.O. Campbell	B.J. McGann	B.J. McGann 3PG	B.J. McGann 2PG,	B.J. McGann 2PG
+J.C. Robbie 2PG	J.C. Robbie 1PG	+D.M. Canniffe	1DG	J.J. Moloney
			D.M. Canniffe	
P.J. Agnew	+P.A. Orr	P.A. Orr		P.A. Orr
+J.L. Cantrell	J.L. Cantrell	J.L. Cantrell	P.A. Orr	J.L. Cantrell
+F.M. McLoughlin	P. O'Callaghan	P. O'Callaghan	J.L. Cantrell	P. O'Callaghan
M.I. Keane	M.I. Keane	M.I. Keane	P. O'Callaghan	M.I. Keane
M.G. Molloy	+B.O. Foley	+R.F. Hakin	M.I. Keane	R.F. Hakin
S.A. McKinney	S.A. McKinney	S.A. McKinney	B.O. Foley	S.A. McKinney
W.P. Duggan	W.P. Duggan	W.P. Duggan	S.A. McKinney	W.P. Duggan
J.F. Slattery	S.M. Deering	S.M. Deering	+H.W. Steele	S.M. Deering
			S.M. Deering	
Lansdowne Road	Parc des Princes	Lansdowne Road	Twickenham	Lansdowne Road
lost 10-20	lost 3–26	lost 9-34	won 13–12	lost 6-15
Ire. 2PG, 1T	Fr. 2G, 2PG, 2T	Ire. 3PG	Eng. 4PG	Ire. 2PG
Aust. 1G, 2PG, 2T	Ire. 1PG	Wales 3G, 4PG, 1T	Ire. 2PG, 1DG, 1T	Scot. 4PG, 1DG
17 January 1976	7 February 1976	21 February 1976	6 March 1976	20 March 1976
		[1]Rep. by +L.A. Moloney		[1]Rep. by +C.H. McKibbin

1976–77

v NZ	v WALES	v ENGLAND	v SCOTLAND	v FRANCE
A.H. Ensor	+F. Wilson	F. Wilson	F. Wilson	A.H. Ensor
*T.O. Grace	*T.O. Grace	*T.O. Grace	*T.O. Grace	*T.O. Grace[1]
C.M.H. Gibson	+A.R. McKibbin	A.R. McKibbin	A.R. McKibbin	+R.G.A. Finn
J.A. McIlrath	J.A. McIlrath	J.A. McIlrath	C.M.H. Gibson 1T, 1C, 2PG	C.M.H. Gibson 1PG
A.W. McMaster	+D. St J. Bowen	D. St J. Bowen	D. St J. Bowen	+A.C. McLennan
B.J. McGann 1PG	C.M.H. Gibson 3PG	C.M.H. Gibson	M.A.M. Quinn 1PG, 1DG	M.A.M. Quinn 1PG
J.C. Robbie	+R.J.M. McGrath	R.J.M. McGrath	J.C. Robbie	J.C. Robbie[2]
P.A. Orr	P.A. Orr	P.A. Orr	P.A. Orr	P.A. Orr
P.C. Whelan	P.C. Whelan	P.C. Whelan	P.C. Whelan	P.C. Whelan
P. O'Callaghan	+T.A.O. Feighery	T.A.O. Feighery	+E.M.J. Byrne	E.M.J. Byrne
R.F. Hakin	M.I. Keane	M.I. Keane	M.I. Keane	M.I. Keane
M.I. Keane	R.F. Hakin[1]	R.F. Hakin	+C.W. Murtagh	R.F. Hakin
S.A. McKinney	S.A. McKinney	S.A. McKinney	S.A. McKinney	H.W. Steele
W.P. Duggan	W.P. Duggan	W.P. Duggan	W.P. Duggan	W.P. Duggan
J.C. Davidson	S.M. Deering	S.M. Deering	J.F. Slattery	J.F. Slattery
Wellington lost 3-11	Cardiff Arms Park lost 9-25	Lansdowne Road lost 0-4	Murrayfield lost 18-21	Lansdowne Road lost 6-15
NZ 1PG, 2T Ire. 1PG	Wales 2G, 2PG, 1DG, 1T Ire. 3PG	Ire. Nil Eng. 1T	Scot. 2PG, 1DG, 3T Ire. 1G, 3PG, 1DG	Ire. 2PG Fr. 1G, 3PG
5 June 1976	15 January 1977 [1]Rep. by B.O. Foley	5 February 1977	19 February 1977	19 March 1977 [1]Rep. by S.E.F. Blake-Knox [2]Rep. by R.J.M. McGrath

1977–78

v SCOTLAND	v FRANCE	v WALES	v ENGLAND
A.H. Ensor[1]	A.H. Ensor	A.H. Ensor	A.H. Ensor
T.O. Grace	C.M.H. Gibson	C.M.H. Gibson	C.M.H. Gibson
A.R. McKibbin	A.R. McKibbin	A.R. McKibbin	A.R. McKibbin
+P.P. McNaughton	P.P. McNaughton	P.P. McNaughton	P.P. McNaughton
A.C. McLennan	A.C. McLennan	A.C. McLennan	A.C. McLennan
+A.J.P. Ward 2PG, 1C	A.J.P. Ward 3PG	A.J.P. Ward 3PG, 1DG	A.J.P. Ward 1DG, 2PG
*J.J. Moloney	*J.J. Moloney	*J.J. Moloney 1T	*J.J. Moloney
P.A. Orr	P.A. Orr	P.A. Orr	P.A. Orr
P.C. Whelan	P.C. Whelan	P.C. Whelan	P.C. Whelan
+M.P. Fitzpatrick	E.M.J. Byrne	E.M.J. Byrne	E.M.J. Byrne
M.I. Keane	M.I. Keane	M.I. Keane	M.I. Keane
+D.E. Spring	H.W. Steele	H.W. Steele	H.W. Steele
+J.B. O'Driscoll[2]	S.A. McKinney	S.A. McKinney	S.A. McKinney
W.P. Duggan	W.P. Duggan	W.P. Duggan	W.P. Duggan
J.F. Slattery	J.F. Slattery	J.F. Slattery	J.F. Slattery
Lansdowne Road won 12-9	Parc des Princes lost 9-10	Lansdowne Road lost 16-20	Twickenham lost 9-15
Ire. 1G, 2PG Scot. 3PG	Fr. 2PG, 1T Ire. 3PG	Ire. 3PG, 1DG, 1T Wales 4PG, 2T	Eng. 2G, 1PG Ire. 1DG, 2PG
21 January 1978 [1]Rep. by L.A. Moloney [2]Rep. by S.A. McKinney 1T	18 February 1978	4 March 1978	18 March 1978

1978–79

v NZ	v FRANCE	v WALES	v ENGLAND	v SCOTLAND
L.A. Moloney	+R.M. Spring	R.M. Spring	R.M. Spring	+W.R.J. Elliott
+T.J. Kennedy	T.J. Kennedy	T.J. Kennedy	+M.C. Finn[1]	C.M.H. Gibson
A.R. McKibbin	A.R. McKibbin	A.R. McKibbin	A.R. McKibbin	A.R. McKibbin
C.M.H. Gibson	P.P. McNaughton	P.P. McNaughton	P.P. McNaughton	P.P. McNaughton
A.C. McLennan	A.C. McLennan	A.C. McLennan 1T	A.C. McLennan 1T	A.C. McLennan
A.J.P. Ward 2PG	A.J.P. Ward 3PG	A.J.P. Ward 3PG, 2C	A.J.P. Ward 1PG, 1DG, 1C	A.J.P. Ward 1PG
+C.S. Patterson	C.S. Patterson	C.S. Patterson 1T	C.S. Patterson	C.S. Patterson 2T
P.A. Orr	P.A. Orr	P.A. Orr	P.A. Orr	P.A. Orr
P.C. Whelan	P.C. Whelan	P.C. Whelan	P.C. Whelan	P.C. Whelan
E.M.J. Byrne	+G.A.J. McLoughlin	G.A.J. McLoughlin	G.A.J. McLoughlin	G.A.J. McLoughlin
M.I. Keane	M.I. Keane	M.I. Keane	M.I. Keane	M.I. Keane
D.E. Spring	H.W. Steele	H.W. Steele	H.W. Steele	D.E. Spring
J.F. Slattery	+C.C. Tucker	C.C. Tucker	W.P. Duggan	W.P. Duggan
W.P. Duggan	+M.E. Gibson	M.E. Gibson	M.E. Gibson	M.E. Gibson
*S.M. Deering	*J.F. Slattery	*J.F. Slattery	*J.F. Slattery	*J.F. Slattery
Lansdowne Road	Lansdowne Road	Cardiff Arms Park	Lansdowne Road	Murrayfield
lost 6-10	drawn 9-9	lost 21-24	won 12-7	drawn 11-11
Ire. 2PG	Ire. 3PG	Wales 2G, 4PG	Ire. 1G, 1PG, 1DG	Scot. 1PG, 2T
NZ 2DG, 1T	Fr. 1G, 1PG	Ire. 2G, 3PG	Eng. 1PG, 1T	Ire. 1PG, 2T
4 November 1978	20 January 1979	3 February 1979	17 February 1979	3 March 1979
			[1]Rep. by T.J. Kennedy	

1979

1ST v AUSTRALIA	2ND v AUSTRALIA
+R.C. O'Donnell[1]	R.C. O'Donnell
J.J. Moloney	J.J. Moloney
C.M.H. Gibson	C.M.H. Gibson
P.P. McNaughton	P.P. McNaughton
T.J. Kennedy	T.J. Kennedy
S.O. Campbell 4PG, 2C, 1DG	S.O. Campbell 2DG, 1PG
C.S. Patterson 2T	C.S. Patterson
P.A. Orr	P.A. Orr
+C.F. Fitzgerald	C.F. Fitzgerald
G.A.J. McLoughlin	G.A.J. McLoughlin
M.I. Keane	M.I. Keane
H.W. Steele	H.W. Steele
*J.F. Slattery	*J.F. Slattery
W.P. Duggan	W.P. Duggan
J.B. O'Driscoll	J.B. O'Driscoll
Brisbane	Sydney
won 27–12	won 9–3
Aust. 1G, 2PG	Aust. 1PG
Ire. 2G, 4PG, 1DG	Ire. 1PG, 2DG
3 June 1979	16 June 1979
[1]Rep. by +F.N.G. Ennis	

1979–80

v ENGLAND	v SCOTLAND	v FRANCE	v WALES
+K.A. O'Brien	R.C. O'Donnell	R.C. O'Donnell	R.C. O'Donnell
T.J. Kennedy	T.J. Kennedy 1T	T.J. Kennedy	T.J. Kennedy
A.R. McKibbin	A.R. McKibbin	+D.G. Irwin	D.G. Irwin 1T
P.P. McNaughton[1]	P.P. McNaughton	P.P. McNaughton	P.P. McNaughton
A.C. McLennan	J.J. Moloney	A.C. McLennan 1T	J.J. Moloney
S.O. Campbell 3PG	S.O. Campbell 3PG, 1C, 1DG	S.O. Campbell 3PG, 1C, 1DG	S.O. Campbell 3C, 1PG
C.S. Patterson	C.S. Patterson	C.S. Patterson	C.S. Patterson
P.A. Orr	P.A. Orr	P.A. Orr	P.A. Orr
C.F. Fitzgerald	C.F. Fitzgerald	C.F. Fitzgerald	C.F. Fitzgerald 1T
G.A.J. McLoughlin	M.P. Fitzpatrick	M.P. Fitzpatrick	M.P. Fitzpatrick
M.I. Keane	J.J. Glennon	B.O. Foley	M.I. Keane
+J.J. Glennon	M.I. Keane 1T	M.I. Keane	B.O. Foley
J.B. O'Driscoll	J.B. O'Driscoll	J.B. O'Driscoll[1]	J.B. O'Driscoll 1T
W.P. Duggan	D.E. Spring	D.E. Spring	D.E. Spring
*J.F. Slattery	*J.F. Slattery	*J.F. Slattery	*J.F. Slattery
Twickenham	Lansdowne Road	Parc des Princes	Lansdowne Road
lost 9-24	won 22-15	lost 18-19	won 21-7
Eng. 3G, 2PG	Ire. 1G, 3PG, 1DG, 1T	Fr. 1G, 2PG, 1DG, 1T	Ire. 3G, 1PG
Ire. 3PG	Scot. 2G, 1PG	Ire. 1G, 3PG, 1DG	Wales 1PG, 1T
19 January 1980	2 February 1980	1 March 1980	15 March 1980
[1]Rep. by +I.J. Burns		[1]Rep. by C.C. Tucker	

1980–81

v FRANCE	v WALES	v ENGLAND	v SCOTLAND
+H.P. MacNeill 1T	H.P. MacNeill 1T	H.P. MacNeill 1DG	H.P. MacNeill
+F.P. Quinn	F.P. Quinn	F.P. Quinn	+K.J. Hooks
D.G. Irwin	D.G. Irwin	D.G. Irwin	D.G. Irwin 1T
P.P. McNaughton	S.O. Campbell	S.O. Campbell 1DG	S.O. Campbell 1PG, 1C
A.C. McLennan	A.C. McLennan	A.C. McLennan	A.C. McLennan
S.O. Campbell 3PG	A.J.P. Ward	A.J.P. Ward	A.J.P. Ward
J.C. Robbie	J.C. Robbie	J.C. Robbie	J.C. Robbie
P.A. Orr	P.A. Orr	P.A. Orr	P.A. Orr
P.C. Whelan	P.C. Whelan	P.C. Whelan	J.L. Cantrell
M.P. Fitzpatrick	M.P. Fitzpatrick	M.P. Fitzpatrick	M.P. Fitzpatrick
M.I. Keane	M.I. Keane	M.I. Keane	M.I. Keane
B.O. Foley	D.E. Spring[1]	B.O. Foley	B.O. Foley
J.B. O'Driscoll	J.B. O'Driscoll	J.B. O'Driscoll	J.B. O'Driscoll
W.P. Duggan	W.P. Duggan	W.P. Duggan	W.P. Duggan
*J.F. Slattery	*J.F. Slattery 1T	*J.F. Slattery	*J.F. Slattery
Lansdowne Road	Cardiff Arms Park	Lansdowne Road	Murrayfield
lost 13-19	lost 8-9	lost 6-10	lost 9-10
Ire. 3PG, 1T	Wales 2PG, 1DG	Ire. 2DG	Scot. 1PG, 1DG, 1T
Fr. 3PG, 2DG, 1T	Ire. 2T	Eng. 1G, 1T	Ire. 1G, 1PG
7 February 1981	21 February 1981	7 March 1981	21 March 1981
	[1]Rep. by M.E. Gibson		

1981

1ST v S. AFRICA	2ND v S. AFRICA
+J.J. Murphy[1]	K.A. O'Brien 1T
T.J. Kennedy	T.J. Kennedy
D.G. Irwin	D.G. Irwin
S.O. Campbell[2] 2C, 1PG	P.M. Dean[1]
A.C. McLennan 1T	A.C. McLennan
+P.M. Dean	M.A.M. Quinn 2PG
R.J.M. McGrath 1T	R.J.M. McGrath
P.A. Orr	P.A. Orr
J.L. Cantrell	J.L. Cantrell
G.A.J. McLoughlin	G.A.J. McLoughlin
+J.J. Holland	J.J. Holland
B.O. Foley	B.O. Foley
*J.F. Slattery	*J.F. Slattery
W.P. Duggan	W.P. Duggan
J.B. O'Driscoll	J.B. O'Driscoll
Cape Town	Durban
lost 15-23	lost 10-12
SA 1G, 3PG, 2T	SA 1PG, 3DG
Ire. 2G, 1PG	Ire. 2PG, 1T
30 May 1981	6 June 1981
[1]Rep. by K.A. O'Brien [2]Rep. by +J.A. Hewitt	[1]Rep. by J.A. Hewitt

1981–82

v AUSTRALIA	v WALES	v ENGLAND	v SCOTLAND	v FRANCE
H.P. MacNeill	H.P. MacNeill	H.P. MacNeill 1T	H.P. MacNeill	H.P. MacNeill
+T.M. Ringland	T.M. Ringland 1T	T.M. Ringland	M.C. Finn	T.M. Ringland
D.G. Irwin	D.G. Irwin[1]	M.J. Kiernan	M.J. Kiernan	M.J. Kiernan
P.M. Dean	P.M. Dean[2]	P.M. Dean	P.M. Dean	P.M. Dean
T.J. Kennedy	M.C. Finn 2T	M.C. Finn	+K.D. Crossan	M.C. Finn
A.J.P. Ward 4PG	S.O. Campbell 1C, 2PG	S.O. Campbell 2PG, 1C	S.O. Campbell 6PG, 1DG	S.O. Campbell 3PG
R.J.M. McGrath	R.J.M. McGrath	R.J.M. McGrath	R.J.M. McGrath	R.J.M. McGrath
P.A. Orr	P.A. Orr	P.A. Orr	P.A. Orr	P.A. Orr
J.L. Cantrell	*C.F. Fitzgerald	*C.F. Fitzgerald	*C.F. Fitzgerald	*C.F. Fitzgerald
M.P. Fitzpatrick	G.A.J. McLoughlin	G.A.J. McLoughlin 1T	G.A.J. McLoughlin	G.A.J. McLoughlin
B.O. Foley	M.I. Keane	M.I. Keane	M.I. Keane	M.I. Keane
+D.G. Lenihan	D.G. Lenihan	D.G. Lenihan	D.G. Lenihan	D.G. Lenihan
J.B. O'Driscoll	J.F. Slattery	J.F. Slattery	J.F. Slattery	J.F. Slattery
W.P. Duggan	W.P. Duggan	W.P. Duggan	W.P. Duggan	J.B. O'Driscoll
*J.F. Slattery	J.B. O'Driscoll	J.B. O'Driscoll	J.B. O'Driscoll	+R.K. Kearney
Lansdowne Road	Lansdowne Road	Twickenham	Lansdowne Road	Parc des Princes
lost 12-16	won 20-12	won 16-15	won 21-12	lost 9-22
Ire. 4PG	Ire. 1G, 2PG, 2T	Eng. 1G, 3PG	Ire. 6PG, 1DG	Fr. 1G, 4PG, 1T
Aust. 3PG, 1DG, 1T	Wales 1G, 1PG, 1DG	Ire. 1G, 2PG, 1T	Scot. 1G, 2PG	Ire. 3PG
21 November 1981	23 January 1982	6 February 1982	20 February 1982	20 March 1982
	[1]Rep. by +M.J. Kiernan [2]Rep. by J.J. Murphy			

1982–83

v SCOTLAND	v FRANCE	v WALES	v ENGLAND
H.P. MacNeill	H.P. MacNeill	H.P. MacNeill 1PG	H.P. MacNeill
T.M. Ringland	T.M. Ringland	T.M. Ringland	T.M. Ringland
D.G. Irwin	D.G. Irwin	D.G. Irwin	D.G. Irwin
M.J. Kiernan 1T	M.J. Kiernan	M.J. Kiernan	M.J. Kiernan
M.C. Finn	M.C. Finn 2T	M.C. Finn	M.C. Finn
S.O. Campbell 1C, 3PG	S.O. Campbell 1C, 4PG	S.O. Campbell 2PG	S.O. Campbell[1] 5PG, 1T, 1C
R.J.M. McGrath	R.J.M. McGrath	R.J.M. McGrath	R.J.M. McGrath
P.A. Orr	P.A. Orr	P.A. Orr	P.A. Orr
*C.F. Fitzgerald	*C.F. Fitzgerald	*C.F. Fitzgerald	*C.F. Fitzgerald
G.A.J. McLoughlin	G.A.J. McLoughlin	G.A.J. McLoughlin	G.A.J. McLoughlin
D.G. Lenihan	D.G. Lenihan	D.G. Lenihan	D.G. Lenihan
M.I. Keane	M.I. Keane	M.I. Keane	M.I. Keane
J.F. Slattery	J.F. Slattery	J.F. Slattery	J.F. Slattery 1T
W.P. Duggan	W.P. Duggan	W.P. Duggan	W.P. Duggan
J.B. O'Driscoll	J.B. O'Driscoll	J.B. O'Driscoll	J.B. O'Driscoll
Murrayfield	Lansdowne Road	Cardiff Arms Park	Lansdowne Road
won 15-13	won 22-16	lost 9-23	won 25-15
Scot. 2PG, 1DG, 1T	Ire. 1G, 4PG, 1T	Wales 1G, 3PG, 2T	Ire. 1G, 5PG, 1T
Ire. 1G, 3PG	Fr. 1G, 2PG, 1T	Ire. 3PG	Eng. 5PG
15 January 1983	19 February 1983	5 March 1983	19 March 1983
			[1]Rep. by A.J.P. Ward

1983–84

v FRANCE	v WALES	v ENGLAND	v SCOTLAND
H.P. MacNeill	H.P. MacNeill	H.P. MacNeill	J.J. Murphy 1C, 1PG
T.M. Ringland	T.M. Ringland	T.M. Ringland	T.M. Ringland
D.G. Irwin	D.G. Irwin	M.J. Kiernan	M.J. Kiernan 1T
+R.J.M. Moroney	R.J.M. Moroney	M.C. Finn	M.C. Finn
K.D. Crossan	K.D. Crossan	K.D. Crossan	K.D. Crossan
S.O. Campbell 4PG	S.O. Campbell 3PG	A.J.P. Ward 3PG	A.J.P. Ward[1]
R.J.M. McGrath	R.J.M. McGrath	+J.A.P. Doyle	J.A.P. Doyle
P.A. Orr	P.A. Orr	P.A. Orr	P.A. Orr
*C.F. Fitzgerald	*C.F. Fitzgerald[1]	H.T. Harbison	H.T. Harbison
G.A.J. McLoughlin	+J.J. McCoy	+D.C. Fitzgerald	D.C. Fitzgerald
M.I. Keane	M.I. Keane	M.I. Keane	M.I. Keane
D.G. Lenihan	D.G. Lenihan	D.G. Lenihan	D.G. Lenihan
J.F. Slattery	+W.R. Duncan	W.R. Duncan	J.B. O'Driscoll
W.P. Duggan	W.P. Duggan	*W.P. Duggan	*W.P. Duggan
J.B. O'Driscoll	J.B. O'Driscoll	J.B. O'Driscoll	+D.G. McGrath
Parc des Princes	Lansdowne Road	Twickenham	Lansdowne Road
lost 12-25	lost 9-18	lost 9-12	lost 9-32
Fr. 1G, 4PG, 1DG, 1T	Ire. 3PG	Eng. 1DG, 3PG	Ire. 1G, 1PG
Ire. 4PG	Wales 1G, 4PG	Ire. 3PG	Scot. 3G,‡ 2PG, 2T
21 January 1984	4 February 1984	18 February 1984	3 March 1984
	[1]Rep. by +H.T. Harbison		[1]Rep. by +H.C. Condon ‡Includes a penalty try

1984–85

v AUSTRALIA	v SCOTLAND	v FRANCE	v WALES	v ENGLAND
H.P. MacNeill	H.P. MacNeill	H.P. MacNeill	H.P. MacNeill	H.P. MacNeill
T.M. Ringland	T.M. Ringland 2T	T.M. Ringland	T.M. Ringland 1T	T.M. Ringland
+B.J. Mullin	B.J. Mullin	R.J.M. Moroney	B.J. Mullin	B.J. Mullin 1T
M.C. Finn	M.J. Kiernan 2C, 1DG, 1PG	M.J. Kiernan 5PG	M.J. Kiernan 3PG, 2C	M.J. Kiernan 2PG, 1DG
M.J. Kiernan 3PG	K.D. Crossan	K.D. Crossan	K.D. Crossan 1T	K.D. Crossan
P.M. Dean	P.M. Dean	P.M. Dean	P.M. Dean	P.M. Dean
+M.T. Bradley	M.T. Bradley	M.T. Bradley	M.T. Bradley	M.T. Bradley
P.A. Orr	P.A. Orr	P.A. Orr	P.A. Orr	P.A. Orr
*C.F. Fitzgerald	*C.F. Fitzgerald	*C.F. Fitzgerald	*C.F. Fitzgerald	*C.F. Fitzgerald
J.J. McCoy	J.J. McCoy	J.J. McCoy	J.J. McCoy	J.J. McCoy
D.G. Lenihan	D.G. Lenihan	D.G. Lenihan	D.G. Lenihan	D.G. Lenihan
+W.A. Anderson	W.A. Anderson	W.A. Anderson	W.A. Anderson	W.A. Anderson
+P.M. Matthews	P.M. Matthews	P.M. Matthews[1]	P.M. Matthews	P.M. Matthews
R.K. Kearney	+B.J. Spillane	B.J. Spillane[2]	B.J. Spillane	B.J. Spillane
+W.J. Sexton	+N.J. Carr	N.J. Carr	N.J. Carr	N.J. Carr
Lansdowne Road lost 9-16	Murrayfield won 18-15	Lansdowne Road drawn 15-15	Cardiff Arms Park won 21-9	Lansdowne Road won 13-10
Ire. 3PG Aust. 3DG, 1PG, 1T	Scot. 4PG, 1DG Ire. 2G, 1DG, 1PG	Ire. 5PG Fr. 2G, 1PG	Wales 1G, 1DG Ire. 2G, 3PG	Ire. 1DG, 2PG, 1T Eng. 2PG, 1T
10 November 1984	2 February 1985	2 March 1985 [1]Rep. by M.P. Fitzpatrick [2]Rep. by +B.W. McCall	16 March 1985	30 March 1985

1985–86

v FRANCE	v WALES	v ENGLAND	v SCOTLAND
H.P. MacNeill	H.P. MacNeill	H.P. MacNeill	H.P. MacNeill
T.M. Ringland	T.M. Ringland 1T	T.M. Ringland 1T	T.M. Ringland 1T
B.J. Mullin	B.J. Mullin	B.J. Mullin 1T	B.J. Mullin
M.J. Kiernan 3PG	M.J. Kiernan 1C, 2PG	M.J. Kiernan 1C, 2PG	M.J. Kiernan 1PG, 1C
M.C. Finn	M.C. Finn	K.D. Crossan	K.D. Crossan
P.M. Dean	P.M. Dean	+R.P. Keyes	A.J.P. Ward
M.T. Bradley	M.T. Bradley	M.T. Bradley	M.T. Bradley
P.A. Orr	+A.P. Kennedy	A.P. Kennedy	P.A. Orr
*C.F. Fitzgerald	*C.F. Fitzgerald	*C.F. Fitzgerald	*C.F. Fitzgerald
J.J. McCoy	D.C. Fitzgerald	D.C. Fitzgerald	D.C. Fitzgerald
D.G. Lenihan	D.G. Lenihan	B.W. McCall 1T	B.W. McCall
W.A. Anderson	J.J. Holland	D.G. Lenihan	D.G. Lenihan
R.K. Kearney	R.K. Kearney	R.D. Morrow	R.D. Morrow
B.J. Spillane	B.J. Spillane	B.J. Spillane	W.A. Anderson
+R.D. Morrow	N.J. Carr	N.J. Carr	N.J. Carr
Parc des Princes lost 9-29	Lansdowne Road lost 12-19	Twickenham lost 20-25	Lansdowne Road lost 9-10
Fr. 1G, 4PG, 1DG, 2T Ire. 3PG	Ire. 1G, 2PG Wales 1G, 3PG, 1T	Eng. 3G,‡ 1PG, 1T Ire. 1G, 2PG, 2T	Ire. 1G, 1PG Scot. 2PG, 1T
1 February 1986	15 February 1986	1 March 1986 ‡includes penalty try	15 March 1986

1986–87

v ROMANIA	v ENGLAND	v SCOTLAND	v FRANCE	v WALES
H.P. MacNeill 1T	H.P. MacNeill	H.P. MacNeill	H.P. MacNeill	H.P. MacNeill
T.M. Ringland	T.M. Ringland	T.M. Ringland	T.M. Ringland 1T	T.M. Ringland
B.J. Mullin 2T	B.J. Mullin	B.J. Mullin	B.J. Mullin	B.J. Mullin 1T
M.J. Kiernan 2PG, 7C	M.J. Kiernan 1T 1C 1PG	M.J. Kiernan 1PG 1DG 1C	M.J. Kiernan 1PG, 1C	M.J. Kiernan 1PG, 2C
K.D. Crossan 3T	K.D. Crossan 1T	K.D. Crossan	K.D. Crossan	K.D. Crossan
P.M. Dean 2T	P.M. Dean	P.M. Dean	P.M. Dean	P.M. Dean 1T
M.T. Bradley 1T	M.T. Bradley	M.T. Bradley	M.T. Bradley 1T	M.T. Bradley
P.A. Orr	P.A. Orr	P.A. Orr	P.A. Orr	P.A. Orr
H.T. Harbison	H.T. Harbison	H.T. Harbison	H.T. Harbison	H.T. Harbison
D.C. Fitzgerald	D.C. Fitzgerald	D.C. Fitzgerald	D.C. Fitzgerald	D.C. Fitzgerald
*D.G. Lenihan	*D.G. Lenihan	*D.G. Lenihan 1T	*D.G. Lenihan	*D.G. Lenihan
W.A. Anderson 1T	J.J. Glennon	J.J. Glennon	J.J. Glennon	W.A. Anderson
P.M. Matthews	P.M. Matthews 1T	P.M. Matthews	B.J. Spillane	P.M. Matthews
M.E. Gibson	W.A. Anderson	W.A. Anderson	W.A. Anderson	B.J. Spillane
N.J. Carr	N.J. Carr	N.J. Carr	P.M. Matthews	N.J. Carr
Lansdowne Road	Lansdowne Road	Murrayfield	Lansdowne Road	Cardiff Arms Park
won 60–0	won 17-0	lost 12-16	lost 13-19	won 15-11
Ire. 7G, 3T, 2PG Rom. Nil	Ire. 1G, 1PG, 2T Eng. Nil	Scot. 1G, 2DG, 1T Ire. 1G, 1DG, 1PG	Ire. 1G, 1PG, 1T Fr. 1G, 3PG, 1T	Wales 1PG, 2T Ire. 2G, 1PG
1 November 1986	7 February 1987	21 February 1987	21 March 1987	4 April 1987

1987 (WORLD CUP)

v WALES	v CANADA	v TONGA	v AUSTRALIA (QUARTER-FINAL)
H.P. MacNeill	H.P. MacNeill 1T	H.P. MacNeill 2T	H.P. MacNeill 1T
T.M. Ringland	T.M. Ringland 1T	T.M. Ringland	T.M. Ringland
B.J. Mullin	B.J. Mullin	B.J. Mullin 3T	B.J. Mullin[2]
M.J. Kiernan 2PG	M.J. Kiernan 5C, 2PG 1DG	D.G. Irwin	M.J. Kiernan 1T, 2C, 1PG
K.D. Crossan	K.D. Crossan 2T	K.D. Crossan	K.D. Crossan
P.M. Dean	A.J.P. Ward 1DG	A.J.P. Ward 3C, 2PG	P.M. Dean
M.T. Bradley	M.T. Bradley 1T	M.T. Bradley	M.T. Bradley
P.A. Orr	P.A. Orr	+J. Langbroek	P.A. Orr
+T. Kingston	+J.P. McDonald	T. Kingston	T. Kingston
D.C. Fitzgerald	D.C. Fitzgerald	J.J. McCoy	D.C. Fitzgerald
*D.G. Lenihan	*D.G. Lenihan	*D.G. Lenihan	*D.G. Lenihan
W.A. Anderson	W.A. Anderson	W.A. Anderson	W.A. Anderson
P.M. Matthews[1]	+P.C. Collins	P.M. Matthews	P.M. Matthews
B.J. Spillane	B.J. Spillane 1T	+N. Francis	N. Francis[1]
D.G. McGrath	D.G. McGrath	D.G. McGrath	D.G. McGrath
Wellington	Dunedin	Brisbane	Concord Oval, Sydney
lost 6-13	won 46-19	won 32-9	lost 15-33
25 May 1987	30 May 1987	3 June 1987	7 June 1987
[1]Rep. by J.J. Glennon			[1]Rep. by B.J. Spillane [2]Rep. by D.G. McGrath

1987–88

v SCOTLAND	v FRANCE	v WALES	v ENGLAND	v ENGLAND (MILLENNIUM MATCH)
P.P.A. Danaher	P.P.A. Danaher	P.P.A. Danaher	H.P. MacNeill	H.P. MacNeill 1T
T.M. Ringland[1]	T.M. Ringland	T.M. Ringland	T.M. Ringland	+J.F. Sexton
B.J. Mullin 1T	B.J. Mullin	B.J. Mullin	B.J. Mullin 1DG	+V. Cunningham
M.J. Kiernan 1PG,	M.J. Kiernan 2PG	M.J. Kiernan 1P, 1C	M.J. Kiernan	B.J. Mullin
2C, 1DG	K.D. Crossan	K.D. Crossan	K.D. Crossan	M.J. Kiernan 1C
K.D. Crossan				
	P.M. Dean	P.M. Dean	P.M. Dean	P.M. Dean
P.M. Dean	M.T. Bradley	M.T. Bradley	M.T. Bradley	+L.F.P. Aherne
M.T. Bradley 1T				
	J.J. Fitzgerald	+T.P.J. Clancy	T.P.J. Clancy	T.P.J. Clancy
J.J. Fitzgerald	T.K. Kingston	T.J. Kingston 1T	T.J. Kingston	+S.J. Smith 1T
T.K. Kingston	D.C. Fitzgerald	D.C. Fitzgerald	D.C. Fitzgerald	
D.C. Fitzgerald	*D.G. Lenihan	*D.G. Lenihan	*D.G. Lenihan	J.J. McCoy
*D.G. Lenihan	W.A. Anderson	W.A. Anderson	+M.M.F. Moylett	*D.G. Lenihan
W.A. Anderson	+D. Whittle	P.M. Matthews	P.M. Matthews	W.A. Anderson
P.M. Matthews	M.E. Gibson	M.E. Gibson	W.A. Anderson	P.M. Matthews
M.E. Gibson	P.M. Matthews	+W.D. McBride	W.D. McBride	M.E. Gibson
W.J. Sexton	Parc des Princes	Lansdowne Road	Twickenham	W. Sexton
Lansdowne Road	lost 25-6	lost 9-12	lost 35-3	Lansdowne Road
won 22-18	20 February 1988	5 March 1988	19 March 1988	lost 10-21
16 January 1988				23 April 1988
[1]Rep. by H.P. MacNeill 1T				

1988–89

v WESTERN SAMOA	v ITALY	v FRANCE	v WALES	v ENGLAND	v SCOTLAND
P.P.A. Danaher	P.P.A. Danaher 2PG	P.P.A. Danaher	+F.J. Dunlea	F.J. Dunlea	F.J. Dunlea 1T
J.F. Sexton 1T,	J.F. Sexton	J.F. Sexton	M.J. Kiernan 3PG	M.J. Kiernan 1PG	M.J. Kiernan 1PG,
1DG	V.J.C. Cunningham	B.J. Mullin 1T	1C	B.J. Mullin	3C
B.J. Mullin 1T	1C	D.G. Irwin	B.J. Mullin	D.G. Irwin	B.J. Mullin 2T
M.J. Kiernan 1T,	B.J. Mullin	M.J. Kiernan 1PG,	D.G. Irwin	K.D. Crossan	D.G. Irwin
2PG, 4C	K.D. Crossan 2T	5C	K.D. Crossan		K.D. Crossan
K.D. Crossan 2T				P.M. Dean	
	P.M. Dean 1DG	P.M. Dean	P.M. Dean 1T	J.F.P. Aherne	P.M. Dean
P.M. Dean	F.F.P. Aherne 1T	L.F.P. Aherne	L.F.P. Aherne		J.F.P. Aherne
L.F.P. Aherne				T.P.J. Clancy	
	T.P.J. Clancy	T.P.J. Clancy	T.P.J. Clancy	S.J. Smith	T.P.J. Clancy
T.P.J. Clancy	S.J. Smith	S.J. Smith	S.J. Smith	J.J. McCoy	S.J. Smith
S.J. Smith	J.J. McCoy	J.J. McCoy	J.J. McCoy	D.G. Lenihan	J.J. McCoy
J.J. McCoy	D.G. Lenihan	D.G. Lenihan	D.G. Lenihan	W.A. Anderson	D.G. Lenihan
D.G. Lenihan	N.P.J. Francis	W.A. Anderson	W.A. Anderson	*P.M. Matthews	N.P.T. Francis
N.P.J. Francis 1T	*P.M. Matthews	*P.M. Matthews	*P.M. Matthews	N.P. Mannion	*P.M. Matthews
*P.M. Matthews[1]	2T	N.P. Mannion	N.P. Mannion 1T	P.T.J. O'Hara	N.P. Mannion
1T	N.P. Mannion	P.T.J. O'Hara	P.T.J. O'Hara	Lansdowne Road	W.D. McBride
+N.P. Mannion	W.D. McBride	Lansdowne Road	Cardiff Arms Park	lost 3–16	Murrayfield
W.D. McBride 1T	Lansdowne Road	lost 21–26	won 19-13	18 February 1989	lost 21-37
Lansdowne Road	won 31-15	21 January 1989	4 February 1989		4 March 1989
won 49–22	31 December 1988				
29 October 1988					
[1]Rep. by +P.J. O'Hara					

1989–90

v NEW ZEALAND	v ENGLAND	v SCOTLAND	v FRANCE	v WALES
+P. Rainey	+K.J. Murphy	K.J. Murphy	K.J. Murphy	K.J. Murphy
K.J. Hooks[1]	M.J. Kiernan	M.J. Kiernan	K.J. Hooks	K.J. Hooks
B.J. Mullin	B.J. Mullin	B.J. Mullin	M.J. Kiernan 4PG	B.J. Mullin
D.G. Irwin	D.G. Irwin	D.G. Irwin	P.P. Danaher	M.J. Kiernan 1C
K.D. Crossan	K.D. Crossan	K.D. Crossan	K.D. Crossan	K.D. Crossan
B.A. Smith 2PG	+P. Russell	B.A. Smith	B.A. Smith	B.A. Smith 1T
F.F.P. Aherne	L.F.P. Aherne	L.F.P. Aherne	L.F.P. Aherne	M.T. Bradley[1]
+N.J. Popplewell[2]	D.C. Fitzgerald	J.J. Fitzgerald	J.J. Fitzgerald	J.J. Fitzgerald
S.J. Smith	S.J. Smith[1]	J.P. McDonald	T.J. Kingston	T.J. Kingston 1T
J.J. McCoy	+G. Halpin	D.C. Fitzgerald	D.C. Fitzgerald	D.C. Fitzgerald
D.G. Lenihan	N.P.T. Francis	*W.A. Anderson	*D.G. Lenihan	*D.G. Lenihan
*W.A. Anderson	*W.A Anderson	D.G. Lenihan	N.P.T. Francis	N.P.T. Francis
P.M. Matthews	P.M. Matthews	P.M. Matthews	W.D. McBride	W.D. McBride 1T
N.P. Mannion	N.P. Mannion	N.P. Mannion	N.P. Mannion	N.P. Mannion
P.T.J. O'Hara	P.T.J. O'Hara	P.T.J. O'Hara[1]	P.T.J. O'Hara	P.T.J. O'Hara
Lansdowne Road	Twickenham	Lansdowne Road	Parc des Princes	Lansdowne Road
lost 6-23	lost 0–23	lost 10–13	lost 12-31	won 14–8
18 November 1989	20 January 1990	3 February 1990	3 March 1990	24 March 1990
[1]Rep. by P.P. Danaher	[1]Rep by J.P. McDonald	[1]Rep. by P.C. Collins		[1]Rep. by L.F.P. Aherne
[2]Rep. by D.C. Fitzgerald				

1990–91

v ARGENTINA	v FRANCE	v WALES	v ENGLAND	v SCOTLAND
K.J. Murphy	K.J. Murphy	+J.E. Staples[1] 1T	J.E. Staples	J.E. Staples[1]
K.J. Hooks 1T	+S.P. Geoghegan	S.P. Geoghegan 1T	S.P. Geoghegan	S.P. Geoghegan 1T
B.J. Mullin[1]	B.J. Mullin	B.J. Mullin 1T	B.J. Mullin	B.J. Mullin 1T
M.J. Kiernan 1T, 4PG	M.J. Kiernan 3PG	+D.M. Curtis	D.M. Curtis	D.M. Curtis
K.D. Crossan	K.J. Hooks	+D.J. Clarke 1T	K.D. Crossan	K.D. Crossan 1T
B.A. Smith	B.A. Smith	B.A. Smith 1C, 1DG	B.A. Smith	B.A. Smith 3C, 1DG
+A.C. Rolland	*+R. Saunders	*R. Saunders	*R. Saunders	*R. Saunders
N.J. Popplewell	J.J. Fitzgerald	J.J. Fitzgerald	J.J. Fitzgerald	J.J. Fitzgerald
J.P. McDonald	S.J. Smith 1T	S.J. Smith	S.J. Smith	S.J. Smith
D.C. Fitzgerald	D.C. Fitzgerald	D.C. Fitzgerald	D.C. Fitzgerald	D.C. Fitzgerald
*D.G. Lenihan	+B.C. Rigney	M.J. Galwey	B.J. Rigney	B.J. Rigney
+P.S.C. Johns	+M.J. Galwey	B.J. Rigney	N.P.J. Francis	N.P.J. Francis
N.P. Mannion	P.M. Matthews	P.M. Matthews	P.M. Matthews	P.M. Matthews
+P.J. Lawlor	+B.F. Robinson	B.F. Robinson	B.F. Robinson	B.F. Robinson 1T
W.D. McBride	+G.F. Hamilton	G.F. Hamilton	G.F. Hamilton	G.F. Hamilton
Lansdowne Road	Lansdowne Road	Cardiff Arms Park	Lansdowne Road	Murrayfield
won 20–18	lost 13-21	drawn 21-21	lost 7-16	lost 25-28
27 October 1990	2 February 1991	16 February 1991	2 March 1991	16 March 1991
[1]Rep. by V.J.G. Cunningham		[1]Rep. by K.J. Murphy		[1]Rep. by K.J. Murphy

1991	
v NAMIBIA	v NAMIBIA
J.E. Staples	J.E. Staples
S.P. Geoghegan[1]	D.J. Clarke
B.J. Mullin 1C	B.J. Mullin
D.M. Curtis	D.M. Curtis
D.J. Clarke	K.D. Crossan[1]
V.J.G. Cunningham	V.J.G. Cunningham
R. Saunders	*R. Saunders
N.J. Popplewell	N.J. Popplewell
S.J. Smith	S.J. Smith
D.C. Fitzgerald	D.C. Fitzgerald
B.J. Rigney[2]	D.G. Lenihan
N.P.J. Francis	N.P.J. Francis[2]
*P.M. Matthews	N.P. Mannion
B.F. Robinson	B.F. Robinson
P.T.J. O'Hara	G.F. Hamilton
Windhoek	Windhoek
lost 6-15 Penalty try	lost 15-26
20 July 1991	27 July 1991
[1]Rep. by +R.M. Wallace	[1]Rep. by +N.M.P. Barry
[2]Rep. by N.P. Mannion	[2]Rep. by M.J. Galwey

WORLD CUP 1991			
v ZIMBABWE	v JAPAN	v SCOTLAND	v AUSTRALIA
J.E. Staples	J.E. Staples 1T	J.E. Staples	J.E. Staples
S.P. Geoghegan 1T	D.J. Clarke	S.P. Geoghegan	S.P. Geoghegan
V.J.G. Cunningham	B.J. Mullin	D.M. Curtis	B.J. Mullin
D.M. Curtis 1T	D.M. Curtis	B.J. Mullin	D.M. Curtis
K.D. Crossan	K.D. Crossan[1]	K.D. Crossan	D.J. Clarke
R.P. Keyes 5PG, 4C	R.P. Keyes 4PG, 2C	R.P. Keyes 4PG, 1DG	R.P. Keyes 3PG, 1C, 1DG
R. Saunders	R. Saunders	R. Saunders	R. Saunders
N.J. Popplewell 2T	J.J. Fitzgerald	N.J. Popplewell	N.J. Popplewell
S.J. Smith	T.J. Kingston	S.J. Smith	S.J. Smith
D.C. Fitzgerald	G.F. Halpin	D.C. Fitzgerald	D.C. Fitzgerald
D.G. Lenihan	M.J. Galwey	D.G. Lenihan	D.G. Lenihan
N.P.J. Francis	N.P.J. Francis	N.P.J. Francis	N.P.J. Francis
*P.M. Matthews	P.T.J. O'Hara 1T	*P.M. Matthews	*P.M. Matthews
B.F. Robinson 4T	N.P. Mannion 2T	B.F. Robinson	B.F. Robinson
G.F. Hamilton	G.F. Hamilton	G.F. Hamilton	G.F. Hamilton 1T
Lansdowne Road	Lansdowne Road	Murrayfield	Lansdowne Road
won 55-11	won 32-16	lost 15-24	lost 18-19
6 October 1991	9 October 1991	12 October 1991	19 October 1991
	[1]Rep. by V.J.G. Cunningham		

1991–92

v ENGLAND	v SCOTLAND	v WALES	v FRANCE	v NZ	v NZ
J.E. Staples	K.J. Murphy	J.E. Staples	K.J. Murphy	J.E. Staples 1T	J.E. Staples[1]
R.M. Wallace	R.M. Wallace 1T	R.M. Wallace 1T	R.M. Wallace	+R. Carey	R. Carey
B.J. Mullin	B.J. Mullin	B.J. Mullin	D.M. Curtis	*P.P.A. Danaher[1]	M.C. McCall
D.M. Curtis	P.P.A. Danaher	D.M. Curtis	P.P.A. Danaher	V.J.G. Cunningham 2T	V.J.G. Cunningham
S.P. Geoghegan	S.P. Geoghegan[1]	K.D. Crossan	S.P. Geoghegan	+J.N. Furlong	J.N. Furlong 1T
R.P. Keyes 1T, 1PG, 1C	R.P. Keyes 2PG	R.P. Keyes 3PG, 1C	+D.R. McAleese 4PG	P. Russell 3C	P. Russell[2] 1C
L.F.P. Aherne	L.F.P. Aherne	R. Saunders	L.F.P. Aherne	M.T. Bradley	*M.T. Bradley
N.J. Popplewell	N.J. Popplewell	N.J. Popplewell	N.J. Popplewell	N.J. Popplewell	N.J. Popplewell
S.J. Smith	S.J. Smith	S.J. Smith	S.J. Smith	S.J. Smith	S.J. Smith
G.F. Halpin	G.F. Halpin[2]	D.C. Fitzgerald	G.F. Halpin	+P. McCarthy	P. McCarthy
M.J. Galwey	M.J. Galwey	D.G. Lenihan	B.J. Rigney	M.J. Galwey	B.J. Rigney
N.P.J. Francis	N.P.J. Francis	N.P.J. Francis	M.J. Galwey	P.S. Johns	P.S. Johns
*P.M. Matthews	*P.M. Matthews	*P.M. Matthews	+P. Hogan	M.J. Fitzgibbon	M.J. Galwey
B.F. Robinson	B.F. Robinson	B.F. Robinson	B.F. Robinson	B.F. Robinson	B.F. Robinson
M.J. Fitzgibbon	M.J. Fitzgibbon	+M.J. Fitzgibbon	M.J. Fitzgibbon	+K.T. Leahy[2]	M.J. Fitzgibbon[3]
Twickenham	Lansdowne Road	Lansdowne Road	Parc des Princes	Carisbrook, Dunedin	Athletic Park, Wellington
lost 38-9	lost 10-18	lost 15-16	lost 12-44	lost 21-24	lost 6-59
1 February 1992	15 February 1992	18 February 1992	21 March 1992	30 May 1992	6 June 1992
	[1]Rep. by D.M. Curtis [2]Rep. by D.C. Fitzgerald			[1]Rep. by +M.C. Call [2]Rep. by B.J. Rigney	[1]Rep. by K.J. Murphy [2]Rep. by D.J. Clarke [3]Rep. by +P. Kenny

1992–93

v AUSTRALIA	v SCOTLAND	v FRANCE	v WALES	v ENGLAND
J.E. Staples	+C.R. Wilkinson	+C.P. Clarke	C.P. Clarke 1DG	C.P. Clarke
S.P. Geoghegan	S.P. Geoghegan	S.P. Geoghegan	R.M. Wallace	R.M. Wallace
*P.P.A. Danaher	V.J.G. Cunningham	V.J.G. Cunningham	V.J.G. Cunningham	V.J.G. Cunningham
V.J.G. Cunningham	P.P.A. Danaher	P.P.A. Danaher[1]	P.P.A. Danaher	P.P.A. Danaher
R.M. Wallace 1T	R.M. Wallace	R.M. Wallace	S.P. Geoghegan	S.P. Geoghegan
P. Russell 4PG	+N.G. Malone 1PG	N.G. Malone 2PG	+E.P. Elwood 3PG, 1C	E. Elwood 2PG, 2DG
L.F.P. Aherne	*M.T. Bradley	*M.T. Bradley	*M.T. Bradley	*M.T. Bradley
N.J. Popplewell	N.J. Popplewell	N.J. Popplewell	N.J. Popplewell	N.J. Popplewell
+J.N. Murphy	S.J. Smith	T.J. Kingston	T.J. Kingston	T.J. Kingston
P.D. McCarthy	P.D. McCarthy	+P.M. Clohessy	P.M. Clohessy	P.M. Clohessy
M.J. Galwey	P.S. Johns	P.S. Johns	P.S. Johns	P.S. Johns
P.S. Johns	+R.A. Costello	N.P.J. Francis	M.J. Galwey	M.J. Galwey 1T
B.F. Robinson	P.J. Lawlor	P.T.J. O'Hara	P.T.J. O'Hara	P.T.J. O'Hara
P.J. Lawlor	N.P. Mannion	M.J. Galwey	B.F. Robinson 1T	B.F. Robinson
G.F. Hamilton	W.D. McBride	W.D. McBride	W.D. McBride	W.D. McBride
Lansdowne Road	Murrayfield	Lansdowne Road	Cardiff Arms Park	Lansdowne Road
lost 17-42	lost 3-15	lost 6–21	won 19-14	won 17-3
31 October 1992	16 January 1993	20 February 1993	6 March 1993	20 March 1993
		[1]Rep. by +B.T. Glennon		

1993–94

v ROMANIA	v FRANCE	v WALES	v ENGLAND	v SCOTLAND
+C.P. O'Shea	C.P. O'Shea	C.P. O'Shea	C.M.P. O'Shea	C.M.P. O'Shea
R.M. Wallace	R.M. Wallace	R.M. Wallace	R.M. Wallace	R.M. Wallace
V.J.G. Cunningham	V.J.G. Cunningham	M.C. McCall	+M.J. Field	M.J. Field
P.P.A. Danaher	P.P.A. Danaher	P.P.A. Danaher	P.P.A. Danaher	P.P.A. Danaher
S.P. Geoghegan 1T	S.P. Geoghegan	S.P. Geoghegan	S.P. Geoghegan 1T	S.P. Geoghegan
E.P. Elwood 6PG, 1C	E.P. Elwood 5PG	E.P. Elwood 5PG	E.P. Elwood 2PG, 1C	E.P. Elwood 2PG
*M.T. Bradley	*M.T. Bradley	*M.T. Bradley	*M.T. Bradley	*M.T. Bradley[1]
N.J. Popplewell[1]	N.J. Popplewell	N.J. Popplewell	N.J. Popplewell	N.J. Popplewell
T.J. Kingston	T.J. Kingston	T.J. Kingston	T.J. Kingston	T.J. Kingston
G.F. Halpin	P.M. Clohessy[1]	P.M. Clohessy	P.M. Clohessy	P.M. Clohessy
P.S. Johns	P.S. Johns	M.J. Galwey	M.J. Galwey	M.J. Galwey
N.P.J. Francis	N.P.J. Francis	N.P.J. Francis	N.P.J. Francis	N.P.J. Francis
M.J. Galwey	M.J. Galwey	B.F. Robinson	B.F. Robinson	B.F. Robinson
B.F. Robinson	B.F. Robinson	P.S. Johns	P.S. Johns[1]	P.S. Johns
W.D. McBride	+K.D. O'Connell	W.D. McBride	W.D. McBride	W.D. McBride
Lansdowne Road	Parc des Princes	Lansdowne Road	Twickenham	Lansdowne Road
won 25-3	lost 15-30	lost 15-17	won 13-12	drawn 6-6
13 November 1993	15 January 1994	5 February 1994	19 February 1994	5 March 1994
[1]Rep. by P.D. McCarthy	[1]Rep. by G.F. Halpin		[1]Rep. by K.D. O'Connell	[1]Rep. by R. Saunders

1994

v AUSTRALIA	v AUSTRALIA
C.M.P. O'Shea[1] 1PG	C.M.P. O'Shea 1PG, 1DG, 1C
S.P. Geoghegan	S.P. Geoghegan
+J.C. Bell	J.C. Bell
P.P.A. Danaher	P.P.A. Danaher
+N.K.P. Woods	N.K.P. Woods
E.P. Elwood 1PG, 1C	E.P. Elwood
*M.T. Bradley	*M.T. Bradley
J.J. Fitzgerald	J.J. Fitzgerald
+K.G.M. Wood	K.G.M. Wood
P.M. Clohessy	P.M. Clohessy 1T
M.J. Galwey[2]	+G.M. Fulcher
N.P.J. Francis	N.P.J. Francis 1T
B.F. Robinson	B.F. Robinson
P.S. Johns 1T	P.S. Johns
+D.S. Corkery	D.S. Corkery
Ballymore, Brisbane	Sydney Football Stadium
lost 13–33	lost 18-32
5 June 1994	11 June 1994
[1]Rep. by M.J. Field [2]Rep. by W.D. McBride	

1994–95

v USA	v ENGLAND	v SCOTLAND	v FRANCE	v WALES	v ITALY
C.M.P. O'Shea 1PG	C.M.P. O'Shea	C.M.P. O'Shea	J.E. Staples	J.E. Staples	J.E. Staples[1]
S.P. Geoghegan 1T B.J. Mullin[1] P.P.A. Danaher J.C. Bell	S.P. Geoghegan *B.J. Mullin P.P.A. Danaher J.C. Bell	S.P. Geoghegan B.J. Mullin 1T P.P.A. Danaher J.C. Bell 1T	S.P. Geoghegan 1T B.J. Mullin[1] P.P.A. Danaher N.K.P. Woods	R.M. Wallace B.J. Mullin 1T P.P.A. Danaher S.P. Geoghegan[2]	R.M. Wallace B.J. Mullin J.C. Bell +D.W. O'Mahony
+A.N. McGowan 3PG, 2C *M.T. Bradley[2] 1T	+P.A. Burke 1PG +N.A. Hogan	P.A. Burke 1PG *M.T. Bradley	E.P. Elwood 2C *M.T. Bradley	E.P. Elwood[1] N.A. Hogan	P.A. Burke 4PG +David O'Mahony[2]
N.J. Popplewell K.G.M. Wood P.M. Clohessy G.M. Fulcher N.P.J. Francis P.T.J. O'Hara P.S. Johns[3] D.S. Corkery	N.J. Popplewell K.G.M. Wood P.M. Clohessy M.J. Galwey N.P.J. Francis[1] +A.G. Foley 1T P.S. Johns D.S. Corkery	N.J. Popplewell K.G.M. Wood P.M. Clohessy P.S. Johns G.M. Fulcher A.G. Foley +B.M. Cronin W.D. McBride	N.J. Popplewell T.J. Kingston P.M. Clohessy +D.A. Tweed G.M. Fulcher +E.O. Halvey A.G. Foley W.D. McBride	N.J. Popplewell *T.J. Kingston P.M. Clohessy D.A. Tweed G.M. Fulcher A.G. Foley P.S. Johns E.O. Halvey	N.J. Popplewell *T.J. Kingston G.F. Halpin D.A. Tweed G.M. Fulcher A.G. Foley P.S. Johns E.O. Halvey
Lansdowne Road won 26-15	Lansdowne Road lost 8-20	Murrayfield lost 13-26	Lansdowne Road lost 7-25	Cardiff Arms Park won 16-12	Treviso lost 12-22
5 November 1994 [1]Rep. by N.G. Malone [2]Rep. by A.C. Rolland [3]Rep. by M.J. Galwey	2 January 1995 [1]Rep. by G.M. Fulcher	4 February 1995	4 March 1995 [1]Rep. by M.J. Field	18 March 1995 [1]Rep. by P.A. Burke 2PG, 1DG, 1C [2]Rep. by M.J. Field	6 March 1995 [1]Rep. by M.J. Field [2]Rep. by A.C. Rolland

1995 WORLD CUP

v NEW ZEALAND	v JAPAN	v WALES	v FRANCE
J.E. Staples[2]	C.M.P. O'Shea	C.P.M. O'Shea	C.M.P. O'Shea
R.M. Wallace B.J. Mullin J.C. Bell[1] S.P. Geoghegan	R.M. Wallace B.J. Mullin M.J. Field S.P. Geoghegan 1T	R.M. Wallace B.J. Mullin J.C. Bell S.P. Geoghegan	D.W. O'Mahony B.J. Mullin J.C. Bell S.P. Geoghegan
E.P. Elwood 2C M.T. Bradley	P.A. Burke 1PG, 6C N.A. Hogan 1T	E.P. Elwood 1PG, 2C N.A. Hogan	E.P. Elwood 4PG N.A. Hogan
N.J. Popplewell *T.J. Kingston G.F. Halpin 1T G.M. Fulcher N.P.J. Francis D.S. Corkery 1T P.S. Johns W.D. McBride 1T	*N.J. Popplewell K.G.M. Wood[1] +P.S. Wallace D.A. Tweed[3] N.P.J. Francis 1T D.S. Corkery 1T P.S. Johns E.O. Halvey[2] 1T	N.J. Popplewell 1T *T.J. Kingston G.F. Halpin G.M. Fulcher N.P.J. Francis D.S. Corkery P.S. Johns W.D. McBride[1] 1T	N.J. Popplewell *T.J. Kingston G.F. Halpin G.M. Fulcher[1] N.P.J. Francis D.S. Corkery P.S. Johns W.D. McBride
Ellis Park, Johannesburg lost 19-43	Bloemfontein won 50-28 2 penalty tries	Ellis Park, Johannesburg won 24-23	King's Park, Durban lost 12-36
27 May 1995 [1]Tem. rep. by M.J. Field [2]Rep. by M.J. Field	31 May 1995 [1]Rep. by T.J. Kingston [2]Temp. rep. by A.G. Foley twice [3]Rep. by A.G. Foley	4 June 1995 [1] Temp. rep. by E.O. Halvey 1T	10 June 1995 [1]Rep. by E.O. Halvey

1995–96

v FIJI	v USA	v SCOTLAND	v FRANCE	v WALES	v ENGLAND
*J.E. Staples 1T	*J.E. Staples	*J.E. Staples	*J.E. Staples[1]	+S.J.P. Mason 2PG, 2C	S.J.P. Mason 4PG
R.M. Wallace 1T	R.M. Wallace 1T	R.M. Wallace	R.M. Wallace		S.P. Geoghegan
M.J. Field[3]	J.C. Bell	J.C. Bell	J.C. Bell	S.P. Geoghegan 1T	J.C. Bell
J.C. Bell	+K.P. McQuilkin	K.P. McQuilkin	K.P. McQuilkin	J.C. Bell	M.J. Field[1]
S.P. Geoghegan 1T	S.P. Geoghegan	S.P. Geoghegan	N.K.P. Woods	M.J. Field	N.K.P. Woods
				N.K.P. Woods 1T	
P.A. Burke 2PG, 4C	E.P. Elwood[1] 3PG, 1C	E.P. Elwood 1PG, 1C	+D.G. Humphreys 1PG, 1C	D.G. Humphreys	D.G. Humphreys 1DG
+C. Saverimutto	C. Saverimutto	C. Saverimutto	N.A. Hogan	*N.A. Hogan	*N.A. Hogan
N.J. Popplewell[4]	N.J. Popplewell	N.J. Popplewell	N.J. Popplewell	N.J. Popplewell	N.J. Popplewell
T.J. Kingston[1]	T.J. Kingston	T.J. Kingston	T.J. Kingston	A.T.H. Clarke	A.T.H. Clarke
P.S. Wallace 1T	P.S. Wallace	P.M. Clohessy 1T	P.M. Clohessy	P.S. Wallace	P.S. Wallace
G.M. Fulcher	G.M. Fulcher	G.M. Fulcher	G.M. Fulcher	G.M. Fulcher 1T	G.M. Fulcher
N.P.J. Francis 1T	N.P.J. Francis	N.P.J. Francis	P.S. Johns	J.W. Davidson	J.W. Davidson
+J.W. Davidson[2]	+V.C.P. Costello	J.W. Davidson	J.W. Davidson	D.S. Corkery 1T	D.S. Corkery
P.S. Johns 1T	P.S. Johns	P.S. Johns	V.C.P. Costello	V.C.P. Costello	V.C.P. Costello
D.S. Corkery	D.S. Corkery	D.S. Corkery	D.S. Corkery	W.D. McBride	W.D. McBride
Lansdowne Road won 44-8	Life College, Atlanta won 25-18	Lansdowne Road lost 10-16 (Penalty try)	Parc des Princes lost 10-45 (Penalty try)	Lansdowne Road won 30-17	Twickenham lost 15–28
18 November 1995	6 January 1996	20 January 1996	17 February 1996	2 March 1996	16 March 1996
[1]Rep. by +A.T.A. Clarke [2]Rep. by W.D. McBride [3]Temp. rep. by +S. McCahill [4] Temp. rep. by +H.D. Hurley	[1]Rep. by P.A. Burke 3PG		[1]Rep. by M.J. Field		Rep. by C.M. McCall

1996–97

v WESTERN SAMOA	v AUSTRALIA	v ITALY	v FRANCE
S.J.P. Mason 6PG, 1C	J.E. Staples[1]	C.M.P. O'Shea	C.M.P. O'Shea
R.M. Wallace 1T	J.A. Topping	J.A. Topping	J.A. Topping
+R.A.J. Henderson	J.C. Bell	J.C. Bell 1T	J.C. Bell
J.C. Bell	M.C. McCall	M.C. McCall	M.J. Field[2]
+J.A. Topping	+D.J. Crotty	D.J. Crotty	D.J. Crotty
D.G. Humphreys	P.A. Burke 4PG	P.A. Burke 8PG	E.P. Elwood 5PG
*N.A. Hogan	+S.C. McIvor	S.C. McIvor	N.A. Hogan
H.D. Hurley	N.J. Popplewell	N.J. Popplewell	N.J. Popplewell
A.T.A. Clarke	*K.G.M. Wood	*K.G.M. Wood	*K.G.M. Wood[1]
P.S. Wallace	P.S. Wallace	P.S. Wallace	P.S. Wallace
M. Galwey	G.M. Fulcher	G.M. Fulcher[2]	P.S. Johns
J.W. Davidson	J.W. Davidson	J.W. Davidson	J.W. Davidson
D.S. Corkery	D.S. Corkery	D.S. Corkery	D.S. Corkery
P.S. Johns	A.G. Foley	A.G. Foley	E.R.P. Miller
W.D. McBride[1]	W.D. McBride	+E.R.P. Miller[1]	W.D. McBride
Lansdowne Road lost 25-40	Lansdowne Road lost 12-22	Lansdowne Road lost 29-37	Lansdowne Road lost 15-32
12 November 1996	23 November 1996	4 January 1997	18 January 1997
[1]Rep. by V.C.P. Costello	[1]Rep. by M.J. Field	[1]Rep. by W.D. McBride [2]Rep. by P.S. Johns	[1]Rep. by A.T.H. Clarke [2]Temp. rep. and then rep. by K.P. McQuilkin

v WALES	v ENGLAND	v SCOTLAND
*J.E. Staples	*J.E. Staples	*J.E. Staples[1]
+D.A. Hickie 1T	D.A. Hickie	D.A. Hickie 1T
J.C. Bell 1T	J.C. Bell	M.J. Field
M.J. Field	M.J. Field	K.P. McQuilkin[2]
J.A. Topping	J.A. Topping	J.C. Bell
E.P. Elwood 3PG, 1C	E.P. Elwood[2] 2PG	D.G. Humphreys 1PG, 1C
N.A. Hogan	N.A. Hogan[3]	B.T. O'Meara[3]
N.J. Popplewell	N.J. Popplewell	+P. Flavin
+R.P. Nesdale	R.P. Nesdale	R.P. Nesdale
P.S. Wallace	P.S. Wallace	P.S. Wallace
P.S. Johns[1]	P.S. Johns	P.S. Johns
J.W. Davidson	J.W. Davidson	J.W. Davidson
D.S. Corkery	D.S. Corkery	D.S. Corkery
E.R.P. Miller 1T	E.R.P. Miller[1]	B.M. Cronin
W.D. McBride	W.D. McBride	W.D. McBride
Cardiff Arms Park won 26-25	Lansdowne Road lost 6-46	Murrayfield lost 10-38
1 February 1997	15 February 1997	1 March 1997
[1]Rep. by G.M. Fulcher	[1]Rep. by A.G. Foley [2]Rep. by D.G. Humphreys [3]Rep. by +B.T. O'Meara	[1]Rep. by C.M.P. O'Shea [2]Rep. by P.A. Burke [3]Rep. by S.C. McIvor

1997–98

v NEW ZEALAND	v CANADA	v ITALY	v SCOTLAND	v FRANCE
+K.W. Nowlan	K.W. Nowlan 2T	K.W. Nowlan	C.M.P. O'Shea	C.M.P. O'Shea
D.A. Hickie	D.A. Hickie	D.A. Hickie	R.M. Wallace	R.M. Wallace
R.A.J. Henderson	R.A.J. Henderson	K.M. Maggs	K.M. Maggs	R.A.J. Henderson
M.C. McCall	M.C. McCall	M.C. McCall	M.C. McCall	K.M. Maggs
+J.P.J. McWeeney[3]	K.M. Maggs 1T	D.W. O'Mahony 1T	D.A. Hickie	D.A. Hickie 1T
E.P. Elwood 1PG, 1C	E.P. Elwood 2PG, 1C	D.G. Humphreys[1] 4PG	D.G. Humphreys 2PG, 1C, 1DG	E.P. Elwood 3PG, 1C
+C.D. McGuinness[4]	C.D. McGuinness 1T	N.A. Hogan	B.T. O'Meara	C.D. McGuinness
N.J. Popplewell	*N.J. Popplewell[1]	R. Corrigan	R. Corrigan	R. Corrigan[1]
*K.G.M. Wood[1] 2T	R.P. Nesdale	*K.G.M. Wood[2]	*K.G.M. Wood	*K.G.M. Wood[2]
P.S. Wallace	P.S. Wallace	P.M. Clohessy	P.S. Wallace[2]	P.S. Wallace[4]
P.S. Johns	P.S. Johns	P.S. Johns	P.S. Johns	P.S. Johns[3]
+M.E. O'Kelly	M.E. O'Kelly	M.E. O'Kelly	M.E. O'Kelly	M.E. O'Kelly
E.O. Halvey[2]	D.J. Erskine	D.J. Erskine[3]	D.S. Corkery	D.S. Corkery
E.R.P. Miller	V.C.P. Costello 1T	E.R.P. Miller	E.R.P. Miller	V.C.P. Costello
+K. Dawson	K. Dawson[2]	+D. O'Grady	K. Dawson[1]	+A.J. Ward
Lansdowne Road lost 15-63	Lansdowne Road won 33-11	Bologna lost 22-37	Lansdowne Road lost 16–17 Penalty try	Stade de France, Paris lost 16-18
15 November 1997	30 November 1997	20 December 1997	7 February 1998	7 March 1998
[1]Rep. by R.P. Nesdale [2]Rep. by +D.J. Erskine [3]Rep. by +K.M. Maggs [4]Rep. by B.T. O'Meara	[1]Rep. by +R. Corrigan [2]Rep. by E.O. Halvey	[1]Rep. by E.P. Elwood 1PG, 1C [2]Rep. by A.T.H. Clarke [3]Rep. by V.C.P. Costello	[1]Rep. by V.C.P. Costello [2] Temp. rep. by N.J. Popplewell	[1]Rep. by N.J. Popplewell [2]Rep. by R.P. Nesdale [3]Rep. by M. Galwey [4]Rep. by P.M. Clohessy

v WALES	v ENGLAND	v SOUTH AFRICA	v SOUTH AFRICA
C.P. Clarke	C.P. Clarke[2]	C.M.P. O'Shea	C.M.P. O'Shea
R.M. Wallace	R.M. Wallace	+J.P. Bishop 1T	J.P. Bishop
K.M. Maggs	K.M. Maggs	K.M. Maggs	K.M. Maggs
R.A.J. Henderson	M.C. McCall[1]	M.C. McCall	M.C. McCall
D.A. Hickie	D.A. Hickie 2T	D.A. Hickie[1]	D.A. Hickie[1]
E.P. Elwood 3PG, 1C	E.P. Elwood 1PG, 2C	E.P. Elwood 2PG, 1C	E.P. Elwood[2]
C.D. McGuinness	C.D. McGuinness	C. McGuinness	C. McGuinness
R. Corrigan	R. Corrigan	+J.M. Fitzpatrick	J.M. Fitzpatrick[3]
*K.G.M. Wood[1]	*K.G.M. Wood	K.G.M. Wood	K.G.M. Wood
P.S. Wallace[2]	P.S. Wallace	P.S. Wallace	P.S. Wallace
P.S. Johns	P.S. Johns	*P.S. Johns[2]	*P.S. Johns
M.E. O'Kelly	M.E. O'Kelly	M.E. O'Kelly	M.E. Kelly
D.S. Corkery	D.S. Corkery	+D. O'Cuinneagain	D. O'Cuinneagain
V.C.P. Costello 1T	V.C.P. Costello	V.C.P. Costello[3]	V.C.P. Costello[3]
A.J. Ward[3] 1T	A.J. Ward	A.J. Ward	A.J. Ward
Lansdowne Road	Twickenham	Bloemfontein	Loftus Versfeld, Pretoria
lost 21-30	lost 17-35	lost 13-37	lost 0-33
21 March 1998	4 April 1998	13 June 1998	20 June 1998
[1]Rep. by R.P. Nesdale	[1]Rep. by +K.P. Keane	[1]Rep. by R.A.J. Henderson	[1]Rep. by R.A.J. Henderson
[2]Rep. by P.M. Clohessy	[2]Rep. by D.G. Humphreys	[2]Rep. by G.M. Fulcher	[2]Rep. by D.G. Humphreys
[3]Rep. by E.R.P. Miller		[3]Rep. by +T. Brennan	[3]Rep. by T. Brennan

1998		
v GEORGIA (WORLD CUP QUALIFYING RD)	v ROMANIA (WORLD CUP QUALIFYING RD)	v SOUTH AFRICA
C.M.P. O'Shea[1] 1T	C.M.P. O'Shea 1T	C.M.P. O'Shea
J.P. Bishop	J.P. Bishop	J.P. Bishop
+P. Duignan 1T	P. Duignan[1]	J.C. Bell
J.C. Bell 1T	J.C. Bell 2T	K.M. Maggs
K.M. Maggs 1T	D.W. O'Mahony	G. Dempsey
E.P. Elwood 10C	E.P. Elwood[2] 2PG, 3C	E.P. Elwood 2PG, 1C
C.D. McGuinness[2]	C.J. Scally[3] 1T	C.D. McGuinness
P.M. Clohessy[3]	P.M. Clohessy	J.M. Fitzpatrick[1]
R.P. Nesdale[4]	A.T.H. Clarke[4]	K.G.M. Wood[2] 1T
P.S. Wallace 1T	P.S. Wallace[5]	P.M. Clohessy
*P.S. Johns 1T	*P.S. Johns	*P.S. Johns
M.E. O'Kelly[5]	M.E. O'Kelly[6]	M.E. O'Kelly[3]
E.R.P. Miller	E.R.P. Miller[7]	D. O'Cuinneagain
V.C.P. Costello[6] 1T	V.C.P. Costello	V.C.P. Costello
A.J. Ward	A.J. Ward 1T	A.J. Ward
Lansdowne Road won 70-0	Lansdowne Road won 53-35	Lansdowne Road lost 13-27
	2 penalty tries	
14 November 1998	21 November 1998	28 November 1998
[1]Rep. by +G. Dempsey 2T	[1]Rep. by K.M. Maggs	[1]Rep. by R. Corrigan
[2]Rep. by +C.J. Scally 1T	[2]Rep. by D.G. Humphreys 3C	[2]Rep. by R.P. Nesdale
[3]Rep. by J.M. Fitzpatrick	[3]Rep. by C.D. McGuinness	[3]Rep. by J.W. Davidson
[4]Rep. by A.T.H. Clarke	[4]Rep. by K.G.M. Wood	
[5]Rep. by J.W. Davidson	[5]Rep. by J.M. Fitzpatrick	
[6]Rep. by D.O'Cuinneagain	[6]Rep. by J.W. Davidson	
	[7]Rep. by D. O'Cuinneagain	

1999

v FRANCE	v WALES	v ENGLAND	v SCOTLAND	v ITALY
C.M.P. O'Shea	C.M.P. O'Shea	C.M.P. O'Shea	C.M.P. O'Shea	C.M.P. O'Shea 2T
J.P. Bishop	J.P. Bishop	J.P. Bishop	J.P. Bishop	J.P. Bishop 1T
K.M. Maggs	K.M. Maggs 1T	K.M. Maggs	K.M. Maggs	K.M. Maggs
J.C. Bell[2]	J.C. Bell	R.A.J. Henderson	J.C. Bell[1]	R.A.J. Henderson[1]
G. Dempsey	N.K. Woods	G. Dempsey	G. Dempsey	G. Dempsey 1T
D.G. Humphreys 3PG	D.G. Humphreys 3PG, 2DG, 2C	D.H. Humphreys 5PG	D.H. Humphreys 2 PG, 1C	E.P. Elwood 4PG, 1C
C.D. McGuinness	C.D. McGuinness	C.D. McGuinness	C.D. McGuinness[2]	C.J. Scally
P.M. Clohessy[3]	P.M. Clohessy[2]	P.M. Clohessy[1]	P.M. Clohessy	J.M. Fitzpatrick[3]
K.G.M. Wood	K.G.M. Wood 1T	K.G.M. Wood	K.G.M. Wood	R.P. Nesdale[4]
P.S. Wallace[1]	P.W. Wallace	P.S. Wallace	P.S. Wallace	P.M. Clohessy
*P.S. Johns	*P.S. Johns[3]	*P.S. Johns	*P.S. Johns	*P.S. Johns 1T
J.W. Davidson	J.W. Davidson	J.W. Davidson	J.W. Davison	J.W. Davidson
E.R.P. Miller	D. O'Cuinneagain	D. O'Cuinneagain	D. O'Cuinneagain	T. Brennan
V.C.P. Costello[4]	E.R.P. Miller[1]	V.C.P. Costello[2]	E.R.P. Miller[3]	D. O'Cuinneagain
D. O'Cuinneagain	A.J. Ward	A.J. Ward	A.J. Ward[4]	V.C.P. Costello[2]
Lansdowne Road	Wembley Stadium	Lansdowne Road	Murrayfield	Lansdowne Road
lost 9-10	won 29-23	lost 15-27	lost 30-13	won 39-30
6 February 1999	20 February 1999	6 March 1999	20 March 1999	10 April 1999
[1]Temp. rep. by J.M. Fitzpatrick	[1]Rep. by V.C.P. Costello	[1]Rep. by J.M. Fitzpatrick	[1]Rep. by R.A.J. Henderson	[1]Rep. by J.C. Bell
[2]Rep. by R.A.J. Henderson	[2]Rep. by J.M. Fitzpatrick	[2]Rep. by E.R.P. Miller	[2]Rep. by C.J. Scally	[2]Rep. by A.J. Ward
[3]Rep. by J.M. Fitzpatrick	[3]Rep. by M.J. Galwey		[3]Rep. by V.C.P. Costello	[3]Rep. by P.S. Wallace
[4]Rep. by T. Brennan			[4]Rep. by T. Brennan	[4]Rep. by K.G.M. Wood

1999

v AUSTRALIA	v AUSTRALIA
C.M.P. O'Shea	G. Dempsey
J.P. Bishop	J.P. Bishop 1T
+B. O'Driscoll	B. O'Driscoll
K.M. Maggs 1T	K.M. Maggs 1T
+M. Mostyn	J.C. Bell
D.H. Humphreys 1GG 1C	D.H. Humphreys 3PG 1C
+T. Tierney	T. Tierney
P.M. Clohessy[2]	P.M. Clohessy[3] 1T
K.G.M. Wood	K.G.M. Wood[1]
P.S. Wallace	P.S. Wallace
P.S. Johns[1]	P.S. Johns[2]
J.W. Davidson	M.E. O'Kelly
*D. O'Cuinneagain	T. Brennan[4]
V.C.P. Costello[3]	D. O'Cuinneagain
A.J. Ward	A.J. Ward
Ballymore, Brisbane	Subiaco, Perth
Lost 10-46	Lost 26-32
10 June 1999	19 June 1999
[1]Rep. by M.E. O'Kelly	[1]Rep. by R.P. Nesdale
[2]Rep. by R. Corrigan	[2]Rep. by J.W. Davidson
[3]Rep. by D.S. Corkery	[3]Rep. by R. Corrigan
	[4]Rep. by D.S. Corkery

PRESIDENTS OF THE IRFU 1923–49

H. Thrift
1923–24

J.J. Coffey
1924–25

F.J. Strain
1925–26

G.T. Hamlet
1926–27

Judge Sealy
1927–28

H.J. Millar
1928–29

T.J. Greeves
1929–30

J.G. Musgrave
1930–31

W.A. Clarke
1931–32

C.S. Neill
1932–33

S.E. Polden
1933–34

J. Wallace
1934–35

Sir S.T. Irwin
1935–36

The Hon. Mr. Justice C. Davitt
1936–37

H.E. Emerson
1937–38

J.J. Warren
1938–45

H.J. Anderson
1945–46

W.A.B. Douglas
1946–47

T.M. McGrath
1947–48

G.P.S. Hogan
1948–49

CAPTAINS OF IRELAND TEAMS 1920–56

W.D. Doherty
1920–21

W.P. Collopy
1921–22

J.K.S. Thompson
1922–23

W.E. Crawford
1923–24

G.V. Stephenson
1924–25

E.O'D. Davy
1928–29

M. Sugden
1930–31

G.R. Beamish
1931–32

J.A. Siggins
1933–34

G.J. Morgan
1936–37

S. Walker
1937–38

C.J. Murphy
1946–47

J.D. Monteith
1946–47

E. Strathdee
1947–48

K.D. Mullen
1948–49

D. O'Brien
1951–52

J.W. Kyle
1952–53

J.S. McCarthy
1953–54

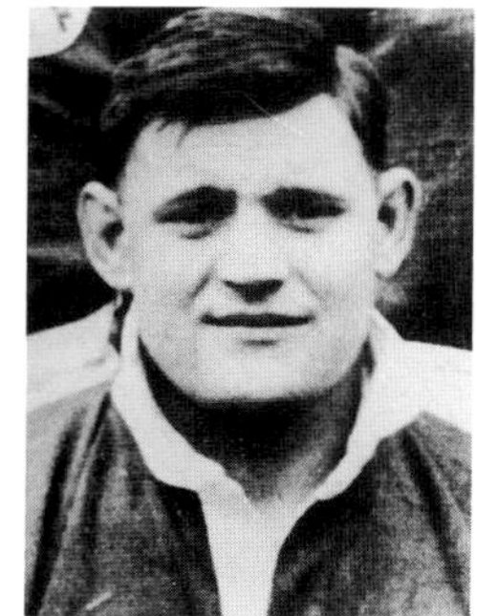
R.H. Thompson
1954–55

J.S. Richie
1955–56

APPENDIX 16

RESULTS

Results of **Ireland**'s International Matches (for which caps were awarded)
Matches against **England**, **Scotland**, **Wales** and **France** are all in the International Championship except where denoted. (X) denotes a non-championship match. (WCM) denotes a World Cup match.

Uniform scoring values of the try, penalty goal and dropped goal have varied as indicated below. A goal from a mark no longer applied when the free kick was introduced.

The scoring values that applied were:

	Try	*Conversion*	*Penalty goal*	*Dropped goal*	*Goal from mark*
1890–91	1	2	2	3	3
1891–92 to 1892–93	2	3	3	4	4
1893–94 to 1904–05	3	2	3	4	4
1905–06 to 1947–48	3	2	3	4	3
1948–49 to 1970–71	3	2	3	3	3
1971–72 to 1991–92	4	2	3	3	3
1992–93	5	2	3	3	–

Ireland v England

1875 The Oval (London) **England** 1G 1DG 1T to 0
1876 Dublin **England** 1G 1T to 0
1877 The Oval **England** 2G 2T to 0
1878 Dublin **England** 2G 1T to 0
1879 The Oval **England** 2G 1DG 2T to 0
1880 Dublin **England** 1G 1T to 1T
1881 Manchester **England** 2G 2T to 0
1882 Dublin **Drawn** 2T each
1883 Manchester **England** 1G 3T to 1T
1884 Dublin **England** 1G to 0
1885 Manchester **England** 2T to 1T
1886 Dublin **England** 1T to 0
1887 Dublin **Ireland** 2G to 0
1888 No match
1889 No match
1890 Blackheath (London) **England** 3T to 0
1891 Dublin **England** 9-0
1892 Manchester **England** 7-0
1893 Dublin **England** 4-0
1894 Blackheath **Ireland** 7-5
1895 Dublin **England** 6-3
1896 Leeds **Ireland** 10-4
1897 Dublin **Ireland** 13-9
1898 Richmond (London) **Ireland** 9-6
1899 Dublin **Ireland** 6-0
1900 Richmond **England** 15-4
1901 Dublin **Ireland** 10-6
1902 Leicester **England** 6-3
1903 Dublin **Ireland** 6-0
1904 Blackheath **England** 19-0
1905 Cork **Ireland** 17-3
1906 Leicester **Ireland** 16-6
1907 Dublin **Ireland** 17-9
1908 Richmond **England** 13-3
1909 Dublin **England** 11-5
1910 Twickenham **Drawn** 0-0
1911 Dublin **Ireland** 3-0
1912 Twickenham **England** 15-0
1913 Dublin **England** 15-4
1914 Twickenham **England** 17-12
1920 Dublin **England** 14-11
1921 Twickenham **England** 15-0
1922 Dublin **England** 12-3
1923 Leicester **England** 23-5
1924 Belfast **England** 14-3
1925 Twickenham **Drawn** 6-6
1926 Dublin **Ireland** 19-15
1927 Twickenham **England** 8-6
1928 Dublin **England** 7-6
1929 Twickenham **Ireland** 6-5
1930 Dublin **Ireland** 4-3
1931 Twickenham **Ireland** 6-5
1932 Dublin **England** 11-8
1933 Twickenham **England** 17-6
1934 Dublin **England** 13-3
1935 Twickenham **England** 14-3
1936 Dublin **Ireland** 6-3
1937 Twickenham **England** 9-8
1938 Dublin **England** 36-14
1939 Twickenham **Ireland** 5-0
1947 Dublin **Ireland** 22-0
1948 Twickenham **Ireland** 11-10
1949 Dublin **Ireland** 14-5
1950 Twickenham **England** 3-0
1951 Dublin **Ireland** 3-0
1952 Twickenham **England** 3-0
1953 Dublin **Drawn** 9-9
1954 Twickenham **England** 14-3
1955 Dublin **Drawn** 6-6
1956 Twickenham **England** 20-0
1957 Dublin **England** 6-0
1958 Twickenham **England** 6-0
1959 Dublin **England** 3-0
1960 Twickenham **England** 8-5
1961 Dublin **Ireland** 11-8
1962 Twickenham **England** 16-0
1963 Dublin **Drawn** 0-0
1964 Twickenham **Ireland** 18-5
1965 Dublin **Ireland** 5-0

1966 Twickenham **Drawn** 6-6
1967 Dublin **England** 8-3
1968 Twickenham **Drawn** 9-9
1969 Dublin **Ireland** 17-15
1970 Twickenham **England** 9-3
1971 Dublin **England** 9-6
1972 Twickenham **Ireland** 16-12
1973 Dublin **Ireland** 18-9
1974 Twickenham **Ireland** 26-21
1975 Dublin **Ireland** 12-9
1976 Twickenham **Ireland** 13-12
1977 Dublin **England** 4-0
1978 Twickenham **England** 15-9
1979 Dublin **Ireland** 12-7
1980 Twickenham **England** 24-9
1981 Dublin **England** 10-6
1982 Twickenham **Ireland** 16-15
1983 Dublin **Ireland** 25-15
1984 Twickenham **England** 12-9
1985 Dublin **Ireland** 13-10
1986 Twickenham **England** 25-20
1987 Dublin **Ireland** 17-0
1988 Twickenham **England** 35-3 (X)
1988 Dublin **England** 21-10
1989 Dublin **England** 16-3
1990 Twickenham **England** 23-0
1991 Dublin **England** 16-7
1992 Twickenham **England** 38-9
1993 Dublin **Ireland** 17-3
1994 Twickenham **Ireland** 13-12
1995 Dublin **England** 20-8
1996 Twickenham **England** 28-15
1997 Dublin **England** 46-6
1998 Twickenham **England** 35-17
1999 Dublin **England** 27-15

Ireland v Scotland

1877 Belfast **Scotland** 4G 2DG 2T to 0
1878 No match
1879 Belfast **Scotland** 1G 1DG 1T to 0
1880 Glasgow **Scotland** 1G 2DG 2T to 0
1881 Belfast **Ireland** 1DG to 1T
1882 Glasgow **Scotland** 2T to 0
1883 Belfast **Scotland** 1G 1T to 0
1884 Raeburn Place (Edinburgh) **Scotland** 2G 2T to 1T
1885 Belfast **Abandoned** Ireland 0 Scotland 1T
1885 Raeburn Place **Scotland** 1G 2T to 0
1886 Raeburn Place **Scotland** 3G 1DG 2T to 0
1887 Belfast **Scotland** 1G 1GM 2T to 0
1888 Raeburn Place **Scotland** 1G to 0
1889 Belfast **Scotland** 1DG to 0
1890 Raeburn Place **Scotland** 1DG 1T to 0
1891 Belfast **Scotland** 14-0
1892 Raeburn Place **Scotland** 2-0
1893 Belfast **Drawn** 0-0
1894 Dublin **Ireland** 5-0
1895 Raeburn Place **Scotland** 6-0
1896 Dublin **Drawn** 0-0
1897 Powderhall (Edinburgh) **Scotland** 8-3
1898 Belfast **Scotland** 8-0
1899 Inverleith (Edinburgh) **Ireland** 9-3
1900 Dublin **Drawn** 0-0
1901 Inverleith **Scotland** 9-5
1902 Belfast **Ireland** 5-0
1903 Inverleith **Scotland** 3-0
1904 Dublin **Scotland** 19-3
1905 Inverleith **Ireland** 11-5
1906 Dublin **Scotland** 13-6
1907 Inverleith **Scotland** 15-3
1908 Dublin **Ireland** 16-11
1909 Inverleith **Scotland** 9-3
1910 Belfast **Scotland** 14-0
1911 Inverleith **Ireland** 16-10
1912 Dublin **Ireland** 10-8
1913 Inverleith **Scotland** 29-14
1914 Dublin **Ireland** 6-0
1920 Inverleith **Scotland** 19-0
1921 Dublin **Ireland** 9-8
1922 Inverleith **Scotland** 6-3
1923 Dublin **Scotland** 13-3
1924 Inverleith **Scotland** 13-8
1925 Dublin **Scotland** 14-8
1926 Murrayfield **Ireland** 3-0
1927 Dublin **Ireland** 6-0
1928 Murrayfield **Ireland** 13-5
1929 Dublin **Scotland** 16-7
1930 Murrayfield **Ireland** 14-11
1931 Dublin **Ireland** 8-5
1932 Murrayfield **Ireland** 20-8
1933 Dublin **Scotland** 8-6
1934 Murrayfield **Scotland** 16-9
1935 Dublin **Ireland** 12-5
1936 Murrayfield **Ireland** 10-4
1937 Dublin **Ireland** 11-4
1938 Murrayfield **Scotland** 23-14
1939 Dublin **Ireland** 12-3
1947 Murrayfield **Ireland** 3-0
1948 Dublin **Ireland** 6-0
1949 Murrayfield **Ireland** 13-3
1950 Dublin **Ireland** 21-0
1951 Murrayfield **Ireland** 6-5
1952 Dublin **Ireland** 12-8
1953 Murrayfield **Ireland** 26-8
1954 Belfast **Ireland** 6-0
1955 Murrayfield **Scotland** 12-3
1956 Dublin **Ireland** 14-10
1957 Murrayfield **Ireland** 5-3
1958 Dublin **Ireland** 12-6
1959 Murrayfield **Ireland** 8-3
1960 Dublin **Scotland** 6-5
1961 Murrayfield **Scotland** 16-8
1962 Dublin **Scotland** 20-6
1963 Murrayfield **Scotland** 3-0
1964 Dublin **Scotland** 6-3
1965 Murrayfield **Ireland** 16-6
1966 Dublin **Scotland** 11-3
1967 Murrayfield **Ireland** 5-3
1968 Dublin **Ireland** 14-6
1969 Murrayfield **Ireland** 16-0
1970 Dublin **Ireland** 16-11
1971 Murrayfield **Ireland** 17-5
1972 No match
1973 Murrayfield **Scotland** 19-14
1974 Dublin **Ireland** 9-6
1975 Murrayfield **Scotland** 20-13
1976 Dublin **Scotland** 15-6
1977 Murrayfield **Scotland** 21-18
1978 Dublin **Ireland** 12-9
1979 Murrayfield **Drawn** 11-11
1980 Dublin **Ireland** 22-15
1981 Murrayfield **Scotland** 10-9
1982 Dublin **Ireland** 21-12
1983 Murrayfield **Ireland** 15-13
1984 Dublin **Scotland** 32-9
1985 Murrayfield **Ireland** 18-15
1986 Dublin **Scotland** 10-9
1987 Murrayfield **Scotland** 16-12
1988 Dublin **Ireland** 22-18
1989 Murrayfield **Scotland** 37-21
1990 Dublin **Scotland** 13-10
1991 Murrayfield **Scotland** 28-25
1991 Murrayfield **Scotland** 24-15 (WCM)
1992 Dublin **Scotland** 18-10
1993 Murrayfield **Scotland** 15-3
1994 Dublin **Drawn** 6-6
1995 Murrayfield **Scotland** 26-13
1996 Dublin **Scotland** 16-10
1997 Murrayfield **Scotland** 38-10
1998 Dublin **Scotland** 17-16

Ireland v Wales

1882 Dublin **Wales** 2G 2T to 0
1883 No match
1884 Cardiff **Wales** 1DG 2T to 0
1885 No match
1886 No match
1887 Birkenhead **Wales** 1DG 1T to 3T
1888 Dublin **Ireland** 1G 1DG 1T to 0
1889 Swansea **Ireland** 2T to 0
1890 Dublin **Drawn** 1G each
1891 Llanelli **Wales** 6-4
1892 Dublin **Ireland** 9-0
1893 Llanelli **Wales** 2-0
1894 Belfast **Ireland** 3-0
1895 Cardiff **Wales** 5-3
1896 Dublin **Ireland** 8-4
1897 No match
1898 Limerick **Wales** 11-3
1899 Cardiff **Ireland** 3-0
1900 Belfast **Wales** 3-0
1901 Swansea **Wales** 10-9
1902 Dublin **Wales** 15-0
1903 Cardiff **Wales** 18-0
1904 Belfast **Ireland** 14-12
1905 Swansea **Wales** 10-3
1906 Belfast **Ireland** 11-6
1907 Cardiff **Wales** 29-0
1908 Belfast **Wales** 11-5
1909 Swansea **Wales** 18-5
1910 Dublin **Wales** 19-3
1911 Cardiff **Wales** 16-0
1912 Belfast **Ireland** 12-5
1913 Swansea **Wales** 16-13
1914 Belfast **Wales** 11-3
1920 Cardiff **Wales** 28-4
1921 Belfast **Wales** 6-0
1922 Swansea **Wales** 11-5
1923 Dublin **Ireland** 5-4
1924 Cardiff **Ireland** 13-10
1925 Belfast **Ireland** 19-3
1926 Swansea **Wales** 11-8
1927 Dublin **Ireland** 19-9
1928 Cardiff **Ireland** 13-10
1929 Belfast **Drawn** 5-5
1930 Swansea **Wales** 12-7
1931 Belfast **Wales** 15-3
1932 Cardiff **Ireland** 12-10
1933 Belfast **Ireland** 10-5
1934 Swansea **Wales** 13-0
1935 Belfast **Ireland** 9-3
1936 Cardiff **Wales** 3-0
1937 Belfast **Ireland** 5-3
1938 Swansea **Wales** 11-5
1939 Belfast **Wales** 7-0
1947 Swansea **Wales** 6-0
1948 Belfast **Ireland** 6-3
1949 Swansea **Ireland** 5-0
1950 Belfast **Wales** 6-3
1951 Cardiff **Drawn** 3-3
1952 Dublin **Wales** 14-3
1953 Swansea **Wales** 5-3
1954 Dublin **Wales** 12-9
1955 Cardiff **Wales** 21-3
1956 Dublin **Ireland** 11-3
1957 Cardiff **Wales** 6-5
1958 Dublin **Wales** 9-6
1959 Cardiff **Wales** 8-6
1960 Dublin **Wales** 10-9
1961 Cardiff **Wales** 9-0
1962 Dublin **Drawn** 3-3
1963 Cardiff **Ireland** 14-6
1964 Dublin **Wales** 15-6
1965 Cardiff **Wales** 14-8
1966 Dublin **Ireland** 9-6
1967 Cardiff **Ireland** 3-0
1968 Dublin **Ireland** 9-6
1969 Cardiff **Wales** 24-11
1970 Dublin **Ireland** 14-0
1971 Cardiff **Wales** 23-9
1972 No match
1973 Cardiff **Wales** 16-12
1974 Dublin **Drawn** 9-9
1975 Cardiff **Wales** 32-4
1976 Dublin **Wales** 34-9
1977 Cardiff **Wales** 25-9
1978 Dublin **Wales** 20-16
1979 Cardiff **Wales** 24-21
1980 Dublin **Ireland** 21-7
1981 Cardiff **Wales** 9-8
1982 Dublin **Ireland** 20-12
1983 Cardiff **Wales** 23-9
1984 Dublin **Wales** 18-9
1985 Cardiff **Ireland** 21-9
1986 Dublin **Wales** 19-12
1987 Cardiff **Ireland** 15-11
1987 Wellington **Wales** 13-6 (WCM)
1988 Dublin **Wales** 12-9
1989 Cardiff **Ireland** 19-13
1990 Dublin **Ireland** 14-8
1991 Cardiff **Drawn** 21-21
1992 Dublin **Wales** 16-15
1993 Cardiff **Ireland** 19-14
1994 Dublin **Wales** 17-15
1995 Cardiff **Ireland** 16-12
1995 Johannesburg **Ireland** 24-23 (WCM)
1996 Dublin **Ireland** 30-17
1997 Cardiff **Ireland** 26-25
1998 Dublin **Wales** 30-21
1999 Wembley **Ireland** 29-23

Ireland v France

1909 Dublin **Ireland** 19-8
1910 Paris **Ireland** 8-3
1911 Cork **Ireland** 25-5
1912 Paris **Ireland** 11-6
1913 Cork **Ireland** 24-0
1914 Paris **Ireland** 8-6
1920 Dublin **France** 15-7
1921 Paris **France** 20-10
1922 Dublin **Ireland** 8-3
1923 Paris **France** 14-8
1924 Dublin **Ireland** 6-0
1925 Paris **Ireland** 9-3
1926 Belfast **Ireland** 11-0
1927 Paris **Ireland** 8-3
1928 Belfast **Ireland** 12-8
1929 Paris **Ireland** 6-0
1930 Belfast **France** 5-0
1931 Paris **France** 3-0
1947 Dublin **France** 12-8
1948 Paris **Ireland** 13-6
1949 Dublin **France** 16-9
1950 Paris **Drawn** 3-3
1951 Dublin **Ireland** 9-8
1952 Paris **Ireland** 11-8
1953 Belfast **Ireland** 16-3
1954 Paris **France** 8-0
1955 Dublin **France** 5-3
1956 Paris **France** 14-8
1957 Dublin **Ireland** 11-6
1958 Paris **France** 11-6
1959 Dublin **Ireland** 9-5
1960 Paris **France** 23-6
1961 Dublin **France** 15-3
1962 Paris **France** 11-0
1963 Dublin **France** 24-5
1964 Paris **France** 27-6
1965 Dublin **Drawn** 3-3
1966 Paris **France** 11-6
1967 Dublin **France** 11-6
1968 Paris **France** 16-6
1969 Dublin **Ireland** 17-9
1970 Paris **France** 8-0
1971 Dublin **Drawn** 9-9
1972 Paris **Ireland** 14-9
1972 Dublin **Ireland** 24-14 (X)
1973 Dublin **Ireland** 6-4
1974 Paris **France** 9-6
1975 Dublin **Ireland** 25-6
1976 Paris **France** 26-3

1977 Dublin **France** 15-6
1978 Paris **France** 10-9
1979 Dublin **Drawn** 9-9
1980 Paris **France** 19-18
1981 Dublin **France** 19-13
1982 Paris **France** 22-9
1983 Dublin **Ireland** 22-16
1984 Paris **France** 25-12
1985 Dublin **Drawn** 15-15
1986 Paris **France** 29-9
1987 Dublin **France** 19-13
1988 Paris **France** 25-6
1989 Dublin **France** 26-21
1990 Paris **France** 31-12
1991 Dublin **France** 21-13
1992 Paris **France** 44-12
1993 Dublin **France** 21-6
1994 Paris **France** 35-15
1995 Dublin **France** 25-7
1995 Durban **France** 36-12 (WCM)
1996 Paris **France** 45-10
1997 Dublin **France** 32-15
1998 Paris **France** 18-16
1999 Dublin **France** 10-9

Ireland v New Zealand (Maoris)

1888 Dublin **New Zealand Maoris** 13-4

Ireland v New Zealand

1905 Dublin **New Zealand** 15-0
1924 Dublin **New Zealand** 6-0
1935 Dublin **New Zealand** 17-9
1954 Dublin **New Zealand** 14-3
1963 Dublin **New Zealand** 6-5
1973 Dublin **Drawn** 10-10
1974 Dublin **New Zealand** 15-6
1976 Wellington **New Zealand** 11-3
1978 Dublin **New Zealand** 10-6
1989 Dublin **New Zealand** 23-6
1992 Dunedin **New Zealand** 24-21
Wellington **New Zealand** 59-6
1995 Johannesburg **New Zealand** 43-19 (WCM)
1997 Dublin **New Zealand** 63-15

Ireland v South Africa

1906 Belfast **South Africa** 15-12
1912 Dublin **South Africa** 38-0
1931 Dublin **South Africa** 8-3
1951 Dublin **South Africa** 17-5
1960 Dublin **South Africa** 8-3
1961 Cape Town **South Africa** 24-8
1965 Dublin **Ireland** 9-6
1970 Dublin **Drawn** 8-8
1981 Cape Town **South Africa** 23-15
Durban **South Africa** 12-10
1998 Bloemfontein **South Africa** 37-19
Pretoria **South Africa** 33-0
Dublin **South Africa** 27-13

Ireland v The Warathas (New South Wales)

1927 Dublin **The Warathas** 5-3

Ireland v Australia

1947 Dublin **Australia** 16-3
1958 Dublin **Ireland** 9-6
1967 Dublin **Ireland** 15-8
Sydney **Ireland** 11-5
1968 Dublin **Ireland** 10-3
1976 Dublin **Australia** 20-10
1979 Brisbane **Ireland** 27-12
Sydney **Ireland** 9-3
1981 Dublin **Australia** 16-12
1984 Dublin **Australia** 16-9
1987 Sydney **Australia** 33-15 (WCM)
1991 Dublin **Australia** 19-18 (WCM)
1992 Dublin **Australia** 42-17
1994 Brisbane **Australia** 33-13
1994 Sydney **Australia** 32-18
1996 Dublin **Australia** 22-12
1999 Brisbane **Australia** 46-10
Perth **Australia** 32-26

Ireland v IRU President's XV

1974 Dublin **Drawn** 18-18

Ireland v Romania

1986 Dublin **Ireland** 60-0
1993 Dublin **Ireland** 25-3
1998 Dublin **Ireland** 53-35 (WCM)

Ireland v Argentina

1990 Dublin **Ireland** 20-18

Ireland v Namibia

1991 Windhoek **Namibia** 15-6
Windhoek **Namibia** 26-15

Ireland v Zimbabwe

1991 Dublin **Ireland** 55-11 (WCM)

Ireland v Japan

1991 Dublin **Ireland** 32-16
1995 Bloemfontein **Ireland** 50-28 (WCM)

Ireland v United States

1994 Dublin **Ireland** 26-15
1996 Atlanta **Ireland** 25-18

Ireland v Fiji

1995 Dublin **Ireland** 44-8

Ireland v Canada

1987 Dunedin **Ireland** 46-19 (WCM)
1997 Dublin **Ireland** 33-11

Ireland v Tonga

1987 Brisbane **Ireland** 32-9 (WCM)

Ireland v Western Samoa

1988 Dublin **Ireland** 49-22
1996 Dublin **Western Samoa** 40-25

Ireland v Italy

1988 Dublin **Ireland** 31-15
1995 Treviso **Italy** 22-12
1997 Dublin **Italy** 37-29
1997 Bologna **Italy** 37-22

Ireland v Georgia

1998 Dublin **Ireland** 70-0 (WCM)

APPENDIX 17

IRELAND A AND B INTERNATIONALS: TEAMS AND RESULTS

NB: B Internationals were designated as A as and from 1992–93

1975–76

v France B, Lansdowne Road, 6 December 1975

L.A. Moloney (Garryowen); J. Fortune (UCD), J. Coleman (Highfield), R. Finn (UCD), H.A. Smith (Cork Con); H.C. Condon (London Irish), D.M. Canniffe (Lansdowne) Capt.; E. Byrne (Blackrock Coll), J.L. Cantrell (UCD), T.A. Feighery (St Mary's Coll), E.J. Molloy (Garryowen), D. Dalton (Malone), A.J. McLean (Ballymena), H.W. Steele (Ballymena), M. Casserly (Galwegians).
Replacement: A. Henry (Sale) for Feighery

Ireland B **9** France B **6**

1976–77

v France B, Dijon, 4 December 1976

F. Wilson (CIYMS); D. St J. Bowen (Cork Con), A.R. McKibbin (Instonians), V.J. Cosgrave (Wanderers), J. Miles (Malone); A.J.P. Ward (Garryowen), R.J. McGrath (Wanderers) Capt.; D. McCann (Dungannon), C.F. Fitzgerald (St Mary's Coll), T.A. Feighery (St Mary's Coll), D.A. Dalton (Malone), C.W. Murtagh (Portadown), J.B. O'Driscoll (London Irish), D.E. Spring (Dublin U), C. O'Carroll (Bective Rangers).
Rep: E.M. Byrne (Blackrock Coll) for Murtagh; M.N. Casserly (Galwegians) for O'Carroll.

France B **16** Ireland B **3**

1977–78

v Scotland B, Murrayfield, 3 December 1977

F.N.G. Ennis (Clontarf); S.D. Dobbin (CIYMS), P.P. McNaughton (Greystones), A.W. Irwin (Queen's U), M.C. Finn (UCC); A.J.P. Ward (Garryowen), C.S. Patterson (Instonians); G.A.J. McLoughlin (Shannon), C.F. Fitzgerald (St Mary's Coll) Capt., M.P. Fitzpatrick (Wanderers), C.M. McCarthy (UCC, Coventry), E.J. O'Rafferty (Wanderers), C.C. Tucker (Shannon), D.E. Spring (Dublin U), A.J. McLean (Ballymena).

Scotland B **3** Ireland B **7**

1979–80

v Scotland B, Lansdowne Road, 1 December 1979

K.A. O'Brien (Broughton Park); K.J. Hooks (Queen's U), D.G. Irwin (Queen's U), G. Barrett (Cork Con), S.G. McComish (NIFC); I.G. Burns (Wanderers), R.H. Stewart (Queen's U); M. Jackman (Old Wesley), I. Kidd (Instonians) Capt., J.J. McCoy (Dungannon), J.J. Glennon (Skerries), D. McCracken (London Irish), R. Kearney (Wanderers), A. O'Leary (Cork Con), N.J. Carr (Queen's U).

Ireland B **13** Scotland B **20**

1980–81

v England B, Twickenham, 6 December 1980

H.P. MacNeill (Dublin U); K.J. Hooks (Queen's U), J.A. Hewitt (NIFC), A.W. Irwin (Queen's U), F.P. Quinn (Old Belvedere); P.M. Dean (St Mary's Coll), J.B. O'Connor (Palmerston); T.F. Kavanagh (Bective Rangers), H.T. Harbison (UCD), A.H. McGuire (St Mary's Coll), J.J. Holland (Wanderers), D.G. Lenihan (UCC), R.K. Kearney (Wanderers), A.F. O'Leary (Cork Con) Capt., N.J. Carr (Queen's U).

England B **20** Ireland B **15**

1982–83

v England B, Ravenhill, 4 December 1982

J.K.P. Barry (Bohemians); P. Haycock (Terenure Coll), C.T. Hitchcock (UCG), R.V. Palmer (Collegians), D.M Aherne (Dolphin); A.D. Goodrich (Ballymena), K.A. O'Regan (St Mary's Coll); N.M. Ryan (Shannon), P.D. Derham (Cork Con), J.J. McCoy (Dungannon), M.M. Moylett (Manchester, Shannon), G.H. Wallace (Old Wesley), C.D. Cantillon (Cork Con), A.F. O'Leary (Cork Con) Capt., N.J. Carr (Queen's U).

Ireland B **6** England B **10**

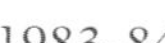

1983–84

v Scotland B, Melrose, 3 December 1983

J.P.K. Barry (Cork Con); J.M. McGeady (Lansdowne), B.J. Mullin (Dublin U), R.J.M. Moroney (Lansdowne), R.V. Palmer (Collegians); H.C. Condon (London Irish), M.T. Bradley (Cork Con); J.G. Langbroek (Blackrock Coll), H.T. Harbison (Bective Rangers), D.C. Fitzgerald (Lansdowne), B.W. McCall (London Irish), M.M. Moylett (Shannon), W.J. Sexton (Garryowen), D.P. Fanning (St Mary's Coll) Capt., D.G. McGrath (UCD).

Scotland B **22** Ireland B **13**

1984–85

v Scotland B, Sports Ground, Galway, 1 December 1984

J.P.K. Barry (Cork Con); T.R. McMaster (Bangor), M.R. Feely (Old Belvedere), J.A. O'Neill (Waterpark), D. Aherne (St Mary's Coll); R.P. Keyes (Cork Con), R.C. Brady (Queen's U); T.P.J. Clancy (Lansdowne), J.P. McDonald (Malone), M.A. D'Arcy (Terenure Coll), M.P. Tarpey (Galwegians), B.W. McCall (London Irish), D.R. Morrow (Bangor), D.P. Fanning (St Mary's Coll) Capt., N.J. Carr (Ards).

Ireland B **23** Scotland B **20**

1989–90

v Scotland B, Murrayfield, 9 December 1989

K.J. Murphy (Cork Con); J.E. Staples (London Irish), J.A. Hewitt (London Irish), P.D. Clinch (Lansdowne), P.V. Murray (Shannon); P. Russell (Instonians), A.C. Rolland (Blackrock Coll); B.M. McKibbin (Instonians), J.P. McDonald (Malone), P.M. Clohessy (Young Munster), B.J. Rigney (Greystones), M.J. Galwey (Shannon), P.C. Collins (London Irish) Capt., B.F. Robinson (Ballymena), P. Kenny (Wanderers).
Rep: P.S. Johns (Dublin U) for Galwey

Scotland B **22** Ireland B **22**

1990–91

v Argentina, Thomond Park, 20 October 1990

C. Wilkinson (Malone); S.P. Geoghegan (London Irish), D.J. Clarke (Dolphin), V.J.G. Cunningham (St Mary's Coll), J.C. Riordan (Wanderers); N.M.P. Barry (Garryowen), M.T. Bradley (Cork Con) Capt.; J.J. Fitzgerald (Young Munster), T.J. Kingston (Dolphin), G.F. Halpin (Wanderers), K.G. Potts (St Mary's Coll), M.J. Galwey (Shannon), K.T. Leahy (Wanderers), P.J. Lawlor (Bective Rangers), W.D. McBride (Malone).

Ireland B **27** Argentina **12**

v Scotland B, Ravenhill, 22 December 1990

C.R. Wilkinson (Malone); D. Hernan (UCD), D.M. Curtis (London Irish), D.J. Clarke (Dolphin), R.M. Wallace (Garryowen); D. McAleese (Ballymena), R. Saunders (London Irish); P. Soden (Cork Con), J. O'Riordan (Cork Con), P. McCarthy (Cork Con), M.J. Galwey (Shannon), B.J. Rigney (Greystones), K. Leahy (Wanderers) Capt., B.F. Robinson (Ballymena), G. Hamilton (NIFC).

Ireland B **16** Scotland B **0**

v England B, Donnybrook, 1 March 1991

C.R. Wilkinson (Malone); R.M. Wallace (Garryowen), M.J. Kiernan (Dolphin), D.J. Clarke (Dolphin), J. Sexton (Lansdowne); N.M.P. Barry (Garryowen), M.T. Bradley (Cork Con) Capt.; N.J. Popplewell (Greystones), J. O'Riordan (Cork Con), P. McCarthy (Cork Con), M.J. Galwey (Shannon), P.S. Johns (Dublin U), P.T.J. O'Hara (Sunday's Well), P.J. Lawlor (Bective Rangers), M. Fitzgibbon (Shannon).

Ireland B **24** England B **10**

1991–92

v Scotland B, Murrayfield, 28 December 1991

C.R. Wilkinson (Malone); N. Furlong (UCG), M. Ridge (Blackrock Coll), M. McCall (Bangor), R.M. Wallace (Garryowen); D. McAleese (Ballymena), A. Blair (Dungannon); P.J. Soden (Cork Con), J. Murphy (Greystones) Capt., P.T. McCarthy (Cork Con), K.G. Potts (St Mary's Coll), G.M. Fulcher (UCD), D. Macartney (Ballymena), B. O'Mahony (UCC), M.J. Fitzgibbon (Shannon).

Scotland B **19** Ireland B **29**

v England B, Richmond, 31 January 1992

C.R. Wilkinson (Malone); R. Carey (Dungannon), M. Ridge (Blackrock Coll), M. McCall (Bangor), N. Furlong (UCG); P. Hennebry (Terenure Coll), A.C. Rolland (Blackrock Coll); J.J. Fitzgerald (Young Munster) Capt., A. Adair (Instonians), P. Millar (Ballymena), B.J. Rigney (Greystones), T. Coughlin (Old Belvedere), K. Leahy (Wanderers), P.S. Johns (Dungannon), D. Macartney (Ballymena).

England B **47** Ireland B **15**

In the 1992–93 season B Internationals were designated A.

1992–93

v Scotland A, Lansdowne Road, 28 December 1992

C.R. Wilkinson (Malone); C.S.D. Leahy (Lansdowne), B.A. Walsh (Cork Con), B.T. Glennon (Lansdowne), N.K.P. Woods (Blackrock Coll); N.G. Malone (Oxford U), R. Saunders (London Irish); P.J. Soden (Cork Con), M.B. Patton (Oxford U) Capt., G.F. Halpin (London Irish), D.A. Tweed (Ballymena), R.A. Costello (Garryowen), L.M. Dineen (Cork Con), W. Cronin (Garryowen), K.J. McKee (Instonians).
Rep: P. Millar (Ballymena) for Halpin

Ireland A **13** Scotland A **22**

v Wales A, Newport, 5 March 1993

J.E. Staples (London Irish); R. Carey (Dungannon), B. Walsh (Cork Con), M.C. McCall (Bangor), N.K.P. Woods (Blackrock Coll); D.G. Humphreys (Queen's U), L.F.P. Aherne (Lansdowne) Capt.; P.J. Soden (Cork Con), W. Mulcahy (Skerries), P. Millar (Ballymena), J. Etheridge (Northampton), D.A. Tweed (Ballymena), K. Potts (St Mary's Coll), N.P. Mannion (Lansdowne), L. Toland (Old Crescent).
Rep: M. Ridge (Blackrock Coll) for Staples

Wales A **32** Ireland A **29**

v England A, Donnybrook, 19 March 1993

A. White (St Mary's Coll); R. Carey (Dungannon), B. Walsh (Cork Con), M.C. McCall (Bangor), N.K.P. Woods (Blackrock Coll); D.G. Humphreys (Queen's U), L.F.P. Aherne (Lansdowne) Capt.; P.J. Soden (Cork Con), W. Mulcahy (Skerries), P. Millar (Ballymena), J. Etheridge (Northampton), D.A. Tweed (Ballymena), K. Potts (St Mary's Coll), N.P. Mannion (Lansdowne), L. Toland (Old Crescent).
Reps: S. McKinty (Bangor) for Mannion; M. Ridge (Blackrock Coll) for Woods

Ireland A **18** England A **22**

1993–94

v Scotland A, Ayr, 28 December 1993

C. Clarke (Terenure Coll); S.P. Geoghegan (London Irish), M.C. McCall (Bangor), D. Dooley (London Irish), N.K.P. Woods (Blackrock Coll); A. McGowan (Blackrock Coll), N. Hogan (Terenure Coll) Capt.; H.D. Hurley (Old Wesley), K.G.M. Wood (Garryowen), P.M. Clohessy (Young Munster), P.J. Rigney (Greystones), D.A. Tweed (Ballymena), E.O. Halvey (Shannon), P.J. Lawlor (Bective Rangers), L. Toland (Old Crescent).

Scotland A **24** Ireland **9**

v Wales A, Donnybrook, 4 February 1994

P. Murray (Shannon); T. Howe (Dungannon), B. Walsh (Cork Con), M. Field (Malone), N.K.P. Woods (Blackrock Coll); P. Burke (London Irish), N. Hogan (Terenure Coll) Capt.; P. Soden (Cork Con), J. McDonald (Malone), P. Millar (Ballymena), J. Etheridge (Blackrock Coll), D.A. Tweed (Ballymena), E.O. Halvey (Shannon), R. Wilson (Instonians), K. McKee (Instonians).

Ireland A **10** Wales A **20**

v England A, Richmond, 18 February 1994

J.E. Staples (London Irish); T. Howe (Dungannon), B. Walsh (Cork Con), M.C. McCall (Bangor), N.K.P. Woods (Blackrock Coll); D.G. Humphreys (Queen's U), A.C. Rolland (Blackrock Coll); P. Soden (Cork Con), J. McDonald (Malone) Capt., P. Millar (Ballymena), J. Etheridge (Blackrock Coll), D.A. Tweed (Ballymena), P. Hogan (Garryowen), R. Wilson (Instonians), K. McKee (Instonians).
Replacement: V.C.P. Costello (St Mary's Coll) for Tweed

England A **29** Ireland A **10**

1994–95

v England A, Donnybrook, 20 January 1995

J.E. Staples (Harlequins); R.M. Wallace (Garryowen), M.C. McCall (Bangor) Capt., M. Field (Malone), D.W. O'Mahony (UCD); A. McGowan (Blackrock Coll), David O'Mahony (Cork Con); J.J. Fitzgerald (Young Munster), W. Mulcahy (Skerries), P.S. Wallace (Blackrock Coll), D.A. Tweed (Ballymena), R. Costello (Garryowen), E.O. Halvey (Shannon), W. Cronin (Garryowen), D.W. McBride (Malone).
Rep (Temp): R. Wilson (Instonians) for Cronin

Ireland A **20** England A **21**

v Scotland A, Myreside, Edinburgh, 3 February 1995

P. Murray (Shannon); R.M. Wallace (Garryowen), L. Boyle (Harlequins), M.C. McCall (Bangor) Capt., D.W. O'Mahony (UCD); A. McGowan (Blackrock Coll), David O'Mahony (Cork Con); J.J. Fitzgerald (Young Munster), W. Mulcahy (Skerries), P.S. Wallace (Blackrock Coll), D.A. Tweed (Ballymena), R. Costello (Garryowen), E.O. Halvey (Shannon), R. Wilson (Instonians), D. Corkery (Cork Con).
Reps: N. Malone (Leicester) for Boyle; C. Clarke (Terenure Coll) for McGowan.

Scotland A **24** Ireland A **18**

v Wales A, Pontypridd, 17 March 1995

C.M.P. O'Shea (Lansdowne); D.W. O'Mahony (UCD), L. Boyle (Harlequins), M.C. McCall (Bangor) Capt., N.K.P. Woods (Blackrock Coll); A. McGowan (Blackrock Coll), David O'Mahony (Cork Con); J.J. Fitzgerald (Young Munster), W. Mulcahy (Skerries), P.S. Wallace (Blackrock Coll), M.J. Galwey (Shannon), N.P.J. Francis (Old Belvedere), S. Rooney (Lansdowne), R. Wilson (Instonians), L. Toland (Old Crescent).

Ireland A **19** Wales A **30**

1995–96

v Scotland A, Donnybrook, 19 January 1996

C.M.P. O'Shea (London Irish); S.J.P. Mason (Orrell), J.A. Gallagher (Blackheath), S.A. McCahill (Sunday's Well), N.K.P. Woods (Blackrock Coll); D.G. Humphreys (London Irish), A.C. Rolland (Blackrock Coll) Capt.; P. Flavin (Blackrock Coll), S.J. Byrne (Blackrock Coll), P.S. Wallace (Blackrock Coll), D.A. Tweed (Ballymena), M.E. O'Kelly (St Mary's Coll), V.C.P. Costello (St Mary's Coll), A.G. Foley (Shannon), E.R.P. Miller (Leicester).
Rep: L. Toland (Old Crescent) for Miller

Ireland A **26** Scotland A **19**

v Wales A, Donnybrook, 1 March 1996

C.M.P. O'Shea (London Irish); R.M. Wallace (Garryowen), R.A.J. Henderson (London Irish), S. McCahill (Sunday's Well), J.A. Topping (Ballymena); E.P. Elwood (Lansdowne), A.C. Rolland (Blackrock Coll) Capt.; P. Flavin (Blackrock Coll), P. Cunningham (Garryowen), A. McKeen (Lansdowne), M.E. O'Kelly (St Mary's Coll), N.P.J. Francis (Old Belvedere), A.G. Foley (Shannon), B. Walsh (London Irish), L. Toland (Old Crescent).

Ireland A **25** Wales A **11**

v England A, Richmond, 15 March 1996

C.M.P. O'Shea (London Irish); R.M. Wallace (Garryowen), R.A.J. Henderson (London Irish), S. McCahill (Sunday's Well), J.A. Topping (Ballymena); E.P. Elwood (Lansdowne), A.C. Rolland (Blackrock Coll) Capt.; P. Flavin (Blackrock Coll), J.S. Byrne (Blackrock Coll), A. McKeen (Lansdowne), M.E. O'Kelly (St Mary's Coll), N.P.J. Francis (Old Belvedere), A.G. Foley (Shannon), B. Walsh (London Irish), L. Toland (Old Crescent).

England A **56** Ireland A **26**

1996–97

v South Africa, Donnybrook, 13 November 1996

D. Crotty (Garryowen); C.M.P. O'Shea (London Irish), B. Walsh (Cork Con), M.C. McCall (Dungannon), N.K.P. Woods (London Irish); E.P. Elwood (Lansdowne), B. O'Meara (Cork Con); P. Flavin (Blackrock Coll), K.G.M. Wood (Harlequins) Capt., A. McKeen (Lansdowne), M.E. O'Kelly (St Mary's Coll), S. Leahy (Lansdowne), A.G. Foley (Shannon), W. Cronin (Garryowen), E.R.P. Miller (Leicester).
Rep: C. Entee (Lansdowne) for O'Kelly

Ireland A **28** South Africa A **25**

v France A, Donnybrook, 17 January 1997

C.P. Clarke (Terenure Coll); D.A. Hickie (St Mary's Coll), B. Carey (Blackrock Coll), K.P. Keane (Garryowen), R.M. Wallace (Saracens); A. McGowan (Blackrock Coll), B.T. O'Meara (Cork Con); H.D. Hurley (Moseley), M. McDermott (Lansdowne), A. McKeen (Lansdowne), M.J. Galwey Capt. (Shannon), B. Cusack (Bath), A.G. Foley (Shannon), W. Cronin (Garryowen), E.O. Halvey (Shannon).
Rep: A. Reddan (Lansdowne) for Carey

Ireland A **23** France A **44**

v Emerging Wales, Pontypridd, 31 January 1997

P.M.C. O'Shea (London Irish); J. Cunningham (Dublin U), A. Reddan (Lansdowne), K.P. Keane (Garryowen), N.K.P. Woods (London Irish); N. Malone (Leicester), B.T. O'Meara (Cork Con); H.D. Hurley (Moseley), M. McDermott (Lansdowne), G. Walsh (Northampton), M.J. Galwey (Shannon) Capt., B. Cusack (Bath), E.O. Halvey (Shannon), A.G. Foley (Shannon), K. Dawson (London Irish).

Emerging Wales **34** Ireland A **14**

v England A, Donnybrook, 14 February 1997

C.M.P. O'Shea (London Irish) Capt.; D.J. Crotty (Garryowen), K. McQuilkin (Lansdowne), K.P. Keane (Garryowen), N.K.P. Woods (Blackrock Coll); P. Burke (Bristol), S.C. McIvor (Garryowen); H.D. Hurley (Moseley), M. McDermott (Lansdowne), G. Walsh (Northampton), S. Jameson (St Mary's Coll), B. Cusack (Bath), S. Duncan (Malone), W. Cronin (Garryowen), K. Dawson (London Irish).
Reps: N. Malone (Leicester) for Burke; A. McKeen (Lansdowne) for Walsh

Ireland A **30** England A **44**

v Scotland A, Myreside, Edinburgh, 28 February 1997

C.P. Clarke (Terenure Coll); D.J. Crotty (Garryowen), B. Carey (Blackrock Coll), M. Lynch (Young Munster), N.K.P. Woods (London Irish); R. Governey (Lansdowne), N.A. Hogan (Terenure Coll, Oxford U); H.D. Hurley (Moseley), M. McDermott (Lansdowne) Capt., A. McKeen (Lansdowne), S. Jameson (St Mary's Coll), B. Cusack (Bath), E.O. Halvey (Shannon), A.G. Foley (Shannon), K. Dawson (London Irish).

Scotland A **33** Ireland A **34**

1997–98

v Canada, Ravenhill, 26 November 1997

C.P. Clarke (Terenure Coll); D.W. O'Mahony (Moseley), P. Duignan (Galwegians), M. Lynch (Young Munster), J.P.J. McWeeney (St Mary's Coll); P.A. Burke (Bristol) Capt., B. Free (Saracens); J. Fitzpatrick (London Irish), W. Mulcahy (Skerries), P.M. Clohessy (Young Munster), G. Fulcher (London Irish), B. Cusack (Bath), S. Easterby (Harrogate), A. Quinlan (Shannon).

Ireland A **26** Canada **10**

v Scotland A, Donnybrook, 6 February 1998

K.W. Nowlan (St Mary's Coll); J. Cunningham (Ballymena), K.P. Keane (Garryowen), M. Lynch (Young Munster), D.W. O'Mahony (Moseley); P.A. Burke (Bristol) Capt., S.T. Bell (Dungannon); J. Fitzpatrick (London Irish), A.T.H. Clarke (Northampton), G. Walsh (Garryowen), M.J. Galwey (Shannon), D. O'Grady (Sale), D. Erskine (Sale).
Reps: G. Longwell (Ballymena) for Cusack; D.P. Wallace (Garryowen) for Quinlan

Ireland A **9** Scotland A **11**

v France A, Quimper, 6 March 1998

K.W. Nowlan (St Mary's Coll); J.P.J. McWeeney (St Mary's Coll), K.P. Keane (Garryowen), M.P. Murphy (Galwegians), D.W. O'Mahony (Moseley); P.A. Burke (Bristol) Capt., S.C. McIvor (Garryowen); J. Fitzpatrick (London Irish), A.T.H. Clarke (Northampton), G. Walsh (Northampton), G.M. Fulcher (London Irish), G. Longwell (Ballymena), E.O. Halvey (Shannon), D.P. Wallace (Garryowen), D. Erskine (Sale).

France A **30** Ireland A **30**

v Wales A, Thomond Park, 20 March 1998

K.W. Nowlan (St Mary's Coll); J.P.J. McWeeney (St Mary's Coll), K.P. Keane (Garryowen), M.P. Murphy (Galwegians), D.W. O'Mahony (Moseley); P.A. Burke (Bristol) Capt., S.C. McIvor (Garryowen); J. Fitzpatrick (London Irish), A.T.H. Clarke (Northampton), G. Walsh (Garryowen), G.M. Fulcher (London Irish), G. Longwell (Ballymena), E.O.

Halvey (Shannon), D.P. Wallace (Garryowen), K. Dawson (London Irish).
Reps: M. Lynch (Young Munster) for Burke; B. Jackman (Clontarf) for Clarke; B. Cusack (Bath) for Longwell; G.S. Leslie (Dungannon) for Walsh; D. Erskine (Sale) for Fulcher

Ireland A **27** Wales A **42**

v England A, Richmond, 3 April 1998

S. McDowell (Ballymena); J.P.J. McWeeney (St Mary's Coll), P. Duignan (Galwegians), M.P. Murphy (Galwegians), N.K.P. Woods (London Irish); B.G. Everitt (Garryowen), S.C. McIvor (Garryowen); J.M. Fitzpatrick (London Irish), B.J. Jackman (Clontarf), G. Walsh (Garryowen), B. Cusack (Bath), G.M. Fulcher Capt. (London Irish), T. Brennan (St Mary's Coll), D. O'Cuinneagain (Sale), K. Dawson (London Irish).
Reps: M. McDermott (Shannon) for Jackman; A.G. Foley (Shannon) for Dawson; D.J. Crotty (Garryowen) for McWeeney; S. Leahy (Garryowen) for Fulcher

England A **40** Ireland A **30**

1998–99

v South Africa, Ravenhill, 1 December 1998

G. Dempsey (Terenure Coll); N.K.P. Woods (London Irish), R.A.J. Henderson (Wasps), P. Duignan (Galwegians), D.W. O'Mahony (Bedford); D.G. Humphreys (Dungannon), C.J. Scally (UCD); R. Corrigan (Lansdowne), R.P. Nesdale (Newcastle), J.J. Hayes (Shannon), M.J. Galwey (Shannon) Capt., J.W. Davidson (Castres), D.S. Corkery (Cork Con), A.G. Foley (Shannon), E.O. Halvey (Shannon).
Reps: S.J.P. Mason (Ballymena) for Woods; A.T.H. Clarke (Dungannon) for Nesdale; E. Byrne (St Mary's Coll) for Hayes; J. Duffy (Galwegians) for Davidson; D.P. Wallace (Garryowen) for Corkery

Ireland A **19** South Africa **50**

v France, Donnybrook, 5 February 1999

G. D'Arcy (Lansdowne); J. McWeeney (St Mary's Coll), S. Horgan (Lansdowne), K. Keane (Garryowen), N. Woods (London Irish); B. Everitt (Lansdowne), G. Easterby (London Scottish); R. Corrigan (Lansdowne), A. Clarke (Dungannon) Capt., A. McKeen (Lansdowne), M. Blair (Ballymena), G. Fulcher (Lansdowne), A. Quinlan (Shannon), A. Foley (Shannon), E. Halvey (Shannon).
Reps: R. Weir (Portadown) for Clarke; D. Corkery (Cork Con) for Halvey; J. Duffy (Galwegians) for Blair; E. Byrne (St Mary's Coll) for McKeen; T. Tierney (Garryowen) for Easterby

Ireland A **26** France A **25**

v Wales, Ebbw Vale, 19 February 1999

G. D'Arcy (Lansdowne); J. McWeeney (St Mary's Coll), S. Horgan (Lansdowne), K. Keane (Garryowen), D. O'Mahony (Bedford); B. Everitt (Lansdowne), G. Easterby (London Scottish); R. Corrigan (Lansdowne), A. Clarke (Dungannon) Capt., A. McKeen (Lansdowne), M. Blair (Ballymena), G. Longwell (Ballymena), A. Quinlan (Shannon), A. Foley (Shannon), D. Wallace (Garryowen).
Reps: J. Hayes (Shannon) for Corrigan; S. Mason (Ballymena) for D'Arcy; P. Duignan (Galwegians) for McWeeney; G. Fulcher (Lansdowne) for Longwell

Wales A **40** Ireland A **29**

v England, Donnybrook, 5 March 1999

S. Mason (Ballymena); J. McWeeney (St Mary's Coll), M. Murphy (Galwegians), S. Horgan (Lansdowne), N. Woods (London Irish); B. Everitt (Lansdowne), T. Tierney (Garryowen); J. Screen (Buccaneers), A. Clarke (Dungannon) Capt., A. McKeen (Lansdowne), G. Fulcher (Lansdowne), G. Longwell (Ballymena), T. Brennan (St Mary's Coll), A. Foley (Shannon), E. Halvey (Shannon).
Reps: P. Duignan (Galwegians) for McWeeney; G. Easterby (London Scottish) for Tierney; J. Hayes (Shannon) for McKeen; M. Blair (Ballymena) for Longwell; D. Corkery (Cork Con) for Brennan

Ireland A **21** England A **28**

v Scotland (Myreside, Edinburgh) 19 March 1999

S. Mason (Ballymena); P. Duignan (Galwegians), S. Horgan (Lansdowne), C. Mahony (Cork Con), D. O'Mahony (Bedford); K. Keane (Garryowen), B. O'Meara (Cork Con); J. Screene (Buccaneers), A. Clarke (Dungannon) Capt., J. Hayes (Shannon), G. Fulcher (Lansdowne), M. Blair (Ballymena), D. Corkery (Cork Cons), A. Foley (Shannon), E. Halvey (Shannon).
Reps: F. Sheehan (Cork Con) for Clarke; D. Hickie (St Mary's Coll) for Duignan; B. Everitt (Lansdowne) for Mahony; M. Cahill (Buccaneers) for Hayes

Scotland A **31** Ireland A **21**

v Italy, Donnybrook, 9 April 1999

S. Mason (Ballymena); J. Topping (Ballymena), M. Mostyn (Begles Bordeaux), M. Mullins (West Hartlepool), D. Hickie (St Mary's Coll); J. Staunton (Garryowen), B. O'Meara (Cork Con); J. Screene (Buccaneers), S. McDonald (West Hartlepool), M. Cahill (Buccaneers), M. Galwey (Shannon) Capt., G. Fulcher (Lansdowne), A. Quinlan (Shannon), A. Foley (Shannon), D. Wallace (Garryowen).
Reps: M. Murphy (Galwegians) for Mullins; R. O'Gara (Cork Con) for Staunton; G. Easterby (London Scottish) for O'Meara; F. Sheehan (Cork Con) for McDonald; J. Hayes (Shannon) for Cahill; G. Longwell (Ballymena) for Fulcher; S. McEntee (Lansdowne) for Quinlan

Ireland A **73** Italy A **17**

Lions Irish Managers, Assistant Managers and Coaches:

J. Siggins Manager 1955 South Africa
O.B. Glasgow Assistant Manager 1959 Australia and New Zealand
H.R. McKibbin Assistant Manager 1962 South Africa
D. O'Brien Manager 1966 Australia and New Zealand
A.R. Dawson Coach 1968 South Africa.
S. Millar Coach 1974 South Africa
S. Millar Manager 1980 South Africa
N.A. Murphy Coach 1980 South Africa.
W.J. McBride Manager 1983 New Zealand

APPENDIX 18

IRELAND UNDER 25 INTERNATIONALS: TEAMS AND RESULTS

v Canada, 27 September 1986

T.P. Lenehan (Bohemians); J.F. Sexton (Dublin U), P.D. Clinch (Lansdowne) Capt., J.A. Hewitt (NIFC), G. O'Kelly (Dolphin); R.P. Keyes (Cork Con), S.D. Cowan (Malone); T.P. Clancy (Lansdowne), T.J. Kingston (Dolphin), M.A. D'Arcy (Terenure Coll), N.P.T. Francis (Blackrock Coll), M.F. Moylett (Shannon), P. Kenny (Wanderers), N.P. Mannion (Corinthians), P.T.J. O'Hara (Sunday's Well).

Ireland Under 25 **26** Canada **20**

v Italy, Ravenhill, 28 December 1988

F. Dunlea (Lansdowne); J.E. Staples (London Irish), R. Hernan (St Mary's Coll), C. Haly (UCC), P. Purcell (Lansdowne); P. Russell (Instonians), M. Bradley (Cork Con) Capt.; N.J. Popplewell (Greystones), T. Kingston (Dolphin), P.M. Clohessy (Young Munster), P.S. Johns (Newcastle-Gosforth), A. Higgins (UCG), C. Pim (Old Wesley), M. Egan (Oxford U), M. Fitzgibbon (Shannon).

Ireland Under 25 **21** Italy **16**

v United States, Thomond Park, 10 March 1990

J.E. Staples (London Irish); D.J. Clarke (Dolphin), P.P.A. Danaher (Garryowen) Capt., V.J.G. Cunningham (St Mary's Coll), P. Murray (Shannon); P. Hennebry (Terenure Coll), A. Blair (Dungannon); N.J. Popplewell (Greystones), J. O'Riordan (Cork Con), G.L. Halpin (Wanderers), P.S. Johns (Dublin U), M.J. Galwey (Shannon), K. O'Connell (Sunday's Well), B.F. Robinson (Ballymena), D.W. McBride (Malone).

Ireland Under 25 **12** United States Eagles **10**

v Spain, Thomond Park, 8 September 1990

S.E. Staples (London Irish); J. Riordan (Wanderers), D.J. Clarke (Dolphin), V.J.G. Cunningham (St Mary's Coll), S.P. Geoghegan (London Irish); N.M. Barry (Garryowen), A.C. Rolland (Blackrock Coll); R. Ward (Blackrock Coll), T.J. Kingston (Dolphin), G.L. Halpin (Wanderers), P.S. Johns (Dublin U), M.J. Galwey (Shannon), K. O'Connell (Sunday's Well), P.J. Lawlor (Bective Rangers), K. Leahy (Wanderers) Capt.

Ireland Under 25 **36** Spain **17**

Ireland has played one Under 23 International

v Holland , Hilversum, 13 October 1979

R.C. O'Donnell (St Mary's Coll); J. Bowen (Cork Con), D.G. Irwin (Queen's U), C. Hitchcock (UCG), J. Crotty (UCC); M.C. Finn (UCC), R.H. Stewart (Queen's U); B. O'Connor (Young Munster), H.T. Harbison (UCD), J.J. McCoy (Dungannon), D.G. Lenihan (UCC), B.W. McCall (Queen's U), D. Hanrahan (Blackrock Coll), D.E. Spring (Dublin U) Capt., N.J. Carr (Queen's U).

Ireland Under 23 **31** Holland **3**

Ireland Development v USA, Sports Ground, Galway, 1 November 1994

C.P. Clarke (Terenure Coll); I.R.H. Gray (Oxford U), S.A. McCahill (Sunday's Well), M.C. McCall (Malone) Capt., D. Wall (St Mary's Coll); D.G. Humphreys (Queen's U), S.C. McIvor (Garryowen); N. Donovan (London Irish), S. Byrne (Blackrock Coll), A.J. McKeen (Lansdowne), M.J. Galwey (Shannon), B. Cusack (Bective Rangers), A.G. Foley (Shannon), R.K. Wilson (Instonians), K. McKee (Instonians).

Reps: P.P.A. Burke (Cork Con) for Humphreys; M. McDermott (Lansdowne) for Byrne (temp)

Ireland Development **13** USA **20**

Appendix 19

Ireland's Overseas Tours

Senior — A Development — Under 21 — Schools

Canada 1899

J.G. Franks (Dublin U) Capt., C.A. Boyd (Dublin U), R.R. Boyd (Lansdowne), J. Byers (NIFC), I.G. Davidson (NIFC), F. Dinsmore (NIFC), B.W. Doran (Lansdowne), I. Grove-Smith (Dublin U), T.A. Harvey (Dublin U), J.C. Lepper (NIFC), H.A. Macready (Dublin U), J.S. Myles (Derry), P.C. Nicholson (Dublin U), B.W. Rowan (Lansdowne), A.C. Rowan (Lansdowne), H. Stevenson (Dungannon), J. Stokes (Lansdowne).

Beat United Services (Wanderers Ground, Halifax) 12 October 10-0
Beat Wanderers (Wanderers Ground, Halifax) 14 October 16-3
Lost to Halifax (Wanderers Ground, Halifax) 16 October 0- 5
Beat Montreal (MAA Ground, Montreal) 19 October 20-12
Beat Quebec City (Quebec) 24 October 8-0
Beat Ottawa (Metropolitan Ground, Ottawa) 28 October 9-3
Beat Brookville (Brookville) 30 October 28-0
Beat Peterborough (Nicholls Park, Peterborough) 2 November 16-3
Beat Hamilton (Hamilton) 3 November 8-0
Beat Argonauts (Toronto) 4 November 23-19
Beat U of Toronto (Varsity Stadium) 6 November 12-6
Tour Record: P11 W10 D0 L1 F150 A51

Argentina and Chile 1952

Backs:
R. Gregg (Queen's U)
M.F. Lane (UCC)
R.R. Chambers (Instonians)
J. Notley (Wanderers)
M. Hillary (UCD)
J.T. Horgan (UCC)
W.J. Hewitt (Instonians)
J.A. O'Meara (UCC)
M. Birthistle (Old Belvedere)

Forwards:
D.J. O'Brien (Cardiff) Capt.
W.J. O'Neill (UCD)
D. Crowley (Cork Con)
J.H. Smith (Collegians)
P.J. Lawler (Clontarf)
A.F. O'Leary (Cork Con)
P.J. Kavanagh (UCD)
J.S. McCarthy (Dolphin)
M.J. Dargan (Old Belvedere)
F.E. Anderson (Queen's U)
P.P. Traynor (Clontarf)
J.R. Kavanagh (UCD)

Manager: G.P.S. Hogan
Secretary: R.W. Jeffares, Jr
Referee: O.B. Glasgow

(All matches played at Buenos Aires except where indicated)
Beat Chilean All-Stars 30-0 (Santiago)
Beat Capital 12-6
Lost to Pucara 6-11
Drew with Buenos Aires Provincial XV 6-6
Beat Argentine A Selection 19-3
Drew with Argentina 3-3
Beat Argentine B Selection 25-3
Beat Argentina 6-0
Beat Buenos Aires University Past and Present 19-11

Tour Record: P9 W6 D2 L1 F126 A43

South Africa 1961

Backs:
T.J. Kiernan (UCC)
A.J.F. O'Reilly (Leicester, Old Belvedere)
N.H. Brophy (UCD)
J.C. Walsh (UCC)
K.J. Houston (London Irish, Oxford U)
W.J. Hewitt (Instonians)
J.F. Dooley (Galwegians)
W.G. Tormey (UCD)
D.C. Glass (Collegians)
A.A. Mulligan (Cambridge U)
T.J. Cleary (Bohemians)

Forwards:
A.R. Dawson (Wanderers) Capt.
S. Millar (Ballymena)
B.G.M. Wood (Garryowen)
J.N. Thomas (Blackrock Coll)
J.S. Dick (Queen's U)
W.A. Mulcahy (UCD)
M.G. Culliton (Wanderers)
C.J. Dick (Ballymena)
N.A. Murphy (Cork Con)
D. Scott (Malone)
J.R. Kavanagh (UCD)
T. McGrath (Garryowen)

Manager: N.F. Murphy
Hon. Assistant Manager: T. O'Reilly

Lost to South Africa (International) 8-24 (Cape Town)
Beat South Western Districts XV 11-6 (Mossel Bay)
Beat Western Transvaal 16-6 (Potchefstroom)
Beat Rhodesia 24-0 (Salisbury)

Tour Record: P4 W3 D0 L1 F59 A36

Australia 1967

Backs:
T.J. Kiernan (Cork Con) Capt.
A.T.A. Duggan (Lansdowne)
F.P.K. Bresnihan (UCD)
J.C. Walsh (Sunday's Well)
N.H. Brophy (Blackrock Coll)
P.J. McGrath (UCC)
J.B. Murray (UCD)
C.M.H. Gibson (NIFC)
B.F. Sherry (Terenure Coll)
L. Hall (UCC)

Forwards:
S.A. Hutton (Malone)
K.W. Kennedy (CIYMS)

S. MacHale (Lansdowne)
P. O'Callaghan (Dolphin)
W.J. McBride (Ballymena)
M.G. Molloy (UCG)
K.G. Goodall (City of Derry)
T.A. Moore (Highfield)
M.G. Doyle (Edinburgh Wanderers)
L.G. Butler (Blackrock Coll)
J. Flynn (Wanderers)
D.J. Hickie (St Mary's Coll)

Manager: E. O'D. Davy
Assistant Manager: D. McKibbin

Beat Queensland 41-8 (Brisbane)
Lost to New South Wales 9-21 (Sydney)
Beat New South Wales County Districts XV 31-11 (Wollongong)
Beat Australia (International) 11-5 (Sydney)
Lost to Sydney 8-30 (Sydney)
Beat Victoria 19-5 (Melbourne)

Tour Record: P6 W4 D0 L2 F119 A80

Argentina

Backs:
T.J. Kiernan (Cork Con) Capt.
B. O'Driscoll (Manchester)
A.T.A. Duggan (Lansdowne)
W. Brown (Malone)
T.O. Grace (UCD)
F.P.K. Bresnihan (London Irish)
F. O'Driscoll (UCD)
H. Murphy (UCD)
B.J. McGann (Cork Con)
J. Moloney (St Mary's Coll)
L. Hall (Garryowen)

Forwards:
J.F. Lynch (St Mary's Coll)
S. Millar (Ballymena)
P. O'Callaghan (Dolphin)
P. Madigan (Old Belvedere)
J. Birch (Ballymena)
W.J. McBride (Ballymena)
M. Molloy (London Irish)
P. Cassidy (Corinthians)
T. Moore (Highfield)
M. Hipwell (Terenure Coll)
R. Lamont (Instonians)
J. Buckley (Sunday's Well)

Manager: E. Patterson
Assistant Manager (Coach): A.R. Dawson

(All matches played at Buenos Aires except where indicated)
Beat Interior Selection 33-11
Beat Rosario 11-6 (Rosario)
Beat Argentine B Selection (Junior Pumas) 9-6
Beat Argentine D Selection 14-3
Lost to Argentina 3-8
Lost to Argentine C Selection 0-17
Lost to Argentina 3-6

Tour Record: P7 W4 D0 L3 F73 A57

New Zealand and Fiji 1976

Backs:
A. Ensor (Wanderers)
L. Moloney (Garryowen)
T. Grace (St Mary's Coll) Capt.
W. McMaster (Ballymena)
J. Brady (Wanderers)
M. Gibson (NIFC)
I. McIlrath (Ballymena)
B. McGann (Cork Con)
M. Quinn (Lansdowne)
D. Canniffe (Lansdowne)
J. Robbie (Dublin U)
R. McGrath (Wanderers) joined tour as replacement

Forwards:
P. Orr (Old Wesley)
R. Clegg (Bangor)
P. O'Callaghan (Dolphin)
T. Feighery (St Mary's Coll)
E. O'Rafferty (Wanderers)
J. Cantrell (UCD)
P. Whelan (Garryowen)
E. O'Rafferty (Wanderers)
B. Foley (Shannon)
M. Keane (Lansdowne)
R. Hakin (CIYMS)
H. Steele (Ballymena)
J. Davidson (Dungannon) joined tour as replacement
S. McKinney (Dungannon)
S. Deering (Garryowen)
W. Duggan (Blackrock Coll)

Manager: K. Quilligan
Assistant Manager (Coach): R. Meates
Medical Officer: T.C.J. O'Connell

Beat South Canterbury 19-4 (Timaru)
Beat North Auckland 12-3 (Whangarei)
Lost to Auckland 10-13 (Auckland)
Beat Manawatu 22-16
Lost to Canterbury 4-18 (Christchurch)
Beat Southland 18-3 (Invercargill)
Lost to New Zealand (Test) 3-11 (Wellington)
Beat Fiji 8-0 (Suva)

Tour Record: P8 W5 D0 L3 F88 A68

Australia 1979

Backs::
F. Ennis (Wanderers)
R. O'Donnell (St Mary's Coll)
M. Gibson (NIFC)
T. Kennedy (St Mary's Coll)
A. McLennan (Wanderers)
P. Andreucetti (St Mary''s Coll)
D. Irwin (Queen's U)
P. McNaughton (Greystones)
O. Campbell (Old Belvedere)
A. Ward (Garryowen)
J. Moloney (St Mary's Coll)
C. Patterson (Instonians)

Forwards:
P. Orr (Old Wesley)
G. McLoughlin (Shannon)
E. Byrne (Blackrock Coll)
M. Fitzpatrick (Wanderers) joined tour as replacement
C. Fitzgerald (St Mary's Coll)
P. Whelan (Garryowen)
B. Foley (Shannon)
M. Keane (Lansdowne)
H. Steele (Ballymena)
W. Duggan (Blackrock Coll)
C. Cantillon (Cork Con)
A. McLean (Ballymena)
J. O'Driscoll (London Irish)
F. Slattery (Blackrock Coll) Capt.

Manager: J. Coffey
Assistant Manager (Coach): N. Murphy
Medical Officer: T.C.J. O'Connell

Beat Western Australia 39-3 (Perth)
Beat ACT 35-7 (Canberra)
Beat New South Wales 16-12 (Sydney)
Beat Queensland 18-15 (Brisbane)
Beat Australia (First Test) 27-12 (Brisbane)
Beat New South Wales Country 28-7 (Orange)
Lost to Sydney 12-16 (Sydney)
Beat Australia (Second Test) 9-3 (Sydney)

Tour Record: P8 W7 D0 L1 F184 A75

South Africa 1981

Backs:
J. Murphy (Greystones)
K. O'Brien (Broughton Park)
K. Crossan (Instonians)
T. Kennedy (St Mary's Coll)
M. Kiernan (Dolphin)
A. McLennan (Wanderers)
J. Hewitt (NIFC)
A. Irwin (Queen's U)
D. Irwin (Queen's U)
O. Campbell (Old Belvedere)
P. Dean (St Mary's Coll)
J. Robbie (Greystones)
R. McGrath (Wanderers)
M. Quinn (Lansdowne) joined tour as replacement
B. O'Connor (Palmerston) joined tour as replacement

Forwards:
P. Orr (Old Wesley)
G. McLoughlin (Shannon)
D. Fitzgerald (Dublin U)
J. Cantrell (Blackrock Coll)
H. Harbison (UCD)
J. Holland (Wanderers)
G. Wallace (Old Wesley)
B. Foley (Shannon)
A. O'Leary (Cork Con, Wanderers)
J. O'Driscoll (London Irish)
R. Kearney (Wanderers)
W. Duggan (Blackrock Coll)
F. Slattery (Blackrock Coll) Capt.
Manager: P. Madigan
Assistant Manager (Coach): T. Kiernan
Medical Officer: M. Little

Lost to SA Gazelles 15-18 (Pretoria)
Beat SA Mining XV 46-7 (Potchefstroom)
Beat President's Trophy XV 54-3 (East London)
Lost to SA Country Districts XV 16-17 (Wellington)
Lost to South Africa (First Test) 15-23 (Cape Town)
Beat Gold Cup XV 51-10 (Dudtshoorn)
Lost to South Africa (Second Test) 10-12 (Durban)

Tour record: P7 W3 D0 L4 F207 A90

Japan 1985

Backs:
P. Rainey (Ballymena)
H. MacNeill (Oxford U, London Irish)
T. Ringland (Ballymena)
K. Crossan (Instonians)
M. Kiernan (Lansdowne, Dolphin)
B. Mullin (Dublin U)
M. Finn (Cork Con)
T. McMaster (Bangor)
J. Hewitt (NIFC) joined tour as replacement
P. Dean (St Mary's Coll)
R. Keyes (Cork Con)
M. Bradley (Cork Con)
R. Brady (Ballymena)

Forwards:
P. Kennedy (London Irish)
M. Fitzpatrick (Wanderers)
J. McCoy (Dungannon)
P. Orr (Old Wesley)
C. Fitzgerald (St Mary's Coll) Capt.
H. Harbison (Bective Rangers)
B. McCall (London Irish)
W. Anderson (Dungannon)
D. Lenihan (Cork Con)
N. Carr (Ards)
P. Matthews (Ards)
B. Spillane (Bohemians)
P. Kenny (Wanderers)
P. Collins (Highfield)

Manager: D. McKibbin
Assistant Manager (Coach): M. Doyle
Medical Officer: J. Gallagher
Beat Kansai 44-13 (Morioka)
Beat Japan B 34-10 (Sendai)
Beat Japan (First Test) 48-13 (Osaka)
Beat Kanto 42-15 (Nagoya)
Beat Japan (Second Test) 33-15 (Tokyo)

Tour Record: P5 W5 D0 L0 F201 A66

Teams in Test matches (Caps not awarded for Tests):
First Test: MacNeill, Ringland, Kiernan, Mullin, Crossan, Dean, Bradley, Orr, Fitzgerald, McCoy, Anderson, Lenihan, Kenny, Spillane, Matthews.

Second Test: MacNeill, Ringland, Kiernan, Mullin, Crossan, Dean, Bradley, Orr, Fitzgerald, McCoy, Anderson, Lenihan, Matthews, Spillane, Kenny.
Replacements: Keyes for Dean, Brady for Bradley.

France May 1988

W.A. Anderson (Dungannon) Capt., P. Danaher (Lansdowne), V. Cunningham (St Mary's Coll), J. Sexton (Dublin U), W. Harbison (Malone), Purcell (Lansdowne), P. Clinch (Lansdowne), A.J. Ward (Greystones), F. Aherne (Dolphin), R. Brady (Ballymena), T. Clancy (Lansdowne), N.J. Popplewell (Greystones), S.J. Smith (Ballymena), J. McDonald (Malone), J. McCoy (Bangor), P. Millar (Ballymena), N.P.J. Francis (Blackrock Coll), M.M. Moylett (Shannon), D. Whittle (Bangor), W.D. McBride (Malone), P. O'Hara (Sunday's Well), M. Gibson (London Irish), N. Barry (Garryowen), M.J. Galwey (Shannon).

Manager K.E. Reid, Coach J.C. Davidson, Medical Officer Dr M.G. Molloy, Masseur J. Doran.

Lost to Côté Basque (Biarritz) 23-33
Beat French XV (Auch) 19-18
Lost to French XV (Lorient) 7-12
Lost to French Barbarians (La Rochelle) 26 – 41

Tour Record: P4 W1 D0 L3 F75 A104

Canada and United States August–September 1989

Backs:
F. Aherne (Lansdowne), N. Barry (Garryowen), M.T. Bradley (Cork Con), P.D. Clinch (Lansdowne), K.D. Crossan (Instonians), P.P. Danaher (Garryowen), F.J. Dunlea (Lansdowne), M.J. Kiernan (Dolphin), P. Haycock (Terenure Coll), J.S. Sexton (Lansdowne, Oxford U).

Forwards:
W.A. Anderson (Dungannon) Capt., T.P. Clancy (Lansdowne), N.P.J. Francis (London Irish), P. Kenny

(Wanderers), T.J. Kingston (Dolphin), N.P. Mannion (Corinthians), P.M. Matthews (Wanderers), W.D. McBride (Malone), J.J. McCoy (Bangor), J.P. McDonald (Malone), P.T.J. O'Hara (Sunday's Well), N.J. Popplewell (Greystones), B.J. Rigney (Greystones).

Manager K.E. Reid, Coach J.C. Davidson, Medical Officer Dr M.G. Molloy, Masseur J.A. Doran.

Beat British Colombia (Vancouver) 30 August 21-18
Beat Canada (Victoria) 2 September 24-21
Beat Mid West (Chicago) 6 September 58-6
Beat USA, Downing Island, New York, 9 September 32-7

Tour Record: P4 W4 D0 L0 F135 A52

Caps were not awarded for Tests

Team v Canada: Dunlea, Sexton, Kiernan, Clinch, Crossan, Barry, Aherne, Popplewell, McDonald, McCoy, Anderson, Rigney, Matthews, Mannion, McBride.
Replacements: Bradley for Aherne; Clancy for Popplewell.

Team v USA: Dunlea, Sexton, Kiernan, Clinch, Crossan, Smith, Aherne, Popplewell, McDonald, McCoy, Anderson, Rigney, Matthews, Mannion, O'Hara.
Replacements: Danaher for Dunlea; Bradley for Aherne; Kingston for McDonald.

Namibia July 1991

Backs:
J.E. Staples (London Irish), K.J. Murphy (Cork Con), S.P. Geoghegan (London Irish), R.M. Wallace (Garryowen), B.J. Mullin (Blackrock Coll), D.J. Clarke (Dolphin), K.D. Crossan (Instonians), V.J.G. Cunningham (St Mary's Coll), N.M.P. Barry (Garryowen), R. Saunders (London Irish), L.F. Aherne (Lansdowne).

Forwards:
J.J. Fitzgerald (Young Munster), N.J. Popplewell (Greystones), S.J. Smith (Ballymena), T.J. Kingston (Dolphin), D.C. Fitzgerald (Lansdowne), G.F. Halpin (Wanderers), B.J. Rigney (Greystones), M.J. Galwey (Shannon), N.P.J. Francis (Blackrock Coll), P.M. Matthews (Wanderers) Capt., P.T.J. O'Hara (Sunday's Well), G.F. Hamilton (NIFC), B.F. Robinson (Ballymena), N.P. Mannion (Lansdowne),* D.G. Lenihan (Cork Con).
* Joined tour as replacement

Manager K.E. Reid, Coach C.F. Fitzgerald, Assistant Coach J.J. Moloney, Medical Officer Dr D. O'Shaughnessy, Fitness Adviser E. O'Sullivan, Masseur J.A. Doran.

Beat Namibia B (Windhoek) 17 July 45-16
Lost to Namibia (Windhoek) 20 July 6-15
Beat Namibia South (Keetmanshoep) 23 July 35-4
Lost to Namibia (Windhoek) 27 July 15-26

Tour Record: P4 W2 D0 L2 F101 A61

New Zealand May–June 1992

Backs:
K.J. Murphy (Cork Con), J.E. Staples (London Irish), R.W. Carey (Dungannon), D.J. Clarke (Dolphin), J.N. Furlong (UCG), R.M. Wallace (Garryowen), V.J.G. Cunningham (St Mary's Coll), P.P.A. Danaher (Garryowen) Capt., M.C. McCall (Bangor), M.P. Ridge (Blackrock Coll), D.R. McAleese (Ballymena), P. Russell (Instonians), L.F.P. Aherne (Lansdowne), M.T. Bradley (Cork Con), D. O'Brien* (Clontarf).

Forwards:
T.P.J. Clancy (Lansdowne), G.F. Halpin (London Irish), P. McCarthy (Cork Con), N.J. Popplewell (Greystones), T.J. Kingston (Dolphin), S.J. Smith (Ballymena), R. Costello (Garryowen), J. Etheridge (Northampton), M.J. Galwey (Shannon), B.J. Rigney (Greystones), M.P. Fitzgibbon (Shannon), P.S. Johns (Dungannon), K.T. Leahy (Wanderers), W.D. McBride (Malone), N.P.S. Mannion (Lansdowne), B.F. Robinson (Ballymena), P. Kenny* (Wanderers).
*Joined tour as replacement

Manager N.A. Murphy, Coach C.F. Fitzgerald, Assistant Coach G. Murphy, Medical Officer Dr D. O'Shaughnessy, Physiotherapist J. Martin, Masseur J.A. Doran.

Beat South Canterbury (Timaru) 13 May 21-16
Lost to Canterbury (Lancaster Park, Canterbury) 16 May 13-38
Beat Bay of Plenty (International Stadium, Rotorua) 20 May 39-23
Lost to Auckland (Eden Park, Auckland) 23 May 7-62
Beat Poverty Bay-East Coast (Rugby Park, Gisborne) 26 May 22-7
Lost to New Zealand (Carisbrook, Dunedin) 30 May 21-24
Lost to Manawatu (Showgrounds, Palmerston North) 2 June 24-58

Lost to New Zealand (Athletic Park, Wellington) 6 June 6-59

Tour Record: P8 W3 D0 L5 F153 A287

Australia May–June 1994

Backs:

M.T. Bradley (Cork Con) Capt., C.M.P. O'Shea (Lansdowne), J.E. Staples (London Irish), S.P. Geoghegan (London Irish), J.C. Bell (Ballymena, Loughborough Coll), N.K.P. Woods (Blackrock Coll), P.P.A. Danaher (Garryowen), M.J. Field (Malone), M.P. Ridge (Blackrock Coll), B. Walsh (Cork Con), E.P. Elwood (Lansdowne), A.C. Rolland (Blackrock Coll), N.A. Hogan* (Terenure Coll).

Forwards:

P.J. Soden (Cork Con), P.M. Clohessy (Young Munster), J.J. Fitzgerald (Young Munster), G.F. Halpin (London Irish), T.J. Kingston (Dolphin), K.G.M. Wood (Garryowen), G.M. Fulcher (Cork Con), M.J. Galwey (Shannon), N.P.J. Francis (Old Belvedere), J.W. Davidson (Dungannon), P.J. Hogan (Garryowen), W.D. McBride (Malone), D.S. Corkery (Cork Con), B.F. Robinson (Ballymena), V.C.P. Costello (St Mary's Coll), P.S. Johns (Dungannon), R.K. Wilson (Instonians), W.M. Cronin* (Garryowen), S.J. Byrne* (Blackrock Coll).
* Joined tour as replacement

Manager F. Sowman, Assistant Manager L. Butler, Coach G. Murphy, Technical Adviser W.W. Anderson, Medical Officer Dr W. Rainey, Physiotherapist J. Martin, Masseur J.A. Doran.

Beat Western Australia (WCCA Ground, Perth) 18 May 64-8
Lost to New South Wales (Waratah Stadium, Sydney) 22 May 55-18
Lost to ACT (Manuka Oval, Canberra) 25 May 9-22
Lost to Queensland (Ballymore, Brisbane) 29 May 26-29
Lost to Australia (Ballymore, Brisbane) 5 June 26-29
Beat New South Wales Country (Lismore) 8 June 20-18
Lost to Australia (Football Stadium, Sydney) 11 June 18-32

Tour Record: P8 W2 D0 L6 F177 A254

South Africa 1998

Backs:

C. Clarke (Terenure Coll), C. O'Shea (London Irish), D. Hickie (St Mary's Coll), J. Topping (Ballymena), R. Wallace (Saracens), J. Bell (Northampton), R. Henderson (Wasps), M. McCall (London Irish), K. Maggs (Bristol), K. Keane (Garryowen), E. Elwood (Galwegians), D. Humphreys (London Irish), D. Hegarty (Terenure Coll), C. McGuinness (St Mary's Coll), B. O'Meara (Cork Con), J. Bishop* (London Irish).

Forwards:

P. Clohessy (Young Munster), R. Corrigan (Greystones), J. Fitzpatrick (London Irish), J. Hayes (Shannon), P. Wallace (Saracens), A. Clarke (Northampton), B. Jackman (Clontarf), K. Wood (Harlequins), G. Fulcher (London Irish), M. Galwey (Shannon), P. Johns (Saracens) Capt., M. O'Kelly (London Irish), T. Brennan (St Mary's Coll), D. Corkery (Bristol), V. Costello (St Mary's Coll), A. Foley (Shannon), D. O'Cuinnegain (Sale), D. Wallace (Garryowen), A. Ward (Ballynahinch), D. Clohessy* (Young Munster).
*Joined tour as replacement

Manager D. Lenihan, Coach W. Gatland, Assistant Coach P. Danaher.

Beat Boland (Wellington) 30 May 48-35
Lost to South West Districts (George) 3 June 20-27
Lost to Western Province (Cape Town) 6 June 6-12
Lost to Griqualand West (Kimberley) 13-52
Lost to South Africa (Bloemfontein) 13 June 13-37
Beat North West (Potchefstroom) 16 June 26-18
Lost to South Africa (Pretoria) 0-33

Tour Record: P7 W2 D0 L5 F126 A214

Australia May–June 1999

D. O'Cuinneagain (Sale) Capt., C. O'Shea (London Irish) Vice Captain, J. Bishop (London Irish), G. Dempsey (Terenure Coll), M. Mostyn (Beglea-Bordeaux), K. Maggs (Bath), M. Mullins (West Hartlepool), B. O'Driscoll (UCD), J. Bell (Dungannon), D. Humphreys (Dunganon), E. Elwood (Galwegians), J. Staunton (Garryowen), T. Tierney (Garryowen), C. Scally (UCD), P. Clohessy (Young Munster), P. Wallace (Saracens), R. Corrigan (Lansdowne), J. Fitzpatrick (Dungannon), K. Wood (Harlequins), R. Nesdale (Newcastle), P. Johns (Sacarcens), J. Davidson (Castres), M. O'Kelly (London Irish), R. Casey (Blackrock Coll), T. Brennan (St Mary's Coll), D. Corkery (Cork Con), A. Ward (Ballynahinch), V. Costello (St Mary's Coll)

Manager D. Lenihan, Coach W. Gatland, Assistant Coach P. Danaher, Fitness Advisor C. White, Technical Officer

S. Aboud, Medical Officer Dr D. O'Shaughnessy, Physiotherapist Miss D. Fanagan, Masseur W. Bennett, Baggage Master P. O'Reilly, Media Officer J. Redmond

Beat New South Wales Country (Woy Woy, Gosford) 31 May 43-6
Lost to New South Wales (Sydney) 5 June 24-39
Lost to Australia (Ballymore, Brisbane) 12 June 10-46
Lost to Australia (Subiaco, Perth) 19 June 26-32

Development Tour South Africa, Namibia and Zimbabwe July–August 1993

BACKS:
C.P. Clarke (Terenure Coll), C.M.P O'Shea (Lansdowne), A. White (St Mary's Coll), I. Gray (Queen's U), N.K.P. Woods (Blackrock Coll), M. Corcoran (London Irish), B. Glennon (Lansdowne), B. Walsh (Cork Con), D. Dooley (Saracens), M.C. McCall (Bangor), P.A. Burke (London Irish), D.G. Humphreys (Queen's U), A. Matchett (Ballymena), N. Hogan (Terenure Coll).

FORWARDS:
P. Soden (Cork Con), H.D. Hurley (Old Wesley), A. McKeen (Lansdowne), P.S. Wallace (Blackrock Coll), A. Adair (Instonians), W. Mulcahy (Skerries), G.M. Fulcher (Cork Con), G. Longwell (Queen's U), B. Cusack (Bective Rangers), E. O'Sullivan (Old Crescent), K. Potts (St Mary's Coll) Capt., P. Hogan (Garryowen), L. Toland (Old Crescent), K. McKee (Instonians), W. Cronin (Garryowen), R. Wilson (Instonians).

Manager N.A. Murphy, Coach G. Murphy, Assistant Coaches H. Williams, D. Haslett, Physiotherapist Denise Fanagan.

Beat Mashonaland 21 July 22-10
Beat Zimbabwe 24 July 20-6
Beat Namibia B 28 July 38-21
Lost to Namibia A 31 July 19-33
Beat SA Central Provinces Development XV 4 Aug 53-15
Beat SA Rural Provinces Development XV 7 Aug 23-18
Beat SA Development Team 11 Aug 44-0

Tour Record: P7 W6 D0 L1 F219 A103

Ireland A: Development Tour to New Zealand and Western Samoa May–June 1997

BACKS:
J. Bishop (London Irish), C. Clarke (Terenure Coll), D. Coleman (Terenure Coll), M. Dillon (Lansdowne), R. Governey (Lansdowne), R.A. Henderson (Wasps), D. Humphreys (London Irish), M. Lynch (Young Munster), K. Maggs (Bristol), A. Matchett (Ballymena), A. McGrath (Shannon), S.C. McIvor (Garryowen), B. O'Meara (Cork Con), C.M.P. O'Shea (London Irish), N.K.P. Woods (London Irish).

FORWARDS:
B. Cusack (Bath), K. Dawson (London Irish), D. Macartney (Ballymena), D. Erskine (Sale), J. Fitzpatrick (London Irish), A.G. Foley (Shannon), G. Fulcher (London Irish), G. Halpin (London Irish) Capt., E.O. Halvey (Shannon), B. McConnell (Bristol), D. Molloy (Wasps), S. Byrne (Blackrock Coll), M. O'Kelly (London Irish), S. Ritchie (Ballymena), R. Sherriff (Shannon), D. Wallace (Garryowen), G. Walsh (Garryowen).

Manager P.C. Whelan, Coach B. Ashton, Assistant Coach D. Haslett, Medical Officer Dr D. O'Shaughnessy, Physiotherapist Denise Fanagan, Masseur W. Bennett, Fitness Adviser A. Clarke, Baggage Master P. O'Reilly.

Lost to Northland (Whangarei) 22 May 16-69
Lost to NZ Academy (Auckland) 26 May 15-74
Lost to Bay of Plenty (Rotorua) 29 May 39-52
Beat Thames Valley (Paeroa) 1 June 38-12
Lost to King Country (Tampo) 6 June 26-32
Lost to NZ Maoris (Palmerston North) 10-41
Lost to Western Samoa (Apia) 14 June 25-57

Tour Record: P7 W1 D0 L6 F169 A337

Ireland Under 21 Tour: Italy September–October 1989

R. Saunders (Queen's U) Capt., I. Gallagher (Collegians), B. Keary (Cork Con), D. Lynagh (Terenure Coll), D.J. Clarke (Dolphin), W. Kearns (London Irish), E.P. Elwood (Galwegians), A. White (Corinthians), J. Harley (Queen's U), G. Lavin (St Mary's Coll), A. Matchett (Portadown), P. Soden (Cork Con), B. Browne (UCD), A. McKean (Lansdowne), D. Bursey (Old Wesley), M. O'Loughlin (Wanderers), K. O'Connell (Sunday's Well), K. Gallick

(Queen's U), R. Finegan (UCD), K. O'Sullivan (Curragh), V.C.P. Costello (Blackrock Coll), B. Barrett (CIYMS), A. Adair (Manchester U).

Manager N.A. Murphy, Coach J.J. Moloney, Assistant Coach C.F. Fitzgerald, Medical Officer Dr D. O'Shaughnessy.

Beat Italian Selection (Arezzo) 34-6
Beat Italy Under 21 (Treviso) 19–9

Tour Record: P2 W2 D0 L0 F53 A15

Under 21 to France November 1998

P. Bracken (Bohemians), D. Broughall (UCD), J. Campbell (Terenure Coll), K. Campbell (London Irish), R. Casey (Blackrock Coll), T. Creegan (Shannon), L. Cullen (Blackrock Coll), B. Cunningham (Bective Rangers), J. Davis (Dungannon), D. Dillon (UCD), A. Dunne (UCD), J. Ferris (Leicester), K. Flanagan (Corinthians), J. Fogarty (Cork Con), K. Hartigan (Garryowen), D. Holt (UCC), M. Horan (Shannon), A. Kearney (UCD), S. Kennedy (Richmond), S. Keogh (Old Belvedere), G. McCullough (Instonians), M. McHugh (Dublin U), S. Moore (UCD, G. Murphy (Leicester), P. Neville (Old Crescent), M. O'Driscoll (UCC), D. O'Callaghan (Cork Con), M. Price (Pontypridd), D. Quinn (Terenure Coll), P. Shields (Instonians), P. Smyth (St Mary's Coll), J. Staunton (Garryowen), P. Stringer (UCC), M. Swift (Richmond), R. Woods (Dublin U).

Manager P. Rainey, Coaches G. Murphy and B. McLaughlin, Medical Officer Dr W. Rainey, Physiotherapist Mary Walsh.

Team A lost to French Selection (Toulouse) 20 November 17–22
Team B lost to French Selection (Toulouse) 20 November 16–20

Tour Record: P2 W0 D0 L2 F33 A42

Ireland Schools Tour to Australia August 1980

G. McMahon (Blackrock Coll) Capt., N. Farren (CBS Monkstown), C. O'Callaghan (CBC Cork), J. Garvey (Blackrock Coll), M. Harvey (Portora Royal), D. Larmour (Bangor GS), P. Russell (RBAI), M. Bradley (PBC Cork), C. McCarthy (Castleknock Coll), P. McIlroy (BRA), D. Barry (St Munchin's Coll), P. Madden (CBC Cork), C. Beverland (Campbell Coll), W. Burns (PBC Birr Community Coll), B. Kennelly (De La Salle Churchtown), J. McGuire (Blackrock Coll), S. Hutton (Belfast HS), P. Horner (Campbell Coll), D. Gaston (Dalriada), B. Waldron (St Michael's Coll), C. Cremin (CBC Cork), N. Kearney (De La Salle Churchtown), R. Kennedy (Campbell Coll), I. Duffy (St Gerard's), B. Hoey (De La Salle Churchtown), E. Brett* (Sligo Grammar).
* Joined tour as replacement

Manager R. Loughead, Coach C.C. Powell, Assistant to Manager Br P.F. O'Reilly, Hon. Medical Officer Dr D. Ivers.

Beat Northern Territory (Darwin) 3 August 37-0
Beat Queensland (Brisbane) 6 August 15-10
Beat NSW Combined High Schools (Oval, Sydney) 10 August 22-19
Lost to ACT (Manuka Oval, Canberra) 13 August 6-7
Beat NSW Combined Associated Schools (Chatswood Oval, Sydney) 16 August 19-13
Lost to NSW (Eastwood, Sydney) 19 August 13-25
Beat NSW Country Schools (Singleton) 23 August 24-0
Beat Victoria (Melbourne) 27 August 32-0
Lost to Australia (Sports Ground, Sydney) 31 August 7-10

Tour Record: P9 W6 D0 L3 F175 A84

Ireland Schools Tour to Australia August–September 1987

N. Barry (Crescent Comp) Capt., I. Gallagher (Methodist Coll), A. White (St Joseph's Coll Garbally), J. Harley (Portora Royal), M. Boyd (Ballymena Academy), G. Murphy (PBC Cork), M. Wilson (Belfast HS), R. Moloney (PBC Cork), G. Ellis (Bangor GS), D. Lynagh (Terenure Coll), R. Saunders (BRA), S. Tracey (St Mary's Coll), J. Lennon (Blackrock Coll), S. Toomey (St Munchin's Coll), A. McKeen (The King's Hospital), P. Byrne (PBC Bray), A. Adair (RBAI), M. Foley (The High School), E. O'Sullivan (Crescent Comp), B. Dean (Coleraine AI), G. Fulcher (Rockwell Coll), K. O'Connell (PBC Cork), D. Todd (RBAI), F. Kenny (Blackrock Coll), R. Finegan (Clongowes Wood Coll), D. Maccartney (Cambridge House), M. Niblock* (Carrickfergus GS)

Manager Noel Turley, Coach D.A. Haslett, Assistant to Manager N. Carpenter, Medical Officer Dr D. O'Shaughnessy.

Beat NSW Combined High Schools (North Sydney Oval) 1 August 12-6
Beat NSW Country Schools (Armidale) 5 August 14-0

Beat Queensland Sec Schools (Ballymore, Brisbane) 8 August 40-0
Beat Queensland (Brisbane) 11 August 8-4
Beat NSW Country W. Zone (Narrabri) 16 August 20-0
Beat ACT (Canberra) 19 August 18-6
Beat NSW (Concord Oval, Sydney) 23 August 12-6
Beat Central Coast (Graham Pk, Gosford) 26 August 41-6
Beat Combined Colls (Oakhill Coll) 29 August 26-3
Beat Australia Div 2 (Shoalhaven) 2 September 18-11
Lost to Australia (Concord Oval, Sydney) 6 September 11-20

Tour Record: P11 W10 D0 L1 F220 A62

Ireland Schools Tour to New Zealand July–August 1992

J. Blayney (Terenure Coll) Capt., B. Begley (Crescent Comp), J. Bell (Coleraine AI), D. Blewitt (Regent House GS), C. Boyd (RBAI), D. Callaghan (Coleraine AI), R. Coveney (Clongowes Wood Coll), R. Cranfield (Blackrock Coll), N. Crowley (Crescent Comp), I. Cummins (PBC Cork), J. Davidson (Methodist Coll), C. Davis (BRA), G. Davis (BRA), A. Foley (St Munchin's Coll), D. De Gascun (Terenure Coll), K. Hilman (RBAI), R. Kernohan (Ballymena Academy), C. McGuinness (St Mary's Coll), D. Moore (Blackrock Coll), J. O'Carroll (Cistercian Coll Roscrea), W. O'Kelly (St Paul's Coll), J. Patterson (Royal School Dungannon), J. Philpott (Belvedere Coll), A. Redpath (Coleraine AI), B. Sheehan (CBC Cork), J. Simon (BRA).

Manager Fr N. Redmond, Coach D. Kidney, Assistant to Manager K. Patton, Medical Officer Dr O. Fogarty.

Beat Southland (Invercargill) 1 August 19-12
Beat Canterbury (Rugby Park, Canterbury) 5 August 26-15
Beat Sheddon Shields (Lansdowne Park, Blenheim) 8 August 18-8
Lost to Hawkes Bay (McLean Pk, Napier) 12 August 23-25
Beat Tairawhite (Rugby Pk, Gisborne) 15 August 30-11
Beat Bay of Plenty (Rotorua) 19 August 40-12
Beat Wellington (Athletic Pk, Wellington) 22 August 57-19
Beat Horowhenua (Levin Pk, Domain) 34-25
Lost to New Zealand (Rugby Pk, New Plymouth) 29 August 25-27

Tour Record: P9 W7 D0 L2 F272 A154

Ireland Schools Tour to Australia July–August 1996

B. Gibney (Blackrock Coll) Capt., S. Best (Portadown Coll), P. Bracken (St Andrew's Coll), T. Cahill (PBC Cork), J. Campbell (Terenure Coll), R. Casey (Blackrock Coll), K. Coleman (Terenure Coll), R. Collins (CBC Cork), L. Cullen (Blackrock Coll), B. Cunningham (Bangor GS), J. David (Belfast HS), C. Dowling (PBC Bray), J. Fogarty (Rockwell Coll), K. Hartigan (St Munchin's Coll), D. Johnson (Blackrock Coll), T. Keating (Blackrock Coll), S. Kennedy (Regent House GS), S. McConnell (Coleraine AI), R. O'Donovan (CBC Cork), B. O'Mahony (CBC Cork), D. Quinlan (Blackrock Coll), C. Scally (Blackrock Coll), P. Smyth (Blackrock Coll), P. Stringer (PBC Cork), E. Travers (Terenure Coll), R. Woods (Blackrock Coll).

Manager G. Kelly, Coach K. Patton, Assistant to Coach-Manager J. McClean, Medical Officer Dr O. Fogarty, Physiotherapist G. Callaghan.

Beat Western Australia Under 19 (Perry Lakes Stadium, Perth) 28 July 15-7
Beat Western Australian Schools (Associates RFC, Perth) 31 July 56-0
Beat South Australian Schools (Brighton RFC, Adelaide) 3 August 92-3
Beat NSW Schools (North Sydney Oval) 7 August 29-15
Beat NSW Combined High Schools (Warathah Stadium, Sydney) 11 August 18-7
Beat ACT Schools (Manuka Oval, Canberra) 14 August 47-17
Beat Victoria Schools (Scotch Coll, Melbourne) 21 August 51-0
Beat NSW Country Schools (Connolly Park, Wagga) 24 August 54-0
Beat Australian Schools (Manuka Oval, Canberra) 28 August 23-21

Tour Record: P9 W9 D0 L0 F385 A70

APPENDIX 20

IRELAND STUDENTS INTERNATIONALS: TEAMS AND RESULTS

v USA Eagles (Thomond Park) 6 March 1990

F. O'Beirn (UCG); J. Harley (Queen's U), B. Glennon (UCD), S. Tormey (Old Belvedere and COMAD), S. Geoghegan (London Irish and London U); N. Barry (Garryowen and Waterford RTC), R. Saunders (Queen's U); R. Ward (Dublin U), P. Kenny (Dublin U), C. O'Brien (Dublin U), P. Johns (Dublin U), J. O'Callaghan (Cambridge U), M. Egan (Oxford U) Capt., K. Gallick (Queen's U), K. Devlin (Old Belvedere and DCU)
Rep: D. Lynagh (Dublin U) for O'Beirn

Irish Students 19 USA 18

v Argentina (Mardyke) 23 October 1990

A. Hewitt (Queen's U); N. Furlong (UCG), B. Glennon (UCD and Lansdowne) Capt., S. Tormey (Old Belvedere and COMAD), D. O'Dowd (Cork Con and Cork School of Commerce); N. Barry (Garryowen and Waterford RTC), S. McIvor (UCD); R. Ward (Dublin U and Blackrock Coll), P. Kenny (Dublin U and Blackrock Coll), G. Leslie (Queen's U), M. O'Driscoll (UCC), J. O'Callaghan (Cambridge U), D. Sheehan (Dublin U), B. Cronin (Waterpark and Waterford RTC), K. Devlin (Old Belvedere and DCU)

Irish Students 6 Argentina 23

v Scottish Students (Edinburgh) 15 March 1991

C. Haly (Oxford U); J. Harley (Queen's U), R. Moloney (Oxford U), A. Burns (UCC and Dungannon), D. Liddy (UCD); N. Barry (Waterford RTC and Garryowen), A. Matchett (UUJ and Portadown); B. Hyland (UUJ and NIFC), M. Patton (Cardiff U and Bangor), F. Griffin (Cambridge U), P. Johns (Dublin U), T. Casey (Bolton St Coll of Technology and Wanderers), S. Rooney (UCD), M. Egan (Oxford U and Terenure Coll) Capt., D. O'Flaherty (UCD)

Scottish Students 16 Irish Students 12

v Scottish Students (Sydney Parade) 14 February 1992

C. Haly (UCC) Capt.; J. Harley (Queen's U), M. Ridge (Stillorgan Business Coll), R. Moloney (Oxford U), N. Woods (Coll of Commerce Rathmines); D. O'Mahony (UCC), A. Matchett (UUJ); L. Murphy (UCC), S. Ritchie (Queen's U), G. Leslie (Queen's U), G. Fulcher (UCD), G. Longwell (Queen's U), D. Macartney (UUC), B. O'Mahony (UCC), L. Toland (Army Cadet Coll)

Irish Students 21 Scottish Students 20

v English Students (Waterloo RFC) 16 April 1992

C. O'Shea (UCD); N. Furlong (UCG), S. Burns (St Mary's Coll Twickenham), A. Burns (UUC), R. Hennessy (St Mary's Coll Twickenham); D. O'Mahony (UCC) A. Matchett (UUJ); J. Horan (Dublin U), M. Patton (Oxford U) Capt., G. Leslie (Queen's U), J. O'Callaghan (King's Inns), G. Duffy (Dublin U), D. Macartney (UUC), P. Johns (Dublin U), D. O'Sullivan (Garda Training Coll).
Reps: R. Finegan (UCD) for Macartney, A. Donovan (UCD) for Patton

English Students 28 Irish Students 19

STUDENTS WORLD CUP, ITALY, JULY 1992

v German Students (Rovigo) 2 July 1992

C. O'Shea (UCD); N. Assaf (UCD), S. Burns (St Mary's Coll Twickenham), D. Lynagh (Paris U), D. Hernan (UCD); N. Malone (Loughborough U), A. Matchett (UUJ); L. Murphy (UCC), M. Patton (Oxford U) Capt., P. Wallace (UCC), G. Fulcher (UCD), J. O'Callaghan (King's Inns), D. Macartney (UCC), B. O'Mahony (UCC), D. O'Sullivan (Garda Training Coll)
Rep: S. Rooney (UCD) for O'Mahony

Irish Students 74 German Students 3

v CIS Students (Padua) 5 July 1992

C. O'Shea (UCD); N. Assaf (UCD), S. Burns (St Mary's Coll Twickenham), D. O'Mahony (UCC), C. Haly (UCC); N. Malone (Loughborough U), A. Matchett (UUJ); L. Murphy (UCC), M. Patton (Oxford U) Capt., P. Wallace (UCC), G. Fulcher (UCD), J. O'Callaghan (King's Inns), S. Rooney (UCD), D. O'Sullivan (Garda Training Coll), D. Macartney (UUC)

Irish Students 35 CIS Students 16

v Italian Students (Rovigo) 8 July 1992

C. O'Shea (UCD); N. Assaf (UCD), S. Burns (St Mary's Coll Twickenham), D. O'Mahony (UCC), C. Haly (UCC); N. Malone (Loughborough U), A. Matchett (UUJ); L. Murphy (UCC), M. Patton (Oxford U) Capt., P. Wallace (UCC), G. Fulcher (UCD), J. O'Callaghan (King's Inns), S. Rooney (UCD), D. Macartney (UUC), R. Finegan (UCD).
Rep: R. Hennessy (St Mary's Coll Twickenham) for O'Shea

Irish Students 6 Italian Students 17

v New Zealand Students (Cagliari, Sardinia) 12 July 1992

C. Haly (UCC); N. Assaf (UCD), S. Burns (St Mary's Coll Twickenham), D. Lynagh (Paris U), R. Hennessy (St Mary's Coll Twickenham); N. Malone (Loughborough U), N. Hogan (RCSI); L. Murphy (UCC), M. Patton (Oxford U) Capt., P. Wallace (UCC), G. Fulcher (UCD), J. O'Callaghan (King's Inns), D. Macartney (UUC), B. O'Mahony (UCC), D. O'Sullivan (Garda Training Coll)

Irish Students 9 New Zealand Students 53

v Scottish Students (Edinburgh) 15 January 1993

C. Haly (UCC); R. Hennessy (St Mary's Coll Twickenham), J. Clarke (Cork RTC), D. O'Mahony (Oxford U), N. Woods (Dublin U); P. Burke (Loughborough U), N. Hogan (RCSI) Capt.; D. Coen (UCD), A. Adair (Queen's U), L. Mooney (Cardiff U), T. Casey (Bolton Street TC), J. O'Callaghan (King's Inns), B. Toland (UCD), B. O'Mahony (Oxford U), K. McKee (Belfast Institute)
Reps: T. Howe (St Andrew's U) for Hennessy, D. O'Sullivan (Garda Training Coll) for O'Mahony

Scottish Students 13 Irish Students 49

v English Students (Anglesea Road) 19 March 1993

C. Haly (UCC); R. Hennessy (St Mary's Coll Twickenham), S. Burns (St Mary's Coll Twickenham), D. O'Mahony (Oxford U), P. Burke (Loughborough U); B. Murphy (Dublin U), L. Murphy (UCC); M. Patton (Oxford U) Capt., P. Wallace (UCC), G. Longwell (Queen's U), J. O'Callaghan (King's Inns), S. Rooney (UCD), B. O'Mahony (Oxford U), K. McKee (Belfast Institute)

Irish Students 19 English Students 6

v English Students (Bournemouth) 18 February 1994

H. Carolan (Maynooth Coll); I. Gray (Queen's U), L. Boyle (Oxford U), S. Burns (West London Institute), R. Hennessy (St Mary's Coll Twickenham); P. Burke (Loughborough U), B. Murphy (Dublin U); L. Mooney (Cardiff U), A. Adair (Queen's U) Capt., J. O'Driscoll (UCC), G. Longwell (Queen's U), K. Murphy (Cork RTC), N. Taylor (Galway RTC), A. Foley (Mid West Business Coll), J. Patterson (UUJ)
Rep: M. Coughlan (Limerick RTC) for Longwell

English Students 23 Irish Students 9

v English Students (Portlaoise) 20 January 1995

R. Hennessy (West London Institute); I. Gray (Oxford U), S. Tynan (Dublin U), J. Clarke (Cork RTC) Capt., D. Crotty (UCC); O. Cobbe (St Mary's Coll Twickenham), N. Assaf (UCD); L. Mooney (Cambridge U), A. Adair (Queen's U), J. O'Driscoll (UCC), M. Coughlan (Limerick RTC), P. Coveney (Oxford U), M. Dobson (Chester Coll of Law), L. Toland (UCG), K. Spicer (UCD)

Irish Students 3 English Students 40

v French Students (Longford) 3 March 1995

R. Hennessy (West London Institute); S. Madigan (U of Limerick), J. Clarke (Cork RTC) Capt., A. Reddan (U of Limerick), D. O'Mahony (UCD); O. Cobbe (St Mary's Coll Twickenham), N. Assaf (UCD); J. Maher (Athlone RTC), R. Kernohan (Queen's U), J. O'Driscoll (UCC), J. Davidson (UUC), M. O'Kelly (Dublin U), K. Spicer (UCD), E. Miller (Waterford RTC), R. Wilson (Queen's U)

Irish Students 18 French Students 20

v Natal Duikers (Mardyke) 4 November 1995

D. Crotty (UCC); J. Topping (Ballymena), A. Reddan (Lansdowne), R. McIlreavy (Dublin U), J. Cunningham (Dublin U); J. Philpott (Old Belvedere), B. Murphy (Old Belvedere) Capt.; I. Cummins (Sunday's Well), P. Curry (Dungannon), P. Flavin (Blackrock Coll), J. Ryan (UCD), K. Walker (UCD), M. Dobson (Sale), R. Wilson (Instonians), F. Twomey (UCC)
Rep: R. West (UUC) for Walker

Irish Students 8 Natal Duikers 12

v French Students (Clermont Ferrand) 16 February 1996

S. Mason (Orrell); D. Crotty (UCC), A. Reddan (Lansdowne), R. McIlreavy (Dublin U), D. O'Mahony (Lansdowne); F. Campion (St Mary's Coll), B. Murphy (Old Belvedere) Capt.; I. Cummins (Sunday's Well), S. Byrne (Blackrock Coll), P. Flavin (Blackrock Coll), G. Webster (Northampton), M. O'Kelly (St Mary's Coll), A. Foley (Shannon), R. Wilson (Instonians), K. Dawson (Bangor)
Reps: P. Curry (Dungannon) for Byrne, A. Thompson (Limerick RTC) for Cobbe (temp)

French Students 42 Irish Students 11

v English Students (Oxford) 15 March 1996

D. Crotty (UCC); D. O'Mahony (Lansdowne), A. Reddan (Lansdowne), R. McIlreavy (Dublin U), J. Cunningham (Dublin U); O. Cobbe (London Irish), R. Saverimutto (Waterloo); B. McConnell (Bristol U), P. Curry (Dungannon), C. Boyd (Currie), G. Webster (Northampton), C. Simpson (Cambridge U), M. Dobson (Sale), K. Spicer (UCD) Capt.
Rep: N. Carolan (Galway RTC) for Reddan

Irish Students 24 English Students 19

STUDENTS WORLD CUP, SOUTH AFRICA, JUNE—JULY 1997

v Welsh Students (Johannesburg) 29 June 1997

S. Mason (Leeds Metropolitan); J. Topping (Queen's U), A. Reddan (U of Limerick), R. McIlreavy (Dublin U), D. O'Mahony (UCD); F. Campion (Account and Bus Coll Dublin), B. Murphy (Griffith Coll); B. McConnell (Bristol U), P. Curry (UUJ), C. Boyd (Edinburgh U), M. O'Kelly (Dublin U), G. Webster (Loughborough U), K. Spicer (UCD) Capt., A. Foley (Mid West Bus Coll), K. Dawson (Queen's U)
Reps: D. Crotty (UCC) for Topping, E. Cobbe (St Mary's Coll Twickenham) for Campion, C. Simpson (Cambridge U) for Webster, L. Toland (UCG) for Dawson

Irish Students 27 Welsh Students 34

v Argentinian Students (Johannesburg) 5 July 1997

S. Mason (Leeds Met); J. Topping (Queen's U), D. Crotty (UCC), A. Reddan (U of Limerick), D. O'Mahony (UCD); D. Humphreys (Queen's U), R. Saverimutto (Leeds Met); B. McConnell (Bristol U), P. Curry (UUJ), C. Boyd (Edinburgh U), M. O'Kelly (Dublin U), C. Simpson (Cambridge U), K. Spicer (UCD) Capt., A. Foley (Mid West Bus Coll), L. Toland (UCG)
Reps: J. Maher (Athlone RTC) for McConnell, R. Weir (Queen's U) for Curry, J. O'Driscoll (UCC) for Boyd, M. Dobson (Chester Coll of Law) for Simpson

Irish Students 37 Argentinian Students 53

v English Students (Johannesburg) 10 July 1997

S. Mason (Leeds Met); J. Topping (Queen's U), R. McIlreavy (Dublin U), A. Thompson (Limerick RTC), D. O'Mahony (UCD); O. Cobbe (St Mary's Coll Twickenham), R. Saverimutto (Leeds Met); J. Maher (Athlone RTC), R. Weir (Queen's U), C. Boyd (Edinburgh U), M. O'Kelly (Dublin U), G. Webster (Loughborough U), K. Spicer (UCD) Capt., A. Foley (Mid West Bus Coll), L. Toland (UCG)
Reps: J. Cunningham (Dublin U) for Topping, D. Crotty (UCC) for Thompson, J. O'Driscoll (UCC) for Boyd, C. Simpson (Cambridge U) for Webster, M. Dobson (Chester Coll of Law) for Toland

Irish Students 26 English Students 21

v Uruguay Students (Pretoria) 12 July 1997

D. Crotty (UCC); J. Topping (Queen's U), R. McIlreavy (Dublin U), A. Reddan (U of Limerick), J. Cunningham (Dublin U); O. Cobbe (St Mary's Coll Twickenham), B. Murphy (Griffith Coll); J. Maher (Athlone RTC), R. Weir (Queen's U), J. O'Driscoll (UCC), G. Webster (Loughborough U), C. Simpson (Cambridge U), K. Spicer (UCD) Capt., A. Foley (Mid West Bus Coll), M. Dobson (Chester Coll of Law)

Irish Students 36 Uruguay Students 9

Ireland finished in ninth place

PRESIDENTS OF THE IRFU 1949–69

W.G. Fallon
1949–50

Air Vice–Marshall Sir
W.Tyrrell 1950–51

D.F. O'Connell
1951–52

V.E. Kirwan
1952–53

J.B. O'Callaghan
1953–54

C.J. Hanrahan
1954–55

H.M. Read
1955–56

Capt. J.R. Ramsey
1956–57

W.E. Crawford
1957–58

J.J. Glynn
1958–59

J.R. Wheeler
1959–60

N.F. Murphy
1960–61

L.B. McMahon
1961–62

J.A.E. Siggins
1962–63

T.A. O'Reilly
1963–64

C.C. Harte
1964–65

P.F. Murray
1965–66

D.G. O'Donovan
1966–67

E. O'D. Davy
1967–68

C.P. Crowley
1968–69

CAPTAINS OF IRELAND TEAMS 1956–91

N.J. Henderson
1956–57

A.R. Dawson
1958–59

A.A. Mulligan
1959–60

W.A. Mulcahy
1961–62

T.J. Kiernan
1962–63

J.C. Kelly
1963–64

R.J. McLoughlin
1964–65

N.A. Murphy
1966–67

M.C.H. Gibson
1970–71

W.J. McBride
1972–73

T.O. Grace
1975–76

J.J. Moloney
1977–78

S.M. Deering
1977–78

J.F. Slattery
1978–79

C.F. Fitzgerald
1981–82

W.P. Duggan
1983–84

D. Lenihan
1986–87

P. Mathews
1988–90

W. Anderson
1989–90

R. Saunders
1990–91

APPENDIX 21

IRELAND UNDER 21 INTERNATIONALS: TEAMS AND RESULTS

v Italy (Lansdowne Road) 24 September 1988

C. Haly (UCC) Capt.; J. Carroll (UCC), D. Lynagh (Terenure Coll), R. McLean (CIYMS), G. Copeland (Ards); N. Barry (Garryowen), B. McGoey (Wanderers); S. Booth (Ballymena), A. Clarke (Dungannon), F. Griffin (UCD), P. Johns (Dungannon), J. O'Callaghan (UCD), J. Dempsey (UCD), P. Hogan (Garryowen), A. Doyle (Blackrock Coll).
Rep: I. Gallagher (Collegians) for Carroll

Ireland 22 Italy 13

v Italy (Treviso) 30 September 1989

A. White (Corinthians); J. Harley (Queen's U), D. Lynagh (Terenure Coll), J. Clarke (Dolphin), W. Kearns (London Irish); E. Elwood (Galwegians), R. Saunders (Queen's U) Capt.; B. Barrett (CIYMS), A. Adair (Manchester U), A. McKean (Lansdowne), E. O'Sullivan (Old Crescent), D. Bursey (Old Wesley), K. O'Connell (Sunday's Well), K. Gallick (Queen's U), R. Finegan (UCD).
Reps: I. Gallagher (Collegians) for White, B. Browne (UCD) for Adair, V. Costello (Blackrock Coll) for O'Sullivan

Ireland 10 Italy 9

v New Zealand Rugby News (Donnybrook) 19 November 1989

A. White (Corinthians); J. Harley (Queen's U), R. Moloney (UCC), J. Clarke (Dolphin), W. Kearns (London Irish); N. Barry (Garryowen), A. Matchett (Portadown); P. Soden (Cork Con), B. Browne (UCD), A. McKean (Lansdowne), E. O'Sullivan (Old Crescent), D. Bursey (Old Wesley), K. O'Connell (Sunday's Well) Capt., K. Gallick (Queen's U), R. Finegan (UCD).
Rep: D. Lynagh (Terenure Coll) for Moloney

Ireland 13 New Zealand 13

v Netherlands (Leiden) 21 September 1990

C. O'Shea (Lansdowne); D. Hernan (UCD), J. Russell (Instonians), N. Murray (Cork Con), R. Hennessy (Lansdowne); N. Malone (Loughborough U), N. Hogan (Terenure Coll); P. Soden (Cork Con), M. Patton (Cardiff U and Bangor) Capt., A. Stewart (Portadown), E. O'Sullivan (Old Crescent), G. Fulcher (UCD), S. Rooney (UCD), B. O'Mahony (UCC), K. McKee (CIYMS).

Netherlands 21 Ireland 7

v England (Moseley) 29 October 1990

C. O'Shea (Lansdowne); D. Hernan (UCD), J. Russell (Instonians), N. Murray (Cork Con), R. Hennessy (Lansdowne); N. Malone (Loughborough U), D. Tobin (Young Munster); P. Soden (Cork Con), M. Patton (Bangor) Capt., S. Tonge (Wanderers), E. O'Sullivan (Old Crescent), G. Fulcher (UCD), S. Rooney (UCD), B. O'Mahony (UCC), K. McKee (CIYMS).

England 16 Ireland 22

v Wales (Newport) 16 October 1991

C. O'Shea (Lansdowne); G. McCluskey (Portadown), M. Ridge (Blackrock Coll), G. Lavin (St Mary's Coll), N. Woods (Blackrock Coll); N. Malone (Loughborough U), N. Hogan (Terenure Coll) Capt.; L. Murphy (UCC), M. McDermott (Blackrock Coll), P. Wallace (UCC), U. O'Callaghan (Highfield), G. Longwell (Queen's U), P. Scott (Dolphin), R. Wilson (Instonians), L. Toland (Old Crescent).

Wales 22 Ireland 15

v England (Donnybrook) 23 October 1991

C. O'Shea (Lansdowne); W. O'Shea (Shannon), M. Ridge (Blackrock Coll), R. Hunter (Loughborough U), N. Woods (Blackrock Coll); N. Malone (Loughborough U), N. Hogan (Terenure Coll) Capt.; L. Murphy (UCC), M. McDermott (Blackrock Coll), P. Wallace (UCC), V. Costello (Blackrock Coll), G. Longwell (Queen's U), S. Rooney (UCD), R. Wilson (Instonians), L. Toland (Old Crescent).
Reps: S. McDowell (Dungannon) for O'Shea, M. Kernohan (Glasgow U) for McDermott

Ireland 19 England 10

v England (Newcastle) 14 October 1992

I. Gray (Queen's U); D. Hernan (St Mary's Coll), R. Hunter (Northampton), S. Tynan (Terenure Coll), G. McCluskey (Portadown); A. McGowan (Blackrock Coll), N. Assaf (Blackrock Coll); M. Carroll (Old Belvedere), K. Wood (Garryowen), P. Wallace (UCC) Capt., G. Longwell (Queen's U), B. Cusack (Bective Rangers), N. Taylor (Old Crescent), L. Toland (Old Crescent), S. Kirkpatrick (Malone).
Rep: D. Sheehan (Shannon) for Hernan

England 39 Ireland 28

v Wales (Donnybrook) 28 October 1992

I. Gray (Queen's U); D. Sheehan (Shannon), R. Hunter (Northampton), S. Tynan (Terenure Coll), G. McCluskey (Portadown); A. McGowan (Blackrock Coll), N. Assaf (Blackrock Coll); M. Carroll (Old Belvedere), S. Byrne (Blackrock Coll), P. Wallace (UCC) Capt., G. Longwell (Queen's U), B. Cusack (Bective Rangers), L. Toland (Old Crescent), R. Wilson (Instonians), D. Corkery (Cork Con).

Ireland 22 Wales 11

v Scotland (Murrayfield) 15 January 1993

H. Carolan (Blackrock Coll); I. Gray (Queen's U), R. Hunter (Northampton), S. Sexton (Greystones), N. Assaf (Blackrock Coll); D. Humphreys (Queen's U), B. Murphy (Old Belvedere); M. Carroll (Old Belvedere), S. Byrne (Blackrock Coll), P. Wallace (UCC) Capt., G. Longwell (Queen's U), B. Cusack (Bective Rangers), L. Toland (Old Crescent), R. Wilson (Instonians), D. Corkery (Cork Con).

Scotland 3 Ireland 18

v New Zealand Rugby News Youths (Donnybrook) 26 October 1993

B. Begley (Old Crescent); I. Gray (Queen's U) Capt., R. Hunter (London Irish), J. Bell (Loughborough U), P. O'Brien (Blackrock Coll); P. Burke (London Irish), N. Assaf (Blackrock Coll); W. O'Kelly (Clontarf), K. Wood (Garryowen), J. Hickey (Shannon), B. Cusack (Bective Rangers), J. Davidson (Dungannon), M. Dobson (Salesians), A. Foley (Shannon), C. Davis (Loughborough U).
Temp. rep: O. Cobbe (London Irish) for Burke.
Rep: Cobbe for Begley

Ireland 6 New Zealand Youths 22

v England (Gateshead) 7 November 1994

J. Bell (Loughborough U); I. Gray (Queen's U) Capt., A. Reddan (Old Crescent), R. Hunter (London Irish), G. Davis (Salesians); P. Burke (London Irish), N. Assaf (Blackrock Coll); W. O'Kelly (Clontarf), N. Mullins (Bective Rangers), J. Hickey (Shannon), J. Davidson (Dungannon), B. Cusack (Bective Rangers), M. Dobson (Salesians), A. Foley (Shannon), L. Toland (Old Crescent).
Reps: D. Scott (NIFC) for Hickey, O. Cobbe (London Irish) for Burke

England 22 Ireland 15

v Wales (Carlow) 4 February 1994

B. Begley (Old Crescent); I. Gray (Queen's U) Capt., R. Hunter (London Irish), J. Bell (Loughborough U), R. Henderson (London Irish); O. Cobbe (London Irish), N. Assaf (Blackrock Coll); W. O'Kelly (Clontarf), R. Kernohan (Queen's U), J. Hickey (Shannon), J. Davidson (Dungannon), B. Cusack (Bective Rangers), M. Dobson (Salesians), A. Foley (Shannon), C. Davis (Loughborough U).

Ireland 5 Wales 27

v Scotland (Anglesea Road) 4 March 1994

J. Bell (Loughborough U); I. Gray (Queen's U) Capt., A. Reddan (Old Crescent), R. Henderson (London Irish), M. Kearin (Lansdowne); P. Burke (London Irish), N. Assaf (Blackrock Coll); W. O'Kelly (Clontarf), R. Kernohan (Queen's U), J. Hickey (Shannon), J. Davidson (Dungannon), B. Cusack (Bective Rangers), M. Dobson (Salesians), A. Foley (Shannon), D. Corkery (Cork Con).

Ireland 24 Scotland 6

v England (Ravenhill) 8 November 1994

S. Mason (Newcastle Gosforth); M. Dillon (Lansdowne), J. Bell (Ballymena), D. Blewitt (Queen's U), R. Kearns (Blackrock Coll); F. Campion (St Mary's Coll), R. Saverimutto (Waterloo); W. O'Kelly (Lansdowne), J. Blaney (Terenure Coll), C. Boyd (Currie), K. Spicer (UCD) Capt., J. Davidson (Dungannon), A. Foley (Shannon), C. McEntee (Greystones), K. Dawson (Bangor).

Ireland 12 England 8

v Scotland (Myreside, Edinburgh) 3 February 1995

S. Mason (Newcastle Gosforth); M. Dillon (Lansdowne), A. Thompson (Shannon), D. Blewitt (Queen's U), R. Kearns (Blackrock Coll); F. Campion (St Mary's Coll), R. Saverimutto (Waterloo); J. Hickey (Shannon), J. Blaney (Terenure Coll), C. Boyd (Currie), K. Spicer (UCD) Capt., J. Davidson (Dungannon), J. Patterson (Dungannon), C. McEntee (Greystones), K. Dawson (Bangor).

Ireland 24 Scotland 22

v Wales (Cardiff) 17 March 1995

B. Begley (Old Crescent); M. Dillon (Lansdowne), A. Thompson (Shannon), D. Blewitt (Queen's U), D. Hickie (UCD); F. Campion (St Mary's Coll), C. McGuinness (St Mary's Coll); W. O'Kelly (Lansdowne), J. Blaney (Terenure Coll), C. Boyd (Currie), J. Davidson (Dungannon), M. O'Kelly (St Mary's Coll), K. Spicer (UCD) Capt., E. Miller (Old Wesley), K. Dawson (Bangor).
Rep: T. Brennan (Bective Rangers) for O'Kelly

Wales 16 Ireland 9

v England (Northampton) 15 November 1995

D. Crotty (UCC); J. Topping (Ballymena), R. McIlreavy (Dublin U), J. Bishop (London Irish), J. Cunningham (Dublin U); F. Campion (St Mary's Coll), C. McGuinness (St Mary's Coll); B. McConnell (Bristol U), C. Egan (Terenure Coll), P. Coyle (UCD), T. McWhirter (Dundee HSFP) Capt., M. O'Kelly (St Mary's Coll), C. McEntee (Lansdowne), E. Miller (Old Wesley), K. Dawson (Bangor).
Rep: A. Bermingham (Garryowen) for Dawson

Ireland 23 England 10

v Scotland (Stradbrook) 19 January 1996

D. Crotty (UCC); N. Carolan (Corinthians), R. McIlreavy (Dublin U), J. Bishop (London Irish), J. Cunningham (Dublin U); F. Campion (St Mary's Coll), B. O'Meara (Cork Con); B. McConnell (Bristol U), C. Egan (Terenure Coll), G. Cully (Bangor), J. Ryan (UCD), T. McWhirter (Dundee HSFP) Capt., D. Evans (Orrell), C. McEntee (Lansdowne), K. Dawson (Bangor).

Ireland 21 Scotland 9

v Wales (Wicklow) 1 March 1996

D. Crotty (UCC); D. Hickie (St Mary's Coll), R. McIlreavy (Dublin U), J. Bishop (London Irish), J. Cunningham (Dublin U); F. Campion (St Mary's Coll), B. O'Meara (Cork Con); B. McConnell (Bristol U), C. Egan (Terenure Coll), G. Cully (Bangor), T. McWhirter (Dundee HSFP) Capt., A. Robinson (Ballymena), C. McEntee (Lansdowne), E. Miller (Leicester), K. Dawson (Bangor).

Ireland 20 Wales 12

v New Zealand Rugby News (Thomond Park) 17 November 1996

G. Dempsey (Terenure Coll); D. Hickie (St Mary's Coll), M. Smyth (Terenure Coll), E. Farrell (Blackrock Coll), A. Park (Blackheath); B. Everitt (Garryowen), S. Bell (Malone); B. McConnell (Bristol), F. Sheahan (UCC), L. Johnston (Ballynahinch), C. McEntee (Lansdowne) Capt., J. Fitzgerald (UCC), D. Wallace (Garryowen), J. Gardiner (Instonians), D. Watt (Ballymena).
Reps: R. Sheriff (Shannon) for Watt, K. Johnson (London Irish) for Dempsey, A. O'Shea (UCC) for Everitt

Ireland 12 New Zealand 6

v France (Anglesea Road) 17 January 1997

G. Dempsey (Terenure Coll); R. O'Neill (Bedford), G. Gannon (St Mary's Coll), M. Smyth (Terenure Coll), A. Park (Blackheath); E. Farrell (Blackrock Coll), S. Bell (Dungannon); B. McConnell (Bristol), F. Sheahan (UCC) Capt., L. Johnston (Ballynahinch), J. Gardiner (Instonians), J. Fitzgerald (UCC), D. Wallace (Garryowen), S. Easterby (Harrogate), D. Watt (Edinburgh U).
Reps: R. Governey (Lansdowne) for Farrell, R. Sheriff (Shannon) for Fitzgerald, E. McCormack (St Mary's Coll) for Bell

Ireland 13 France 40

v Wales (Bridgend) 31 January 1997

G. Dempsey (Terenure Coll); R. O'Neill (Bedford), S. Coulter (Ballymena), M. Smyth (Terenure Coll), A. Park (Blackheath); E. Farrell (Blackrock Coll), S. Bell (Dungannon); B. McConnell (Bristol), F. Sheahan (UCC) Capt., L. Johnston (Ballynahinch), R. Sheriff (Shannon), J. Fitzgerald (UCC), J. Gardiner (Instonians), S. Easterby (Harrogate), D. Wallace (Garryowen).
Reps: C. O'Kane (Heriot's FP) for Sheahan, A. O'Shea (UCC) for Smyth

Ireland 16 Wales 44

v England (Dr Hickey Park, Greystones) 14 February 1997

G. Dempsey (Terenure Coll); R. O'Neill (Bedford), S. Coulter (Ballymena), G. Gannon (St Mary's Coll), A. Horgan (Cork Con); R. Governey (Lansdowne), S. Bell (Dungannon) Capt.; B. McConnell (Bristol), C. O'Kane (Heriot's FP), L. Johnston (Ballynahinch), R. Sheriff (Shannon), J. Gardiner (Instonians), L. Cullen (Blackrock Coll), D. Wallace (Garryowen), D. Watt (Edinburgh U).
Reps: E. Farrell (Blackrock Coll) for Gannon, A. McSweeney (UCC) for Johnston, E. McCormack (St Mary's Coll) for Bell

Ireland 28 England 27

v Scotland (Myreside, Edinburgh) 28 February 1997

G. Dempsey (Terenure Coll); R. O'Neill (Bedford), S. Coulter (Ballymena), G. Gannon (St Mary's Coll), A. Park (Blackheath); R. O'Gara (Cork Con), S. Bell (Dungannon); B. McConnell (Bristol), F. Sheahan (UCC) Capt., L. Johnston (Ballynahinch), R. Sheriff (Shannon), J. Gardiner (Instonians), L. Cullen (Blackrock Coll), S. Easterby (Harrogate), D. Wallace (Garryowen).
Reps: E. Farrell (Blackrock Coll) for O'Neill, P. Coyle (St Mary's Coll) for Johnston, A. McSweeney (UCC) for McConnell

Ireland 31 Scotland 0

v Scotland (Castle Avenue, Clontarf) 6 February 1998

T. Keating (Blackrock Coll); M. McNamara (Lansdowne), S. Horgan (Lansdowne), C. Mahony (Dolphin), C. Kilroy (Garryowen); R. O'Gara (Cork Con), T. Tierney (Garryowen); M. Horan (Shannon), F. Sheahan (Cork Con), M. Cahill (Bohemians), J. Duffy (Galwegians), M. O'Driscoll (UCC), A. McCullen (Lansdowne), L. Cullen (Blackrock Coll) Capt., B. Gibney (Blackrock Coll).
Reps: D. Watt (Melrose) for McCullen, I. McLaughlin (London Irish) for Horan, S. McConnell (Currie) for Cahill

Ireland 23 Scotland 7

v France (La Roche sur Yon) 6 March 1998

T. Keating (Blackrock Coll); M. McNamara (Lansdowne), S. Horgan (Lansdowne), C. Mahony (Dolphin), G. McCullough (Instonians); B. Cunningham (Bective Rangers), T. Tierney (Garryowen); M. Horan (Shannon), F. Sheahan (Cork Con), M. Cahill (Bohemians), J. Duffy (Galwegians), M. O'Driscoll (UCC), D. Blaney (Terenure Coll), L. Cullen (Blackrock Coll) Capt., B. Gibney (Blackrock Coll).
Reps: S. Coulter (Ballymena) for McNamara, S. Spence (Newcastle) for Horan, P. Smyth (Blackrock Coll) for Sheahan, S. McConnell (Currie) for Cahill, D. Watt (Melrose) for Gibney

France 36 Ireland 28

v Wales (Donnybrook) 20 March 1998

T. Keating (Blackrock Coll); M. McNamara (Lansdowne), S. Horgan (Lansdowne), C. Mahony (Dolphin), G. McCullough (Instonians); B. Cunningham (Bective Rangers), T. Tierney (Garryowen); M. Horgan (Shannon), F. Sheahan (Cork Con), M. Cahill (Bohemians), M. O'Driscoll (UCC), J. Duffy (Galwegians), D. Blaney (Terenure Coll), L. Cullen (Blackrock Coll) Capt., D. Watt (Melrose).
Reps: A. McCullen (Lansdowne) for Watt, R. Ormond (St Mary's Coll) for Cunningham, I. McLaughlin (London Irish) for Cahill

Ireland 27 Wales 25

v England (Richmond, London) 3 April 1998

T. Keating (Blackrock Coll); S. Coulter (Ballymena), S. Horgan (Lansdowne), C. Mahony (Dolphin), G. McCullough (Instonians); R. O'Gara (Cork Con), T. Tierney (Garryowen); M. Horan (Shannon), F. Sheahan (Cork Con), M. Cahill (Bohemians), M. O'Driscoll (UCC), J. Duffy (Galwegians), A. McCullen (Lansdowne), L. Cullen (Blackrock Coll) Capt., D. Wallace (Garryowen).
Rep: S. McConnell (Currie) for Cahill

England 7 Ireland 9

v France (Musgrave Park) 5 February 1999

G. Murphy (Leicester); D. Quinlan (Blackrock Coll), K. Hartigan (Garryowen), B. O'Driscoll (UCD), T. Keating (Blackrock Coll); B. Cunningham (Bective Rangers), P. Stringer (UCC); M. Horan (Shannon), P. Smyth (St Mary's Coll), S. Best (Newcastle), M. O'Driscoll (UCC), R. Casey (Blackrock Coll), P. Neville (Old Crescent), L. Cullen (Blackrock Coll) Capt., R. Woods (Dublin U).
Reps: J. Campbell (Terenure College) for Best, J. Staunton (Garryowen) for Cunningham

Ireland 24 France 9

v Wales (Caerphilly) 19 February 1999

G. Murphy (Leicester); D. Quinlan (Blackrock Coll), K. Hartigan (Garryowen), B. O'Driscoll (UCD), T. Keating (Blackrock Coll); B. Cunningham (Bective Rangers), P. Stringer (UCC); M. Horan (Shannon), P. Smyth (St Mary's Coll), S. Best (Newcastle), R. Casey (Blackrock Coll), M. O'Driscoll (UCC), P. Neville (Old Crescent), L. Cullen (Blackrock Coll) Capt., R. Woods (Dublin U).
Reps: J. Campbell (Terenure College) for Best, J. Staunton (Garryowen) for Cunningham, J. Davis (Dungannon) for O'Driscoll, D. O'Callaghan (Cork Con) for Casey

Wales 24 Ireland 18

v England (Templeville Road) 5 March 1999

G. Murphy (Leicester); D. Quinlan (Blackrock Coll), K. Hartigan (Garryowen), B. O'Driscoll (UCD), T. Keating (Blackrock Coll); J. Staunton (Garryowen), P. Stringer (UCC); M. Horan (Shannon), P. Smyth (St Mary's Coll), J. Campbell (Terenure Coll), M. O'Driscoll (UCC), R. Casey (Blackrock Coll), P. Neville (Old Crescent), L. Cullen (Blackrock Coll) Capt., R. Woods (Dublin U).
Reps: S. Barretto (Terenure Coll) for Campbell, D. O'Callaghan (Cork Con) for Neville.

Ireland 23 England 5

v Scotland (Stirling) 19 March 1999

G. Murphy (Leicester); D. Quinlan (Blackrock Coll), K. Hartigan (Garryowen), B. O'Driscoll (UCD), T. Keating (Blackrock Coll); J. Staunton (Garryowen), P. Stringer (UCC); M. Horan (Shannon), P. Smyth (St Mary's Coll), J. Campbell (Terenure Coll), R. Casey (Blackrock Coll), M. O'Driscoll (UCC), P. Neville (Old Crescent), L. Cullen (Blackrock Coll) Capt., R. Woods (Dublin U).
Reps: J. Fogarty (Cork Con) for Smyth, S. Best (Newcastle) for Campbell, D. O'Callaghan (Cork Con) for O'Driscoll, S. Barretto (Terenure Coll) for Horan

Scotland 13 Ireland 22

v Italy (Ravenhill) 9 April 1999

G. Murphy (Leicester); C. Dowling (Greystones), D. Quinlan (Blackrock Coll), K. Hartigan (Garryowen), T. Keating (Blackrock Coll); M. McHugh (Dublin U), P. Stringer (UCC); M. Horan (Shannon), P. Smyth (St Mary's Coll), S. Best (Newcastle), R. Casey (Blackrock Coll), P. Neville (Old Crescent), L. Cullen (Blackrock Coll) Capt., R. Woods (Dublin U).
Reps: J. Davis (Dungannon) for Murphy, D. McCombe (Instonians) for McHugh, C. Campbell (London Irish) for Stringer, N. Brady (Dungannon) for Horan, D. Blaney (UCD) for Smyth, D. O'Callaghan (Cork Con) for Casey, A. Kearney (UCD) for Neville

Ireland 57 Italy 14

v Argentina July 1999

L. Cullen (Blackrock Coll) Capt.; T. Keating (Blackrock Coll); J. Davis (Dungannon); D. Quinlan (Blackrock Coll); S. Horgan (Lansdowne); K. Hartigan (Garryowne); A. Dunne (Old Belvedere); M. McHugh (St Mary's Coll); J. Staunton (Garryowen); B. Cunningham (Bective Rangers); K. Campbell (London Irish); S. Barretto (Terenure Coll); A. O'Brien (UCD); S. Best (Newcastle); N. Treston (Blackrock Coll); A. Flavin (London Irish); J. Flannery (UCC); R. Casey (Blackrock Coll); M. O'Driscoll (UCC); D. O'Callaghan (Cork Con); P. Neville (Garryowen); A. Kearney (UCD); D. Dillon (UCD); A. Hughes (Dungannon); M. Haslett (Instonians); S Keogh (Old Belvedere); P. Wallace (UCD); S. Moore (UCD).
Manager E Wigglesworth; Coach B. McLaughlin; Assistant Coach H. Kurger; Technical Advisor M. McDermott; Medical Officer Dr W. O'Flynn; Physiotherapist Miss M. Walsh; Baggage Master P. O'Reilly

APPENDIX 22

IRELAND YOUTHS INTERNATIONALS (UNDER 19): TEAMS AND RESULTS

FIRA WORLD YOUTHS (UNDER 19 CHAMPIONSHIP)

ALL MATCHES IN BUENOS AIRES

Tour Manager D. Crowley, Team Manager J. Glennon, Coach D. Kidney, Assistant Coach B. Fannin, Medical Officer Dr W. Mulcahy, Physiotherapist Mary Costello

v PORTUGAL 24 MARCH 1997

T. Keating (Blackrock Coll); D. Nolan (Greystones), G. McCullough (RBAI), R. Wallace (Dublin U), M. Price (Blackrock Coll); B. Cunningham (Dublin U) Capt., I. Knox (Instonians); S. Keane (Sunday's Well), H. Byrne (Tullow), E. Scullion (Ballymena), R. Casey (Blackrock Coll), B. Dineen (Cistercian Coll Roscrea), S. Kennedy (London Irish), P. Neville (Old Crescent), J. Hogan (Lansdowne).
Reps: G. Murphy (Naas) for Cunningham, S. Best (Newcastle) for Scullion, M. O'Driscoll (UCC) for Dineen, L. Cullen (Blackrock Coll) for Neville

Ireland 39 Portugal 20

v SCOTLAND

T. Keating (Blackrock Coll); J. Davis (Dungannon), K. Hartigan (Garryowen), D. Quinlan (Blackrock Coll), M. Price (Blackrock Coll); G. Murphy (Naas), I. Knox (Instonians); M. Haslett (BRA), S. Elkinson (Terenure Coll), S. Best (Newcastle), R. Casey (Blackrock Coll), M. O'Driscoll (UCC), S. Kennedy (London Irish), L. Cullen (Blackrock Coll) Capt., R. Hussey (Lansdowne).
Reps: G. McCullough (RBAI) for Keating, S. Keane (Sunday's Well) for Keating, B. Cunningham (Dublin U) for Murphy

Ireland 22 Scotland 8

v ARGENTINA 28 MARCH 1997

G. McCullough (RBAI); J. Davis (Dungannon), K. Hartigan (Garryowen), D. Quinlan (Blackrock Coll), M. Price (Blackrock Coll); G. Murphy (Naas), I. Knox (Instonians); E. Scullion (Ballymena), S. Elkinson (Terenure Coll), S. Keane (Sunday's Well), R. Casey (Blackrock Coll), B. Dineen (Cistercian Coll Roscrea), S. Kennedy (London Irish), M. O'Driscoll (UCC), L. Cullen (Blackrock Coll) Capt.
Reps: K. Becker (St Michael's Coll) for Knox, H. Byrne (Tullow) for Elkinson, P. Neville (Old Crescent) for Kennedy, B. Cunningham (Dublin U) for Murphy

Ireland 0 Argentina 42

v WALES 30 MARCH 1997

G. McCullough (RBAI); J. Davis (Dungannon), K. Hartigan (Garryowen), R. Wallace (Dublin U), D. Nolan (Greystones); B. Cunningham (Dublin U), K. Becker (St Michael's Coll); M. Haslett (BRA), H. Byrne (Tullow), S. Best (Newcastle), D. Dineen (Cistercian Coll Roscrea), M. O'Driscoll (UCC), P. Neville (Old Crescent), J. Hogan (Lansdowne), L. Cullen (Blackrock Coll) Capt.
Reps: S. Kennedy (London Irish) for Neville, R. Hussey (Lansdowne) for Hogan, S. Elkinson (Terenure Coll) for Best, I. Knox (Instonians) for Becker

Ireland 17 Wales 35

v ITALY (MCDOWELL PARK, SUTTON) 14 FEBRUARY 1998

D. Rossi (Clontarf); J. Reynolds (Watsonians), S. Moore (UCD), A. Considine (Bective Rangers), D. Holt (UCC); B. O'Driscoll (UCD), K. Campbell (London Irish); A. O'Brien (UCD) Capt., A. Flavin (London Irish), F. Roche (Bohemians), D. O'Callaghan (Cork Con), A. Kearney (St Mary's Coll), C. Fitzgerald (Garryowen), C. McCarey (Ballymena), N. Coughlan (UCD).
Reps: E. Benham (Coventry) for Moore, B. McCracken (CIYMS) for Considine, D. Mescal (Ballina/UCG) for Campbell, R. Keane (Old Belvedere) for O'Brien, B. Powell (Lansdowne) for Flavin, C. Schofield (Bangor) for Roche, S. Walsh (Old Belvedere) for Fitzgerald

Ireland 26 Italy 19

v Spain (Upritchard Park, Bangor) 16 March 1998

D. Rossi (Clontarf); M. Cuppitt (Instonians), B. O'Driscoll (UCD), B. McCracken (CIYMS), J. Reynolds (Watsonians); P. Wallace (Campbell Coll), D. Mescal (Ballina/UCG) Capt.; C. McMahon (Castleknock Coll), B. Urquhart (Methodist Coll), C. Schofield (Bangor), D. O'Callaghan (Cork Con), D. Broughall (UCD), B. Cahill (UCC), A. Kearney (St Michael's Coll), N. Coughlan (UCD).
Reps: S. Moore (UCD) for McCracken, K. Campbell (London Irish) for Mescal, A. Bohane (Highfield) for McMahon, F. Roche (Bohemians) for Schofield, C. McCarey (Ballymena) for Kearney

Ireland 63 Spain 0

IRB-FIRA WORLD YOUTHS CHAMPIONSHIP

Manager H. McKibbin, Coach D. Kidney, Assistant Coach B. Fannin, Medical Officer Dr Bill Mulcahy, Physiotherapists Mary Costello and Maeve Mitchell

v USA (Lombez) 4 April 1998

P. Wallace (Campbell Coll); D. Rossi (Clontarf), S. Moore (UCD) Capt., B. McCracken (CIYMS), M. Cuppitt (Instonians); B. Ronan (CBC Cork), D. Mescal (Ballina/UCG); C. Schofield (Bangor), B. Urquart (Methodist Coll), F. Roche (Bohemians), D. Broughall (UCD), A. Kearney (St Michael's Coll), B. Cahill (UCC), C. McCarey (Ballymena), J. Sheahan (UCC).
Reps: K. Campbell (London Irish) for Rossi, C. Goode (RBAI) for Roche, D. O'Callaghan (Cork Con) for Broughall, C. Fitzgerald (Garryowen) for Cahill

Ireland 47 USA 13

v South Africa (Samatan) 6 April 1998

D. Rossi (Clontarf); M. Cuppitt (Instonians), S. Moore (UCD) Capt., B. O'Driscoll (UCD), D. Holt (UCC); P. Wallace (Campbell Coll), K. Campbell (London Irish); A. O'Brien (UCD), A. Flavin (London Irish), F. Roche (Bohemians), D. O'Callaghan (Cork Con), D. Broughall (UCD), C. McCarey (Ballymena), A. Kearney (St Michael's Coll), N. Coughlan (UCD).
Reps: B. Urquhart (Methodist Coll) for Flavin, C. Schofield (Bangor) for Roche

Ireland 17 South Africa 17

Ireland lost penalty shoot-out 3-4 but South Africa were disqualified for using an ineligible player in shoot-out.

v Argentina (Colomiers) 9 April 1998

Semi-final

D. Rossi (Clontarf); M. Cuppitt (Instonians), S. Moore (UCD) Capt., B. O'Driscoll (UCD), D. Holt (UCC); P. Wallace (Campbell Coll), K. Campbell (London Irish); A. O'Brien (UCD), A. Flavin (London Irish), F. Roche (Bohemians), D. O'Callaghan (Cork Con), D. Broughall (UCD), C. McCarey (Ballymena), A. Kearney (St Michael's Coll), N. Coughlan (UCD).
Reps: J. Reynolds (Watsonians) for Cuppitt, A. Considine (Bective Rangers) for O'Driscoll, B. Urquhart (Methodist Coll) for A. Flavin, C. Schofield (Bangor) for Roche, C. Fitzgerald (Garryowen) for Broughall

Ireland 18 Argentina 3

v France (Stade Toulousain) 12 April 1998

Final

D. Rossi (Clontarf); M. Cuppitt (Instonians), S. Moore (UCD) Capt., B. O'Driscoll (UCD), D. Holt (UCC); P. Wallace (Campbell Coll), K. Campbell (London Irish); A. O'Brien (UCD), A. Flavin (London Irish), F. Roche (Bohemians), D. O'Callaghan (Cork Con), D. Broughall (UCD), C. McCarey (Ballymena), A. Kearney (St Michael's Coll), N. Coughlan (UCD).
Reps: J. Reynolds (Watsonians) for Holt, A. Considine (Bective Rangers) for O'Driscoll, D. Mescal (Ballina/UCG) for Campbell, C. Goode (RBAI) for O'Brien, B. Urquhart (Methodist Coll) for Flavin, C. Schofield (Bangor) for Roche, C. Fitzgerald (Garryowen) for Coughlan

Ireland 18 France 0

v Italy (Treviso) 16 January 1999

G. Brady (Ballina); G. Hayes (Dublin U), R. Murphy (Bective Rangers), D. D'Arcy (Lansdowne), G. Rossi (St Paul's Coll); P. O'Reilly (Wasps), M. Best (Banbridge); R. Flanagan (Bruff), G. Hickie (St Mary's Coll) Capt., N. Treston (Blackrock Coll), D. Browne (Galwegians), D. Dillon (UCD), D. Danaher (London Irish), D. O'Loughlin (UCD), J. O'Connor (Corinthians).
Reps: M. Meenan (Leicester) for O'Reilly, D. Spence (Queen's U) for Best, S. Byrne (Cistercian Roscrea) for

Flanagan, A. Hickey (UCC) for O'Loughlin, R. McGrath (Cork Con) for Treston

Italy 11 Ireland 18

IRB-FIRA Under 19 World Cup (Wales) March–April 1999

Manager H. McKibbin, Coach D. Kidney, Assistant Coach B. Fannin, Physiotherapists M. Costello and M. Mitchell, Doctor W. Mulcahy

D. Barbour (Malone); N. Breslin (Mullingar), K. Cowman (Suttonians), D. Danaher (London Irish), D. Dillon (UCD) Capt.; R. Flanagan (St Enda's Comm Sch and Bruff), D. Browne (Galwegians); G. Hickie (St Mary's Coll), P. Malone (St Munchin's and Bruff), I. McKee (Old Wesley), R. McGrath (Cork Con), J. O'Connor (Corinthians), D. O'Kane (Portadown), J. O'Sullivan (Newbridge Coll), N. Treston (Blackrock Coll), G. Brady (Ballina), C. McKibbin (Instonians), A. Cahill (Blackrock Coll), M. Meenan (Leicester), R. Murphy (Bective Rangers), M. O'Kelly (Dublin U), D. Popplewell (Wesley Coll), G. Rossi (St Paul's Coll), D. Spence (Queen's U), J. Staunton (Garryowen), J. Downey (Belvedere Coll).

v Georgia (Dunvant) 28 March 1999

Cahill; Rossi, Murphy, Browne, Brady; Meenan, Spence; Cowman, Hickie, McGrath, Barbour, Breslin, Danaher, Dillon Capt., O'Connor.
Reps: Popplewell for Cahill, Staunton for Meenan, McKee for Hickie, Malone for Dillon

Ireland 48 Georgia 3

v Italy (Dunvant) 1 April 1999

Meenan; Brady, O'Kelly, Downey, Cahill; Staunton, Spence; Flanagan, McKee, Treston, Brown, Danaher, Malone, Dillon, O'Kane.
Reps: Popplewell for Spence, Rossi for Staunton, O'Sullivan for Malone, Breslin for Brown, McGrath for Treston, Hickie for McKee

Ireland 24 Italy 15

(Semi-final)

v New Zealand (Bridgend) 1 April 1999

Meenan; Brady, O'Kelly, Downey, Cahill; Staunton, Spence; Flanagan, McKee, Treston, Breslin, Danaher, Malone, Dillon Capt., O'Connor.
Reps: Rossi for Downey, O'Kane for O'Connor, O'Sullivan for O'Kane, McGrath for Treston

New Zealand 21 Ireland 15

(Play-off for third and fourth place)

v South Africa (Stradey Park) 4 April 1999

Meenan; Brady, Downey, O'Kelly, Cahill; Staunton, Popplewell; Flanagan, McKee, Treston, Breslin, Danaher, Malone, Dillon Capt., O'Connor.
Reps: McKibbin for Meenan, Rossi for Downey, McGrath for Treston, Hickie for McKee, Cowman for Flanagan, O'Sullivan for Malone

South Africa 27 Ireland 20

APPENDIX 23

IRELAND SCHOOLS INTERNATIONALS: TEAMS AND RESULTS

Where a replacement is named it indicates that the player came on during the course of a match.

v England (Lansdowne Road) 29 March 1975

M. Quaid (Rockwell); J. Bowen (PBC Cork), J. Molloy (Castleknock), J. Murphy (PBC Bray), A. McKibbin (RBAI); M. Finn (PBC Cork), J. Sexton (Castleknock); J. Langbroek (Blackrock), H. Harbison (Blackrock), J. McCoy (Portora Royal), W. Howard (Wallace HS), B. Clifford (PBC Cork), G, Molloy (Blackrock), D. Spring (Cistercian Roscrea) Capt., H. Donnelly (Dungannon RS).
Rep: R. Kearney (Newbridge)

Ireland 3 England 6

v Scotland (Lansdowne Road) 3 April 1976

H. MacNeill (Blackrock) Capt.; S. Morris (Methodist), P. Loughran (Castleknock), A. McKibbin (RBAI), P. McCormack (Clongowes Wood); B. Murphy (De La Salle Churchtown), H. Simpson (BRA); J. McCoy (Portora Royal), P. Derham (Castleknock), P. Curran (Rockwell), L. Browne (BRA), L. Monahan (Blackrock), C. Armstrong (Dungannon RS), K. O'Loane (Rainey Endowed), W. Sexton (Castleknock)

Ireland 16 Scotland 4

v Wales (Aberavon) 10 April 1976

H. MacNeill (Blackrock) Capt.; S. Morris (Methodist), P. Loughran (Castleknock), A. McKibbin (RBAI), P. McCormack (Clongowes Wood); B. Murphy (De La Salle Churchtown), H. Simpson (BRA); J. McCoy (Portora Royal), P. Derham (Castleknock), P. Curran (Rockwell), L. Browne (BRA), L. Monahan (Blackrock), C. Armstrong (Dungannon RS), K. O'Loane (Rainey Endowed), W. Sexton (Castleknock).
Rep: D. Leonard (Limerick CBS)

Wales 26 Ireland 10

v Wales (Lansdowne Road) 26 March 1977

H. MacNeill (Blackrock) Capt.; M. Keogh (CBC Monkstown), T.R. Shiels (Rainey Endowed), J. Duggan (Rockwell), R. Millar (Regent House); P. Dean (St Mary's), P. Melville (Wallace HS); P. Connor (Blackrock), J. Hartnett (Blackrock), I. Johnston (Methodist), D. Lenihan (CBC Cork), B. McCall (Armagh RS), P. Matthews (Regent House), K. O'Loane (Rainey Endowed), M. MacWhite (Castleknock).
Rep: T. Brown (Armagh RS)

Ireland 4 Wales 10

v England (Gloucester) 6 April 1997

H. MacNeill (Blackrock) Capt.; K. Hooks (Bangor GS), T.R. Shiels (Rainey Endowed), J. Duggan (Rockwell), R. Miller (Regent House); P. Dean (St Mary's), P. McDonnell (St Mary's); P. Connor (Blackrock), J. Hartnett (Blackrock), I. Johnston (Methodist), D. Lenihan (CBC Cork), B. McCall (Armagh RS), P. Matthews (Regent House), K. O'Loane (Rainey Endowed), M. MacWhite (Castleknock).

England 37 Ireland 7

v Australia (Thomond Park) 17 December 1977

R. Hopkins (Terenure); P. Nowlan (Wesley), B. Keogh (CBC Monkstown), P. Bauress (Blackrock), K. Hooks (Bangor GS); P. Dean (St Mary's), P. McDonnell (St Mary's); W. Iveston (Regent House), J. Douglas (Methodist), R. Blair (Methodist), M. Moylett (Castleknock), P. Collins (CBC Cork), P. Matthews (Regent House) Capt., A. Blair (High School), C. Jennings (St Gerards).
Rep: K. Forkin (St Michael's)

Ireland 10 Australia 12

v England (Lansdowne Road) 1 April 1978

R. Hopkins (Terenure); P. Nowlan (Wesley), B. Keogh (CBC Monkstown), P. Bauress (Blackrock), K. Hooks (Bangor GS); P. Dean (St Mary's), P. McDonnell (St Mary's); W. Iveston (Regent House), J. Douglas (Methodist), R. Blair (Methodist), M. Moylett (Castleknock), P. Collins (CBC Cork), P. Matthews (Regent House) Capt., A. Blair (High School), T. Crotty (CBC Cork).

Ireland 22 England 16

v Scotland (Inverleith, Edinburgh) 7 April 1978

R. Hopkins (Terenure); P. Nowlan (Wesley), B. Keogh (CBC Monkstown), P. Bauress (Blackrock), K. Hooks (Bangor GS); P. Dean (St Mary's), P. McDonnell (St Mary's); W. Iveston (Regent House), J. Douglas (Methodist), R. Blair (Methodist), M. Moylett (Castleknock), P. Collins (CBC Cork), P. Matthews (Regent House) Capt., A. Blair (High School), C. Jennings (St Gerard's).

Scotland 7 Ireland 21

v Wales (Arms Park, Cardiff) 7 April 1979

D. Hooks (Bangor GS); O. Crotty (CBC Cork), J. Hewitt (Carrickfergus GS), M. Kiernan (PBC Cork), C.G. Maxwell (Bangor GS); G.K. Graham (RBAI) Capt., N. Malcolmson (Methodist); G. McMahon (Blackrock), W. Burns (Clongowes Wood), B. McKibbin (RBAI), J. Malone (CBC Monkstown), C. Jenkinson (Newbridge), D. Webb (Terenure), N. Ridgeway (Wesley), F.W. Vincent (RBAI).
Rep: N. McLaughlin (Carrickfergus GS)

Wales 20 Ireland 15

v Scotland (Lansdowne Road) 14 April 1979

D. Hooks (Bangor GS); O. Crotty (CBC Cork), J. Hewitt (Carrickfergus GS), M. Kiernan (PBC Cork), N. McLaughlin (Carrickfergus GS); G.K. Graham (RBAI) Capt., N. Malcolmson (Methodist); G. McMahon (Blackrock), W. Burns (Clongowes Wood), B. McKibbin (RBAI), J. Malone (CBC Monkstown), C. Jenkinson (Newbridge), D. Webb (Terenure), N. Ridgeway (Wesley), C. Cremin (CBC Cork).

Ireland 19 Scotland 0

v Wales (Thomond Park) 29 March 1980

N. Farren (CBC Monkstown); M. O'Connor (Rockwell), J. Garvey (Blackrock), M. Harvey (Portora Royal), D. Larmour (Bangor GS); P. Russell (RBAI), G. Neill (Grosvenor HS); G. McMahon (Blackrock) Capt., W. Burns (PBC Birr), B. Kennelly (De La Salle Churchtown), J. McGuire (Blackrock), S. Hutton (Belfast HS), P. Horner (Campbell), D. Gaston (Dalriada), C. Cremin (CBC Cork).
Rep: P. Madden (CBC Cork).

Ireland 7 Wales 13

v England (Twickenham) 12 April 1980

N. Farren (CBC Monkstown); C. O'Callaghan (CBC Cork), J. Garvey (Blackrock), M. Harvey (Portora Royal), D. Larmour (Bangor GS); P. Russell (RBAI), M. Bradley (PBC Cork); G. McMahon (Blackrock) Capt., W. Burns (PBC Birr), B. Kennelly (De La Salle Churchtown), J. McGuire (Blackrock), S. Hutton (Belfast HS), P. Horner (Campbell), D. Gaston (Dalriada), P. Waldron (St Michael's).
Rep: P. McIlroy (BRA)

England 12 Ireland 7

v Australia (Sydney Sports Ground) 31 August 1980

N. Farren (CBC Monkstown); D. Larmour (Bangor GS), J. Garvey (Blackrock), M. Harvey (Portora Royal), C. O'Callaghan (CBC Cork); C. Beverland (Campbell), M. Bradley (PBC Cork); G. McMahon (Blackrock) Capt., W. Burns (PBC Birr), B. Kennelly (De La Salle Churchtown), J. McGuire (Blackrock), S. Hutton (Belfast HS), C. Cremin (CBC Cork), D. Gaston (Dalriada), B. Hoey (De La Salle Churchtown).
Rep: N. Kearney (De La Salle Churchtown)

Australia 10 Ireland 7

v Scotland (Braidholm, Glasgow) 11 April 1981

J. Gardiner (Blackrock); S. Meharg (Campbell), B. Mullin (Blackrock), M. Davidson (Dungannon RS), R. Anderson (Coleraine AI); P. Bell (Castleknock), M. Bradley (PBC Cork) Capt.; N. Hastings (Rainey Endowed), B. O'Connell (St Michael's), D. Dowling (De La Salle Churchtown), S. Hutton (Belfast HS), N. Francis (Blackrock), D. Crawford

(RBAI), R. Clarke (PBC Cork), D. Sheehan (Clongowes Wood).
Rep: E. Coulter (Bangor GS)

Scotland 6 Ireland 14

v England (Lansdowne Road) 18 April 1981

J. Gardiner (Blackrock); S. Meharg (Campbell), B. Mullin (Blackrock), M. Davidson (Dungannon RS), R. Anderson (Coleraine AI); P. Bell (Castleknock), M. Bradley (PBC Cork) Capt.; M. Connolly (Gonzaga), M. Quaid (St Munchin's), D. Dowling (De La Salle Churchtown), S. Hutton (Belfast HS), N. Francis (Blackrock), D. Crawford (RBAI), R. Clarke (PBC Cork), D. Sheehan (Clongowes Wood).

Ireland 11 England 16

v Australia (Donnybrook) 1 January 1982

E. Murphy (Newbridge); M. Ennis (CBC Monkstown), B. Mullin (Blackrock) Capt., G. O'Reilly (PBC Cork), R. Anderson (Coleraine AI); S. Reid (Methodist), J. Moloney (Crescent Comprehensive); J. Livesey (PBC Cork), T. Kingston (CBC Cork), D. Dowling (De La Salle Churchtown), T. Lowry (Rainey Endowed), N. Francis (Blackrock), M. Semple (Grosvenor HS), M. Fitzgibbon (Rockwell), J.E. Coulter (Bangor GS).
Rep: J. Ahern (St Munchin's).

Ireland 0 Australia 24

v Wales (Neath) 3 April 1982

P. Murray (St Munchin's); N. Matthews (Portadown), B. Mullin (Blackrock) Capt., S. Hall (Portadown), M. Ennis (CBC Monkstown); D. Bryce (King's Hospital), J. Moloney (Crescent Comprehensive); M. Reynolds (BRA), T. Kingston (CBC Cork), D. Dowling (De La Salle Churchtown), J. Ahern (St Munchin's), N. Francis (Blackrock), M. Fitzgibbon (Rockwell), J.E. Coulter (Bangor GS), G. Flanagan (Belfast Model).
Rep: D.B. Hyland (PBC Cork)

Wales 17 Ireland 9

v Scotland (Musgrave Park) 10 April 1982

P. Murray (St Munchin's); M. Ennis (CBC Monkstown), D. Marrs (BRA), B. Mullin (Blackrock) Capt., S. Hall (Portadown); D. Bryce (King's Hospital), B. O'Shaughnessy (PBC Cork); M. Reynolds (BRA), T. Kingston (CBC Cork), D. Dowling (De La Salle Churchtown), N. Francis (Blackrock), J. Ahern (St Munchin's), A. Kinsella (Belvedere), M. Fitzgibbon (Rockwell), G. Flanagan (Belfast Model).

Ireland 42 Scotland 0

v England (Moseley) 2 April 1983

M. Mahon (CBC Monkstown); C. Campbell (Rainey Endowed), N. Johnston (Campbell), C. McLaughlin (Blackrock), C. Poole (Clongowes Wood); P. Danaher (St Munchin's), K. O'Farrell (Clongowes Wood); M. Reynolds (BRA) Capt., P. Shields (RBAI), G. Halpin (Rockwell), S. Greer (Bangor GS), M. Feely (De La Salle Churchtown), D. McBride (Belfast Model), S. Fraser (Regent House), M. Fitzgibbon (St Enda's).
Reps: G. Cross (St Mary's), N. Muldowney (De La Salle Churchtown).

England 16 Ireland 0

v Wales (Musgrave Park) 9 April 1983

M. Mahon (CBC Monkstown); C. Campbell (Rainey Endowed), N. Johnston (Campbell), C. McLaughlin (Blackrock), S. Stewart (RBAI); P. Danaher (St Munchin's), K. O'Farrell (Clongowes Wood); M. Reynolds (BRA), N. Muldowney (De La Salle Churchtown), G. Halpin (Rockwell), S. Greer (Bangor GS), M. Feely (De La Salle Churchtown), T. O'Connor (St Munchin's) Capt., G. Cross (St Mary's), D. McBride (Belfast Model).
Rep: M. Fitzgibbon (St Enda's).

Ireland 10 Wales 24

v Scotland (Braidholm, Glasgow) 7 April 1984

D. Larkin (St Munchin's); M. Costello (Terenure), B. Glennon (De La Salle Churchtown), A.P. Archer (Dungannon RS), J. Riordan (Rockwell); R. Cullen (RBAI), R. Montford (PBC Bray); B. Rhodes (Ballymena Acad) Capt., P. Madden (CBC Cork), G. Halpin (Rockwell), L. Dinneen (Crescent Comprehensive), P. Coleman (CBC Cork), D. Madigan (Gonzaga), B. McFarland (BRA), K. Leahy (Crescent Comprehensive).

Scotland 13 Ireland 26

v England (Ravenhill) 14 April 1984

D. Larkin (St Munchin's); M. Costello (Terenure), B. Glennon (De La Salle Churchtown), A.P. Archer (Dungannon RS), J. Riordan (Rockwell); R. Cullen (RBAI), R. Montford (PBC Bray); B. Rhodes (Ballymena Acad) Capt., P. Madden (CBC Cork), G. Halpin (Rockwell), L. Dinneen (Crescent Comprehensive), P. Coleman (CBC Cork), D. Madigan (Gonzaga), B. McFarland (BRA), K. Leahy (Crescent Comprehensive).

Ireland 15 England 7

v New Zealand (Musgrave Park) 5 January 1985

D. Larkin (St Munchin's); M. Webb (Bangor GS), A.P. Archer (Dungannon RS), B. Glennon (De La Salle Churchtown), K. Murphy (CBC Cork); M. McCall (Bangor GS), R. Montford (PBC Bray); B. Hyland (PBC Cork), P. Madden (CBC Cork), S. Ferguson (RBAI), L. Dinneen (Crescent Comprehensive) Capt., P. Coleman (CBC Cork), W. Pollock (Coleraine AI), K. Potts (Templeogue), B. McFarland (BRA).

Ireland 3 New Zealand 17

v Scotland (Lansdowne Road) 6 April 1985

D. Larkin (St Munchin's); P. Chambers (Coleraine AI), D.P. Lynch (St Mary's), B. Glennon (De La Salle Churchtown), C. Foley (St Mary's); M. McCall (Bangor GS), R. Montford (PBC Bray); S. Porter (King's Hospital), C. Wylie (BRA), S. Ferguson (RBAI), L. Dinneen (Crescent Comprehensive) Capt., K. Potts (Templeogue), W. Pollock (Coleraine AI), B. Walsh (Crescent Comprehensive), D. O'Flaherty (Blackrock).

Ireland 3 Scotland 9

v Wales (St David's) 13 April 1985

D. Larkin (St Munchin's); P. Chambers (Coleraine AI), D.P. Lynch (St Mary's), B. Glennon (De La Salle Churchtown) Capt., C. Foley (St Mary's); V. Cunningham (St Mary's), C. Stewart (Wallace HS); S. Porter (King's Hospital), M. Brady (PBC Cork), F. Griffin (Blackrock), L. Dinneen (Crescent Comprehensive), M. Wilson (King's Hospital), W. Pollock (Coleraine AI), K. Potts (Templeogue), D. O'Flaherty (Blackrock).

Wales 7 Ireland 10

v Australia (Ravenhill) 1 January 1986

C. Haly (PBC Cork); N. Barry (Crescent Comprehensive), J. Clarke (Rockwell), A.G. Hoey (St Mary's), J. Carroll (PBC Cork); M. McCall (Bangor GS) Capt., B. MacGoey (Rockwell); S. Booth (Ballymena Acad), A. Clarke (Dungannon RS), F. Griffin (Blackrock), P. Johns (Dungannon RS), N. Sweeney (Wesley), K. O'Connell (PBC Cork), B. Walsh (Crescent Comprehensive), D. Todd (RBAI).
Rep: R.S. Temple (RBAI)

Ireland 9 Australia 13

v England (Nottingham) 2 April 1986

C. Haly (PBC Cork); N. Barry (Crescent Comprehensive), J. Clarke (Rockwell), P. Grealy (Blackrock), P. Pollock (RBAI); M. McCall (Bangor GS) Capt., B. MacGoey (Rockwell); R.A. Semple (RBAI), M. Foley (King's Hospital), G.J. Coughlan (CBC Cork), P. Johns (Dungannon RS), N. Sweeney (Wesley), K. O'Connell (PBC Cork), B. Walsh (Crescent Comprehensive), M. O'Donoghue (Crescent Comprehensive).
Rep: J.G. Prendergast (Crescent Comprehensive)

England 13 Ireland 6

v Japan (Lansdowne Road) 5 April 1986

I.S. Gallagher (Methodist); N. Barry (Crescent Comprehensive), J. Clarke (Rockwell), P. Grealy (Blackrock), P. Pollock (RBAI); M. McCall (Bangor GS) Capt., B. MacGoey (Rockwell); S. Booth (Ballymena Acad), A. Clarke (Dungannon RS), F. Griffin (Blackrock), P. Johns (Dungannon RS), N. Sweeney (Wesley), K. O'Connell (PBC Cork), B. Walsh (Crescent Comprehensive), M. O'Donoghue (Crescent Comprehensive).

Ireland 16 Japan 6

v Wales (Sports Ground, Galway) 19 April 1986

C. Haly (PBC Cork); N. Barry (Crescent Comprehensive), J. Clarke (Rockwell), P. Pollock (RBAI), M. McCall (Bangor GS) Capt.; B. MacGoey (Rockwell), R.A. Semple (RBAI); M. Foley (King's Hospital), G.J. Coughlan (CBC Cork), P. Johns (Dungannon RS), N. Sweeney (Wesley), K. O'Connell (PBC Cork), B. Walsh (Crescent Comprehensive), M.

O'Donoghue (Crescent Comprehensive).

Ireland 17 Wales 3

v Scotland (Myreside, Edinburgh) 11 April 1987

I. Gallagher (Methodist); J. Harley (Portora Royal), M. Wilson (Belfast HS), R. Moloney (PBC Cork), M. Boyd (Ballymena Acad); N. Barry (Crescent Comprehensive) Capt., S. Treacy (St Mary's); J. Lennon (Blackrock), M. Foley (High School), A. McKeen (King's Hospital), E. O'Sullivan (Crescent Comprehensive), B.G. Dean (Coleraine AI), F. Kenny (Blackrock), D. Macartney (Cambridge House), A. Crowther (Bangor GS).
Reps: A. White (St Joseph's Garbally), R.A. Finegan (Clongowes Wood)

Scotland 9 Ireland 13

v England (Thomond Park) 18 April 1987

I. Gallagher (Methodist); J. Harley (Portora Royal), M. Wilson (Belfast HS), R. Moloney (PBC Cork), M. Boyd (Ballymena Acad); N. Barry (Crescent Comprehensive) Capt., A. Matchett (Portadown Coll); J. Lennon (Blackrock), A. Adair (RBAI), A. McKeen (King's Hospital), E. O'Sullivan (Crescent Comprehensive), B.G. Dean (Coleraine AI), R. Finegan (Clongowes Wood), D. Macartney (Cambridge House), A. Crowther (Bangor GS).

Ireland 12 England 12

v Australia (Concord Oval, Sydney) 6 September 1987

I. Gallagher (Methodist); J. Harley (Portora Royal), R. Moloney (PBC Cork), D. Lynagh (Terenure), G. Murphy (PBC Cork); N. Barry (Crescent Comprehensive) Capt., R. Saunders (BRA); J. Lennon (Blackrock), A. Adair (RBAI), A. McKeen (King's Hospital), E. O'Sullivan (Crescent Comprehensive), B. Dean (Coleraine AI), K. O'Connell (PBC Cork), D. Macartney (Cambridge House), D. Todd (RBAI).

Australia 20 Ireland 11

v Scotland (Ravenhill) 31 March 1988

J. Hayden (Newbridge); S. Fitzpatrick (CBC Cork), A. Hewitt (Sullivan Upper), D. Hernan (Cistercian Roscrea), S. Butler (Blackrock); L. Mahon (CBC Monkstown), N. Hogan (Terenure); P. Soden (CBC Cork), D. Rock (Clongowes Wood) Capt., A. Stewart (Friends Sch), E. O'Sullivan (Crescent Comprehensive), B. Dean (Coleraine AI), S. Rooney (St Michael's), D. Widger (St Michael's), S. Crowther (Bangor GS).

Ireland 25 Scotland 16

v England (Grange Road, Cambridge) 6 April 1988

J. Hayden (Newbridge; S. Fitzpatrick (CBC Cork), A. Hewitt (Sullivan Upper), D. Hernan (Cistercian Roscrea), S. Butler (Blackrock); L. Mahon (CBC Monkstown), N. Hogan (Terenure); P. Soden (CBC Cork), D. Rock (Clongowes Wood) Capt., A. Stewart (Friends Sch), E. O'Sullivan (Crescent Comprehensive), B. Dean (Coleraine AI), S. Rooney (St Michael's), D. Widger (St Michael's), S. Crowther (Bangor GS).
Rep: N. O'Kelly (St Mary's)

England 21 Ireland 10

v Wales (Lansdowne Road) 9 April 1988

J. Hayden (Newbridge); S. Fitzpatrick (CBC Cork), A. Hewitt (Sullivan Upper), G. Lavin (St Mary's), D. Hernan (Cistercian Roscrea); L. Mahon (CBC Monkstown), N. Hogan (Terenure); P. Soden (CBC Cork), N. O'Kelly (St Mary's), A. Stewart (Friend's Sch), E. O'Sullivan (Crescent Comprehensive), D. Dean (Coleraine AI), S. Rooney (St Michael's), D. Widger (St Michael's), S. Crowther (Bangor GS) Capt.

Ireland 18 Wales 16

v Zimbabwe (Lansdowne Road) 20 December 1988

J. Dunn (Belvedere); G. McCluskey (Portadown College), D. Hernan (Cistercian Roscrea), M. Ridge (Blackrock), T. Moran (St Munchin's); P. Allen (High School), K. Hodgen (Campbell); L. Murphy (PBC Cork), C. Twomey (CBC Cork), A. McDonald (CBC Cork), V. Costello (Blackrock), S. Kirkpatrick (Sullivan Upper), S. Rooney (St Michael's), D. Widger (St Michael's) Capt., S. Liston (St Munchin's).

Ireland 22 Zimbabwe 0

v England (Musgrave Park) 25 March 1989

R. Davidson (Dungannon RS); G. Anderson (Bangor GS), G. Lavin (St Mary's), M. Ridge (Blackrock), D. Hernan (Cistercian Roscrea); N. Malone (Methodist), N. Hogan (Terenure) Capt.; L. Murphy (PBC Cork), M. Kernohan (RBAI), D. Cole (High School), S. Kirkpatrick (Sullivan Upper), V. Costello (Blackrock), S. Rooney (St Michael's), D. Widger (St Michael's), J. Callaghan (Wallace HS).

Ireland 10 England 19

v Wales (Aberystwyth) 1 April 1989

R. Kelleher (CBC Cork); G. Anderson (Bangor GS), G. Lavin (St Mary's), M. Ridge (Blackrock), D. Hernan (Cistercian Roscrea); N. Malone (Methodist), N. Hogan (Terenure) Capt.; L. Murphy (PBC Cork), M. Kernohan (RBAI), P. Wallace (Crescent Comprehensive), S. Kirkpatrick (Sullivan Upper), V. Costello (Blackrock), S. Rooney (St Michael's), D. Widger (St Michael's), J. Callaghan (Wallace HS).
Rep: T. Moran (St Munchin's)

Ireland 9 Wales 6

v Scotland (Galashiels) 5 April 1989

R. Kelleher (CBC Cork); G. Anderson (Bangor GS), G. Lavin (St Mary's), M. Ridge (Blackrock), D. Hernan (Cistercian Roscrea); N. Malone (Methodist), N. Hogan (Terenure) Capt.; L. Murphy (PBC Cork), M. Kernohan (RBAI), P. Wallace (Crescent Comprehensive), S. Kirkpatrick (Sullivan Upper), V. Costello (Blackrock), S. Rooney (St Michael's), D. Widger (St Michael's), J. Callaghan (Wallace HS).
Rep: K. Martin (Methodist)

Scotland 12 Ireland 27

v Wales (Ravenhill) 6 April 1990

R. Garvey (De La Salle Churchtown); D. O'Dowd (Rockwell), B. Cotter (St Mary's), R. Hunter (Methodist), G. Collins (Methodist); D. Humphreys (Ballymena Acad) Capt., F. Downes (Crescent Comprehensive); P. Parker (RBAI), I. Blake (Terenure), P. Wallace (Crescent Comprehensive), N. Nolan (Cistercian Roscrea), R. Wilson (RBAI), L. Toland (St Clement's), F. Butler (Blackrock), A. Deyermond (Methodist).
Reps: G. Purdy (Regent House), F. Fitzgerald (Rockwell)

Ireland 12 Wales 10

v Scotland (Lansdowne Road) 14 April 1990

R. Garvey (De La Salle Churchtown); D. O'Dowd (Rockwell), B. Cotter (St Mary's), R. Hunter (Methodist), G. Collins (Methodist); D. Humphreys (Ballymena Acad) Capt., F. Downes (Crescent Comprehensive); P. Parker (RBAI), I. Blake (Terenure), P. Wallace (Crescent Comprehensive), N. Nolan (Cistercian Roscrea), R. Wilson (RBAI), L. Toland (St Clement's), F. Butler (Blackrock), A. Deyermond (Methodist).

Ireland 14 Scotland 10

v England (Iffley Road, Oxford) 18 April 1990

R. Garvey (De La Salle Churchtown); D. O'Dowd (Rockwell), R. Casey (CBC Cork), R. Hunter (Methodist), G. Collins (Methodist); D. Humphreys (Ballymena Acad) Capt., F. Downes (Crescent Comprehensive); P. Parker (RBAI), G. Purdy (Regent House), P. Wallace (Crescent Comprehensive), N. Nolan (Cistercian Roscrea), R. Wilson (RBAI), L. Toland (St Clement's), F. Butler (Blackrock), A. Deyermond (Methodist).

England 6 Ireland 15 (Ireland won Triple Crown)

v Australia (Thomond Park) 5 January 1991

I. Gray (RBAI); M. Kearin (Newbridge), R. Casey (CBC Cork) Capt., R. Hunter (Methodist), J. O'Carroll (Cistercian Roscrea); O. Cobbe (PBC Bray), N. Assaf (Blackrock); C. Keown (Omagh Acad), R. Kernohan (Ballymena Acad), J. O'Driscoll (PBC Cork), G. Tuohy (PBC Cork), S. Rose (CBC Cork), D. Corkery (CBC Cork), A. Foley (St Munchin's), T. Murphy (Cistercian Roscrea).

Ireland 9 Australia 13

v England (Thomond Park) 30 March 1991

I. Gray (RBAI) Capt.; M. Kearin (Newbridge), M. Young (RBAI), A. Reddan (Crescent Comprehensive), J. O'Carroll (Cistercian Roscrea); O. Cobbe (PBC Bray), A. Gallagher (Dungannon RS); C. Keown (Omagh Acad), R. Kernohan (Ballymena Acad), J. O'Driscoll (PBC Cork), G. Tuohy (PBC Cork), S. Rose (CBC Cork), D. Corkery (CBC Cork), A. Foley (St Munchin's), T. Murphy (Cistercian Roscrea).

Ireland 0 England 15

v Wales (St Helen's, Swansea) 15 April 1991

I. Gray (RBAI) Capt.; M. Kearin (Newbridge), M. Young (RBAI), A. Reddan (Crescent Comprehensive), J. O'Carroll (Cistercian Roscrea); O. Cobbe (PBC Bray), A. Gallagher (Dungannon RS); C. Keown (Omagh Acad), R. Kernohan (Ballymena Acad), J. O'Driscoll (PBC Cork), G. Tuohy (PBC Cork), S. Rose (CBC Cork), D. Corkery (CBC Cork), A. Foley (St Munchin's), T. Murphy (Cistercian Roscrea)

Wales 14 Ireland 11

v Scotland (Kelso) 12 April 1991

I. Gray (RBAI) Capt.; M. Kearin (Newbridge), M. Young (RBAI), A. Reddan (Crescent Comprehensive), J. O'Carroll (Cistercian Roscrea); O. Cobbe (PBC Bray), A. Gallagher (Dungannon RS); C. Keown (Omagh Acad), D. Crossan (Terenure), J. O'Driscoll (PBC Cork), G. Tuohy (PBC Cork), S. Rose (CBC Cork), D. Corkery (CBC Cork), A. Foley (Crescent Comprehensive), T. Murphy (Cistercian Roscrea).
Reps: J. Doddy (St Michael's), M. McNicholas (St Michael's), B. Begley (Crescent Comprehensive)

Scotland 9 Ireland 17

v Scotland (Sports Ground, Galway) 4 April 1992

J. Bell (Coleraine AI); G. Davis (BRA), C. de Gascun (Terenure), D. Blewitt (Regent House), J. O'Carroll (Cistercian Roscrea); G. Gamble (BRA), C. McGuinness (St Mary's); W. O'Kelly (St Paul's), J. Blaney (Terenure) Capt., C. Boyd (RBAI), D. Moore (Blackrock), R. Coveney (Clongowes Wood), J. McGovern (Terenure), A. Foley (St Munchin's), C. Davis (BRA).

Ireland 17 Scotland 6

v Wales (Musgrave Park) 11 April 1992

J. Bell (Coleraine AI); B. Begley (Crescent Comprehensive), C. de Gascun (Terenure), D. Blewitt (Regent House), J. O'Carroll (Cistercian Roscrea); G. Gamble (BRA), C. McGuinness (St Mary's); I. Cummins (PBC Cork), J. Blaney (Terenure) Capt., C. Boyd (RBAI), D. Moore (Blackrock), R. Coveney (Clongowes Wood), J. McGovern (Terenure), A. Foley (St Munchin's), C. Davis (BRA).

Ireland 7 Wales 9

v England (Bedford) 15 April 1992

J. Bell (Coleraine AI); B. Begley (Crescent Comprehensive), C. de Gascun (Terenure), D. Blewitt (Regent House), J. O'Carroll (Cistercian Roscrea); J. Philpott (Belvedere), C. McGuinness (St Mary's); I. Cummins (PBC Cork), J. Blaney (Terenure) Capt., C. Boyd (RBAI), D. Moore (Blackrock), J. Davidson (Methodist), A. Foley (St Munchin's), R. Coveney (Clongowes Wood), C. Davis (BRA).

England 15 Ireland 9

v New Zealand (Rugby Park, New Plymouth) 29 August 1992

J. Bell (Coleraine AI); B. Begley (Crescent Comprehensive), C. de Gascun (Terenure), D. Blewitt (Regent House), G. Davis (BRA); J. Philpott (Belvedere), K. Hilman (RBAI); I. Cummins (PBC Cork), J. Blaney (Terenure) Capt., C. Boyd (RBAI), D. Moore (Blackrock), J. Davidson (Methodist), J. Patterson (Dungannon RS), A. Foley (St Munchin's).
Rep: J. O'Carroll (Cistercian Roscrea)

New Zealand 27 Ireland 25

v Wales (Ebbw Vale) 3 April 1993

J. Cunningham (Bangor GS); J. Topping (Ballymena Acad), G. Brennan (PBC Bray), R. McIlreavy (Wesley), D. Hickie (St Mary's); F. Campion (St Mary's), C. McGuinness (St Mary's); B. O'Doherty Campbell (Terenure), C. Egan (Terenure), S. Waterworth (Methodist), R. Powell (King's Hospital), J. Ryan (Blackrock), T. O'Connell (PBC Cork) Capt., E. Miller (Wesley), K. Dawson (Bangor GS).
Reps: A. Turtle (Campbell), A. Bermingham (St Munchin's)

Wales 0 Ireland 8

v Scotland (Balgray, Glasgow) 10 April 1993

J. Cunningham (Bangor GS); J. Topping (Ballymena Acad), G. Brennan (PBC Bray), R. McIlreavy (Wesley), D. Hickie (St Mary's); F. Campion (St Mary's), C. McGuinness (St Mary's) Capt.; B. O'Doherty Campbell (Terenure), C. Egan (Terenure), S. Waterworth (Methodist), R. Powell (King's Hospital), J. Ryan (Blackrock), A. Bermingham (St Munchin's), E.Miller (Wesley), K. Dawson (Bangor GS).

Scotland 9 Ireland 21

v England (Ravenhill) 14 April 1993

J. Cunningham (Bangor GS); J. Topping (Ballymena Acad), G. Brennan (PBC Bray), R. McIlreavy (Wesley), D. Hickie (St Mary's); F. Campion (St Mary's), B. O'Doherty Campbell (Terenure); C. Egan (Terenure), S. Waterworth (Methodist), R. Powell (King's Hospital), J. Ryan (Blackrock), T. O'Connell (PBC Cork) Capt., E. Miller (Wesley), K. Dawson (Bangor GS).

Ireland 13 England 8 (Ireland won Triple Crown)

v Wales (Templeville Road) 30 March 1994

J. Lowe (Ballyclare HS); S. Doggett (St Mary's), J. Lacy (Clongowes Wood), M. Smyth (Terenure), K. McNamee (St Mary's); R. Governey (Clongowes Wood), S. Bell (Friends Sch); A. Sweeney (CBC Cork), R. Sands (Dungannon RS), J. Spence (Dungannon RS), R. Sheehan (St Jospeh's Garbally), J. Fitzgerald (PBC Cork), D. Lane (PBC Cork), E. Miller (Wesley), P. Lynch (Clongowes Wood) Capt.
Reps: G. Gannon (St Mary's), D. Shanley (St Michael's).

Ireland 14 Wales 13

v Scotland (Thomond Park) 4 April 1994

J. Lowe (Ballyclare HS); S. Doggett (St Mary's), J. Lacy (Clongowes Wood), M. Smyth (Terenure), D. Hickie (St Mary's); R. Governey (Clongowes Wood), S. Bell (Friends Sch); A. Sweeney (CBC Cork), R. Sands (Dungannon RS), J. Spence (Dungannon RS), R. Sheehan (St Joseph's Garbally), J. Fitzgerald (PBC Cork), D. Lane (PBC Cork), E. Miller (Wesley), P. Lynch (Clongowes Wood) Capt.

Ireland 30 Scotland 5

v England (Durham City RFC) 13 April 1994

J. Lowe (Ballyclare HS); S. Doggett (St Mary's), L. Lacy (Clongowes Wood), M. Smyth (Terenure), D. Hickie (St Mary's); R. Governey (Clongowes Wood), S. Bell (Friends Sch); A. Sweeney (CBC Cork), R. Sands (Dungannon RS), R. Sheehan (St Jospeh's Garbally), J. Fitzgerald (PBC Cork), D. Lane (PBC Cork), E. Miller (Wesley), P. Lynch (Clongowes Wood) Capt.

England 23 Ireland 8

v Australia (Lansdowne Road) 23 December 1994

D. O'Brien (PBC Cork); S. Doggett (St Mary's), J. Lacy (Clongowes Wood), C. Mahony (CBC Cork), S. Coulter (BRA); E. Farrell (Blackrock), G. McCullough (RBAI); R. McCormack (St Mary's), P. Smyth (Blackrock), J. Spence (Dungannon RS), P. Murphy (Methodist), R. Leahy (Crescent Comprehensive), I. Girvan (Dungannon RS) Capt., D. Shanley (St Michael's), D. Blaney (Terenure).
Rep: R. Ormond (St Mary's) for Coulter

Ireland 3 Australia 27

v Scotland (Balgray, Glasgow) 8 April 1995

K. Johnston (Methodist); S. Doggett (St Mary's), S. Coulter (BRA), C. Mahony (CBC Cork), J. Keenan (St Munchin's); R. Ormond (St Mary's), K. Murphy (CBC Cork); M. Horan (St Munchin's), P. Smyth (Blackrock), R. McCormack (St Mary's), P. Murphy (Methodist), R. Leahy (Crescent Comprehensive), I. Girvan (Dungannon RS), D. Blaney (Terenure) Capt., L. Cullen (Blackrock).

Scotland 23 Ireland 29

v England (Sports Ground, Galway) 15 April 1995

C. Kilroy (Crescent Comprehensive); S. Doggett (St Mary's), S. Coulter (BRA), C. Mahony (CBC Cork), J. Keenan (St Munchin's); R. Ormond (St Mary's), K. Murphy (CBC Cork); M. Horan (St Munchin's), P. Smyth (Blackrock), R. McCormack (St Mary's), P. Murphy (Methodist), R. Leahy (Crescent Comprehensive), I. Girvan (Dungannon RS), D. Blaney (Terenure) Capt., L. Cullen (Blackrock).
Reps: E. Farrell (Blackrock) for Mahony, G. McCullough (RBAI) for Doggett, M. Finlay (Methodist) for K. Murphy

Ireland 6 England 17

v Wales (Dunvant) 21 April 1995

E. Farrell (Blackrock); D. Johnson (Blackrock), S. Coulter (Belfast RA), C. Mahony (CBC Cork), J. Keenan (St Munchin's); R. Ormond (St Mary's), M. Finlay (Methodist); M. Horan (St Munchin's), P. Smyth (Blackrock), R. McCormack (St Mary's), P. Murphy (Methodist), R. Leahy (Crescent Comprehensive), I. Girvan (Dungannon RS), D. Blaney (Terenure) Capt., L. Cullen (Blackrock).
Reps: C. Kilroy (Crescent Comprehensive) for Mahony, J. Lane (St Mary's) for Smyth

Wales 28 Ireland 20

v Scotland (Mardyke) 6 April 1996

T. Keating (Blackrock); J. Davis (Belfast HS), E. Travers (Terenure), K. Hartigan (St Munchin's), C. Dowling (PBC Bray); B. O'Mahony (CBC Cork), C. Scally (Blackrock); S. McConnell (Coleraine AI), P. Smyth (Blackrock), S. Best (Portadown), P. Bracken (St Andrew's), R. Casey (Blackrock), T. Cahill (PBC Cork), L. Cullen (Blackrock), B. Gibney (Blackrock) Capt.
Rep: J. Fogarty (Rockwell)

Ireland 37 Scotland 12

v England (Hull) 10 April 1996

T. Keating (Blackrock); J. Davis (Belfast HS), E. Travers (Terenure), K. Hartigan (St Munchin's), S. Dowling (PBC Bray); B. O'Mahony (CBC Cork), C. Scally (Blackrock); S. McConnell (Coleraine AI), P. Smyth (Blackrock), J. Campbell (Terenure), P. Bracken (St Andrew's), R. Casey (Blackrock), T. Cahill (PBC Cork), L. Cullen (Blackrock), B. Gibney (Blackrock) Capt.

England 9 Ireland 12

v Wales (Ravenhill) 17 April 1996

T. Keating (Blackrock); J. Davis (Belfast HS), E. Travers (Terenure), K. Hartigan (St Munchin's), C. Dowling (PBC Bray); B. O'Mahony (CBC Cork), C. Scally (Blackrock); S. McConnell (Coleraine AI), P. Smyth (Blackrock), J. Campbell (Terenure), P. Bracken (St Andrew's), R. Casey (Blackrock), B. Gibney (Blackrock) Capt.
Rep: S. Kennedy (Regent House)

Ireland 13 Wales 12 (Ireland won Triple Crown)

v Australia (Canberra) 28 August 1996

T. Keating (Blackrock); J. Davis (Belfast HS), E. Travers (Terenure), K. Hartigan (St Munchin's), C. Dowling (PBC Bray); B. Cunningham (Bangor GS), C. Scally (Blackrock); S. McConnell (Coleraine AI), P. Smyth (Blackrock), J. Campbell (Terenure), P. Bracken (St Andrew's), R. Casey (Blackrock), T. Cahill (PBC Cork), L. Cullen (Blackrock), B. Gibney (Blackrock) Capt., R. O'Donovan (CBC Cork).

Australia 21 Ireland 23

v England (Lansdowne Road) 29 March 1997

C. Dowling (PBC Bray); D. Willmott (Coleraine AI), S. Moore (Belvedere) Capt., B. O'Driscoll (Blackrock), D. McCombe (RBAI); A. Dunne (Belvedere), C. Scally (Blackrock); N. Brady (Dungannon RS), D. Blaney (Terenure), P. Hanlon (CBC Cork), D. O'Callaghan (CBC Cork), G. Lloyd (St Mary's), N. Coughlan (Blackrock), A. Hughes (Dungannon RS), C. McCarey (BRA).
Reps: B. Quigley (Clongowes Wood), P. Callanan (Clongowes Wood)

Ireland 9 England 16

v Wales (Maesteg) 5 April 1997

C. Dowling (PBC Bray); D. Willmott (Coleraine AI), S. Moore (Belvedere) Capt., B. O'Driscoll (Blackrock), S. Conway (Crescent Comprehensive); A. Dunne (Belvedere), B. Quigley (Clongowes Wood); N. Brady (Dungannon RS), D. Blaney (Terenure), P. Hanlon (CBC Cork), D. O'Callaghan (CBC Cork), P. Callanan (Clongowes Wood), N. Coughlan (Blackrock), A. Hughes (Dungannon RS), C. McCarey (BRA).
Reps: S. McCullough (Clongowes Wood), G. Lloyd (St Mary's)

Wales 25 Ireland 27

v Scotland (Ayr) 12 April 1997

C. Dowling (PBC Bray); D. Willmott (Coleraine AI), S. Moore (Belvedere) Capt., B. O'Driscoll (Blackrock), S. Conway (Crescent Comprehensive); A. Dunne (Belvedere), B. Quigley (Clongowes Wood); N. Brady (Dungannon RS), D. Blaney (Terenure), P. Hanlon (CBC Cork), D. O'Callaghan (CBC Cork), G. Lloyd (St Mary's), N. Coughlan (Blackrock), A. Hughes (Dungannon RS), C. McCarey (BRA).
Reps: P. Magee (Dungannon RS), B. McCracken (Campbell), N. Wilson (Campbell), A. O'Brien (Terenure)

Scotland 11 Ireland 48

v Scotland (Thomond Park) 7 April 1998

G. Darcy (Clongowes Wood); J. Norton (St Mary's), K. Lewis (St Mary's), R. Miliken (Bangor GS), D. McCombe (RBAI); A. Dunne (Belvedere), D. Spence (Wallace HS); N. Brady (Dungannon RS), G. Ryan (Clongowes Wood), N. Treston (Blackrock), D. Dillon (Clongowes Wood), P. O'Connell (Ard Scoil Ris), A. Hickey (CBC Cork), D. O'Loughlin (Cistercian Roscrea), A. Hughes (Dungannon RS) Capt.
Reps: N. Beggs (Campbell Coll), A. Cullen (Belvedere)

Ireland 49 Scotland 0

v Wales (Sports Ground, Galway) 11 April 1998

G. Darcy (Clongowes Wood); J. Norton (St Mary's), K. Lewis (St Mary's), R. Miliken (Bangor GS), D. McCombe (RBAI); A. Dunne (Belvedere), D. Spence (Wallace HS); N. Brady (Dungannon RS), G. Ryan (Clongowes Wood), N. Treston (Blackrock), D. Dillon (Clongowes Wood), P. O'Connell (Ard Scoil Ris), A. Hickey (CBC Cork), D. O'Loughlin (Cistercian Roscrea), A. Hughes (Dungannon RS) Capt.
Rep: R. Henson (St Mary's)

Ireland 11 Wales 13

v England (Stourbridge) 18 April 1998

G. Darcy (Clongowes Wood); J. Norton (St Mary's), K. Lewis (St Mary's), R. Miliken (Bangor GS), D. McCombe (RBAI); A. Dunne (Belvedere), D. Spence (Wallace HS); N. O'Connor (Clongowes Wood), R. Henson (St Mary's), N. Treston (Blackrock), D. Dillon (Clongowes Wood), P. O'Connell (Ard Scoil Ris), A. Hickey (CBC Cork), D. O'Loughlin (Cistercian Roscrea), A. Hughes (Dungannon RS) Capt.
Rep: R. McGrath (CBC Cork)

England 26 Ireland 22

v Australia (Ravenhill) 22 December 1998

P. Drew (Blackrock); J. Norton (St Mary's), K. Lewis (St Mary's), C. O'Sullivan (PBC Cork), F. Baynes (St Michael's); D. Crotty (Belvedere), P. McCarthy (CBC Cork); B. Young (Ballymena Acad), H. Bourke (Clongowes Wood) Capt., J. Montgomery (Blackrock), A. Maher (St Joseph's Galway), G. Brown (Armagh RS), D. Leamy (Rockwell), S. Jennings (St Mary's), H. McMillan (BRA).
Reps: E. Reddan (Crescent Comprehensive), G. Duffy (Cistercian Roscrea)

Ireland 11 Australia 24

v England (Musgrave Park) 3 April 1999

P. Drew (Blackrock); J. Norton (St Mary's), G. Brown (Blackrock), C. O'Sullivan (PBC Cork), F. Baynes (St Michael's); G. Duffy (Cistercian Roscrea), P. McCarthy (CBC Cork); B. Young (Ballymena Acad), H. Bourke (Clongowes Wood) Capt., J. Montgomery (Blackrock), A. Maher (St Joseph's Galway), M. McCullough (Ballymena Acad), D. Leamy (Rockwell), S. Jennings (St Mary's), T. Carter (Terenure).
Reps: I. Kidd (CBC Cork), E. Reddan (Crescent Comp)

Ireland 8 England 6

v Wales (Ebbw Vale) 10 April 1999

P. Drew (Blackrock); J. Norton (St Mary's), G. Brown (Blackrock), C. O'Sullivan (PBC Cork) Capt., S. Baynes (St Michael's); G. Duffy (Cistercian Roscrea), P. McCarthy (CBC Cork); B. Young (Ballymena Acad), H. Bourke (Clongowes Wood), J. Montgomery (Blackrock), A. Maher (St Joseph's Galway), M. McCullough (Ballymena Acad), D. Leamy (Rockwell), T. Carter (Terenure), S. Jennings (St Mary's).
Reps: E. Reddan (Crescent Comp) for McCarthy, J. Coughlan (CBC Cork) for Maher

Wales 0 Ireland 41

APPENDIX 24

IRELAND YOUTHS INTERNATIONALS (UNDER 18): TEAMS AND RESULTS

v Scotland (Sports Ground, Galway) 11 April 1992

R. Larkin (Curragh); D. Carolan (Dundalk), P. Koschinley (Ballynahinch), G. Nolan (Tuam), S. Kennedy (Carrickfergus); V. Middleton (Curragh), D. Daly (Kilkenny); R. Faith (Limavady), D. Ryan (Highfield) Capt., J. Hickey (Thomond), M. King (Ballymena), T. Brennan (Barnhall), B. Turley (Corinthians), M. Hill (Omagh), R. Heaslip (Curragh).

Ireland 0 Scotland 4

v Scotland (Ayr) 10 April 1993

B. Roche (Highfield); D. Batch (Carrickfergus), R. Larkin (Curragh), G. Foley (Sligo), B. Everitt (Nenagh Ormond); C. Burke (Clonmel), T. Tierney (Richmond); R. Thomas (Cork Con), R. McGarrigle (Limavady), L. Johnston (Dromore), E. Gannon (Ballina), L. Moore (Limavady), C. McEntee (Naas), A. Quinlan (Clanwilliam) Capt., I. Dillon (Young Munster).

Ireland 14 Scotland 20

v Wales (Bridgend) 3 April 1994

O. Moran (Bohemians); G. Foley (Sligo), T. Lane (Clonmel), P. Connellan (Ennis), G. Corless (Tuam); A. Finney (Portadown), T. Tierney (Richmond); L. Johnston (Dromore), R. McGarrigle (Limavady), R. McArdle (Youghal), M. Mullan (Monaghan), E. Cullen (Wexford), R. Cogan (Highfield) Capt., G. Sloan (Dromore), M. Crowley (Highfield).
Reps: G. Williamson (Clogher Valley) for Crowley, R. Doyle (Old Christians) for Corless, A. Patterson (Ballymena) for Cullen

Wales 6 Ireland 12

v Scotland (Ravenhill) 9 April 1994

O. Moran (Bohemians); G. Foley (Sligo), T. Lane (Clonmel), P. Connellan (Ennis), G. Corless (Tuam); A. Finney (Portadown), T. Tierney (Richmond); L. Johnston (Dromore), R. McGarrigle (Limavady), R. McArdle (Youghal), M. Mullan (Monaghan), E. Cullen (Wexford), R. Cogan (Highfield) Capt., G. Sloan (Dromore), M. Crowley (Highfield).
Reps: A. Patterson (Ballymena) for McArdle, P. Humphreys (Richmond) for McGarrigle

Ireland 10 Scotland 5

v Wales (Thomond Park) 2 April 1995

K. Mullen (Clonakilty); J. Finegan (Drogheda), K. O'Riordan (Youghal), I. Dunne (Tullamore), N. Johnston (Dromore); M. Maguire (Banbridge), T. Tierney (Richmond) Capt.; M. Cahill (Bohemians), I. Ryan (Richmond), T. Clifford (Bohemians), J. Wilson (Ballynahinch), P. Bracken (Tullamore), D. Duggan (Thurles), R. Dickson (Banbridge), P. Hehir (Kilkenny).
Rep: B. Buckley (Thomond) for Dickson

Ireland 12 Wales 17

v Scotland (Millbrae) 8 April 1995

K. Mullen (Clonakilty); J. Finegan (Drogheda), K. O'Riordan (Youghal), I. Dunne (Tullamore), N. Johnston (Dromore); M. Maguire (Banbridge), T. Tierney (Richmond) Capt.; M. Cahill (Bohemians), I. Ryan (Thomond), T. Clifford (Bohemians), J. Wilson (Ballynahinch), P. Bracken (Tullamore), D. Duggan (Thurles), R. Dickson (Banbridge), P. Hehir (Kilkenny).

Scotland 11 Ireland 15

v Spain (Under 19) (Pepe Rojo Stadium, Valladolid) 10 March 1996

A. Ponaird (Monivea); R. Hartmann (Corinthians), O. Geoghegan (Thurles), S. Horgan (Drogheda), M. Crothers (Dromore); M. Maguire (Banbridge) Capt., J. Aiken (Dromore); R. Bolger (New Ross), A. Keaveney (Ballina), E. Scullion (Ballymena), D. O'Kane (Ballymena), B. O'Connor (Skerries), A. O'Gorman (Newport), K. McKinley (Mullingar), J. Shanks (Ballynahinch).

Spain 23 Ireland 6

v Scotland (Sports Ground, Galway) 30 March 1996

A. Ponaird (Monivea); R. Hartmann (Corinthians), O. Geoghegan (Thurles) Capt., S. Horgan (Drogheda), M. Crothers (Dromore); M. Maguire (Banbridge), I. O'Gorman (Old Crescent); R. Bolger (New Ross), A. Keaveney (Ballina), E. Scullion (Ballymena), D. O'Kane (Ballymena), B. Kelleher (Dolphin), A. O'Gorman (Newport), K. McKinley (Mullingar), B. O'Connor (Skerries).
Rep: A. Morrissey (Highfield) for Geoghegan

Ireland 17 Scotland 18

v Wales (Cardiff Arms Park) 27 April 1996

A. Ponaird (Monivea); R. Hartmann (Corinthians), O. Geoghegan (Thurles) Capt., S. Horgan (Drogheda), M. Crothers (Dromore); M. Maguire (Banbridge), I. O'Gorman (Old Crescent); R. Bolger (New Ross), A. Keaveney (Ballina), E. Scullion (Ballina), D. O'Kane (Ballymena), B. Kelleher (Dolphin), A. O'Gorman (Newport), K. McKinley (Mullingar), B. O'Connor (Skerries).
Reps: D. Quinlan (Clanwilliam) for O'Connor, D. Lillis (Corinthians) for Scullion, C. Lyons (Clogher Valley) for Keaveney, S. Keane (Highfield) for Bolger

Wales 21 Ireland 16

v Wales (Anglesea Road) 9 March 1997

A. Morrissey (Highfield); R. O'Donovan (Cobh), A. Considine (Ennis), S. Horgan (Drogheda), A. Bell (Malone); M. McHugh (Drogheda) Capt., S. Cahill (Portadown); M. Mulhaire (Thurles), P. Whateley (Dundalk), G. Fusco (Barnhall), D. Marmion (Dundalk), D. Broughall (Cill Dara), J.P. Walsh (Westport), E. Daly (Naas), S. Madigan (Shannon).
Reps: N. Foxe (Kilkenny) for Mulhaire, D. Murray (Cork Con) for Whateley, D. Quinn (Drogheda) for Walsh

Ireland 11 Wales 10

v Scotland (Stirling RFC) 5 April 1997

A. Morrissey (Highfield); R. O'Donovan (Cobh), A. Considine (Ennis), S. Horgan (Drogheda), A. Bell (Malone); M. McHugh (Drogheda) Capt., S. Cahill (Portadown); N. Foxe (Kilkenny), D. Murray (Cork Con), G. Fusco (Barnhall), D. Marmion (Dundalk), D. Broughall (Cill Dara), E. Daly (Naas), D. O'Kane (Portadown), D. Quinn (Drogheda).
Reps: M. Mulhaire (Thurles) for Foxe, A. Bohane (Highfield) for Fusco, S. Madigan (Shannon) for Broughall

Scotland 5 Ireland 22

v Italy (Merrion Road) 10 January 1998

G. Brady (Ballina); G. Duggan (Richmond), B. Davis (Boyne), D. Dunne (Athy), C. Blanchfield (Athy); J. Staunton (Garryowen), M. Walls (Mullingar); N. Foxe (Kilkenny) Capt., P. Whateley (Dundalk), G. Horan (Portarlington), T. Hogan (Nenagh), G. Logan (Guinness), D. Quinn (Boyne), J. Walsh (Westport), P. Fitzgerald (Shannon).
Rep: A. Hanley (Athlone) for Quinn

Ireland 14 Italy 11

v Wales (Llandovery) 28 February 1998

G. Brady (Ballina); I. Murray-Tait (Ballymena), B. Davis (Boyne), D. Dunne (Athy), C. Blanchfield (Athy); J. Staunton (Garryowen) Capt., M. Walls (Mullingar); N. Foxe (Kilkenny), P. Whateley (Dundalk), G. Horan (Portarlington), T. Hogan (Nenagh), K. Dowling (Skerries), D. Quinn (Boyne), J. Walsh (Westport), D. O'Kane (Portadown).
Rep: C. Richardson (Thurles) for Dunne

Wales 0 Ireland 15

v Scotland (Ravenhill) 11 April 1998

G. Brady (Ballina); I. Murray-Tait (Ballymena), B. Davis (Boyne), C. Richardson (Thurles), C. Blanchfield (Athy); J. Staunton (Garryowen) Capt., P. Jennings (Westport); N. Foxe (Kilkenny), P. Whateley (Dundalk), G. Horan

(Portarlington), T. Hogan (Nenagh), K. Dowling (Skerries), D. Quinn (Boyne), J. Walsh (Westport), D. O'Kane (Portadown).
Reps: D. Hunt (Athlone) for Richardson, B. Walsh (Portarlington) for Jennings, F. Farrell (Monivea) for Foxe, P. Flanagan (Athlone) for Whateley, D. Vennard (Portadown) for Horan, O. Collings (Boyne) for Walsh

Ireland 25 Scotland 16

Italy (Congegliano Venetto, Treviso) 27 February 1999

N. O'Brien (Monivea) Capt.; D. O'Riordan (Youghal), B. Lynn (Wicklow), D. Cantley (Dromore), B. Burke (Barnhall); R. Glennon (Edenderry), R. Farrell (Tullamore); D. Witherow (City of Derry), I. Campbell (Limavady), J. Roche (Highfield), B. Prenderville (Abbeyfeale), C. Finnerty (Tullamore), D. Maguire (Longford).
Reps: J. Boyd (Malone) for Prenderville, M. McPhail (Corinthians) for Burke, C. Prime (Banbridge) for Roche

Italy 10 Ireland 9

v Wales (Glasgow) 3 April 1999

B. Burke (Barnhall); J. Gill (Westport), E. Lynn (Boyne), D. Cantley (Dromore), D. O'Riordan (Youghal); F. Lynch (Guinness), R. O'Farrell (Tullamore); D. Witherow (City of Derry), I. Campbell (Limavady), C. Prime (Banbridge), T. Barker (Malone), J. Murphy (Highfield), J. Boyd (Malone), C. Finnerty (Tullamore) Capt., D. Maguire (Longford).
Reps: B. Lynn (Wicklow) for E. Lynn, R. Glennon (Edenderry) for Gill, M. Chambers (Banbridge) for O'Farrell

Wales 15 Ireland 10

v Scotland (Stirling) 6 April 1999

B. Burke (Barnhall); M. McPhail (Corinthians), L. Barry (Wicklow), D. Cantley (Dromore), N. O'Brien (Monivea); R. Glennon (Edenderry), M. Chambers (Banbridge); A. Nash (Roscrea), P. Smyth (Midleton), C. Prime (Banbridge), C. Murphy (Corinthians), J. Murphy (Highfield), B. Prenderville (Abbeyfeale), C. Finnerty (Tullamore) Capt.
Reps: F. Lynch (Guinness) for Glennon, D. O'Riordan (Youghal) for McPhail

Ireland 19 Scotland 5

v England (Murrayfield) 9 April 1999

B. Burke (Barnhall); D. O'Riordan (Youghal), B. Lynn (Wicklow), D. Cantley (Dromore), N. O'Brien (Monivea); F. Lynch (Guinness), M. Chambers (Banbridge); A. Nash (Roscrea), P. Smyth (Midleton), J. Roche (Highfield), C. Murphy (Corinthians), J. Murphy (Highfield), J. Boyd (Malone), C. Finnerty (Tullamore) Capt., N. McCordick (Ballynahinch).
Reps: C. Prime (Banbridge) for Roche, D. Witherow (City of Derry) for Nash, T. Barker (Malone) for J. Murphy, B. Prenderville (Abbeyfeale) for Boyd, J. Gill (Westport) for Burke

England 15 Ireland 12

PRESIDENTS OF THE IRFU 1969–89

J.W.S. Irwin
1969–70

E. Patterson
1970–71

D.A. Dineen
1971–72

The Hon. Mr. Justice
J.C. Conroy
1972–73

I.F. Mahony
1973–74

H.R. McKibbin
1974–75

J.J. Keane
1975–76

J.A.D. Higgins
1976–77

J.F. Coffey
1977–78

K.J. Quilligan
1978–79

J. Montgomery
1979–80

R. Ganly
1980–81

J.J. Moore
1981–82

J.E. Nelson
1982–83

G.F. Reidy
1983–84

M.H. Carroll
1984–85

D. McKibbin
1985–86

Sir Ewart Bell
1986–87

P.F. Madigan
1987–88

T.J. Kiernan
1988–89

CAPTAINS OF IRELAND TEAMS 1990-97

T.J. Kingston
1990–91

P.A. Danaher
1991–92

M.T. Bradley
1992–93

B.J. Mullin
1994–95

N.J. Popplewell
1994–95

J.E. Staples
1994–95

N.A. Hogan
1995–96

K.G.M. Wood
1996–97

P.S Johns
1998–99

D. O'Cuinneagain
1999

Committee of the Union 1999

APPENDIX 25

SEVENS

(Ireland Squads and Results in Sevens Tournaments)

Scotland Rugby Union Centenary Sevens (Murrayfield) 7 April 1973

V.A. Becker (Lansdowne), S. Dennison (Garryowen), A.W. McMaster (Ballymena), C.M.H. Gibson (NIFC) Capt., T.A. Moore (Highfield), D.M. Canniffe (Cork Con), J.F. Slattery (Blackrock Coll), P.C. Whelan (Garryowen), K. Mays (UCD)

Results: Ireland 22 New Zealand 18; Ireland 16 Australia 4; Ireland 24 Scotland 12. Final: Ireland 18 England 22

Hong Kong Sevens 27–28 March 1993

A. Rolland (Blackrock Coll) Capt., V. Cunningham (St Mary's Coll), B. Glennon (Lansdowne), E. Elwood (Lansdowne), R. Wallace (Garryowen), J. Garth (Wanderers), P. Johns (Dungannon), W. Mulcahy (Skerries), D. McBride (Malone), M. Galwey (Shannon)

Results: Ireland 7 Italy 5; Ireland 24 Hong Kong 0; Ireland 12 Australia 17

Rugby World Cup Sevens (Murrayfield) 16–18 April 1993

D. McBride (Malone) Capt., J. Garth (Wanderers), P. Johns (Dungannon), V. Cunningham (St Mary's Coll), A. Rolland (Blackrock Coll), E. Elwood (Lansdowne), R. Wallace (Garryowen), B. Glennon (Lansdowne), W. Mulcahy (Skerries), M. Galwey (Shannon)

Results: Ireland 21 South Korea 12; Ireland 17 France 9; Ireland 45 Netherlands 0; Ireland 7 New Zealand 24; Ireland 38 United States 0; Ireland 17 Western Samoa 0; Ireland 14 Tonga 12; Ireland 7 Fiji 31. Semi-final: Ireland 19 Australia 21

Hong Kong Sevens 26–27 March 1994

D. McBride (Malone) Capt., B. Robinson (Ballymena), P. Johns (Dungannon), E. Halvey (Shannon), A. Rolland (Blackrock Coll), E. Elwood (Lansdowne), A. McGowan (Blackrock Coll), B. Walsh (Cork Con), I. Gray (Queen's U), P. Danaher (Garryowen)

Results: Ireland 40 Singapore 0; President's VII 22 Ireland 7; USA 14 Ireland 12

Hong Kong Sevens 25–26 March 1995

M. McCall (Bangor) Capt., N. Woods (Blackrock Coll), B. Walsh (Cork Con), A. Rolland (Blackrock Coll), N. Assaf (Blackrock Coll), R. Wilson (Inst), J. Garth (Wanderers), E. Miller (Old Wesley), J. Davidson (Dungannon), M. Ridge (Blackrock Coll)

Results: Ireland 12 Portugal 12; Ireland 19 Namibia 26; Ireland 14 Japan 19

Melun Sevens 6–7 May 1995

D. Hickie (UCD), I. Gray (Inst), B. Walsh (Cork Con), A. McGowan (Blackrock Coll) S. Smyth (City of Derry), N. Doak (NIFC), S. McKinty (Bangor), J. Garth (Wanderers) Capt., J. Hastings (Dungannon), M. Ridge (Blackrock Coll)

Results: Ireland 14 England 26; Ireland 26 Holland 12; Ireland 5 France 32; Ireland 40 Wales 47

Hong Kong Sevens 29–31 March 1996

P. Burke (Cork Con), D. Corkery (Cork Con), V. Cunningham (St Mary's Coll), J. Garth (Wanderers), N. Hogan (Terenure Coll), P. Johns (Dungannon), W.D. McBride (Malone) Capt., J. Topping (Ballymena), R. Wallace (Garryowen), N. Woods (Blackrock Coll)

Results: Ireland 43 Malaysia 5; Ireland 21 Namibia 15; Ireland 14 Western Samoa 14. Quarter-final: Ireland 0 New Zealand 49

World Cup Sevens (Hong Kong) 21–23 March 1997

W.D. McBride (Malone) Capt., J. Bell (Northampton), W. Cronin (Garryowen), K. Dawson (London Irish), D. Hickie (St Mary's Coll), D. Humphreys (London Irish), N. Malone (Leicester), E. Miller (Leicester), R. Wallace (Saracens), N. Woods (London Irish)

Results: Ireland 22 Argentina 31; Ireland 5 South Africa 38; Ireland 5 South Africa 34; Ireland 5 Hong Kong 26. Ireland failed to qualify.

Bowl — Quarter-final: Ireland 33 Portugal 5
Semi-final: Ireland 22 Japan 24

Hong Kong Sevens March–April 1999

S. Horgan (Lansdowne), J. McWeeney (St Mary's Coll), F. Campion (St Mary's Coll), D. Crotty (Garryowen), B. Carey (Blackrock Coll), D. Wallace (Garryowen), B. Everitt (Lansdowne), D. Corkery (Cork Con), K. Nowlan (St Mary's Coll), J. Topping (Ballymena)

Manager A. Rolland (Wanderers), Coach D. McBride (Malone), Physiotherapist, J. Martin

Results: Ireland 22 Hong Kong 14; Ireland 15 Croatia 14; New Zealand 26 Ireland 0; Japan 32 Ireland 22

APPENDIX 26

RECORDS

The highest scores recorded by Ireland at the various levels of international rugby are:

Full international level: 70 v Georgia (Lansdowne Road) 14 November 1998

A:	73 v Italy A (Donnybrook) 9 April 1999
U 25:	36 v Spain (Thomond Park) 8 September 1988
U 23:	31 v Holland (Hilversum) 13 October 1979
Development:	44 v South Africa (Cape Town) 11 August 1993
U 21:	57 v Italy (Ravenhill) 9 April 1999
U 19:	63 v Spain (Upritchard Park, Bangor) 16 March 1998
U 18:	25 v Scotland (Ravenhill) 11 April 1998
Academy:	76 v Canada U21 (Donnybrook) 20 September 1998
Schools:	41 v Wales (Musgrave Park) 10 April 1999

The highest scores recorded against Ireland are:
Full International level: 63 v New Zealand (Lansdowne Road) 15 November 1997

A:	77 v Western Samoa (Apia) 1997
U 25:	20 v Canada (Lansdowne Road) 27 September 1986
U 23:	3 v Holland (Hilversum) 13 October 1979
Development:	33 v Namibia A (Windhoek) 31 July 1993
U 21:	40 v France (Anglesea Road) 17 January 1997
U 19:	42 v Argentina (Buenos Aires) 26 March 1997
U 18	Spain (Valladolid) 10 March 1996
Academy:	29 v Canada (Donnybrook) 20 September 1998
Schools:	37 v England (Gloucester) 6 April 1977

Most points by a player in a full international: 24 by P. Burke v Italy (Lansdowne Road) 1997
Most tries by an Ireland player in an international: 4 by B. Robinson v Zimbabwe (Lansdowne Road) 1991
Most tries by an Ireland player in international rugby: 17 by B. Mullin in 55 internationals between 1984 and 1995
Most penalty goals by an Ireland player in an international: 8 by P. Burke v Italy (Lansdowne Road) 1997
Most conversions by an Ireland player in an international: 10 by E.P. Elwood v Georgia (Lansdowne Road) 1998
Most dropped goals by an Ireland player in an international: 3 by D. Humphreys v Wales (Wembley) 1999; 2 by C.M.H. Gibson v Australia (Lansdowne Road) 1967; 2 by W.M. McCombe v France (Lansdowne Road) 1975; 2 by S.O. Campbell v Australia (Sydney) 1979; 2 by B.E.P. Elwood v England (Lansdowne Road) 1993
Most points by an Ireland player in internationals: 308 by M.J. Kiernan in 43 internationals
Most capped Ireland player: C.M.H. Gibson (69) 1964–79
Most capped Ireland back: C.M.H. Gibson (69) in three positions, wing, centre and outside half
Most capped Ireland forward: W.J. McBride (63) all in second row 1962–75
Most internationals as Ireland captain: T.J. Kiernan (24) 1963–73
Most points by Ireland in Five Nations Championship in a season: 71 (1982–83)
Most points by an individual for Ireland in Five Nations Championship series: 52 by S.O. Campbell 1982–83

Ireland Academy

v Canada (U 21) Donnybrook 20 September 1998
T. Keating (Blackrock Coll), D. McCombe (Inst), S. Moore (UCD), D. O'Sullivan (Skerries), J. Davis (Dungannon), M. McHugh (DU), C. Scally (UCD), K. Flanagan (Corinthians), D. Blaney (UCD), N. Treston (Blackrock Coll), R. Casey (Blackrock Coll), M. O'Driscoll (UCC), A. Kearney (UCD), L. Cullen (Blackrock Coll), P. Shanley (UCD).
Reps: A. Dunne (UCD) for Keating, G. D'Arcy (Lansdowne) for McCombe, C. Campbell (London Irish) for Scally, A. O'Brien (UCD) for Flanagan, S. Best (Newcastle) for Treston, C. McCarey (Ballymena) for Kearney

Ireland 76 Canada 29

APPENDIX 27

IRISH PROVINCES: RESULTS IN EUROPEAN COMPETITIONS

Cup 1995–96

Pool Matches

Cardiff 46 Ulster 6; Ulster 16 Begles Bordeaux 29; Munster 17 Swansea 13; Castres 19 Munster 12; Milan 21 Leinster 24; Leinster 23 Pontypridd 22

Semi-final: Leinster 14 Cardiff 30

Cup 1996–97

Pool Matches

Llanelli 34 Leinster 17; Leinster 10 Leicester 27; Scottish Borders 25 Leinster 34; Leinster 25 Pau 23

Caledonia 34 Ulster 41; Ulster 15 Harlequins 21; Neath 15 Ulster 13; Ulster 6 Brive 17

Munster 25 Milan 5; Cardiff 48 Munster 18; Munster 49 Wasps 22; Toulouse 60 Munster 19

Conference

Connacht 34 Padova 12; Dunvant 29 Connacht 9; Connacht 11 Northampton 31; Toulon 44 Connacht 10; Connacht 30 Orrell 18

Cup 1997–98

Pool Matches

Leinster 25 Toulouse 24; Leinster 16 Leicester 9; Milan 33 Leinster 32; Leicester 47 Leinster 22; Leinster 23 Milan 6; Toulouse 38 Leinster 19

Ulster 12 Glasgow 18; Swansea 33 Ulster 16; Wasps 56 Ulster 3; Ulster 28 Swansea 20; Ulster 31 Wasps 38; Glasgow 30 Ulster 15

Harlequins 48 Munster 40; Cardiff 43 Munster 23; Munster 17 Bourgoin 15; Munster 32 Cardiff 37; Bourgoin 21 Munster 6; Munster 23 Harlequins 16

Conference

Pool Matches

Connacht 43 Northampton 13; Nice 20 Connacht 16; Begles-Bordeaux 9 Connacht 15; Connacht 28 Nice 25; Connacht 22 Begles-Bordeaux 15; Northampton 5 Connacht 20

Connacht won pool

Quarter-final: Agen 40 Connacht 27

Cup 1998–99

Pool Matches

Ulster 38 Edinburgh Reivers 38; Toulouse 39 Ulster 3; Ebbw Vale 28 Ulster 61; Ulster 29 Toulouse 24; Ulster 43 Ebbw Vale 18; Edinburgh Reivers 21 Ulster 23

Ulster won Pool

Quarter-final: Ulster 15 Toulouse 13

Semi-Final: Ulster 33 Stade Français 27

Final: Ulster 21 Colomiers 6

Munster 20 Padova 13; Munster 34 Neath 10; Perpignan 41 Munster 24; Neath 18 Munster 18; Munster 13 Perpignan 5; Padova 21 Munster 35.

Munster runners-up in pool

Quarter-final: Colomiers 23 Munster 9

Llanelli 27 Leinster 23; Leinster 17 Stade Français 28; Leinster 9 Begles-Bordeaux 3; Stade Français 56 Leinster 31; Begles-Bordeaux 31 Leinster 10; Llanelli 34 Leinster 27

Shield

Newport 12 Connacht 31; Connacht 29 Perigueux 28; Rovigo 20 Connacht 21; Connacht 26 Narbonne 38; Caerphilly 39 Connacht 8; Connacht 14 Racing Club 19

APPENDIX 28

INTERPROVINCIAL CHAMPIONSHIP RESULTS

The first interprovincial took place between Leinster and Ulster in 1875–76. However, the four provinces Interprovincial Championship did not start until the 1946–47 season. The Exiles played in the Championship for a four year period between 1992–93 and 1995–96. In 1998–99 the provinces met each other twice on a home and away basis.

The results in the series to date are:

Leinster v Ulster

1946–47 Ulster 16-8
1947–48 draw 0-0
1948–49 Leinster 8-0
1949–50 Leinster 8-0
1950–51 Ulster 10-3
1951–52 Ulster 17-14
1952–53 Leinster 5-3
1953–54 Ulster 3-0
1954–55 Leinster 5-3
1955–56 Ulster 21-6
1956–57 Ulster 17-8
1957–58 Ulster 24-13
1958–59 Leinster 16-12
1959–60 Leinster 16-6
1960–61 draw 9-9
1961–62 Leinster 8-3
1962–63 Ulster 11-8
1963–64 Leinster 12--8
1964–65 draw 8-8
1965–66 Leinster 8-6
1966–67 Ulster 8-6
1967–68 Ulster 9-5
1968–69 Ulster 14-8
1969–70 Ulster 8-3
1970–71 Ulster 6-3
1971–72 Leinster 12-10
1972–73 Leinster 11-6
1973–74 Leinster 20-13
1974–75 Ulster 22-9
1975–76 Leinster 16-9
1976–77 Ulster 36-21
1977–78 Leinster 29-18
1978–79 Leinster 9-3
1979–80 Leinster 18-12
1980–81 Leinster 39-9
1981–82 Leinster 19-6
1982–83 Leinster 15-9
1983–84 Leinster 20-16
1984–85 Ulster 16-3
1985–86 Ulster 19-13
1986–87 Ulster 14-12
1987–88 Ulster 22-9
1988–89 Ulster 18-17
1989–90 Ulster 14-6
1990–91 Ulster 13-6
1991–92 Ulster 22-21
1992–93 Ulster 12-8
1993–94 Leinster 25-0
1994–95 Leinster 12-6
1995–96 Leinster 31-3
1996–97 Leinster 35-25
1997–98 Leinster 26-25
1998–99 Ulster 34-12
1998–99 Leinster 35-11

Leinster v Munster

1946–47 Leinster 15-11
1947–48 Munster 14-11
1948–49 Leinster 6-0
1949–50 draw 3-3
1950–51 Leinster 8-6
1951–52 Leinster 12-9
1952–53 Munster 3-0
1953–54 draw 0-0
1954–55 Munster 9-8
1955–56 Leinster 12-9
1956–57 Leinster 19-9
1957–58 Munster 19-12
1958–59 Leinster 32-0
1959–60 Munster 18-14
1960–61 Leinster 14-9
1961–62 Leinster 6-3
1962–63 Munster 14-6
1963–64 Leinster 10-6
1964–65 Leinster 14-3
1965–66 Munster 6-3
1966–67 Munster 9-5
1967–68 Leinster 8-5
1968–69 Munster 12-8
1969–70 Leinster 12-6
1970–71 Leinster 10-0
1971–72 Leinster 9-0
1972–73 Munster 17-9
1973–74 Munster 13-3
1974–75 Leinster 9-6
1975–76 Munster 9-0
1976–77 Leinster 12-6
1977–78 Munster 15-10
1978–79 Munster 12-3
1979–80 Leinster 4-3
1980–81 Leinster 18-9
1981–82 draw 15-15
1982–83 Munster 9-6
1983–84 Leinster 22-13
1984–85 Leinster 15-9
1985–86 Leinster 15-6
1986–87 Leinster 15-3
1987–88 Munster 10-3
1988–89 Leinster 23-12
1989–90 Munster 10-3
1990–91 Munster 27-12
1991–92 Munster 20-3
1992–93 Leinster 21-20
1993–94 Munster 21-19
1994–95 Munster 36-14

1995–96 Leinster 19-15
1996–97 Munster 45-40
1997–98 Munster 15-12
1998–99 Leinster 24-18
1998–99 Munster 25-10

Leinster v Connacht

1946–47 draw 5-5
1947–48 Leinster 15-0
1948–49 Leinster 3-0
1949–50 Leinster 31-3
1950–51 Connacht 10-6
1951–52 Leinster 39-3
1952–53 Leinster 35-0
1953–54 Leinster 34-14
1954–55 Leinster 6-3
1955–56 Connacht 8-6
1956–57 Leinster 19-3
1957–58 Leinster 9-3
1958–59 Leinster 9-3
1959–60 draw 3-3
1960–61 draw 0-0
1961–62 Leinster 13-9
1962–63 Leinster 18-17
1963–64 Leinster 11-6
1964–65 draw 6-6
1965–66 Leinster 13-6
1966–67 Leinster 26-3
1967–68 Leinster 24-11
1968–69 Leinster 15-6
1969–70 Leinster 26-6
1970–71 Leinster 11-3
1971–72 Leinster 12-6
1972–73 Leinster 13-0
1973–74 Leinster 20-13
1974–75 Leinster 12-3
1975–76 Leinster 7-0
1976–77 Leinster 21-7
1977–78 Leinster 30-9
1978–79 Leinster 13-6
1979–80 Leinster 25-10
1980–81 Leinster 18-9
1981–82 Leinster 20-10
1982–83 Leinster 13-7
1983–84 Leinster 29-6
1984–85 Leinster 14-3
1985–86 Connacht 9-6
1986–87 Leinster 41-6
1987–88 Leinster 20-19
1988–89 Connacht 11-10
1989–90 Leinster 16-12
1990–91 Leinster 20-18
1991–92 Leinster 24-9
1992–93 Connacht 28-9
1993–94 Leinster 15-11
1994–95 Connacht 20-19
1995–96 Leinster 41-9
1996–97 Connacht 22-13
1997–98 Leinster 23-6
1998–99 Leinster 29-24
1998–99 Connacht 24-23

Leinster v The Exiles

1992–93 Leinster 16-14
1993–94 Leinster 13-8
1994–95 Leinster 20-18
1995–96 Leinster 42-26

Ulster v Munster

1946–47 Ulster 6-3
1947–48 draw 6-6
1948–49 Ulster 13-6
1949–50 Ulster 11-0
1950–51 Ulster 6-3
1951–52 Ulster 16-3
1952–53 draw 0-0
1953–54 Munster 11-6
1954–55 Ulster 3-0
1955–56 Ulster 6-3
1956–57 Ulster 5-3
1957–58 Munster 11-6
1958–59 Ulster 8-6
1959–60 Munster 18-0
1960–61 Ulster 13-3
1961–62 Ulster 26-3
1962–63 Munster 11-0
1963–64 draw 0-0
1964–65 Munster 9-8
1965–66 Munster 13-6
1966–67 draw 3-3
1967–68 Ulster 13-6
1968–69 Munster 17-9
1969–70 draw 3-3
1970–71 Ulster 8-3
1971–72 Ulster 13-6
1972–73 Ulster 4-3
1973–74 draw 6-6
1974–75 draw 6-6
1975–76 Ulster 9-7
1976–77 Ulster 27-24
1977–78 Ulster 9-6
1978–79 Munster 11-6
1979–80 Munster 15-11
1980–81 Munster 21-10
1981–82 Ulster 18-16
1982–83 Ulster 19-10
1983–84 Ulster 13-12
1984–85 Ulster 14-6
1985–86 Ulster 23-3
1986–87 Ulster 17-6
1987–88 draw 10-10
1988–89 Ulster 12-9
1989–90 Ulster 13-10
1990–91 Ulster 19-15
1991–92 Ulster 37-22
1992–93 Ulster 12-11
1993–94 Ulster 24-21
1994–95 Munster 17-16
1995–96 Ulster 14-10
1996–97 Munster 27-24
1997–98 Ulster 22-12
1998–99 Ulster 29-12
1998–99 Munster 31-9

Ulster v Connacht

1946–47 Ulster 26-3
1947–48 Ulster 19-0
1948–49 Ulster 30-6
1949–50 Ulster 12-3
1950–51 Ulster 26-3
1951–52 Ulster 13-0
1952–53 Ulster 28-3
1953–54 Ulster 11-3
1954–55 Connacht 14-6
1955–56 Connacht 12-9
1956–57 Connacht 6-3
1957–58 Ulster 23-12
1958–59 Connacht 14-5
1959–60 Ulster 9-3
1960–61 Connacht 6-3
1961–62 Ulster 11-0
1962–63 Ulster 19-6
1963–64 Connacht 13-3
1964–65 Connacht 13-3
1965–66 draw 3-3
1966–67 Ulster 9-8
1967–68 Ulster 14-12
1968–69 Ulster 11-9
1969–70 Ulster 20-0
1970–71 Ulster 42-0

1971–72 Ulster 13-0
1972–73 Ulster 37-6
1973–74 Ulster 17-14
1974–75 Ulster 29-6
1975–76 Ulster 6-3
1976–77 Ulster 13-3
1977–78 Ulster 18-3
1978–79 Ulster 11-4
1979–80 draw 6-6
1980–81 Ulster 13-12
1981–82 Ulster 6-3
1982–83 Ulster 22-21
1983–84 Connacht 9-4
1984–85 Ulster 28-6
1985–86 Ulster 12-6
1986–87 Ulster 37-6
1987–88 Ulster 20-3
1988–89 Ulster 16-3
1989–90 Ulster 38-3
1990–91 Ulster 16-9
1991–92 draw 10-10
1992–93 Ulster 19-6
1993–94 Ulster 39-10
1994–95 Ulster 20-6
1995–96 Ulster 27-9
1996–97 Ulster 32-27
1997–98 Connacht 27-12
1998–99 Connacht 21-18
1998–99 Ulster 36-6

Ulster v The Exiles

1992–93 Ulster 16-13
1993–94 Ulster 21-3
1994–95 Ulster 42-16
1995–96 Ulster 29-3

Munster v Connacht

1946–47 Munster 13-10
1947–48 Munster 24-3
1948–49 Munster 20-6
1949–50 Munster 6-5
1950–51 Munster 12-8
1951–52 Munster 28-3
1952–53 Munster 8-0
1953–54 Connacht 3-0
1954–55 Munster 8-3
1955–56 Munster 8-3
1956–57 Connacht 10-3
1957–58 Munster 3-0
1958–59 Munster 9-0
1959–60 Munster 6-0
1960–61 Munster 5-0
1961–62 Munster 11-3
1962–63 Munster 6-0
1963–64 Munster 12-8
1964–65 draw 5-5
1965–66 Munster 9-3
1966–67 Munster 12-6
1967–68 Munster 11-9
1968–69 Munster 12-3
1969–70 Munster 22-0
1970–71 Munster 9-0
1971–72 Munster 10-0
1972–73 Munster 12-3
1973–74 Munster 29-7
1974–75 draw 6-6
1975–76 Munster 16-6
1976–77 Munster 13-6
1977–78 Munster 10-6
1978–79 Munster 19-3
1979–80 Connacht 20-16
1980–81 Munster 16-0
1981–82 Munster 21-18
1982–83 Munster 9-7
1983–84 Munster 29-7
1984–85 Munster 15-9
1985–86 Munster 16-9
1986–87 Connacht 11-9
1987–88 Munster 17-12
1988–89 Munster 25-10
1989–90 Munster 14-10
1990–91 Munster 19-18
1991–92 Munster 15-9
1992–93 Munster 20-10
1993–94 Munster 15-9
1994–95 Munster 60-20
1995–96 Munster 46-11
1996–97 Munster 45-28
1997–98 Munster 29-9
1998–99 Munster 18-13
1998–99 Munster 21-7

Munster v The Exiles

1992–93 The Exiles 19-13
1993–94 Munster 34-19
1994–95 Munster 46-8
1995–96 Munster 20-14

Connacht v The Exiles

1992–93 The Exiles 17-12
1993–94 The Exiles 41-12
1994–95 The Exiles 35-9
1995–96 The Exiles 28-22

APPENDIX 29

ALL IRELAND LEAGUE

AIB League

(The winners, runners-up and relegated teams in the All Ireland League)

The league was inaugurated in the 1990–91 season. It was not sponsored in the initial season, but subsequently was sponsored for six years by Insurance Corporation and for the last two years by Allied Irish Banks and is now known as the AIB League.

1990–91

Division One
Winners: Cork Constitution; Runners-up: Garryowen
Relegated: Wanderers and Malone

Division Two
Winners: Old Wesley; Runners-up: Young Munster
Relegated: NIFC, Athlone, Corinthians

Promoted after round robin play-off between provincial league winners: Blackrock College, Dungannon, Dolphin

1991–92

Division One
Winners: Garryowen; Runners-up: Shannon
Relegated: Lansdowne, Instonians

Division Two
Winners: Dungannon; Runners-up: Greystones
Relegated: Malone, Sunday's Well, CIYMS

Promoted from round robin play-off between provincial league winners: Clontarf, Galwegians, Old Crescent

1992–93

Division One
Winners: Young Munster; Runners-up: Cork Constitution
Relegated: Ballymena

Division Two
Winners: Lansdowne; Runners-up: Wanderers
Relegated: Clontarf

1993–94

Division One
Winners: Garryowen; Runners-up: Cork Constitution
Relegated: Greystones, Wanderers

Division Two
Winners: Instonians; Runners-up: Sunday's Well
Relegated: Galwegians, Ballina

Division Three
Winners: UCD; Runners-up: Bective Rangers
Relegated: Portadown, Collegians, Sligo

Division Four
Winners: Monkstown; Runners-up: Waterpark

1994–95

Division One
Winners: Shannon; Runners-up: Blackrock College
Relegated: Dungannon, Sunday's Well

Division Two
Winners: Old Belvedere; Runners-up: Ballymena
Relegated: UCD, Bangor

Division Three
Winners: NIFC; Runners-up: Clontarf
Relegated: Corinthians, Ballina

Division Four
Winners: Bohemians; Runners-up: Skerries

1995–96

DIVISION ONE
Winners: Shannon; Runners-up: Garryowen
No relegation due to restructuring of league

DIVISION TWO
Winners: Old Crescent; Runners-up: Dungannon
Also promoted: Terenure College

DIVISION THREE
Winners: Monkstown; Runners-up: City of Derry
Also promoted: Highfield, DLSP, Skerries and UCC

DIVISION FOUR
Winners: Portadown; Runners-up: Dublin University
Also promoted: Collegians, Queen's University and Corinthians
Promoted from the Provincial Junior leagues: Suttonians, Ballynahinch, Creggs and Richmond (UCG withdrew from the competition)

1996–97

DIVISION ONE
Winners: Shannon; Runners-up: Lansdowne
Relegated: Old Wesley and Instonians

DIVISION TWO
Winners: Clontarf; Runners-up: Dolphin
Relegated: NIFC, Highfield

DIVISION THREE
Winners: Buccaneers; Runners-up: Galwegians
Relegated: Bangor, Waterpark

DIVISION FOUR
Winners: Suttonians; Runners-up: Ballynahinch
Relegated: Armagh and UCG
Promoted from the Provincial Junior leagues: Carlow, Omagh Academicals

1997–98

DIVISION ONE
Winners: Shannon; Runners-up: Garryowen
The title was decided on a knock-out competition between the top four clubs. Shannon had finished top of the division with Garryowen second, Young Munster third and St Mary's College fourth. In the semi-finals Shannon defeated St Mary's College 28-21 and Garryowen defeated Young Munster 24-10. In the final at Lansdowne Road, Shannon defeated Garryowen 15-9.
Relegated: Dungannon, Dolphin, Old Crescent, Old Belvedere

DIVISION TWO
Winners: Galwegians; Runners-up: Buccaneers
Relegated: Monkstown, Instonians

DIVISION THREE
Winners: Portadown; Runners-up: Ballynahinch
Relegated: Collegians, Suttonians, Queen's University

DIVISION FOUR
Winners: Carlow; Runners-up: Richmond
Relegated: Sligo, Creggs
Promoted from Provincial Junior leagues: Midleton and Banbridge

1998–99

DIVISION ONE
Winners: Cork Constitution; Runners-up: Garryowen
Yet again the title was decided on a knock-out competition between the top four clubs in the league section. Garryowen finished top of the division on points difference from Cork Constitution and Buccaneers after all three clubs had finished on 16 points. St Mary's College, on 14 points, finished in fourth place on points difference from Lansdowne, who also had 14 points.
In the semi-finals Garryowen defeated St Mary's College and Cork Constitution defeated Buccaneers. In the final Cork Constitution defeated Garryowen after extra time 14–11.
Relegated: Galwegians and Blackrock College

DIVISION TWO
Winners: Dungannon; Runners-up: DLSP
Relegated: Old Wesley, Ballynahinch and Skerries

DIVISION THREE
Winners: UCD; Runners-up: NIFC
Relegated: Dublin University and Highfield

DIVISION FOUR
Winners: Midleton; Runners-up: Ballina
Relegated: CIYMS and Collegians
Promoted from Junior League: Barnhall and Thomond

APPENDIX 30

SCHOOLS CUP WINNERS

Ulster Schools Senior Cup Winners

1876	Armagh RS
1877	Armagh RS
1878	Methodist Coll
1879	Armagh RS
1880	Armagh RS
1881	Armagh RS
1882	Methodist Coll
1883	Armagh RS
1884	Coleraine AI
1885	Armagh RS
1886	Coleraine AI
1887	Coleraine AI
1888	RBAI
1889	Methodist Coll
1890	RBAI
1891	Methodist Coll
1892	Methodist Coll
1893	Methodist Coll
1894	Coleraine AI
1895	RBAI
1896	Methodist Coll
1897	Coleraine AI
1898	Campbell Coll
1899	Methodist Coll
1900	Foyle Coll
1901	Methodist Coll
1902	Methodist Coll
1903	RBAI
1904	Methodist Coll
1905	Portora RS
1906	Portora RS
1907	Dungannon RS
1908	Portora RS
1909	Portora RS
1910	Campbell Coll
1911	Not completed
1912	RBAI
1913	Campbell Coll
1914	Methodist Coll
1915	Foyle Coll
1916	RBAI
1917	Campbell Coll
1918	RBAI
1919	RBAI
1920	Coleraine AI
1921	Campbell Coll
1922	Campbell Coll
1923	Campbell Coll
1924	Campbell Coll
1925	Coleraine AI
1926	Campbell Coll
1927	Methodist Coll
1928	Methodist Coll
1929	Methodist Coll
1930	RBAI
1931	Campbell Coll
1932	Campbell Coll
1933	RBAI
1934	RBAI
1935	RBAI
1936	Methodist Coll
1937	Methodist Coll
1938	RBAI
1939	Coleraine AI
1940	Portora RS
1941	Portora RS
1942	Portora/RBAI (shared)
1943	RBAI
1944	RBAI
1945	RBAI
1946	RBAI
1947	RBAI
1948	RBAI
1949	Methodist Coll
1950	Campbell Coll
1951	RBAI
1952	Methodist Coll
1953	Methodist/Campbell (shared)
1954	Campbell/RBAI (shared)
1955	Campbell Coll
1956	Campbell Coll
1957	RBAI
1958	Annadale GS
1959	RBAI
1960	Campbell/RBAI (shared)
1961	Campbell Coll
1962	BRA/RBAI (shared)
1963	BRA/Rainey (shared)
1964	BRA/Campbell (shared)
1965	Campbell Coll
1966	Campbell Coll
1967	Rainey Endowed
1968	Campbell Coll
1969	Bangor GS
1970	RBAI
1971	Belfast Model
1972	Ballymena Academy
1973	Ballyclare HS
1974	Methodist Coll
1975	Methodist Coll
1976	Methodist Coll
1977	Armagh RS
1978	Bangor GS
1979	Methodist Coll
1980	Campbell Coll
1981	Ballymena Academy
1982	Rainey Endowed
1983	Grosvenor HS
1984	Methodist Coll
1985	Bangor GS
1986	Bangor GS
1987	Methodist Coll
1988	Bangor GS
1989	Methodist Coll
1990	Methodist Coll
1991	Methodist Coll
1992	Coleraine AI
1993	Campbell Coll
1994	Regent House
1995	RBAI
1996	Regent/Methodist (shared)
1997	BRA
1998	RBAI
1999	Campbell Coll

Ulster Schools Medallion Winners

1910 Methodist Coll
1911 RBAI
1912 RBAI
1913 RBAI
1914 Methodist Coll
1915 RBAI
1916 RBAI
1917 RBAI
1918 Dungannon RS
1919 Dungannon RS
1920 RBAI
1921 RBAI
1922 RBAI
1923 RBAI
1924 Methodist Coll
1925 RBAI
1926 RBAI
1927 Methodist Coll
1928 Methodist Coll
1929 Methodist Coll
1930 RBAI
1931 RBAI
1932 Methodist Coll
1933 RBAI
1934 Methodist Coll
1935 Coleraine AI
1936 Bangor GS
1937 Coleraine AI
1938 Coleraine AI
1939 RBAI
1940 Methodist Coll
1941 Methodist Coll
1942 RBAI
1943 RBAI
1944 Coleraine AI
1945 Methodist Coll
1946 Methodist Coll
1947 Methodist Coll
1948 Methodist Coll
1949 Methodist Coll
1950 Coleraine AI
1951 Ballymena/RBAI (shared)
1952 RBAI
1953 RBAI
1954 Annadale/Methodist (shared)
1955 RBAI
1956 RBAI
1957 Methodist Coll
1958 RBAI
1959 RBAI
1960 Annadale/RBAI (shared)
1961 RBAI
1962 Methodist Coll
1963 Coleraine AI
1964 Methodist Coll
1965 BRA
1966 Bangor GS
1967 Annadale/BRA (shared)
1968 BRA
1969 Ballymena/BRA (shared)
1970 Ballymena Academy
1971 Methodist Coll
1972 Methodist/RBAI (shared)
1973 Methodist Coll
1974 Methodist Coll
1975 Coleraine AI
1976 Regent House
1977 Rainey Endowed
1978 BRA
1979 BRA
1980 RBAI
1981 RBAI
1982 RBAI
1983 Methodist Coll
1984 Campbell Coll
1985 Bangor GS
1986 Methodist Coll
1987 Regent House
1988 Methodist Coll
1989 Coleraine AI
1990 Ballyclare HS
1991 Methodist Coll
1992 RBAI
1993 Campbell Coll
1994 Dungannon RS
1995 Methodist Coll
1996 Methodist Coll
1997 RBAI
1998 Regent House
1999 Methodist Coll

Leinster Schools Senior Cup Winners

1887 Blackrock Coll
1888 Blackrock Coll
1889 Corrig
1890 Blackrock Coll
1891 Rathmines
1892 Corrig
1893 Blackrock Coll
1894 Blackrock Coll
1895 Blackrock Coll
1896 Blackrock Coll
1897 Blackrock Col
1898 Wesley
1899 St Columba's
1900 Blackrock Coll
1901 Blackrock Coll
1902 Blackrock Coll
1903 Blackrock Coll
1904 Blackrock Coll
1905 Blackrock Coll
1906 St Andrew's
1907 Blackrock Coll
1908 Blackrock Coll
1909 Blackrock Coll
1910 Blackrock Coll
1911 St Andrew's
1912 Blackrock Coll
1913 Castleknock
1914 Mountjoy
1915 Blackrock Coll
1916 Blackrock Coll
1917 Blackrock Coll
1918 Blackrock Coll
1919 Blackrock Coll
1920 Castleknock
1921 St Andrew's
1922 St Andrew's
1923 Belvedere
1924 Belvedere
1925 Blackrock Coll
1926 Clongowes
1927 Blackrock Coll
1928 Blackrock Coll
1929 Blackrock Coll
1930 Blackrock Coll
1931 Castleknock
1932 PBC Bray
1933 Blackrock Coll
1934 Blackrock Coll
1935 Blackrock Coll
1936 Blackrock Coll
1937 Castleknock
1938 Belvedere
1939 Blackrock Coll
1940 Blackrock Coll
1941 Newbridge
1942 Blackrock Coll

1943 Blackrock Coll
1944 Castleknock
1945 Blackrock Coll
1946 Belvedere
1947 Castleknock
1948 Blackrock Coll
1949 Blackrock Coll
1950 Blackrock Coll
1951 Belvedere
1952 Terenure
1953 Blackrock Coll
1954 Blackrock Col
1955 Blackrock Coll
1956 Blackrock Coll
1957 Blackrock Coll
1958 Terenure
1959 Castleknock
1960 Blackrock Coll
1961 St Mary's
1962 Blackrock Coll
1963 Blackrock Coll
1964 Blackrock Coll
1965 Castleknock
1966 St Mary's
1967 Blackrock Coll
1968 Belvedere
1969 St Mary's
1970 Newbridge
1971 Belvedere
1972 Belvedere
1973 High School
1974 Blackrock Coll
1975 Blackrock Coll
1976 CBC Monkstown
1977 Blackrock Coll
1978 Clongowes
1979 Terenure
1980 Terenure
1981 Blackrock Coll
1982 Blackrock Coll
1983 De La Salle Churchtown
1984 Terenure
1985 De La Salle Churchtown
1986 Blackrock Coll
1987 Blackrock Coll
1988 Clongowes
1989 Blackrock Coll
1990 Blackrock Coll
1991 Clongowes
1992 Terenure
1993 Terenure
1994 St Mary's
1995 Blackrock Coll
1996 Blackrock Coll
1997 Terenure
1998 Clongowes
1999 Blackrock Coll

Leinster Schools Junior Cup Winners

1909 St Andrew's
1910 Blackrock Coll
1911 Blackrock Coll
1912 Blackrock Coll
1913 Belvedere
1914 Belvedere
1915 Castleknock
1916 Belvedere
1917 Belvedere
1918 Belvedere
1919 Belvedere
1920 Castleknock
1921 Castleknock
1922 Castleknock
1923 Blackrock Coll
1924 Castleknock
1925 Belvedere
1926 Castleknock
1927 Blackrock
1928 Castleknock
1929 Belvedere
1930 PBC Bray
1931 Belvedere
1932 Blackrock Coll
1933 Blackrock Coll
1934 St Mary's
1935 Blackrock Coll
1936 Blackrock Coll
1937 Belvedere
1938 High School
1939 Roscrea
1940 Belvedere
1941 Blackrock Coll
1942 Blackrock Coll
1943 Blackrock Coll
1944 Clongowes
1945 Blackrock Coll
1946 Blackrock Coll
1947 Clongowes
1948 Blackrock Coll
1949 Clongowes
1950 Newbridge
1951 Blackrock Coll
1952 Clongowes
1953 Blackrock Coll
1954 Blackrock Coll
1955 Terenure
1956 Blackrock Coll
1957 Blackrock Coll
1958 Terenure
1959 Blackrock Coll
1960 Belvedere
1961 Belvedere
1962 Blackrock Coll
1963 St Mary's
1964 Blackrock Coll
1965 Blackrock Coll
1966 Castleknock
1967 Terenure
1968 Blackrock Coll
1969 Blackrock Coll
1970 Blackrock Coll
1971 St Mary's
1972 Blackrock Coll
1973 Blackrock Coll
1974 St Mary's
1975 PBC Bray
1976 Terenure
1977 Terenure
1978 Terenure
1979 Blackrock Coll
1980 Blackrock Coll
1981 Blackrock Coll
1982 Blackrock Coll
1983 Terenure
1984 Blackrock Coll
1985 PBC Bray
1986 Blackrock Coll
1987 Blackrock Coll
1988 PBC Bray
1989 Terenure
1990 PBC Bray
1991 St Michael's
1992 St Mary's
1993 Blackrock Coll
1994 Belvedere
1995 Blackrock Coll
1996 Belvedere
1997 St Mary's
1998 Blackrock Coll
1999 Belvedere

Munster Schools Senior Cup Winners

1909 CBC Cork
1910 Rockwell
1911 Rockwell
1912 Rockwell
1913 CBC Cork
1914 Rockwell
1915 Rockwell
1916 CBC Cork
1917 Rockwell
1918 PBC Cork
1919 CBC Cork
1920 PBC Cork
1921 The Abbey, Tipperary
1922 CBC Cork
1923 No Competition
1924 CBC Cork
1925 CBC Cork
1926 CBS Limerick
1927 PBC Cork
1928 Rockwell
1929 Rockwell
1930 Rockwell
1931 CBS Limerick
1932 PBC Cork
1933 CBS Limerick
1934 CBS Limerick
1935 PBC Cork
1936 CBC Cork
1937 Rockwell
1938 PBC Cork
1939 PBC Cork
1940 Rockwell
1941 Mungret
1942 Rockwell
1943 CBC Cork
1944 CBC Cork
1945 PBC Cork
1946 PBC Cork
1947 Crescent
1948 PBC Cork
1949 Crescent
1950 Rockwell
1951 Crescent
1952 PBC Cork
1953 Rockwell
1954 PBC Cork
1955 Rockwell
1956 CBC Cork
1957 PBC Cork
1958 PBC Cork
1959 Rockwell
1960 Rockwell
1961 Rockwell
1962 CBC Cork
1963 Crescent
1964 Rockwell
1965 PBC Cork
1966 PBC Cork
1967 Rockwell
1968 St Munchin's
1969 PBC Cork
1970 Rockwell
1971 CBC Cork
1972 CBC Cork
1973 CBC Cork
1974 CBC Cork
1975 PBC Cork
1976 CBC Cork
1977 CBC Cork
1978 PBC Cork
1979 CBC Cork
1980 CBC Cork
1981 PBC Cork
1982 St Munchin's
1983 Crescent Comp
1984 CBC Cork
1985 Rockwell
1986 Crescent Comp
1987 PBC Cork
1988 CBC Cork
1989 Crescent Comp
1990 Crescent Comp
1991 PBC Cork
1992 PBC Cork
1993 PBC Cork
1994 Crescent Comp
1995 PBC Cork
1996 PBC Cork
1997 CBC Cork
1998 CBC Cork
1999 CBC Cork

Munster Schools Junior Cup Winners

1932 CBS Limerick
1933 PBC Cork
1934 Rockwell
1935 Rockwell
1936 Rockwell
1937 Rockwell
1938 CBC Cork
1939 Mungret
1940 Mungret
1941 Mungret
1942 Rockwell
1943 Rockwell
1944 PBC Cork
1945 PBC Cork
1946 PBC Cork
1947 Rockwell
1948 Rockwell
1949 Rockwell
1950 Crescent
1951 PBC Cork
1952 Crescent
1953 CBC Cork
1954 PBC Cork
1955 Rockwell
1956 Rockwell
1957 PBC Cork
1958 Rockwell
1959 Rockwell
1960 PBC Cork
1961 Crescent
1962 CBC Cork
1963 PBC Cork
1964 PBC Cork
1965 PBC Cork
1966 PBC Cork
1967 Rockwell
1968 Rockwell
1969 CBC Cork
1970 St Munchin's
1971 CBC Cork
1972 Rockwell
1973 PBC Cork
1974 Rockwell
1975 CBC Cork
1976 PBC Cork
1977 PBC Cork
1978 CBC Cork
1979 PBC Cork
1980 PBC Cork
1981 CBC Cork
1982 Rockwell
1983 PBC Cork
1984 PBC Cork
1985 PBC Cork
1986 PBC Cork

1987 St Munchin's
1988 PBC Cork
1989 St Munchin's
1990 CBC Cork
1991 Crescent Comp
1992 PBC Cork
1993 St Munchin's
1994 CBC Cork
1995 PBC Cork
1996 CBC Cork
1997 Rockwell
1998 St Munchin's
1999 CBC Cork

Connacht Schools Senior Cup Winners

1913 St Joseph's Garbally
1914 St Joseph's Garbally
1915 St Joseph's Garbally
1916 St Joseph's Garbally
1917 No competition
1918 St Joseph's Galway
1919 Ranelagh Athlone
1920 No competition
1921 No competition
1922 St Joseph's Galway
1923 Ranelagh Athlone
1924 Colaiste Iognaid
1925 Colaiste Iognaid
1926 St Joseph's Garbally
1927 Colaiste Iognaid
1928 Colaiste Iognaid
1929 St Joseph's Garbally
1930 St Joseph's Galway
1931 St Joseph's Garbally
1932 Collegians/St Joseph's Galway (shared)
1933 No competition
1934 No competition
1935 No competition
1936 St Joseph's Garbally
1937 St Joseph's Garbally
1938 St Joseph's Garbally
1939 St Joseph's Garbally
1940 St Joseph's Garbally
1941 Galway GS
1942 St Joseph's Garbally
1943 to 1948 No competition
1949 St Joseph's Garbally
1950 St Joseph's Garbally
1951 Collegians
1952 St Joseph's Garbally
1953 St Joseph's Garbally
1954 St Joseph's Galway
1955 St Joseph's Garbally
1956 St Joseph's Garbally
1957 St Joseph's Garbally
1958 St Joseph's Garbally
1959 St Joseph's Galway
1960 St Joseph's Galway
1961 Sligo GS
1962 Sligo GS
1963 Sligo GS
1964 St Joseph's Galway
1965 St Joseph's Galway
1966 Wilson's Hospital
1967 No competition
1968 No competition
1969 Sligo GS
1970 St Joseph's Galway
1971 St Joseph's Garbally
1972 St Joseph's Garbally
1973 St Joseph's Garbally
1974 St Joseph's Garbally
1975 Clifden Community School
1976 St Joseph's Garbally
1977 Marist Athlone
1978 St Joseph's Garbally
1979 Colaiste Iognaid
1980 Sligo GS
1981 St Joseph's Galway
1982 St Joseph's Garbally
1983 St Joseph's Garbally
1984 St Joseph's Garbally
1985 Colaiste Iognaid
1986 St Joseph's Garbally
1987 St Joseph's Garbally
1988 St Joseph's Garbally
1989 St Joseph's Garbally
1990 St Joseph's Garbally
1991 St Joseph's Garbally
1992 St Joseph's Garbally
1993 St Joseph's Galway
1994 St Joseph's Galway
1995 St Joseph's Garbally
1996 St Joseph's Garbally
1997 St Joseph's Garbally
1998 St Joseph's Garbally
1999 Sligo GS

Connacht Schools Junior Cup Winners

1915 Galway GS
1916 St Joseph's Garbally
1917 Ranelagh Athlone
1918 Colaiste Iognaid
1919 Ranelagh Athlone
1920 to 1923 No competition
1924 St Joseph's Galway
1925 St Joseph's Garbally
1926 Ranelagh Athlone
1927 St Joseph's Garbally
1928 St Joseph's Galway
1929 Ranelagh Athlone
1930 St Joseph's Galway
1931 St Joseph's Garbally
1932 and 1933 No competition
1934 St Joseph's Garbally
1935 Sligo GS
1936 No competition
1937 St Joseph's Garbally
1938 St Joseph's Garbally
1939 St Joseph's Garbally
1940 St Joseph's Garbally
1941 St Joseph's Garbally
1942 to 1948 No competition
1949 St Joseph's Garbally
1950 St Joseph's Garbally
1951 St Joseph's Garbally
1952 St Joseph's Garbally
1953 St Joseph's Garbally
1954 St Joseph's Garbally
1955 St Joseph's Garbally
1956 St Joseph's Garbally
1957 St Joseph's Garbally
1958 Galway GS
1959 Sligo GS
1960 St Joseph's Galway
1961 Sligo GS/St Joseph's Galway (shared)
1962 Sligo GS
1963 St Joseph's Galway
1964 St Joseph's Galway
1965 No competition
1966 Sligo GS
1967 and 1968 No competition
1969 Galway Voc Sch
1970 St Joseph's Garbally
1971 St Joseph's Garbally
1972 St Joseph's Garbally

1973	St Joseph's Garbally
1974	St Joseph's Garbally
1975	St Joseph's Galway
1976	Clifden Comm Sch
1977	St Joseph's Garbally
1978	Colaiste Iognaid
1979	St Joseph's Garbally
1980	St Joseph's Garbally
1981	Colaiste Iognaid
1982	St Joseph's Garbally
1983	St Joseph's Garbally
1984	St Joseph's Garbally
1985	St Joseph's Garbally
1986	St Joseph's Galway
1987	Colaiste Iognaid
1988	St Joseph's Garbally
1989	Sligo GS
1990	St Joseph's Galway
1991	St Joseph's Galway
1992	St Joseph's Garbally
1993	St Joseph's Garbally
1994	St Joseph's Garbally
1995	St Joseph's Garbally
1996	St Joseph's Garbally
1997	Portumna Community Sch
1998	St Joseph's Garbally
1999	St Joseph's Garbally

PRESIDENTS OF THE IRFU 1990–98

A.R. Dawson
1989–90

N.J. Henderson
1990–91

Dr. A.D. Browne
1991–92

C.A. Quaid
1992–93

M. Cuddy
1993–94

K.E. Reid
1994–95

Dr. S. Millar
1995–96

R.M. Deacy
1996–97

N.H. Brophy
1997–98

N.A. Murphy
1998–99

W.H. Lavery
1999–2000

INDEX OF NAMES IN MAIN TEXT

ACKNOWLEDGMENTS

The publishers are grateful to the following for permission to reproduce photographs listed on the pages below:

Associated Press Photography pp 147, 154; Bob Thomas Sports Photography p. 145; colorsport pp 123 (bot.), 129, 130, 148, 168; The Clinch family, The Examiner p. 85; Frank Fennell Photography pp 211, 452 (last two photos); Gareth Miller Photography p. 216; Inpho: pp 162, 173, 196, 201, 205, 232 (top), 234 (Billy Stickland), pp 180, 192, 193 (Allsport); John Sheehan Photography pp 251, 255; Lafayette Photography p. 66; Mike Brett Photography p. 152; Museum of Rugby, Twickenham p. 91; National Library of Ireland p. 10; Robert Allen Photography p. 15; Sport and General Press Agency Ltd pp 104 (top and bottom), 112 (top and bottom), 114, 116, 126; Sportsfile: pp 194, 228 (top), 232 (bottom), 242 (David Maher), pp 195, 230 (Ray McManus), pp 221, 227, 228 (bottom), 229, 236, 237 (Brendan Moran), p. 222 (Dave Doher); pp 235, 239, 258, 276 (Matt Browne); The Irish Times pp 95, 127 (top and bottom), 132, 133, 137; Trinity College Dublin p. 32 (bottom). For all other photographs the publishers are grateful to the Irish Rugby Football Union.

Despite their best efforts the publishers were unable to trace all copyright holders prior to publication of this book. They would be glad to hear from additional copyright holders after publication.